Essays on

ACCOUNTANCY

by A. C. Littleton

SECOND PRINTING, 1963

© 1961 by the Board of Trustees of the University of Illinois. Manufactured in the United States of America. Library of Congress Catalog Card No. 60-8341.

FOREWORD

A. C. Littleton's many valuable contributions to accounting literature during the past four decades have furnished guidance, inspiration, and thought-provoking ideas to thousands of readers. His books on *Accounting Evolution to 1900, Introduction to Corporate Accounting Standards*, written with W. A. Paton, and *Structure of Accounting Theory* were augmented by many articles published in the *Accounting Review, Journal of Accountancy*, the *Harvard Business Review*, the *Illinois Certified Public Accountant*, the *New York Certified Public Accountant*, and other periodicals.

The essays contained in this book are for the most part extracts from his articles. They are brief and are somewhat independent of each other and therefore may be read in a random fashion, or in any order selected by the reader. They do not attempt an integrated or a chronological development of subject matter; yet they are sorted into topical categories. Accordingly the reader may, if he wishes, devote his attention to a group of essays related to a particular aspect of accounting.

The essays are grouped according to four principal areas, namely, accounting history, accounting theory, the profession, and accounting education, with several subgroups under each of these, as indicated in the Table of Contents.

Accountants will find excursions into these short essays invigorating and varied. Some of the essays will be enlightening, some will encourage further reading, some will contain ideas with which the reader agrees, some will express points of view with which the reader dissents, and all will be thought-provoking.

They will also prove extremely useful to accounting students as a basis for classroom discussions, as a source of topics to be explored further, as a storehouse of ideas for expansion into written assignments, into articles, and into theses, and as an aid to exercises in constructive and imaginative thinking.

Professor Littleton prepared most of the articles from which these essays were extracted while he was teaching and developing graduate courses in accounting theory and history at the University of Illinois. After spending several years in public accounting, he taught at the University of Illinois from 1915 until his retirement in 1952. Under his direction a program leading to an M.S. degree in accountancy was developed in 1922, and the first Ph.D. program in accountancy in the United States was developed, with the first degree being awarded in 1939. Professor Littleton has always been very active in professional organizations. He was president of the American Accounting Association in 1943, director of research from 1940-42, and editor of the *Accounting Review* from 1943-47. He also served on the Committee on Accounting Procedures of the American Institute of Certified Public Accountants, and on other committees of the institute.

Like hundreds of his other students, I was always greatly impressed, and in fact awed, by the many ideas he projected in his graduate classes and by his numerous outstanding contributions to the literature of accounting; yet fundamentally he was always modest and humble. He has sometimes expressed surprise that he ever became a teacher, and particularly that he found his thoughts acceptable for publication. He seems to be the sort of person Heskith Pearson speaks of in *The Man Whistles:* "A modest man often seems conceited because he is delighted with what he has done, thinking it better than anything of which he believed himself capable."

The author has asked that acknowledgment be made of his indebtedness to the many students, teachers, writers, and practitioners whose thoughts inescapably have been threaded into these essays. He has often mentioned that he is particularly grateful to Professor Hiram T. Scovill, who introduced him to professional and academic work, who gave him continued encouragement in his endeavors, and who opened many doors for students and for members of his faculty as well. Special acknowledgment is made to the Haskins and Sells Foundation, Incorporated for its co-operation and financial assistance in making possible the publication of this book.

C. A. Moyer

University of Illinois
Urbana, Illinois
March, 1959

CONTENTS

PART ONE *On Accounting History*

RELATIVITY IN HISTORY

1. The Nature of History

The opinions of some very wise men on this topic are an inspiration. Aristotle expressed it this way: "If you would understand anything, observe its beginnings and its development." Ernst Jäger, who in 1876 translated Paciolo into German, might have been influenced by Aristotle when he wrote: "Wer tiefer in eine Wissenschaft eindringen will, muss auch ihre Geschichte kennen lernen." Accounting is only one area of knowledge (Wissenschaft) but, as in other areas, if one wishes to delve deeply into it he must, as Jäger says "come to know its history." Perhaps these ideas apply to accountancy as well as other subjects.

At some moment during the educative process one realizes for the first time that the occurrences which he has been calling history are effects rather than mere events. The voyage of Columbus is to us only an attempt to find a water route to India and China, until we realize that there was a tremendous need to reach the East. Some book or some teacher completes the circuit of understanding by linking events of 1492 to antecedent events of 1453. And we thrill to the glimpse given us of the relation of effects to prior events.

But history is useful as well as inspiring. In meeting conditions as they arise it is helpful to start with a consciousness of the fact that change is a permanent element now as always. Whence better than from history could that consciousness come?

History also creates perspective. Direct observations of men and events of the present, if unchecked against some knowledge of men and events of the past, may prove an inadequate basis of wise choices today. The reason is that current events are necessarily disconnected and fleeting. The evidence is fragmentary; and a legion of inconsequential elements will be intermixed with the few which in the sequel will prove to have been important. Events may seem to be marching forward, but it is not easy at the time to detect the real direction they are taking. Many a seemingly useful idea may have been tried in some earlier generation and found wanting. Many a poorly timed proposal might have been halted by better perspective.

With accounting history, as with general history, interdependence of events runs throughout the story, and change is a permanent feature. In this special field the need for perspective is perhaps not so great as in

3

affairs of state. But accountancy is still evolving—we may even now be in
the midst of its greatest movement—and we are poorly equipped to understand its trend if our perspective is weak. We are badly poised to assist
the wiser movements if the trend is too dimly perceived.

A history book perhaps deserves to be characterized as one person's
reading of a design which time is continually perfecting. If this one be
judged to have revealed something of the pattern which diverse forces
have been weaving in the development of bookkeeping and accounting,
and if it affords the reader a glimpse of the intermingling of economic
forces, business institutions, industrial methodology, and social growth
with men's ambitions, ideals, plans, and failures, it will have justified its
existence.

This story of a portion of the evolution of accounting has intended to
furnish one more picture of the effects of expanding commerce and
changing economic conditions. The high lights are in the fifteenth century, when, under pressure from rapidly growing trade, men expanded
account-keeping into double entry; and in the nineteenth century, when
a similar pressure from industry led men to expand bookkeeping into
accounting. It is one more small cross section of the unending stream of
history wherein ". . . all events, conditions, institutions, personalities,
come from immediately preceding events, conditions, institutions, personalities" (Cheyney).

(from the preface and conclusion of the author's
Accounting Evolution to 1900, American Institute Publishing Co., 1933)

2. Ingredients of Accounting

Bookkeeping under the microscope consists of arithmetic digits written
in a certain arrangement. In essence it seems very simple, but in fact it is
quite complex. Those digits, however neatly marshaled, are only symbols
that need interpretation. They refer to a bewildering array of different
things—lands, goods, money, capital, debts, savings, losses, promises,
wages, and a legion of other elements. But to sense complexity in the
constituent elements is only the beginning of understanding. If we turn
the microscope upon the several elements themselves—the antecedents
without which there could be no bookkeeping—it will perhaps illuminate
the origins of double entry better than if we look steadily at the complex
whole.

The antecedents of double entry—those factors which in time became
so interwoven as to render double entry inevitable—are all familiar quantities; some of them are very old, and some are very obvious, but all of
them are indispensable. They are given below in a rough sort of sequence.

The *art of writing* is an indispensable antecedent, since bookkeeping
is before all else a record; *arithmetic* is essential also, since bookkeeping

is a sequence of simple computations, even though they are cast into certain forms; *private property*, since bookkeeping is concerned only with recording the facts about property and property rights; *money* (i.e., a money economy), since bookkeeping is useless except as it reduces all transactions in properties or property rights to a common denominator; *credit* (i.e., incompleted transactions), since there would be little impulse to make any record whatever if all transactions were completed and closed on the spot; *commerce*, since a merely local trade would never have created enough pressure (volume of business) to stimulate men to co-ordinate various ideas into a system; *capital*, since without capital, commerce would be trivial and credit would be inconceivable.

We can recognize these elements as essential to the formation of double entry; had any of them failed to appear, the appearance of double entry would have been problematical. If either property or capital were not present, there would be nothing for records to record. Without money, trade would be only barter; without credit, each transaction would be closed at the time; without commerce, the need for financial records would not extend beyond governmental taxes. If either writing or arithmetic were absent, the "vehicle" of bookkeeping would not exist. All of these items are antecedent elements to bookkeeping; we could not dispense with any of them and expect to see double entry remain.

But indispensable though they are, even these elements could not produce bookkeeping by merely appearing together historically. All of them were present in some form throughout the era of ancient history, but the ancient civilizations failed to produce double entry.

Writing, for example, is as old as civilization itself; yet bookkeeping is more than a writing, although always written.

Arithmetic as we understand it—the easy and systematic manipulation of number symbols—did not exist in the ancient world. The lack of an easy means of computation must have been as strong a deterrent to financial record-making at this time as its later appearance was a favorable factor.

Property is an indispensable antecedent to bookkeeping, of course; for without the right to possess, enjoy, and dispose of articles of property there would be little reason indeed to "keep books." But property rights under the ancient civilizations were not of the kind to inspire other conditions necessary to bookkeeping. The highest early need for bookkeeping would be satisfied with a sort of "stores accounting" which would merely tell what property was available. The accounting of the Egyptians extended no further than that.

Even the addition of the factor, *money,* to the art of writing and private property could not produce double-entry bookkeeping. These three factors made possible a written record of private properties which could be expressed in terms of a common denominator, money of account. But the incentive to convert a possibility into an actuality was lacking.

Credit was used too, such as that extended by the ancient moneylenders. Money was not loaned commercially but against necessity, that is, for consumptions rather than production. Personal account records would suffice. Nor was the *commerce* of the ancient world the kind to stimulate such a thing as bookkeeping. Barter did not need systematic, integrated records. The commerce which was required to foster the formulation of double entry was a large-scale and *profitable* commerce, for a profitable commerce alone creates a fund of *capital* which can be re-employed productively and thus give rise to additional capital in turn.

Here, in the opinion of the writer, is the principal explanation of why the ancient world did not produce bookkeeping. It did not have the conception of productive business capital; it lived throughout its era in an agricultural stage of development where there was no occasion to consider capital as a factor in production. This stage was to be followed long afterward by an era of handicraft and of commerce, and still later by an industrial era. These later stages were better suited to the development of bookkeeping, but neither of them had been reached when the doors closed upon ancient history.

(Accounting Review, June, 1927)

3. Importance of Nominal Accounts

In recent years the income statement has been given increasing recognition. This recognition is a recent development; yet the importance of income and the accounts related thereto is as old as double-entry bookkeeping.

Anyone who drew most of his knowledge of accounting from personal acquaintance with the early traditional auditing procedures, or from a study of statutory and case law as they touched accountancy, could hardly escape the conviction that the income statement was distinctly secondary to the balance sheet in general importance. Bookkeeping textbooks usually gave the two statements co-ordinate rank; some authors even labored to teach that the statements were significantly interlocked. The literature of auditing, however, from its beginning has emphasized the balance sheet almost to the point of ignoring the determination of income.

Yet income determination rather than determination of solvency has always been the central feature of double entry, the very heart and soul of the system. Think what fifteenth century double-entry bookkeeping would have been if income determination were omitted. Dropping out the profit and loss summary account and the expense accounts would only partly ruin the system, since goods accounts would remain with costs on the debit and revenues on the credit. But drop goods accounts out too and nothing would remain but assets, liabilities, and capital. Profit determination could then be nothing more than an appraised figure derived from comparison of balance sheets. What was left of the system certainly could not be called double entry without overthrowing all connotations of that term.

If we reverse the process and think of the elements of record-keeping which were amalgamated to produce double entry, the indispensability of income determination as part of the system will again be clearly revealed. The first element in use which later made up part of "books of account in the Italian manner," was personal accounts, that is, detached records of debts payable (and paid) and debts receivable (and received) that grew out of the use of bills of exchange. Some "double" entries were already possible in these records, but not "double-entry" bookkeeping. Next, goods accounts came into use in addition to personal accounts; possibly goods accounts originated in the experience of agent-traders. Since a goods account recorded costs (purchase) on the debit and revenues (sales) on the credit, the number of "double" entries was greatly increased. Yet this did not produce "double-entry" bookkeeping.

Later, after expense accounts, profit and loss account, and capital account were added to the pattern, the formulation of double-entry bookkeeping was complete. The several parts of the integrated system that we now know and use had been fitted together in the third stage of accounting development. Not until nominal accounts and closing entries for profit and loss items were invented into the pattern of record-keeping were all enterprise transactions translatable into debits and credits. Only then were "double entries" complete enough so that the phrase could be applied to an integrated system—double-entry bookkeeping.

From historical evidence it must be concluded that income determination by matching cost and revenue has for 500 years been the central feature of double entry.

It is reasonable that it should be the chief characteristic. Traders employed their capital productively in commerce, that is, they chose among risks for gain. They sought to make saved capital reproduce itself (plus something for themselves) by offering buyers the service of desirable goods brought from a distance. The traders could not avoid wishing to learn what the gain or loss amounted to, for that knowledge was the basis for judging the wisdom of having risked capital in a certain manner. In such a setting it seems inevitable that the real substance of the system of record-keeping that must finally emerge would have to be a proprietor's calculation of the gains (revenue credits) resulting from ventured capital (revenue debits).

Because the proprietor's relation to every transaction played a prominent part in early transaction analysis, and because the accounts were kept for his (proprietorship) information, double entry came to be considered as "ownership accounting." But strictly speaking it was "enterprise accounting" even though some proprietors might include household expenses in their bookkeeping. Every use of accounting for a separate venture, and for every partnership, gives support to that conception.

In order to see by means of records how enterprise property came to fruition, economic (nominal) accounts had to be invented to provide an "opposite" for economic transactions, that is, for those transactions which were more than an obvious exchanging of equivalent quantities at the moment (as a promissory note for a bank deposit). Without the use of goods accounts, expense accounts, and a summary profit and loss account, the fruitfulness of particular activities, such as one line of goods or another, could not be read from the record. Nor could diverse activities be marshaled into an array to epitomize the whole.

Without nominal accounts a coherent scheme of interrelated accounts converging into capital account would not be possible. Without this scheme, the operations that we now call double-entry bookkeeping could not be carried on, and statements designed to analyze the economic activities that constitute the reason for the existence of an enterprise could not be constructed. Here, therefore, lies the essence of enterprise accounting. Even though in auditing this essence has often been by-passed, and even though in legal situations this essence has not been considered material to the issues under examination or subject to control, matching of costs and revenues is nevertheless the focal center of accounting now as it always has been.

(editorial, *Accounting Review*, July, 1945)

4. Some Notes on Systems

Paciolo's text of 1494 described three books: daybook, journal, and ledger. This trilogy so impressed Europeans as the Italian tradition was transmitted that in some countries statutory law came to require that all ledger entries be derived from posting a journal—a practice which spread to Latin-American countries. Even where the force of law did not support the three-book system, it was universally the basis of textbook explanations, and usually still is. But these conditions should not obscure the fact that more "system" than this was needed, and was developed very early.

Only a few writers have pointed out that old business records preserved from the fifteenth and sixteenth century clearly show that men engaged in textile manufacture used other records, some being posting mediums and others auxiliary records. Some examples are as follows: a book of loans (cf. accounts payable ledger and notes payable book); a book of invoices (cf. sales book); a book of materials bought and used (cf. stores ledger); a book of materials delivered to workmen (under the household system of manufacturing); a book of wages due and paid; a book for finished textiles returned by workmen, for listing wage and material costs.

Some of these records, such as those for wages, included separate books for wool washers, spinners, weavers, etc. Sometimes a workmen's ledger was used to show charges and credits to individuals. Often these provided source material for forming into regular journal entries. Occasionally their use was so well interlocked with ledger accounts that the basic records could be posting mediums.

One particularly interesting example was called a book of income and outgo—in reality a subdivided cash book for posting to ledger accounts. This book had four sections: (1) cash receipts from all sources, (2) purchases and partners' withdrawals, (3) workers' services received (measured by wages due, hence expressing wage cost, not disbursement for wages), (4) money paid out.

These reflected very early some basic cost accounting ideas. Here was recognition of the separateness of costs by processes, of the need for uniting material and labor costs, of the distinction between labor cost and wage disbursements.

Perhaps these various records were not often all used by a given manufacturer; perhaps those used by one person often were not closely enough knit together to constitute an "accounting system," either separate from or in conjunction with daybook, journal, and ledger. But the structural elements of "a system" were clearly present, and the desire existed in the minds of enterprisers for basic "cost information." Sooner or later such desires and such structural elements were bound to be so firmly united as to produce a real cost system. The history of cost accounting has not yet been fully written. But when it is, its roots will be found reaching a long way back in time. And the wonder will be that, with such a start, it could take so long to evolve into the still un-co-ordinated cost accounting procedures that were typical of the nineteenth century. It is easier to recognize the factors which in the twentieth century produced an extraordinary acceleration in the development of accounting systems in general and cost accounting in particular, than it is to understand why a good start was so slow in gathering momentum.

Loose-leaf and columnar records before 1900 played a part in the later acceleration; and the growth of industry and mass production had a role, as did also the quiet blooming of professional accounting. But the taproot of "systems" reaches back 500 years. Loose-leaf records need not detain us here. Their primary usefulness, other than for convenient separation of filled pages, was their adaptability to machine-made records. This phase as systems places the present in startling contrast to the distant past.

The foundations for machine accounting were laid in the double decade of the 1880's and 1890's. Most of the necessary inventions had been made before 1900. In the years that followed the devices were perfected, production techniques were developed, cost reduced, and the usefulness of office machines was sold to the business public. Selling the idea was probably the hardest task.

About fifty years later there now is talk of adapting electronics to applications in office and accounting machines. But immediate results are unlikely; the same old problems will need to be met again: perfecting the devices, reducing first cost, selling the usefulness.

When Blaise Pascal built a mechanism that could be made to add and subtract, when Gottfried Wilhelm Leibnitz announced a machine for multiplying and dividing as well as adding and subtracting, and when Henry Mill was granted a patent for a machine "for the impressing or transcribing of letters singly or progressively," all of them no doubt had high hopes for the future of their devices. But even the inventors' dreams could hardly anticipate the developments of their ideas that had taken place by the late nineteenth century—to say nothing of the twentieth century adaptations. For the time was 1642 for the Frenchman Pascal, 1671 for the German Leibnitz, and 1714 for the Englishman Mill.

After machines that could add and machines that could write had been developed separately, it was natural that the two faculties should be combined in one device. Together they make an accounting machine.

In America a key-driven device for adding was patented in 1850, and one for typing in 1872. The Remington typewriter was first marketed in 1874. The Burroughs adding machine was first exhibited in 1884 (figures printed on a tape were included in 1888). In 1891 two men—Cawford Elliott and Robert J. Fisher—patented different machines to write on flat surfaces, thus making it possible to type records in bound books at about the same time that loose-leaf account books were laying another foundation under machine accounting.

After 1900, adding and writing were put together. In 1908 the Wahl adding register was attached to the Remington typewriter, making the machine useful for bookkeeping purposes (using loose-leaf sheets) as well as for separate writing or adding. The Moon-Hopkins billing and bookkeeping machine was first marketed in 1909. Elliott-Fisher accounting machines date from 1913.

Collateral to these are numerous office machines which, while useful for their purposes, are not so directly "bookkeeping machinery" as those named above. These include the cash register (1884), addressograph (1893), and various calculators such as Comptometer (1886), Marchant (1908), Monroe (1912).

Punch-card sorting and tabulating machines are in a class apart. Bookkeeping requires writing and adding for its records. Originally these functions were done by hand (this need not imply that adding was done on the fingers); later the processes were greatly speeded up by the use of machinery having finger-depressed keys (so adding was done by the fingers after all). But bookkeeping is also statistical in nature; its major contribution comes from sorting and classifying the facts that come under the jurisdiction of its rules. Sooner or later this aspect would be recognized and mechanized.

The present-day applications of the Hollerith electric tabulating machines to mass accounting classifications are familiar. Herman Hollerith spent a decade in experimenting to produce a "census machine." His patent was granted in 1889; but it was not until long afterward that there was a sufficient mass of accounting data within a given enterprise to justify this type of mechanization. Most accounting data serve their purpose in a single use. When this is the case much of the advantage of punch-card records would go unused.

Mechanization would prove more useful if business firms engaged in more research that used accounting data. Or put the other way, if businessmen were research-minded about the data accumulating in their accounts, further mechanization of their accounting processes would be indicated, perhaps even the employment of ultra-high-speed electronic posting and tabulating.

The results probably would soon reach the point of canceling the attendant cost. For really high-speed methods could make the cumulative account balances of today available at once for the financial statements of tomorrow; and between statement dates could pour out analytical data enough to keep an "accounting research department" busy searching for clues to relationships between policies and results, between enterprise conditions and economic conditions.

If electronic devices are to be effectively employed in accounting it may be necessary to make further changes in the classification side of accounting. It used to be the custom to note in the ledger account the name of the contra account involved in each entry. The aid this could be in later analyzing a given account is now obvious. But the practice fell into disuse probably at the time that complex, combined journal entries came into use making this notation more difficult. Yet such cross-classification is basically characteristic of double-entry accounting. Perhaps the full exploitation of the analytical possibilities lying in this fact is only waiting the development of ultra-high-speed tabulation of data and the resulting summarization of details into a multitude of subclasses.

In their day, loose-leaf records and the simpler accounting machines were spectacular changes. When they were eighteen years old, we can see now, they were still struggling through their beginning. The compacting of records has indeed made progress: bulky invoice books, loose-leaf carbon copies, tabulating machine cards, microfilm rolls.

But in some ways the most spectacular development came long ago— double-entry bookkeeping itself. It has not been necessary to change its basic ideas in 500 years. It is as suitable for integrating business transactions today as it was long before the time of Columbus. The early Italian record-keepers could have had no notion whatever of how spectacularly successful and infinitely adaptable their methods would prove to be.

(editorial, *Accounting Review*, October, 1946)

5. Capital and Trade

There was capital in the sense of wealth in the ancient world, but the mere existence of wealth does not inevitably give rise to conditions suitable to the formation of double entry. It is not wealth in marble palaces and secret hoards which calls up a co-ordinated system of financial recording. Only wealth can do that which is in the form of merchandise and ships, wealth which is active, turning over under management, ever changing in the processes of producing more.

Wealth in that form creates questions and doubts and hopes, and men in striving to find answers slowly evolve methods of recording to serve their needs. Wealth in the ancient world did not possess the energy to become capital in a sense to make it an antecedent of double entry. In fact all of the elements which we accept as indispensable antecedents of bookkeeping were already present in the ancient civilizations. Yet they failed to produce then what the same elements later did produce— double-entry bookkeeping, the ancestor of accounting. The prime factor in working this change in the power of these elements was the new atmosphere in which men lived and worked in the next historical era—the medieval world between the years 1200 and 1500.

The very ancient institutions of money, property, and the art of writing took on a new vitality in the new surroundings. But in the other items in the list of antecedents to bookkeeping, even greater changes appear. *Commerce, capital, credit,* and *arithmetic,* all partake of the spirit of the Renaissance which surrounded them; they seem animated by a new life in comparison with that seen in ancient history. Of these, commerce attracts first attention, because the others are not a little influenced by it.

Because ancient civilizations lived, for the most part, in an agricultural stage of economic development, with large slave or serf classes which had no purchasing power, barter was the usual method of exchange, and traders were hardly more than "peddlers."

The wealth of the ancient civilizations was static in the form of palaces rather than active in the form of ships. But in the city-republics of Italy, between the years 1200 and 1500, wealth was urged into productiveness. Trading was the vocation of large and small; the wealthy owned their own ships and ventured their capital in goods to fill them; those in more moderate circumstances went adventuring as active partners upon the capital of silent partners. Others chose the safer road of lending money upon the security of the ships themselves, or of lending to various governments. Here was the beginning of real *credit* transactions.

All through this period of 300 years, *arithmetic* had been quietly playing its appointed part along with the other antecedents of bookkeeping. The ancient world had been greatly handicapped by inability to make computations easily; the literal symbols used for numbers by the Greeks, and the even more faulty system used by the Romans, did not lend themselves readily to calculations. But in the Middle Ages, Europe began to learn arithmetic from the Arabs, and this condition was in the way of being remedied.

There is small doubt that Italian traders knew the essentials of early commercial arithmetic before the material appeared in Europe in manuscripts; their contacts with the Arabs of northern Africa and in Constantinople would indicate this. And in 1202, Arabic numerals and methods of computation were introduced into Europe in book form by Leonardo of Pisa. This book had chapters on addition, subtraction, prices of goods, barter, partnership, and the like, and would be of interest to merchants because of this type of contents as well as because it made use of the new system of ten numerals, including a zero.

Such a system lent itself naturally to computations and had already been applied by the Arabs to a great number of arithmetical problems of trade. This knowledge the Italians acquired early in this period, and it seems very probable that it opened the way for systematizing the record-keeping made necessary by bills of exchange, as nothing else could have done. This connection would not be easy to prove to the satisfaction of a critical historian, however, and no attempt is made here to go into the argument.

It is evident from all this that the circumstances surrounding commerce, capital, and credit in the Middle Ages were very different from those surrounding the same elements in the period of ancient history. And it must become increasingly evident that these surrounding conditions so changed the extent and kind of commerce and the purposes for which capital and credit were employed, that these elements could now become the vitalized antecedents of bookkeeping where before they could not.

Let us draw a figure of speech here from the nurseryman's practice among his fruit trees. He grafts the buds taken from one strain of cherry tree on the hardy rootstock of another strain, and thus produces a tree which combines the hardy life of the parent root and the engaging characteristics of the engrafted stock.

The hardy rootstock you will recognize at once is double-entry bookkeeping. What buds have been grafted onto that root, and what has the combination produced? Here is just a suggestion; there is time for no more.

One of the buds grafted on the parent stock has been the philosophy of economics. From this younger discipline, bookkeeping acquires a body of concepts and a language which has been invaluable in producing a new hybrid of far greater value to business than the parent alone. From this source came our concepts of cost and of income, for example, and the distinction between current and fixed capital. Another engrafted bud has been secured from the science of law in the form of the limited liability, joint stock corporation. From this source comes the distinction between initial capital and reinvested profits, the concept of permanent capital investment and dividends only out of profits. A third bud has been grafted on to the hardy root from the art of business management. From this source come certain practical necessities of the executive, such as the periodicity of financial statements, with all that implies in the way of valuation, accruals, depreciation, etc. and such practical necessities of management as cost accounting, budgeting, and the like.

Each of these three graftings has changed the fruits of the parent stem. Where for nearly 500 years men saw merely bookkeeping—financial records leading at best to little more than a calculation of profits—they now see accounting—a scientific procedure of inestimable value to society through the service it performs in facilitating sound business management.

We have reason, therefore, to be proud of double entry, though we should at all times carry our pride with humility. We have reason to feel that double entry lacks nothing in either remote ancestors or in parents and associates. Few indeed are the other institutions which were so soundly established in their beginning that they have continued for 500 years as little altered in their essentials as double entry. We have reason to be proud too of the results of uniting bookkeeping and other disciples —in other words, of accounting. Accounting has had a large part in the world of affairs recently, and it bids fair to continue to give increasing service. But just as the accounting of today is clearly a product of evolution, influenced by many men and many forces, so the accounting of tomorrow will be but a continuation of that evolution, influenced still by all of the circumstances which may surround it. This process is called the relativity of history. It is a productive interweaving of existing elements that produces change, growth, and progress.

(*Accounting Review,* June, 1927)

6. Relativity of Development

All accounting development has been conditioned by the times. This is not difficult to demonstrate.

Ancient wealth was not productive; it was not capital. It originated in tribute and the spoils of war. Wealth needed the pressure of an extensive and profitable commerce to give it real productivity. Such a commerce appeared in the Middle Ages largely as a result of the Crusades. Wealth began to grow from active trading exchanges. The purpose of the employment of capital and credit was changing from consumption and display to use in gainful enterprises in supplying newly felt wants with goods from distant sources.

This was the fertile soil from which double entry grew. But there was need for sun as well as soil; the "sun" was proprietorship.

The early records of medieval commerce were merely "agency book-keeping"—the records necessary to enable an agent or the active partner of a specific venture to report intelligently upon his activities. These, together with the records needed by bankers' dealings in exchange, brought personal debt accounts into extensive use.

However, when continuing partnerships replaced single ventures and occasional agreements, the recording problem passed from that associated with an irregular reporting by an agent to that occasioned by a continuing investment of capital variously employed and periodically summarized. The new burdens expanded the account-procedure of agency bookkeeping into proprietorship bookkeeping. Not until bookkeeping was thus called upon to serve the enterprise as a unit were its full possibilities achieved.

Whereas wealth in antiquity was stagnant, wealth employed in medieval trade became capital actively striving to reproduce itself. This was the first step toward true commercial proprietorship. The "master's account" of agency bookkeeping foreshadowed the "capital account" of the next step, but note that it was not thus converted until proprietorship had expanded and refined the need for account-keeping.

Another good illustration of the interrelation of surrounding conditions and the development of accounting is found in the rise of theory. Double-entry bookkeeping, as expounded in a long line of early texts, was singularly devoid of the theoretical discussions. The presentation was almost entirely descriptive—a verbal picture of bookkeeping routine. This in later years was supplemented by a multitude of rules of thumb for resolving transactions into debits and credits. But occasionally in the nineteenth century a bookkeeping teacher appeared who perceived the inadequacies of the learning of methods and rules by rote and who tried to supplement rules with reasons. These few men saw more in bookkeeping that a clerical routine and more in transaction analysis than a process of account personification. Practical business experience gave them a consciousness of the ultimate purpose of bookkeeping which the mathematicians and writing masters of an earlier day did not have. And some deep instinct for good teaching seemed to have led them to seek ways and means of bringing out the clear logic which was inherent in bookkeeping.

The clue to bookkeeping logic (theory) lay in "proprietorship." When the teacher began to speculate about the nature of proprietor's expense accounts and about the relation of the enterpriser to his enterprise, theory began. In the nature of proprietorship is the basis for that fundamental distinction between asset and expense which underlies so much of the theory of accounts. Here too is revealed the necessity for a grouping together of like accounts which can be viewed in contrast to other groups with differing characteristics. This is recognized as the foundation of much of the value which financial statements possess; it is the basis of the technique of marshaling an array of figures into an enlightening display.

The nineteenth century development of professional auditing in Great Britain is another good illustration of the way antecedent conditions produce subsequent results. It is not sufficient merely to point to the statutory audit as the basis for the growth of professional experts, for the question immediately arises: Why was such a statute proposed and passed by Parliament? There are several parts to the answer.

In the early nineteenth century an increasing pressure was apparent in England in favor of freedom of incorporation. The resistance of the government slowly weakened, and an approach was made in the second quarter of the century to permission for incorporation through compliance with a general statute. That constitutes the first point: the pressure of expanding commerce leads to incorporation by statute.

But the statutes prescribed an annual audit. The second point therefore is that England's unpleasant experience with fraudulent stock promotions in the early eighteenth century—the so-called Bubble period—leads to certain safeguard clauses in the corporation statutes of the nineteenth century, such as an audit in the interest of the inactive shareholders of the directors' various activities.

Why is the thing prescribed an audit instead of some other protective device? This then is a third point: England's experience in feudal days contained a suitable method for effectively supervising delegated responsibilities—the audit, or review of the records of the various officials of the feudal baron's household.

The device had been quite effective and could easily be adapted to the nineteenth century need. The audit which was prescribed for all joint-stock companies was therefore not without precedent.

It is noteworthy that the British government played an important part throughout this development. The publicity sections of the corporation statutes and the audit provision had the purpose of protecting stockholders from "stock-jobbing" promoters and fraudulent practices by company directors. Here are clear examples wherein organized society (government) undertakes to limit individual action in the interest of unorganized society, the latter being here represented by creditors and stockholders.

This illustrates very well the fact that the development of accounting has been relative to society's own development. It is unlikely that professional auditing would have appeared when and where it did if England had lacked a parliament, or had one which was unresponsive to the social needs of the time. Professional accounting, in the nineteenth century sense, could not have appeared in fifteenth century England, for the earlier age did not have the right kind of problems to call it forth. And it would be quite as unreasonable to expect to see fifteenth century Charge and Discharge accounting satisfying the accounting needs of the nineteenth century.

(*Journal of Accountancy*, October, 1933)

7. Relativity of Theory

The many problems created by corporations have generated much discussion, and hence probably influenced theory more than did the teachers of bookkeeping.

The corporation's contribution to accounting theory is threefold. Because of limited liability there was a legal obligation to retain in the business the amount of the capital contribution. It became important therefore to be able to make an accurate calculation of the amount of assets which could safely be distributed. The necessity for such calculations gave added importance to knowledge enabling one properly to distinguish asset and expense.

Because the incorporation of an enterprise resulted in a definite continuity of economic existence (although with changeable membership), there was an economic obligation to maintain the productive power of the enterprise. Here was a further use for sound theory to guide the management in making periodic calculations of the profits. Here, for example, was a practical justification for following the theory of treating depreciation as a necessary cost of production instead of as a voluntary reservation of profits.

Furthermore, because corporations were aggregates of capital under delegated management, it was necessary to substitute "figure knowledge" for personal acquaintance with detail by investors. Financial statements thus became the medium of stockholders' knowledge of their affairs, and this gave added importance to well-chosen account classification and grouping which would make the statements clear and understandable.

These various conditions had conspired to improve the underlying theory by means of which business facts were analyzed for bookkeeping records and to increase the clearness with which financial facts were presented to the understanding. This was clearly a refinement of bookkeeping definitions and concepts and grew out of the needs of the time.

Some of these same conditions, together with others which were more deeply social in nature, created a need for expert professional services and at the same time produced a body of men capable of performing these services. This was auditing—a method of scrutinizing and evaluating bookkeeping data. Still other circumstances brought about a very great advance in the technique of bookkeeping itself which we call cost accounting.

Our familiarity with the machine age makes it somewhat difficult to realize the "revolution" which is hidden in cost accounting. Just as double-entry bookkeeping was a revolution in account-keeping, so costing, which is a complex process of calculating for one's self the cost-make-up of his product, was a revolution in commercial bookkeeping wherein an article's cost was simply the purchase price complete.

When double entry was developing, and for many generations afterward, business was commercial rather than industrial; it was trade, not manufacture. Production was at first handicraft work in the family; it was a way of making a living rather than production for later distribution at a profit above cost. There were "costs," of course—raw materials gathered or grown and the labor of the family—but there were no factories, few employees, and very little invested capital. There was no need here for cost bookkeeping.

Costing problems began to appear when men began to work for money wages under enterprising masters who brought workmen and material together under one roof. This was the "factory system." Its cost bookkeeping where any was attempted was mainly in regard to kinds of material and quantities of articles produced. But there was a real need to ascertain money costs (material prices, wages paid) in order to test the adequacy of selling prices. This was satisfactorily done in a general way quite easily, for "wool" and "wages" could still be treated with the account simplicity found in trading expenditures.

The soil in which cost accounting grew was the factory system of production. But it needed the sun of the Industrial Revolution to help it grow toward its destiny. With the Industrial Revolution came power machinery, first water wheels, then steam, and with machinery came the costing problems of fixed assets, depreciation, overhead, etc. Later the nature of costing became more clearly evident and its calculations better refined. Methods of allocating cost units to product units were devised with such skill that cost accounting has finally become a veritable symphony of analysis and synthesis, and thereby acquired much of its usefulness in aid of managerial control. But its modern origins are the intricate origins of the Industrial Revolution, the movement away from the land to the towns, the commutation of traditional services into wages, and the invention of machines which applied power to productive processes. Costing therefore, like auditing and accounting theory, was a product of the surrounding conditions of its time. And for costing, like double entry, its earliest background must be sought in conditions and practice existing several centuries before the English industrial revolution.

(*Journal of Accountancy*, October, 1933)

8. Relativity of Purpose

For nearly a generation an increased emphasis upon income has been evident in the literature of accounting. Taking this clue as a hint an attempt will be made to formulate a hypothesis as to the central purpose of accounting. Surely the chief purpose will not be so limited as that of making a record. Accounting is more than a recording. Accounting data are important because, as summarized in financial statements, they supply valued information to enterprise managements and to investors. Yet a great deal of essential data to guide decisions is beyond the ability of accounting to furnish. If the furnishing of informative data shall be considered the function of accounting, it must be a limited type of data. And if limited, then wherein is it limited or where peculiar in that, though limited, it reflects the essence of accounting?

The hypothesis could be that the extensive need for dependable determinations of periodic net income makes the income statement the most important product of enterprise accounting.

If the hypothesis can be justified, its theme can then be converted in form to express more closely a central principle of accounting. Perhaps it could take this form:

For many uses the most important data from accounting are the revenue charges and the revenue credits by means of which enterprise efforts are periodically matched against enterprise accomplishments.

The relativity of accounting purpose comes into view here. Purpose can not stand alone; it can only be understood as a relationship. If the basic ideas of accounting are related to the basic ideas of a business enterprise, we have relativity. Accounting purpose is what it is because enterprise is what it is. Accounting is tightly tied to enterprise; the latter's purposes therefore will condition accounting purpose, and the discharge of accounting function will further the purposes of business enterprises. There is a close interconnection between the concept "enterprise" and the concept "accounting." This will be explored.

The concept of enterprise can be outlined by four "enterprise principles." Strictly speaking these are not accounting principles since they do not state significant relationships about that economic-statistical system which we call accounting. Rather they are business principles, or perhaps principles of enterprise economics, which lie close enough to the heart of accounting to throw light upon the nature of accountancy. These four principles may be given names for ready reference: Enterprise Service, Enterprise Entity, Enterprise Periodicity, Enterprise Effort and Accomplishment.

The principle of enterprise service is this: Business enterprises are accepted and used because they perform effective economic functions in supplying goods (for living) and employment (for earning).

This idea suggests that business enterprises make a desirable contribution to society and it implies that, by and large, the contribution is worth what it costs. It also involves the thought that here is a public-service aspect to the use of accounting data. Large corporations, for example, are public institutions in a very real sense though they are operated by private interests, and even though sometimes some of them appear to exist solely for the benefit of private interests. The need, public and private, for dependable accounting data is clear, especially as to those facts which show how the enterprise is fulfilling its basic functions of providing goods and giving employment to people and to capital.

Accountancy arose to provide information to the owner-investor. Even after a long evolution it still is strongly colored with that use. Yet this service to the owner-investor, important and indispensable as it must be, is not as fundamental as the more obscure but very vital purpose of aiding in the fulfillment of economic functions of an enterprise that are broader than that of earning a profit.

The principle of enterprise entity may be stated this way: Each business enterprise is treated in our industrial society as if it were a cohesive economic entity in its own right, or a self-contained and impersonal operating unit, rather than a grouping of persons.

Accounting-wise, a distinction between an enterprise and the persons concerned is inescapable. Enterprise costs are not the personal expenses of enterprise owners; and enterprise revenues are not the personal incomes of the owners. To hold otherwise would throw accounts into utter confusion. Since accounts are essentially statistical in method, close attention is necessary to the relevancy of the facts classified, and the first question of relevance is: Relevant to which enterprise? An enterprise therefore is the basis of the first classification of business transactions. If facts are entered in the accounts of one enterprise that are relevant only to another, factual truth cannot be stated in the accounts for either one.

Next is the principle of enterprise periodicity: In the functioning of a business enterprise there is a rhythm of seasons and activities, a cycle of events, which furnishes a framework for compressing the flow of enterprise data into comparable time segments.

The mass of facts that exists in any but a small enterprise becomes unintelligible unless the facts are treated statistically to make an understanding of them possible. Accounting is the instrument used to treat a mass of enterprise facts in such a manner that the flow of transactions becomes intelligible. In addition to compressing like transactions into a small number of classes, accounting utilizes the framework of seasonal rhythm to introduce a comparison of data period by period. It is hard to overestimate the contribution to understanding made by compressing a mass of facts and by setting up the resulting data in ways that permit comparisons to be made. The mind cannot grasp many separate facts at once, and figures lose most of their significance unless the eyes can quickly see whether they are larger or smaller now than they were.

The principle of enterprise effort and accomplishment is the most important of the four: The data of primary significance to all parties sharing in the proceeds of enterprise or in controlling enterprise operations are those facts which express enterprise efforts made and accomplishments secured.

Many parties have an interest in a given enterprise: creditors (loans and interest), workers (employment and wages), customers (goods and prices), managers (prestige and profits), stockholders (investment and dividends), government (productivity and taxes). All of these are concerned about the continued success of the enterprise with which they are associated. It is important to all interests that the enterprise continue to be financially healthy and economically productive. The facts most directly keyed into these conditions are the ones that make possible an intelligent comparison of enterprise efforts with enterprise accomplishments. These are the cost-and-revenue facts which accounting presents in the income statement. The balance sheet has its place—a place of importance for some uses— but it cannot come as near being all things to all men as the income statement.

The four enterprise principles form a progressive sequence which can graphically be set in layers to form a pyramid. At the bottom is the reason for enterprise existence; at the top is the element that points an arrow directly toward accounting. This places the concept of an enterprise directly in support of the central purpose of accounting as stated above in the form of an hypothesis and a principle. The concept of an enterprise gives a clue to the need that exists for people to have an understanding of enterprise activities. The proper concept of accounting purpose will be one that gives a clue to the way enterprise activities in the mass are made understandable, thus joining accounting (the means) to enterprise activities (the ends).

(adapted from Chapter 2, *Structure of Accounting Theory*, American Accounting Association, 1953)

CHARACTERISTICS OF DOUBLE ENTRY

1. Before Paciolo

Two years after Columbus landed on an island in the Western Hemisphere a little book on geometry and arithmetic was printed in Venice. This was Paciolo's *"Summa"*; it included a section on double-entry bookkeeping "according to the Method of Venice. . . ."

An interesting part of the introduction to Baldiun Penndorf's translation is the section devoted to an outline of the early bookkeeping practices out of which a teaching text finally emerged. It is especially noteworthy that all of the characteristics of double entry were well developed more than one hundred years before Paciolo's book appeared.

Paciolo, it appears, not only wrote long after double entry had been established but he did not present all of the things which seem to have been good practice several generations earlier. In this connection Professor Penndorf has made good use of the Datini archives in Florence which contain some five hundred old account books of a merchant of the years 1358-1412, Francesco di Marco.

The practices reflected therein are in some respects in advance of Paciolo's simple explanations of bookkeeping mechanics. Inventories are usually found priced at cost, but if the cost were unknown it was stated that one should use the opinion of experienced persons or the average of several. In one case in 1412 the inventory was taken as less than cost because, as the notation said, "the vineyard was ruined." In another case the quotation accompanying a loss entry recites a fall in prices as the explanation. In 1406 the "Profits on Goods Account" showed a loss item of 14 fl. because utensils deteriorated (*sono pegiorate*) during the year. About the same time loss is debited for a bad debt (*cattivo debitore*). Even before 1400 entries appear for accruals (*resierbo*), for fees in arrears (an asset), and for unpaid wages (a liability).

Here too is very early mention (1393) of records related to manufacturing processes—a wage book for spinners, weavers, and dyers and a spinning book with a page for each spinner showing memoranda of the weight and price of wool given each worker, weight of yarn returned, and the spinner's wages. In 1395 an old day book lists the details of the costs of producing two bolts of woolen cloth: wool, yarn, and the wages for carding, spinning, weaving, cleaning, clipping, dyeing, etc. (The next we hear of any such records is 1817 in France in a textbook by Payen and in 1818 in England through a text by Cronheim.) Paciolo and his successors do not mention such aspects of industrial accounting, and the world was a long time in developing them anew.

(book review, Accounting Review, December, 1933)

2. Basic Technology Unchanged

From the very beginning—say before the middle of the fifteenth century —certain basic peculiarities have been associated with double entry. These fundamental characteristics still persist and form the principal means of setting bookkeeping apart from other fact-manipulating systems. A characteristic technical manner of operating is one of the peculiarities which has undergone no basic change with the passing centuries.

In its operation, bookkeeping is essentially a classifying mechanism, but it is more, because simple classification (the sorting into pigeonholes) does not go far enough. Simple classification is fully accomplished when segregation is complete; that is, classification has served its purpose by bringing like things together. But segregation of like quantities is alone not sufficient for bookkeeping; both "likes and opposites" must be brought into the classes (accounts) to fulfill the requirements of bookkeeping. Classification looks toward class totals; bookkeeping requires class "balances." In bookkeeping every class (account) may receive increasing and decreasing elements; in ordinary statistical sorting there are no decreasing elements.

This peculiarity of the data of business makes a bilateral form in the basic record practically inevitable, the item of primary importance being always the balancing remainder. In thus working for balances, subtraction comes to be indicated by contraposition; that is, items placed in juxtaposition are thought of as having a natural "oppositeness" which leads to subtraction. This underlying character within business transactions is the basis of "equal debts and credits."

Bookkeeping for many years has possessed a characteristic technology and theory. The underlying theory must be read, so to speak, between the lines of Paciolo, for he takes up no space in philosophizing. His purpose was practical: "To give sufficient rules to enable them to keep all their accounts and books in an orderly manner." He was describing the manner in which records were kept by the method employed in his time and place.

On the surface the bookkeeping described seems to hinge upon the duality of the entries. "Thus for each entry in the Journal you will write two in the Ledger," he says. "Of this entry, as we have said, and of any entry in the Journal, a duplicate must always be placed in the Ledger twice, that is, first to debit and the other to credit. . . ." Or it seems to rest upon the opposition of debit and credit. "The debitor's entry is placed on the left side and that of the creditor on the right."

But this is not theory; this is not the essence of double entry; it is simply methodology. The double posting and opposition of debit and credit are merely incidental. They produce an equilibrium of amounts, it is true, but the real virtue of bookkeeping is not in this weak insurance against errors. The real essence of bookkeeping lies deeper.

Beneath the surface of the methodology is the unquestionable recognition of the fact that every transaction has a dual aspect, just as a coin has "heads and tails." This is much more fundamental than the mere recording of facts "in double" to get as a test an equality of totals. Yet this is the essence of the theory of transaction analysis which pervaded all of the fifteenth century practices and which is still considered a basic concept in accounting. However, the mere search for means of increasing arithmetical accuracy could hardly have produced impersonal accounts and nominal accounts in that day when little beyond the personal accounts of moneylending records was in existence. There could scarcely have been standards of accuracy at that time sufficient to prompt the devising of such a symbolic thing as an expense account. But it could easily result when each transaction was seen to present two aspects, both of which businessmen wished to have recorded.

It is very probable that the application of bankers' personal account methods to trading affairs brought into prominence the fact that the proprietor was a frequently recurring factor in the transactions; that he owed this person and was owed by another; that certain transactions brought him gains and others brought losses, or constituted merely equivalent exchanges of such advantages as the future should determine. This consciousness of the proprietor and of proprietorship is much more fundamental than equality of total debits and total credits. A well worked out statistical methodology could conceivably sort all the necessary financial elements into properly classified records without the intervention of "debit and credit" at all. But we can conceive of no procedure capable of bringing all of the financial elements of trade into the records which did not make use of the proprietorship concept. The proprietorship idea comes before debit and credit—not before the idea of debitors and creditors, of course, but before the idea of an equilibrium of classified entries.

With the proprietor made a party to many of the transactions, the way is opened to the analysis and record of every type of transaction where before only personal debts could be recorded. Or, putting it the other way around, the realization that every transaction had two distinct aspects made the introduction of "proprietorship" into the reasoning an inevitable step.

The treatment of nominal accounts in relation to the capital account is so consistent that it is obvious that Paciolo had a very clear conception of the relation of the proprietor to every transaction. And we cannot follow his descriptions of method without feeling that merchants who kept accounts must have been well aware of the fact that every transaction, even those which we now call closing entries, had a dual aspect within them regardless of the technicality of trial balance equilibrium.

(*Accounting Review*, June, 1928)

3. Additions Since Paciolo

Bookkeeping as such has not changed a great deal in its basic aspects. What then has been added? The form of the ledger account is only changed in the direction of simplifications; the ledger now is much more abbreviated in its record—a tabulation of figures with posting references, in place of a rather complete copy of the several transactions concerned. The form of the journal entry is changed only in the direction of further abbreviation—technical phrases like "*per*" and "*a*" are replaced by a technology of position which gives significance to the mere indentation in the writing of certain items, or to the location of figures in columns. To these changes have been added the subdivision of the books of original entry, the introduction of loose-leaf practices, and the principle of total posting.

But time has not left the recording functions in business unaltered even though the technique of recording is little changed. As business grew in size and complexity, its records took on added importance. Simple records, for so long entirely adequate to all managerial uses, were no longer fully satisfactory, and within the last one hundred years or perhaps even less important refinements have been added—refinements not so much of methodology as of theory.

It will be noted in reading Paciolo that his practice makes no provision for financial statements. The reason for this omission is not far to seek: proprietors were in personal contact with their affairs and the occasional computation of a profit and loss account in the ledger was ample for their needs. This means that no particular importance was attached to "periodical closing" or to the careful apportionment of costs and income as between successive comparable periods. In fact, even periodical inventories are not mentioned by Paciolo. When these things began to receive attention, "theory" followed as a matter of course. Out of financial statements emerges the theory of organized accounting data, i.e., the idea that sequence of items could have significance and that the grouping of like elements and the contrasting of opposites could be interpretative; out of "periodicity" grew those refinements of apportionment which produce deferred charges, accruals, and the like, and perhaps inventories themselves and all of the modern problems of burden distribution as well.

In producing the business corporation with its far-flung ownership and limited liability, moderns placed upon accounting such burdens as the ancients did not dream. Periodic determination of profits, for example, becomes a matter of prime importance where "dividends out of capital" becomes a critical matter. Under the simple early proprietorships withdrawals of capital and profit could be made at the same time.

Business is now regarded as a continuous process rather than as a group of disjointed transactions. This is expressed by our development of the terms "earnings" and "income" in contrast with "profits." No such abstractions were thought of until recent times. We are anxious to associate with earnings the cost of producing those specific returns. Consequently we use cost accounting extensively and give due recognition to depreciation as a cost. The ancients did neither. In fact, fixed asset accounts played very little part in the old books, and wages were of minor importance. With us wages and salaries count heavily in all computations of cost and expense; and our breakdown of expenses into subclasses far outdoes anything thought of in the earlier day.

Attention to close definitions and to extensive subdivisions of bookkeeping data is a modern addition. The distinction between fixed and current assets is an interpretative element only associated with very modern financing; capital and revenue expenditures grew out of our desire to determine net profits carefully; reserves of surplus appear only after conservatism becomes a virtue in corporation finance. These things troubled Paciolo and his contemporaries not at all; and there was no need that they should.

New times have brought new conditions, and these in turn have wrought some changes. We note how different modern accounting is from the practices of the fifteenth century, how broad is its field, how closely refined its definitions and concepts have become. A profession has appeared. Yet we seldom realize that we have added to the basic elements little but a body of theory and made certain adaptations of methodology in our search for efficiency and for sharply calculated periodic results. We have indeed added techniques for auditing and for cost-finding. Yet the best and the most we can show cannot compare, as a real contribution, to the first steps taken so long ago. Accounting is now conditioned by its modern setting, as bookkeeping was conditioned by its surroundings. The outstanding fact throughout is evolution. Even the basic characteristics of double entry evolved up to a stage from which further evolution, even into the twentieth century, became possible.

(*Accounting Review*, June, 1928)

4. Early Transaction Analysis

Early writers on bookkeeping were intent upon giving instruction in the practice of the day and indulged in very little theorizing. Even in connection with transaction analysis the underlying reasoning must be surmised from the practices described. An attempt will therefore be made to find the reasoning in the phraseology used in the entries of the day.

Two unrelated items are taken from the ledger 1519-27 of Thomas Howells for analysis.[1]

(a)

John de Lassys and de Rowso of Muros in Galicia ought to give an Acc't of Broadcloth shipped in S't Maria de Rodys. . . . £74, 0s, 0d.

(b)

R. Donnington ought to have in barbing of a short Plonket that Th. Petter delivered to you. . . . 8d.

It will be noted that each entry expresses a complete thought. Very likely the wording is much as if the thought had been spoken; it probably would have been easily understood by anyone who heard it so phrased.

Perhaps the completeness of the thought expressed will be clearer if the old entry is rendered more freely.

L. and R. "ought to give" me an accounting in money or in goods for the broadcloth shipped in their care . . . etc. ....$74.
D. "ought to have" $.50 from me for fuller's work done on my cloth. ......$.50.

In addition to being framed here in complete sentences, all of the entries, it will be observed, contain certain "words of accountability," that is to say, words which apparently were regarded as just as indispensable in making an accounting entry out of an otherwise straightforward sentence as in modern times the words of negotiability (as "or order") are regarded as indispensable to a bill of exchange. Other similar verb forms are found in or translated from other authors as below.

For Debits:	For Credits:
must give	must have
shall give	shall have
ought to give	ought to have

These phrases all express the same basic idea; the differences are only variations in emphasis. Clearly the idea of "give," i.e., return to the proprietor or agent, was directly associated with debits, and "have," i.e., receive from the proprietor or agent, with credits. The debit side of a

[1] Quoted in *The History of the Worshipful Company of Drapers of London*, by Rev. A. H. Johnson, Vol. II, p. 253.

bilateral account was the "give" side, and the credit side was the "have" side.[2]

It is also to be observed that the records were stated in the future tense. "Must give," "shall have," "ought to give" are phrases which look to the future. This sense of futurity is brought out more clearly in the entries as restated.

The old ledger entries, then, contain these three characteristics:

1. The entries are complete sentences expressing complete ideas.

2. The entries were written from the point of view of the proprietor or agent in question, i.e., his accounts with others.

3. The entries were definitely stated as memoranda of expected future occurrences, not of present happenings.

How would these ideas of framing ledger entries be stated in a general rule? We do not know; none of the early writers tried to reduce the process to a general rule. The nearest they came to it was to have rules for specific accounts such as: "Goods Account is debited for Purchases." Since they stated no general rules we may frame some for ourselves. The following hypothetical rules are offered in the attempt to reduce to simple concise statements the ideas of transaction analysis which seem to have been at the basis of the formulation of double-entry bookkeeping:

(1) A sum is to be entered in the record as "shall give," if the person involved is obliged to return to me at a later date an equivalent of what he has just now received from me.

(2) A sum is to be entered in the record as "shall have," if the person involved is entitled to receive from me at a later date an equivalent of what he has just now given me.[3]

These statements of principle may be abbreviated somewhat as follows:

(1) X shall later give what he now receives—(i.e., Dr. X.).

(2) Y shall later receive what he now gives—(i.e., Cr. Y.).

(Accounting Review, September, 1931)

---

[2] It is interesting to note that this basic concept is preserved in the designations given to the two sides of an account in Italian, French, and German.

in Latin		in Italian	
Debent dare	Debent habere	Dare	Avere

in French		in German	
Doit	Avoir	Soll	Haben

Each term used for debit and credit either is, literally "give" and "have" or can be traced to these verbs. Note also that the "rule of thumb" for analyzing debits and credits which was so much used by later writers is not unrelated to these technical terms. The rule was in two parts: (1) "Debit what is received," that is to say: what I now receive I must give back; (2) "Credit what is given," that is to say: what I now give I must have returned to me.

[3] Compare with the following German explanation of the technical terms Debit and Credit: "Der Empfänger eines Wertes wurde als Schuldner, der einen Gleichwert geben soll, mit 'Soll,' der Geber eines Wertes hingegen als Gläubiger, der."

5. Fable in Dialogue[4]

On a certain day in the early thirteenth century an old Lombard money-changer was seated at his table in a little stall in the market place of Florence. Another Florentine, Antonio by name, enters the booth with a companion and lays a bag of coins upon the table before the old man.

Antonio: Lombard, I go presently upon a journey to Venice and would leave these two hundred ducats in your hands for safekeeping. Do you accept them and in the presence of this witness, Ludovico, pledge to hold them in my name and return them at my pleasure?

Lombard: Yes, I do that for noble gentlemen sometimes. It is a great risk in these days for so small a fee as six denari. But I will do it. (Turning to Ludovico.) I take you to witness, noble sir, that I say Antonio shall have two hundred ducats from me at his pleasure. See, I write it so on my tablets. Now the pledge is good before all judges according to very ancient rule and custom.

Antonio: Enough. I know the forms you think you have to follow. So be it. (Exiunt.) (Enter Francisco, a young gentleman of Florence.)

Lombard: How may I serve your lordship?

Francisco: Lombard, I have a present need for a hundred ducats. Have you that much in hand?

Lombard: Barely, barely, my lord. You will give it back soon? Give it to me at my pleasure, eh? With something more, eh?

Francisco: Yes, yes, of course. But this is only talk. Give me the money.

Lombard: At once, at once. (Calls.) Simione! A witness, just a witness as is the ancient custom. Here is the money in the bag. See, I write down what you pledge. (Writes and reads.)

> "Francisco shall give[5] 100 ducats to me at my pleasure
> for money this day given to him. . . . . 100 D."

That is what you pledge, is it not, my lord? You witness, Simione. It now is all according to rule and custom.

Francisco: Yes, yes, that is what I pledge. Give me the money.

Lombard: In this bag—except for the interest—good, full count; good gold coins.
•

[4] A fanciful dialogue designed to suggest how men in the Middle Ages might have talked of transactions in phraseology the essence of which became incorporated in the bookkeeping records of the day—records which gradually evolved into systematic double entry.

[5] It is only natural to expect such early memoranda to be couched substantially in the words of the conversation which gave rise to the transaction and the agreement, because the art of abbreviating the record of a transaction is a product of long evolution and could hardly be expected to appear at the beginning of men's attempts to record financial transactions.

The beginning of traditional phrases (later to become technical terms) are well illustrated by the words "shall give" (he owes, i.e., debit) and "shall have" (he has a claim, i.e., credit) which are found in one form or another, in practically all of the old ledger entries shown in the histories. With quite understandable variations in spelling, even within one language, the Latin *debet dare* became in Italian *dee dare,* in German *soll geben,* and (probably) in French *doit rendre;* the Latin *debet habere* became *dee avere* in Italian, *soll haben* in German, and (probably) *doit avoir* in French. Vestiges of these phrases are still preserved in the ledger headings which correspond to our abbreviations, Dr. and Cr.; the Italian being *dare* and *avere,* respectively; the German *soll* and *haben;* and the French, *doit* and *avoir.*

Come again, my lord. (Exit F.) It is the third time since his father died. Well, a ship of his may yet win through. (Exit.)

Some months elapse, during which time Antonio has made his journey to Venice and returned. Again the Lombard is seated at his table in the market place, and to him come Antonio and Francisco.

Antonio: You lately pledged that I should have two hundred ducats at my pleasure. Give them to me now.

Lombard: As you will; just as you wish. Yes, surely I pledged; I remember it well. Besides it is written on the tablets. But you find me now a little short. So much to Benevetto yesterday on his venture in spices. (Craftily.) If only my lord Francisco could give me as he promised some of the money he had of me in coins. Why then, Antonio—

Francisco: (Interrupting.) Is it not enough that you send your cringing messenger three times to whisper in my ear and set my guests chattering?

Antonio: (Quieting him.) My lord! Hush, my lord! (To the Lombard.) Give me the money as you pledged. Let his lordship rest; you will be paid. I will myself see to it if necessary.

Lombard: Ah, that's different, that's different. Your pardon, my lord, pardon. (To Antonio, insinuatingly.) You do now ask this money perhaps to pay upon the sum my lord is pledged to give me at my pleasure?

Antonio: (Again interrupting.) My lord Francisco, please to step here by the window. You will—(They confer in whispers apart and return to the table)—It will be best. Let me do the talking.

(To the Lombard.) I all but lose my patience. You seize my very words and turn them out of their meaning. I came not to pay you for my lord Francisco's pledge, but to have my own money of you. Yet—yet, I think I *will* discharge him to you —for my own reasons, mark you, Lombard, not because it seems to suit *your* purpose.

Lombard: Yes, yes, surely. It shall be done then. You will stand in his stead— all according to the ancient rules and customs. Do you, Antonio, discharge me of the two hundred ducats owing to you? Do you agree they shall be held at my lord Francisco's pleasure instead?

Antonio: That is my intention, Lombard.

Lombard: Yes, yes, I only state it in careful language so there will be no mistake —no mistake. Yes. And I then in turn do here discharge my lord Francisco of two hundred of the ducats he has pledged to give me. Do you understand it thus, my lord?

Francisco: I am discharged of two hundred ducats. Yes—but little thanks to you.

Antonio: Put this matter on the tablets before we leave.

Lombard: I was about to do so. (Writes and reads.)

> "Antonio shall give to me 200 ducats this day placed
> at the pleasure of my lord Francisco. . . . . 200D"

You understand, Antonio, that I write, "You shall give me" as if I owed you nothing, because this writing only cancels the former writing wherein I pledged that you should have two hundred ducats of me. That is right?

Antonio: I understand; but have done.

Lombard: In a moment, in just one moment more. The ancient customs must be followed. Now I write again. (Writes and reads.)

> "My lord Francisco shall have of me 200 ducats placed
> this day at his pleasure by Antonio—200 D."

That is clear, is it not, my lord? You shall have two hundred ducats as I have written, *if you are not already pledged to give me that much.* As it is, this money which by this writing you shall have is only an offset against what you pledge to give me on the former writings. That is it, is it not?

Francisco: (A little bewildered.) That is what you meant, Antonio? It is all right? (He nods.) Well, if you say so. All right, Lombard. But Antonio, the present need. You know I spoke—.

Antonio: Of that later. We have finished here. Come. (Speaking privately.) There is another Lombard I know who holds you in high regard. . . . (Exiunt.)

This seemingly cumbersome roundabout way of analyzing a transaction and of framing an agreement in particular words for the record may have its base in old Roman practices, a tradition of which may conceivably have been preserved in local custom throughout and beyond the Dark Ages.

MacLeod tells in his *Theory of Credit* of definite procedures for contracting a binding debt, including a set form of preliminary conversation. There was an equally definite procedure for transferring a debt to a third party. The creditor and debtor and transferee met together, and the creditor, with assent from the debtor, transferred his right to the third party by word of mouth. The creditor by word of mouth released the debtor, and the transferee, also by word of mouth, released the creditor.

(*Accounting Review*, December, 1927)

6. Er Soll Gaben

The journal entry is an important bookkeeping mechanism which serves as a means of converting a nontechnical statement of transaction into a species of technically formed, intermediate statistical record. It is, moreover, particularly characteristic of double entry—more characteristic perhaps than the ledger—because it so clearly expresses the inevitable duality which lies within all transactions. For this reason, undoubtedly, journalizing has always been a very important element in the teaching of double-entry bookkeeping; and in some countries, it is a legal requirement that all entries shall pass through the journal.

The earliest journal entries were not what one would perhaps be inclined to expect in view of the early characteristics of the ledger account. Ledger entries were at first complete sentences—whole transactions entered twice *in toto.* But the earliest journal entries that we know were not sentences to be rewritten in the ledger. On the contrary, they were even in the first appearances quite technical in form and phrasing. The uninitiated might understand a ledger entry, for the wording expressed a complete thought, but they could hardly grasp the meaning of a journal entry unaided, for the expression of thought was very much abbreviated.

The absence of any authority showing how the technical phrases in

journal entries came about throws the matter open to conjecture. The
question is intriguing enough to be dwelt upon for a few paragraphs.

A hint of a possible starting place may be found in the phrasing of
some of the early German journal entries. The dates of the German
examples are later than those of many of the Italian entries in the established form. However, these particular German entries are not cast
into the same technical form. The following is a sample entry[6] by
Mathew Schwartz, the chief bookkeeper for the famous Fugger family
of German merchants. It is dated 1516:

Uns soll herr Jacob Fugger duc. 85, die *sollen wir* a Cassa, umb souil hat Matheus
Schwartz hie zu Venedig fur sich gebraucht . . . dc 85. *To us* Mr. Jacob Fugger
shall [give] 85 ducats, which *we shall* [give] to cash, for as much as Mathew
Schwartz has used here at Venice . . . dc 85.

The italicized words are the ones which have technical significance;
the words in brackets in the translation are added to the original to
complete the obvious meaning. Thus completed, the journal entry assumes the form of a simple sentence, quite devoid of technicalities and
therefore understandable to anyone who reads it. The word "give" is
not in the original entry of 1516; without that word even this entry
becomes semitechnical, since a missing word is to be implied.

In 1440-44, however, unsystemized memoranda of the time contained
the phrases *"er sol geben," "ich hab im gegeben"* ("he shall give," "I
have given him"), and the like. Thus it seems clear that the Germans
had started with complete sentences, but by 1516, had begun to drop
words out of the bookkeeping entry so that the record was already becoming technical. The process had not yet gone so far as to make the
full sentence hard to reconstruct.

By 1549, however, some entries had become more technical. For example:

Für Ingwer an Nutz und Schaden für Nutz und Gewin ich au dem Ingwer
gehabt—fl. 6.
[By Vinegar, to Profit and Loss, for loss and gain I have had on Vinegar. . . . fl.
6.]

This phraseology is too technical for the unimitated to understand.
The entry is not a complete sentence, whereas the entry of 1516 was
almost complete. Possibly the Italian form, shown just above, did not
make itself felt in Germany until some time after its early use in Italy
(1430).

One of the most interesting facts about the old practices of double-
entry bookkeeping is the existence at the same time of two strikingly
different types of journal entry, one of which has already been presented
here. Yet, different as they are in wording and technicalities and different

[6] Penndorf, *Geschichte der Buchhaltung in Deutschland,* p. 50.

undoubtedly also as they are to origin, they nevertheless could serve the same function equally well without, apparently, introducing any confusion.

This other form of entry may prove to be even more interesting than the one first discussed. It is closer to modern forms; and the modern journal entry in English seems to evolve more naturally out of this form than out of the "by and to" type of entry.

(1491)[7]

Faro debetore Tomasone del Buono e *creditore* spese di mercanzie di s. iiij d'oro per spese fatta a un fardello di panno corsato mandato da Lucca da Bonaccorsi a Libro 203/100 lib—siij d—.
[I *make debtor* Tomaso del Buono and *creditor* Merchandise Expenses for 4 s. in gold, for expenses incurred on a bale of cloth sent by Lucca da Bonaccorsi in the book 203/100 lib.—54—d.]

(1550)[8]

Cassa *est debiteur* adj—ditto L. 987.13.4 Je Pierre du Mont ay receu de mon maistre Micolas de Reo en argent contant L. 987.13.4 pour luy seruir au train de marchandise dieu me donne la grace de bien servir.

Micholas de Reo
   est Creditor   **L. 987.13.4**

[Cash *is debtor* on this day (for the) L. 987.13.4. I, Pierre du Mont have received from my master Micolas de Reo, L. 987.13.4 in ready money to be employed for him by way of business. (May) God give me grace to serve well.

Nicholas de Reo
   Is Creditor   **L. 987.13.4**]

These entries say, in essence, "I make A debtor and B creditor," or "A is debitor, B is creditor." Other examples, not here shown, present additional variations in phraseology, which seem to say: "A is debitor to B," or "A owes to B."

These latter forms are particularly unsuitable because they seem to say that one account or person owes another account or person. Yet person A, debited in the records of person X, does not now owe person B, who is there credited. A's debt runs to X. And it is surely faulty reasoning to say that cash (debited) owes person D, who has just paid money to the person whose cash account is affected.

What happened seems to be the following. Early entries (ledger and journal) were stated in complete sentences wherein certain phrases gave the key: "er soll geben" (he shall give to me, the proprietor); or "Ich hab im gegeben" (I, the proprietor, have given to him, hence he must later give to me). The German verb phrase "soll geben" (shall give) obviously carries the sense of the English verb "owes." Moreover, the phrase was presently contracted to "soll" but still carried the sense of "he shall give back," i.e., he owes. Note too that the Latin *debet* from *debeo,* the Italian *dere* from *dovere,* and the French *doit* from *devoir*

---

[7] Fabio Besta in *La Ragioneria,* Vol. III.
[8] *Ibid.*

all mean "he must (give back)"; hence all are the technical equivalent of "he owes." [9]

It is clear that these entries are radically different from the first example in both form and phrasing. The first type was probably devised from the wording of the ledger entries of the time and obviously led to the use, much later, of "to" in the debit and "by" in the credit of the English ledger entries. The second type of journal entry, on the other hand, would seem to be one to grow more naturally out of the "day-book" record of personal account transactions; it is quite clearly a closer antecedent of modern journal entries than is the first type.

(*Accounting Review*, December, 1928)

7. Anglicizing Italian Terms

Double entry spread rapidly from Italy throughout Europe in the sixteenth century and has remained unchanged in its essential features throughout the centuries. In Great Britain, however, the adoption of the Italian method was accompanied by certain modifications in the manner of analyzing transactions, even though most of the basic ideas and practices were accepted as designed. This modification is less surprising when it is recalled that Great Britain was the only country in Europe to have specific accounting methods of its own at the time it received the Italian system. The "charge and discharge" system of accounting had been in use there long before the newer ideas reached the island. But as a system it was clearly inferior to double entry in flexibility, and consequently it was finally superseded by the more useful methods.

It is the present purpose to indicate the change in point of view which took place during the process of "Anglicizing" the Italian ideas of record-keeping and to suggest, as a plausible explanation, that pre-existing local ideas may be expected to give something of their own color to those which may be imported.

In our English ledger of 1519, the key words are "ought to give" (for the debit), and "ought to have" (for the credit). There is clear similarity here in the sixteenth century to the ledger terms found in the Italian records of the previous century: *de dare* (shall or must give); *de havere* (shall or must have).

[9] In 1396, *"debet dare"* (he must give) indicated the debit side of the ledger (see the *Accountant*, March 27, 1926, p. 484). And in 1494, "dee [deve?] dare," the medieval Italian phrase, indicated the same thing (see Geijsbeek's reproduction of Paciolo's "De Computis" in *Ancient Double Entry Bookkeeping*). The debit side of the modern French ledger is "doit," and of the German ledger is "soll," both clearly derived from "he shall give." The Italian ledger, however, indicates the debit side by "dare" (give) rather than "deve" (shall), but the English ledger uses "Dr" (debtor). This English form is clearly different from all the rest; yet those journal entries which used the word "owe" imply the sense of "he shall give" more directly than do those entries which use the word "debitor."

These phrases all express the same basic idea; the differences are only variations in emphasis. Clearly the idea of "give" was directly associated with debits and "have," with credits. The debit side of a bilateral account was the "give" side, and the credit side was the "have" side.

These ledger entries reflect three characteristics: (1) They were complete sentences. (2) They were written from a proprietor's own point of view. (3) They were memoranda of expected future events.

How would these ideas of framing ledger entries be stated as a general rule? We do not know; none of the early text writers reduced the process to a general rule.

Since they stated no general rule, we shall then frame one for ourselves. The following hypothetical rules are offered in the attempt to reduce to simple, concise statements the ideas of transaction analysis which seem to have been at the basis of the formulation of double entry:

(1) A sum is to be entered as "shall give," if the person involved is obliged to return to me at a later date an equivalent for what he has just now received from me.

(2) A sum is to be entered as "shall have," if the person involved is entitled to receive from me at a later date an equivalent of what he has just now given me.[10]

These statements of principle may be abbreviated somewhat as follows:

(1) X shall give what he now receives, i.e., Dr. X.

(2) Y shall receive what he now gives, i.e., Cr. Y.

Still further shortened, the rule becomes:

(1) Debit what shall be given (to me).

(2) Credit what shall be received (from me).

By a process of deduction, we conclude that the early medieval Italians *might have* analyzed business transactions by the help of some such rules. Whether they did or not, we do not know; yet to us it would seem logical from the way the ledger entries themselves were stated.

In contrast with these "deduced" Italian rules, notice the clearly stated general rules which appear when the Italian method is first made available in the English language.

ENGLISH GENERAL RULES
Oldcastle (1543), Peele (1569), Mellis (1588)[11]

There is a rule . . . to be learned by rote as by reason . . . all things received or the receiver must owe to all things delivered or to the deliverer.

.

[10] Compare with the following German explanation of the technical terms Debit and Credit: "Der Empfaenger eines Wertes wurde als Schuldner, der einen Gleichwert geben soll, mit 'soll,' der Geber eines Wertes hingegen als Glaeubiger, der einen Gleichwert zu empfangen hat, mit 'hat,' Besw. 'Haben,' bezeichnet."—"Buchhaltungslexikon," by Stern, p. 560.

[11] Quoted by P. K. in *Accountant*, January 16, 1926.

Dafforne (1660)[12]

Whatsoever cometh to us [whether money or wares] for proper, factorope, or Company account, the same is Debitor.
Whatsoever goeth from us [whether money or wares] for Proper, Factorope, or Company account, the same is Creditor.

In essence the role is: debit what is received by me; credit what is given by me. Compare the time-focus of the essence of the earlier Italian entry phrasing: debit what shall be given to me; credit what shall be received from me.

It is not mere chance that the Italians emphasized the future in their technical "words of accountability" (shall give), while the English emphasize the present (what is received). Neither nation could hardly have taken another point of view and been consistent with the environment in which their accounting first developed.

Italian bookkeeping began with the records of moneylenders and dealers in exchange. Mere detached memoranda sufficed—records of unclosed transactions were written on the spot. Records of expectations and obligations were a necessity for lenders and depositors. An exchange of one type of coins for those of another country needed no records. The moneylender's vital interest lay in the future; his thoughts constantly ran in that direction. His memoranda, couched in the words of his thought and interest, therefore naturally laid stress on such future-pointing phrases as "shall give" and "shall have."

The whole fabric of British thought, however, was very different. At the time their first accounting methods were being developed, they were not yet a nation of traders. Money exchange was not an important function as it was with the Italians who were traders. Early British accounting—charge and discharge—was developed within the self-sufficing communities of the feudal days. There, not external trade for profit, but control of internal operations within the extensive manor house and landed estates was the objective. Events happening at the time were therefore more important to record than events expected to happen in the future.

(*Accounting Review*, June, 1926)

8. Stewardship or Proprietorship

Although Great Britain, like all other countries, ultimately adopted Italian methods of bookkeeping, the English had made extensive prior use of "charge and discharge" records. This system was well suited to local needs in the thirteenth and fourteenth century, when accounting problems were centered in the control of a multitude of internal activi-

[12] Geisjbeek, *Ancient Double Entry Bookkeeping,* quoting entries from Dafforne that were dated 1630-34.

ties in the self-contained British landed estates. When trade and commerce became important, Italian bookkeeping proved more suitable.

The feudal system was closely knit for all of its self-sufficing manors and villages. The essence of the system was an unbroken chain of "fealty" extending from the king through the whole of society down to the humblest serf and artisan. Authority extended from the top downward, and all of the authority and privileges which were parceled out to those lower on the scale carried definite obligations in return. Everyone had a well-developed sense of dependence upon another and of being responsible to him. Everyone felt himself accountable to an immediate superior and acted as if he were in some degree the latter's agent.

This social background, so different from the life of the individual in Italy, produced a very different kind of "recording-need" and a very different attitude toward the ends to be accomplished by the records.

Feudalism produced an atmosphere of "agency" and "stewardship" rather than "ownership" and "proprietorship," as in the more commercial Italy. None but the king was absolute sovereign over his property with full and free power to dispose of it without consulting the plans or will of another. The nobles held their lands under the king's pleasure, and the peasant tenants held such land as they used solely under their noble master's pleasure. English "business" in the thirteenth and fourteenth centuries was confined to small artisans and peddlers—nothing to call up any sort of record-keeping. The largest activity was the maintenance of the manor house and its self-sufficing community.

The only "big business" of the day was the management of the nobles' estates and their large households. The management of the noblemen's manors was delegated to stewards or bailiffs. The relationship between baron and bailiff was that of principal and agent.[13] While the steward was an important dignitary in the nobleman's household, the limitation of his powers was well defined. Although he might possess, control, and dispose of various kinds and amounts of assets, he did so only through delegated authority. The property itself was not his; he held no lawful title to any of it. The use and disposition of what he controlled was not according to his own discretion but according to his master's instructions.

The steward could not be said to be indebted for whatever he might hold. Not owning it, he could not owe for it; not having borrowed, he could not be pressed for an equivalent. He was under no necessity of paying for what he held. He could return what was placed in his charge, or he could report it as consumed in the natural course of events. In a

[13] See P. V. B. Jones, *The Household of a Tudor Nobleman,* University of Illinois Studies in Social Science, Vol. VI, No. 4 for an intimate picture of English life built largely upon information in household account books between 1462 and 1640. By this time the function of "bailiff" or "steward" had been expanded in many establishments to include a chamberlain, a steward, a treasurer, and a comptroller. The duke of Norfolk, for example, in 1483 had a "receiver" who collected the rents, etc. and an "auditor" for "taking the accompt," as well as a steward and a comptroller.

word, property placed in his control and profits coming to him through the use of property were not his own, but only his *to account for.*

These were the characteristics of "stewardship" and grew naturally out of the activities of the times and the type of social organization then prevalent. *The man who borrowed* from a moneylender in medieval Venice was a debtor in fact; but the steward in medieval England was far from being a debtor. The steward was put *in charge* of property, of incomes, of expenditures; he was *charged* with whatever he was made responsible for. A *charge* was something to be explained; a satisfactorily explained charge was called for a *discharge.* When the steward could satisfactorily explain how he had disposed of his responsibilities, he was *discharged* of what he had been previously *charged.*

Observe that a discharge was inconceivable before a charge had taken place; one could not be discharged if he had never been charged. Under the charge and discharge system of records, what we would call a credit could not appear first, because a credit (discharge) could only explain what had happened to something previously given under this system.

A tabular statement of some of the various transactions which would produce a charge to the steward and of some of the acts which would discharge him will help to summarize the characteristics of stewardship.

The steward would

Charge himself for:	*Discharge* himself by:
1—Items of Property put in his care.	1—Old items of property given in even exchange.
2—New items of property received in even exchange.	2—Items consumed (finally or in production).
3—Natural increases, as in crops, cattle, etc.	3—Gifts, etc. (authorized).
4—Gifts, etc.	4—Losses by accident, disease, or exchange.
5—Gains and profits on exchanges of property.	5—Return of the property intact (inventory).

Clearly, the charges were values which were *received* by the one doing the recording and not values for which the person charged must pay ("shall give"). The point of view of the one making these records was that of one who had received the charges;[14] the point of view of the one making the early Italian entries in accounts with persons, on the other hand, was that of one who records the obligation of another ("he shall give" rather than "I have received").

In a similar way, the discharges summarized above were values *given up* by the one doing the recording and not values which the recorder

[14] An English writer in the late thirteenth or early fourteenth century says: "He who renders account ought to swear that he will render a lawful account and faithfully account for *what he has received* of the goods of his lord, and that he will put nothing in his roll save what he has, to his knowledge, spent lawfully and to his lord's profit." Woolf, *A Short History of Accountants and Accountancy,* p. 85, quoting from Lamond's edition of Walter of Henley's "Husbandry." The italics are by the present writer.

(as a creditor) would later have to pay. The point of view of the one making these entries in England was that of one who had given up (discharged) a responsibility; on the other hand, the point of view of the one making the (credit) entry in Italy was that of one who records the expectations of another ("he shall have" rather than "I shall give").

The English steward was intent upon keeping "my" account so that "I" may be able to report properly to my lord, the Earl of Whatnot. The Italian moneylender, however, was intent upon keeping "his" account (an account with "him," another person) so that the debtor, if need arose, could be confronted with *his* account, that is, the acknowledgment of the debt practically in his own words, e.g., "I, Francesco, shall give—etc." In case the creditor should later lay claim to more than he had deposited, the money-changer could confront the creditor with *his* account stated practically in the words of the verbal transaction.

As a result of this background, a "debit" in Great Britain came to mean a charge and since a charge was something received, therefore the rule: "Debit what is received."

That kind of rule for handling the Italian methods was understandable on the basis of previously conceived ideas and was, for that reason, easier to grasp than strange new ideas about "debitors" and "creditors."

The conclusion is nothing momentous—men thought differently and very much according to the circumstances under which they lived. Their ideas were relative to the time and place of their activities.

Italy had its own environment and its own type of activities; Great Britain had its type. Each country produced a good method for recording those financial occurrences which to the people concerned seemed to warrant recording. It is not surprising that the methods were different, although originated at about the same time, and that pre-existing ideas should color imported ideas. This is to be expected. That the two systems should so well fit together when finally laid side to side, however, is something of a surprise.

The systems existed side by side for many years; even today the heritage of charge and discharge records is found in executor accounting, where it still is quite appropriate. But only the fittest survive among methods as well as among plants and animals. Italian double entry was the more flexible, the more fitted to survive. Double entry was basic and it was broad; charge and discharge was suited only to certain rather limited conditions. Double entry survived early competition from the British system and it has survived later competition from other systems —Logismorgraphy, Statsmorgraphy *et al.*—as well. We can now see that it is suitable under all sorts of conditions and is capable of tremendous expansion in respect to physical volume of material recorded. Yet, throughout all of the many situations in which we find double entry useful and throughout all of the expansion we have ever seen or can conceive of, there runs a thread of fundamental logic which is unescapable and which unites what would otherwise be chaotic memoranda into a harmonious whole. Therein lies its superiority.

The same thread of logic ran through the first completed structure of double entry in the fourteenth century just as it does today. No alterations in basic fundaments have taken place since that time. This is not the case because the world that has used double entry since the Middle Ages has been so conservative that it has not tinkered to improve its instrument. Tinkering there has been in plenty, but that tinkering has resulted only in the improvement of the technique of operation, in the clarity of the description of the processes, and in the extension of accounting's sphere of usefulness. Experimentation and adaptation have never disturbed the fundamental logic. The old Italian moneylenders and traders got out a "basic patent," and that was about 500 years ago. It was, and still is, basic because their problem was to record most usefully the facts about the trading activities of profit-seeking proprietors. They succeed because, somehow, they hit upon account categories which integrated asset and liability transaction effects with the effects of loss and gain transactions. Since profit-seeking enterprises continue to exist and function, the integration of data about financial transactions and economic transactions is still highly useful—perhaps more necessary today than ever before. Under such circumstances double entry can still serve society well. Its virtue is not age, but continued usefulness.

(*Accounting Review,* June, 1926)

9. Early Managerial Techniques

As an approach to comparing the old and the new, we might first take note of some familiar modern ideas about good management and adequate accounting.

In order to operate an enterprise well, management will need to plan future operations and maintain close control over materials and activities. One of the most useful techniques of planning is forward budgeting. Its figures will be based on known intentions decided by high-level authority and on knowledge of the results of prior activities that grew out of prior planning. This necessary knowledge derives from detailed records, i.e., accounting, periodically compacted into summary reports.

Of the many techniques of managerial control, several can perhaps be called essential. (1) Set up an operating organization and carefully provide for subdivided duties. It may be helpful if production standards are established as a guide to workers and supervisors. (2) Provide trained personnel, plus suitable supervision, frequent inspection, etc. (3) Tie record-keeping into the operating activities. This will call for establishing a system of internal check and a systematic testing of the interlocking records. (4) Supplies will need to be kept under lock and key when not

under the eye of responsible employees. (5) Separation will be maintained
between the activities of recording the collection and disbursement of
cash on the one hand and those of reporting on income-producing activities and the authorization of payments. (6) Periodical inventories will
be taken that can be traced back into cash transactions. (7) Set up internal audit procedures for employees and provide for re-audit of the
results of dependable and skilled representatives of management.

This outline obviously is not a complete indication of the relation
between modern management and modern accounting. No mention is
made above of independent professional accountants. This was premeditated, because the period selected to reveal the old ideas is clearly different from the present in this respect. Another notable difference lies in
the fact that the factory system and mass production had not yet appeared. Important as the differences are, they nevertheless are overshad-
owed by many similarities, in spite of the intervening four centuries.
If the above outline of management planning and control is reasonably
indicative of present practice, we are in a position to look for some details about these similarities.

The reader may be surprised to find the essence of so many of these
modern practices reflected in the activities of so long ago. The elapsed
four hundred years would take our thought back to a period centering
about 1553. The time would be close to the date of the voyages of
Columbus.

The notes which follow about early practices trace back to a bibliography consisting in large part of household account books and estate
management instructions preserved from use in sixteenth century England. The records, with some overlapping and some empty periods, extend from 1462 to 1640. These old records and much other material were
examined more than thirty years ago by Paul V. B. Jones, now professor
emeritus of history at the University of Illinois. His analysis was published in 1917 by the University under the title, *The Household of a
Tudor Nobleman*.[15]

Items from this fascinating account have been selected in order to give
point to the thought that many of the nobility of that time were good
businessmen, although they did not operate commercial enterprises. They
were forced by circumstances to become good administrators. In maintaining their way of life, they had to make a business out of managing
productively their large land holdings and controlling effectively the
activities of possibly two hundred employees. Since most nobles of that
time had important responsibilities associated with the activities of king
and court, they had to build an organization at home that could operate
dependably in their absence. To establish and control an active organization, even through trusted officers, calls for an amount of good man-

[15] Studies in the Social Sciences, Vol. VI, No. 4.

agerial judgment that is not often revealed to us in our usual sources of knowledge of the people of this era—the books we read, the plays we see.

Note first the chief officers of a typical sixteenth century landed estate. Below the earl or duke who owned the estate under the king were the following. The receiver-general (a man we probably would call treasurer) collected the land rents, paid cash to other household officers on the duke's warrant, and kept a record of his receipts and payments. Note that his payments were covered by written authorization and that his collections were made verifiable by the work and records of another officer, the surveyor. The latter had the duties of judging the character and usefulness of all sections of the nobleman's land, of reporting to the duke on current and prospective employment of the lands, and of preparing a book of rentals and other incomes.

Just below these officers were steward, comptroller, and auditor. The steward paid the wages and fees as directed, using funds supplied by the receiver-general. The comptroller might today be called inspector or perhaps supervisor of internal control. As to the auditor, he was described in an old record in these words: "He is to bee judge betwixte the lords and his accomptants, and to deale trulie for and betweene all parties, and upon the determination of his audite, to presente to his lorde by books or breviate, all his receipts, expenses, imprests, whatsoever, with the remaines of money, if any bee . . ." (from p. 143 regarding accounts audited by Thomas Clay in 1612). More about the auditor later.

These officers were not clerks, but executives with clerks to assist them. Frequently they were knights, and some were earls' sons who were in training for managerial responsibilities on their home estate. Many employees with smaller responsibilities, as we shall see, also had clerical assistants. The officers were expected to guard against extravagance and to exercise careful control over supplies. These duties involved a daily tour of inspection into each department—at unannounced hours, let it be noted—and they were to report to the duke both "misdemeanors" and "zealous painstaking."

Several modern business practices are clearly foreshadowed in this type of organization. There was a carefully selected and experienced group of executives working under a single leader who was himself active in the affairs at hand. Plainly visible is a logical separation of the duties and the responsibilities of each executive; yet the duties of all dovetail, and the responsibilities of all are interrelated. Persons charged with responsibilities kept detailed records of pertinent facts and actions. The records were audited by a third party who, even four hundred years ago, stood without bias between two parties at interest "to deale trulie for and betweene all parties."

To me the fascinating part of history is found in such spots as these which show us that some of the present is not so new after all, and in those parts which help us to see that the old is not merely reproduced generation after generation. Thus we come to realize that the practices of today are not good or bad because they are old. Then, as now, the actions taken in business and accounting were taken because they were judged in their particular setting to be useful and adequate. If judged no longer useful, they will be dropped; if no longer adequate, they must be modified. We may well be proud of the present, provided we can be sure we are improving when a change is made.

We should now look at the lower echelons of the old manor house organization. Most of the names of the work places are self-explanatory and easily converted into the titles of the respective workers. Stable, woodyard, granary, butchery—these terms tell of a rural setting, of fields, animals, and forest. Here are some others: armory, wardrobe, larder, bakehouse, brewhouse, kitchen—these are divisions within the manor house itself.

More puzzling terms are those of "buttery," "ewery," "catery." The butler in the buttery was not in charge of butter, but beer. The ewerer had the care of towels and basins used at table for washing the hands before and after meals—this being before the day of forks. In addition, the ewerer was responsible for a valuable inventory of pewter and silver plate. The cator (caterer?) was expected to provide and care for the supply of fresh vegetables, dressed poultry, eggs, fish, etc.

These locations were not only work areas (production centers?), but recording centers as well. All provisions brought in, all that were used, and the amounts left at the end of each day, week, and year became a matter of record. Would we not call this "perpetual inventory?"

The following is part of an instruction for clerks of the kitchen. "Affore they maik any barganne for provisions [they] shall maik my Loorde privvy thereto . . . to the entent that they may know whether his Lordship will agre to the said prices or not. . . ." Each day's use of provisions was on specific order, and the instruction book tells us ". . . none dared under penalty to issue another thing from his stock but by special command." Except during hours of service the supplies were always under lock and key; all "keis" were brought to the countinghouse after each meal. If an servant's stock issue passed beyond normal, he was called to task. Another quotation tells us all supplies "that are boght [must] be entered forthwith in the Journall Booke when thei ar boght." Clerks of the kitchen made a constant round of inspection of operations and records. This was to see "that the service that is appointed in the Booke of Direcions . . . be observed and kept without abridgement."

These old practices clearly have modern equivalents. Our work specialization in production centers has progressed far, but only in extension of a principle. Work in progress is still inspected and checked against production standards, but not always against a "Booke of Direcions," as in the sixteenth century. Control today is exercised by a flow of work orders and other directives rather than by a manual of instructions. Perpetual inventories are now commonplace; valuable tools and materials are as carefully safeguarded as ever, although the "keis" will not be delivered into our equivalent of the "countinghouse."

Perhaps some day historians will bring together in sequence the story of the many stages through which business methodology has passed. It would be fascinating reading, and no doubt would indicate that progress comes less from inspired inventions than bit by bit out of adaptations and improvements.

The remaining topic for these notes touches more closely upon accounting as such. The countinghouse, as already indicated, was a department in its own right. But lest accountants sigh for the good old days, let me point out that bookkeeping operations began at 7 A.M. and continued to 8:30 P.M.

Today we regard internal check very highly. So did these men of affairs four hundred years ago. It was not unusual for independently kept records to be matched as a test or proof. For example, the gentlemen ushers supervising meal service in the great hall made records of the food used at each meal. These facts could then be compared with issue records kept in the kitchen and other departments. And the issue records could be matched at any time against the same person's record of incoming provisions and unused inventory. Moreover, the records of baker and pantler were expected to agree as to bread delivered and used. Brewer and butler crosschecked as to beer; the slaughterman was checked against the larderer (as to meat), against the glover (as to hides), and against the "chaundler" (as to tallow for candles). Furthermore, the baker, the larderer, and the brewer must produce a predetermined amount of bread, meat, and beer out of a stated amount of materials received. Surely this tells of both internal check and production standards.

Faced with managerial craftsmanship such as this, we will not be surprised to see them use budgeting also. We are told it was customary to estimate a year in advance the need for food, cloth, fuel, and other commodities. The duke and his council approximated the price of all supplies and scheduled the times at which stated amounts of money should be transferred to designated household officials. As if this planning (budgeting) was not enough, the duke and council determined the menus of all meals for the next year, with specified extra dishes for the feast days. These decisions, no doubt, were the basis for supervisors in the kitchen to calculate daily requirements in provisions issue.

Along with forward budgeting and close control over planned operations, frequent inventories enabled management to observe the extent to which procurement and issue were kept faithful to the budget. Clerks of the kitchen, spicery, granary, etc. made monthly summaries and inventories for their departments under the eyes of the comptroller's clerks. The countinghouse clerks assembled these reports into a total of household expenses and a "Bill of Remainder," the latter being described as "the Remaineth of such Stuf as remains unspent provided and bought in the year aforesaid."

The arrangement of monetary data in statement form before audit showed a simple, if detailed, contrasting of receipts and disbursements. First were the rents collected from tenants; then receipts were listed from sale of wood, hay, etc. Following these, the expenses were reported; the details were grouped in subsections. Under each group of details and for the totals and balance, the auditor indicated his verification by writing "Ex per T.C. auditor" (examined by Thomas Clay, auditor). Part of the year-end procedure was called "declaration of audit" and was carried out in the presence of the duke, the receiver, the surveyor, the auditor, and the other members of the domestic council. In attendance were representatives from each department, for example, "the Yoman of the Beddes that staunds charged with my Lord his wardrobe Stuf." Each was presumably present to answer questions and perhaps orally to substantiate the facts of his department from personal knowledge.

It is not unlikely that this assembly was instituted to enable the council to study the cash transactions, serving reports, and remaining stock of supplies, in relation to the budget and "Booke of Direcions" provided to guide operations. The scheme of internal check and departmental records led naturally to an inventory report as proof of compliance. And the cash warrants for money transferred to officers tied the cash reporting to physical facts reflected in the inventory, the latter being that part of authorized disbursements not yet consumed. The whole of the data there assembled not only served for review purposes but also provided the basic information for the duke and council to use in making estimates for the next year, thus to start the operating cycle once more.

Accountants of today are familiar with the "charge and discharge" form of statement, since this is often used now in reporting to the courts on the management of a trusteed estate. It is, therefore, not difficult mentally to project backward such a scheme of reporting and catch a glimpse of the same kind of reporting four centuries ago.

The kind of recording, of control and audit here described, antedated English knowledge of Italian double-entry records, although this had been in use in Italy for some time. Even after an English textbook made double entry available (1553), it seems to have been put in use but slowly during the next one hundred years.

Management of the household of the typical Tudor nobleman therefore was skillfully conducted without benefit of the antecedent of modern bookkeeping. In some respects, however, the English method was superior to the Italian. In the latter there was at that early day very little of financial statement arrangement, of internal check, or independent audit. After Italian methods were adopted in England came the wedding of English managerial accounting and Italian business accounting. The issue from that union we call "modern accounting" and include in that term not only accounting for mercantile business but for estates, governmental divisions, manufacturing corporations, and other organizations as well.

We may justly take pride in our intricate modern techniques and the professional status of our independent auditors. Yet we can well afford now and then to acknowledge a large intellectual debt to generation after generation of unknown contributors to our art. Perhaps it is not inappropriate to add that future generations will be able to thank the men of today for striving in their turn to make accounting ever more dependable and increasingly of service to management as well as to investors. Improvements from the past fifty years plainly indicate continuing development. What reason could we find for believing that accounting development is now complete?

(*Accounting Review*, April, 1954)

10. Bookkeeping by Rule

The first bookkeeping texts did not generalize upon transaction analysis to the extent of stating rules for resolving transactions into debits and credits. And it is doubtful whether the early authors resorted to personification of impersonal accounts. But later such rules and personification of accounts became the mainstay of text-writers, especially those writing in English.

With the use of the old terminology, personification would be quite unnecessary; the term "shall give" is clearly equivalent to "yield up"; thus even an impersonal moneychest account could "yield up" what had been placed in it and could "receive back" ("shall have") what had earlier been abstracted—all this without resort to analogy to a person owing or being trusted.

However, when the left side of every account came to be called, in translation, "debitor" and the right "creditor," personification was implied in the words themselves; and rules appeared which directed that transactions affecting impersonal accounts be resolved into debits and credits, as if each account represented a person. No doubt transaction data of the day found its way into the proper accounts by use of this artificial reasoning. Yet much of the clear logic embodied in the Italian technical terms of ledger accounts was lost for generations in a sea of specific rules.

Simon Stevin (1604) introduces personification in his textual explanations in this manner: "Suppose that someone by the name of Peter owed some money on account of which he paid me 100 L. and I put the money in a cash drawer just as if I gave it the money for safekeeping. I then say the cash drawer owes me that money, for which reason [just as if it were a human being] I make it debtor." [16]

Richard Dafforne (1636) makes a similar phrasing of the explanation of the entry for cash invested: "Q—How booke you the Ready money after the way of Debitor and Creditor? A—Cash Debitor to Stock. Q—Why make you Cash Debitor? A—Because Cash [having received my money unto it] is obliged to restore it again at my pleasure: for Cash representeth [to me] a man to whom I [only upon confidence] have put my money into his keeping; the which by reason is obliged to render it back or give to me an account what is become of it. . . ." [17]

Impersonal accounts in an early day would undoubtedly have been hard to teach as abstractions. Cash account as an abstraction, that is, as a more or less statistical subdivision of enterprise total property, would be more difficult to grasp than an arbitrary analogy to the account of the person owning the enterprise. The simple and logical manner of the presumably customary transaction analysis of the Italian method became much obscured when the apparently conscious inclusion of "proprietor" in every transaction analysis fell into neglect in translation. Perhaps a sort of simplification of analysis was thus achieved, even though logical reasoning suffered in the process. Yet this was no more than artificial simplification, for no amount of fiction can successfully make a fundamentally complex process actually simple.

The formulation of many rules of thumb was one of the results of this approach to teaching double entry. This development was particularly evident in the texts of the seventeenth and eighteenth centuries.

One of the early writers (Joannes Buingha, 1627)[18] presents his rules in the following compact tabulation:

Who the Debitor [or oweth] is:	Who the Creditor [or must have] is:
1. What we have	1. Whence it arriveth
2. Who so receiveth	2. Whoso giveth out
3. What we buy	3. Of whom we buy
4. Unto whom we sell	4. That which is sold
5. For whom we buy	5. They of whom we buy
6. Who so must pay	6. They that must have
7. For whom we pay	7. Wherewith we pay
8. What we cause to be insured	8. The assuror
9. For whom we insure	9. Insurance reckoning
10. Whither-wards we send	10. What we send away
11. That which is gained upon	11. That which is lost
12. Profit and losse	12. Profit and Losse

[16] P. Kats, *Institute of Bookkeeper's Journal* (London, September, 1927).
[17] Richard Dafforne, *Merchant's Mirror,* bound with Malynes, *Lex Mercatoria* (3d ed., London, 1686).
[18] H. J. Eldridge, *Evolution of the Science of Bookkeeping* (London, 1931), p. 34.

The greater part of the usual text that emphasized the use of rules consisted of rehearsing individual transactions in great variety and showing them made into debitors and creditors by application of a cited rule. The student had to learn transaction analysis not by reason, but by rote.

John Mair[19] compressed his rules into six, including such as these: "A thing received is Debtor to the thing given for it; In cases where personal and real Debtors and Creditors are wanting, the defect [sic] must be supplied by fictitious ones."

Following these rules, the author devotes fifty pages to applying the rules to many different situations. The aim, apparently, was to include every conceivable type of transaction in domestic and foreign trade. Mair's transactions distinguish seven situations involving purchase of goods; seven situations for goods sold; for barter, four; for money received, twelve; for money paid, fourteen.

Despite what may today seem dreary formalism through the application of rules and personification of impersonal accounts, progress was evident. Textbooks have always served as teaching devices; and progress in text-writing has been evidenced whenever increased effort has been expended to reach the student's understanding. Texts of the fifteenth century were purely descriptive. Paciolo presented "the method of Venice." There was no theory and very little explanation of the thought processes involved. Presumably the latter was the function of the teacher to provide, out of his experience, to supplement the text. Perhaps many teachers, even of that day, would be content if their students learned to do the necessary without pressing for excursions into the reasoning processes back of the expected actions. Very likely double entry seemed very complicated in the fifteenth century, at a time when solving a problem in long division was the work of a professor of mathematics (as Paciolo was).

Double entry is still complex, as any beginning student in the subject will testify. It would be easier now if, as in an earlier day, one had only to memorize some rules. The direction of educational evolution, however, has been toward revealing the thought process by means of which a wide variety of transactions may be understood, and systematically and logically translated into quasi-statistical categories called accounts. Because thought processes are revealed, the modern study of accounting becomes one more avenue for stimulating mental development and clear reasoning.

The text-writers who, in the seventeeth and eighteenth centuries moved from pure description into rules for analyzing transactions into debits and credits were improving on the teachability and understandability of the earlier textbooks. Yet there was room for still further improvement. The method did not do much to develop a power of logical rea-

[19] John Mair, *Bookkeeping Methodized* (8th ed., Edinburgh, 1765).

soning and of thinking with abstractions. Yet rules are generalizations, that is, abstractions compressed out of a mass of experiences. Learning to recognize the applicability of a rule to a transaction is a step forward and is learning to think convincingly. The "mysteries" of double entry tend to retreat where accounts become carefully defined statistical categories, and where transaction analysis becomes a matter of rationally and reasonably sorting transaction data into a scheme of account—categories designed to make an incomprehensible mass of data more intelligible and thus more useful.

(Chapter 4, *Accounting Evolution to 1900*)

11. Accounts Become Categories

As soon as similar transaction data were recorded on a designated page, that page became in fact a statistical category. Yet it may well be doubted that the page was clearly perceived in this light. Ledger accounts began as memory aids of items having future significance, e.g., "he shall give." A separate page was merely a convenient aid to finding an item in the record associated with a certain person. This conception was so thoroughly attached to ledger accounts that, when impersonal and nominal accounts came into use, personification of these was used by text-writers in teaching students to convert transaction data into ledger entries. Only in relatively modern times, and after a slow evolution in ways of thinking, was an account consciously considered as a classification category and transaction analysis taught accordingly.

The development through which the ledger account passed presents several stages, each with its own distinguishing characteristics. The first period extends from 1396, the date of the earliest ledger account to come to the writer's hand, to about 1600. Three examples of ledger accounts are available, dated 1396, 1436, and 1588. These will be reproduced and discussed in order.

(A Ledger Account of 1396)
MCCCLXXXXVI

Joint gains and losses of the firm of J . . . . . D . . . . . and M . . . . . S . . . . . at C . . . . . , should give (*debet dare*) for joint expenses incurred on behalf of the firm on Dec. 28, written in the credit (*scriptos in credito*) of M . . . . . S . . . . . at folio 6 . . . . £12, s17, d14

Joint gains and losses should have (*debet habere*) for partable gains in Milan from 46 bales of cloth sent to L . . . . . D . . . . . in exchange, on Dec. 28, written in the debit (*scriptos in debito*) of M . . . . . S . . . . . at folio 6 . . . . £52, s10, d . . .

This is a part of the profit and loss account from a mercantile partnership ledger found in the Duomo of Milan.[20] The extract contains a charge to joint account for certain expenses incurred by one of the

[20] Free translation of the Latin by P. K. in *Accountant*, March 27, 1926.

partners and a credit for merchandise gains. It will be observed that the entries are stated in complete sentences and contain clear references to both aspects of the transaction. Each ledger entry therefore contains the essentials of a complete journal entry and is not merely the posting of one side of a transaction.

The terms which have particular technical significance are translated literally, the Latin of the original being shown in parentheses. These words or their derivatives are used in most examples of ledger accounts but do not usually appear in journal entries. In the latter debit and credit were usually indicated by *per* (by) and *a* (to). It will be noted that the contra reference in a debit entry does not make use of *debet habere* as we would expect. Instead the phrase *scriptos in credito* (written in the credit side) is used together with the title of the account there concerned. Thus it appears that *debito* and *credito* were used as nouns naming the respective sides of an account; *debet dare* and *debet habere* were verb forms used to indicate the action expected of the account or person involved.

(A Ledger Account of 1436)[21]

G . . . . . B . . . . . must give (*de dare*) on 8th March s4, d4 per G . . . . . V . . . . . , to whom credited on folio 13 . . . . . £ . . . . . , s4, d4	G . . . . . B . . . . . must have (*den avere*) on 8th March £19, s11, d11, by the B . . . . . Co. of London, debited to them, folio 4 . . . . . £19, sll, dll

This portion of an account is from the ledger of the London branch of a large Italian firm, *Filippo Borromeo e comp.*, and is stated in very much the same form as the previous example, being a complete statement of the transaction with the usual contra references. In this account, however, the title is repeated in the first entry on the credit side but is not repeated in subsequent entries in the same account either on the debit or credit side.

The verbs, which were in the process of becoming technical phrases, are in this example unchanged in meaning although differently spelled. This is due to the fact that the 1396 account was stated in Latin while the 1436 account was in Italian. The terminology is contrasted below.

Debit	Credit
Latin: *debet dare* (should give)	Latin: *debet habere* (should have)
Italian: *de dare* (must give)	Italian: *den avere* (must have)

This is an interesting example of the evolution of terminology. The Italian form is directly descended from the Latin. In modern Italian bookkeeping the left side of a ledger account is still called *Dare* and the right, *Avere*.

The next example is from a text by John Mellis (England, 1588). There is some reason for thinking that Mellis did little but reprint an earlier work by one Hugh Oldcastle (1543). If this be true, the following

[21] Extract by P. K. in *Accountant*, January 16, 1926, from an article by Dr. Gerolamo Biscaro in *Archivo Storico Lombardo* (Milan, 1913).

ledger account can be traced back to this, the earliest known work on double entry written in English.

A Ledger Account of 1588 (1543?)[22]

1587 Folio 1	1587 Folio 1
Aug. 8—Chest or Ready Money ought to give me (or is Debtor to Stock) £, s, d for so much ready money in gold and silver I have this day in stock, as in credit, folio.......£, s, d	August. 12—The account of the Chest or Ready Money is due to have £, s, d, and is for so much lent R. B. as in his account in Debtor, folio ... £, s, d

Probably the most interesting feature in this example is the inclusion of both the older and the newer phraseology in the same entry. The account debited is mentioned at the beginning of the paragraph, and the contra account is mentioned at the end. The parenthetical expression in this ledger entry is nearly an identical copy of the phrasing of the journal entry from which the ledger entry was posted. Mellis' journal entry was as follows: "Chest or Money is Debtor (or owes) to Stock belonging to me. . . ."

In his ledger Mellis translates the technical terms *dee dare* and *dee havere* quite literally into English as "ought to give" and "is due to have." Yet, feeling no doubt that such a translation might not clearly carry the meaning to English readers, Mellis (or Oldcastle) also uses the very different alternative phrase "is debtor to." Elsewhere in his text he says, "all things received must owe all things delivered, as Money owes to William Hall." This rendition into English seems to have introduced a novel idea. It is questionable whether the older writers in saying, "Cash shall give to Peter," meant to imply that Cash owed Peter. It seems more likely that their thought was—Cash shall give [to the proprietor], and Peter shall have [from the proprietor]. The phrases here in brackets would probably be implied, since they were not written in the entry or explained in the textbooks.

Early in the next century certain modifications of the ledger account became evident in a manner suggesting that accounts were evolving in the direction of a simplified and abbreviated arrangement.

(A Ledger Account of 1604)

(Left Folio)				(Right Folio)			
Notes Debit	Year	1600		Notes Credit	Year	1600	
	£	s	d		£	s	d
30 Jan.				30 May			
Per capital fol. 3	144	0	0	Per Peter DeWitt			
28 March				fol. 10................	334	16	0
Per David Roels fo. 15	95	4	0	4 Aug.			
				Per pepper fol 16	20	0	0

[22] From a reproduction of Mellis' "Brief Instruction," by P. K. in *Accountant*, May 1, 1926.

Here, for the first time, the account begins to take on a modern appearance—to give less the appearance of narrative paragraphs and more the effect of tabulations.

The title of the account is definitely separated from the body of the entry and placed above the details. Together with the title stand the technical terms *debet* and *credit,* now clearly "labels" to the respective sides of the tabulation and no longer merely the verbs of complete sentences. Yet, it is to be noted, the words and phrases employed are not entirely without grammatical relationship, in spite of their altered spacial relationship. If we but substitute for "debet" the original verb form, "shall give," the left entry may be made to read: "Notes shall give [is debited], per capital credited on page 3." So the essence of the older practice of using complete sentences is still present, although perhaps somewhat obscured by the altered location of the significant words and by the translation of *dee dare* (shall give) as Debet and *dee havere* (shall have) as Credit.

The next example is from the English again and shows similarities both to Mellis (English) and to Stevin (Dutch), although the author, Richard Dafforne, refers directly in his preface only.to his indebtedness to Stevin. The book went through several editions between 1634 and 1648, and probably very definitely influenced later writers. The following ledger account is from the third edition.

(A Ledger Account of 1660)

Left Folio

Cash is Debitor		s	d
1 Jan. To Stock for several coynes of money	1000	15	7
27 Feb. To Jacob Symonson, his account current	328	10	11

Right Folio

Cash is Creditor			
4 Jan. By George Pinchback, paid in part	144	—	—
13 March. By Figs in Company, 3/5 R.R., 2/5 for me	8	7	6

It is clear from this example that the account title, even though set apart as a heading, is to be read with each entry thus making a complete sentence which states not only the debit but the contra credit as well. Thus the first entry on the debit side above is read:

    Cash is Debitor (in title)   to Stock (in entry)

Reading the heading of the credit side along with the entry gives:

    Cash is Creditor (in title)   by George Pinchback (in entry)

This is as much as to say for the credit: Cash is trusted by Pinchback; and for the debit it is as much as to say: Cash is indebted (owes) to Stock (i.e., Capital). Here again a too literal translation from Italian into English (via the Dutch, no doubt) has failed to reveal the essence of transaction analysis which rests within the old technical phrases. My cash cannot be said to *owe* Pinchback because he has now paid part of his prior debt to me. He has intrusted cash to me, the proprietor, trusting that I will forthwith reduce his debt accordingly.

From this point the evolution of the ledger account moves rapidly towards recognition as a classification category. The English practices were now fixed, and for two hundred years changes were few and unimportant. An account was written on two folios; account titles were established as page headings; the arrangement was less narrative and more in the nature of tabulations than formerly. By the middle of the nineteenth century the account was compacted to appear on one page, much as the following example.

(The 19th Century Type of Ledger Account)

Dr.			Bills Receivable			Cr.
1847				1847		
May 10	to Wm. Johnson	150.00		Nov. 10	by Cash	150.00

For over fifty years this was the prevailing type of account.[23] Indeed, it may be said to be still in use. The simple omission of the Dr. and Cr. abbreviations in the title and of the "to" and "by" references in the explanation columns will produce the ledger accounts in the form used in most ledgers in this country today where bookkeeping machines are not in use.

Clearly there was a growing tendency in this later period to treat the account as a tabulation of facts related to the title. Such details as were still entered in the body of the account seem to have been used more as brief explanations to the amounts rather than as avowedly cross references to the contra accounts concerned.

With the disappearance from most ledgers at about the turn of the century of the explanations, "to so and so" and "by so and so," there passed out of sight the last tangible suggestion in the ledger itself that each entry in an account expresses a complete thought resolvable into a grammatical sentence.

This, perhaps, is the most significant change in the evolution of the ledger account. Although at first sight it seems a very simple and natural alteration, it definitely marks the transition from a *personification* concept of accounts to a *statistical* concept. Accounts with cash, notes, etc., are no longer "debtors," much less "debtor to stock" or "debtor to John Doe," and the like. Accounts now show on their face nothing but title, date, posting reference, and amount. They are little more than the resting place of certain data, accumulated and tabulated perhaps without those most concerned having much knowledge of the whole of bookkeeping.

Indeed, in some cases modern twentieth century practice goes even

·

[23] Accounts of this kind are used in the illustrations in the following texts: Thos. Jones (New York, 1841); Duff (New York, 1848); Bryant and Stratton (Chicago, 1861); Mayhew (Detroit, 1870); and Bandy (New York, 1885).

beyond this and abandons the ledger account as a *form* entirely. In its place are statistical summaries which bear not the faintest physical resemblance to left- and right-sided ledger accounts. Figures are tabulated on long sheets and in columns for subclassifications, and maybe are thought of as "blacks" and "reds" instead of "debits" and "credits." Yet the results finally appear in financial statements not distinguishable from those differently derived.

The twentieth century is thus seen to be less concerned with form and more with substance; modern bookkeeping is less formal and yet more technical than the accounting of earlier days. As a result, bookkeeping no longer aims at classifying somewhat artificial *debt-relationships,* but at statistically, i.e., economically and accurately, *tabulating the changes* occurring in a great variety of those financial elements which in summary will reveal financial condition and the course of earnings.

It may well be that this important change in the point of view of bookkeeping derives largely from the searching analyses into bookkeeping method and philosophy made during the last quarter of the nineteenth century by such men as Charles E. Sprague in the United States, and J. F. Schär in Germany. Without the loosening of the chains of formalism which these writers helped so much to bring about, it seems doubtful whether the bookkeeping of a generation or two ago, if unchanged, would have been elastic enough to have served modern conditions effectively and to have facilitated the development of such aids to management as cost-finding, budgetary control, and the like.

Thus there has been a distinct evolution of the ledger account, as there has been of all bookkeeping in fact. That evolution has brought us very far indeed—farther than the meager outline of these paragraphs would indicate. Now that the fundamentally statistical nature of modern bookkeeping is definitely and widely perceived, the evolution of accounting will probably be further accelerated far beyond that witnessed in the past five hundred years.

(*Accounting Review,* December, 1926)

NINETEENTH CENTURY THEORY

1. Cronhelm and Jones

The nature of double entry and the place of its origin combine to suggest that a concept of proprietorship was an element of great importance in the creation of "records by the Italian Method." Early transaction analysis probably made extensive use of "proprietor" in bridging the chasm that we now see separating the reasoning behind simple account records of personal debt and the reasoning involved in proprietary bookkeeping in terms of integrated real and nominal accounts. All of the procedures of Italian double entry were directed toward the computation of proprietary profits and proprietary capital—which is to say, toward a measurement of the obviously related means of producing income and the income produced as a result of use of those means. Stated that way makes it clearer that double entry has always been a technical methodology serving a very significant purpose; it still serves the same purpose very well many centuries later under vastly different economic conditions.

The development of double entry that took place after Italian methods had been accepted into British usage was first one of formulating a multitude of rules for analyzing transactions into debts and credits. And, under the impact of a realization that the antecedent of Italian double entry had been personal accounts of debts receivable and/or payable, the rules devised by some authors personalized even impersonal accounts (e.g., "cash," as the account of Mr. Cashier) in an effort to make transaction analyses simple for learners.

By the nineteenth century a few text-writers recognized the pedagogical limitations in the current formalization of procedure into a multitude of rules. They began to seek out the logic and reasonableness which their knowledge of bookkeeping and their intuition told them must be buried in its procedures. Their rationalization of the fundamental nature of double entry probably was the real beginning of accounting theory. Their search for the keynote led them to proprietorship as the basic concept and the inspiration back of the peculiarities of bookkeeping methodology.

Two men in the eighteenth century (Alexander Malcolm, 1718; Hustcraft Stevens, 1735) pointed the way forward by writing briefly of the distinction between the totality of a proprietor's capital and the constituent parts—obviously a very useful perception of the nature of the balance sheet. They also saw that some transaction exchanges expressed

55

only changes among assets, or assets and debt, without change in quantity of proprietorship wealth; other transactions affected proprietorship "total capital" as increase or decrease at the same time that assets were affected.

Another author writing early in the nineteenth century (F. W. Cronhelm, 1818) gave his reader many lucid passages that reached into the logic lying within double entry.[1] He was convinced that "the clear and simple principle of the equality of the whole to the sum of its parts" was the basis of bookkeeping. In his second chapter he distinguishes "partial" and "complete" bookkeeping. In the former approach, capital is found simply by noting its known constituent parts and striking a total; under the other, proprietor's capital is computed by two distinct processes: (1) by finding the sum of the various parts of the proprietor's property; (2) by looking to the capital account for the figure telling of the whole property. The first of these elements obviously refers to the real accounts of the balance sheet; the second to the balance sheet net worth, that is, proprietor's investment plus and minus the gains and losses. We still use his idea that some of the constituent parts of property are "positive property," and some are "negative property." He then is in a position to indicate, and he does indicate, the presently familiar "balance sheet equation": positive property minus negative property equals stock. He does not use the modern phraseology since he is interested in pointing out that this equivalence between properties and capital shows that expense and income accounts are created to avoid the inconvenience of recording in proprietor's capital account every transaction which alters proprietorship total.

The essence of accounting theory reflected over a century ago in Cronhelm's writing is the concept of income as net increase in proprietorship. The later significance of this concept is that it is often used to lend support to later contentions that value increments (appreciation, price-level change) produce an increase in proprietorship; hence they possess the essential characteristics of profit.

In 1841, a New York accountant and teacher named Thomas Jones published a bookkeeping text, *Principles and Practices of Bookkeeping*, which marks him as an accounting pioneer whose insight into the logic of double entry was in notable contrast with that of most writers on the subject.

"The Theory of bookkeeping teaches the simplest and most intelligible method of recording and arranging financial transactions . . . the method of double entry enables us to unravel any mass of data and dispose of it in such a manner as to afford a clear and concise statement of the result of each and any successive steps of the merchant's progress."

The term "balance sheet approach" in 1927 had been in our vocab-

[1] For extracts, see *Accounting Evolution to 1900*, Chapter 11.

ularies but a scant half dozen years; yet this teacher of bookkeeping began his first chapter some eighty-five years earlier by stressing statements as a goal. And he shows from the beginning that bookkeeping is wholly focused upon that goal—"embracing only such facts as are absolutely indispensable—to a statement of the merchants' Resources, Liabilities, Gains, Losses, and Original Capital."

We pride ourselves upon our modern conception of bookkeeping as a special form of statistical methodology. Jones speaks of "mass of occurrences" and of the necessity of a "plan of arrangement" for them. Again, he mentions "mass of data" to be disposed of thus and so, and he speaks of "collections of facts" indispensable for certain purposes. Clearly he considered his material as statistical data and his method as one of the statistical classification.

In another place he compacts his view of the essence of double entry into two propositions:

The arrangement of double entry is based upon the following propositions. (1) If we can ascertain our resources and liabilities at any stated time, their comparison will determine the position of our affairs at that time. (2) If we determine the position [net worth?] in which our affairs stood at the commencement of any period of time and our gains and losses during that period we can therefore [thereby?] determine our position at the end of the period. [Net worth?]

Double entry then embraces two distinct plans of arranging the facts that have transpired in a business, each plan involving a distinct set of accounts [nominal and real?]; the one set fulfilling the conditions of the first proposition, the other those of the second; the agreement in the result of the two constitutes what is called the balance of the books.

Jones is here pointing to the fact that the profit and loss statement is co-ordinate (integrated) with the balance sheet. In the seventeenth century, Simon Stevin (1608) called the former calculation "proof of my estate," thus giving the balance sheet (Stevin called it "State of my Capital") a clear priority in importance. Jones makes a definite contribution to theory when he makes it clear that the two accounting statements are calculations designed to reach the same result by different paths. Net worth will be the same figure and constitute a test of the bookkeeping, when calculated as assets minus liabilities, and when calculated as prior net worth minus and plus summarized losses and gains. Today we would call the second calculations "income and surplus report." But the century of intervening time has not changed the fundamental characteristic of double entry so clearly perceived in 1841. When we examine the essential aspects of double-entry procedure back to Paciolo's day (1494), it is easy to see that the real essence behind the methodology had escaped the text-writers for many generations.

Jones must have impressed his readers with a realization of the significant interrelation of real and nominal accounts. Expenses and revenues were not mere plus and minus modifications, item by item, of proprietor's capital to him. Hence his concept of profit does not seem to have been that of proprietorship increase, as seems implicit in other writings. Thomas Jones must have believed that, instead of looking to the change in amount of assets for the clue to profit, we should seek to know profit by a calculation using recorded elements (nominal accounts) which would present the various factors expressive of profit causation as well as profit measurement. Clearly, two balance sheets calculating increase in net worth at different dates can only present a measured total of change. Such limited information could not adequately serve proprietorship, i.e., management, with useful information relative to the efforts made to produce desired increases in net assets.

In his third chapter, Jones makes this penetrating explanation: "Equality of debits and credits is the distinguishing feature of double entry; but instead of being, as commonly represented, a primary principle, it is a consequence of such as have been already discussed; without the help of which [equilibrium] necessarily cannot be established or demonstrated." Jones follows this exposition with a demonstration which convincingly reveals how he realized that the use of nominal accounts, rather than a duality of entry, is the really basic characteristic of double entry.

(Certified Public Accountant, June, 1927)

2. Hautschl, Augspurg, and Kurzbauer

This is not, as it may seem, the firm name of an accounting partnership in Germany. These are the names of three Europeans whose writings on bookkeeping show interesting common characteristics. They also show a thread of ideology not unlike that so well presented in the nineteenth century by the British author F. W. Cronhelm (1818) and the American author Thomas Jones (1841), and hinted by a few other writers of bookkeeping textbooks.

The element that makes these writings of interest at this time is the fact that in them we can see the beginnings of accounting theory as such —theory which we see even today epitomized in the equation "assets minus liabilities equals capital," or sometimes in a simplified form closer to the earlier ideas: "Property Kinds equal Total Proprietor Capital."

These writers were not conceiving a new basic idea; their contribution is related to their ability to frame verbal explanations of practices long in use. This, surely, is writing theory. No one acquainted with modern accounting and reading these explanations by nineteenth century writers can fail to see at once the same theory essence reflected, but not explained, in Paciolo's labored description in 1494 of the items and treatment of an entry for opening a set of account books. He directed that each individual item (property and debts) should be posted first to its own separate account and second, item by item, the same information should be brought into proprietor's capital account. Clearly, the idea (theory) back of the described practice was: "property kinds equals proprietor capital."

Franz Hautschl wrote a text (Vienna, 1840) which had a few pages of this kind of early theory. In translation, two of these areas follow: "At the beginning of business the merchant is doubly represented: (1) in the capital account where final gains and losses join the original assets and liabilities; (2) in the balance account where the latest assets and liabilities appear." The balance account has now fallen into disuse, but for some years it received year-end, real account balances in the same way that the profit and loss account received nominal account balances. By this device within the ledger (not by columnar worksheets as today), the elements of the two basic accounting statements were assembled and compactly presented to the reader.

The other two German authors presented more comprehensive explanations and, as a result, make the theory more understandable. Their texts were epitomized in 1898 by a Swiss author (Hügli-Buchhaltungstudien) who became interested in bookkeeping history. Any quotations used below are translations; some of the terms, as is to be expected, are not easily rendered into our terminology.

Hügli says that the two authors, G. D. Augspurg of Brennen (first edition, 1852) and George Kurzbauer of Vienna (editions in 1850 and 1867), "have hit upon the way to a natural theory of double-entry bookkeeping which is in full agreement with existing facts and is free from fictions and suppositions." We can readily agree with this conception of theory. Explanations (agreeing with the facts) present a kind of "theory" which is quite different from "theory" consisting of imaginative hypotheses (fiction). Yet it should be added the latter approach to understanding may sometimes of necessity have to be the first step towards theory that does explain known facts. Each kind of theory therefore has its own kind of usefulness.

Augspurg pointed out that double-entry bookkeeping consists in keeping side by side two sets of accounts. This view received the designation *Zweikonten Theorie* from the fact that one of the two sets of accounts presented proprietorship net properties (*reine Vermögen*) and the other presented the individual items of property (*Vermögensbestandteile*).

The reciprocal agreement of the two totals was considered to prove the arithmetical correctness of the records. This explanation is more helpful than usage described without explanation; yet it will be noted that "prove" is too strong a term since the only thing tested by a trial balance is whether every transaction debit has had a credit of equal amount. Such arithmetical accuracy is of vastly less significance than is accuracy of classification—every item in the proper account. No doubt this may not have been so important a distinction in the fifteenth century, at a time when mathematics was new and difficult and perhaps beyond most people, as it is in the twentieth century, where complexity of transaction effects poses far greater problems of classification than does our machine-made arithmetic.

Augspurg was also concerned with a peculiarity of double entry which may still bother instructors of elementary accounting, that is, the fact that some account balances are increased by debit entries while in other accounts increases fall into credit. He says: ". . . just as it is impossible to deliver the same article to two different people at the same time, it is impossible to debit an article at the same time to two different accounts. Because the aspects of a transaction have to express an opposite effect and a systematic control over each other, they are reciprocally related." But it would take more theory than this to explain why the plus and minus characteristic of assets and expenses are alike and those of liabilities and proprietorship are alike, but different from assets.

Out of his analysis of oppositeness, Augspurg concludes ". . . we establish as the basis of the whole system the principle that the account for the investment as a whole, called capital account, stands as creditor opposite to the accounts of positive property, and as debitor opposite to the negative property." In another place he makes this penetrating observation: "Strictly speaking the property accounts are stewardship accounts since basically they represent loans from a capital account. In opening a set of books one can imagine that at first the whole of the property is united in the possession of the capital account, and that the administration of the assets and liabilities is given over to the property accounts."

From the vantage point of modern ideas about accounting theory, it is not difficult to see that the principal deficiency in these explorations of theory a century ago lay in the neglect to dig deeper into the nature and function of nominal accounts. For example, it must be clear that the development of cost accounting was fostered by a desire to know more about that side of a manufacturing enterprise which is represented in the nominal accounts whose balances for so many generations have merely been passed into a summary profit and loss account.

A contemporary of Augspurg also explained how two groups of accounts constituted the essence of double entry. This was George Kurzbauer. His text on mercantile bookkeeping appeared in 1850; other editions appeared in 1867 and 1882. In the preface to the edition of 1867, he proposes to present a concise statement of a theory of bookkeeping having great usefulness for teachers. He rejects personification of accounts as a means of determining debits and credits and observes that it is seldom enough to ask which account receives, which gives. In dealing with classification of accounts, he disapproves of saying there are accounts with things and personal accounts. He wants the classification to be derived from the essential purposes of bookkeeping.

Books are kept either for the purpose of learning from them from time to time the amounts of the different kinds of property and of having a record of the changes therein, or for the purpose of learning what results (profits or losses) have been produced by particular divisions of the business. From this purpose came two essentially different kinds of bookkeeping. The ledger of the first kind contains real accounts (*Vermögensbestandteile*) in which are entered the properties acquired and given up; the ledger accounts of the second kind denote phases of the business and in them are entered the receipts (incomes?) and payments (expense?) which these phases of the business give rise to.

"Each of these types of bookkeeping is a simple one. Of course the second kind of bookkeeping [*Erfolgsbuchhaltung*, i.e., results bookkeeping] is not practiced in business for itself alone since the merchant must of necessity keep records also of his assets [*Bestandbuchung*]. But in order to attain both objects at the same time, both kinds of bookkeeping are brought into a close union in one system, and out of this arises the purport as well as the form of double entry bookkeeping."

Here we see a more positive indication than other authors give of the separateness of the function of nominal accounts and a hint that they constitute an indispensable factor for making bookkeeping records complete. Yet still lacking is a rational explanation of the tight interrelation between nominal and real accounts. If this were successfully accomplished, it would make clear that equilibrium of a trial balance is not the basic characteristic of double entry, but only the consequence of the insertion of nominal accounts into the scheme of records in order to report needed data not readable from real accounts alone. Nominal accounts are not best explained as elements of proprietorship split from that account for convenience. For this would suggest that incomes and expenses are in fact direct increases and decreases in proprietorship. Rather, nominal accounts are measurements of certain aspects of transactions touching assets of great interest to management; yet they cannot be read from records of asset exchanges.

An interesting point can be made from observing the expressiveness of some German accounting terms, and it may advance our understanding of bookkeeping theory.

In one section Kurzbauer writes of *Bestandconten* (literally, accounts of remainders) as one group and of *Erfolgsconten* (accounts of results) as the companion group. We call these real accounts and nominal accounts. Yet expenses are real enough to deserve a name of different connotation than "nominal"; and balance sheet accounts are not so superior in significance as to warrant elevation to prior ranking as "real." Our terminology therefore is either biased by, or makes us biased in favor of, a supposed superiority in usefulness of balance sheet data. This would be equivalent to believing that solvency, i.e., financial position, is more important than demonstrated earning power, i.e., operation effectiveness. Of course there are occasions when solvency is the major issue. Yet it can be said that effective operation is always an issue right up to the appearance of a condition of insolvency. Surely it is not realistic to state our basic theory in a way which implies that insolvency is always just around the corner.

The German terminology is much more directly expressive of an operating point of view. "Accounts of Remainders" tells us on its face of prior investments made for operation uses but not yet thus used. "Accounts of Results" brings to mind, without effort on our part, the efforts being made to operate an enterprise successfully. The word "results" can lead us to think of the mixed content of the income statement. Here measured efforts and measured accomplishments are so associated that we may see the net results of positive and negative factors.

(adapted from the *Certified Public Accountant,*
February, 1927; June, 1927; July, 1928)

3. Proprietorship Point of View

The first half of the nineteenth century showed the beginning of accounting theory. Writers of bookkeeping texts tried to explain the basic nature of double entry so students might learn to analyze transactions into debits and credits without resorting to personification of impersonal accounts or relying upon a multitude of rules of thumb. The outstanding fact apparent in these explanations was the recognition given to proprietorship as the central idea of double entry. This was a distinct contribution although the fact was present in the methodology from its earliest day. Possibly it was the primary force that produced nominal accounts and integrated them with personal and other real accounts. It was the proprietor's need for information on the location of his losses and gains which made nominal accounts inevitable.

The writers of the early nineteenth century however did not analyze the nature and purpose of nominal accounts as the chief peculiarity of double entry. They only went as far as explaining the arithmetical features of the system by examining the proprietor's interest in his capital. They saw his wish to know his capital situation in detail as to kinds of property, both positive (assets) and negative (liabilities), and also to know what the amount of his claim (capital) would be if creditor claims were fully met first. These writers therefore explained that bookkeeping involved two series of accounts of proprietor capital: property standing in various forms; proprietor's stock, i.e., net worth. In equation form this view is today expressed as assets less liabilities equals net proprietorship.

It is to be noted that both the theory and the equation relate to the balance sheet; they do not contrast real and nominal accounts as such. The latter approach was before long followed by other writers and, as we can now see, it laid the foundation for the modern conception of the central features of double entry. But most writers for a long time seemed greatly impressed by a surface characteristic of bookkeeping, that is, by the fact that journal entries always showed equal amounts debited and credited, and by the fact that a correct summary of ledger accounts always showed equal debit and credit totals.

An American writer and a German writer in the last quarter of the nineteenth century resorted to equations by the score in attempting to probe deeply into the mysteries of double-entry methodology. Earlier text-writers had tried to explain double entry by showing how the proprietor's desire for detailed and totaled information regarding his property could make the purpose of bookkeeping procedures more understandable. Writers a generation or so later seem to have been more directly concerned with techniques as such, that is, with the duality within journal entries and the way this feature produced duality in the summarized results at the end of a period of making entries and posting them. It is not clear whether or not these later writers knew about the "two-series-of-accounts" explanations of other writers. If they did, perhaps they were consciously attempting to supplement those explanations by systematizing the student's understanding of the more or less mechanical features of the methodology. If they did not, their analyses nevertheless constituted a supplement to prior explanations. Taken together they reflect the then current "proprietorship theory" of double entry.

The American writer was Charles E. Sprague. In 1880, he contributed a series of articles to *The Bookkeeper,* a New York periodical, under the title "Algebra of Accounts." Some twenty-five years later these were elaborated into his book *Philosophy of Accounts* (New York, 1907). This was a few years after New York University began to offer courses in preparation for the CPA examination. Sprague was a member of the initial faculty.

He considered "the science of accounting as a branch of mathematics" and explained its procedures by use of algebraic equations. "I teach," he wrote, "that no matter what peculiar form is employed in the presentation of facts, if the equation is preserved, implicitly or explicitly, it is true bookkeeping."

He considered all procedures as aimed at transforming this basic equation: "What I have plus what I trust equals what I owe plus what I am worth." In symbols this was shortened to $H + T = O + X$.

It will be noted that his use of the terms "trust" and "owe" reflects the continuing influence of the personal account antecedent of double entry and the tendency of teachers of that day, and later, to attach particular significance to a more or less literal rendering of the Latin derivation of the terms *debit* and *credit* (he owes, he trusts). As a matter of fact, the persistence of the effort to make double entry understandable by reaching back to foreign words has long been a handicap. For too many generations it tied thinking to aspects of recording that relate only to personal accounts. Moreover, "owe" and "trust" as technical terms do not success-fully transmit the essential meaning of the earliest terminology of double entry.

The sense of the left side of a debtor's account is better rendered by "he shall give"; the right side of a creditor's account, by "he shall receive." An account in Latin then would be written on the one side "debet dare," on the other "debet habere." Here "debet" was closer to "shall" than to "owe." The Italian terms were "dare" and "avere," that is, "give" and "have." The German rendition was still more confusing: "soll" (shall or must) for the debet side and "haben" (have) for the credit. It would no doubt have been better if the technical terms from the original had been recognized as such, and in translation been given similar connotations. The procedure could be more readily grasped, then and now, if accounts had "lefts" and "rights," and if journal entries showed some transaction data as "lefts" and others as "rights." Explanations could then rest upon the plus and minus characteristic of each major account-type.

It has taken long years of slow evolution to bring us to see the elements of accounting methodology and ideology in clear relation to purpose and objectives. It is this development that has slowly made it possible to bring reason rather than rote into play when we teach or learn to translate transaction events into data for classification into significant categories.

In spite of his use of words from personal accounts (owe, trust), Sprague pushes open the door a little way toward viewing accounts as statistical categories and journal entries as indicating plus and minus changes in categories.

"There are only two kinds of change: increase and decrease, more and less, + and −. More gives four modes of increase: I have more, I trust more, I owe more, I am worth more. Less gives four modes of decrease: I have less, I trust less, I owe less, I am worth less."

These elements of "the equation of value in motion" Sprague then sets in two columns.

Debits	Credits
Have more	Have less
Trust more	Trust less
Owe less	Owe more
Worth less	Worth more

"These tables," he says, "are a complete rule for balance sheets or statements of financial condition, and a complete rule, for ascertaining the debit and credit in any transaction or shifting of values." A little later in the text Sprague says, "Debit and credit mean simply left hand side and right hand side of the equation." Here he drops the literal meaning of debit and credit. Although he introduces the reader to the terms through use of "owe" and "trust," finally he abandons them. They might therefore never have been put into the student's thought. Today we go at once to plus and minus changes in accounts. And we show very early in the first that assets and expenses are alike in plus and minus characteristics because they are cousins by nature. We also show that incomes, liabilities, and capital are similar in plus and minus, but find it difficult to relate them by their nature. Perhaps this is, in part at least, because we still feel the influence of earlier ideas which stressed the distinction between enterprise liability to outsiders and to insiders (debts and capital), although there is much more significance, accounting-wise, in their similarity.

The German writer was Johann Friedrich Schär. In 1889, in teaching the elements of bookkeeping to mature engineers, lawyers, and chemists, he tried to adapt his explanations to his audience and attacked the problems from a mathematical point of view not unlike that followed by Sprague. His materials were published as a pamphlet in 1890 and later in a larger book.

Schar made use of an opening equation similar to Sprague's elements of an opening balance sheet. Then, using a variety of letter symbols (V for debtors, Q for creditors, K for merchandise, R for bills payable, etc.), he sets typical transactions into equation form, instead of technical journal entry form. These are listed in a table in two columns and are then added algebraically after canceling out identical items in opposite colunms. The result is an equation of symbols for the usual balance sheet items. Of course the equation is identical with the opening equation except in the spots where outright increase or decrease in wealth was involved. The opening equation was $A - P = K$; the equation after the algebraic process was $A^1 - P^1 = K^2$.

Today we would not labor to demonstrate convincingly that equals added to equals will produce totals which are also equal although larger than initially was the case. Nor would we labor in any try to prove this as the outstanding characteristic of bookkeeping. Why not? Probably because we now can see that the clue to double entry lies in the nature of nominal accounts. Presenting the subject compactly to mature people, we now could with benefit begin with the nature of enterprise profit and the interest most people have in measurements thereof. There we could discuss the elements in the calculation of net income, and the arrangement of the income statement. Third, we could examine the interest of some people in a solvency picture of debt-paying capacity. From this balance sheet and income statement it is but a step back into account categories for collecting the data desired. The matter of analyzing transaction events into the scheme of categories could be approached in typical examples from the point of view of the effect of the event upon various elements in both or in only one of the financial statements. The transaction facts are then to be entered in such account categories as will presently contribute the desired statement information from the account's total or its remainder.

But we may need to note that we are able to make such a compact and understandable presentation because other men long ago struggled with the problem of making a relatively new technology understandable, and little by little succeeded. We can do no less for complications introduced by the complexities of modern business.

(Chapter 12, Accounting Evolution to 1900)

4. Theory of Enterprise Entity

Many explanations of the characteristics of double entry emphasize proprietorship as the chief clue. This was a distinct advance since the earliest writers merely described sequential procedures in detail. Yet proprietorship always lay beneath the descriptions of practice. Other types of transaction recording lacked this feature. Early records of medieval commerce were merely in aid of an agent's reporting to a principal on the results of a trading venture. The charge and discharge records used on British landed estates in the sixteenth century were designed to present details of servant accountability rather than changes in the nobleman's wealth.

Double entry evolved out of simple records of debts receivable and payable. Records of debts were sufficient for money-changers (bankers?), but a merchant needed to know more than his debts; he wanted factual records of his property as well as his debts, records of costs of goods and expenses, as well as the sale price received. In a word, the merchant, being at once investor and manager, wanted to be able to measure his managerial accomplishments in terms of money price, and to have available compact records of the kinds and totals of his business investment. No doubt these felt needs gradually stimulated merchants to devise records that seemed likely to supply answers. And when the as yet unknown steps of evolution were complete, proprietorship was necessarily a central feature, the records having been created to aid proprietors to make later decisions.

Text-writers were entirely correct therefore when, in undertaking to make bookkeeping processes more understandable, they wrote of two series of accounts, one for the various forms in which a proprietor's wealth existed, and another, coming to the same total, for calculating the proprietor's wealth as a total. But these writers of theory did not stand alone. Other writers, with similar intentions of explaining the nature of double entry, followed other paths to the same goal. Perhaps they were consciously trying to improve upon other explanations they had heard. The new point of view we can now call "the entity theory," for certain writers were pointing toward the separateness of the enterprise as an institution and the proprietor as a person. Bookkeeping under this view was concerned with transactions between the enterprise and all the rest of the world. All property recorded had been intrusted to the enterprise from outside its boundaries and had thus become dedicated to its purposes. Under this view there would be no place in the records of an enterprise for a proprietor's private transactions—such as gambling losses, household expenses, etc. which should be part of a complete record of a person's financial activities and properties. The proprietorship explanation of bookkeeping considered the records as being those of that person. This was but following the precedent of 1494; Paciolo at that time showed that a merchant would include his household assets and personal expenses and losses along with his business assets and expenses.

But the distinction between the two types of explanations lies deeper than this, although the early writers on the entity theory did not reach down so far. Capital, according to a proprietorship theory, was that person's investment; hence it was measured by total assets less liabilities as negative assets. Under an entity theory, capital would be the total property active in the enterprise from whatever source derived. Here loans from nonproprietors and proprietor investments were both sources of all the capital which was detailed by the list of enterprise assets. Profit in the first theory would be a noninvestment increase in the net figure for positive and negative assets. By the second theory, profit would be conceived as flowing from enterprise operations as measured by proceeds recovered in excess of the outlays (costs and expenses) advanced to carry on the purposes of the enterprise. In one case, profit would be any and all increments to proprietorship. In the other, the concept leans toward the view that net income is the result of managerial skill rather than a result merely of proprietary ownership. The first theory produces a balance sheet equation expressive of its concept of capital: "assets — liabilities = proprietorship." The second produces another equation to express the concept of capital: "assets = investments," or "asset kinds = asset sources."

It is interesting to note that the entity theory seems to reach back into agent accountability for its keynote. The enterprise, being a separate entity distinct from the sources of the assets it holds, is like an agent holding another's property without true ownership and owing to these owners a duty of careful stewardship and full reporting. Perhaps the greatest significance today of this nineteenth century entity theory is the fact that it fits modern conditions and the limited liability corporation much better than would an extension of the proprietorship theory of the nature accounting.

How early did the entity concept appear? Some hints are found here and there in nineteenth century literature, but there are few elaborations. Leo Gomberg (*Histoire Critique de la Theorie des Comptes*, Geneva, 1929) cites several authors—Lodovico Crippa, 1638 and an unknown writer in London, 1869—as believing that the capital account is essentially the trader's own personal account with the enterprise. A French writer (J. G. Courcelles—Seneuil, Paris, 1870) is quoted as saying that "all commercial capital is a capital intrusted to a firm to manage . . . the firm has an account with the merchant as if he were a stranger."

A German writer (Manfred Berliner) in a magazine article in 1887 stressed the separateness of a merchant's private life and activities and correspondingly the separateness of his private property and his business capital. Commercial bookkeeping was concerned only with the latter. Profit or loss in an enterprise indicated the value of services of the proprietor—manager. Expenses were not losses but part of the cost of goods. In a later book, Berliner stated that he had taught these views to students since 1870.

The principal usefulness of these theories of the nature of double entry in their day, as is the case with all theory today, lay in the fact that they began to make it clear to students that accounting procedures were the outward expression of an inward purpose, namely, from collected transaction data to distinguish clearly and quantitatively between capital and income, the tree and the fruit, was very necessary if management, whether proprietor or hired executive, is to have definite knowledge where prior decisions had proved productive or nonproductive.

It is noteworthy that both theories held that the essence of double entry was its ability to serve enterprise management with managerial information. The entity theory did not have a monopoly on this theme. The proprietor was also manager and in need of managerial information. Even if an enterprise were an entity separate from its sources of capital, factual information about that entity was needed for use of the humans who made its decisions.

The entity theory, however, made a distinct contribution by carrying accounting still more towards its impersonal, statistical, reporting functions; it thus continued an evolution began when proprietorship theory helped break up the notions that bookkeeping was purely a clerical routine and that nominal accounts had to be personified in order to make transaction analysis understandable. Time has shown how the entity theory is not only expressive of the very early managerial focus of bookkeeping but, in a modern continuation of that focus, how well it is constituted to reflect the separateness of today's corporation management and that corporation's stockholding and bondholding investors. Proprietorship as such is not a useful concept in explaining the nature of a corporation; therefore it is not a useful approach to explaining corporation accounting. Furthermore, today's consciousness of the entity theory helps us realize that the "center of gravity" of accounting is and has always been in the nominal accounts (income determination) rather than in the real accounts (solvency determination). This does not mean that the balance sheet should be a mere formality, as seems probable if index number adjustment of the income statement breaks up the integration of the two reports. And surely this rational entity theory does not support the assignment of an exaggerated emphasis upon the balance sheet as the report of chief usefulness as seems inherent in the balance sheet audit and in the "balance sheet approach" so often met in elementary texts today.

(Chapter 12, *Accounting Evolution to 1900*)

5. The Logic of Accounts

This was the appropriate title for the text in which an American, E. G. Folsom, made a praiseworthy attempt two generations ago to show the student that bookkeeping procedures reflect rational purposes and implement reasonable and understandable objectives. His pedagogical intention clearly was one of easing the learner's task by teaching him the thought processes behind the technical features of double entry. In this approach he displays a penetrating insight into the weakness inherent in learning a technology by memorizing rules for dealing with typical situations.

Recognition of this same distinction between pedagogical methods was, a generation later, an important factor in gaining the acceptance of accounting as subject matter appropriate for college level classes. College courses which make no more contribution to the student's mental development than that involved in learning rules by heart and applying them clerically to routine situations, do not deserve a place in college catalogs. The reason is not found in the subject matter but in the method by which the teaching materials are used. Since higher education exists to foster higher mental development, every subject plus its teaching method should contribute to that goal. A review of the changes taking place over a half century will show that this conception has been steadily at work in accounting instruction and that the usefulness of the subject for stimulating mental development has been steadily improved at the same time that instruction in its technical aspects has kept pace with growing needs in business for increased accounting technology.

Perhaps Folsom was conditioned by his education to attempt the broadening of instruction in bookkeeping. He signed his book as a master of arts and displays an acquaintance with the economics of his day far beyond that reflected in contemporary textbooks on bookkeeping. He was not the first to try to break away from the time-favored descriptive approach, but he seems to have succeeded better than others. For example, he utilized his understanding of economic theory—he mentions Mill and Carey specifically—to undertake to rest the student's grasp of accounting upon some certain concepts from economics. In doing this he put more discussion (theory?) into his text than others had done. About one-fifth of the total pages were used in this way.

In both editions (New York, 1873, 1881) he lays stress throughout upon the concepts of capital, of value, of service. Not all property, he points out, is capital. To be capital, property must be devoted exclusively to some business enterprise with a view of realizing profit. Capital thus set apart constitutes a business which from its beginning establishes relations between itself and all parties dealing with it.

Here Folsom plainly indicated the separateness of the enterprise itself and the sources of enterprise capital. Elsewhere he strongly stresses service as the principal factor responsible for operational increases and decreases of enterprise capital. Thus he associates the concept of profit with reward for services rendered. His nominal accounts are labeled "received service" on the debit (expense) side and "gave service" on the credit (revenue) side. Since the proprietor can only serve and be served, as the author writes, we may now add the thought that the proprietor looks to his expense and goods accounts to learn the extent to which he is being served by possessing the means of serving others, and to his sales revenue and other earning accounts to learn the extent to which he has served others.

While Folsom did not develop his ideas this far, his mind nevertheless convincingly reached into the entity concept of capital and profit: the enterprise is a separate entity; it holds all assets (capital) for enterprise purpose regardless of the source of assets; net profit comes to the enterprise before it reaches those who supplied assets; enterprise profit comes, not from holding assets or from revaluing them as prices rise, but from the service rendered to customers that is made possible by the possession and exchange of enterprise property (capital).

It seems very unlikely that Folsom would have been receptive to modern ideas about replacement costs being reported in the financial statements, or to the use of appraisal surplus as a basis for cash dividends. The conditions which long after his time generated such ideas were not present early enough to disturb this author's logic. But because this thoughtful writer presented the essence of double-entry theory with so much logical insight, and because the logic inherent in double-entry objectives and methods has gradually become better understood, we need not in 1955 be so easily persuaded towards an expedient concept of enterprise net income, and toward viewing the financial statements resulting from double-entry technology as so loosely integrated that, as has sometimes in recent years been intimated, they need not be interlocked at all.

One of Folsom's aims in writing his text, like that of many other authors, was to teach the student how to analyze transactions into debits and credits for entry into double-entry ledger accounts. Although he logically rests his explanations upon useful concepts from economics, he gets tangled up (in the 1872 edition), as others had, by an inherited terminology wherein debit meant "owe" and credit meant "trust." Thomas Jones before him and Charles Sprague after him escaped this trap and taught that these terms of Latin derivation no longer meant what they did originally. Folsom gave examples of transactions reduced to equations;

but he did not teach students to think of entries in accounts merely as arithmetical increases and decreases in carefully defined categories.

His equations are based on his principle that "all transactions have their origin in an exchange of values" and "in all transactions there is a coequal receiving and giving of values." These ideas he develops (in the 1881 edition) into six equations of values exchanged, using three basic terms as the equation members. These terms are tied to the concept of service. "Commodity" is stored service of the past; "claim" is service promised for the future; "service" itself is "incorporeal and unembodied." This last phrase, perhaps unconsciously but nonetheless clearly, reflects the sense of the word "nominal" as now applied to one group of ledger accounts. Yet we can now see that the information in these accounts instead of being insubstantial ("nominal") is very real and useful to management.

His equations are these:

Service	= Service	Service	= Commodity
Service	= Claim	Commodity	= Commodity
Commodity	= Claim	Claim	= Claim

Every transaction can be expressed in one of these forms.

Like other authors he stumbles over the problem of distinguishing between expense and loss. This is another instance of the difficulty of shaking off the influence of earlier modes of thought. The importance of "proprietor" in proprietary bookkeeping was so great (in comparison to agency records without ownership) that expense and income were traditionally explained as loss and gain to proprietor. As such, they could be fitted into journal entry equations, and students finally learned thereby to translate familiar transaction data into ledger account data. Now we see that nominal account debits do not speak of proprietorship loss, and nominal account credits do not speak of proprietorship gain. Instead nominal accounts tell of certain active types of increase or decrease in enterprise net wealth, sharply different from those changes in wealth which come from loans or investments. Such explanation helps us today to face the pedagogical problems of preparing students from their first courses to understand cost accounting entries when they meet them later.

This is a page where Folsom has something for us even though he misses the concept of expense by calling it loss, which is paying for a service that is not exchangeable. He mentions interest, rent, and commissions. Along with rent, etc. he includes the consumptive use of materials, fixtures, and other incidentals. He therefore does realize that costs can attach to product. In connection with the above phrase "consumptive use of materials, etc." he adds, "these are in the nature of losses unless services of these kinds are treated as embodied in the merchandise and are charged in with it as enhancing its value." Cost accounting in Folsom's day was not well developed, but here he expressed the conception that costs and appropriate expenses attach to the merchandise purchased. That is part of his "accounting logic." It was likewise logical—when the time came—for relevant manufacturing costs and expenses to attach to the product manufactured.

Folsom, without developing the matter, seems almost on the point of drawing the very modern distinction between cost, expense, and loss. When and if an author succeeds in making these distinctions for his reader, it may be taken as an indication that he has pushed his mind behind the clerical procedures of bookkeeping and into an appreciation of the real essence of double entry, namely, the meaning and usefulness of impersonal accounts, especially those for cost, expense, and loss which we now so ineptly call nominal accounts.

Like some other text-writers of the nineteenth century, Folsom is carrying on a part of the step-by-step evolution of bookkeeping (and accounting) theory. He therefore has contributed to a gradual broadening and deepening of our ability to understand what accounting really is and how it could possess great usefulness over several centuries, and more and more usefulness as its evolution continues. Although this author, like his contemporaries, misses many opportunities to speed up accounting theory, this does not detract from the valuable insight he was able to pass on to his students. It must have often lodged in fertile soil, this striving to tie accounting into economics. To those of his students who wished to understand more than the formation of journal entries, it must have been helpful to read in an early page that we gain in business because we bring newborn value into the sphere of exchange. With that idea as a basis, students have an exceptional opening for developing an interest in and understanding of the nature and usefulness of nominal accounts. With such a start, the small technical aspects of double entry can readily be made understandable. We are still learning how to use this logical approach to understanding double entry. Later years show progressive improvement in accounting theory largely because earlier writers aspired to help students to understand rather than being content to push them to remember rules.

(*Accounting Review*, January, 1955)

6. Assets and Equities

In explanations of the nature of double entry the focal point has gradually shifted over the years from the proprietor to the enterprise. Each point of view has been particularly appropriate to the climate surrounding it. The major distinction between accountability, as typified by the charge and discharge records on English landed estates in the sixteenth century, and ownership, as indicated in Italian double entry at about the same time, can be represented by the terms "agency" for one system and "proprietorship" for the other. An agent expects to report on his stewardship of property intrusted to him; a proprietor expects to calculate the net results of his productive employment of capital in the hope of gain.

It is quite understandable therefore that the concept of proprietorship should permeate textbook explanations and descriptions of double-entry procedure. The recording methodology was designed to collect information of interest and use to a proprietor, information as to the actions he had taken in the past since it would be a very desirable aid in making new decisions.

Earlier writers did little more than describe the procedure of making transaction memos and translating these into the debits and credits of ledger accounts. In the nineteenth century, however, some writers, seeking to present students with the essence of double entry that underlies procedures, drew attention to the way bookkeeping was focused toward a proprietor. It was his capital that was at work; the gains and losses were his gains and losses because he owned the assets at the beginning and at the end. His interest in the assets was to know from records the amount of each kind of property he controlled. He did not own all of the assets if he owed debts to other people; therefore he must view debts payable as negative property. A proprietor was interested in the total of his proprietorship as well as in the variety of kinds in his property. As a kind of headline, or epitome of the proprietor's two lines of interest, some writers compressed the theory into a compact equation. F. W. Cronhelm (1818) used the form: $(a + b + c) - l - m - n = S$ to represent (positive property) − (negative property) = proprietor's stock.

Such an equation not only emphasized the proprietor as the center of interest but served as a useful point of reference in demonstrating the inevitable equality of debits and credits in double-entry records.

Thomas Jones (1841) does not compress his explanation of bookkeeping equalities into a symbolic equation. He states his ideas in illustrative calculations.

Position of Our Affairs

Cash in our possession	15,000	Bills payable	3,000
Bills receivable	4,000	We owe J. S.	6,000
W. J. owes us	3,000		
	$22,000		$9,000

$22,000 less 9,000 leaves $13,000, our present worth.

Change in Our Position

On Jan. 1 our net capital was	10,000
During the year we gained	3,000
Our clear worth at the end of the year is	$13,000

This determination is made independent of any references to resources and liabilities. "Double entry," he writes, "embraces two distinct plans of arranging the facts that have transpired in a business, each plan involving a distinct set of accounts . . . and the agreement in the result of the two constitutes what is called the balance of the books."

While Jones does not use an equation of symbols here, he nevertheless makes the same point in very illuminating fashion.

A German writer in 1850 and 1882 (A. D. Kurzbauer), instead of using simplified accounting statements, characterizes double entry as two separate series of accounts (*Zweikontenreiken*) and names the two opposing series accounts of remainders (*Bestandconten*) and accounts of results (*Erfolgsconten*). His verbal picture is very much the same as that conveyed by others who use different modes of expression. All of them however are thinking in terms of a proprietary emphasis, a view later expressed in modern symbols as $A - L = P$.

Charles E. Sprague (1880) proposes "to work out still another way of looking at the principle of debit and credit. Treating the science of accounts as a branch of mathematics [which it is] I reduce it to an algebraic notation. All operations of double entry bookkeeping are transformations of the following equation: What I have + what I trust = What I owe + what I am worth. Symbolically written: $H + T = O + X$."

It is noteworthy that Sprague's equation is a departure from the others since he places both liabilities and proprietorship in the right side of the formula. He thus pictures to the reader the essential structure of a balance sheet and so is able to explain transaction analysis in terms of the effect the event would have on the basic equation.

Here too we may see reflected the basic idea behind the entity concept of the nature of double entry. Instead of leading up to the distinction between real and nominal accounts, as the two-series-of-accounts theory does, the entity theory points to the separateness of the enterprise and the proprietor; the accounts are records of enterprise activities not those of a proprietor. Hence it is logical to view liabilities to creditors and ownership investments as very closely related (sources of assets) and therefore proper to be added together in a balance sheet.

In 1870 a French author (J. G. Courcelles—Senenil) wrote that "the firm has an account with the merchant as if he were a stranger. . . ." A German writer (Manfred Berliner, 1887) was clearly of the opinion that a merchant's private life and property were separate from his business activities and business capital. Commercial bookkeeping therefore was only a mirror of dedicated capital. E. G. Folsom (1873, 1881) touched the same theory in indicating that capital invested constitutes a business enterprise which from the beginning establishes relations between itself and all parties dealing with it.

Later writers, notably W. A. Paton (*Accounting Theory*, 1922), made use of the equation "assets equal equities" to epitomize the balance sheet. This expression seems particularly appropriate to modern legal theory that a corporation is an entity in its own right quite separate from creditors and all classes of security-holders. Although the modern view was foreshadowed in the ideas of a number of writers in the nineteenth century, it cannot be said that the entity theory of double entry had achieved full stature before 1922.

The entity approach to explaining the nature and function of double entry is well suited to the corporation as the predominant form of modern business enterprises. But it has other significance in its twentieth century setting. It makes it reasonable to associate assets and expenses as different means of carrying out enterprise functions. Expenses express current services expended in enterprise activities; assets express latent services awaiting call to make their productive contributions. Thus basic accounting ideology approaches contact with economic ideas.

The enterprise is an economic institution; property dedicated to its activities by various types of investors can be considered as capital advanced and expected to be repaid if it has been profitably employed in the meantime (managed within the enterprise) in providing goods or services to satisfied customers. Profit comes to the enterprise primarily because skillful management renders acceptable service at a cost kept below the price the market will pay in the form of enterprise revenue. The accounting process therefore serves two major functions: (1) that of providing needed data regarding prior managerial commitments so current managerial decisions may be factually based, and (2) that of providing a means of dependably computing the recovery from customers of the capital advanced in the form of product costs and operating expenses, thus to approach the calculation of enterprise earnings as a first step in compensating the suppliers of capital for their service and risk.

The proprietorship theory was entirely appropriate to its day. The typical enterprise was not incorporated; the proprietor and the business were not legally distinct. In the modern setting, "ownership" looses its force; the assets are corporation property; ownership consists in certain rights to ultimate liquidation of prior investments and of interim rights to share in enterprise earnings at the discretion of shareholder-elected directors. The entity concept is much more appropriate to twentieth century conditions. Both views are deeply rooted in the past; both have much logic to support them. The two theories are not basically antagonistic; both describe very well the basic features of double entry. They merely approach the same landscape from a different angle. A full appreciation of the scene will best follow exploration along both paths. Both excursions will be illuminating; but one path will be judged more suitable for travel today. And we will know it is more suitable from knowing that many thoughtful people trod out the other path first.

That is the way of history; events are relative to their surroundings but derive from their antecedents.

(Chapter 11, *Accounting Evolution to 1900*)

7. Terminable or Permanent Investment

The corporate form of business organization is so well known that its most significant features are taken for granted. But there was a time when large business enterprises were not treated as if they had continuous life; investments by stockholders were not easily transferable; periodic profits were not calculated from enterprise accounting records.

Individual proprietorships were continuing enterprises only under a maximum run of the lifetime of the proprietor. Simple partnerships could run longer by bringing in new partners. Double-entry bookkeeping evolved to serve this form of enterprise. Even the use of double entry did not necessitate regular, periodic closing of the books or an annual calculation of enterprise net profit. The persons most concerned could watch the progress of the business by frequently examining the ledger accounts; perhaps in most cases the proprietor or a partner made the entries and thus kept in constant touch with the profit situation.

Individual merchants from very early days also engaged in occasional terminable ventures in foreign trade on a relatively small scale. In such cases, as Paciolo explained in 1494, careful records were kept so that the details of operation and the final outcome could be determined separately from the other business activities of the merchant.

Evidently, record-keeping methods were adapted to the type of operation, whether as more or less continuous, or as terminable ventures. While the records as such may have looked very much alike, except for the volume and variety of transactions, the basic ideology back of each type of business was different enough to have influenced later accounting ideology in different ways.

Business in the early days usually was "venturing for profit," a series of speculations even in the case of a small trader. It is significant, for example, that separate goods accounts were kept for each type of merchandise, e.g., Pepper, Eastern Silk, etc. Modern business is more stable; we speak of "merchandising a stock," meaning continuous operation by replenishing the inventory frequently and use of more or less standard types. This is an operation yielding a regular return from turning over a continuing investment. In contrast, a great deal of earlier business brought irregular, sporadic profits from separate ventures.

The East India Company is an outstanding example of large-scale trading operations carried on for a long time by numerous separate ventures. Newly discovered countries possessed many useful commodities which the people would barter for things they did not possess. Possible end profits were tempting, and men combined forces to secure some of the fruits of trade by contributing goods to a "joint stock" in order to share later in the proceeds when the venture was liquidated after the ship returned to home port. The venturers received not a "dividend" out of venture profit, but a "division," that is, to each his contracted share in the whole proceeds, capital and profit. The company's bookkeeping therefore was moulded to suit this kind of operation.

For more than half a century (1600-1657) the East India Company operated under a system of terminable joint stocks. Between 1600 and 1617, there were 113 distinct voyages, each with a separately subscribed capital; the assets brought back were divided between the "partners" when the voyage terminated. Obviously different assets had to be separately valued. Otherwise some venturers might receive more valuable returns than others. Here perhaps is an early source for a long-lived idea— the idea that accounting must necessarily involve the valuation of assets. The modern conflict of ideas, so compactly indicated by the phrase "cost or value," therefore is an ancient one even though the conflict is much sharper now than earlier.

Of course many ventures were terminated by sale of goods to distributing merchants for such prices as bargaining produced. In that case ready money would soon be in hand for dividing among the venturers. But it should be noted that a partner received, not enterprise profit, but a share of liquidating capital. If he received more capital back than he had contributed, he could easily measure his profit. That is still one concept of profit, but another concept is more suitable to modern conditions; it too had an early background—one that reached beyond the bookkeeping practice of individual proprietorship. Or perhaps we should say, the concept of profit most suitable to modern conditions came from an extension of the operating practices of proprietorship.

In 1657, the East India Company secured a new charter in which a clause provided that, after seven years, the stock was to be valued at the end of each three years thereafter. On the basis of that valuation any shareholder was entitled to have his place taken by another who wished to join the company. Before this, in order to get an interest in a venture, one had to subscribe to a new undertaking or buy a fraction of a share from a present member. Under the new charter a very modern feature appeared, transferable shares in a continuing operation.

It is significant also that in 1661 the governor (president?) of the company stated that future distributions would consist of profits earned rather than of liquidating "divisions" as in the past. Clearly this development made it very necessary to distinguish sharply, in theory and in practice, between capital and income. No such necessity was involved in the accounting for the operation of a terminable venture. Thus a great forward step was taken in arranging the conditions under which modern corporations operate and modern accounting assumes some of its greatest responsibilities.

The theory and practice of permanency of investment pushed the theory and practice of terminable ventures out of use by large business enterprises and sharply modified accounting practice, for collateral to permanent investment was the idea of periodic and severable enterprise profit. If capital investment is permanent (except as a buyer is found for a transferable share), then separation of income is an economic and a financial necessity. It is a highly significant fact that Italian double entry, already well developed and in a sense awaiting its larger destiny, provided a technology for accomplishing the careful separation of these two elements, capital and income, under very diverse and, as later centuries were to demonstrate, unanticipated circumstances. It seems as if joint-stock companies (corporations) were the catalyst in whose presence the permanent investment in enterprise assets was united with a mechanism for sharply measuring periodic enterprise income.

Certain evidence in support of the above conclusion is available in a number of nineteenth century cases and statutes in English law. In one case in 1856, it was held fraudulent to declare a dividend out of capital since such action would decrease the security of the creditors. In 1864 (and in 1882), an attempt to pay "interest" on capital when there were no profits met opposition in the courts. The proposal was held improper because it would be equivalent to diverting capital from the objectives of the enterprise. Obviously the points at issue were the proper distinction between capital and (divisible) income, as well as the contractual priorities of creditors.

Other evidence reveals a belief in a relation between the balance sheet and enterprise profit. The bylaws of a company (1864) stated that the balance sheet "shall contain a true account of the capital, credits, and property belonging to the company, and the debts, gains and losses of the company . . . and shall show the balance remaining after payment of all expenses of maintaining and working the railway, which balance shall be designated the net revenue."

Today, in order to convey this idea, we would have to refer to both balance sheet and income statement. Perhaps this was the intention of the bylaw above. Yet in the language of some countries from which the British derived double entry, "the balance of the books" meant the reports produced from balancing the books. Possibly the foreign phrase referred more directly to the two summary ledger accounts, the balance account (real accounts summarized) and the loss and gain account (nominal accounts summarized). But the essence of the phrase "the balance of the book" is the same in both cases since financial statements began as copies of these two summary accounts.

The English interpretation of "balance sheet" is further illustrated in two cases a few years later than the bylaw mentioned. The court said, "The first step would be to make good the capital by taking stock and putting a value upon all the assets of the company and of deducting therefrom all the liabilities, including contributed capital, and the surplus if any remaining of the gross receipts would be net profit." In another case the court said, "The object of the clause in the by-laws was that the directors should produce a balance sheet in order to show the assets of the company and their value and on the other hand the liabilities of the company; because it is only on this sort of statement that you can draw any rational conclusion as to whether there is a profit."

Do these statements suggest a concept of profit that is associated with a liquidation of company assets and termination of the enterprise? Would such a concept be more closely related to the pattern shown in terminable ventures or to that reflected in the use of double entry for a continuing enterprise? Was not "cost or value" already an issue a century ago?

It is no fault of nineteenth century theory that it drew heavily upon earlier ideas and practices or that it does not fully meet twentieth century needs. Instead of being critical of earlier ideas, it would be more helpful to realize that twentieth century needs are currently so dimly perceived that we are still trying to make too many nineteenth century notions suffice for today. This is not to say that there is no usefulness in the earlier ideas. There is much usefulness in them. But the contributions they can make are not to be derived from transferring them out of their natural setting. Rather we should seek to understand them in their setting in order that we may adapt the best of them as may be suitable to the new setting.

(Chapter 13, *Accounting Evolution to 1900*)

8. Enterprise Continuity

Today, midway in the twentieth century, the limited liability corporation is such a familiar feature of business that the influence of the ideology (theory) behind this institution is seldom considered. Yet the idea had great effect upon developing accounting out of double-entry bookkeeping.

The concept of enterprise entity (separateness from owners) was inherent even in fifteenth century proprietorship enterprises although there was no occasion then for the idea to come to attention. It was sufficient to the needs of the time to build bookkeeping ideas about the proprietor as an individual. Under modern developments, accounting ideology draws as many concepts, perhaps more, from corporation theory than from concepts peculiar to proprietary enterprises. Particularly important is the concept of enterprise entity which is such a prominent feature of the corporation.

The separateness of the corporation as an entity provides the logic back of limited liability. Limited liability in turn brings about a legal and moral obligation to preserve invested capital intact against impairment from dividends, and this requirement makes very necessary a most careful calculation of distributable profit, including clear recognition of depreciation as a factor in computing enterprise net income. Double entry, expanding under pressure of this new responsibility, provided a completely adequate framework upon which accounting as we know it today was gradually constructed. The reason this development could take place was the fact that double entry was already an instrument of proven usefulness for recording and classifying the occurrences of business in such a manner as to make possible a dependable computation of enterprise net income. Double entry could do this, not because of a rule that "for every debit there must be an equal and opposite credit," but because through its system of account relationships it had long ago succeeded in integrating nominal accounts (summarizing economic activities) and real accounts (summarizing financial activities). By systematic use of these distinctly different but integrated categories, accounting makes possible a consistent and understandable separation of capital (the tree) and income (the fruit). It is of particular importance in limited liability corporations that this distinction be dependably and constantly kept in mind by management. Hence it is plausible to believe that double-entry accounting can make a greater contribution to corporate enterprises than it can to proprietary enterprises.

Much of the contribution that accounting makes to the success of the corporation as a social institution is of relatively recent appearance. This is true because the inherent potentialities of this form of organization have been brought into play for the most part only in the twentieth century. It is significant to the expanded use of double entry, however, that the ideological roots of corporations and hence of modern accounting theory reach far back of the twentieth century.

One of those ideological roots is enterprise limited liability as such. The concept of limited liability for corporations is a product of economic and social evaluation. The idea of an organizational entity separate from organization members, which is the parent idea, is much older than limited liability. Pollock and Mailland (*History of English Law*) tell us that lawyers in the Middle Ages recognized this characteristic of separateness as early as the thirteenth century. Men drawn together by common religious beliefs, as in the early Christian church, felt in the church a unity which was separate from an individual person and more than the sum of all the personal membership. Men drawn together into trade fields (craft guilds) for mutual protection in their occupations felt themselves limited in an organization that was outside of but included the individual members. When medieval municipalities began to appear, people felt there was a "town" in addition to the individual inhabitants.

None of these three institutions sprang into existence fully endowed with "separateness." This was a concept rather than a form, and it grew into conscious shape in men's minds only with the passage of time. Yet here was the essence of the concept we later label with the term "entity" wherein the essential idea is separateness.

When business enterprises were able to take the form of corporations—when the basic idea had spread and legal permission had become statutory—it was inevitable that the relation of creditors to the corporation and/or its members should come into question. When the issue arose, the way to solution was found to be already prepared. As soon as separateness of corporation and members is accepted, it must follow as a matter of logic and justice that corporate property could not be available to the creditors of members. The reason is that members had no more direct property rights in the assets of the active corporation than they would have had if they had sold their original possessions to another human being. In like manner creditors of the corporations could not in logic and justice expect to reach the private property of members to satisfy corporation debts.

It will be observed that "separateness," "entity," and "limited liability" are not original with the lawmakers. The ideas expressed by these terms antedate governments and law as we know them. The ideas arose out of surrounding conditions without premeditation or deliberate intent of the people. Law, being merely statements of man-made and man-accepted rules, could recognize or ignore the existence of "entity," but it could not of itself originate the thing the term connotes or the concept of which the word speaks.

The establishment of a practice of investing capital in enterprise (as distinct from terminable joint ventures) gave strong emphasis to a careful separation, in the record, of enterprise capital and enterprise income. The recognition of limited liability in corporations made the same aspect of record use even more important. A permanent capital investment (enterprise continuity) made separate computation of capital and income an economic necessity; the statutory recognition of limited liability made that separation a legal necessity.

From both points of view, business is concerned as a continuing activity. Hence economic capital must be maintained in order that the economic power of the enterprise may be unimpaired. And in order to have the basic data about maintained capital, we must separate capital and income in the record. But the requirements of the situation are even more complex than this statement seems to imply. Legal capital also must be preserved intact; this is in order that the rights of parties outside of the entity—shareholders and creditors—may be duly protected.

Failure to maintain enterprise economic power would result in loss of productivity and earning power, thus affecting workers, customers, investors, and government. Failure to protect legal capital likewise entails undesirable consequences following upon the resulting condition of insolvency. Both kinds of failure affect some parts of society adversely. It is clear therefore that a social, as well as a managerial, responsibility rests upon accounting to provide dependable data concerning the separateness and present status of enterprise capital and income.

Since economic capital and legal capital are not identical concepts, a complication of theory may arise when we see that two computations may be necessary in order to see whether both types of capital are unimpaired. The controversies of the 1940's and 1950's, related to the responsibility for modern accounting to compute one kind of maintenance or the other, cannot be explored here where the thought is directed toward some of the background of modern theory. But it would seem clearly evident, however, that the basic data for judging maintenance of both economic and legal capital must derive from the integrated nominal and real accounts of enterprise double-entry records. Where is there an equal source of knowledge about enterprise capital and income?

Certain ideas related to enterprise continuity have been considered above. The statutory implementation in the nineteenth century of continuity, entity, and limited liability should also be briefly noted.

In England the Companies Act of 1855 enabled enterprises registered under the Statute of 1844 to obtain certificates of limited liability for their shareholders. The prior act (1844) did not go that far. This statute grew out of testimony before a Parliamentary Committee (1841-43) about the auditing of insurance companies. The object of the statute was to protect the stability and financial soundness of companies. In a later consolidation of several statutes, the Companies Act of 1862 provided, among other things, for limited liability of shareholders as that factor would be defined in the original memorandum of association.

In the United States permission to form corporations by complying with provisions stated in a general statute was first extended to ecclesiastical, educational, and literary associations in five states between 1778 and 1791. Business incorporations were authorized state by state from 1795 (North Carolina) and 1811 (New York); between 1845 and 1851, six states passed general incorporation statutes wherein limited liability was a feature from the beginning.

It is significant that the most extensive adoption of double entry came in the twentieth century, that is, only after the business corporation had been made widely available under general statutory authority, and after it had had time to demonstrate its capacity to serve society productively for customers and safely for investors. When viewed in retrospect, it seems as if double entry, though long in use, waited its full destiny for centuries. When the nineteenth century merged into the twentieth, many deeply planted roots put forth new shoots into the sunshine of commercial and industrial progress. The adaptability of this methodology, in view of its simple beginning, is nothing short of amazing. And the end is not yet.

(Chapter 15, *Accounting Evolution to 1900*)

9. Nineteenth Century Depreciation

Some day the years in the middle of the twentieth century can be viewed in perspective. They will then be observed to have been marked, among other things, by a not inconsiderable discussion of depreciation and ways of reporting it. In the center of the swirl of argumentation will lie the proposal that depreciation expense as reported in the income statement should be an amount reflecting current price equivalents rather than an amortized portion of prior invested cost price.

By the time such a backward perspective becomes possible, there may perhaps be even less interest in ideas about depreciation in the middle of the nineteenth century than is now the case. Since at the moment we stand in the middle of the twentieth, the present cannot be viewed in retrospect, but the middle of the nineteenth century can. It too was a period of differences of opinion about depreciation. Yet out of those differences a pretty general consensus emerged: that depreciation expense was a factor in the calculation of periodic net income; that depreciation expense should be recognized and reported even though its inclusion turned a net profit into net loss; that depreciation calculations expressed amortizations of past invested cost into present expense, rather than constituting reservations of revenue to provide replacements.

The last doctrine is the one under challenge in the 1940's and 1950's. The essence of the present debate is not new; amortization versus reservation was a point of contention a century ago. Only the application of index-numbers is new. The basic issue has always been—it still is— the nature of net income. The earlier consensus resolved the matter as indicated above and showed a marked preference for the related conception of the nature of income. The heart of the belief was the idea that fixed assets contributed service, and for that reason the cost of that service should be part of the net income calculation along with other service charges (expenses). That point is not denied today; it is the determination of the amount chargeable that has become an issue.

It is not the present purpose to discuss the current issue. But while that issue is still a live one, it may be of interest to restate some general conclusions regarding depreciation ideas of the nineteenth century.

Depreciation was an old idea even in the nineteenth century. In his text of 1588, John Mellis credits "Implements of householde" account for the amount judged to be "consumed and worn," and debits "profit and loss" account for the same amount, "lost by decay of householde stuff." In 1690, Stephen Monteage's text illustrated an account for horses; it had on the credit side an item "lost by their use." The account for "loss and gain" is debited.

The preferred theory and method of today are both very similar. As to theory, the consensus is that depreciation is a periodic expense. That was the idea in these examples from the sixteenth and seventeenth centuries. As to method, we credit a "reserve" rather than the depreciating asset account itself. But teachers explain the "reserve" relating to depreciation as designed to preserve the credit items separate from the asset debits in order to report a cumulative total of "charge off" that will

---

be deducted in the balance sheet from the original invested cost of the asset concerned. The so-called "reserve" is not an appropriation of surplus or an amount measuring a sum held back for replacement; it delays the direct association of an asset and a logical credit to that asset until the balance sheet is constructed. At that time we deduct the amount of depreciation credit, as Mellis and Monteage did more directly.

The distinction between "loss" and "lost" is not clear in the earlier treatment of depreciation. A debit found its way into loss and gain account on the theory of "wear and tear" as we would say. The horse account in Monteage's illustration, after the posted depreciation credit, shows "By balance resting, 6 horses valued at 7£." The original asset debit was for 6 horses valued at 8£ each. Obviously this represents an asset account brought to a balance by insertion of a repriced inventory of the remaining items. John Mair (1768 edition) explains the treatment of a ship account as if it were a mixed merchandise account: ". . . first give the account credit by balance for the value of the ship and then close the account with Profit and Loss."

This "inventory approach" to recognition of depreciation in the accounts continued into the nineteenth century. Under this view depreciation of a ship would be no different, in principle, from the loss of a ship in a storm. May it not have been recognition of an essential difference in these two situations which gave rise to the idea of "capital loss" and to a different treatment of this item in the accounts?

The inventory view of a depreciating asset, however, underwent a noteworthy change toward the middle of the nineteenth century. The appearance of steam railroads at that time directed attention as never before to fixed assets and their associated problems of maintenance, renewal, and improvement. Out of the discussion and experience which followed, new ideas took form and the ground was prepared for a better comprehension of the nature of depreciation.

As early as 1841, an article in a British railway magazine gave emphasis to the necessity for careful and periodical ascertaining of "the precise comparative degree of wear and tear" so that only bona fide net income would be apportioned to the shareholders. Depreciation here comes close to being considered cost rather than a loss ascertained by inventory. But practice varied. Some railroads adopted an annual valuation method, that is, using an inventory approach. Others formed a "depreciation fund" by setting aside "for repairs an annual percentage above the ordinary charges."

American railroads also faced the depreciation question in several ways. The Baltimore and Ohio (report of 1833) used a twelve-year annuity to estimate tie renewal expense. The Reading Railroad (1839) lumped depreciation and repair of engines at an estimated 25 per cent. As might be expected, the idea was also held by some people that a company "annually stored away in times of prosperity while their work [assets] are new, at least six cents an engine mile" (*American Railroad Journal*, 1843). Others favored ignoring depreciation if repairs were considered sufficient to make good the wear and tear; or they preferred to charge certain capital expenditures to expense if repairs expense had been inadequate to cover depreciation. Surely such variety of treatment called for some striving toward a consensus.

In the 1880's, the discussion of depreciation began to expand beyond railroad circles and to be considered in connection with manufacturing companies as well. Edwin Guthrie, when lecturing to the Manchester Students Society in 1883, pointed out that all costs of goods and services consumed in producing manufactured goods must be fully known before "the recoupment of capital outlay" could be ascertained; he specifically classed machinery and building as consumable over a period of years. A series of articles in the next year by Ewing Matheson was published as a book, *The Depreciation of Factories*. A great many ideas, now generally accepted, were either indicated or foreshadowed there. The author considered unsound the theory that maintenance will balance depreciation and thought periodic revaluations were not a feasible approach to depreciation. He does not approve using a fixed percentage of profits, his reason: "deterioration goes on even if no profits are being earned." The best method he believes is to charge all maintenance to revenue and calculate depreciation as a percentage of the capital value "as it was left at the previous reviews." This has most of the characteristics of the declining-balance method. In spite of his grasp of much of the depreciation problems, Matheson does not fully associate depreciation with factory cost of production. It was characteristic of the early years of cost accounting to include depreciation among other "establishment charges" in the expense section of the profit and loss statement. Later writers, including J. S. Lewis (1896), Garcke and Fell's (1893) *et al.*, treated depreciation less thoroughly although they were writing on cost accounting as such.

Since the idea of depreciation was known at least as early as the sixteenth century, one might question why it did not receive greater development until the middle of the nineteenth, and why then.

Some of the answer may be found in surrounding circumstances that differed materially in the early years and the later. Business units were small ones with few strong incentives for proprietors sharply to refine the calculation of enterprise profit. A small number of large units, such as the overseas trading companies (East Indies Company, Hudson's Bay Company *et al.*) did in fact overshadow proprietorship in size, but size did not bring recognition of depreciation. Company profits then were very ample; of creditors there were few or none; many shareholders before long were strongly attracted to the new pastime of trading in company shares—under these conditions little incentive appeared for sharpening the calculation of net profit.

The circumstances most likely to have created a new incentive seem to have been (1) popularization of limited liability companies endowed with relative permanency of status, (2) perception of the fact that a corporation was an entity separate from its shareholders and creditors, and (3) a consequence of the first two, the necessity for protecting capital stock against impairment from excessive dividends. Measuring correctly the amount available for dividends called for new niceties in the calculation of periodic net income. The somewhat dormant knowledge of the fact that long-lived assets were eventually worn out from services rendered in each year came strongly to life. Under the new circumstances the service rendered by fixed assets slowly emerged as their strongest characteristic. Today it is commonplace to compact this conception into the thought that fixed assets are in effect deferred charges against revenue. However the idea may be phrased, the concept, as soon as men became aware of it, made it necessary to treat depreciation as an expense, and later as a cost of production of goods that were on their way to take part in the periodic calculation of enterprise net income.

Looking even briefly at depreciation ideas over the centuries from the sixteenth to twentieth century can make us not only aware of its long development but also of the fact that depreciation, perhaps more than any other aspect of accounting theory and practice, brings us closest to the heart land of double entry. Depreciation accounting and its many theoretical facets force us to think sharply of the continuing significance of the integration of real and nominal accounts, and of the amazing adaptability—flexibility with strength—of this very old technology.

(Chapter 16, *Accounting Evolution to 1900*)

10. Change in Financial Statements

A listing of property possessed and debts owed could be made without benefit of double entry merely by counting and valuing the items and consulting some kind of record of debts owing and owed. The assembled figures would lead to a calculation of net worth as the difference between the two totals. Usage to the contrary notwithstanding, such a listing hardly deserves the designation "financial statement"; it is a valuation calculation of solvency. More meaning lies in the phrase "financial statement" than this.

The principal superiority of real financial statements, in the best sense of that term, is the fact that the data reported have been objectively derived in the first instance. The count-and-appraise approach will result in a much more subjective report because many items will be open to evaluation (pricing) by the party most at interest. Financial statements as such rest upon objectively determined invested costs, which have been recorded and classified by the rules of double entry. Appraisal statements on the other hand rest upon subjective opinion of values, and as a result, are beyond verification review or testing by reference to collateral data.

The essential purpose of financial statements has changed little over the centuries. That purpose has long been the presentation of a compact summary of the established facts about a business enterprise, set up in a manner designed to picture in money figures (1) the relation existing at the moment between property and debt, and (2) the relation between income earned and expense incurred. One presentation portrays financial status and degree of solvency; the other measures economic progress and net income produced. And the two reports, since the data came from double-entry records, integrate one with the other just as the real and nominal accounts in a double-entry ledger are integrated; and thus they support and validate each other.

Although purpose has not changed, ways of implementing purpose have changed over the years. Financial statements of today are the result of evolutionary change; consequently they may become more understandable from viewing them in historical perspective.

As soon as double-entry methodology had been worked out, probably by trial and error under many hands, the ledger included a profit and loss account which received the transfer of nominal account data in summary form. A copy of this account became, when need arose, a profit and loss statement. To judge by some early texts, modern readers might conclude that no similar ledger source was provided which, when copied on separate paper, might be considered a statement of assets and liabilities. Other contemporary writers however have indicated that this was not the case; their texts included what we now would call an "assets and liabilities summary account," but was at that time called a "balance account," or "the balance (balancing?) of the books."

Since the principal features of double entry persist to this day, we can readily surmise what once was a fact, namely, that the balance account received summarizing transfers from all property and debt accounts. Today such data would produce a "post-closing trial balance," but this summary would not have a place within the ledger. Here we see an old and still useful idea under another name. How old? Gotlieb, 1546; Pietra, 1576; Dafforne, 1635; and Liset, 1684, the latter being English texts. In these cases, and probably in general practice, the summaries within the ledgers sufficed. The parties at interest were proprietors or partners who had access at will to the accumulating entries in the regular ledger accounts and needed no separate copies of summary accounts. In fact, it was customary in many enterprises for long intervals to omit a formal closing of nominal accounts to profit and loss, for often several years or perhaps not until a change took place in the members of the partnership.

It seems to have been a Dutch author (Simon Stevin, 1608) who made a point of separating both sets of data, real accounts and nominal ac-

counts, from the ledger and using the two resulting tabulations to demonstrate the outstanding characteristic of double entry, namely, the integration of real and nominal accounts, the mutual tie-in of the two
financial statements. The matter is such an important feature of modern
accounting that it will be of interest to give this author's idea in some
detail, using a translation published in the *Institute of Bookkeeper's
Journal* (London, December, 1927).

> . . . I collect together the accounts of money, wares, debtors . . . such things
are taken of which it is usual to make up an estate on a certain day. . . . Thus
the estate would appear as follows:

The Estate of Derick Roose
made up on the last day of December 1600

Estate of Capital debit	£ s d	Estate of Capital credit	£ s d
Per Arnold Jacobs	51- 8-0	per nuts	60-13-2
Balance debit, put here in		per pepper	20- 0-0
order to close this statement	3140- 9-1	per Omar de Sevarte	513-12-0
		per Adrian de Winter	150- 6-0
		per Peter de Witte	448- 0-0
		per Jack de Somer	54-18-6
		per cash	1944- 7-5
Total....	3191-17-1	Total	3191-17-1

The remainder of the year is 3140- 9-1
At the beginning of the year it was 2153- 3-8

Increase during the year 987- 5-5

Proof of the Estate

In order to make certain that the above Estate is correct I collect all remainders of accounts increasing or decreasing capital.

Estate of Capital debit	£ s d	Estate of Capital credit	£ s d
Per trading expenses.	57- 7-0	Per profit on cloves	75- 4-7
Per household expenses.	107-10-1	Per profit on nuts	109- 7-2
Total	164-17-0	Per profit on pepper	18-19-0
Remaining credit being		Per profit on ginger	41- 8-4
profit agreeing with the		Per Profit and Loss	907- 3-4
above statement	987- 5-5		
	1152- 2-5		1152- 2-5

> 'Since the profit ascertained in this way is equal to that found in the Estate,
viz £987-5s-5d, this may be taken as the Proof of the work.'

Stevin in this presentation shows a better grasp of the heart of double
entry than many authors whose texts appeared later. It is interesting as
a collateral note that Stevin's balance sheet (the Estate) stands in the
form now used in Great Britain, assets on the right, liabilities and capital
on the left.

It is a matter of speculation to try to state the concepts which underlie this arrangement and to decide whether the Dutch presentation furnished the model adopted into British practice. The "Estate" statement

would seem not to be a fair copy of a ledger account which had received transfers from all asset and liability accounts, for in that case, assets would stand on the debit side in the balance account and in the copied statement. It may be possible that the statement data came out of a transfer journal entry from which the real accounts were posted and closed. If the liability-asset arrangement did not derive from double-entry methodology, the reason for the order becomes even more obscure. It would seem obscure, even though a similar arrangement of assets and debts were found antedating double entry, to have been used by lawyers in connection with trustee reports to the early courts in stating the discharge of the trustees' responsibilities under a deceased person's will and testament.

It may be farfetched to cite a practice in the middle of the nineteenth century as related to this earlier left-right arrangement. Yet both this and the later usage could stem from the same concepts, whether in bookkeeping or law. The British bankruptcy act of 1861, in schedule 16, prescribed a form of statement of accounts designed for use by trustees in bankruptcy in reporting to the courts on the state of affairs of a bankrupt merchant. On the left side of the form is presented a list of secured creditors, unsecured creditors, creditors to be paid in full, and any contingent liabilities on discounted bills. On the right are debtors, classified good, doubtful, or bad, and the property given up to the assignees or trustees in bankruptcy. Clearly this is the forerunner of the modern statement of affairs. But it is not equally clear whether this statutory form reflects prior accounting usage, prior legal usage, or some combination of the two which antedated Stevin's arrangement of "The Estate of Derick Roose" in 1608.

Might it not be that early trustees, whether lawyers, accountants, or laymen, may have reasoned by analogy in trying to decide originally how to report on their responsibilities? One could reason this way: If I were a merchant reporting on property received from another, I would show that I owed him the amount of property received. To owe, is to credit. When reporting on the discharge of my responsibility, I would then report a debit in cancellation of the prior credit. It would be clear reporting therefore if I, as trustee, report as credit the property received (assets) from the estate and as debit (discharge of responsibility) the disposition I must make or have made of the property intrusted to my care, but not report on my ownership. Even though I as trustee do not hold the property in ownership possession and though I am not liable as a debtor is liable, I nevertheless have a somewhat analogous responsibility for and possession of the property involved. Because of the similarity, though not the identity, of the merchant's situation and of mine as trustee, it will be understandable reporting if I show as credit the assets intrusted and as debits the discharge or duty to discharge the trust obligations respecting the assets.

When men copied on separate sheets the details of the two summary accounts from a double-entry ledger, financial statements began. The development thereafter was in the direction of experimental arrangements of the figures and refinements of classification.

Lest we think that columnar worksheets are a modern invention, we may note that Dafforne's texts (1635, 1686) illustrated a six-column treatment of what he termed "survey of the general balance, or Estate reckoning," three columns being used for debits and three for credits. The first pair of columns reported a trial balance of totals, the middle columns a trial balance of balances, and the last columns contain the residual assets, liabilities, and capital. There were no columns for assembling expenses and gains. Was this omission deliberate and designed to give emphasis to the "Estate," i.e., balance sheet, alone? Such choice of emphasis was in any event a particular feature of accounting practice for corporate enterprises in the nineteenth century and later. Indeed, strong emphasis upon the importance of the income statement emerged only after one-third of the twentieth century had passed. Later texts (Goddard, 1834; Colt, 1838) included the profit and loss column in the worksheet illustrations.

Usually in the nineteenth century the statements were presented in the same form as ledger accounts, thus following earlier custom. In Hamilton's text (1788) one was called "profit and loss sheet," the other "balance sheet." This is an early, perhaps the first, use of the latter term. Colt's text refers to his columnar presentation as "balance sheet"; but Harris (1842) applies the term to the listing in account form of assets, liabilities, and capital. This arrangement persisted into the twentieth century; the basic structure of the balance sheet is still that of contrasting left and right sections.

However, a writer in 1848 (Peter Duff) used another arrangement, for instructional purposes at least. He required the student "to list his effects" from the ledger and strike a total; then list his debts and strike a total; subtracting produced a remainder, "my present net capital." Comparison of this statement with the balance account in the ledger will give "a clearer insight into the nature and object of that account than all the rules that bookkeepers have ever written about it." The modern income statement is now usually presented in the vertical report form. Why this statement developed that way and the balance sheet did not is difficult to say.

More important changes were taking place than over-all structural arrangement, particularly in the matter of grouping data into subsections. In the nineteenth century the naming of the major classes of accounts was much debated. Some people suggested primary and secondary, or real and representative. In three-way classifications, some preferred to classify items as material property, personal accounts, and profit and loss; others liked real, personal, and imaginary (or fictitious) accounts.

Apparently the major stumbling block was the naming of the group we now call "nominal accounts." Before that term was generally accepted, we find "secondary," "representative," "imaginary," and "fictitious." Settling for "nominal" was not very logical; neither this nor any of the other terms characterize the true nature of accounts for cost, expense, and revenue. But there is no need to cling to old terms if more expressive ones can be found. In the middle of the twentieth century a good deal of discussion of terminology has appeared. But the term "nominal" is still vague, but for texts and teaching it is much more in need of modernization than some other terms under current discussion.

Progress has been slow. The present subdivision of the balance sheet into current assets, fixed assets, intangibles, deferred charges, current liabilities, long-term debt, capital stock, reserves, and surplus evolved only slowly within the twentieth century as an accompaniment, it seems, to the growth and expansion of the corporate form of enterprise.

The late nineteenth century also saw the beginning of the refinement in financial statements now commonly known as accruals and deferments. The idea itself is met earlier here and there, but it lay relatively dormant for a long time as far as general usage was concerned. For example, out of fifty textbooks scattered over the years between 1788 and 1899, only some 10 per cent attempted to teach accruals. Those few used items such as the following: interest due the bank; wages due a clerk (1788); bad debts at 3 per cent of sales (1840), interest payable on mortgage (1861); rent due or paid in advance, fuel unconsumed (1877).

In the present day, accounting adjustments seldom fail to give special consideration to fixed assets and merchandise inventory in order to separate balance sheet aspects and income statement aspects. Before the twentieth century, however, fixed assets were few, and text discussions of depreciation were infrequent. The usual approach was by inserting an inventory in the fixed asset account and transferring any debit remainder to profit and loss. Even if this method was described, the basis of pricing the fixed assets was seldom made clear. Presumably the price was a matter of personal judgment. We may conclude therefore that the price could be made high or low if the choice were made consciously to influence the remainder and thus affect calculated net profit. A more direct statement is sometimes met (as in J. G. Pilsen's text, 1877) to the effect that we "take off a percentage for wear and tear" of property not for sale but listed as inventory. But even such a directive fails to make the point clear that depreciation is a true cost of operation rather than the result of a valuation of an inventory at the owner's discretion.

In regard to merchandise inventory, text-writers had more to say, but here too the problem of pricing (valuing?) the items appeared to be most strongly influenced by need for a balance sheet item. Ideas were various. In 1837, B. F. Foster estimated the value of property unsold; in 1842, Harris (*Practical Bookkeeping*) used a value no more or less than the property could be sold for; in 1854, Fleming (*Bookkeeping by Double Entry*) valued merchandise in proportion to its first cost.

The outstanding changes in financial statements over the years can be compacted into a few sentences. First, the data of property and capital and the data of income and expense came to be reported separately from the ledger; the balance account disappeared, although the profit and loss account still remains. Second, the early arrangement of the reported data, reflecting the form of an account with left and right sides clearly indicated, underwent some reorganization—some balance sheets, while holding to the account form, reported assets on the left; others showed assets on the right side; and most statements began to group related items into subsections. Third, a beginning was made in refining the data reported in financial statements. This was accomplished by giving increased recognition to accrued and deferred items, to fixed asset depreciation, and to rational pricing of merchandise inventories.

It must be said that progress was made in improving financial statements, even though it was slow. From the vantage point of later years and of ideas now generally accepted, the following extract from a text early in the eighteenth century (Jacques Savary, 1712) seems strikingly modern. "If this merchandise is commencing to deteriorate, or go out of style, or is that which one judges he could find at the factory or wholesalers at 5% less, it must be reduced to this price."

This idea is now headlined as "cost or market, whichever is lower," and persists (in spite of modern critics) some 250 years later. But the idea's prestige during most of the intervening time does not seem to have been very strong, for it is very seldom reflected in the contemporary literature of the nineteenth century.

(Chapter 9, *Accounting Evolution to 1900*)

PUBLIC ACCOUNTING

1. Experts in Accounts

It is a convenient bench mark in the evolution of public accounting to note that Scottish accountants formed a professional society in 1854, and that English accountants between 1870 and 1880 formed similar local societies in various English cities. But these dates do not mark the beginning of public accounting; before professional societies appeared, professional accountants had been serving their public for many years.

City directories in the fourth quarter of the eighteenth century listed a few men as holding themselves out to the public for accounting work. Some examples are the following: Edinburgh, 1774 (14); Glasgow, 1783 (6); Liverpool, 1796 (10); London, 1799 (11). In the early nineteenth century the numbers increase somewhat: London, 1811 (24), 1820 (44); Edinburgh, 1821 (58); Bristol, 1830 (28); Manchester, 1831 (32). Beginning in 1840, however, growth in the number of professional accountants increased: London, 1845 (210), 1860 (310), 1870 (467); Liverpool, 1860 (91), 1870 (139); Manchester, 1861 (84), 1871 (159). In a single generation between 1811 and 1847, the number of accounting firms in the London directories increased almost eightfold; total population did not quite double in this interval. In another generation—up to 1883—the number of London accountants increased four and one half times.

No profession grows by willing growth to come; a social need must first come into existence that can be served by a class of experts. The need generates the response. The British people had gained considerable experience with audits before public accounting had appeared. The chamberlain of London in 1298 was audited by a committee of aldermen, sheriffs, and certain other people. The city of Dublin in 1316 required the collectors of taxes to render account of receipts and payments "before the commonalty of their auditors." The Pewterer's Guild provided in its book of ordinances (1564) that "foure Audytours" be chosen every year "to audit the crafts accompts." On the English landed estates in the fifteenth century it was the usual practice to have the extensive records dealing with estate operations audited by an experienced man on the nobleman's council. In one directive dated 1605, this item appears: "The auditor being the laste of all officers, is to bee judge betwixte the lorde and his accomptants."

In all of these early examples it will be noted that the auditors were "middlemen" charged with a double duty and standing independent between parties having differing, perhaps conflicting, interests. The professional public accountant today is still a "moderator" with a duty running to both parties at interest.

In later years in certain types of legal situations a need appeared for men of integrity and business experience having an expert knowledge of accounts. As executors of estates and trustees in bankruptcy, the individuals often had to face large responsibilities and complex situations. Their duties as a fiduciary placed them also between parties with possible conflicting interests, as life tenant and remainderman, or as bankrupt merchant and his creditors. At first these men were not professionals offering services to the general public; yet they were not "internal accountants" for one of the parties concerned. In a sense they linked the past to the present; they marked a transition between the auditor who was a member of a nobleman's council and the present-day chartered accountant holding out his services to the general public.

The linkage between the twentieth century and the sixteenth is also to be observed in the arrangement of the facts in the financial report of the present-day executor of an estate. He charges himself with the items of estate property intrusted to his administration and with additions thereto during his term of responsibility; he discharges himself with estate property disposed of as directed in the will and shows as balance the estate property still in his possession at the date of report. This is essentially the same arrangement of data made by every person in the typical English landed estate of the sixteenth century who had a responsibility for certain property, e.g., the cook for food materials received, cooked, and passed to the servers in the great hall. It was also the form in which the accounts for the whole establishment were cast at the end of a year; it was the "financial statement" which the nobleman's "awdy tour" carefully checked against other reports and records and signed if correct.

Trustees in bankruptcy were often used in nineteenth century England. Between 1815 and 1866, there were half-a-dozen industrial and financial crises as a result of changing economic conditions. Many merchants, under those conditions, could not pay their debts as due. The tendency of the time was to consider the businessman rather than economic conditions as responsible for the sad state of his affairs and for the actual or potential loss to his creditors. As a result, seven statutes on bankruptcy were passed between 1825 and 1883; all were concerned with the administration of the bankrupt's affairs in the interest of his creditors or with realization of his assets and the disposition of the proceeds among his creditors.

The statute of 1861 required among other things that the trustees in bankruptcy furnish the creditors a statement of account every three months and file with the court a complete statement of account before final discharge. The form of this statement of account is still in use under the title "statement of affairs," supplemented by a "deficiency account." The first statement set up a contrast between (1) creditors classified as to secured, unsecured, or preferred status, and (2) property in the hands of the trustees, debts receivable classified as good, doubtful, or bad, and ended with the amount of the deficiency. The other statement, even as today, contrasted the various losses and the firm's capital, leading to a balance of "deficiency" as in the statement of affairs.

According to contemporary opinion, the number of bankruptcies over the years and the complexities of carrying the analytical report back to a time when the merchant could show he was solvent, created a not inconsiderable demand for expert services. One chartered accountant who began practice near the middle of the century was of the considered opinion that the period 1847-49 (crisis of 1847, bankruptcy law of 1849) "did more than anything else to place professional accountancy on a solid and substantial basis." The work of some accountants of the time undoubtedly derived almost entirely from business failures. Other observers were of the opinion that preparation of statements for bankrupts, as required by the statute of 1849, "brought many well known accountants into prominence and repute." There is some basis for the belief therefore that professional auditing could also be traced back in part to examinations and statements connected with composition with creditors or liquidation of firms in financial difficulty.

(Chapter 16, *Accounting Evolution to 1900*)

2. Statutory Audits

A significant development related to public accounting took place in England during the first half of the nineteenth century. The statutory controls then erected over joint-stock companies in the public interest made extensive use of accounting and auditing.

British experience with joint-stock companies in the eighteenth century had not been a happy one. Extensive frauds in the midst of wild speculation in company shares brought such a severe reaction in Parliament that company formation was banned during the next one hundred years. Slowly, in the first half of the nineteenth century, the advantages of joint-stock companies were impressed upon the Parliament, with the result that, after preliminary legislation in 1825 and 1837, laws were passed in 1844 and 1845. These laws set up the conditions under which companies with a joint stock might be formed by complying with statutes wherein particular care had been taken to establish safeguards against fraudulent actions by promoters and directors which earlier had done so much to foster speculation in company shares.

In addition to requiring public registration of companies, a check upon directors was provided by requiring accounts to be kept and the appointment of auditors who would be representatives of the shareholders and report to them, and by directing that the balance sheet and the auditors' report be sent to the registrars of joint-stock companies as well as to the shareholders before the general meeting.

This statutory foundation for setting a check upon business companies was effectively supplemented by the Companies Act of 1862. The main accounting features of the prior statutes were continued and strengthened by additional provisions, including several which more precisely set forth the responsibilities and duties of the auditor to examine the accounts and report. The antecedent of the present audit certificate is found here, where the statute stated that the auditors were to report "whether in their opinion the balance sheet is a full and fair balance sheet containing the particulars required by these regulations and properly drawn up so as to exhibit a true and correct view of the state of the company's affairs."

The main purposes of these laws, as indicated more briefly above, were to establish (1) some degree of public control over company formation and (2) some check upon the directors' discharge of their managerial and fiscal responsibilities. The first was accomplished by registration of the relevant facts and careful scrutiny thereof by a public registrar who had power to deny registration to unfit projects. The second purpose was achieved by requiring the shareholders, or their representatives, to audit the records and financial statements of the directors. Through knowledge thus made available to them, the shareholders were given the basis for judging the actions of the directors and holding the latter responsible for the results of their actions.

It will be noted that the audits here required by statute were not particularly related to a lender's problem of granting credit to a company. The auditor's attention, therefore, was not so strongly pointed toward testing the ability of the company to repay short-term loans (as indicated by the relation of current assets and current liabilities) as was the case in nonstatutory American practice. The intention back of the British requirements was that of putting in the hands of shareholders dependable information regarding the results of the actions of company directors elected by them to operate the company in the shareholders' interest.

In framing the companies acts, Parliament undoubtedly had public welfare in mind and the need to protect shareholders against fraudulent promotions and directors' mismanagement. To insure such protection would be good public policy. Because knowledge of the usefulness of adequate and audited records had been transmitted from feudal days, it would have been surprising if provision for accounts and audits had been omitted from the companies acts when these were under development.

It was quite incidental that these laws should aid in the formation of a definite profession of public accounting whose practitioners would be independent experts. The original expectation had been that a few shareholders would check the records of the directors and report to their colleagues. But the seeds of a profession had earlier lodged in fertile soil and had already begun to grow. Even before the nineteenth century, men had gained expert experience with accounts. Some of these, no doubt, had already been helpful to shareholders in companies organized under letters patent. Such men and their technical knowledge would be remembered; their capacity to be helpful would be recognized by shareholders who were selected as audit committees under the law of 1844.

Some such idea must have been present; in the next year the law was elaborated in certain particulars, especially in the fact that it made specific the privilege of shareholder—auditors to employ "accountants" as outside assistants equipped with technical knowledge. This was perhaps but meager recognition of the experts in accounts of that day; but the way was opened, the men were available, and their service soon demonstrated their capacity to take larger responsibilities. It is possible to trace through the succession of companies acts the gradual recognition of this fact. As a result of demonstrated ability to serve and to grow in that ability, more demands were made for service, more responsibility was lodged, and more independence granted. Soon professional societies were formed and given control over admission of individuals into professional service. Today it is a statutory requirement in Britain that the auditor must be an independent professional as indicated by his membership in a recognized professional society.

These nineteenth century developments, in thus extending the sphere of service of double-entry bookkeeping, were quite consistent with England's past. In fact, in the light of surrounding conditions, the professionalization of auditing seems a most natural consequence. The need for independent check (inspection or audit) lies deep in human nature. When persons were given designated fiscal responsibilities whether in relation to government revenue, manorial estate management, or craft guild operation, some type of "audit" had long since been brought into use. The financial responsibilities resting upon the directors of joint-stock business enterprises in industrial Britain were not basically different from those delegated to the officers in a feudal lord's household. Only the setting was different, and a profit motive was attached to the operations. Yet the similarity was long overlooked. The shock of frauds and huge speculative losses which resulted from uncontrolled stock promotions finally left responsible government no alternative but to seek ways and means to protect the public interest. Bad experience thus provided evidence of need for controls; earlier good experience suggested the means of putting company promotion and operation under check and restraint.

It is perhaps particularly significant that the exercise of safeguard controls must rest upon adequate knowledge of relevant enterprise facts. It is in the nature of accounting to provide relevant facts, and it is the nature of auditing to test the adequacy (dependability) of those facts. These technologies therefore could and did serve the public interest.

(Chapter 18, *Accounting Evolution to 1900*)

3. Public Accounting in the United States

One of the characteristics of "public" accounting is that its practitioners "hold themselves out," that is, offer their services to the general public rather than accept employment in a simple enterprise. Men like George Watson (d. 1723) and Alexander Chalmers (d. 1759) often placed their knowledge at the disposal of others than their employers. But they were not public accountants; one was cashier of a large mercantile firm; the other was accountant for the city of Edinburgh. When men began to list their names as accountants in the city directories, they were offering their services at large. In the directories of Edinburgh before 1800, a small number of names appear: 1773 (7), 1774 (14), 1778 (14). The number increased later: 1821 (58), 1834 (80); Glasgow, 1801 (6), 1821 (16); London, 1776 (1), 1840 (107); Liverpool, 1796 (10), 1860 (91).

City directories in the United States reflect similar growth trends but from a later start. Three cities, New York, Chicago, and Philadelphia, listed totals as follows in sample years: 1870 (28), 1880 (49), 1885 (91), 1890 (125), 1894 (208), 1899 (332).

Although the time periods were different, the pattern of growth was similar in both Great Britain and the United States. In the former the increase was very gradual until about 1840; in the next thirty years the number of listed public accountants increased approximately fourfold. The change in both countries is noticeably associated with periods of rapid increase in the number of business corporations.

In 1870, the listings were as follows: New York (12), Chicago (2), and Philadelphia (14); in 1884, the numbers were 47, 13, and 21 respectively; in 1890, 66, 24, and 35; in 1899, 183, 71, and 74.

The turnover of listed personnel was considerable; many names soon disappeared. Some appeared in as many as 20 or more annual directories. New York, 6 names; Philadelphia, 4. Some names appeared 15 times. New York, 17; Philadelphia, 8. For Chicago, only 10 names appear 10 times or more; close to 53 per cent appeared only once. In Philadelphia, there was a similar showing, and 66 names appeared only twice. New York did better; 305 individuals, almost 45 per cent, appeared only once and 110 only twice. For the three cities, 1850-99, a total of 1,370 different individuals or firms were listed; of this number, 662 appeared only once; thus about one half gave up the attempt to reach the public in this manner. Perhaps many were qualified only to keep books.

The subsequent history of those who survived is interesting. Out of 1,370 individuals or firms, 886 names appeared only once or twice. Of the 484 names appearing three times or more, almost one half (211) later obtained the CPA certificate. Of the 211 who later became CPA's, 31 first listed their names in the 1870's; 28, in the 1880's; and 145, in the 1890's—most of these in 1895, 1896, and 1897.

An upsurge in the last decade is evident here. But the increase was not evenly distributed. Except for 1895, the rate was close to 16 names a year; in 1895, however, 44 new names appeared; in the three years 1895-97, 65 names were added. The first CPA law (New York, 1896) may have had an influence; it was under consideration in 1895, and the first examination was given in 1897. It would seem probable from the upsurge in listings that more people than named in the directories were giving other people accounting service besides that rendered to a single employer and were ready to hold themselves out generally if enough clients seemed available.

Another view of the growth of public accounting in the United States can be had from the advertising pages of the old city directories. Some extracts typical of the period before 1885 are as follows:

1851. Practical bookkeeper and accountant. Books opened, closed, posted. Book-keeping taught.

1875. Prepared to make statements for executors; examine corporation, partner-ship, industrial books and accounts of every description. Books posted monthly and trial balance taken at a trifling cost.

1880. The rigid investigation of complicated and debated matters, and the clear presentation of the results divested of technicality, a specialty. Particular attention given to the books of insurance companies, and the accounts of executors, estates in trust and bankrupt estates.

The following extracts come from directories after 1885:

1889. Public auditor and accountant. Over twenty years practical experience. Balance sheets proved and verified. Banks and railway accounts a spe-ciality.

1889. Fellow of American Association of Public Accountants with twenty years of experience. Prepared to arrange books for any business. Partnership and disputed accounts adjusted. Competent assistants furnished to write up accounts.

1891. Public accountant and auditor. Consulting accountant. Fifteen years prac-tical experience. Complications a specialty. Highest testaments for accu-racy and simplicity of labor saving systems.

1896. Public accountants and auditors. Periodical expert examinations a spe-cialty. Investigation in matters of defalcation. Balance sheets and state-ments of profit and loss prepared, certificates as to profits.

Back of these samples lies the implication that periodic audits were relatively infrequent before the turn of the century. The greatest im-pulse toward regular audits came later in the United States. No statutory requirements for audits existed here. Public accounting made its way without statutory aids. The service rendered bankers and other lenders through "balance sheet audits" seemed particularly appreciated and proved during the first quarter of the twentieth century to be an important steppingstone to the development of the profession in the United States.

(University of Illinois, Bureau of Business Research,
Bulletin No. 40, October 13, 1942)

4. American Audits

Robert H. Montgomery's long career in public accounting touched the early days of American auditing as well as the years of its modern aspects. It was as a contemporary to the circumstances that he expressed the opinion in 1912 (*Auditing Theory and Practice*) that most early audits were "bookkeeper audits." The program of examination, he indicated, usually consisted of vouching all cash disbursements, checking all footings and postings, checking the ledger to the trial balance, and the latter to the financial statements (p. 80). He estimated that three-fourths of the audit time was spent on footings and postings, whereas experience showed that three-fourths of the defalcations were hidden by failures to account for income or cash receipts (p. 258). Later (*Fifty Years of Accountancy*) he expressed the view (p. 316) that the auditor of fifty years earlier had no recognized professional status largely because the matters referred to him were relatively unimportant and this tended to reduce him to the level of a clerk.

Although early American audit programs may now seem overly simplified, they nevertheless expressed a planned and critical approach to the facts in the case. Wherein they proved faulty, in due time they were changed; wherein they proved satisfactory, they fostered in the auditor a detached and independent point of view and supported a conscious effort to avoid personal bias. Today, if we look at auditing thoughtfully, it is possible to see something of a scientific attitude of mind at work and to see in the skilled auditor some of the marks of a scientific investigator.

Possibly this kind of development was inherent in the materials of accounting. For, without ever aspiring to the status of a science, accounting is much more than "keeping books." It is, in fact, an important method of thinking factually about a business enterprise. And an auditor is more than one man of a team engaged in calling back book entries to documents. "He alone of professional men," a president of the American Institute of Accountants once said, "occupies the unique position of interpreter and arbiter among parties of opposing interests in financial transactions, serving simultaneously creditor and debtor, management and investor, taxpayer and tax collector, the regulator and regulated."

The audit function is not unique to accounting. The architect's supervision of a building under construction and the engineer's critical inspection of road-building are "audits" in their intention and effect.

So too are the physician's clinical tests and the chemist's analysis of unknown compounds. Each expert follows techniques peculiar to his own field, but a necessary part of each of these "audits" is to know before judging.

Inspection, examination, review, analysis, test, verification—these words may connote different methods of attack in different kinds of scrutiny. Yet behind them all are the same questions: What are the facts? Are the apparent facts complete and dependable? What significance attaches to a particular grouping or timing of the facts?

From an examination of auditing literature it is evident that American practice in the first decade of the twentieth century was compressing the procedures of a general audit in various ways in order to produce a program better suited to local conditions. Out of the efforts of many people came a type of program that soon was called a balance sheet audit. It is not clear where the name started. Some of the earlier writers seemed to be thinking of this sort of program but did not call it by name. However, by 1912 the pattern was well enough established to be described at length under the present characteristic name.

In Montgomery's 1912 preface the author indicated the American point of view as a departure from the procedures described in typical British texts. He indicated that for our purposes the detection of fraud and error must take second place to the ascertainment of actual financial condition and earning of an enterprise. All parties at interest would benefit: proprietors, stockholders, managerial executives, prospective investors, and bankers considering short-term loans on promissory notes. Statements certified by disinterested and competent persons could assure users of the fairness and accuracy of all essential particulars. Such statements thus become particularly useful as a basis for credit ratings by mercantile agencies and for loan decisions by bankers or note-brokers.

The approach indicated by these ideas is not at all the one most suited to finding carefully concealed evidence of speculations. It requires less experience and judgment to set up a program to uncover a defalcation than to plan an audit in such a way as to deal well with "the more important branches of the auditor's duties." By this phrase Montgomery refers to "higher frauds," and to all the professional services an auditor can render beyond following in the figure footsteps of the client's bookkeepers.

Without saying it in so many words, Montgomery is indicating in his early chapters that American auditors were beginning to look upon their work as "researching" rather than "rechecking." And that is as it should be in a profession.

It is noteworthy that the purpose stressed is to ascertain the financial condition and earnings of the concern under audit. It is considered more important to devote audit time to the search for possible evidence of "higher fraud" than for employee thefts.

These considerations help to shape the preferred audit procedure away from a pattern that would take the auditor through the bookkeeper's sequence of operations. Since a possible misinterpretation of accounting principles is considered more significant than errors in posting, it is understandable that analysis of account content is given a higher usefulness than checking vouchers, postings, and footings.

Since an auditor is more than a technician, he should cultivate judgment-guided procedures rather than depend on simpler methods built around checking. Analysis directed toward the most likely spots takes judgment; calling back postings merely takes close attention. Reasonableness has an important place in the audit. Are the inventory quantities reasonable in view of average consumption? Is the volume of receivables reasonably in line with that of other concerns in the auditor's experience? Is the cash balance excessive? The presence of ideas like these in Montgomery's program indicates that he considered every audit a research project.

The American type of audit also received editorial consideration in the *Journal of Accountancy* in March, 1907. The examination is considered more expeditious, and because it is broader in scope, possesses greater administrative value. Tests are used throughout the audit; if these give an impression of irregularities, the details get further examination. American auditors, it is pointed out, give a great deal of attention to the composition of the accounts (by means of account analysis) and to the relation of important accounts to each other.

A concise description of the beginning of change in American practices is given by a professional accountant[1] who had extended experience with both types of programs. A few sections are quoted below because they characterize so well the methods indicated by much of the earlier literature.

. . . The detailed auditor verified, by reference to required vouchers so far as possible, all entries in the original records; checked, or substantially tested, all footings or recapitulations in these original records; checked the postings therefrom to the general ledger (and sometimes tested them to the subsidiary ledgers); and footed and balanced the general ledger.

. . . In the course of his work the detailed auditor devoted a not inconsiderable amount of time to investigating the possibility that there might be transactions which had never been entered upon the books. In fact, he regarded this as the greatest risk, since his methods were such as to insure reasonable accuracy after transactions had been recorded. Having finished this work, the detailed auditor was disposed to assume that the resulting trial balance was correct and he therefore devoted but little time to proving that the results shown by the accounts were correct.

. . . I do not mean to imply that he devoted no time to an independent examination of these results. He did, but it was of distinctly minor importance and it was devoted principally towards such items as inventories and other

[1] Frank G. Shorts, *Journal of Accountancy*, September, 1940.

year-end adjustments which were incapable of proof from the accounts kept during the year.

Thus the author concisely describes the first stage of American auditing. But these procedures, being found unsuited to American business conditions, were gradually changed until a characteristically American audit emerged.

The second stage came about because the detailed audit was considered "unduly expensive for the benefits derived from it," and as a result there was pressure to reduce the amount of work done. The changes made in the program did not bring at first any change in the point of view taken by the auditor. He merely incorporated the idea that in most cases "it was not necessary to make a detailed examination of every entry, footing, and posting during the period in order to get the substance of the value which resulted from an audit. . . . The second phase of the development of auditing retained the view point of the detailed auditors, but resulted in a smaller total quantity [and cost] of detailed audit work."

The second stage produced the test audit. The third stage produced the balance sheet audit—Short called it "our present common analytical examination." Here was reflected an entirely new concept in auditing—"that the results shown by accounts were capable of a substantial degree of proof without the necessity of auditing the individual transactions which produced the results."

This idea was rapidly accepted and widely applied because it embodied a wholly valid conception and one that was particularly suited to American conditions. As a consequence, "more and more emphasis was laid on the analytical approach to the results and less upon the remaining features of the detailed audit, until finally detailed audits and test audits almost completely disappeared from our practice."

To this epitome of the three stages of our auditing development only one point of emphasis will be added. The keynote of the American audit lies in a phrase used above—"analytical approach." That phrase clearly says that our audit is not a clerical procedure. It tells readers that we aim to conduct an audit in a research frame of mind; that we seek to rest our conviction and professional opinion on facts; that professional procedures will be selected and applied with careful judgment; that we will seek convincing evidence by the shortest dependable route.

(unpublished manuscript, late 1940's)

5. Certified Balance Sheets

Two facts about American certified balance sheets are well known: they have rendered important service to business borrowers and bank leaders; they rest upon audit procedures that are peculiarly American in many aspects. But the reasons for these facts are not so well known. What characteristics of American business made the balance sheet audit an effective means of supplying credit information? The answer lies somewhere in American practices of borrowing and lending.

Business credit may rest on personal acquaintance; the local lender knows the borrower as a neighbor of good character and as a businessman of ability. Or credit may pass through an intermediary. The seller knows the buyer; the latter accepts the former's time draft; the bank knows the seller and buys the two-name paper. That trade acceptance thus becomes part of the circulating medium. In later developments a great deal of credit in the United States came to be extended on a more impersonal basis. Where adequate personal knowledge was lacking, the decision had to rest largely on other information—at first, on the opinions of other businessmen and a self-prepared property statement from the borrower; later, on verified accounting statements.

The focus of credit information is ability to repay loans. Personal acquaintance with the borrower may not alone be evidence enough. The best intentions may be defeated by outside conditions. A property statement alone may not be enough supplementary information. Experience has shown that the statement may be biased, overoptimistic, sometimes false. A certified balance sheet gives the banker-lender a better view of ability to repay. For the statement representation has passed under the scrutiny of an independent auditor. But a certified balance sheet may not be enough in itself. Even with respect to short-term loans the statement should be supplemented by the banker's analyses of trends reflected in a series of statements and by his knowledge of the place of the present in the pattern of changing economic conditions.

Although American procedures were derived from British methods, the principal aim of their auditing was not fully repeated here. Whereas British practice could be called a general audit, American practice could only be called a credit audit. It is probably a matter of general accounting knowledge that, in one case, an audit was required because it was public policy to put the corporation directors' stewardship of stockholder property under independent scrutiny. In the United States an audit was voluntary on the part of the client; and the work of the public accountant came to be called a balance sheet audit, meaning a credit investigation leading to a certified balance sheet. Such a distinction does not just happen; there must have been conditioning circumstances which gave little stress to credit audits in one country and much in another.

Balance sheet audits form part of the American way of making credit investigations. These investigations were fostered by the same conditions that favored the use of direct personal loans over other methods of short-term borrowing, such as using bills of exchange and trade acceptances. This direct method of financing current operations began to appear before the war between the states and was accentuated by postwar conditions. The preference for financing with personal promissory notes was greatly stimulated during the war years of the 1860's and the depression years of the 1870's. Ultimately the use of promissory notes became so firmly established by long use that commercial paper was made a basis for our monetary system in 1915.

The war produced an inflation represented by 450,000,000 "greenbacks" —printing press money that was neither redeemable in gold nor held within the monetary needs of the time. Gold went to a premium; depreciated greenbacks became the principal medium in circulation. The fact that the currency was of questionable soundness collaborated with typically American postwar optimism in bringing about something like a boom. Then came depression; the panic of 1873 was the turning point; bad times lasted for seven years.

These surrounding conditions of war and inflation produced marked changes in the financial practices of business, practices that today are so familiar as to seem to have always been part of our methods. Both factors introduced uncertainties into the currency system and price structure. These uncertainties cast a shadow over the practice of financing merchandise purchases with retailers' six-month notes payable. Wholesalers therefore shortened their credit terms and tried to get closer to a cash basis. Substantial discounts for quick payment of open accounts receivable were part of this effort. It was a persuasive inducement. The buyer who could borrow from local banks on single-name paper not only transferred his debt into his own community but gained the difference between the interest paid and the cash discount granted. The proceeds from sale of the goods acquired would pay off the local loan; if sales were unexpectedly slow, extension of part of the loan was easier to arrange by personal contact locally than if the debt were held some place else.

Short-term credit has long been an important aspect of business finance; the mechanics of credit may change, but the need continues. When credit arrangements were made face to face by acquaintances, perhaps neighbors, a minimum of "credit information" was necessary. But this did not last. As lending became more impersonal and changing business conditions made lenders increasingly sensitive to nonpersonal risk factors, the mechanics of credit were expanded to include more and better investigation of borrowers.

Business depressions, financial insolvencies, currency of doubtful stability, and such conditions as these cast a shadow over the unsupported promissory notes of borrowers. Buyers of commercial paper in the open market became more wary. Note-brokers experienced increasing competition and sales resistance and began to advance part of the funds to borrowers they knew. Before 1890, many brokers were buying paper outright and reselling it. Credit information beyond that represented by personal acquaintance grew increasingly useful. Brokers therefore accumulated files of information about their regular customers to help resell the paper.

Banks too felt a need for information. By the 1880's the purchase and sale of commercial paper grew into a distinct phase of banking. In spite of changing business conditions, there was a marked increase of financing by the use of single-name paper. Such notes came through the depression days of the early 1890's with a good record of safety. Good credit information in the bank's file was a vital element in forming the lender's judgment and thus a factor in giving such loans a history of safety.

In the 1870's, The Mercantile Agency distributed its first standard information blank. Spaces were provided for data regarding assets (merchandise, receivables, personal property, real estate) and liabilities (on real estate, on merchandise purchased from home creditors and other creditors). In addition, the amount of insurance carried was to be shown. The method thus devised for increasing credit information was destined to experience a great expansion. This development later came to be particularly important to the profession of public accounting.

A few banks early in the 1880's had a credit department to pass upon loans to strangers. At first these departments relied on accumulated personal knowledge (by the staff or a note-broker) of the character and ability of the borrowers, plus information from correspondent banks. In addition the bank credit men kept in touch with directors of the bank who had a broad knowledge of specific lines of business and of the people engaged therein. Borrowers were tactfully urged to supply signed financial statements. Many declined, but gradually the prejudice was overcome. Bankers continued to desire the statements for two reasons: (1) If a borrower after default had to be charged with fraud, his signed property statement might prove to be an important part of the bank's evidence; (2) A statement of assets and liabilities would show the liquid position of the borrower. This ratio was considered almost as important to the lender as an honest intention on the part of the borrower, for it gave a clue of the margin of safety behind a new debt.[2]

Banks probably first made single-name loans, based on an analysis of financial statements, in the decade of the 1870's.[3] This was not standard practice for some time, but as the use of single-name paper grew, the need for this type of information grew also. By 1900, the use of single-name paper was a recognized American banking practice—"a practice unique among the banking systems of the world."[4]

.

[2] Bankers' interest in the borrower's current position was due to the idea that the relation of current assets to current liabilities was a gauge to the margin of safety, as it was in a bank. Judging the significance of similar relationships within his own enterprise was an everyday experience for a banker. His demand liabilities and his liquid assets were in a state of constant change, and a drift toward an unsound relationship might be at any time.

[3] Foulke, *Practical Financial Statement Analysis* (1945), p. 12.

[4] *Ibid.*, p. 19.

As short-term borrowing and lending outgrew the limitations inherent in local contracts and personal acquaintance, the information obtainable from borrowers' property statements assumed increasing importance. Credit in the last analysis rests upon the debtor's solvency. The creditor, therefore, needs to study data reflecting the former's ability to pay his debits when due. This is more a question of the relation of current assets to current liabilities than one of the relation between total assets and total liabilities, which indicates legal solvency. A statement of assets and liabilities supplied the essential information, particularly if the accounts reflecting current position were separately classified. But the experience of lenders began to show that more was needed—a verified statement. By 1903, some balance sheets certified by public accountants were available; by 1913, they were fairly common. Clearly this was an important decade for professional accounting. Public accountants were prepared by their training to render the important service of independent verification. Much of the impulse to make use of that service came from bankers who saw benefit in it for both borrower and lender.

A sampling of informed opinion made by the American Association of Public Accountants in 1913 showed strong support for the use of audit certificates in connection with loan requests. Out of 850 replies to a questionnaire, only 20 were opposed to certification, and 200 were non-committal; 630 replies were clearly favorable.

By this sampling of opinion, several things were made clear. A great many loans by commercial banks at this time rested on financial statements. Human optimism made the typical borrower overestimate his important current assets. The banker needed a third party's opinion in considering the typical credit risk. He needed something more than a certificate that the statements were in accordance with the books. He needed the certificate of a competent and reliable public accountant who had done some independent verifying of inventories and receivables. Evidence of competence and reliability would be found in the accountant's personal reputation and in the public recognition accorded him by the restricted title, Certified Public Accountant.

Certified financial statements slowly became customary. Their usefulness grew out of the wishes of individual bankers and note-brokers, out of the needs of individual enterprises for short-term loans, and out of the competence of professional public accountants. Accounting practice was therefore greatly influenced by the financial practices of businessmen and bankers.

This discussion of American financial methods points to the conclusion that local conditions rather than precedents transmitted from Great Britain directed the early growth of professional accounting in the United States. The distinction between "a general audit," typical in Great Britain, and "a balance sheet audit," typical in the United States, lies less in details of procedures than in concepts of audit function.

British audits were essentially examinations of the stewardship of corporation directors, with a collateral interest in possible employee embezzlements. Stewardship was a very old idea; it went back into feudal days and the charge and discharge accounting of that time. Possible mismanagement by directors also had an early background in the years of excessive speculation in corporation securities that preceded the prohibition in 1720 of joint-stock company promotions and sale of shares.

America had no background of this kind. For a long time it was a new country where business enterprises were individual and small and where after Colonial days there were very few agent-managed landed estates. Under these circumstances it would have been strange indeed if general audits to examine reports on director stewardship had become customary. Since American local conditions did not long support the British conception of audit function, our concept of audit purpose came to be quite different. Our audit was a "credit investigation." This phrase received no more than a few pages of consideration in Dicksee's *Auditing*. Although this British author provided no special program of procedure, the idea was clearly expressive of a type of audit service that would be well suited to the American pattern of business finance which had slowly emerged out of a period of Civil War with its cycles of inflation and deflation.

Our use of single-name paper for short-term loans was unique in the banking world; yet it proved unexpectedly useful, flexible, and safe. Perhaps the American audit was not equally unique; its procedures were variants of procedures used in general audits. But it did demonstrate an important characteristic of auditing techniques—adaptability. It marked a change of emphasis rather than a weakening of professional standards.

                                                          (unpublished manuscript, late 1940's)

6. A Long-Lived Textbook

Two thoughts come to mind upon examining the seventeenth edition (1951) of this famous book, Dicksee's *Auditing*. One is that professional accounting in the United States was greatly influenced by antecedent professional developments in Great Britain. The other is that many changes of significance to accounting have taken place in England during the decade between the sixteenth edition (1940) and the seventeenth (1951).

The formation in 1880 of the Institute of Chartered Accountants in England and Wales provided a strong impulse felt here and throughout the world for building national organizations of professional accountants. British capital invested in many enterprises in the United States brought British auditors and audit programs to this country at a time when our local auditors did not have the needed preparation or experience. British textbooks provided the initial materials for much of our early efforts to acquire an accounting education to accompany or precede learning by practical experience.

These inheritances were not merely transmitted and absorbed. Rather, they were received and gradually modified to fit American conditions. Here the dual system of governmental organization separated the powers of the states and the federal government. Recognition and regulation of the professions were powers assigned to the separate states. Hence, examination and certification of CPA's were functions of the several states.

It is also characteristic of the American pattern that the passage of time and the accumulation of diversified experience should foster, by a variety of methods, a useful degree of co-ordination among different views. For example, the American Bar Association is constantly studying this kind of problem and recommending desirable changes looking toward greater uniformity without complete similarity in designated sections of state statute law. It was therefore inherent in the situation that a strong national organization of professional accountants should sometime emerge in this country and that it would make much of its contribution through mutuality of objectives with state societies of CPA's. Perhaps the most outstanding evidence of successful fostering of mutuality is the nationwide CPA examination prepared by a board of examiners in the American Institute of Accountants and used by state boards of examiners in testing local candidates for state-granted certificates.

In time the visiting auditors from Europe were replaced by resident auditors who built their staffs and partnerships from both American and British personnel. Many individuals brought European training and experience to this country and followed up by becoming American citizens and leaders in the profession. Their work and character attracted more and more American-born citizens toward professional accounting. At the same time, the technical service made available became more widely recognized and sought. The audit program was itself gradually modified to suit American conditions, particularly in ways that made it practicable for bankers to ask borrowers for certified balance sheets in support of the direct short-term loans which had become a customary feature of our financial methods.

Slowly we developed our own technical literature and educational methods, particularly those associated with preparation for the CPA examination. In 1905, Robert H. Montgomery edited an American edition of Dicksee's *Auditing*. Until 1912, when Montgomery's *Auditing Theory and Practice* appeared, there was no substantial text that was distinctly American in content and point of view.

There are two interesting side lights on this phase of the development of American accounting literature. A reviewer of Montgomery's "Dick-see" expressed the view in 1910 that there was more Montgomery than Dicksee in the book. The present reviewer some years ago made a page-by-page comparison of the two books and came away with the clear conviction that the American editor had been entirely faithful to the British text except where he had changed the money figures and eliminated British case law and statutory rules.

The other circumstance indirectly supports the same conclusion. A paper on auditing procedure by Walter Staub (later a partner with Montgomery) was presented before the Congress of Accountants in St. Louis, 1904, and a paper by Montgomery on the work of the auditor appeared in the *Journal of Accountancy* for April, 1906. In these two items are early indications that an American-type modification of the traditional audit program was underway. These developments were not even suggested in the American edition of Dicksee. The articles indicated some of the ideas then taking root here which ripened in 1912 into Montgomery's *Auditing Theory and Practice*.

At about the same time instruction in accountancy was creeping into American universities. Night classes were available in New York University, Columbia University, University of Pennsylvania, and Northwestern University. And general texts on accountancy by American authors were beginning to appear—further indication of adaptation and modification. As examples, mention may be made of the text in 1907, by Professor Sprague of New York University; of the book in 1908, by Professor Cole of Harvard; and that of Professor Hatfield of the University of California in 1909.

Dicksee's *Auditing* is a famous book in its own right and in the author's own country. Seventeen editions, several since the author's death, are evidence of that. It has been in demand for sixty years; the number of copies printed has run into five figures in the midst of other important British books on auditing. Its content well deserves the attention of any reviewer, even though, as in this instance, it will not be appropriate to try to judge the book's usefulness to its own public.

The work is almost a handbook. Within its 896 pages, 353 are text. Besides verification procedures, this section includes consideration of peculiarities of different lines of business, profits and dividends, auditor liabilities, holding companies, and investigations. Three appendixes account for 532 pages; extracts from statutes and regulations, 220 pages; court cases of professional interest, 280 pages; recommendations on accounting principles issued by the Institute of Chartered Accountants in England and Wales, 32 pages.

The decade of the 1940's was not only beset by war but by vast economic and political changes as well. Some of the effects of these conditions upon British accountancy are reflected in many pages of this edition.

Under nationalization of many industries, the long-established traditions of proper accounts and independent audits were continued. The new statutory agencies for operating various industries were required to keep proper records and accounts, to prepare financial statements in such form as the minister concerned directed, and to have the accounts audited by appointees of the appropriate minister. In connection with the audit, assurance was given and made effective that appointees would be reputable and qualified auditors. Under some statutes (as that for gas in 1947 and that for electricity in 1948) the requirement added that the auditor must be a member of a recognized professional body. There was, however, a certain amount of displacement of independent auditors due to the fact that a small number of new statutory agencies took the place of a larger number of independent companies. Some of the effects of this displacement were balanced by the establishment of internal auditing departments in some industries (pp. 8, 9, 23-25).

Until recently, secret reserves were often considered "desirable, even essential" in the best interests of the stockholder as a means of equalizing dividends and promoting confidence and stability. The Royal Mail Case (Rex v. Kylsant, 1931) may be considered as the turning point of change. The Institute's recommended principle (1943) is the profession's considered attitude on the matter. The phrasing of appropriate sections of the Companies Act of 1948 (in substance, the Institute's recommendation) sets statutory approval upon the new concept. The abandonment of "undisclosed reserves" is reflected in a stated distinction between a reserve and a provision. The latter is to refer to amounts set aside to meet liabilities, diminution of asset value, and specific commitments; the former term refers to "revenue reserves" that are free and available for distribution as dividends. These reserves should be disclosed in the balance sheet. However, the Institute also recommended (1943) that, in case disclosure of a particular provision would clearly be detrimental to the interests of the company, the item might be included under another heading, and a general statement in the report narrative would be made of this treatment (pp. 187, 836-37, 871).

The impact of price-level change upon depreciation has been felt in Great Britain as well as in the United States. It is of interest to note that the profession's attitude has been essentially the same in both countries.

Several pages in the book are used to present (1) the Institute's analysis of the impact of price changes and high taxes on business operations, on maintenance of capital, and upon financial statement reporting; and (2) a summary of the pros and cons of a change in accounting ideology. Recommendations in 1949 were three: (a) amounts to finance high replacement costs are not provisions before net income but transfers of net to reserves; (b) such reserves should be treated as capital reserves not available for dividends; (c) fixed assets should not be written up on the books on the basis of estimated replacement costs, especially in the absence of stability in price level (pp. 871-73).

A few other matters may be briefly indicated as interestingly similar to or different from American ideas.

As to the lower of cost or market for pricing inventories, market is explained as the price that can be realized under consideration of abnormal and obsolete inventory, trend of the market, and prospect of disposal. No mention is made of last-in, first-out (p. 864). Renewal reserve (for depreciation) is not commonly used in industrial and commercial companies (p. 862). The Companies Act of 1929 contained no requirement as to the form of the income statement. Under the Companies Act of 1948, the auditor is required to report on the income statement and certify whether it "gives a true and fair view of the profit and loss of the year" (p. 214).

For taxation purposes a company may deduct an initial 40 per cent of plant and machinery. Some companies adjust their financial statements accordingly. But the council of the Institute has recommended "that for accounting purposes, normal depreciation methods of depreciation should be maintained . . ." (p. 152).

The American reader may not have much professional interest in a textbook presentation of another country's audit procedure. But this book is more than that. Many sections can improve our knowledge of the way other professional men have reacted to conditions like those which do or may affect us also. We can get a new insight into those areas of professional interest where thought in America and Great Britain is drawing closer together. We may find new strength for our confidence that accountancy will long continue to render effective public service and that it will grow and develop with passing time, but this will be only if we take careful thought lest society lose important existing benefits while reaching hopefully toward hypotheses of possible future benefits.

(book review, *Accounting Review,* July, 1952)

7. Balance Sheet Prominence

If, as it seems, income determination is the central feature of double-entry bookkeeping, why is the balance sheet given more attention than the income statement?

There is not much evidence in the early history of bookkeeping pointing to an emphasis upon balance sheet data. In fact, although income data were clearly compacted in every ledger that had a profit and loss account, it was a long time before solvency data were compactly assembled into a "balance account."

It is true that at times in the middle of the fifteenth century double-entry records were used as a basis for self-assessed property taxes. And it is true that early in the seventeenth century Simon Stevin, after heading the balance sheet with the titles, "Estate of Capital Debit" and "Estate of

Capital Credit," gave income data such a minor place as to permit that statement to be called merely "Proof of the Estate." But such usage, even if it had been widely extended, would not be enough to explain the strong emphasis given later to the balance sheet in auditing and in law.

There are more plausible surmises as to the origins of this emphasis. The British use of auditing for the purpose of putting nineteenth century corporations under scrutiny probably had its inspiration in the use made of auditing on feudal estates of an earlier day. It seems equally probable that certain persisting concepts of accounting were established at the same time, that is, before Italian methods came into use in England. One idea having such an origin is the view that financial statements were essentially reports of stewardship. The charge and discharge statement certainly reflected that view very early; and the balance sheet, when it came into use much later, was regarded as being more in the nature of a report of director stewardship than a profit and loss statement could be. Add to this the idea, probably fully justified by nineteenth century competitive conditions, that the intimate details usually placed in the profit and loss statement were confidential private information, and the result may explain the fact that British auditing practice, without neglecting examination of profit and loss data, gave primary emphasis to examination of balance sheet data.

From the point of view of verification, this procedure is satisfactory. The profit and loss statement necessarily cannot contain a complete summary of the effect of all transactions that need expert scrutiny; the reality of costs and of revenues needs to be tested with reference to counterparts lying among assets and liabilities; assets, whether derived from loans or from profit-making sales, can be more objectively confirmed than can revenue figures, since the latter merely say something quantitative about enterprise contacts with customers. It is understandable therefore that auditing should give strong emphasis to the balance sheet. This was particularly true in the United States at the time when auditing was closely concerned with the examination of balance sheets in support of short-term bank credit.

But the exigencies of British and American auditing practice did not determine the characteristics of double entry; the basic features of double entry, including the primary importance of income determination, were permanently etched into the pattern long before investor-protecting auditing had evolved.

The prominence of balance sheets has also been fostered by various statutory provisions and numerous court decisions. Here it should be noted that accounting came into contact with law only in special situations, usually situations which could as easily be satisfied by data from an appraisal statement of assets and liabilities as by a balance sheet from double-entry accounts.

When the law has been invoked in accounting matters, it usually has been in connection with a contest in regard to the rights of contending persons. In order to approach a just resolution of the issue, the problem often has to be considered in terms of values rather than of book-recorded prices. Thus, dividend suits and bankruptcy cases turn on the issue of solvency, and solvency is measured by the usefulness of the assets for discharging liabilities or paying dividends rather than use for producing future revenue.

For these and many other legal uses the *sine qua non* of double-entry bookkeeping (the matching of revenues and costs) would not be relevant. Yet income determination has remained the focal point of accounting because of characteristics designed into it in its initial creation. Any other emphasis merely illustrates the wide usefulness that is inherent in accounting and utilizes accounting-supplied data without drawing upon the "basic patent," so to speak, which makes double entry what it is.

The recent tendency of auditors to recognize the primacy of the income statement is in effect acknowledgement that audits are special cases in the utilization of accounts rather than activities which determine the basic character of accountancy. Whether law, except for income tax determinations, will follow suit and similarly emphasize income is still an open question.

The central purpose of accounting, in the midst of many uses, is to make possible the periodic matching of costs and revenues. This concept is the nucleus of accounting theory and a bench mark that affords a fixed point of reference in accounting discussions.

From its very nature a central purpose should be the controlling factor in the ordering of accounting procedures. If other uses of the resulting data do appear, they are clearly secondary and derivative uses; the data may therefore need interpretative modification to be appropriate. But if modification is made, it is a change from that which is basic, and not a change to produce something basic.

For example, if a deferred charge in a balance sheet is ignored in making certain legal determinations, the result is an adjustment away from accounting as a base, rather than an adjustment made to fit the balance sheet better to the accounting base. Again, since the double-entry balance sheet was not originally designed into the system to furnish current information for short-term credit uses, an inventory adjustment, when considered necessary, should be made by reserve rather than by valuation at the lower of cost or market. The former procedure is preferable, for one reason among others, because it keeps that balance sheet item in harmony with its function as one of the income-determining elements of the next period; at the same time, by means of a legitimate device of interpretation, it puts the grantor of short-term credit on notice in regard to a condition of considerable interest to him.

It is not brashness, therefore, that leads public accountants to assert their professionalism. The things accountants believe to be important are not stressed just because they are believed; but rather they are stressed because experienced accountants have a deep sense of their social mission in the midst of inescapable limitations, and because, in their special area, they are an essential part of informed public opinion. It must be historical conviction rather than the eagerness of a new profession that underlies a recent editorial statement in the *Journal of Accountancy*.

"It is the business of accountants to determine what expenditures are costs and how they may best be allocated to reflect properly the operations of a specified period of time. No amount of legislation can create a cost which does not actually exist, nor allocate a cost properly to a period of time to which it is applicable."

The strength of the common law is that it is common to the times and therefore changing. In the same way the strength of professional accounting is that it rests upon the accepted, but changing, accounting practices common to the times. It is particularly significant, however, that the deepest rights of men that are expressed in the common law and the most significant objectives of accounting are both unchanging in the midst of change.

(Accounting Review, July, 1945)

8. An Epitome of Growth

It is a small volume of 168 pages (*Fiftieth Anniversary, 1898-1948*) which outlines for partners and staff members the history of the firm of Lybrand, Ross Brothers, and Montgomery. But readers outside of that personal relationship can see in it an epitome of the growth of American professional accounting and a revealing sample of typical organization spirit and accomplishment.

A layman would no doubt expect a book of this kind to have chapters about the professional activities of the firm. This expectation is fulfilled by brief descriptions of half a dozen of the firm's unusual engagements and a chapter dealing with committee and leadership activities within state and national professional societies.

But these are not the most significant chapters. Professional service obviously makes up most of professional life; educational activities would seem secondary at best, as they are of course in point of man-hours spent. Yet the sections of the book which show that a steady flow of technical literature came from these men and that they maintained a continuing pressure toward improving the educational preparation of accountants, seem to the reviewer to be of high significance. For the facts and attitudes these sections present do a great deal to demonstrate, by this sample, that public accountants have long been keenly aware of the duty they owe to their profession as a profession, a duty which is of higher social importance than their own individual fee-earning activities. The layman might not expect this consciousness of an educational obligation (to transmit understanding and to encourage improvement against the future) to reveal itself so clearly in so young a profession.

Since 1920, the firm has published its own *Journal*. About one half of the articles listed in twenty-eight pages of bibliography had appeared in this publication. Much of the material was effective in keeping the firm and staff informed as to tax changes and other current developments. Clearly this is an educational activity for both the contributors and their readers. The other material listed had appeared in various publications of general circulation and in numerous books. A count here shows slightly more than 500 items, including short articles and large books. This is a surprising output to flow from the extracurricular activities of busy men. It is noteworthy too that the number of items put in general publications has been accelerating in recent years. This accords with the generally evident fact that accountants as a whole are now more articulate than ever before. They are well prepared by education and experience to have reasonable and constructive ideas; and their past services to society have earned them the right to speak out their judgment.

The increased output of accounting literature also reflected the growth in this firm's staff. In 1898, there were 4 partners, one staff assistant, and one clerical assistant; in 1948, the partners numbered 56, and the staff, 1,192. Most of this growth in numbers, like the growth of accounting literature and the demand for professional services, came in the past twenty years. In its first thirty years the firm made seven new partners; in the next twenty years, fifty-one.

The two chapters that deal directly with accounting literature by partners and staff make up about one third of the book. One chapter briefly presents the principal titles according to individuals: Robert H. Montgomery, William M. Lybrand, T. Edward Ross, Walter A. Staub, Homer N. Sweet, Prior Sinclair, Norman J. Lenhart. In the other, under the title "Published Articles of Lasting Interest," five articles are reprinted in full. Robert H. Montgomery's "Professional Standards" heads the chapter. It was published in the *Journal of Accountancy*, Vol. 1, No. 1 (November, 1905) and undoubtedly laid the groundwork for the development of our concrete rules about professional conduct. The other articles are by Gilbert R. Byrne (a prize-winning essay), T. Edward Ross (his spritely character, Ripley V. Winkle, views accounting in 1941 with astonishment through the eyes of an accountant of 1891), Donald P. Perry, and Prior Sinclair.

These samples, as is also the case with many other articles in accounting literature, are full of good ideas clearly and forcefully presented. These and many others illustrate the fact that figures and financial statements are not the accountant's only medium of expression. If all accountants had confined themselves to the details of verification and certification, the advancement of the profession, in capacity to render a service to society, would have been slow and halting indeed. Whenever the accountant exerts himself to conceive good ideas and to clothe them in convincing language, he is rendering an extra service. And it would be a service of education, although acting as educator may have been far from the author's mind. "The extent to which the members of the profession create [accounting] literature is, in a sense, a mark of their professional development" (*The Journal of Accountancy*).

Members of this firm, from an early day, did even more for accounting education than contribute to literature; they went into the classroom to work directly with students. In 1902, a few years after their CPA law was passed, the Pennsylvania Institute organized evening classes in accounting. Of the four teachers, two (Lybrand and Montgomery) were from this firm. A few years later local instruction in public accounting subject matter achieved academic status thereby being offered in the University of Pennsylvania. Before long the firm instituted summertime courses of practical study for its staff to supplement the more theoretical preparations currently or previously taken in college. Presently it was necessary to divide the staff so this sort of preparation could be different for those who had or those who had not had college classes in accounting. "This program was an interesting and valuable experience. The results indicated that the non-technically trained laymen generally took four or five years to attain equal rank with those who had received technical training in college before employment."

Although opportunities for formal education have been greatly expanded, there still is a need for organized staff training within accounting firms. By including a chapter on "Staff Education, Selection and Training," this firm indicates not only the existence of a long-standing policy of staff training, but of an intention to continue the policy and improve the technique. Schoolmen will approve; they are fully aware of the limitations of textbooks and classroom exercises. But they are convinced, as are many practitioners as well, that most people planning to enter the profession would be better prepared for the long pull in their career if they could secure a college education. Yet we would do well to advise the aspirant that the long pull is not down hill and a college education does not provide one with roller skates for the road to success.

(book review, *Accounting Review*, July, 1949)

9. The Past Reaches Forward

Walter A. Staub's little book, *Accounting Developments During the Present Century* (1942), is a compact and inspiring picture of present-day auditing by an author having special qualifications for the task. His forty years in public accounting, nearly all of them as a member of the firm, and his extended service in professional organizations have put him in personal touch with all of the important developments of the period. Within the limits of his time and space available for these Dickinson lectures, the author could not be expected to present a complete history of American auditing, even though he has been very much in and of it. Nor would such an approach have been appropriate to the occasion. Those who heard the lectures must have felt that the material was well selected and organized with notable skill. They would perceive, as the reader does, that here is an excellent description of the characteristics and present-day purposes of auditing. We are taken behind the scenes and shown that, despite popular misconceptions and regardless of inherent limitations too often overlooked, public accounting does make a definite contribution to social welfare. By skillfully interweaving comments about earlier conditions while giving major attention to present-day matters, the author very effectively brings the reader to the conviction that the events of recent years indicate a distinct growth in the professional stature of public accountants.

From the author's observations on the evolution of auditors' certificates, it is clear that the changing phrasing of this report has signified important developments in the professional accountant's responsibilities. No doubt this is not unrelated to the concurrent evolution of controllership and internal control. As fast as competent internal auditing staffs are organized within large corporations which can conduct a continuous and extensive verification of transactions and records as a safeguard against speculation, the independent public accountant gains a counterbalancing freedom to devote more of his time to study of the corporation's consistent application of accepted accounting principles and to consideration of the manner in which disclosure is made in the financial statements. The professional auditor in this way can direct most of his energies toward guarding the corporation and the public against undesirable accounting policies.

The public interest in the dependability of published financial statements is now widely recognized, and the necessity for auditor independence is increasingly stressed. But this has not always been the case. The author points out that at the time he began his professional career, financial statements were seldom under examination. The public accountant was most often retained to conduct a cash audit in order to examine the fidelity of a cashier or treasurer. In the late nineties an era of corporation consolidation brought with it the need for a more general accounting examination. As a result, financial statements assumed new importance, and because of the volume of transaction details which made selective tests necessary, the "balance sheet audit" became standard procedure. Soon after the turn of the century this procedure proved to have additional usefulness. Banks were then developing credit departments wherein the procedure of passing upon applications for loans included a study of the borrower's balance sheet. The usefulness of an independent report on that statement was obvious, and the balance sheet continued to be the focus of the auditor's examination.

By 1917 federal income taxation had developed to the point where business felt impelled to give closer attention to the determination of net income. Depreciation expense, for example, now became a reality for many to whom it had before been only a vague theory. In addition, the war made people security conscious, and that interest being transferred to general securities after peace gave still further impetus to the reporting of income. The time was passing when the balance sheet could be the principal object of the auditor's examination and the main source of public information about a corporation. These developments not only showed that a public welfare aspect of public accounting already existed —which led to the inclusion of certain accounting provisions in the securities and exchange legislation of 1933-34—but they also gradually led to changes in audit procedure. A few of the items of this sort that the author mentions may be indicated here.

Early published financial statements were highly condensed; today statements are much improved both as to form and substance. Until recent years the auditor seldom had any physical contact with inventories and only infrequently sought confirmations from people outside the enterprise under audit. Furthermore, relatively little attention was given to the verification of fixed assets at a time when cash was the center of interest. As fixed assets came to bulk ever larger in the balance sheet and as the whole statement came under examination, this attitude changed. Another item of considerable significance was internal check. Ever since selective tests came into prominence, the auditor has considered that the absence of good internal check was cause to modify the extent of his examination in some respect. This question has grown in importance in recent years, and now it is quite usual for the public accountant to make an extensive and critical examination of all phases of the client's system of control.

This epitome of the developments of forty years would be incomplete without mention of another feature. The author's experience makes him clearly competent to observe that the accomplishments of accounting in enterprises under direct regulation of government have seldom measured up to what has been done through accounting elsewhere. Banks and insurance companies, for example, have lagged behind trade and industry in the full utilization of accounting and the skills of accountants. But in these fields the pattern was established before public accounting was recognized in this country. And because the type of regulation and scrutiny then implanted has been continued, financial institutions such as banks and insurance companies have seldom had the benefit of regular and critical contact by professional accountants. It may be noted, however, that this has not been the case in Britain and Canada.

The author supports this thesis also by citing instances tending to show that prescribed uniform accounts for railroad companies have not been a satisfactory substitute for the independent audits which at one time were customary here as well as in Great Britain. There is no necessary clash between prescribed accounts and independent audits. This is indicated by the fact that public utility companies, while regulated by state and federal governments, are for the most part audited by certified public accountants.

It is the reviewer's opinion that no one who is in the least aware of the pressure of work under which public accountants have struggled for a long time could believe that convictions such as these could be prompted by a self-seeking complex on the part of accountants. The fact of the matter is that clear concepts of public welfare are very strong in the minds of responsible public accountants and have been for a long time. In speaking of the benefits of accounting they are no more self-seeking than the physician who urges the establishment of a department of public health. Since the early days of certified public accountant laws, detractors of accounting as a profession have sought to establish the idea that the sponsors of such legislation were monopolists at heart, seeking only their own advancement. We are now far enough from this early legislation to realize that the pioneers of statutory recognition had the public interest at heart at a time when there was little public interest supporting their views.

Only two criticisms come to mind concerning this volume, and both of these are minor. Many students will regret that the author has given us but sketchy glimpses of the earliest days of the four decades. But since he had to choose his material with care for the purpose at hand, he probably could do no other than to stress the present at the expense of the past. Those who wish to look further into past details are referred to a prize paper by the same author entitled "Mode of Conducting an Audit," published in the proceedings of the first International Congress of Accountants and reprinted in the *Accounting Review*. It impresses one not only as fully worthy of the prize it won, but also as being a distinct contribution to American auditing literature at the early date of 1904.

The other criticism is possibly sponsored by the reviewer's own prejudices. It has to do with frequent reference to the cost or market rule, even though there is good reason to believe that the rule is probably on its way out of the auditor's lexicon. Even in the beginning it never was anything more than a banker's rule for valuing collateral, extended by analogy to inventory and accepted by accountants who prepared balance sheets for credit purposes. It is doubtful that the rule ever was a true part of accounting as such, or ever had any real validity in connection with the vital matter of a careful calculation of enterprise periodic income.

These are indeed small matters in comparison with the real contribution the author has made. But if a critic can find fault with nothing, he may as well confess, as this reviewer does, to the wish that he could have had the background to have written the book himself.

(book review, *Accounting Review,* April, 1943)

10. Serving the Public Interest

Part of the evidence of progress in the profession takes the form of effective recognition of the fact that the public interest is deeply involved in the work of public accountants.

The public interest is involved, for example, in the long-run solution of the problem of recruiting for the profession. An inflow of men with high talents for success in this field will be a long-run benefit to the profession; but this will be so primarily because such men will be fertile in finding new ways to serve more clients in harmony with the needs of business and of society.

Some observers will interpret the growing tendency in the profession to favor restrictive legislation as indicating one more area where monopolistic ideas are hard at work. Actually this movement is the most tangible evidence to appear in fifty years that large numbers of professional accountants are becoming increasingly alive to the existence of two underlying facts: that the success of the profession as a whole amounts to more than the sum of the successes of its members; that the welfare of the profession (and through it, of individuals) is closely bound up with the contribution it makes to public welfare. Since dependable accounting information is indispensable in a modern industrial and capitalistic democracy, it is in the public interest that such information shall be inspected by independent, competent, and impartial experts. It then becomes a matter of public interest that the competency of the "inspectors" shall be tested and that the "inspecting" shall be restricted to the competent. This is the essence of the idea back of restrictive legislation for public accounting. And support by professional societies of this legislative development is more by far an indication of recognition that the public interest can best be served by competent individuals who are under the restraints of professional discipline than it is a sign of big ideas of occupational monopoly.

Recognition of the public interest is also evidenced by the willingness of practitioners these days to speak out when issues are at hand on which their training and experience have qualified them to have responsible views. Indeed, they form a section of public opinion that is particularly well informed in certain areas of thought and action. It is reassuring that they are loosening some of the natural inhibitions of professional men. This does not come easy to most of them. The fact that some do speak up is evidence that they do so from knowledge and conviction; it seldom would be from personal preference.

Past progress therefore has in part been based upon detecting the public interest underlying the profession and acting in line with that knowledge. It is reasonable to expect that it would be helpful to future progress also to continue the attempts to devise suitable ways of serving the public interest.

It would serve the public interest to contribute steadily to the education of the public, especially in the direction of eradicating misconceptions.

It is a misconception to favor a high degree of uniformity of accounting methods that may smother the natural distinctions between enterprises. It is a misconception to think of balance sheet figures as expressing values, and to talk of profit as if it were a sum of disbursable cash. It is a misconception, to say the least, to believe that independent certified public accountants are subservient to their clients' financial whims ("hired checkers [who] never win any arguments for a different presentation"), or to imagine that truthful accounting allows for one, and only one, treatment of a given situation.

It would serve the public interest to foster technical competence in every conceivable way.

Rightly or wrongly, the view seems widely held that a very small percentage of candidates with the specified education and experience succeed in passing the accounting practice section of the usual CPA examination. To this view might be added another thought: Holding an overly tight rein on examination (whether by way of entrance restrictions, re-examination privileges, selection of problems, or system of grading) probably is one of the least effective ways of trying to increase average competence in the profession. Examinations constitute a negative approach at best.

A positive approach to greater competence, on the face of it, should be much more promising. Undoubtedly, recognition of this fact is the supporting foundation of the Institute's growing program of research, debate, and publication dealing with professional ideas, objectives, terminology, techniques, and education. And it seems likely that far more can be accomplished in the public interest, and more quickly, by striving to increase the competence of those who have already passed the qualifying examination than by using a fine-mesh screen to find the most promising new material to work upon. Nevertheless, the latter should not be neglected.

It is in the public interest to extend and improve technical education.

One of the best ways practitioners can help the schools prepare men to enter into and to grow with the profession is to supply teaching materials. There are no trade secrets among physicians. Whatever one doctor learns that could be helpful to others soon finds its way to them—by personal contact, clinical lectures, published papers. This productivity and this communication serve the public interest more than they do the individual.

Alert accounting teachers will see and use new educational materials as fast as they can mold them to classroom needs. Therefore, when professional men write papers, bulletins, books, committee reports, and speak at group meetings and conventions, they are likely to reach a wider audience than they might imagine. Indeed, that is a strong reason for more practitioners to be vocal in this way.

But education does not end with school or when one passes the CPA examination. And continuation education often will not be all that it could be, if its plan is left wholly to the initiative and resourcefulness of the individual. The need is not only for continued technical education. Many men on the way up the ladder would benefit as much from gaining a working acquaintance with such collateral subjects as economics, finance, management, and even broader subjects such as rhetoric, psychology, government, history, etc.

Perhaps all too often the need for continued technical education is considered to be satisfied by accretions from the day's work. The value of experience and observation is unquestionable. But a great deal of this value takes a great deal of time to come within range. For that reason organized education (supplementary adult education) should somehow be made available to staff members.

Some of this could be done within firm offices. For new second assistants (juniors) there could be transitional training in accounting techniques and standards as well as drill in the needed skills; for first assistants and seniors, separate discussion groups to consider field problems, novel situations, knotty issues, new literature. Beyond that? Why not a leave of absence for supplementary studies having particular objectives? Many a man would fit himself to render better service by making a thorough study of the problems involved in controlling the finance of business, of the techniques of organizing for efficient production within industrial enterprises, of the intricacies of public-utility depreciation and rate-making problems, or of the economics and politics of taxation.

The public interest is also in the individual's best interest to a larger extent than is usually realized.

(*Accounting Review*, January, 1947)

11. Accounting Adaptability

The collapse of American prices late in the 1920's came as a tremendous shock to most people. And as a result, the depressed conditions of the early 1930's were widely attributed to a philosophy, believed to permeate business, of maximizing profits with little or no regard for the effects

upon society as a whole. Yet there was much that was sound in the practices and ideas of an era which was the nearest approach up to that time
to the conquest of the art of volume production and to a high standard
of living for all. The ideals of full production and abundant living were
not lost in the perplexities and emotions of the 1930's. Even under those
distressing conditions we accepted as still attainable what seemed so
nearly within our grasp in 1928 and seemed to many so hopelessly unattainable in 1932, namely, high wages, low cost of production, joy in
working, and leisure for spending.

Out of this background, consisting of prior speculative excesses which
culminated in a collapse of prices and an earlier experience in high productivity linked with high standards of living, came the belief in the
1930's that recapture of favorable conditions would follow if excessive
individualism in business were put under tighter rein. This was not the
first time that the idea had been advanced of putting business under
governmental restrictions in the public interest and of using accounting
as one of the means of instrumenting that policy. The 1930's, therefore,
need to be viewed as a phase of the evolution of our industrial society—
evolution, whether in social government, national economics, business
finance, political ideas, industrial arts, or in accountancy. At the moment
we are interested primarily in the last item, for accountancy is being
again affected, as many times in the past, by the interplay of economic
conditions and the ideas of men. And since accountancy will unescapa-
bly continue in the future to be affected by the atmosphere surrounding
its use, it may be appropriate to epitomize the stages already visible
through which accountancy has been developing up to the time of our
securities legislation of the early 1930's.

The first phase was the largest to date and included two movements;
the earliest was concerned with the formation of double-entry technology.

It is doubtful whether we shall ever learn step by step just how double
entry was put together within the shadows of the Middle Ages; but from
materials still preserved we can see that records kept in a manner suitable to personal loans and deposits slowly began about the fourteenth
century to be adapted to other uses. In later years records appear in which
we can recognize the beginning of co-ordination of elements into a system. By the early fifteenth century men began to perceive the usefulness
of impersonal accounts and then to note that these accounts, while serving purposes different from those served by personal accounts, were also
interrelated with them. Transactions were observed to affect both classes
of accounts. When the interrelations between real and nominal accounts
were perceived and so integrated in use that a trial balance finally became
possible, double entry was born.

This was clearly a system of actual and logical relationships between
categories of transaction facts, not an accidental discovery of equality of
debits and credits. It is because the elements within transactions are

various and yet similar that a co-ordinated system of categories could be
designed that would untangle the interrelations in a manner which would
permit subsequent summaries to be made for presenting a compact yet
intelligible view of enterprise status and progress to interested parties.
Order and understanding thus could emerge out of a mass of detail—
quite an accomplishment in itself but even more astonishing in its inherent adaptability to vastly different uses in later centuries.

A long interval followed this first part of the first phase of the evolution of accountancy—an interval of some four hundred years while
double-entry techniques were slowly spreading over the civilized world.
The second part of this phase made accounting out of bookkeeping; perhaps we should say, built a structure now called accounting upon the
foundation called double-entry bookkeeping.

The elements thus added, including accounting theory, justifiably
constitute parts of a superstructure. Theory came partly because teachers
felt a need to present bookkeeping procedures as logical steps toward a
known goal rather than as mere application of yardstick rules to typical
business transactions. Theory was also greatly stimulated by the need to
refine the apportionment of revenues and expenses between fiscal periods.
Professor Hatfield was of the opinion that nine tenths of the problems
of accounting arise from this objective of reporting by fiscal periods.

Another element in the superstructure was cost accounting. While periodicity of accounting reports necessarily gave rise to problems of apportionment, a sharp calculation of the cost of product units made necessary
even greater attention to apportionment. Here as never before attention
was centered upon rationally associating income earned with relevant
costs of producing that income; the over-all objective was to provide management with quickly available data in aid of current decisions. Bookkeeping technology, while retaining long-established basic ideology, was
surely being revolutionized in this phase of its evolution in adaptability.
Imagine Paciolo, a contemporary of Columbus, being confronted with
standard cost accounting!

Clearly the first phase of development was not accounting in the public
interest. Double entry first was used to serve the needs of medieval businessmen for managerial information about their activities. On the foundation of such bookkeeping, accounting was erected to serve the needs of
later generations of businessmen facing new problems of enterprise
operation. However, a facile instrument such as accounting was presently recognized as having other than private uses. The form taken in
this second phase of development was that of sharing enterprise financial
data with the public. This would be nearer to accounting in the public
interest, yet without going all the way. It was an adaptation of accounting; that is, it was an added use of the facts developed primarily at the
initiative of enterprise management for management's use.

From a mere memory-aiding record of debts, bookkeeping became an aid to later decisions and actions by means of systematically summarizing and analyzing the effects on an enterprise of prior decisions and actions, thus placing data regarding the accomplished past in direct and useful contact with future planning.

But businessmen's control over their business activities have not escaped criticism. Men at times have come to believe that individual control, using accounting entirely for private interest, has sometimes been shortsighted to say the least, perhaps even unsocial if the thought be stronger phrased. Unrestrained competition between enterprises under private initiative has at times seemed to have had unfortunate results. Such a conviction is not a recent one or one found only in America.

The British more than a century ago faced the problem of finding a way to restrain certain types of individualism that seemed unsocial in effect. They had tried in 1720 to protect society (investors) from the results of fraudulent promotion of joint-stock companies and unrestrained speculation in company shares. In furthering this idea, the formation of joint-stock companies—distinguished from companies chartered by act of Parliament—was prohibited. This lasted for one hundred years.

About a century later great pressure appeared in favor of freedom to incorporate. The subsequent legislation, between 1825 and 1862, was middle-of-the-road in the sense that it avoided a continuation of the old prohibition by repealing the Bubble Act of 1720 and thus restored freedom of incorporation. The essential point for present purposes in this legislative action was the decision to call for accounting in the public interest, or more precisely the adaptation of existing accounting data to social uses. The public was to be better protected against future fraudulent promotions by breaking the privacy of financial statements and by government-enforced publicity (company registration) regarding the capital, purpose, and personnel of proposed corporations. Investors were to be further protected by an enforced keeping of accounts by the company and by a compulsory examination by representatives of the shareholders of the director's accounting reports.

Until recently there was no comparable effort in the United States to compel the adaptation of accounting to the public interest. Some uniformity in accounts has been prescribed from time to time under the authority given to regulatory commissions, such as the Interstate Commerce Commission, beginning in the 1880's and by later rules of state utility commissions or the Federal Power Commission. These requirements were prepared in the public interest because the enterprises involved were considered natural monopolies whose rates for service must therefore be controlled by public authority. The background for this legislative development was another example of a period of excessive individualism among businessmen with adverse effects or prospective adverse effects upon the general public. It will be noted that commission use of uniform accounting statements as an aid in rate-making did not include prescribed audits.

Incorporation of companies was controlled by separate state laws which did not specifically require accounting or audits. Many states however have supplemented their laws with the so-called "blue-sky laws" wherein additional publicity of financial data relative to new issues of securities was required. Federal securities legislation of 1933 was formulated with much the same intention. However, it was better implemented than state laws in the direction of enforcing improved standards of disclosure in published financial statements and of strengthening the independence of certifying auditors. This legislation made use of accounting for the public interest. And although professional accountants at first resented some of the regulations of the commission, the methods of enforcing the statute have been satisfactorily developed in full co-operation with the profession of public accounting.

Our securities law did not go as far as British statutes and prescribe independent audits for all corporation reports. No doubt this was not done in part because a tradition had long existed of extensive reporting on company affairs in the annual report and of voluntary wide distribution of the reports, including the certificate of independent auditors. The legislation of the 1930's, in the public interest, therefore had only to reinforce and strengthen existing practice regarding audits and financial publicity.

The principal fact emerging from this viewing of the major stages of accounting development is the adaptability of accounting. It began as a systematic procedure of untangling for a business enterprise the facts regarding the interrelation of enterprise capital at work and the enterprise income which resulted. On that foundation of methodology a superstructure was slowly erected which we now call accountancy. But accountancy, as with bookkeeping before it, was operated in the interest of the enterprise. This was an example of the adaptability of double entry, but the area of service was the same.

The adaptability of accounting techniques established so long ago was more fully demonstrated when, in relatively recent years, accounting procedures and the resulting data were called upon to serve the public interest quite directly. Some of the sharing of data was made compulsory, as in the British companies acts, the American "blue-sky laws," and the uniform accounting required by public-utility commissions. Sharing of company financial data in the United States grew extensively on a voluntary basis, prompted no doubt in a large measure by a belief that widespread ownership of corporation securities was a desirable source of company finance and by a conviction that wide distribution and publicity of audited annual financial reports would encourage investment. Federal legislation creating the Securities and Exchange Commission constituted

a sort of superstructure upon the established fact of wide publicity of
company accounting data and extensive public investment in company
securities. The commissions requirements as to use of good accounting,
full disclosure, and independent audits were clearly designed to strengthen
accounting in the public interest. Basically the legislative intent was very
similar to that back of the British series of companies acts in the first
half of the nineteenth century, that is, protection of the investing public
against deceit by company management.

In both instances it is noteworthy that a wider public interest was
served than that represented by investors alone. Undoubtedly better corporation management also resulted, and as a consequence all segments of
society benefited. Thus, indirectly as well as directly in furnishing internal data necessary to sound managerial decisions, accounting enters
the public service and in so doing demonstrates an almost incredible
adaptability in a technology some five hundred years old.

It is evident from this brief survey (1) that accountancy has shown
great adaptability and (2) that this feature has often made possible the
use of accountancy directly in the public interest. The federal securities
legislation of the 1930's was therefore neither premature in conception nor
a new idea conceived under the spur of existing conditions. This legislation clearly was part of a continuing evolution—an evolution of social
controls in the public interest and in evolution in accounting adaptability.

(*Accounting Review*, December, 1933)

12. But Is It Accounting?

Although accounting began centuries ago as a system of private records
in aid of enterprise management, its rare capacity for rendering varied
services eventually produced accounting in the public interest. This was
not merely a reshaping of the list of ledger accounts to produce the fund
accounting which has proved so serviceable in untangling the interrelations between government revenues, appropriations, and disbursements.
The public interest was more directly served when in various ways enterprise accounting data came to be open to public scrutiny: enforced publicity of financial statements (as by the British companies acts); critical
scrutiny of company financial disclosures (as by the American Securities
and Exchange Commission); by means of voluntary publication and wide
distribution of company annual reports to attract funds and report to
the large number of people holding corporation securities.

Various other proposals have been made for accounting in the public
interest. Some of the ramifications of these deserve to be examined. They
may have been conceived in the public interest, but sometimes a question
might be raised whether they are accounting.

One of the doctrines of government function prevalent during the 1930's was that the strength of the federal government should be used to bring the nation out of the depth of economic depression. The strength of government was not only that associated with the ability to pass laws, levy taxes, appropriate funds, change the monetary base, etc.; but it lay also in the ability of officials to stimulate men to conceive of ideas for vesting additional power in the central government to direct the nation's activities of production, consumption, and finance along lines considered to be in the public interest. Policy decisions of great significance had to be made almost day by day. The centralization of making decisions gave important emphasis to the factual bases available for consideration. A good deal of use naturally was made of nationwide statistics, since many decisions were to be nationwide in effect.

Economic statisticians had for years been interested in data of national wealth and national income. Such data now assumed new importance. Their known defects, such as incompleteness of original sources, lack of uniformity in methods of reporting original data, need for better integration of data under analysis, etc. were cause for more than ordinary concern. Improvement and reform of data and wider use and wider understanding of statistics became outstanding objectives.

This movement has a relationship with accounting evolution since much of the most important data of national income originate directly in the accounts of business enterprises and indirectly from the daily economic activities of the people as a whole. Since statistics of national income, among other data, would be helpful to decisions and policies entered upon in the public interest, the accounting data that entered into such statistics could be viewed as data affected with a public interest. This is quite a modern extension of the significance of accounting and apparently is without earlier parallel.

A good deal of statistical material relevant to national income was already available but for most effective use in aid of policy-making it needed to be better integrated. Out of this need came the methodological development now called "social accounting." In essence the method involved establishing subgroups of economic statistics which could produce interrelated subtotals and intermediate summaries designed to make the great mass of data more comprehensible. This objective is clearly the same statistical objective that has prevailed in double-entry bookkeeping from its beginning to the present. Masses of factual data, wherever an understanding of their message is important, must be simplified by classification and compression. In this respect there is a similarity between aggregates of statistics of national income and wealth on the one hand and aggregates of transaction data concerning the wealth and income of a business enterprise on the other.

However, it does not follow that the two systems of classifying and integrating data for these two very different uses can both be appropriately said to produce "double-entry records." Over-all objectives of arranging data into understandable form are not enough to make the two methods sufficiently identical as to justify describing them by the same phrase.

The methodology of "social accounting" or of almost any other large segment of statistical data can be so arranged as to produce subsections and make use of duplicate entries in a manner which will yield a summary of results showing equal grand totals or zero results, if contras are used. In a purely literal sense the entries have been "double"; hence the summaries of totals are bound to be equal, also in a purely literal sense. Yet these equal totals can no more be given an informative, descriptive name than can the totals of a trial balance from the accounts of a commercial enterprise.

A more significant fact however is overlooked in reasoning by analogy from enterprise "double-entry bookkeeping" to "social accounts": the analogy is not persuasive because the "doubleness" of commercial accounting is not the essence of that technology. The trial balance has never been more than an inadequate testing in summary of duality in detail of the debit (left) and credit (right) aspect written into each entry in the basic records. And the duality within each entry was only an accidental result of an early perception of the fact that a significant relation existed between real accounts (expressing wealth) and nominal accounts (expressing expense efforts made to produce revenue from enterprise performance). Enterprise management is vitally concerned to have knowledge of the cost of relevant efforts made and of the associated revenue accomplished by those effort-costs—almost a cause-and-effect relationship.

Two points of dissimilarity between social accounting and business accounting are here discernible. (1) There is no counterpart in our national economy to management in enterprise operation. (Or is such repudiation of "a managed economy" to be considered treasonable?) (2) National wealth and national income are not integrated in the way capital at work in an enterprise is integrated with enterprise income as the fruit of effort. One reason the integration is different lies in the fact that national well-being is not satisfactorily measured by aggregate national income and national wealth is not assembled or used exclusively in producing national income. In a business enterprise wealth is like a cultivated fruit tree; it is dedicated to the production of fruit. The fruit may be consumed, sold, or "reinvested" as seed for future production capital. This is not the picture of the nation's circle of existence. Preservation of our way of life could be vastly more important to national welfare than maintenance of a high standard of living, that is, a high net income for the whole nation derived from a centrally managed national economy.

Since the analogy is so imperfect, the phrase "double-entry social accounts" is misleading. It seems to try to draw prestige from the long use and versatile adaptability of accounting technology without approaching the latter's logical foundation. It is perhaps evidence of recognition of the wide service rendered by accountancy and of a growing desire to further extend that service in the public interest. But accountancy is not statistics, though it follows the statistical objective of truthful classification. And it would be reasonable to believe that statistics is not accountancy. The limitations inherent in the latter would be a handicap to the services statistics can render as statistics. In a similar way the flexibility of statistical methodology, if incorporated into accounting as accounting, would constitute a handicap in rendering the accountancy type of service.

Statistical analysis such as has been called "social accounting" is indeed material prepared in the public interest; and properly used it can serve the public interest even when strongly centralized government control over economic activities does not prevail. But it would seem wiser to use other terminology to headline the methodology, since accounting has been evolving for a very long time into a technology that is necessarily different in most respects from statistics in techniques and service functions.

It must be added, however, that criticisms relative to a title such as "social accounting" for a purely statistical operation do not attach to the adaptation of business accounting ideas and procedures to use within governmental divisions. Since business operation has clearly derived increasing aid over many generations from the use of accounting technology, it must be reasonable to believe that operation of the federal government—the largest operating enterprise in the nation—would be aided if business accounting could be suitably adapted to this service. The need for adaptation rather than outright adoption is clear from the fact that measurement of money profit is not involved there but is an essential aspect of accounting service to business enterprises. Another way of putting the point is to note that, since profit is not available in government divisions as a sign of effective accomplishment, the other features of business accounting, for that reason, are even more necessary in governmental operations. The other features of accounting of particular usefulness in this setting include well-designed and effectively used record procedures, planned control over expenses, integration of budget and data from past operating experience, and use of internal check and internal audit.

One of the most promising recent tendencies in operating the federal government has been an energetic movement in the direction of incorporating business accounting methods into the operation of many government divisions. Controllers, in the accounting sense of technical assistants in business management, are being installed in many spots and are being given appropriate responsibilities. Surely all this is highly desirable in government—the nation's most extensive business operation. In fact it deserves clear characterization as accounting in the public interest. Perhaps it may also be significant that this development is being implemented by accounting-trained men and that it has not been labeled "social accounting" or been given any other headlining phrase. No doubt it is considered by those concerned as just accounting, or at most as an illustration of the adaptability of accounting technology. It might also be said that this new use of accounting carries implication of some limitations inherent in that technology. There are so many similarities between a business enterprise and an operating division of government, even though the profit motive is lacking in the one, that the accounting methods of one can be employed by the other without doing violence to the ideology and schematic operations of that technology. This is the reason that the use of accounting can be extended in this manner and be "in the public interest."

Another activity affecting accounting is currently undergoing analytical debate and is favored by its advocates partly on the ground that adoption of its ideas into accounting would be in the public interest. The proposal to modify the historical cost data in accounts by applying index-number adjustments thereto in effect poses another test to the adaptability of double-entry technology.

The new proposals seem to have been generated primarily (1) by the persistent rise in price levels for a longer stretch of years than has previously been characteristic of our economy, and (2) by an expressed belief that the possible adverse effects of this continuing economic phenomenon may not be realized by enough people to change the trend or to be prepared for eventualities.

The facts of the trend are unmistakable; and the example of excessive price inflation abroad some years ago is indeed disturbing if a similar outcome is considered possible in the United States. It is obviously advisable for businessmen to give careful consideration in making their business decisions to the significance at the moment and for the near future of price-level trends. They should be alerted by all suitable means to the fact that "money" profits are, because of rising prices, not identical with "real" profits.

In the same direction the people generally should be constantly reminded that money wages are not real wages unless the purchasing power of the pay check is relatively stable. Most workers no doubt have reason to be pleased with the present relation of the wages they earn and the cost of living they pay. Perhaps businessmen similarly feel confident of the future. Both parties may be right as to the essential features of the future of this country. Yet both may not benefit from their attitude as expected; mistaken policies in their private and business planning during the present may stand in the way.

Perhaps it is this line of reasoning that leads some forward-thinkers, economists and economic statisticians particularly, to advocate use of various ways and means of alerting business management, governmental policy-makers, and the producing and consuming public to conditions shaping present economic trends and to possible undesirable consequences of unchecked speed and direction of change.

Yet some of the suggestions of methods, especially those for alerting businessmen to the need for carefully viewing the future while planning in the present, may well be questioned inasmuch as they could involve, if fully implemented, a very serious modification of the very characteristics of today's business accounting which have long been rendering highly effective aid to managerial and investment decisions. Because the well-being of the economy would be gravely affected by a long-continued and rapid price inflation, the proposal for the use of index-number series to translate the familiar historical costs of accounts into current price equivalents seems to be considered a further extension of "accounting in the public interest."

The chief charge of "distortion" made against historical costs, especially costs expressed by depreciation expense, is that the established accounting processes fail to eliminate from the net results of the income statement calculation the inflationary effect of rising price levels. The theory seems to be that use of statistical procedures (clearing of price effects) would eliminate this "distortion" in the income calculation and thus prove to be "in the public interest." It is a fact that the public interest would benefit from a dampening of the trend for prices to rise. But there is little or no basis for drawing a defensible conclusion that the proposed direct modification of accounting procedures would contribute materially to the needed modification of price-level change.

Those who are convinced that most businessmen throughout a long past have quite successfully made business decisions in the presence of a reasonably realistic judgment of probable future conditions will find it difficult to believe that the proposed "reform" of established accounting thought and practice is necessary to keep businessmen making good judgments of the near future. It is reasonable to believe that about as many may be confused into poor planning by lack of historical costs reflecting past decisions as are likely to be brought to wiser decisions by ignoring historical costs (and past actions) in favor of their substitute, "current price equivalents." After all, these "equivalents" are only the resultant of statistical assumptions and processes that are a greater mystery to more people than are the technicalities of accountancy. Moreover, "current price" is a useful guide to decisions affecting the enterprise in the future, only to the extent that future prices are similar or correctly diagnosed as trending higher or lower. There can be little doubt that many unfortunate decisions have arisen from incorrect assumptions that current conditions will continue forward, whereas presently the conditions moved very differently.

It seems too much to expect that index-numbers applied to accounting operations could nationally improve a businessman's faculty for correctly previewing future trends. If he still has to make this effort by using other means, it would seem that solving his most difficult problem would not be helped by modification of his accounts. Therefore, a question arises as to how effectively this modification could extend the capacity of accounting to serve the public interest.

The federal government and some of the larger business enterprises employ trained economists to analyze and undertake to interpret economic trends as well as accountants to analyze and interpret enterprise facts resulting from prior managerial decisions. Perhaps it would be a more constructive suggestion to advocate rapid expansion of the use of economists within enterprises, either as employees or as regular consultants. At least such a development would avoid the emasculation of managerial accounting in the attempt to bring the impact of economic conditions to management's attention. Management could then have the benefit of expert staff assistance on both sides. Making decisions is an executive function; it is a difficult art at best and at worst, mere hopeful guessing. It is reasonable to believe therefore that better aid to decisions would emerge from a separation rather than a merging of the two best "intelligence services" available to enterprise managers. Through aid to better enterprise management such a development would indeed be in the public interest.

(*New York Certified Public Accountant,* November, 1954)

13. Government Regulation of Accounting

In the book entitled *Financial Accounting* (1943), George O. May has distilled his long experience and wide contacts with the growth of professional accounting into an interesting series of essays and enriched it with an abundance of historical facts and numerous expressions of personal views.

Six of fourteen chapters are strongly historical in flavor, especially in the area of depreciation and governmental regulations. Here the theme seems to express the view that accounting must in a large measure be as individual as the enterprise and the management it reflects. For this reason accounting regulations devised outside the enterprise and uniformities imposed through power given to governmental agencies may fail adequately to take into consideration the extent and the complexity of the diversities inherent in a system of free enterprise within a profit and loss economy. The author believes that the effect of diversities can best be met by full freedom to act according to the judgment of the businessmen and professional accountants concerned. He therefore looks with some disfavor upon most accounting regulatory activities as being likely to overstress the expected benefits of uniformity of practice.

Some readers may feel that the author's major reaction to the historical development of accounting during the past generation is made somewhat unduly pessimistic by the extensive consideration given to the actions and attitudes of governmental agencies, such as the Public Utility Commission, the Bureau of Internal Revenue, and the Securities and Exchange Commission. It is the author's view (p. 69) that "accounting influence rose to a high point" in connection with the revenue acts and regulations of 1917 and 1918, that income tax laws as a whole deserve to be called "a towering monument to legalism," and (p. 71) that "if 1918 saw the authority of the accounting body in America at a peak, the years 1933 and 1934 saw it at a low point."

There may be grounds indeed for pessimism in connection with many specific actions by governmental agencies. Most of their people are so thoroughly convinced of their mission and seriously conscious of their authority that they may sometimes have overreached themselves. But it is also fair to say that in the years during which some of these agencies have been functioning, a new high point has been reached in the variety and importance of the public services rendered by American professional accountants and in the public recognition of the independent position and technical knowledge which make that service possible. Thus governmental agencies seem not to have been much of a handicap to the profession.

The three chapters on depreciation are in a large measure a contrasting of the treatment of this expense in industrial accounting and in the controlled accounting of regulated companies. Being historical in its approach, the material gives the reader an excellent basis for sensing the complexities which pile one upon another as a result of government's assuming the task of substituting its fiat for the control of prices, costs, and profits by the ordinary forces of economic conditions.

The treatment of depreciation by industry as cost amortization is pictured as flowing out of the merger period of 1896-1903. In order to study a group of companies under comparable accounting conditions, it often was necessary in those days to eliminate the effect of the (conservative) prior practice of charging many new capital items to expense and then to substitute income charges of systematic depreciation. The depreciation practice thus established was usually carried over into the accounting of the new corporations. By 1906, straight-line depreciation was in fairly general use, and by 1918, depreciation accounting was fully established in unregulated industry.

In regulated companies, on the other hand, depreciation was for many years a highly controversial subject, to which the author devotes the larger part of two important chapters.

In the earlier cases the courts did not distinguish between provisions for future replacement and amortizations of past cost. By 1913-14, the common-law view was that depreciation was a function of value. The usual practice was to provide retirement reserves a few years in advance for the cost of property soon to be retired. But in 1920 the Interstate

Commerce Commission sought to introduce amortization into railway accounting. This would result (1) in substituting cost for value in rate regulation, and (2) in associating the depreciation thus charged as operating expense with the deductions used in computing the rate base. But it was over twenty years before a modified straight-line form of depreciation accounting was put in effect. Some of the delay had been due to the controversies which the proposal stirred up, and some had been due to temporary suspension of the depreciation order during the depression years.

In 1922 the National Association of Railroad Utilities Commissioners gave approval, through their standard classification of accounts, to retirement reserve accounting for fixed assets. But it was not until 1936 that they advocated depreciation accounting such as had so long before been recognized in taxation and general accounting.

The course of development to this point thus gives the appearance of gradually evolving in the direction of wide agreement to use depreciation accounting in regulated as well as unregulated companies. But actual agreement was not so easily achieved, as the present situation amply demonstrates.

The author also gives considerable attention to the historical background of the Securities and Exchange Commission. It was evident in the middle 1920's that some corporations needed to be pushed to improve certain unsatisfactory financial and accounting practices. The New York Stock Exchange took the initiative in 1926 by appointing a committee on stock list to campaign for improvement. In 1930, a special co-operating committee was appointed in the American Institute of Accountants. The essence of the proposal which emerged in 1932 from these committees was that the listed companies should disclose the accounting methods employed by them and public accountants should report whether the financial statements conformed with the representation made.

At about the same time the Depression reached its depths in the midst of a political campaign. There were heavy losses in the security markets and loud calls for protective legislation. In spite of the fact, as the author believes, that inadequate or misleading financial statements played a relatively unimportant part in causing those losses, the Securities Act of 1933 and the Securities Exchange Act of 1934 were passed by Congress to put the issuance of securities under regulation and to use accounting as one of the important statutory instruments to that end.

In regard to this legislation the author makes a number of observations. The laws were not a result of prior judicial inquiry; rather they were statutes passed "under pressure of public indignation." They ran counter to "some of the most firmly established principles of English practice"; their penalty provisions, for example, were harsher than under English law. The laws impaired the professional status of public accountants; they took the responsibility for accounting rules out of the hands of the profession and placed it in the hands of a policy-making body; the grant of power to prescribe accounting procedures was "as unwise and unnecessary as it was inadequately considered." Yet, he agrees that later experience has shown that the commission has exercised with restraint its power to prescribe accounting rules and usually has consulted with the American Institute before accounting rules have been published.

Up to 1933 the stock exchanges were the arbiters of "reasonable disclosure," having always in mind the relatively different information desired by long-term investors and short-term traders in securities. This jurisdiction was then transferred to the Securities and Exchange Commission. As a result, the author points out, a body is established that is vested with the duty of preparing policy-making regulations and is given functions suitable to a quasi-judicial institution. It is this body which sometimes seeks freedom from legal restraints by asserting the higher authority of accounting principles laid down by it; and sometimes, as a matter of regulatory expediency or administrative policy, it seeks to relax the applications of such principles.

In the light of these and other historical origins and legal circumstances, the author urges professional accountants to try to extend their public service through the Institute (1) by intervening to aid the courts since these bodies are not expert in accounting matters and (2) by cooperating with regulatory bodies and by accepting responsibility for the maintenance of complete individual independence in relation both to clients and to government commissions.

(book review, *Accounting Review*, July, 1946)

14. A Practitioner's View of Principles

A considerable part of George O. May's book, *Financial Accounting,* is concerned in one way or another with theory. Those chapters are good reading particularly because they bring certain aspects into clear focus. Such an approach will surely prove an aid to understanding why there are issues—a first step toward resolving them.

Sometimes the results of financial accounting are misunderstood because some users do not realize that the statements were not made up especially for them and that reports are in fact a compromise made to give them a maximum usefulness for purposes as diverse as taxation, governmental supervision and price regulation, internal fiscal policy, dividend action and dividend legality, granting of credit, and evaluation of investments. Accounting is utilitarian, it is true, but this cannot be taken to mean that it can be all things to all men.

Misunderstanding may also arise from failure to realize that accounting is conventional. Being influenced by the social and economic concepts of the time as well as by statutes and court decisions, accounting reflects at once both current habits of thought and customary types of action. Underlying an accounting debate there will often be found a question as to the extent to which customary ideas are being replaced by new ideas, or should be so replaced.

This basing of accounting on convention apparently leads to the author's skepticism as to the existence of "accounting principles" (pp. 37-38). The phrase is considered inappropriate also because in earlier days it was likely to be used merely to awe a client into accepting a certain accounting treatment and furthermore, because of late it has been used by utility commissions to avert judicial review of their decisions and to give an impression of permanence and inevitability to their ideas. The fact is, he points out, accounting rules are mere postulates, derived from experience and reason, that have proved useful and acceptable. They are like the rules of common law in many respects—changing as further experience brings greater wisdom, flexible to meet the peculiarities of many situations that seem alike yet vary in some significant way.

Though this is the nature of accounting, the trend of forty years has been away from the common-law mode of thought in accounting and toward the civil code point of view of prescriptions and regulations. This growing emphasis on uniformity of methods and administrative convenience may prove to be a real disservice if it submerges the general usefulness of accounts in favor of some specific usefulness, and if it prevents the true individuality of enterprise and management from being clearly reflected in the financial statements.

Another source of misunderstanding is the evolutionary shift in the focus of accounting from an emphasis on the balance sheet (for short-term credit) to an emphasis on the income statement (for long-term investment). This may create a conscious or unconscious conflict between customary ideas and new ideas. The same can be said of the persisting idea that the balance sheet should be expected to reflect values. This it cannot do because "the value of the enterprise is seldom a material fact," and if it were a fact, "it can only be measured by looking ahead" (p. 8). He would be uninformed indeed who considered financial statements as "looking ahead."

Users must bear in mind that financial statements are not reports of facts but rather the conclusions reached from applying a body of conventions to events and transactions. Statements cannot therefore be successfully made up according to a complete set of rules. This is true primarily because the accounts are in part "a reflection of the temperament and modes of thought of those responsible for their preparation" (p. 246).

Other topics in theory are given due consideration. The author views *Lifo* with some skepticism, and sees the debate over the cost-or-market rule as arising from the contact of older uses (balance sheet emphasis) and newer uses (income emphasis).

Lifo is a variant of the base-stock method. This base was resisted by the Treasury Department when its use was urged as a countereffect to the rise in prices (from an index of 100 to 250) in the decade after 1913. As a result of the Department's stand, taxes were collected at that time on "large nominal profits due merely to increases in price level" (p. 48). In the decade after 1934, a discrete change in terminology was advanced and "last-in, first-out" has gradually come to be accepted by the Treasury Department.

The use of the *Lifo* method "no doubt serves to protect against the illusion of prosperity" derived from a rise in price levels (p. 176), but its use may nevertheless obscure the dangers inherent in the results of a fall in price levels.

If the primary reason that *Lifo* is growing in favor is the prospect of using it to reduce taxes in a period in which prices and tax rates are rising, it could be added that skepticism as to its fundamental soundness is fully justified. Yet it does not stand alone as an example of the way in which taxation influences accounting out of its natural framework of operation. If taxes cannot be determined by close adherence to the ideas that control the usual accounting computations of corporation net income, it perhaps would be just as well that the tax calculation should become a determination in its own right outside the framework of enterprise-managerial-investor accounting.

As to the cost-or-market rule, considerations of soundness and reasonableness "point to a restatement of the rule as requiring only a measurement of the cost that may properly be carried forward" (p. 183). In the discussion of "measurement" that then follows, a doctrine of "normal usefulness" of inventory and "minimum normal profit" on its sale is advanced as the clue to the amount that may properly be carried forward.

It is not made clear, however, why all amounts not thus carried forward should automatically fall into cost of goods sold. It seems a classification fallacy to treat an amount representing price shrinkage of goods that are not sold in a way to send it to join purchase cost of goods that are sold. And a doctrine of "normal profit" can hardly be a sufficient reason for creating a disagreement between the clear meaning of the name of a statistical category (cost of goods sold) and the content in dollars of that category.

It is puzzling that there is so little sentiment among accountants for making the income statement more truthful (as to the cost-of-sales item) by the device of an inventory reserve in the balance sheet. Perhaps it is because the Treasury Department is disinclined to accept the deduction of a flat percentage shrinkage of inventories. But the reserve could conceivably be calculated otherwise and with as much accuracy as the allowance for bad debts is calculated. Perhaps it is because the cost-or-market rule was brought into tax regulations at the insistence of accountants and they hesitate to reverse themselves. But ideas change in twenty years; inventory valuation is one of them. Undoubtedly, if accountants really believed the application of the rule did materially misstate the cost of goods sold, they could succeed in convincing the tax authorities to accept a carefully calculated reserve to be deducted from the inventory item on the face of the balance sheet. A change in tax practice was one accomplished in connection with allowance for uncollectible accounts. Is another change beyond expectation?

Although the cost-or-market rule has long been established and "continues to occupy the leading position," the author clearly indicates that fixed rules to be observed by all companies may not be appropriate (p. 174). He suggests a research program (p. 183) for classifying industry according to the type of business carried on. Uniform methods of valuing inventory would no doubt fall into disfavor when the real diversity of circumstances was clearly revealed.

It may be noted that recent studies of the inventory question show that many complications in applying the rule conspire to shake the confidence of all but the most ardent advocates of cost or market. And the most bothersome question is why the figures of a current period should be adjusted for the purpose of assuring a profit in the next period's use of the inventory. Surely the objectives of accounting do not go so far as to direct that present profit be computed with a calculating eye turned toward assuring a profit at the next calculation. The profit calculation of the future must in the nature of the case depend primarily upon conditions prevailing then, not upon those of the present. It is clear that accounting calculations do not make profit; they can only reveal what is there, and that only in so far as the natural limits of accounting processes permit. When accounting presses upon this example of some of its several limitations, it is time to use the technique designed for such occasions—reserves.

The problem of appreciation gets its share of attention in chapter V. American thought for some time followed the British tendency to give a strong emphasis to recording fixed assets at cost without prohibiting the recording of appreciated values. But in recent years the propriety of recognizing appreciation comes to be questioned in America. Under the influence of a long, sustained rise in price levels from 1896 to 1922, a belief developed that cost figures for fixed assets had gradually lost their significance. Under the influence of an apparently stabilized price level in the 1920's, a theory arose that the economy was operating upon a permanently high level of prices. Since these theories weakened the cost conception of accounting function, the value conception was correspondingly strengthened. As a result it seemed desirable that accounting should reflect the changes in the value of the monetary unit; the mechanism selected for accomplishing this was the increased depreciation charges resulting from write-up of fixed assets.

The reaction was clear. Wholesale write-ups produced unacceptable mixtures in the surplus accounts; appraisal surplus and earned surplus had to be segregated. There also was a tendency to look with disfavor upon asset write-up even when surpluses were carefully segregated. Later on past write-ups were condemned "as if they had been originally violations of a fundamental principle instead of being merely something that is outmoded today."

A complete exploration in the context of fixed asset accounting would no doubt call for more than a few paragraphs dealing with the subsequent problem of write-down, which occasioned a good deal of discussion in the 1930's. It also might call for further consideration of possible counterarguments to the effect that recognition, however early, of appreciation (if it were allowed to affect undivided profits) was even then objectionable as a violation of the fundamental concept of profit and that if there was no prohibition of its recognition at the time, this was merely because customary rules reflected usual situations and ignored the few exceptional situations as being without special significance. When the exception (asset write-up) became so common and so large in amount as to generate misrepresentation, perhaps even deceit, the former complacency in the face of infrequent violation of principle could no longer sustain itself.

It therefore seems that if something was outmoded, it was not an earlier good practice now out of favor, but an earlier failure to give exceptions a rightful place in their current accounting theory and practice.

(book review, *Accounting Review*, July, 1946)

15. On the Writing of History

Two books dealing with the development of organizations representing professional accountants recently appeared: Webster, *The American Association of Public Accountants;* and Stacey, *English Accountancy, 1800-1954*. They are examples of one kind of historical writing; this approach is summarized below. Another kind of historical writing—one not yet given much attention in accounting literature—also receives passing comment in this review.

Because accountancy is a technology with professional overtones, its history could be presented from either of two points of view. As a technology, accountancy has a record of service extending over nearly five centuries; it has shown an amazing versatility of application, particularly in its modern setting. An historian might view this long technical evolution of service and undertake to find, in the surrounding economic atmosphere over the centuries, some explanations for the appearance of these techniques and for the changes therein which have widened its usefulness so greatly.

The first approach would examine technical characteristics interpretatively as to origins and significant uses; the second would focus attention upon technicians banded into organized groups which, under the impact of modern social conditions, eventually became professional bodies having a recognized function and a statutory status.

Both authors named above have cast their work in the mould of the second and more limited objective; the one writes about accountants in Great Britain; the other writes about accountants in the United States.

Mr. Webster declaims authorship as such by signing his title page, "compiled by Norman E. Webster, Chairman, Committee on History." His presentation is limited to the period from 1886, the time of the organization of the American Association of Public Accountants (ancestor of the present American Institute of Certified Public Accountants), to the year 1906. The latter date was selected because thereafter ample materials are available "from which a well organized history of those years may be written . . . at some future time."

This book may therefore be considered a public-service action of the American Institute in making available the factual details of the first twenty years of organized activity of American public accountants. The book is moreover a monument to the vast patience and unceasing persistence of an editor who had developed those qualities through a long career in public practice and then, at a time when most of us would have chosen an easy chair in a shady spot with a good view, applied his talents to a long search for widely scattered, nearly forgotten original data and to the laborious task of sorting and classifying an astonishing mass of documentary materials and periodical items. The same editor gave much the same service to the New York State society of CPA's in connection with its *Ten-Year Book*.

In Webster's book we find no editorializing, no philosophizing as to causes or effects; we find only organized factual data and extensive but selected quoted extracts from organization minutes, relevant correspondence as available, and pertinent editorial or news paragraphs from contemporary periodicals and newspapers. The people who were active in accounting matters during those years receive abundant consideration. The seventy-five pages of biographical data for more than 200 individuals clearly indicate that the editor has maintained an interest in people although for many years immersed in a sea of accounting figures. Late in the book he writes: "There is a voluminous literature on the technical aspects of the profession but only a little space on the shelves is necessary for storage of the works on the human side of accounting practice, its individual firms, societies, etc., the side to which an effort has been made in the preparation of this story of the first twenty years of the Association."

Mr. Stacey, the British author, is a relatively young man who has had considerable contact with British accountancy through his activities as assistant secretary of the Association of Certified and Corporate Accountants, and as editor of the *Accountants Journal*. His pages also indicate a wide acquaintance with social and economic history, an aspect of his preparation for this writing which was no doubt reinforced by a period recently spent in lecturing and research in the graduate school of business at Columbia University. His approach to his subject is suggested by the phrasing of the title, *English Accountancy, 1800-1954* and his subtitle, "a study in social and economic history."

If one may believe that the American book is by design something less than a history of a time segment of the profession in the United States, it is appropriate to say that the British book is somewhat more than a history of organizational activities; it is largely concerned with the impacts upon business of the circumstances and ideas inherent in economic development, which impacts, being transmitted through business to accounting, became casual factors tending to make understandable both the growth in the use of accounts and the clash of conflicting ideas among various organized bodies of British accountants.

A project such as this obviously necessitated a vast amount of research and studied consideration, not only of the facts about organizational actions and attitudes, but also about the facts and the significance of events characteristic of the developmental phases of modern economic society.

Although the period involved covers only a century and a half, it marks a time of great changes in the economy of the nation and the empire. It was a time therefore likely to generate conflicts between people strongly saturated with the way things had been and people strongly influenced by the way conditions have changed.

Perhaps the essence of the book could be compacted into these sentences: British productive activities in the nineteenth century constituted a part of world trade carried on by large corporations. Statutory audits arose a century ago as a means by which government, acting for society, undertook to protect security investors against a repetition of early frauds and misrepresentations by company promoters and/or directors. In relatively recent years efficient production and effective company management have become a matter of such concern that earlier accounts, even though they still are thoroughly audited, no longer sufficed for the needs of the times. The basis for an expanded and improved use of accounting lies in this sequence of development. The same sequence indicated the framework in which a statutory profession of auditing appeared and later expanded, not without some of the friction natural to a dynamic and democratic security.

The book may seem hard reading in spots because of the extensive consideration given to economic conditions, social changes, and statutory developments. Yet it may well be that these aspects are the ones which constitute the author's major contribution. Accountancy is what it now is because of conditions that existed in the past, and today's industrial economy is what it now is because accounting technology has contributed to its development.

Stacey gives the reader a frank preview in the preface of his forthright attitude toward his subject. Accounting development, he points out, has been strongly conditioned by its economic climate. It is therefore necessary for an historian to appraise the natural and artificial obstacles to its progress. He prepares the reader early for the interpretative criticisms which appear throughout the work. In the preface the author writes: ". . . accountancy is too important a professional service to be left solely in the hands of its practitioners" because they are "too preoccupied with the esoterics of their work" to plan how better to focus their art in aid of solving contemporary problems. He sees accountants, because of preoccupation with their craft, becoming divorced from conscious contact with economics of which accountancy is a part. This interpretation is supported by the slowness of British practitioners to orient accountancy toward aid to enterprise management while continuing to serve investors by providing audited balance sheets. There also seems to have been an unfortunate lack of interest for research in accounting theory, accompanied by an overemphasis upon pragmatic and traditional ways.

In the same vein the author writes (p. 38): "By the middle of 1880 the art of accountancy showed signs of stratification, a state in which it remained, at least in some respects, until the twentieth century. . . . In two aspects in particular this dead hand of conservation survived an incredible length. These are accountancy training and education, and the evolution of dynamic, management accountancy. In a sense one is the corollary of the other." The essence of an important later section of the book, one dealing with the period 1940-54, seems to be that toward the middle of the twentieth century technical education and the art of managerial accounting had made a substantial beginning, yet one which, in the author's opinion, still leaves much for the future to accomplish.

If a reader of Webster's book wished a sample of its essence, he would find it between pages 163 and 325. Here in about one half of the volume is presented the important work of the American Association in connection with early CPA legislation, ideas and achievements in technical accounting education, and types of co-operation with other societies of accountants.

Similar areas of activity can also be seen reflected in the British book. Legislative success and failures were experienced in both countries: in Britain nationally through the long series of companies acts which gave status to auditing; in the United States through CPA laws in the individual states. Accountancy recognition through the companies acts extended from 1862 to the statute of 1948 and the present time; recognition in America, to the extent of exclusive use of the title "CPA" and in some states including registration of practitioners and restriction of practice to those registered, extends from the first CPA law in New York in 1896 to the present time.

Competing societies of accountants appeared in both countries. Perhaps this came to be a smaller problem here than abroad because we had state societies with functions distinct from those of a national body. At times state society prerogatives were strongly advocated by separate national organizations (such as the Federation 1902-5, and the American Society of CPA's in the 1920's) even when this brought disagreement with other contemporary national groups (such as the American Association and later the American Institute). In Britain differences between societies of accountants arose out of opinions regarding admission requirements, field of primary professional service, and statutory status. Most of the problems between American organizations were resolved by the time the Institute and the Society merged in the 1930's and a council of state society presidents was given a place in the work of the Institute. The examination service provided by the Institute since 1917 (and now used by all state boards of examiners) was a major factor in modifying existing interstate friction growing out of differing CPA laws and board regulations.

Both authors give considerable attention to education for accountants, each according to circumstances peculiar to his respective country and the time period involved. Because of the terminal date in Webster's book, education is there considered only in connection with an abortive attempt in the 1890's by the Association to establish a technical accounting school and with the successful launching of an evening school of accounts at New York University in 1900. Just as the CPA law of New York established the pattern of subsequent state legislation, so too this school established a pattern for part of the later expansion of technical education.

Soon, however, full-time colleges of commerce were offering degree programs which associated accounting studies with other business subjects and with a substantial content of general education. This has come to be the typical pattern here and one which brings an increasing flow of broadly prepared personnel into public and private accounting work. Degree graduates who have accountancy and business administration as their major subjects are in strong demand from professional firms and business corporations. Many of these employing organizations now have continuation training programs designed quickly to erect a bridge between classroom study and direct contact with accounting in the respective settings.

Stacey clearly indicates various aspects of British attitudes which long delayed the offering of appropriate education in science and in business in the universities. Some of the same attitudes, evidenced by excessive conservatism and complacency, he considers to have stood in the way of a more rapid development of the arts of enterprise management suitable for modern conditions. In other places he does not hesitate similarly to criticize attitudes which led men to resist proposals to unify and modernize accountant societies.

To some readers the British author may seem overly critical. Yet it should be observed that frank criticism, after the fact as well as at the moment, is a very useful aid to the satisfactory working of a democracy. Such for example is the result of the attitude of Her Majesty's loyal opposition. Hence a writer may regret slowness to change and opportunities missed and at the same time contribute to ultimately satisfactory outcomes by pointing in history to a succession of disappointments which, viewed in retrospect, reveal neglected opportunity for a swifter transition. Perhaps knowledge of earlier delayed transitions may smooth out or speed up present and later transitions. The need for adaptability will not disappear with the solution of present problems.

As an earnest historian, Stacey does not hesitate to be interpretative. The attitudes of the time, the failures and successes in nineteenth century British business and accountancy, were what they are now known to have been because of the economic and social setting that constituted the then surrounding atmosphere. He is helpfully interpretative not only in uncovering specific influences but in pointing as well to the reverse—the beneficial effect that required accounts and audits had upon the continuing success of business enterprise. His major point is that it would seem to have been perfectly possible for accounts and business management to have evolved faster in the direction we now see them moving.

It is obvious throughout this work that the author is deeply conscious of the forces and movements which affected British life and industry over the past century and a half. Perhaps it is this fact which enables him to make the largest contribution of the book: the interweaving of threads of technology and professionalism into a fabric of industrial, economic, social, and political change. If one reads first the 1940-54 sequence, he will probably find himself caught up in the essential theme —the interrelation between an economy and a technology. He will then wish to read the prior sections, decade by decade, dealing with the gradually developing interaction of the two factors over several generations.

This 1940-54 sequence is particularly rewarding, for in eighty-six pages it epitomizes the problems faced in accountancy throughout most of a century and a half and reports upon the present status of those problems. Subsections deal with effects of the war, managerial accounting, influence of and on company law, professional progress, education, and outlook toward the future.

In this section, as elsewhere, the author courageously criticizes a continued slow approach toward modernization and is frankly critical of earlier conservatism and complacency in both business management and professional accountancy. For example, after many years of debate, a

plan of unification for the profession, under registration for public practice, acceptable to the established accountant organizations seemed
achieved in 1945. Yet in the revision of company law in 1948, this plan
became an accomplished fact only in a very disappointing degree. "Pro-
vincialism," he writes at page 240, "in the ranks of the councils of the
various bodies" stood in the way though seeming to have agreed to the
draft proposal. "If the profession wishes to assure its continued ascendancy, it must speak with one voice." Thus the author indicates his own
present disappointment.

It will be evident to American readers that even this failure constitutes
a much closer approach to nationwide restriction of public practice to
registered qualified accountants than has been achieved in the United
States, where only a few individual states have such legislation. Here
registration has been advocated only in connection with professional
auditing. In Britain the proposal asked statutory recognition of several
nonaudit organizations of accountants which gave qualifying technical
examinations for admission. This seems to express the broader concept
of "professional accounting." When one thinks of the service to society
rendered by administrative accounting and accountants through aid
given to improved techniques of enterprise management and likewise
notes the increasing use of technically trained accountants in governmental divisions, where in the United States at least commercial accounting technology is being adapted to new uses, it becomes apparent that
a broad concept of "professional accounting" would be appropriate here
also.

There is no space in a book review to examine into the similarities
and differences in the problems faced by accountants in the two countries. Stacey's book will provide abundant materials on his side for someone to draw upon who is familiar with the major problems on our side.
Webster's book only takes us to 1906. Yet even in this double decade
similar situations appear; and other similarities together with elements
of difference are known to characterize our years between 1907 and 1954.
We ought not have to wait for a full presentation of the American story
now that the British story is available. A solid analytical article could
reinforce our natural feeling of kinship while our own history was being
written.

The development of accountancy is an intricate fabric that has great
length and complexity. The warp and woof have been woven; yet, for the
lack of written history, we can only dimly know the unfolding pattern,
each one according to his own small contact with the facts. It has been
outside the intention of these authors to attempt to present the whole
of the pattern. They have taken a more or less limited and modern
segment under examination. Other explorers of parts of the whole pattern should be encouraged to sharpen a spade and dig. Out of an accumulation of separate studies such as these two, gradually will come

the power to comprehend and picture forth what really lies within this service technology and within the profession which has done and can still do so much to make accounting an effective instrument in the service of modern industrial society.

We particularly lack historical studies of the evolution of the technical aspects of accounting as a technology. We have a sizable literature on accounting technique, but no history of its beginnings and advances. It is important that this technology with its large potentials for expanded service shall steadily grow in capacity to serve. Written history can provide perspective from the facts of past changes and the settings in which new applications of that day grew by use from ideas of the day before. We may hesitate to consider economics a technology; and compared with the antiquity of the basic methodology of accountancy, we note that it is of more recent origin as an organized discipline. Yet many authors have contributed significantly to our ability to understand an economic society by laboring to present economic ideology in an historical setting of prior contemporary thought and action.

It is not enough to know the facts about actions taken and the men responsible for the actions, interesting as this may be. No historian is willing to indulge in pure speculation regarding cause and effect. Yet, if history of the past is to contribute to the development of the present, readers at the later date must be able to catch some glimpses of those prior conditions and ideas which stimulated known actions, and glimpses of the way that these actions subsequently stimulated ideas, favorable or corrective. We would like to have some idea at least whether a present need exists for continuation of past attitudes, or for new attitudes. This we might learn from the past—if its story were available to us.

It is true that power to penetrate causation is not given to men. But there must be some middle ground above unsubstantiated speculation. Perhaps that would be the area, so skillfully used by this British author, of thoughtful interpretation of antecedent circumstances and ideas as having possibly and plausibly conditioned later ideas and events in not unreasonable ways. At least we have to say that at any given time even laymen must of necessity try to surmise a plausible near future out of whatever materials they may possess.

The historian will be better equipped than any layman to see some distance into the interrelation of causative factors and subsequent actions, for he has factual knowledge of both the earlier part and the then future. Would it not seem therefore that the historian would most help his readers by developing and exercising a skill in interpretatively, even if inconclusively, looking at events and ideas against a background of antecedent conditions and thought?

Stacey concludes his book with some helpful observations in the later pages as to the future.

The major emphasis, he thinks, may shift from audits to wider services, such as helping keep peace between management and labor; umpiring between company, shareholders, and the state; and assisting in avoidance of economic upheavals and social unbalance. Change in economic climate and various social imitations, he believes, must inevitably bring the ordering and balancing of production and distribution under decisions made by officials in a welfare state. The vehicle of such control is careful forward planning; an important instrument in aid of this planning is an accountant applying his special techniques.

In the United States we have not had practical experience with nationalized industries. Yet some American writers on the methods of assembling and presenting statistical data regarding national product and income have begun to call that arrangement of figures "social accounting." Such statistical tables may be "social" in significance, but they hardly deserve the other descriptive term "accounting." This shows a term taken over from one technology and applied regardless of its other connotation to a different technology.

It is sometimes urged these days that accounting technology should be modified in the hope that in its new form it would become of even greater service to society—that is, to governmental management of society—than it now renders through the accounts of individual business concerns. If the profession of accountancy is to inherit large responsibility in attempting to modify accounting in the hope that this may then help society achieve a desired degree of economic stabilization, it might be advisable, perhaps necessary, to greatly accelerate the accountant's education in economic theory and statistical methodology, perhaps to a total amount substantially equal to the best (technical, present) education in accountancy as such. How long would it take, in either country, to achieve this goal? Assuming it could be and was achieved in due time, would the modified accounting technique be able to make its presumed contribution to economic stabilization in the face of forces and factors beyond the reach of these techniques, whatever their design might be? Future historians may have to examine such questions in retrospect. We might save them and many other people some headaches if we pondered similar problems thoroughly in the present.

(*Accounting Review*, January, 1955)

HISTORY OF THEORY

1. Accounting Rediscovered

Although the literature of accounting has deep roots in the distant past, little of it reflects an interest in the growth of its ideology. Yet the formative actions which originally produced accounting, and later matured it toward larger service, necessarily appeared in association with ideas and intentions. And these motivating elements in turn were necessarily related to problems and conditions of the times in which the evolutionary actions took place.

A relativity theory of the way ideology evolves is not new, but it has not been applied to accounting history. Economists have long realized that over the years much of the impulse to write anew about economic principles originated in the mood of the times. This awareness of the relativity of economic thought to its time of appearance has produced a special literature—history of economic doctrine.

The focus of interest in accounting however has for centuries been turned toward its usefulness in practical affairs. Its evolutionary development has been strongly influenced by that fact. Its service from the beginning has been that of expressing and systematically organizing the data of economic acts and business decisions stated in quantitative terms. The acceptability of that kind of service has been so positive that the literature has been concerned with improved technology and the professionalization of independent auditing.

Here too a principle of relativity has been at work. But in this case the working of that principle is not easily detected in the literature. No procession of accounting authors has been analyzing the accounting acts and ideology of their time and earlier, and putting their reasoning and conclusions into print. Idea evolution remains to be discovered—mined from beneath the thick overburden of described practices.

Accounting itself was not "discovered"; it did not exist in nature or human nature awaiting an explorer. Nor was the initial technology—which later was to be repeatedly "rediscovered"—a happy invention out of a flash of insight. The basic framework evolved in the course of perhaps three centuries out of the trial-and-error experiences of traders who were sensitive to such economic relations as those which joined capital productively employed and the income that was the fruit of that employment.

Although the recording methodology which developed into accounting is usually called double-entry bookkeeping, a much more descriptive name would be "Italian capital-income accounting." That phrase carries a deeper significance than duality. For dual entry and equality of trial balance totals are very superficial aspects of accounting technology. The real essence of the Italian contribution lies in the skillful integration of real and nominal accounts. It is this technical aspect which makes visible, in account figures, the interrelation of capital in use and the income which results from management's supervision of that use.

After Italian capital-income accounting had slowly spread throughout the world, there came a time when acquaintance with its techniques stimulated discovery of previously unsuspected potentialities. In this sense, accounting has been repeatedly discovered. It is significant of the vitality originally built into early bookkeeping that most "rediscoveries" have come within the last one hundred years.

One of these rediscoveries can be dated in the first half of the nineteenth century and placed in Great Britain. In retrospect, it seems the result of a real inspiration that men should see in accounting, which was a technology traditionally dedicated to use in private business, an instrument capable of serving the public interest of that day. Yet there were contemporary circumstances which make the outcome a completely logical answer to the contemporary problem.

It was clearly in the public interest to help British investors gain protection in the future against past types of fraudulent company promotions, thus to encourage the productive employment of savings in the development of public-utility services. The protective mechanism chosen was publicity for company affairs—as to company promotion and company operation. To implement that policy, companies were required by statute to keep accounts and to prepare annual balance sheets from them (in a newly devised, interpretative form). These reports of directors' stewardship must be audited and sent to all shareholders.

This effective solution of a pressing social and economic problem was no fabrication of a lively imagination. British historical background revealed the nature of stewardship responsibilities, the usefulness of audits, and provided ideas which could lead to an interpretative arrangement of balance sheet data.

A second rediscovery of accounting took place some distance into the twentieth century in the United States and at a time when businessmen discovered unexpected potentialities in capital-income accounting for extensive new services in aid of decision-making in large manufacturing operations.

When the American economy had developed in the direction of mass production and mass markets, men found ways of expanding the managerial service of accounting. Large investments in fixed assets and the competitive significance of low-unit cost of products gave added importance to close control over operations. As a result, accounting evolution took another step; presently we see the outcome taking form: standard cost accounting, industrial budgeting and operation planning, control-

lership, research in analysis techniques and in methods for use in shop
and office.

At about the same time university schools of business were improving
their programs of training for careers in business. Accounting was early
recognized as an important tool in aid of business decisions and as the
technical basis for the growing profession of public accounting.

Perhaps the major American contribution to the modern evolution of
accounting could be compacted into the term "administrative accounting." By mid-century the administrative potential of business accounting
was recognized as also adaptable to improving the administration of divisions of the federal government. The term administrative accounting
therefore is taking on a broad meaning, and the scope of the contribution is expanding.

The third rediscovery of accounting is quite recent. It is perhaps an
oversimplification to say it came about as a by-product of war, depression, war; but there is a discernible relationship. Information derived
from "social accounts" proved so helpful to deciding important matters
of public policy under those conditions that the statistical tabulations
which acquired this name may appropriately fall under the broad category of administrative data. Obviously the data are from "accounts" only
in a special sense of that word, and they have an administrative focus,
in a special sense of that phrase.

Certain surface characteristics of business accounts and financial statements, e.g., dual entry, equality of summary totals, are useful for classifying and presenting data about national product and income. But this
much adaptation would not duplicate the essence of capital-income accounting. Integration of balance sheet (capital) and profit and loss statement (income) is lacking in this scheme of national statistics. The analogy
to business accounting therefore is clearly tenuous, even though the tabulations supply data useful in the formation of governmental policy.

Because these data have greatest significance to economists and public
servants and the methodological adaptation has been devised by economists, it is not unreasonable to think of this development as indicating
a third "rediscovery" of accounting, this time by economists. An increasing number of contributions to the current literature has come from
economists who, in one way or another, evidence an interest in accounting matters. Some seem interested in reform of accounting ideas; others
in certain educational aspects of accounting theory.

One line of discussion centers upon an asserted unreality in the usual
calculation of enterprise net income—a condition which, it is said, could
be corrected by clearing revenue charges, especially those for fixed asset
depreciation expense, of the effect of changes in the purchasing power
of the dollar. The other line of discussion centers upon a perceived relation between economics and accounting, the latter being conceived as
a universally useful instrument for the classification and quantitative

measurement of data. The second kind of interest in accounting will be considered presently.

The asserted need for correcting the accounting calculation of business income seems directly related to certain data desired for use in the statistics of national income. If adjustment for changing purchasing power were made by all whose income data find their way into social accounts, the message of those tabulations would more closely reflect the economist's idea of "income." Useful as such adjusted figures might well be for some purposes, a difficulty arises when a proposal is made or implied that established accounting procedures might well be modified in order to produce directly income figures cleared of the effect of price-level change.

Use of collateral, interpretative data reflecting the calculated impact of price-level change raises no objections from accountants. They realize how much users of account data need a variety of interpretative presentations to help them penetrate to the significance of the results of accounting processes. Growth in this aspect of accounting is one of the noteworthy achievements of its evolutionary development. But outright modification of account-keeping has been hard to get accepted.

It would seem that beneath the literature of this discussion of reality in accounting lies a measure of failure to take sufficient note of the justifiable relation of accounting ideas to the necessary preoccupation of accountants with individual concerns. In view of economists' preoccupation with philosophy and public policy, this oversight on their part is understandable. Concern over public policy points up a desire for the best possible basic data for interpreting changes in the nation's economy. Concern for philosophical truths in the area of economics may account for a critical reaction toward practical business and accounting judgments, in the belief that they are shot through by expediencies and conventions, and that therefore they are quite unscientific from not resting upon a conclusion logically drawn from a chain of stated premises.

In the *Journal of Accountancy* recently (May, 1957), emphasis was given to the limited function of accounting by printing an excerpt from Oswald Knauth's book of last year, "Business Practice, Trade Position and Competition."

The aim of accounting is not so much to arrive at eternal truth as to present a useful working tool, a guide for judgement. The postulates assumed in accounting . . . are not adopted because they are universally true but because they are useful.

In the same number of the *Journal of Accountancy*, Professor Norton M. Bedford gives evidence of a thorough understanding of economic reasoning and a clear knowledge of accounting theory and practice by making a careful and enlightening examination of certain points of disagreement between economic ideas and accounting ideas. He includes this observation (p. 58) regarding managerial use of account data:

If past activity was performed in an atmosphere of changing prices and it is assumed that the same atmosphere will prevail in the future, unadjusted data may be more useful than adjusted data as a basis for planning and control decisions.

Now that the flurry of discussion about adjusted account figures seems to be tapering off, the time may be ripe for contributions to the current literature on other phases of economics for accountants and accounting for economists. If the ideological base standing beneath generally accepted practices were uncovered and clearly described, such material would be very useful for students of accounting and economics alike.

For many years the schools which make up the membership of the American Association of Collegiate Schools of Business have done more than may be realized abroad to keep economics and accounting in close contact in the same programs. The later growth of postgraduate work in these schools, including that leading to the doctorate, has substantially advanced that contact. Although modern trends in the teaching of economics in these schools may have generated some dissatisfaction (from an apparent disproportion of time devoted to social economics in contrast to business economics), no concerted movement is discernible to bring about a reconstruction of economics teaching in the light of the needs of students of business, useful as some change might be. Yet some writers, mostly economists, press for ideas which imply, if they do not directly state, that the methods and therefore the teaching of accounting are not in tune with the times.

It is well known, and significant, that contact between economics and accounting was recognized in the literature a generation ago or more by such writers as Irving Fisher, J. M. Clark, J. B. Canning. Indications now appear that further "rediscovery" of accounting is under way.

The contacts between managerial accounting and the economics of the firm have been recently examined in such works as "Economics of Industrial Management" (Villars), "Managerial Economics" (Dean), "Economies of Business Enterprise" (Doyle). Still more recently several articles on the relation of economics and accountancy have been contributed to the *Accounting Review,* to mention only one periodical where controversial material often appears. The sample from that source includes the following:

"The Constellation of Accountancy and Economics" by Professor Richard Mattessich—ACCOUNTING REVIEW, October, 1956.
"Macroaccounting and Some of its Basic Problems" by Professor S. C. Yu—ACCOUNTING REVIEW, April, 1957.
"The Theory and Practice of Accounting" by H. McCredie—ACCOUNTING REVIEW, April, 1957.
"Detail for a Blueprint" by Professor R. J. Chambers—ACCOUNTING REVIEW, April, 1957.

These several recent items show a certain kinship by showing indications of how economists are becoming increasingly aware of an educational usefulness within accounting beyond that of providing some technical methods for the analytical classification of data regarding national income. Apparently accounting can be viewed as an area neighboring upon economics, and one which also may have potentialities for use as an intellectual discipline outside of the study of its technical and professional aspects. It is not yet clear whether this latest "rediscovery" includes recognition of the possibility that much of such potential may reside in technical features not expressed by "conventions" and in the ideas beneath the ideals and standards of professional accountants.

Perhaps the contact economists have had in teaching business students —in the United States the bulk of their enrollment usually is in this category—and the reading necessarily done in research and in teaching "economic accounting" to economics majors have made teachers of economics increasingly acquainted with some of the literature of accounting, even though they probably would have passed by its technical problems and deeper professional aspects.

The articles mentioned make much of a discovered similarity between a popular present-day pattern for the main functional areas of economics and a possible reorientation of the functional areas of accounting into a like pattern. Two of the articles offer an extensive explanation of an asserted parallelism. Accounting for business enterprises is named "microaccounting," and accounting for a region or an economy is named "macroaccounting" (Yu, p. 260). These items are graphically matched with microeconomics and macroeconomics in the well-documented article by Professor Mattessich. His compact diagram, however, does not use the terms microaccounting and macroaccounting (p. 554).

> Business Accounting.....................Microeconomics
> National Accounting.....................Macroeconomics
> Balance of Payments.....................Foreign Trade
>   Accounting   Economics

All of these categories except "business accounting" are clearly aspects of economics. Although the word "accounting" is attached to several items, the purposes of such a diagram could also be served if the three items were named "business enterprise statistics," "national economy statistics," and "balance of payments statistics." This usage would also avoid an implication inherent in using the term "business accounting" in the pattern, namely, that account data need purification (elimination of effects of price-level change) before they would be completely appropriate as a conceptual companion to economics (from their relation, through macroaccounting, to macroeconomics).

Along a somewhat different but not unrelated line of discussion, some parts of the several articles seem directed toward formulating a single positive theory of the function of accounting which, if desired, could then become a framework for the critical examination of the "conven-

tions" of accounting practice. The breadth of the conception involved
is illustrated in the following paraphrase of four propositions called
"the most general and the most fruitful" for use as a basis for the desired
theory (Chambers, p. 209).

1. A wide variety of entities exists because of the will of the co-operating parties.

2. These entities are managed rationally in accord with the demands
of the parties concerned.

3. Rational management is facilitated by statements in monetary terms.

4. Such statements are prepared purely as a service function.

This simplification of the chain of four propositions helps to reveal
a significant thread of meaning. Because financial statements are purely
a service rendered on demand in whatever kind of entity, the conclusion
would follow that the statements resulting from business accounts should
present whatever data the respective managements might demand. However, a stumbling block to the implementation of such a logical conclusion would need to be removed. Could such monetary statements for
business enterprises be certified by professional accountants? This kind
of hurdle would be avoided if the exigencies of the practice of accounting were ignored and accounting were redefined simply as a tool of
analysis of universal application to any data whatsoever.

A conception of universality of service would give accounting a field
of operation practically as wide as that of statistics. And if this concept
of function prevailed, then either accounting technology as widely used
would have to be completely remade to fit its new statistical responsibilities, or the use of account data in the freer manner of statistics would
have to be separated sharply from the kind of reports to which professional accountants could attach their certificates indicating accord with
"generally accepted accounting principles."

Perhaps realization of this kind of alternative may in some measure
explain the diminished flow of discussion about index-adjusted accounts.
However that may be, a number of ideas appear in these articles which
could be considered as pointing a new direction for accounting education. Teachers in the United States should think these matters through.
For we have long been committed to college education for careers in
business and in accounting; and we have now before us for study and
debate a significant report on "Standards of Education and Experience
for Certified Public Accountants."

A selection of brief quotations from this group of recent articles, even
though out of context, can perhaps serve to indicate something of the
scope and direction of the educational theories involved. For the best
appraisal, the articles should be read as a group.

". . . majors in economics may be required to have more training in accounting, because an adequate knowledge of accounting is indispensable before studying macroaccounting [National income accounting]. . . . It should be added
that to train accounting students only in the field of microaccounting [business

accounting] with the objective of making CPA's of them, seems to lose sight of the true meaning of college education." (Yu, p. 272.)

"We have to consider both accountancy and economics as parts of a more comprehensive body of 'economic science.'" (Mattessich, p. 553.)

"The whole structure of accounting as a theory can be set up to precede the structure of accounting as practiced . . . there are what may be termed fundamental premises from which accounting practice develops." (McCredie, p. 222.)

"When accountancy emerges as the incarnation of economics, the rational decision-maker will be able to take optimal advantage of the achievements of economic science." (Mattessich, p. 262.)

"The absence of 'pure' accounting in contrast to the large bulk of 'applied' has severely handicapped all of the profession." (p. 223) "Recorded experience does not form part of any theory of accounting . . ." (p. 217). "It is essential for the advancement of accounting that the subject be studied in theory and that proposition be formulated which can eventually be tested by practical use. . . . The 'pure' aspect is the ideal method, or 'ought,' and the 'applied' is the expedient, or the 'is'. . . . In 'pure' accounting the changed social and economic environments must be taken into account to see if these in any way affect the propositions in use" (p. 218). (McCredie, pages as indicated.)

One of the methods for "verifying the correctness of bold guesses or patiently worked out hypotheses . . . is reasoning, logical reasoning about the relationships between observed phenomena or concepts . . . reasoning leads to generalizations, principles and laws, the general body of which constitutes the science." (p. 206) A theory of accounting can be built which "will be internally consistent, since it proceeds by logical steps to reasoned conclusions." (p. 211) "The scientist, or theorist, as such is unconcerned whether practitioners use [his conclusion] or ignore it." (p. 210) "The student is free to consider many possible modes of action, many combinations of facts and many hypothetical propositions in his search for knowledge. He is not constrained by the necessity of making any of his theoretical models work in practice." (p. 206) "There are, of course, no natural limitations; accounting is what it is made." (p. 213) "But the study of the subject and the practice of the art will be hamstrung unless this preoccupation [with corporate affairs] is tempered with critical and imaginative comparisons of different entities and different accounting methods" (p. 215). (Chambers, pages as indicated.)

Along with the demonstrated exercise of imagination, these writers are quite realistic in including mention of deficiencies in their programs which may or may not be overcome. For example: "Needless to say, a national balance sheet is urgently needed because the usefulness of the income statement [national product and income] cannot be fully explored without the balance sheet . . . the two statements should be considered the backbone of the whole system [of macroaccounting]." (Yu, p. 267.)

It would seem this conclusion implies that the analytical potential of economic accounting derives from the same kind of integration of data as we see in business accounting. It remains to be seen whether this can be demonstrated. It is integration between enterprise real and nominal accounts which, in business, makes measurable and visible the interrelation between enterprise capital productively employed and the income produced by management's supervision of that employment. Are the "liabilities" of a national economy debts which we owe to ourselves and can therefore omit from a national balance sheet? Are the assets of a national economy under "management" control by the federal government in its three branches? Are the balance sheet assets to be valued on the basis of their productivity of a net return? If not, wherein is there an informative interrelation of the two statements for macroaccounting?

Also recognized are some difficulties to the integration of accounting into economics or of economics into accounting.

"Both branches [of economic science] are trying to reproduce economic reality in a certain system of concepts . . . accounting as the mother plant, rooting in the soil of reality, and economics, as the father, is turned toward mathematics and philosophy." (Mattessich, p. 553.)

Later, as part of his conclusion, the same author writes: ". . . economists will realize that accountancy cannot be learned from books alone, but requires contact with actual practice." For the other side he writes: ". . . one can hardly require a practicing accountant [or a career student?] to take courses in advanced economic theory and analysis, mathematical economics, econometrics, statistical inference, set theory, matrix algebra, game theory, linear programing, etc." (Mattessich, p. 563.)

Ideas of the kind indicated by these quotations, however philosophical, imaginative, theoretical they may seem—or perhaps because of these qualities—should be thought-provoking and serve a constructive purpose, even if they stimulate only criticism. And probably they will do just that; while they deal with accounting, they seem to avoid consideration of the rational bases and inescapable limitations which justify and explain a very important part of accounting—professional practice and education in preparation for that kind of career. Surely there must be a close interrelation between the practices of accounting as generally accepted in business and the "generally accepted accounting principles" which underlie the American audit certificate.

It is clear, however, from these articles as well as elsewhere in the recent literature, that the nature of accounting education, both in the United States and abroad, is a topic of increasing interest. It may well be, from the vantage point of a decade or two later, that this broadening awareness of the significance of appropriate education in accounting may come to be the hallmark of the latest "rediscovery" of accounting. If this should prove to be the case, it could be considered the most recent phase of the long evolutionary development of accounting.

It is not unreasonable to believe that wide benefits could flow from an expanding literature on various phases of accounting education, including consideration of the "relativity" of educational developments to conditions in different places. Similar significant benefits would be unlikely from attempts to change the considered view held in the profession that modifications in accounting technology, designed to bring its results into closer harmony with the concepts of economists, are neither necessary nor acceptable under present conditions.

If accounting education becomes a leading subject of discussion, some of the issues may have been foreshadowed in recent articles.

1. Should university preparation for a career in professional accounting consist of the broadest kind of liberal education (including much technical economics) with accounting being studied later in private and in conjunction with employment which provides experience?

2. Should preparation be concentrated in the study of accounting technology, professional standards and techniques, and closely related subjects of business administration, business finance, business economics, business statistics, business policy? Should this be done in specialized schools where the accountants' own interpretation of economics, finance, statistics, etc. would prevail, thus following the precedent of agricultural economics, educational statistics, accounting for law students, etc.?

3. Should preparation preferably be built on the foundation already existing in the schools where throughout the program the pattern shows a judicious mingling of the essentials of liberal education, business education, accounting education?

If subject matter were intermingled for four years, a fifth year for a master's degree could be specially designed to carry the student beyond CPA problems and audit programs into some of the desirable "higher plateaus" which could not be crowded into an undergraduate program, or be well digested by undergraduate students. Some possible examples: historical and theoretical bases of accounting; ethical aspects of business management and professional accounting; micro and macro phases of economic analysis; methods for making administrative decisions; practice in communication by interpretative arrangement of data and by forceful written English.

The educational ideals underlying the articles epitomized above do not seem very useful for university programs for accounting careers, for they lack contact with professional matters. These ideas, however, might appropriately be called into play in the United States at the postgraduate level in the schools of business. The profession here more than ever looks to university programs as the primary source of its recruits. These schools therefore feel a continuing moral commitment for giving a directly useful bent to the programs for accounting majors. Professional men and educators alike are coming to recognize the additional benefits of postgraduate work in accounting, following a substantial major in undergraduate accounting and business. The results, in added maturity of thought, intellectual initiative, ability to grow rapidly with experience, are often astonishing to the participating parties.

The closing thought for these ideas is taken from Fritz Eichenberg's "A Plea for a Middle Ground," in *The American Artist* of June, 1957 (p. 89). "It seems that we need the extremist as urgently as we need the traditionalists as check points and deterrents for the wildest excesses."

(*Accounting Review*, April, 1958)

2. An Accounting Inheritance

Out of the many riches we moderns have inherited from the Middle Ages, one is of particular interest to accountants. Over the centuries it has been called by various names, such as account-keeping by the method of Venice (1494); account books in the Italian manner (1543); keeping double accounts (1636). But most often in later years we have called it "double-entry bookkeeping," [1] usually with little realization that this was the name of a rich inheritance.

The term persists although belief has been growing that the phrase is not very descriptive of the essence of accounting. The essence is the real inheritance, whatever name may be given it, and that essence is not simply a matter of record methodology. Perhaps in the phrase "enterprise accrual accounting" we can see an attempt to be more descriptive. Yet it may be useful to dig deeper than trite titles; headlines can seldom tell the real story.

Let us first try to describe this inheritance somewhat more broadly.

"Accounting is an ingenious arrangement of interrelated classification categories. The elements in this arrangement are so skillfully articulated as to measure and make quantitatively visible the inescapably close integration of enterprise capital and income—an integration which is an economic fact of life even in the absence of conscious recognition or systematic measurement."

This improvised statement reads so like a complex definition that it will be advisable to treat it only as a text to be analyzed and appraised rather than as a complete indication of the essence which constitutes our earliest accounting inheritance.

The principal difference between the indicated textbook titles and the above descriptive phrasing about the central accounting objective lies in the fact that the former refers to aspects of the mechanism we use; the latter refers to something more significant, namely, the economic service the mechanism has been able to render in varying degrees for more than five centuries.

That economic service is not difficult to recognize. For it is related to the tight interrelation between capital (as the tree) and income (as the fruit). Saved income begets capital; capital productively employed begets income; this income can be consumed as fruit or can be put back to work as seed.

These relationships are not new. They are age-old facts of economic life. They were known by traders centuries before economic literature was written. They were known to businessmen long before enterprise accrual accounting was formulated. Disorganized written memoranda were rendering effective aid to enterprise management before records

[1] A much more descriptive name would be "Italian Capital—Income Accounting."

were knit into a planned relationship which we now call "system." But the elements of system can only be parts of mechanism and methodology. The result of the use of the mechanism—the information made available —was more significant to businessmen than the means by which the data were organized and arranged. The one was the means to an end; the other was the reason for having a methodology.

If we may believe the early traders were rational men, we can surmise that they gradually tied together various parts of their disorganized records in a conscious effort to secure more and more useful information about their business affairs. The kind of information which rational men would gradually come to realize they needed would be objective, measurable facts about capital productively at work and about the fruits of that employment. The reason businessmen would desire such information would be that they could not avoid knowing from experience how closely interrelated capital and income were; and they would not fail to know that their personal plans and decisions had helped to effect changes both in the kinds of capital employed and in the income of the enterprise.

It would seem reasonable to believe businessmen realized that more complete information about past business decisions and the related results—good or bad—would provide an improved basis for subsequent decisions.

Clearly there would have been ample motives even centuries ago for men to wish systematically to assemble facts about their business affairs. But wishing would not be enough; a practical problem had to be solved. In retrospect, we can see the key to the solution, but we do not know how men thought their way to that key.

When nominal accounts (expense and revenue categories) were finally injected into an existing framework of real accounts (asset and liability categories) the "ingenious arrangement of interrelated classification categories" was well on the way to becoming the central feature of "the method of Venice," and of modern accounting. Those categories—real and nominal accounts—were indeed "skillfully articulated" since as a result of technical arrangements, the data accumulated therein could "make quantitatively visible the close integration of capital and income."

Experience had indicated that such an interrelation existed in real life; this belief (theory) was finally given practical form and dimension. Known facts, such as exchange-priced transactions (historical costs) which permeated every phase of enterprise activities under management, could then be marshaled into informative categories, and the totals and balances of these categories could picture in arithmetical symbols the diversities of enterprise capital (positive and negative) and the reasons for enterprise expenses and revenues.

Note that this "picture in symbols" (account data in terms of money price) which was so useful as an aid to managerial decisions, both ancient and modern, came into being because traders centuries ago knew that capital and income were interrelated as is a tree and its fruit; and because, somehow, the same men found the key by means of which these economic aspects of business activities could be brought quantitatively into interrelated, analytical categories. The key was real and nominal accounts, integrated.

It must be clear that the essence of bookkeeping, the ancestor of accounting, lies within this particular arrangement of co-ordinated and analytical categories. Our inheritance cannot be suggested by inadequate phrases such as "double-entry bookkeeping," "enterprise accrual accounting," etc. Slowly men are coming to realize that accounting is not the use of a collection of clerical records. Bookkeeping even in its early days was a true technology because it was more than a mechanism. Accounting today is more than methodology, i.e., systematic procedure, because its methods are expressive of a basic philosophy which furnishes the ends and aims for which the mechanism is the means. The means would not exist except in conjunction with perceived ends, whether perception was clear and positive or vague and uncertain.

When appraising the social service accounting can render as of today, with its roots reaching five hundred years deep, we should include appreciation that this service became possible because of strongly original contributions made to its technology by businessmen at a very early date. It was a magnificent accomplishment to have fabricated so early such a satisfactory means of serving their own ends that the same basic mechanism could continue to serve the same kind of ends under the unimaginably different conditions in which accounting is used today.

This accounting inheritance could have been rejected after it was received. No compulsion existed which could explain the way Italian accounting replaced contemporary recording methods now called "charge and discharge accounting." The latter were adequately serving the needs of English landed estates. Or no one could explain the way the use of the Italian system spread over the world. Clearly the inheritance was accepted for us long ago. But having been accepted, it could have been dissipated later, as personal inheritances sometimes are. The fact that this has not taken place can be considered significant of the strength of the underlying ideology and the recognized usefulness of the organized methodology.

It is therefore disturbing to see at this late date a small cloud of misunderstanding on the horizon which from its conformation seems as if it could become a twister, capable of beginning to weaken the tight integration of real and nominal accounts and the interrelation of the major financial statements. If such a weakening were to become progressive, it would indeed dissipate the inheritance.

If index-adjusted revenue charges are not restricted to an interpretative status outside of the trial balance and supplementary to the usual income statement, the resulting modified revenue charges could hardly be considered other than as consisting in part of a forcefully injected, ir-relevant element. It would be irrelevant, that is, in the sense the charge did not derive from transactions to which this enterprise was a party. It certainly cannot be a transaction party to the data entering an index of general wholesale prices.

Since the advocates of adjusted revenue charges do not propose a similar adjustment for assets, the acceptance of income statement adjust-ment alone would have the effect of interfering with the natural in-tegration of the two primary accounting statements. And since statement integration is only an expression of the unbreakable interrelation of capital and income, a forced disintegration of that bond would be a repudiation of the central core of early bookkeeping and a violation of the chief accounting function inherited by modern accounting.

This conclusion could hardly be changed by a second arbitrary adjustment—one made in some "capital adjustment" account in the balance sheet to offset the extraneous charge injected in the revenue debits of the income statement. For that action would merely indicate acceptance of equality of totals as the basic characteristic of capital-income accounting.

A similar offset injection of extraneous data was proposed and debated a generation ago. The proposed use of imputed interest as an expense would call up a contra-credit to "theoretical interest earned." The idea was finally rejected. The best we could say for either of these two pro-posals is that each would force extraneous, hypothetical, interpretative data into a body of living data traceable back to unquestionable exchange-priced transactions of this enterprise. If the earlier proposed injection of interpretative data were rejected for cause, surely there is even more reason for rejecting the later suggestion. For the latter would even more seriously becloud the interrelation of capital dedicated to the work of an enterprise and the earning power of that investment as reflected by trans-actions in which this enterprise was clearly a party.

Outright dissipation of inheritance has been rejected when suggested; its acceptance and proper use have been amply demonstrated by modern accounting. It is particularly fitting therefore to inquire whether the heirs have succeeded in multiplying the inheritance.

They have indeed done so; they have by modifications practically made over the original methodological pattern. Yet they have never smothered early originality with modern ingenuity. This however does not furnish a reason for moderns to feel they have been more creative than their tech-nical ancestors. Theirs was a basic patent; ours were but improvements suited to the times.

Today, and indeed throughout five centuries, men have been so pre-occupied with extension and improvement of accounting mechanics and procedure that they generally have failed to see into the heart of their technical riches. It almost seems as if we continue to show relatively little interest in matters of theory merely because writers of early textbooks did not include descriptions of beliefs and motivations which furnished the internal cement necessary to bind procedures into a unity deserving the name of technology.

We have, to be sure, enlarged the inheritance as wise beneficiaries should. We may have been more impressed by the adaptability to new uses which lay in bookkeeping methods than by the interpretative significance of the integration of real and nominal accounts. Nevertheless we have expanded the inheritance considerably by adapting and refining accounting techniques to the needs of large-scale business and financial operations, and to many noncommercial uses. As a result, some aspects of accountancy have become truly professional (e.g., public accounting), and others (e.g., administrative accounting) have become highly technical occupations.

Yet, throughout the slow expansion of early methodology, a conviction seems implied that equality is the keynote. Today the mental process of converting transaction facts into items in account categories seems for the most part little more than variations on early textbook themes, such as "debit what comes in; credit what goes out," "every debit must have an equal and opposite credit," "equal totals for the columns of a trial balance indicate that the basic rule of double entry has been followed throughout."

There is more than that. The balanced arrangement of a ledger account—items on the left, opposed by items on the right—seems to have been elevated to a significance which is not justified. Or perhaps we should say, some parts of the inheritance have been preserved intact in a highly literal sense. In this respect the modern income statement puts interpretative arrangements ahead of traditional form. The balance sheet does show considerable modification of details and subtotals. Yet it usually preserves the left-right form of a ledger account. And this has sometimes seemed an unimaginative adherence to equality of grand totals. Note how some items, being ledger debits, find their way into tabular association with earnings (e.g., fixed asset appraisal credits in general surplus account). Surely this illustrates mechanical aspects more than logical arrangements.

Accounting methodology was originally formulated through slow steps of practical trial and error. No central philosophy of capital-income interrelation was first worked out and then implemented by suitable techniques. It is not surprising, therefore, that later developments should come from following a similar approach. Yet this need not stifle curiosity as to whether any inner essence of purpose exists which has been and is influencing the choice between alternatives often faced in trial-and-error use.

The fact may be full of significance that nearly all methodological improvements in capital-income accounting—possibly in some measure without having been consciously planned—have been essentially faithful to the central theme of accounting, that of rendering quantitatively visible the inescapable interrelation of enterprise capital and income earned by its employment under management decisions.

And it is likewise quite significant that modern verbal formulations of basic accounting concepts—without starting from a conscious premise of capital-income integration—will be found upon analysis to supplement and support the thesis that accounting serves a useful purpose primarily because its classified data bring into view objectively measured enterprise facts which are analytically useful for appraising prior business decisions regarding enterprise capital and income in comparison with subsequent, related events.

The following accounting beliefs surely tell us that modern ideas give support to the thesis indicated above.

"1. Belief that a business enterprise is conceptually an individual entity, a segment of capital productively employed within a definable economic and/or legal framework."

A man of wealth in the early days would often have several branch managers representing him, or he would be partner with different men in various enterprises. Thus one man's capital would be strategically divided and separately dedicated to business activities in different ways and in several localities. Consequently, he would have a variety of sources of profit or loss from the employment of his own capital.

Conceivably such a man might have tried to keep accounts for all of his capital and income as if his activities were confined to one enterprise. Merely to think now of such an operation is enough to convince anyone that no rational man would have attempted it. It was simpler and quite adequate to keep separate sets of accounts for separate enterprises.[2]

The next mental step was inevitable: each enterprise came to be considered, for accounting and for policy, as a separate entity.

In an economic sense (productivity) and in an administrative sense (managerial responsibility) each business enterprise, even in an early day, would be conceptually separate and different from all others, particularly because each had its own identifiable capital and a measurable income peculiarly its own. And this situation would exist long before the idea of a limited liability corporation made it necessary to endow that kind of operating unit with statutory status as an entity separate from its security-holders, its creditors, and its management.

"2. Belief in the fundamental significance of account data stated in terms of exchange-priced transactions."

This concept of the accounting usefulness of money price is a corollary of the concept of an enterprise entity possessed of capital and earning income. Because each enterprise is an entity, only transactions of which

---

[2] We are not more rational today, only more ingenious in using consolidated statements; but even these derive from separate sets of accounts.

this enterprise is a party could be relevant to the record of its capital and income. Because enterprise transactions would be of many kinds, they needed to be rendered homogeneous so the elements could be combined in various informational arithmetical totals and balances. This would be essential in order that interpretative understanding of capital and income should become possible. Transactions recorded in terms of the exchange price of each bargain would very satisfactorily meet this requirement of homogeneity. Restricting the record to those transaction facts also would give assurance that the capital and income data would consist only of facts definitely relevant to this enterprise. In this way quantitative representation of the various transactions of this enterprise, in addition to being assuredly relevant, would also be objective and reviewable, that is, not imaginative or hypothetical, and would be supported by documentary evidence.

The key to satisfying these needs is the exchange-priced transaction. Capital-income data having such a basis become quantitative from being expressed in units of the appropriate local money system. Transactions related to capital and income are demonstrably real because they are tied to the exchange bargaining of two independent parties, thus excluding irrelevant and unilateral determinations. If supporting evidence does not show that the transaction is clearly relevant to this enterprise, its use in connection with this segment of capital and income is questionable to say the least. An enterprise entity is obviously the first classification category involved in any systematic capital-income accounting. If falseness creeps into the data entering this major category, no amount of subclassification or disclosure can obviate the misleading effect upon reader understanding of the capital and income thus subverted.

And only transactions which are exchange-priced by co-operation of this enterprise have a satisfactory quality of objectivity and reviewability. If imaginative, irrelevant, or extraneous events seem likely to have some impact upon management, and thus indirectly upon the enterprise, they are suitably considered only as collateral evidence or conditioning factors leading to managerial action. Such events have no place within the accounting framework until they have induced measurable managerial action within this enterprise and within the authority of this management.

"3. Belief that a business enterprise, regardless of its legalistic character, has continuity of existence and operation from formation to termination."

There is no available evidence that this concept of continuity was consciously held by pioneers in the formulation of capital-income accounting. Yet the time came in the seventeenth century when the great East India Company gave recognition to continuity of operation and periodicity of reporting by abandoning its prior practice of accounting for each voyage as a separate terminable trading venture. This change clearly expresses a preference for a concept of profit as a periodic measurement in the midst of continuing operations, as against a concept of profit as part of liquidation proceeds, the size of which each venture participant decided for himself according to the relation of his share in the proceeds to his original investment.

The Italian method of accounting was ideally suited to use under a concept of operational continuity. This is particularly true since this accounting made it possible to see illuminating details of the factors making the profit figure what it was, whereas no such interpretative data were made available by dividing the whole proceeds of a venture among the participants. Although annual closing of the accounts was not uniformly practiced, it is found often enough in old records still preserved to indicate that not all business activities were conducted and accounted for as separate ventures.

A known amount of capital dedicated to certain kinds of business operations under management would indicate the fiscal boundaries of a given business entity. And so long as the same human element (management) continued in control (this being before the day of corporations) an obvious continuity would exist, and with it the administrative need to view operations and results, through account data, at regular or irregular intervals. It would have been irrational management indeed which, except for ventures of short duration, would wait for years to learn the outcome of prior decisions and actions, particularly outcome presented in terms of measured positive factors (revenues) and negative factors (expenses, costs, losses).

The concept of enterprise continuity and its use long ago include recognition of the usefulness of periodic computations which could make visible the interrelations running between capital and income.

"4. Belief that the financial soundness of an enterprise and the effectiveness of its management can be read from the interrelations among data summarized in the major financial statements; and that change in financial conditions and change in managerial effectiveness can be read in comparative figures from the reports for a series of fiscal periods."

This phrasing undertakes to state the ultimate usefulness of the data assembled and classified by accounting technology. Some such use-objective, however vaguely perceived, must have lain beneath even the earliest experimental evolution of record-keeping into a co-ordinated system. Even in these days traders would wish to have a means of measuring the effectiveness of their business decisions (enterprise earning power) and of gaining understanding of their financial conditions (capital status).

And the same use-objective, however it may be phrased, provided over the years the basic motivation for improving upon and extending the inherited accounting mechanism; for improving the methods of using and teaching the use of the mechanism and understanding the related ideology; for modernizing the methods of reporting and analyzing the accumulated data; for creating a profession of the work of testing the dependability of the data reported and the completeness of disclosure.

The chief usefulness of account data, whether in the fifteenth or the twentieth century, derives from the fact that accounting technology is able to make visible the interrelations running between enterprise capital and enterprise income. But classification technology cannot indicate the significance of data or the import of data interrelations. There is a point at which technology has completely rendered its service; at that point men must undertake to make the most of the material which technology has made available. For example, financial soundness or unsoundness has to be read out of data, dependable data. If "soundness" were arbitrarily written into the accounts, only deception could result from the fraud which introduced false interrelations.

An opinion regarding managerial effectiveness must also be interpretatively read out of the results of accounting technology. If the reader is unfamiliar with at least the ideological core of this technology, he will be handicapped in seeking to extract meaning from the most completely integrated data. His power of analysis will be weak; his ability to gain from data an understanding of a given enterprise will be deficient.

From its early days, accounting has provided interrelated data which, when the interrelations have been intelligently interpreted, can make the enterprise understandable. Understanding can emerge because a business enterprise is a segment of dedicated capital; because managerial decisions regarding the employment of that capital play a very important part in generating enterprise income; because at the core of accounting technology lie integrated real and nominal accounts which, by reporting interrelated elements as quantitative sums, provide highly informative facts about a given enterprise.

It is a significant part of the modern improvements in the "basic patent" formulated so long ago that the interpretative significance of account interrelations has been extensively recognized and increasingly put to use.

Analysis, for example, can detect diversion of working capital into permanent improvements, thus explaining a chronic condition of insufficient cash to take discount on purchase invoices—this in spite of a showing of attractive periodic profit. A gradual increase in the relation of debt payable to total assets can indicate a drift in the direction of insolvency. A disproportion of insurance expense to book figures for investment in inventory was the initial clue which led to uncovering an extensive and well-hidden embezzlement.

A systematic analysis of the rates of investment movement around the working capital cycle can present many significant indications. Goods bought on credit pass into inventory, thence upon sale into receivables. As receivables are collected in cash, payments are made on the accounts payable. Then another turn about the circle begins. A changed rate of flow at any of these "points of exit and entry" in the cycle may be a significant clue to an undesirable condition, a symptom of probable trouble unless proportionality is restored by managerial detection, decision, and action.

Our inheritance from long ago has indeed been carefully preserved. Modifications and extensions have gradually been made; but these changes have been adaptations made necessary or useful by modern conditions. On the whole the inheritance has been enriched; but not enriched to the limit of the possibilities.

No doubt a good deal more could be done to improve and extend the techniques of interpretative analysis. This is perhaps the least developed area of accounting. And it would be fallacious to think this area is not within the boundaries of accounting. In order to understand an enterprise from data, analysis is necessary. If analysis is inadequate, understanding is handicapped, and technical improvements in system, in procedure, and in communication will be of little benefit.

Few areas of data collection have been so well served by classification methodology as has accounting. From the very beginning a core of highly significant interrelations was made available to informed readers of the data. Today the possibilities are enormous for more extensive analysis of interrelated account data. A few textbooks on financial statement analysis have pointed the way. Yet the reader audience therein visualized consists primarily of investors and investment analysts, and the analytical techniques there used are necessarily designed for application to published, or personally submitted, financial statements.

The area of analysis available to internal accountants is much greater because significant data are lodged in both sides of every account, whereas only account balances are reported in the statements. These data probably could be usefully analyzed further than is usually done. Such possibilities, as well as present analytical practices, exist because the modern industrial world has a classification technology which is centered upon making visible the interrelations between enterprise capital employed and enterprise income earned under the perceptions and decisions of enterprise management.

The basic ideology and methodology worked out some five centuries ago in Italy have indeed proved to have the aspects of a notable inheritance, one deserving to be carefully preserved and further enriched.

(unpublished manuscript, 1956)

3. Accounting Adapted to the Public Interest

A particularly significant aspect of all professional accounting is the fact that, although accounting evolved originally in the service of private traders and is closely suited to that use, it nevertheless proved to be a technology which could be effectively used to serve the public interest as well.

A good case could be made for believing that even if accounting were used only to facilitate business management, it would at the same time be serving the public interest. We can see more clearly now than perhaps was possible long ago that information derived from accounts has helped enterprise management steadily to improve production efficiency and increase managerial good judgment. These factors have brought cumulative benefit to society in general.

It is another aspect of public service, however, which is to be explored here. How and why was accounting technology made into an instrument to help protect the public consisting primarily of people who had funds which were or could be invested in productive industry?

Obviously, a suitable technology would first have to exist or be improvised for that purpose out of whole cloth. Improvisation was not necessary because an adaptable technology was already in existence. The fact needs no elaboration here that double-entry bookkeeping was inherited from Italy—a technology best described perhaps as capital-income accounting. And it is clear that the essence of accountancy's large capacity for rendering varied service has from the beginning been centered in the unique integration of real and nominal accounts, the accounts which respectively reflect enterprise capital and enterprise income—a very significant inheritance in itself.

It was this inherited technology which British ingenuity early in the nineteenth century enriched and adapted to the service of the public interest, an action made manifest at the time in a remarkable series of statutes. Because the early literature of accounting on the continent did not describe any more auditing than "ticking the trial balance," it becomes a matter of interest to inquire how Italian capital-income accounting came to be required of British joint-stock companies—although "charge and discharge" accounting had earlier served British landed estates very satisfactorily—and why an audit of company accounts was prescribed by statute.

Several significant questions in accounting history are involved here. What public interest triggered this development? Why at that time? Why was it accounting which was called upon to serve this public interest? What precedents, lacking in Italian bookkeeping, provided ideas which, when united with the basic techniques of double entry, helped to create an instrumentality very directly suited to serve the public interest?

The reason some action was needed in the second quarter of the nineteenth century was twofold. Excessive speculation in the days when readily transferable company shares were a new institution (late seventeenth century) ultimately brought about such extensive losses to the investing public that the government prohibited the formation of joint-stock companies. The reason for such legislation was that the investing public clearly needed some kind of protection against fraudulent stock issues.

Early in the nineteenth century it became evident that business enterprise, being still restricted to a few parliamentary companies and to partnerships or proprietorships, was operating under a degree of handicap in securing expansion capital. This was the second reason new legislation seemed called for. It would now be in the general public interest if incorporation of limited liability companies were more widely permitted. The legislation which emerged gives the clue in its content to other reasons for the companies acts. Since full freedom to issue transferable shares had generated unfortunate consequences, new permissive legislation would need to include safeguards against another era of wild speculation in company shares.

It was completely in character for the English people, through their Parliament, to resolve the dilemma by attempting to make it possible for investors (the public in this case) to reach sound decisions about investing or disinvesting their savings. The government undertook only to provide assurance that dependable company information would be available from which individual judgments could derive.

This assurance was given by requiring (1) financial publicity from the people who proposed new registered companies, (2) adequate accounts to be kept by all registered companies, and (3) annual distribution of an audited balance sheet to all shareholders and the government registration office.

This adaptation, directly in behalf of a public interest, was a great and lasting contribution; a technology which had evolved in business usage had been given a new function. Perhaps it is not too much to say that this was a contribution to modern society second only to that made by the original formulation much earlier of Italian capital-income accounting methodology.

The legislation which constituted the companies acts of this period also makes it clear Parliament had recognized that mere repeal of the earlier "Bubble Act" would not alone be satisfactory; and that a requirement for keeping accounts would by itself be an insufficient safeguard, since there was little in Italian bookkeeping practice to suggest a usefulness beyond the needs of business management.

Since the British contribution was greater than would have been the case if only these two devices had been employed, some other precedents or experiences must have furnished additional ideas. It was particularly significant, for example, that financial statements were at that time given new emphasis; that the statements themselves took on a novel and very useful form; that beneath the statements and the associated audit lay a constructive and appropriate theory of management responsibilities and of the related function of the balance sheet.

It is not difficult to believe that certain definite ideas underlay these parliamentary actions, although they may not have taken on the following specific phraseology: Ideas that investment of savings in productive enterprises would be encouraged if joint-stock companies were again permitted to exist; that publicity of company affairs would enable investors to protect themselves by decisions which could rest upon dependable financial information regularly communicated to them; that double-entry accounts would be a useful source of basic data about company affairs; that pre-audit of the distributed balance sheets would increase the dependability of the communicated information.

Beneath the statutory requirements lay an important theory, namely, belief that publicity of the facts involved would be a strong deterrent to the formation of spurious enterprises and to later putting out insufficient or misleading information about the stewardship of company management. The key words here are "publicity" and "stewardship"; and they are not unrelated.

The idea of stewardship—personal responsibility to others, duty to be faithful to trust, obligation to report honestly on the discharge of responsibilities received—had a long development in English history. It is therefore reasonable to believe such a background would make itself felt in the presence of the new dilemma. Acceptance of responsibility (stewardship) strongly implies acceptance of a related accountability (publicity). Company directors accept responsibility for supervising the employment of other people's invested funds; hence directors should be held accountable to the investors; and a balance sheet from double-entry accounts is a suitable public presentation of that accountability. Making such ideas into the law of the land is but a matter of authoritatively communicating a considered legislative consensus to the people to whom the ideas will have special significance.

Such ideas as these were not without early precedent. Collectors of city taxes centuries earlier received responsibility, and they publicly reported before the assembled citizens on the discharge of that responsibility. Similar action was taken by treasurers of the early craft guilds. And in the administration of feudal landed estates, an elaborate system of stewardship accounting was developed by means of which the interrelated services of numerous operating departments were reported and a correlation between department records was made evident.[3]

Another precedent for the stewardship concept, perhaps the most significant one, is found in the ideas and practices developed in connection with some of the legal aspects of property inheritance. Here it was often necessary, according to a testator's will, to place the control of an estate in the hands of a trustee who held the property, not in ownership, but in trust for the interest of designated beneficiaries. A reporting of accounts

.

[3] "Old and New in Management and Accounting," *Accounting Review*, April, 1954.

would of course be necessary—a reporting of responsibilities received and discharged.

It is worth noting that this background of the theory of the nature of company directorship has significant overtones beyond simple steward-ship duties. The trustee for the heirs of a landed estate was frequently and quite early faced with an added duty of properly distinguishing between estate corpus and estate income. For the one was the concern of a re-mainderman; for the other was the concern of a life tenant; and the trustee's stewardship extended to both interested parties. He was there-fore often presented with the same basic problem as that involved in early traders' accounts in Italy: that of separately and appropriately classifying the effect of enterprise transactions on economic capital and on operation earnings. In traders' accounts this kind of necessity was responsible for making a clear distinction between real and nominal accounts; in trustees' accounts, the distinction was between the accounts of estate corpus and the accounts of income.

Ownership accounting and stewardship accounting, therefore, are more alike than might have been supposed. Nevertheless, the British contribu-tion to the development of accountancy is undiminished; perhaps it is even enhanced. For their accomplishment in adapting ownership ac-counting methodology to serve the public interest was highly rational beyond the minimum needed to secure reportable data about company directors' stewardship. It is not inconceivable, for example, that use of a charge and discharge type of recording could have provided data for use in reporting on directors' stewardship. The added factor of company in-debtedness could also have been usefully dealt with by charge and dis-charge methods.

Although this methodology was not used, the basic theory of such reporting persisted. The methodology required by statute was Italian double entry; but the theory of the balance sheet report was that this statement was to tell of directors' stewardship. It is clear, moreover, that the form of the balance sheet report was not to be a simple copy of the real accounts as they stood in a double-entry ledger. The required steward-ship report presented liabilities and shares on the left side of the sheet, with assets on the right.

This arrangement is not what one would expect to emerge from a use of Italian bookkeeping. Yet the presentation is not illogical when the circumstances of its probable origin are brought into view. The essential fact of the matter undoubtedly is that the men, who more than a century ago were innovating an instrumentality for protecting investors, would be more concerned about a form of report which on its face would speak of stewardship than a form of statement which was mechanically, left and right, in harmony with the ledger accounts resulting from Italian double entry.

It is not difficult to believe that in a report on stewardship the items of first interest to the usual reader would be those for the responsibility received by the reporting party. For reader benefit, placement of those items would logically be at the left top of the document. The items of next interest would be those indicating the way responsibility had been discharged. Placement of these at the right top would be logical. In that way the two classes of items would be graphically shown to be closely related and opposite in nature.

It would not be unreasonable to consider that the first responsibility given to directors would be represented by the amount of authorized shares put in their hands to be exchanged for investors' funds; and that the first discharge of responsibility received would be represented by the funds converted into assets appropriate to the company's operating objectives. The top section of the stewardship report would then logically present on the left the authorized share capital (and indebtedness, if any) and on the right, the permanent assets currently possessed by reason of the investors' permanent contribution to a going concern. Proceeds from shares in excess of the amount converted into fixed assets would be indicated by an item brought down into the lower section of the statement. New short-term debt and profits available for dividends would ultimately follow on the left. On the lower right would be reported the disposition of these funds among the several working assets.

This left and right arrangement would use placement of account data to suggest receipt and discharge of stewardship responsibilities. The division of the report into a top and bottom section would use statement form to indicate an important major classification of company assets as between permanent and working assets. Perhaps this second aspect of report arrangement may have reflected contemporary economic ideology, for economists of that era made a point of sharply distinguishing permanent and circulating capital. It was inherent in this distinction (1) that only actively circulating capital could by use generate profits, (2) that replacements related to permanent economic assets would be a charge against revenue, and (3) that reacquisition of replacements for circulating assets would be made from the proceeds in hand received from customers.

The economic logic of this distinction in types of capital was supported within the next generation by legalistic logic in some court decisions to the general effect that unrealized price fluctuation for assets possessed should not become a factor in determining company profits available for dividends. This economics-founded, law-supported concept in more recent years acquired the name "realization principle." [4]

.

[4] Economics, law, and accounting a century ago seem to have been in a state of harmony as to the calculation of divisible profits. In recent years, however, that harmony of thought has been challenged by a theory that the effect on calculated business net profit of rising price levels should be eliminated by adjusting important accounting elements through application of an index series for average prices. It may be significant

This analysis indicates that the British people have made two notable contributions to accountancy. The first was the adoption of Italian account technology to the purpose of protecting absentee shareholders. The second and related contribution was the introduction of interpretative arrangements into balance sheets which were to be circulated to all shareholders.

By the first contribution, a new function was given to the capacity inherent in Italian methodology for collecting and segregating into account categories the transaction-based data about enterprise capital and income. The second contribution drew upon the basic fact of the close interrelation between the integrated accounts which was so characteristic of Italian accounts, and by data arrangement in the balance sheet, skillfully extended the capacity for interrelated account figures to convey their message to report readers.

It is possible to generalize even further. This development in Britain long ago is an indication of the ability of reasonable men to improve and adapt to new and different conditions a capacity for effective service which had very early been built into the original technology of capital-income accounting. The development described is also greatly to the credit of British common sense. Only such a factor as this could have so effectively interwoven useful ideas out of the nation's historical background with technical features from a foreign recording methodology.

America in turn has received an enriched inheritance. We received, by virtue of British prior usage and technical literature, the basic technology of capital-income accounting; an introduction to interpretative arrangement of financial statement data; the idea of publicity for company financial affairs as a matter of social policy; a foundation for an American profession of independent, qualified auditors.

It has, of course, been necessary to adapt this inheritance to American conditions. Some parts of this may be briefly noted here.

From the 1880's to the present, various regulatory commissions have been devised to serve the public interest. Examples are the Interstate Commerce Commission and the Federal Power Commission. For the most part such instruments of public policy have been conceived and used to preserve an equitable balance between the interest of investors and the interest of the consumers of the specific services. Since the basic data upon which many regulatory decisions are rested are account-derived, suitable accounts and standardized reports have been prescribed.

In commerce and manufacturing, the accounts and financial state-

that this doctrine comes upon the scene in an era of sharply rising price levels accompanied by currency devaluations, and that the theory, if it is not to be purely expedient, still has to face a test of usefulness under a period of falling price levels. The earlier economic-legal-accounting doctrine was possessed of some built-in logic from the fact that both unrealized profits and unrealized losses were ruled out of the concept of divisible profits.

ments have traditionally been unregulated. Yet voluntary publicity for corporation annual reports came to be widespread, and voluntary audits came to be commonplace. These developments are the results of reactions to specific American conditions; yet they reflect the same basic recognition of the existence of public interest as that which characterized the antecedent developments in Great Britain.

Regulatory commissions first appeared in response to excessive and unethical competition among early railroad companies. The same social device was later used to bring the operations and mergers of power companies under scrutiny. Wide distribution of corporation annual reports grew out of a gradual recognition by management that expanded industrialization could be secured by attracting savings of a great many people into investment in corporation securities. Whether distribution of company reports is by statutory requirement or is voluntary, the underlying concept is the same—a public reporting on the use company management makes of investor funds.

Professional audits in the United States first became customary and took on special functions because, out of a variety of American circumstances, the current financing of merchants came to be a matter of borrowing from local banks, on single-name promissory notes, the funds needed to pay merchandise invoices promptly, thus to benefit from an offered "discount for cash." The auditing profession's early growth was much strengthened by the need bankers felt for an independent scrutiny of their borrower's current financial position. The question then at issue was not so much the trustworthiness of a report on stewardship as in the dependability of the figures reflecting the relationship between the current assets, as the source for repayment of loans, and the current liabilities, as an important indication of future demands against later current assets.

The creation of the Securities and Exchange Commission (early 1930's) extended to industrial corporations the use of account scrutiny by a regulatory body and publicity for company financial affairs. This extension of the doctrine of financial publicity in the public interest appeared because an era of security speculation in the 1920's had been charged with responsibility for the collapse of prices in 1929-32. Both the origins and the outcome here are obviously similar to the collapse of a speculative house of cards in eighteenth century Britain and to the subsequent prohibitory legislation thought to be in the public interest at the time. The SEC legislation made necessary an extensive use of accounting data as a basis (1) for regulatory decisions regarding financial reporting, (2) for auditor independence, and (3) for adequacy of corporate publicity accomplished through full disclosure of pertinent information in the financial statements issued in support of sales of securities to the general public.

More recently a new line of development has appeared for use of accounting in the public interest. Many divisions of the federal government have been adapting business accounting ideas and methods in order to improve efficiency and economy in their operations. Here the public at interest is the whole body of taxpayers. In connection with voluntary audits for credit purposes, the public directly at interest was represented by the lender; the public indirectly at interest consisted of consumers who stood to benefit from economically and safely financed business enterprises.

These developments, all of which use accounting in the public interest, also have in their over-all impact certain indirect results which are socially significant. They have helped to foster high standards of business morality; they have encouraged investment in the country's productivity from all sections of the general public; they have helped build dependable, factual bases for decisions in a wide and fluid money market.

The people of the United States have reason to be proud to have received an inheritance with the potential for such developments, and to be pleased that they could see ways for satisfactorily adapting those potentialities to the exigencies of local conditions. Americans as a rule seem not much inclined to reach toward adjustments and progress through the help of historical perspective. Nevertheless, the results which emerge often indicate definite historical continuity. We may well believe that Henri Bergson, in *The Creative Mind,* stated a significant truth when he wrote ". . . it is the flux, the continuity of transition, it is change itself that is real"; and again when he refers to ". . . an evolution whose continuous phases penetrate one another by a kind of internal growth. . . ."

The extensive expansion over the centuries in the uses of accountancy could not have been visualized by the people who evolved from trial and error the technology of capital-income accounting. Nor could the men who participated in the British accounting innovations of the nineteenth century realize the future significance to society at large of their ideas and actions. Yet it must be clear that the past, if we but realize the fact, is full of situations, ideas, and actions which can stimulate rational and useful reactions to contemporary problems, thus to extend "the continuity of transition."

But rational continuity is unlikely to emerge on the spur of the moment out of pure inspiration. A most fruitful source of useful ideas for moments of transition can be a prior absorption, perhaps not consciously recalled at the time, of some of the lessons from history: lessons on perceiving a difficulty, on assembling an assortment of possibly useful ideas towards a solution; on selecting, rejecting, modifying, until a rational, even though incomplete, solution evolves.

(unpublished manuscript, 1959)

4. The Search for Accounting Principles

The phrase "accounting principles" has often been used in the title of textbooks. Yet the authors seldom have attempted to select and compactly phrase items which might then deserve that designation. Perhaps a text on procedures is not the proper place for such a presentation. Nevertheless, the search has been underway. If we think back over a period of twenty-five years (1958 to 1933) it will be noted that a good deal of consideration has been given to the problem of verbal formulation of accounting principles. It should be of interest therefore briefly to note the present status of this aspect of accounting theory in evolution.

Dictionary definitions usually tend to emphasize the distinctions between several uses of the word "principle." For present purposes however it may be more useful to try to indicate the essence of the word in its accounting context. We may choose to consider accounting principles simply as important accounting ideas that have been more or less compactly verbalized for convenient use. The usefulness of such material would be twofold: (1) to serve as guideposts for extension of accounting knowledge and deepening understanding of this area, and (2) to serve as springboards for thinking toward appropriate accounting actions.

At the present time much of the material on accounting principles, exclusive of a considerable output of articles in the periodicals, is available in rather compact form in a few sources.

The American Institute of Certified Public Accountants has issued Accounting Research Bulletin (ARB) No. 43 which rearranges the research work of relevant Institute committees (1933-53) into a compact restatement of the considered views of the committees on a variety of topics. Five Bulletins (numbered through 48) were subsequently issued. Other Institute research committees in this period also have produced significant materials not directly concerned with accounting principles as such. Mention should be made especially of the work on audit standards and technical auditing procedures and programming.

The American Accounting Association's recent pamphlet presents the latest report (1957) of the committee on accounting concepts and standards and compactly restates the essence of certain of the views of several preceding committees. Also included are reprints of earlier reports: 1936, 1941, 1948, and eight supplementary statements amplifying the 1948 report. The complete title of this pamphlet is "Accounting and Reporting Standards For Corporate Financial Statements and Preceding Statements and Supplements." Association Monograph No. 3 ("An Introduction to Corporate Accounting Standards" by W. A. Paton and A. C. Littleton; 1940). It is essentially an elaboration, by the authors, of the ideology compactly embodied in the 1936 committee's "Tentative Statement of Accounting Principles." Before each chapter, brief "headlines" highlight many of the points made therein. In Association Monograph No. 5

("Structure of Accounting Theory" by A. C. Littleton; 1953), the author undertakes, in chapters 9, 10 and 11, to formulate a number of principles, each of which associates some aim or objective of accounting with a well-known means of attaining the indicated objective.

It is clear therefore that both organizations have been interested in accounting principles, although from different points of view. The publications of the professional accountants (The AICPA) present the considered judgments of experienced practitioners regarding preferred practices in connection with situations met in professional experience. The publications of the accounting teachers (The AAA) present the attempts by committees and the monograph authors, guided primarily by consideration of the accumulated literature, compactly to express the ideological essence beneath the whole of accountancy.

This section of the literature indicates some of the reactions of thoughtful men to their times. In order to point up the fact that ideas usually have a definite relativity to contemporary circumstances, brief consideration should be given first to some aspects of relevant background.

Most of the 1920's was marked by an upward spiral of activities and prices which culminated in a strong speculative movement, especially in the stock market. In October, 1929 came the collapse; the depressed decade of the 1930's followed. In the postwar decade following 1946, a persistent inflation of prices raised anew the specter of a possible duplication of the late 1920's. Along with this development appeared a division of opinion as to whether existing aspects of a managed economy were responsible, or whether economic planning by the central government was the way to prevent another boom and collapse. The conditions so briefly suggested here represent two screens, standing nearly a generation apart, against which to project some of the reactions which stimulated research in the formulation of accounting principles.

Slowly during the earlier period, dissatisfaction grew in the minds of many informed people regarding the appraisal of fixed assets and the related treatment of surplus in those booming years. Certain deficiencies in the dividend base as stated in some corporation statutes were a matter of contemporary concern, particularly where issues of no-par stock were permitted and where the asset appreciation credit had not been clearly excluded from surplus available for cash dividends.[5]

A few accounting articles and committee reports in 1930, 1931, and 1932 already reflected a growing concern. Soon thereafter the impact of recent observation and experience began to produce more specific actions. Two of these are particularly relevant here—the securities and exchange

---

[5] Writing of the evolutionary development of audit certificates, George Cochrane makes this point regarding reactions to the stock market crash of 1929: "Demands arose from the public, professional and layman alike, that methods be formulated which would avoid the repetition of the misleading financial reporting practices of the past years." (*The New York Certified Public Accountant*, May, 1951, p. 321, reprint—from *The Accountant* of Nov. 4, 1950.)

legislation and the publication at about the same time of correspondence between a committee of the American Institute of Accountants and officers of the New York Stock Exchange.

A significant feature of this new legislation was the optional authority granted the new commission to issue regulations affecting corporation accounts and financial statements. Two significant features of the published correspondence were (1) new wording for audit certificates (including use of the phrase "generally accepted principles of accounting"), and (2) formulation of five rules (reprinted on pages 11 and 12 of ARB No. 43) designed to narrow permissible charges and credits to surplus, thus collaterally pointing up the major significance of the income statement.

Two of these rules strongly reflect the influence of some of the background conditions mentioned above. "Unrealized profit should not be credited to income account . . . [even by indirect means]." "Capital surplus, however created, should not be used to relieve the income account . . . of charges which would otherwise fail to be made thereagainst." If the practices here frowned upon were freely open to use, company management could slyly influence upward the company's reported net income and/or the figure for surplus apparently available for dividends. The stand taken by the profession of public accounting and the New York Stock Exchange on these points is clear indication of recognition that the public interest was involved in financial reporting.

In retrospect it is evident that these events and these actions laid down a groundwork for the subsequent development of a literature dealing with accounting principles. The pages which follow here will present, as far as space permits, some indications of the nature of the principles which have been suggested and something of the similarities and differences in the points of view expressed in the literature referred to above.

The ideas expressed in the first two rules stated by the Institute in 1933 are also reflected in the Association's 1936 statement, under item 17—"Neither paid-in surplus nor surplus reserves should be availed of for the absorption of losses. . . ." In neighboring paragraphs the content of the paid-in surplus and earned surplus accounts is described. In Monograph 3 (1940) on page 112, is this statement—"There is serious objection . . . to the practice of absorbing sweeping and arbitrary writedowns to property accounts through capital account, directly or indirectly, particularly if the principal purpose is the reduction of operating charges and the making of a more favorable income showing in subsequent periods." On page 114, the following—". . . no losses can be so absorbed [into capital accounts] in the presence of earned surplus."

The literature on principles from the Institute and from the Association each include several items not presented by the other group. The 1957 revision by the Association committee includes a section entitled "Underlying Concepts" and subsections explain "business entity," "enterprise continuity," "money measurement," and "realization." These items are presented as basic ideas lying beneath the conventions, derived from practical experience, which give form and substance to enterprise financial statements. Monograph 3, chapter 2, also presents most of these concepts and includes in addition, "costs attach," "effort and accomplishment," "verifiable, objective evidence." [6]

In Monograph 5 (1953) chapter 11, ten of the twenty-three items there formulated into accounting principles were included under the conviction that the principles of double-entry bookkeeping form a part of the principles of accounting. These ten items are related "to such matters as truthful distinctions between categories, truthful translation of enterprise events into account data, truthful classification of account data into suitable account-categories" (p. 194).

It is perhaps significant of the necessary and useful differences in the points of view of practitioners and teachers that the literature from the latter, but not of the former, includes sections which try to verbalize underlying concepts and to relate the technical features of bookkeeping to the structure (accounting) which has been erected on that foundation. The reverse is also natural; some sections of ARB No. 43 deal with matters not found in the Association statements: government contracts and foreign exchange are examples; items given a more extensive treatment include taxes, pensions, stock options, lease disclosure, etc.

The relative amount of space given to specific topics is not an indication of relative importance. Yet this would perhaps indicate the areas of greatest contemporary interest or items of considerable complexity. In the Accounting Research Bulletins, greatest interest centers in financial statements and depreciation; together they count for an estimated 51 per cent of the space; depreciation, 10 per cent; capital accounts, 18; balance sheet, 23 (current assets, particularly inventory, constitute approximately one-half of this last item). As a convenient though incomplete test of topic space, the more detailed presentation made in the Association's eight statements supplementing the 1948 revision shows the following distribution: Impact of price-level change, 43 per cent, about equally divided between inventory and financial statements in general; another 11 per cent is divided between disclosures, consolidated statements and retained income. Together, these subdivisions account for approximately 54 per cent of the space.

It is clear that the results from the research deliberations of committees of the respective organizations admirably supplement each other. This is a desirable development. And it is already evident that publications such as these make for better-informed professional accountants and better-prepared accounting graduates from the schools of business.
•

---

[6] In that chapter's conclusion is this thought: "The fundamental concepts or propositions of accounting . . . are in themselves assumptions in considerable measure. . . ." The present writer is beginning to wonder whether most, if not all, of the accounting ideas usually labeled "assumptions" would be more closely described as "the better choices among alternatives."

The remaining pages of this article will be devoted to a consideration
of the ideology presented in these reports relative to the impact of price-
level change because this complex subject epitomizes the difficulties inherent in the search for accounting principles. The influence of contemporary conditions[7] upon the formulation of accounting principles is
clearly evident throughout this literature. And naturally so, for men cannot escape the impact of their surroundings; and their reactions not infrequently indicate a desire, perhaps a determination, that the future
should be different. We need therefore to look beneath the wording of
"principles."

As previously suggested, the five rules formulated in 1933 by an Institute committee clearly reflect reaction to certain earlier financial practices which subsequent events showed were in need of abatement. Reactions thus stimulated, continued. In 1940 (ARB No. 43, Chapter 9, Sec.
A), depreciation on appreciation was considered with the result that a
certain course of action was recommended as expressing a generally accepted accounting principle: When appreciation has been entered on the
books "income should be charged with depreciation computed on the
written-up amounts." Three members of the committee, while assenting
generally, believed the opinion should also indicate "that increase in
property valuation should become a permanent credit item, not available
for subsequent transfer to earned surplus as realized through depreciation
or sale."

Associated with these pronouncements in significance and in originating impulse was the Institute's work in defining earned surplus. These
activities appeared at a time when state legislatures, which had also become aware of undesirable financial practices of the era, were amending
the corporation statutes in order to clarify the statement regarding the
cash dividend base, especially as to excluding appraisal surplus.

Apparently, physical science is not the only area in which action can
produce reaction. The above is a case in point. And it is not unreasonable
to consider the Association's brief "tentative statement" of 1936 also as a
research reaction to prior conditions and practices. Perhaps the same
could be said for Monograph 3 (1940), although both items undoubtedly
were in considerable measure inspired by the decision in the Institute to
associate certification with generally accepted principles.[8]

[7] In referring to the changes which have taken place over the past twenty-five years in
American auditing, George Cochrane wrote (in the article referred to above): "The
changes . . . have been designated largely by concrete economic circumstances, intermixed with important ethical conditions flowing out of changing ideas about managerial responsibilities to the public."

[8] The same article by George Cochrane (p. 320) outlines the events leading up to the new
form of certificate. The primary importance of the income statement was indicated in
the Institute's bulletin of 1929 on audit procedure. In September, 1932, an Institute
letter to the Committee on Stock List of the New York Stock Exchange repeated that
view of the income statement and urged the desirability of broad recognition by corporations "of certain broad and generally accepted principles of accounting . . ." (p.
322).

The Association's pamphlet of 1957 reflects the first committee's reaction as of 1936 (p. 61). "If values other than unamortized costs are to be quoted, they should be expressed in financial statements only as collateral notations for informative purposes." "Present procedure is unsatisfactory in that it permits periodic revaluation of assets, up or down, in accordance with current price levels and expected business developments."

In the reprint of the 1941 revision, the developing ideology appears again: "Values other than costs applicable to future periods should be treated in balance sheets as supplementary data . . ." (p. 54). "Appreciation or enhancement resulting from changing market prices of existing units of property does not represent realized revenue" (p. 55).

These ideas came largely as reactions to asset write-up and write-down which were so often observed in the 1920's and 1930's. A more recent era has also witnessed reaction to contemporary conditions. That era includes the significant fact of a postwar inflation. One reaction to inflation brought assertions of unreality in accounting computations of enterprise net income. The consequent reaction of accountants is related to an idea inherent in this criticism, namely, that the asserted unreality could be avoided if depreciation expense were adjusted to represent the current purchasing power of the dollar. The series of statements by Association committees from 1936 to 1957 gives some insight into the evolution of antecedent ideas over a period of time.

In the 1936 and 1941 reports these comments appear: "A history of cost and cost amortization [being a consistent record of actual occurrences measured according to an intelligible formula] constitutes an essential starting point in financial interpretation" (pp. 62, 54). "An extreme [marked] change in the value of money might vitiate [impair] the usefulness of cost records . . ." but price-level changes in the last half century "have afforded insufficient reasons for [repeated] adjustment of asset values" (pp. 61, 54); parenthetical wording represents changes in the 1941 statement.

In the 1948 report, these expressions of accounting ideology were further clarified by expanding the phraseology. "There should be no departure from the cost basis to reflect the assets of an enterprise at amounts higher than unassigned costs." There still is need for "a historical record in terms of the consistent, objective basis of cost." In a footnote (p. 14) repeating earlier phrases about marked changes in the value of money, the term "recent years" is substituted for "the last half century." Added is this sentence: "Accounting concepts and standards appropriate for the reflection of a drastic and permanent change in prices would need to be developed in the event of such a change."

Between the 1948 statement and the 1957 statement, a decade of expanded research study produced eight "supplementary statements," two of which are related to the theme of price-level change. The essence of these has been extracted by the latest committee and included in the more compact statement of 1957. A few relevant extracts will reflect the present state of this section of accounting principles.

From the 1957 report: "Nor can it be assumed that price is necessarily a final and thoroughly objective measure of value. . . . Despite these limitations, price is at least indicative of value at time of exchange, and as such is a great aid in the quantification of business data for accounting purposes" (p. 3). "Adjusting for price level change, for instance, can be made meaningful only when the underlying asset amount is objectively stated" (p. 5). As to interperiod and intercompany comparability: ". . . the principle barriers . . . are distortions resulting from price fluctuations and variations in accounting methods." "Uniformity of accounting method is neither expected nor necessarily desirable, but reasonable comparability of reported data is essential." ". . . supplementary data would be helpful in evaluating the significance of price fluctuations in the interpretation of financial reports of the particular enterprise" (p. 9).

A few items must suffice to sample the ideology reflected in the supplementary statements, using for that purpose Supplementary Statement No. 2 (1951) dealing with price-level changes and financial statements.

"No specific objective method of measurement and adjustment applicable to all situations has been devised and widely accepted . . ." (p. 24) for estimating and disclosing the effect of price-level change upon a given business enterprise. "In periodic reports to stockholders, the primary financial statements, prepared by management and verified by an independent accountant, should, at the present state of accounting development, continue to reflect historical dollar costs" (p. 24). A final item from Supplementary Statement No. 8 (1954) dealing with disclosure: There is need for ". . . a reemphasis of the complexity of price-level effects and the difficulty encountered by highly skilled analysts in coping effectively with them unless granted full access to the underlying corporate records. Analysis of these pervasive effects must, for all practical purposes, be accomplished within the reporting company" (p. 50).

Research committees sponsored by the American Institute of CPA's also have studied the impact on accounting of rising price levels. A large committee (composed of accountants, businessmen, economists, accounting teachers) was organized in 1948 and spent several years considering some of the problems which economic conditions were creating. The results of their deliberations were published in 1952 in the book, *Changing Concepts of Business Income.*

The Committee on Accounting Procedure in 1947 issued ARB No. 33, "Depreciation and High Costs." Succeeding committees reaffirmed the prior opinion in 1948 (ARB No. 43, p. 69) and in 1953 (ARB No. 43, p. 67) expressed "approval of the basic conclusions," and placed the subject "on its agenda for further study." In support of ARB No. 33, the essence of the majority view in committee was that responsibility devolves upon company management rather than on the professional accountant in the matter of reporting on the impact of price-level change. Management should meet the immediate problem (1) by taking into consideration, when formulating operating and financial policy, the probability of higher replacement cost of plant, (2) by preparing to meet higher replacement cost through annual appropriations out of net profit or surplus, and (3) by use of supplementary financial schedules, explanations and footnotes to explain the need for retaining funds out of earnings to help cover higher replacement costs.

By their contrasting views, six dissenting committee members pose the issue which lies within this particular problem. They believe (1) that accepted accounting practices should comprehend "financial statements . . . designed to reflect those concepts of cost and net income . . ." which are implied in the above recommendations to management, and (2) that in addition to historical depreciation "a supplementary annual charge to income should be permitted, with corresponding credit to an account for property replacement and substitutions. . . ." (ARB No. 43, pp. 70, 71.)

A few items from the larger committee's report will serve to epitomize the views of the majority of its members.

For measuring costs to be deducted from revenues "the choice of units of measurement seems to lie between monetary units of changing purchasing power and units of equal purchasing power. . . ." (*Changing Concepts of Business Income*, p. 104.) "It is believed that statements of business income in which revenue and charges against revenue would be stated in units of substantially the same purchasing power would be significant and useful for many purposes. . . . For the present, it may well be that the primary statement of income should continue to be made on bases now commonly accepted." But the larger corporations "should be encouraged to furnish information that will facilitate the determination of income measured in units of approximately equal purchasing power . . ." (p. 105).

The report also includes some ideas expressing dissent or comment. The relevant essence is suggested by the following notes.

Footnotes about price-level change might be erroneously considered by some financial statement readers as within the scope of the auditor's formal opinion (p. 110). Some sections of the committee's conclusions imply that financial statements as now prepared are improper (p. 111). The report "does not give enough recognition to the substantial arguments . . . in which adherence to historical cost is favored and index adjustments opposed" (p. 117). The measurement of money income is a "useful and necessary task"; it is important to indicate "the difference between historical cost and current revenue, irrespective of changes in price levels" (p. 121).

It is unwarranted to believe that "financial statements based on historical cost . . . are inappropriate for and of limited value to investors" (p. 122). "Books must be kept in the established monetary unit. Any attempt to adjust the books to conform to the value of the monetary unit . . . will not be beneficial either to our business institutions or to our national economy" (p. 125). "The accounting process is a poor and helplessly inadequate tool to deal effectively with the economic evils of inflation and deflation. In fact, the application of this tool in the manner suggested in certain parts of the report would be harmful rather than helpful" (p. 127). "An important result will have been achieved if the report leads to more general acceptance of the view that business income has two components which are separable and possess different significances . . ." (p. 139).

The items herein selected to epitomize the search for accounting principles can reflect only a small part of the research studies of these two accounting organizations. Yet it may be that enough material has been presented to demonstrate the relativity of ideas to contemporary circumstances.

In the 1920's and the 1930's, economic boom and economic depression produced widespread repercussions; accountants, among others, were brought to consider anew some of their prior views. In the decade just past, during the years of postwar "creeping inflation," the impact of conditions has again stimulated thought about accounting ideas and methods. The sequel to that decade is still hidden; and the present and near future are still of deep concern to all segments of the nation. Accountants could not ignore the situation presented to view. But representing only a small segment as they do, accountants could contribute, at best, but little power toward modifying the forces producing the clearly evident results. Yet their discussions and publications may have served in some measure to help alert the people of the nation to continuing conditions. At the very least, accountants have probably learned a good deal recently about modern economic ideas; and, no doubt, economists were in a position to learn something about the limitations under which accountants render service to society. Perhaps the greatest good lies right there; increased mutual understanding, like the usual business transaction, is advantageous to both parties.

Beneath issues posed in this recent literature lie some fundamental differences in concepts and in basic methodology. Clearly it would be most difficult indeed to justify a basic modification of account technology (which uses invested costs of transactions that are directly relevant to a given business enterprise) in favor of adopting into account-keeping certain aspects of statistical technology (which makes use of averages, trends, price-index series) that are so definitely suited to economists' use as to be indisputable in economic analysis.

Moreover, two different types of communication are involved. Reports reflecting invested costs standing under management's responsibility, and at the same time reflecting results of management's decisions, cannot be abandoned or strongly modified without risking greater confusion than now prevails. Economic analysis is so often prompted by a desire to search deeply for evidence of causation beneath observed changes in economic data, and the search is so complex that every technique is acceptable which will help to separate mixed causes. Index series of price averages, where applied to raw statistical data about the nation's economic activities, modify those data into residuals which can be considered as quantitative expressions of physical movement of goods and services that could not be measured directly. This has obvious interpretative usefulness.

A fundamental difference between economics and accountancy becomes visible at this point, and it seems to account for the essence of the indicated results of accounting research discussions in the area here considered.

Accountants are convinced that their technology should hold fast to directly measurable, objectively determined, clearly reviewable data which are inescapably associated with the enterprise concerned. Whatever conclusions they may formulate into principles will be found tied into this conviction.

Many significant aspects of business do not come within the indicated range of accounting technology and should be examined by other techniques than those of accountancy. Exploring only one avenue of analysis is not likely to lead to the best decisions. A management problem examined by differing techniques will very likely come to be seen as presenting a choice among alternatives. Neither one technology nor several can offer help beyond this point on the road to managerial decisions.

If the attempt should be made to extract from this part of recent accounting literature a single principle dealing with the central issue, it probably should in some way make the point that these new interpretative data would be adequately communicated by means of schedules supplementary to the usual financial statements.

Disclosure of the impact on an enterprise of sustained price-level change is, in this day, a moral obligation. And accounting principles are not unrelated to moral considerations. When accounting had only the function of serving private interests, formulation of "principles" was not necessary; good technique was enough to make accounting objective and accurate for management's use. And a simple decision by a proprietor or a change of partners could directly lead to a restatement of financial position.

A century ago in England, the early series of companies acts gave clear evidence that accountancy could also serve the public interest. And during the last twenty-five years in the United States, the doctrine of full disclosure in financial statements has arisen because the public interest is deeply involved in corporation affairs. Supplementary schedules re-flecting financial statement data as adjusted by application of some price-index series can be an effective instrument in support of full disclosure, and thus can adequately serve the public interest within the framework of accountancy's limitations.

(*New York Certified Public Accountant*, April, 1958)

PART TWO *On Accounting Theory*

BASIC IDEOLOGY

1. Money of Account

When the French discovered the present named Gulf of St. Lawrence and the long river beyond, they found the neighboring Indians well supplied with a variety of rich furs, and the natives saw that the white men were equipped with such desirable things as knives and iron pots. Since each party coveted some of the possessions of the other, trade was inevitable, even without a common language or the aid of money. If the European was astonished at the number of beaver skins offered as the price of a knife, the savage was equally astonished that the white man should be willing to accept skins at all—beaver were everywhere; they were free to the one who took them. But sharp knives and strong hatchets, these were nowhere to be had.

Naive as the Indian's "valuations" may have been, his practice of trading something given for something received was as natural as were unsatisfied wants. He gives what he wants but little, in order to receive what he wants very much. If one has no unsatisfied wants or if he possesses nothing that someone else wants, there is no basis for an exchange. But if an exchange is effected, each party is satisfied with the results even though the trade seems to an onlooker as uneven as a cheap knife for five beaver skins. The reason for this, even though it may not be clearly perceived by the parties, is that each has gained in total utility as seen from his own point of view. Both, we would say, have "profited."

Here then, in primitive barter, is the basic concept of profit: *Profit is an individual's opinion of the increase of total utility, usefulness, or value-in-use that is his as the result of an exchange.*

From this it will be noted that a concept of profit does not need to be associated with money, accounts, or formal calculations of any kind. Expected profit from consumption is simply a judgment of relative usefulness read into the goods received in barter; and accomplished profit, the test of the prior judgment, is the excess of consumptive satisfactions flowing out of the use of the thing received. If appearances of probable usefulness were deceptive or if one party's judgment were faulty, the exchange may of course yield a "deficiency" of satisfactions, a sort of negative "profit."

In barter for re-trade, expected profit is a judgment regarding relative subsequent exchangeability of the new thing possessed in comparison with other, as yet, unpossessed desirable things. The test of this prejudgment comes when the anticipated re-exchange is accomplished. If, subsequent to the first barter-exchange, no third person finds a prospective

utility in the goods held for re-exchange, there is no second exchange
and no accomplished profit for the trader; also if after a second barter-
exchange, the goods then newly received should prove not to have the
expected utility, there can be no accomplished profit.

In this analysis of barter certain characteristics of profit appear without the intervention of money or accounts. The first of these is that profit
is a highly intangible, inconclusive element, depending for a trader upon
an almost unending chain of events for its validity. Profit is not a thing
in itself, nor is it a specific condition among things; it is an intellectual
concept only and varies from person to person and from time to time.

Because profit is thus an extremely illusive element, two conclusions
follow:

(1) Reality of profit should not be read into a situation too soon or
upon inadequate evidence. This is the basis of the so-called "realization
principle." When an objective test has verified a personal hope, conviction of reality may safely follow, but not before. Anticipated profits are
mere opinions and therefore subject to individual bias and mistaken
judgment. Realized profits on the other hand have met an objective test,
under conditions by which the utility of the goods has been further
attested by the independent judgment of a subsequent receiver in an
exchange. But even such "realization" may prove to be an incomplete
test of reality because today's gains may be consumed by tomorrow's
losses if the goods prove useless.

(2) Valuation is a part of the process of exercising sound judgment in
consuming or trading, and it forms the basis for all production and
merchandising operations. The ability to make sound judgments regarding consumption wants and uses, or of trade opportunities, often exists
independent of records as such.

Barter transactions carried with them a concept of profit. And presently a need appeared to attempt a calculation that might give quantitative measurement to an accomplished profit. Traders wished such a
computation so it could serve as a check today against an earlier judgment that the earlier purchase had profit potentialities. To get such a
test it was necessary to find a way to express a great diversity of transactions in terms of a common denominator which would make all of
them suitable for use in arithmetical additions, subtractions, and comparisons.

This important progressive step was taken in the Middle Ages when
merchants began to combine (1) a standard money of account by which
differing commodities, etc. could be translated into a single, local system
of monetary price, and (2) a scheme of systematic records by means of
which completed and incomplete exchange transactions could be con-
veniently arranged for reference and quantitative summary.

Since the money price involved in a bargaining transaction reflects the
individual's mental judgment of prospective value-in-use and current

value-in-exchange, money price can be used to replace the mental concept of use value with a quantitative measurement of exchange value. Since double-entry bookkeeping is a record methodology particularly designed to make effective use of money price, it is clear that bookkeeping is primarily an instrument for producing a quantitative measurement of profit (income statement) and that a statement of wealth in possession and debts (balance sheet) is in essence a secondary intention.

As modified by this development, the above formulated concept of profit may be restated this way: *Quantitatively expressed profit is the excess of money prices received in bargaining exchanges over money prices previously given.*

The assumptions underlying this idea are that bargained prices can and do reflect the individual's judgment of relative utilities and that a comparison of judgments thus rendered quantitative will be more serviceable than mere mental images of the advantages of a series of exchanges. If the attempt to express profit in quantitative terms does not come near enough to the full truth to constitute a useful substitute for mental images, then bookkeeping could have no function but to record uncompleted transactions (debts) as a memory aid.

Out of this development of the concept of profit come several conclusions:

(1) A uniform money of account (not to be confused with money said to have a "stable" value) can be used to render diverse elements quantitative and homogeneous so that comparison and summation become possible.

(2) Bookkeeping is an instrument of "quantification." In order to render profit estimates quantitative, bookkeeping systematically records the bargained prices, in terms of a standard money of account, of things given and things received.

(3) The use of these two processes does not change the illusive nature of profit or make its inconclusive characteristics more definite. Caution in accepting profit figures is still as necessary with money of account as it was in judging the utilities involved in direct barter-exchange.

(Accounting Review, March, 1936)

2. Income Accounting

Substantial and significant progress has been made in establishing dependable and verifiable periodic calculations of enterprise net income. It may therefore be appropriate to examine the continuing theme of double-entry bookkeeping for possible further means of refinement.

The central theme of enterprise accounting has always been income determination. Refinements of the original methodology have produced modern accrual accounting. But this term is not properly considered to mean profit accounting, if profit is thought of merely as the difference between two specific prices. Accrual accounting is better described as income accounting for the reason that accounting is a method of computing the net result produced by two price streams rather than a way of comparing pairs of individual prices. One stream is the outflow of services given; the other is the inflow of services received.

It is only as a practical expedient for securing a common denominator that these service streams are expressed in money prices and called "revenue" and "expense" respectively. The essential thought is the comparison, as it were, of two physical streams, one tending to raise the level of a lake and the other to lower the level. Insofar as accounting operates from the capital or balance sheet point of view, it looks at the lake levels at different dates. But business is much more concerned with the income point of view which looks at the waxing and waning influences themselves. It is a case of the dynamic versus the static; accounting must be primarily dynamic because business is dynamic.

Accrual accounting has two important parts. One of them directs us in distinguishing expense from disbursement, and income from receipt; the other directs us in the careful separation of assets and expenses. Both of these elements of accrual accounting are parts of the process of allocating cost outlays to time periods where they will meet income revenues similarly allocated to time periods.

But accruals according to the periods wherein benefit is conferred and realization takes place may not be enough to show the full facts. The emergence of revenue and the incidence of expense are stressed in accounting in order to bring together the elements which belong together. But what is the clue to "belonging?" [1] Is periodic revenue when linked with periodic cost an association of cause and effect that is as close as would be desirable?

The intent of accrual accounting is to associate *related* costs and revenues; allocation to equal fiscal periods is the present accepted method. But occasionally the impression arises that we use time periods for this association merely because more positive means are lacking for linking cost more directly with the revenue it helped to produce.

It therefore seems probable that the principle of distinguishing incomes from receipts could be further refined by rules for better classifying income by sources, for sources provide a clue to causes. One of the principles of accrual theory is that income is considered valid only after it has been tested as to its reality—the rule of realization. Would it not

[1] Alfred Marshall mentions a report on the income tax by a committee of the British Association as early as 1878 wherein deductions from gross income were referred to as "the outgoings that belong to its production." *Principles of Economics*, 8th ed., p. 72. John B. Canning gives point to the problem in this question, "How much of any given dollar of outlay is spent to obtain any particular dollar of receipt?" *Econometrica*, January, 1833, p. 57.

be a desirable refinement to distinguish earned income produced and derived profit received?

In order to distinguish these two, we may say that a concern earns income to the extent that it produces revenue which may reasonably be considered to have arisen because of the costs currently incurred in the performance of the enterprise's particular economic function. And we may say it receives derived profit merely by alienation of property, adjustment of debts or capital structure, or other activities unrelated to the direct performance of the enterprise's particular economic function.

Because of the obviously different indications that these two kinds of realized gains give of managerial skill and activity, they should be separately reported in the first instance. Probably only one of them should be lodged in earned surplus so that the balance of that account will reflect only undistributed earned income which was produced as the result of outlays made with the intent of generating earned income. Earned surplus thus treated will not be strictly analogous to the older concept of undivided, realized profits. Rather, in the interest of distinguishing earned income and realized profits, it will be a new extension of the normal accounting impulse to break down every complex into its constituent elements.

It is also probable that the principles which distinguish asset and expense can be further refined by suitable rules for drawing a more careful distinction between expense and loss and between different kinds of losses.

It is no doubt an acceptable generalization to say that cost allocation is the fundamental process of accounting. And it is clearly recognized that original outlay costs may be deferred (as assets), amortized (as expenses), or abandoned (as losses). It is the duty of accounting theory in this connection to lay down the rules and reasons for making these distinctions. By the present treatment of original costs the clue to the status of a given item is its relation to a time period. It would be better if the clue were the relation of a particular cost cause to its corresponding revenue source. Thus original outlay costs should become deferred costs only when they may reasonably be considered as being causally related to future revenue sources; they should become amortized costs only when they may reasonably be considered as being causally related to current revenue sources; and they should become abandoned costs only when they may reasonably be considered as unlikely ever to be causally related to the production of any revenue. If reasonable causal connections are established between revenue sources and cost causes, the allocation of costs and revenues to equal time periods becomes incidental rather than the controlling feature of the calculation of net income.

But it is an open question whether even this basis for associating revenue and its cost would alone serve to carry the refinement of accrual theory far enough to distinguish also between different kinds of losses. Therefore certain other sharp distinctions must be added.

An abandoned item of equipment represents one type of loss; another and quite distinct type of loss is a deficiency of current revenue to cover the cost which must be currently charged against that revenue. The latter loss is definitely related to the performance of the enterprise's particular economic function and is significant of the unacceptability in the market of the economic service offered, or of a failure to keep the supply cost below the demand price which the market affords. On the other hand, costs abandoned or disposed of other than in a way to affect the appearance of earned income currently or later, are significant of a managerial change of capital policy—a decision not to try to enter the market with an output derived from that particular outlay.

If these distinctions are made, we would then have something that could be called "earned net loss" (to parallel "earned net income") and something that could be called "derived net loss" (to parallel "derived profit"). A deficiency of reserve, or an earned loss, should logically be entered in earned surplus; an abandoned cost, or derived loss, could probably be best recorded in an account reflecting reserved surplus.

(*Accounting Review*, March, 1937)

3. Accrual Accounting

It is a characteristic of the concept of profit that the clue to the existence of profit is *relative utility*. Any conclusion concerning relative utility necessitates a judgment based upon a comparison of the thing received and the thing given. Perhaps this is the key to the surprising vitality of the very old rule of thumb: Debit what is given; credit what is given. It continues to live, not because it is an adequate guide to transaction analysis, but because we subconsciously recognize that accounts are essentially no more than records of give-out and take-in. Only by receiving one thing for another can we, and they, benefit from specialization in the production of use-values. And it is only by exchanging one service potentiality for another service potentiality that differing ideas of relative utility operate to create a concept of profit and thus generate a need for an instrument to compute profit quantitatively.

The use of a standard money of account and records of price transactions made it possible to deal with heterogeneous elements of business in arithmetical calculations as if they were physically homogeneous. Hence we may say that accounting has helped business to make definite progress in acquiring something like a scientific methodology. While it is clear that bookkeeping has thus made a distinct social contribution, it should not be forgotten that the elements thus rendered homogeneous in the record are still the utilities of things given and things received.

The refinements of the old bookkeeping analysis of receiving and giving (now called accrual accounting) were the next contribution of accounting to scientific business methodology.

The practice of recording all transactions in terms of a standard money of account had the natural result of leading uncritical businessmen to confuse money with cash. They thus came to think of the accounts as showing cash collected (or cash to be collected from debtors) and cash disbursed (or to be disbursed to creditors). By an unconscious drift through a long period of time, the fundamental processes of business thus came to be thought of as collecting and disbursing rather than giving and receiving goods or services.

What accrual accounting did was to correct that mistaken conception. Those who used accrual accounting recognized the fact that bargained purchase price, and not cash disbursed, was the element used to represent the thing received; that bargained sale price, and not cash collected, was the element used to represent the thing given. This much could be deduced from those transactions which involved deferred payments. A further correction was made when it was also perceived that it was utilization of goods or services, and not the act of acquisition, which marked the appearance of expense; and that alienation of goods or the act of rendering a bargained service, rather than the receipt of an object in exchange, marked the appearance of revenue.

Here was a truly scientific separation of the substance from the shadow. All that was received, though coming in, was not income; all income, though taken in, was not in the form of cash collections. Not all disbursements, though going out, were expenses; not all expenses, though they were going out, were represented by cash disbursements.

Thus it gradually became evident, as accrual accounting developed, that the basic elements of business, so long thought of simply as things received and given, were in reality income earned and expense incurred or the potentialities of income and expense. Although accruals are usually explained as year-end adjustments made to produce a more accurate balance sheet, it is nearer the real fact to say that accrued assets are recognized primarily in order to secure a more sharply correct calculation of periodic earned income, and that accrued liabilities are recognized primarily in order to secure a more sharply correct calculation of periodic expense. In a similar manner, deferred charges are used as an indirect calculation of the consumed portion of previously acquired expense factors, and deferred credits are used as an indirect calculation of the earned portion of income already received.

The accounting problems treated under the head of "capital and revenue charges" are but subproblems of accrual accounting's major problem of associating revenue and its relevant costs. In a similar way, cost accounting constitutes a series of subdivisions of the same major objective. Costing is clearly a part of the larger problem of accrual accounting, since both serve as aids for judging the adequacy of services rendered by comparing the price which the service commands with the cost of rendering the service.

The central purpose of accrual accounting is to bring into contrast the inflowing services acquired and used (as measured by expenses and costs) and the corresponding outflowing services rendered (as measured by income and earnings). With this as the concept profit may be phrased somewhat in this manner:

Profit (net income) is the result of providing an output of economic services (thereby causing an in-flow of gross revenue) which services are valued by the purchaser at an amount higher than the in-put of economic factors (brought about by an out-flow of expense) required to produce the services put out.

Out of this concept comes the conclusion that, by becoming a refinement of the analysis of things given and things received, accrual accounting makes it possible to approach closely a direct comparison between services rendered to another and the disservices experienced in preparing to do so. In other words, the utility to the producer (as judged by his cost price outlays) is, by means of accrual accounting, set against the utility to the purchaser (as judged by his buying price outlay). The presence of profit in this comparison of exchange prices indicates to the producer that his economic service has proved acceptable in the market. The presence of a loss in the calculation indicates that he has not been successful in providing an economic service of a kind desired at a price acceptable in the market.

It is difficult to conceive of an instrument for qualitative measurement more useful than this to the formation of good business judgments, and through these good decisions, very beneficial to workers and consumers, that is, to society in general.

(*Accounting Review*, March, 1936)

4. Recognition of Cost and Revenue

The appearance of enterprise revenue marks the accomplishment of the principal objective of the business concern, namely, placing new utilities in the hands of consumers. The tests by which we judge the reality of the profit or loss that may be embedded in revenue are two: (1) economic tests—service has been rendered by a producer, utility has been accepted by a purchaser, a price has been determined by independent bargaining; (2) legal tests—delivery has been completed, title to product has been passed, producer's claim for payment in due course is "property."

A sale as marked by these tests is the climax of the operating cycle; it is "accomplishment." A sale, by the action and judgment of the purchaser, corroborates the producer's opinion that utility has been added, and it thus provides verifiable, objective evidence that a profit (or loss) has now appeared and may be reported as such for the current period.

It is an important accounting standard that recognition of revenue for reporting purposes shall rest upon verifiable, objective evidence.

Revenue is a measure of the current assets received in exchange for product or service. After properly allocated costs and losses are deducted, the remaining revenue is called net income. When first recorded, revenue therefore already contains an element of profit (or loss); the income statement is a calculation to determine the net amount. But the correctness of this calculation is conditioned by the reality of the revenue figure for the period. Hence, it is necessary to have some objective test of the realization of income. Without an objective test serving to corroborate one's own opinions, there is danger that profit will be read into a situation where bias fails to detect a lack of reality.

The usual objective test of the reality of a profit or loss which is sanctioned by accounting is transfer of title attending a bona fide sales transaction consummated by independent parties at a mutually acceptable price. The objectivity of the test is destroyed, and with it the confidence in the reality of the profit, if one of the parties is not in fact independent, if he is coerced, or if the stated exchange price is, for any other reason, a false representation of the parties' actual value judgments at the time.

Since the association of revenue with performance is basic to the concept of revenue, accounting standards should preserve that association: recognition of revenue should neither anticipate performance nor be delayed beyond performance.

In a few situations a variation from this standard is usual. In the case of installment sales, economic performance is complete when possession and use of the property pass to the purchaser. But the risk of uncollectible installments or loss from repossession is so great that we may be justified in declining to accept this economic performance as the test for reporting the revenue involved. Furthermore, legal performance, transfer of title, usually is here delayed until all installments are paid. Yet the businessman hesitates to delay recognition of revenue until legal performance is complete because his service has been rendered and the risk of loss diminishes as each succeeding installment is paid. As a result, it is an acceptable deviation from standard to recognize revenue from installment sales in proportion to collections, and to recognize revenue from long-time contracts in proportion to degree of completion. In both cases the acceptability of this deviation depends upon certain collateral conditions (1) that ultimate payment is relatively assured by the margin "held back" (in construction contracts) or by chattel mortgages (rights of repossession in installment sales), (2) that the completed portion of costs can be satisfactorily computed and reported along with the revenue portions, and (3) that the partial payments are planned in the original agreement.

Like revenue, cost must be measured according to definite standards if accounting data are to be dependable and relevant. Like revenue, cost must be subject to a test of objectivity and rest upon a bona fide exchange transaction consummated by independent parties at a mutually acceptable price. As is the case with revenue, the reality of "cost" might be questioned, for example, in an exchange between legally distinct corporations which are nevertheless so dominated by a single interest that no actual change in beneficial interest has been effected by the transaction. Reality of cost is also difficult to determine in cases where the transaction is essentially barter. It should be the universal practice of the contracting parties to price such transactions in money; only in this way can an accounting quantity be established which will make each party's record of the transaction a counterpart of the other's. Where this has not been done in particular cases any record made will be a departure from standard and will have to be justified by (1) clear inability to follow the standard and (2) a conscientious attempt to approximate the standard in a fair and equitable manner.

If an enterprise being merged has no records which permit an accurate determination of the cost of assets still in use, the application of accounting standards may have to date from a selected point of time rather than cover all past transactions. Once that start has been made however, the consistent use of accounting standards over a period of years will eventually yield accounting statements in which asset figures derive from the single basic postulate of cost, original or unamortized, and do not derive from uncertain and inconsistent accounting policies.

The objective test for the recognition of cost is not cash disbursed, since the intervention of the credit system may give us control over services before payment. The test is much the same as that for revenue because "service acquired" is but our side of another's "service rendered." This means that we may not measure a cost in terms of our own uncorroborated judgment alone.

There are occasions in a competitive economy when it is the part of common sense to reorganize not only the financial structure of an enterprise but the property structure as well. But it is not "reorganization" to decide that costs are high and shall be lowered by devaluing plant so that depreciation charges will be smaller. This merely converts real costs (of the past or future) into a lump-sum charge to surplus, perhaps to capital. The point is that cost (especially depreciation expense) is not whatever we choose to say it is, but what the best obtainable objective evidence shows it to be. Accounting standards for the recognition of cost are designed to guide business away from arbitrary or personal decision and toward an impersonal, quasi-scientific attitude toward the computative problems of a going concern.

(Accounting Review, March, 1939)

5. Matching Cost and Revenue

The central problem of accounting is to bring into association, in the present, the revenues identified with the present and their related costs, and to bring into association, in the future, the revenues identified with the future and their related costs. In solving this problem those who use accounting are, in effect, matching enterprise efforts and accomplishments. Some efforts are effective in the present; they are measured by the costs (effort) currently deductible from revenue (accomplishment); they are the revenue costs of the present. Other efforts are expected to be effective in the future; they are measured by the costs that are deferred as being revenue costs of the future (assets). Some efforts prove ineffective in the present and are judged unlikely to be effective in the future; they are measured by the costs that must be currently deducted from revenue as recognized losses.

The fundamental problem of accounting therefore is to cut through a continuing stream of costs and correctly assign portions to the present and to the future. The instruments for reporting the division of the stream as between present and future are (1) nominal and real accounts and (2) the income statement and the balance sheet. Both are essential; the income statement reports the assignment to the present, the balance sheet the assignment to the future. The balance sheet thus serves as the means of carrying forward unamortized acquisition prices, the not-yet-deducted costs; it stands as a connecting link that joins successive income statements into a picture of the income stream. This conception of the balance sheet has no place for "valuation" in the sense of subjective judgment of utility, probable replacement price, or sales price.

The emphasis upon unamortized costs does not deny the propriety of financial reorganization and the attendant realignment of assets and equities when this is accomplished under proper limitations as to bona fide and unbiased consideration of all facts and interests. Nor does it deny that information beyond unamortized historical costs may be of great usefulness. It merely denies such information a settled place within the framework of double-entry bookkeeping. Outside that framework, accounting sets no limits whatever upon the extent to which pertinent, collateral information may be supplied.

There are many devices of reporting by which figures in addition to unamortized costs may be given for informative purposes. Collateral notations may be made in footnotes, in text accompanying account titles, in parenthetical figures, or in supplementary tabulations—all of these illuminate the cost figures. If desired, extra columns may be inserted to reflect the effect of weighting by index-numbers. Significant ratios and percentages may be shown to advantage, and supporting exhibits may be referred to in the statements. But these are interpretative devices;

and to be fully useful they should have a known "basing point," i.e., cost. They come into play after accounting has brought its subject matter to a focus within the framework of a consistent theory of historical cost.

If "values," whether by appraisal, the cost-or-market tradition, or by index-number adjustments, are brought into the statements by account-keeping processes, the ultimate result is likely to be the complete submergence of the only objectively determined quantities that accounting has to work with—unamortized historical costs. However, if such "values" are brought to attention by interpretative action, the objectively determined quantities are preserved, with illuminating additions.

(Accounting Review, March, 1939)

6. Leveling of Profits

The author, Henry W. Sweeney, has chosen a short title, Stabilized Accounting. But a reviewer may choose a more comprehensive headline. For example: "An accountant's technique for calculating stabilized profits" would as a title at once show the reader that the book deals with a type of profit calculation rather than possible new bookkeeping procedures. This would be reassuring to most readers. "A method for re-expressing financial statements in terms of the current general price level," would as a title give a direct clue to the element now so cryptically covered in the word "stabilized." This too would be reassuring, for a considerable number of people may at first interpret "stabilized accounting" as meaning legislated uniformity in accounting procedure or something equally artificial and restrictive.

It should be said at once, however, that the author does not propose any change in recording methodology or valuation base. It is only incidental that he favors replacement value over original cost, for he makes his interpretive technique applicable to whatever valuation base is used. The book, therefore, is a notable supplement to a somewhat meager literature on the interpretation of accounting data and to the debates on replacement value versus original cost.

It is not stable prices that the author discusses, nor regimented accounting procedure, but leveled profits. The effect of the proposed technique would be to narrow the calculated profit margin on the upswings of the general price level and widen it on the downswings. In a sense, therefore, the idea is to produce a methodology—and a philosophy—for accomplishing systematically what some managements have long tried to do by increasing depreciation and maintenance in good times and decreasing them in bad times, or by building up surpluses and reserves out of high profits to be used to absorb subsequent losses when the tide had turned.

There are not a few people who have strong convictions about artificially leveling the data for naturally fluctuating elements, holding that
the function of statistics and accounting is to reveal existing variations
rather than to conceal them. There are others who will say that the
search for "stabilization" is a result of depression psychology, that the
term only means "stop the downward trend"; that there will be no
stabilization urge on the upswing—in a word, that stabilization, or artificial leveling, is not only undesirable but undesired.

Chapter I is entitled "Where Accounting Always Goes Wrong." Since
a better understanding of the limitations of orthodox accounting is given
as one of the main reasons for studying stabilization technique, the
reader will do well to give particular attention to this chapter, for therein
accounting as we know it is said to be irrelevant to the real reason for
keeping accounts, to be mathematically unsound because of combining
unhomogeneous elements, and to be incomplete in its failure to display
all of the helpful information it could easily do.

In considering this basic chapter, however, the reader may find it
advantageous to keep certain questions in mind. Is the reason for keeping accounts more closely related to progress toward greater power over
consumption goods in the hands of individuals, or to the attempt on
the part of producers of goods and services to pierce a little the veil
separating cause from effect in their activity and judgments? Is greater
homogeneity to be obtained from making comparable all the elements
in a financial statement as of a specific date by translating them into
current general price equivalents, or by making comparable all statements of whatever date by keeping them expressive of actual transactions
stated in terms of actual outlay costs? Will a greater service be rendered
management and investors by bringing under the aegis of accounting
itself all possible interpretive devices, or by refining and improving accounting for original cost to such an extent that it may serve as a fully
dependable base for whatever interpretation the individual concerned
may be capable of bringing to it.

It may be true that the lay public tends to consider original cost
figures in a balance sheet as if they were present value figures. But there
exists another corrective besides one of interposing an analytical methodology which can convert actual outlays into what the lay public thinks
it is reading. That other corrective would be stubborn repetition of the
inescapable limitations of accounts expressed in their natural medium
of original cost. This would be a constant reminder to the reader to
make his own interpretation or apply for enlightenment to someone
skilled in such interpretation.

If the relatively simple concept of balance sheet assets as unamortized
costs must forever be confused by many readers with present value, it
seems that the addition of new and strange distinctions in the kinds of

losses and gains would have better than an even chance of further confusing more people than it would enlighten.

The author's answer to the objection of "too complicated" is that (p. 96) "the present basis on which conventional accounting rests . . . must unfortunately be looked upon as having become much too simple a one for satisfactory use in an economic system of many fluctuable prices," and the completely stabilized accounting "must be looked upon as a necessary accompaniment of the complicated economic structure" which is characteristic of modern industrial society.

This, in effect, merely asserts the inevitability of increasing complexity. If this is inescapable, so too is further confusion inevitable for most of us. For the few—those who can follow statistical involutions easily and who are well grounded in the economics of price—this new technique can perhaps be enlightening. But one will ask whether this specially equipped group includes the large number of the business executives who guide our enterprises, the investors who own the concerns, the bankers who lend to them, and the officials of the governments which tax them. Yet who else constitutes the readers of financial statements?

(book review, *Accounting Review*, September, 1936)

7. Creating a Profit

The very extensive use of double-entry bookkeeping (an art using an income-and-expense method of calculating enterprise net profit rather than following the increase-in-proprietorship theory of profit associated with single entry) may be considered as evidence that business practice favors the former concept of profit. But we must look to economics to find consideration being given to the forces which generate profit or loss.

It is often held that risk is the principal element which accounts for profit and that profit is necessary to induce enterprisers to appear and accept risks. The risks in question are mainly the risk of failure to get a return and the risk of a loss of capital. The risk is a very real one and largely because, under competition, buyers (consumers) have such a large advantage over sellers that many important factors are beyond the latter's control. For example, the enterpriser contracts for fixed payments for rent, interest, and wages. For good or ill, he has agreed to stand the shock of changing conditions. He is prompted to do this by the expectation that his skillful judgment will enable him to keep his costs, expenses, and losses within the boundaries of his income.

The risks of the enterpriser are real enough; they press in upon him from both buyer's and labor's side, and some inducement (such as a profit) is perhaps necessary to get done the things society needs to have done. But are we entitled to consider risk as the factor which generates profit?

The real function of the enterpriser is not merely to serve as a "shock absorber" between changing conditions and labor, but rather his true purpose is to overcome naturally speculative conditions and to avoid losses. This would let it seem that profit would come to the enterpriser in proportion to his skill in dodging the effect of risks rather than in proportion to the size of the risk itself.

The emphasis would seem to lie with choosing risks wisely, if profit is to emerge. If one is too venturesome, loss results; if one is not venturesome enough, there may be but meager profits, if any. A middle course is indicated, and the distance one may safely stray from the path depends largely upon that person's ability to overcome successfully the obstacles which are sure to be found in great abundance in and alongside the path. It may be concluded, therefore, that "risk influences the dimensions of profit but is not necessarily a cause." To this might well be added the thought that ability in meeting the conditions imposed by risky situations is at least as important in generating profit as the existence of circumstances abounding in potential profit.

It is sometimes said that profit arises from the changes which are constantly taking place in actual life as compared with the unchanging conditions which theoretically might exist. If society were stationary and free from all progress, although perfectly organized, and if labor and capital were perfectly mobile, then competition would also be perfect and consequently there would be no price changes; that is, selling price would always be just equal to the cost of production, and there would be no profit.

This highly imaginative condition of society is, of course, merely an artificially simplified point of departure for economic reasoning about real conditions. Society is not stationary and is not lacking in all progress. Theoretically society could be in a wholly static, profitless condition were it not for change and uncertainty.

It would seem, however, that uncertainty and change produce only an opportunity to profit, that they call management into being, and that it is management which converts a mere possibility into a real actuality. Uncertainty might exist for a long time without profit appearing unless some enterpriser saw a way to turn it to an advantage—that is, to gain a profit.

It is much the same with change. In times of change there are indeed many opportunities to profit. The enterpriser flourishes among favorable opportunities; he perhaps sees the need in one place for high-bred livestock, or he locates fertile lands lacking only sufficient water; it may be that he merely sells the town's whole stock of oilcloth to a football crowd for makeshift capes in a sudden rainstorm. The important fact, however, is the seizure of the opportunity. Without seizure the possibility comes to naught. Without opportunity there is nothing to seize. Which blade of a pair of shears does the cutting?

Yet, seizure merely determines who gets the profit; and not even opportunity plus seizure—picking the fruit ready to hand—explain profit
itself. What creates the apple? What generates the profit? It must be
something at the root of the tree, something that conditions the opportunities. Is it not generated in the very foundations of the economic
system: division of labor, money economy, subjective valuations of utility?
I want an object; division of labor keeps me from furnishing it myself,
but you can supply it; I express its relative utility in a price. You had
anticipated just such a desire on my part, because I was busy doing other
things. You produced the article at a price (cost). When your price (cost)
is less than my price (the measure of utility to me), there is profit. But
is it not this whole situation which creates the profit? Any and all factors which influence either of these two prices in any way, are they not
conditioning or generating factors, each partially responsible, however
indirectly, for the actual appearance of profit?

(Accounting Review, September, 1928)

8. Price and Profit

In a very definite sense enterprise profit is tied into enterprise prices as
these are tied into the whole of society's price structure. Fluctuating
commodity prices—from maladjustments of supply and demand—must
perforce influence very profoundly such a price-made phenomenon as
profit. One who holds a commodity through a rise in its price sees, when
he sells, a profit generated in large measure without much effort on his
part. When war causes a shortage in certain supplies, when monopoly
squeezes the last penny, price is not under the control of usual conditions, and unusual profits may result when transactions take place. Under
ordinary conditions of commodity price movements or under exceptional
conditions, the enterpriser feels the change first. And because it is evident
that he is not personally responsible for the change, he is not usually
credited with any responsibility for the resulting profit. But when we
look closely at business, we see that short supplies or increased demands
are *conditions precedent* and that the specific profit, when finally it
emerges, is as much attributable to the enterpriser's judgment of probable future markets or to his service in preserving a supply, as it is to
the fluctuations in market price as such. The skill of the businessman
in making the most of fluctuations, in keeping his profits ahead of the
losses, and in his ability to choose the proper moment for purchase or
sale, is a very positive factor in the size of the profit.

Often profit is traced simply to a difference in prices (cost and selling),
but upon occasion there is wide fluctuation in selling prices. Here again
profit is for the most part not merely the result of outside conditions

and a passive attitude on the part of the enterpriser; rather it is the result of outside conditions and a very active part played by the business-man. Prices may fluctuate widely, but unless someone is in the right market at the right time with the right goods, and unless a sale is made, the fluctuations are mere variations in "bid prices," and do not generate profits at all. Profit made at such times is to be largely attributed to the enterpriser's ability to anticipate conditions, or to be ready for that which is unexpected by the mass, and to be able quickly to adjust himself to whatever circumstances shall rule at the moment.

After price there comes the question of costs and their relation to profit. There is much to indicate that this is a very vital element. Profit may be explained as due to the enterpriser's struggle to reduce outlays, enlarge the plant, decrease costs, and increase quality and quantity. This profit, it may be pointed out, is governed by the technical laws of in-dustry and responds to a given positive effort of the enterpriser in the technical process of production. A good manager is like good farm land —unusually productive from the use of a given amount of labor. Here the emphasis is placed upon efficiency and high productivity in business management as the most important element in the explanation of profit.

The relation of management to profit is clear. The forces of compe-tition tend to bring price and cost of production together and thus to wipe out profits. Management expends its energies in keeping these two apart and thus in creating profit where there easily might have been none. The task in modern times is extremely difficult and calls for ability of high order, if it is to be done well. Securing a profit is not so simple a thing as outbargaining labor or retaining an undue share of the results of advances in the arts. Profit is much more nearly described as the *out-come of work*—the strenuous activity of searching out an opportunity for profit and then even more strenuously struggling to keep selling price and cost apart.

All proposals for explaining profit, it will be noted, have a "mana-gerial" aspect. It would seem that management always plays a very vital part in profit, whatever the other aspects of the explanation may be. And it is to be observed that management, or the enterpriser, is mainly concerned in grasping intelligently the opportunities which he can locate, or in creating conditions which will produce a margin for himself. This is essentially the income statement view of what profit is—a spread be-tween revenue derived and the costs and expenses assignable thereto.

It is for sound and logical reasons therefore that accountants tend to cling to cost prices for accounting and financial statement purposes. *Cost* is definite and once expended is an unchangeable quantitative fact. It will afford a basis for a profit calculation whenever the other element (sold price) is also known. But *value* is indefinite and as changeable; it can never be the starting point of a calculation of factual profit.

(*Accounting Review*, September, 1928)

9. Capital and Income

A survey of accounting literature would probably lead most observers to the conclusion that capital received more attention in accounting than income.

Ever since bookkeeping expanded into accounting, most of the literature being derived from or related to auditing practices has been preoccupied with the balance sheet—the capital statement. The reason apparently was because this statement reflected the most accessible evidence of the concern's ability to pay its debts. This report was important to American bankers lending to enterprises on single-name paper. But it was given strong emphasis by British practices long before balance sheet audits for credit purposes developed in the United States.

A writer in the *Accountant*[2] indicated that the Companies Act of 1844 made the balance sheet alone the main object of the accounting sections because, in Parliament's concern for the prevention of fraud by directors, it desired to place emphasis on the evidence of stability and financial soundness. It had less interest in the company's earning power or the operating competence of the officers—aspects which would be suggested to the shareholders by the income statement. These early regulations applying to business enterprises would not constitute denial that revenue and expense rather than assets and liabilities were the central theme of enterprise account-keeping. They merely mean that government regulation need not go so far as to be concerned with reporting the income calculations.

Another explanation of emphasis on the balance sheet as the report on status of enterprise capital is found in certain developments in the common law. For a century there has been considerable litigation involving the capital statement although the chief issue usually had to do with dividends and directors' liability. In general, court decisions have limited legal dividends to those declared out of profit. But in England these divisible "profits" were evidenced by a balance sheet item which expressed the excess of assets over debts plus capital stock rather than by a profits statement as such. Such a balance sheet item was of course indicative of undivided past and/or present profits—in American terminology, "Surplus."

Accounting literature may therefore seem to be mainly concerned (1) with the capital statement as revealing financial soundness (ability to pay debts), or (2) with the sum available for dividend disbursements as determined by two capital elements, namely, total quantity of economic capital (assets) compared with total legal indebtedness (liabilities and capital stock).

The study of the periodic profit out of which asset accumulations

.

[2] George F. Todd on Sept. 5, 1936.

grow did not play an important part in auditing or in court decisions on dividends. Solvency and director liability were not questions of enterprise earnings in relation to assets employed, but were concerned with the relation between debts and the asset means of paying them. In addition, profit and loss information was generally considered in Britain as confidential information unsuitable for general publication available to the eyes of competitors and stock-speculators.

But deeper there was another idea. It was generally believed in the day when these practices were being laid down that the key amount would be the same whether undivided profit was calculated as the balancing item among enterprise assets and debts, or as an accumulation of prior undivided profit now increased or decreased by the net results of the current fiscal period.

This conception was reasonable enough in its day and in Britain. But a few generations later, and in the United States, after no-par stock, revaluation surplus, and paid-in surplus had blossomed forth, the results calculated by the two familiar methods so characteristic of double entry could no longer be depended upon to produce identical sums.

Fundamentally income produced, not capital in use, is the central theme of accounting-keeping, as indeed it is the central theme of a business enterprise's activities. Asset capital is only a means to an end; income is that end.

The recent tendency to emphasize income is apparent in the attention given by the American Institute of Accountants to a careful defining[3] and distinguishing of earned surplus and capital surplus (including paid-in and revaluation surplus). The wish is clearly evident here to re-establish as much as possible the accord between the two traditional calculations of identical sums by the use of (1) assets and debts, (2) revenue and related costs and expenses.

The same tendency is shown in another publication of the Institute[4] where this phraseology appears: ". . . the real value of the assets of any large business is dependent mainly on the earning capacity of the enterprise (p. 6). It is probably fairly well recognized by intelligent investors today that earning capacity is the fact of crucial importance in the valuation of an industrial enterprise, and that therefore the income account is usually far more important than the balance sheet" (p. 10).

(Accounting Review, March, 1937)*

10. Income Is Primary

Early in the 1930's the American Institute of Accountants recommended a new wording for auditors' certificates. This form has become accepted

[3] *Year Book*, American Institute of Accountants, 1930, p. 173.
[4] *Audit of Corporate Accounts*, 1934.

practice. The clause of major significance is the one which rests the auditor's opinion of the financial statements upon their accord with "generally accepted principles of accounting."

This form of certificate can do a great deal in the midst of the complexities of modern finance to help us to recapture the original essence of double-entry bookkeeping. "Accepted principles of accounting" are more than the customary practices of professional accountants making balance sheet audits. The phrase must reach far enough to include those principles which have been fundamental to double-entry bookkeeping for many centuries and those principles which have been so serviceable in refining bookkeeping into accrual accounting, that is, accounting wherein income earned is sharply distinguished from cash received, and expense incurred from cash disbursed.

The outstanding characteristic of double-entry bookkeeping is not the equality of debits and credits but the systematic inclusion in the record of data expressing incomes and expenses. "Nominal accounts" for expenses and incomes were added some five hundred years ago to the then very incomplete debt records. That addition made the financial recording mechanism complete; since that time only refinements have been added to the system. It likewise seems to be clearly evident that accrual accounting is concerned more directly with the calculation of correct income and expense than with securing refinements for the statement of assets and liabilities, although the two results always appear together.

The emphasis given in publications by the American Institute of Accountants to the importance of correct income determination and to the isolation of earned surplus joins with the new form of audit certificate to indicate a return to basic first principles. Profit, being the focal center of business enterprise, is likewise the focal center of account-keeping. This fundamental thought has never been divorced from double-entry bookkeeping and has been much elaborated by cost accounting procedure. It had however drifted into relative obscurity in much of the accounting literature through the tendency of both balance sheet audits for credit purposes and judicial consideration of the dividend problems of limited liability corporations to stress the balance sheet almost to the exclusion of the income statement.

It is a good indication of the fundamental vitality of the principles upon which account-keeping rest that our period of apostasy should finally come to a reaffirmation of fundamental truth. Income *is* primary.

One of the keenest critics of accounting theory has said with much justification that "accountants have no complete philosophical system of thought about income." [5] That statement is all too true. Accountants, like businessmen, are too deep in practical affairs to be philosophers. But that does not prevent accounting records from giving expression, piecemeal as it were, to definite concepts of profit and income.

[5] J. B. Canning, *The Economics of Accountancy*, p. 160.

Bookkeeping has given quantitative expression to various aspects of profit ever since income and expense accounts have been used, and that has been at least for five hundred years. Few indeed are the companion disciplines which have served more effectively for as long with so little change in their fundamental doctrines or methods.

Businessmen and accountants have been rather inarticulate in expressing a theory of profit. They have left it to economists to explain why there was such a thing as a profit margin, and to jurists to say how dividends shall be based in order to protect creditors of limited liability corporations. Businessmen, however, along with bookkeepers working within the limits of their tradition, have for a very long time been living a theory of profit even though they wrote little about it. They, not economists or jurists, undertake day by day to quantify profit. It has been necessary that they do this since they are unable to await the outcome of ultimate liquidation before making business decisions. Businessmen cannot escape acting with regard to profit one way or another, and this without having much time to rationalize their acts in advance.

Accounting, which we may well call the art of keeping accounts, is the primary means of giving definite quantitative expression to many accepted customs of business. And public accountants are constantly scrutinizing the details of these "profit customs" and criticizing their reasonableness in the light of sound principles. Accountants therefore supplement business activities. If their service proves useful to investors, creditors, and tax collectors, such service first of all must rest on a dependable record.

Bookkeeping is a record methodology for an economic enterprise as a producing unit. And since accounting is but expanded and refined account-keeping, we must conclude that the true base of the most useful ideas of accounting is economic rather than judicial, even though accountants as well as businessmen are under the necessity of conforming to the law of the land. The concept of income, then, which underlies accounting will lie closer to those found in economics than to those expressed in statutory law or court decisions.

(Accounting Review, March, 1937)

11. Economic and Financial Condition

A clear concept of profit (net income) is inherent in double-entry bookkeeping as the latter has been refined into accrual accounting. It is a concept interpreted out of business customs and accounting practices, and lived day by day within all areas of business activities. Back of this concept there lies a differentiation between the economic condition of an enterprise and its financial condition.

Whenever debtors and creditors enter into contractual relationships, the "financial conditions" of the debtor become an important consideration. This relationship is largely a legal matter. Yet a business enterprise is more basically an economic unit than it is legalistic creature. That this is true is shown by the fact that enterprise debt (finance) is clearly secondary to the primary economic activity of producing an output acceptable to customers. It is possible therefore to say that economic condition, not financial condition, is of first importance in a business enterprise.

The appearance of output is not the result of the simple speculative adventuring of an investment, although very early that was an important aspect of trade. And income is more than the chance realization of a gain arising out of an ownership now transferred to another.

The assembly and union of selected elements of input form the units of final output by an enterprise. Presumably the manipulative processes add new utility beyond the sum of utilities of the previously separate elements. The amount thus added can be tested only by the market's acceptance or rejection of the product at the price asked. Insofar as money costs can measure sacrifices made in producing the output, it may be said that the calculated cost of production expresses the sum of the utilities previously embodied in the separate input elements. This sum (cost), when compared with market (buyer) opinion regarding output utility (revenue), presumably can be accepted as producing a measure of the utility added by the productive processes.

We may say therefore that the point of view of the businessman is (1) that *output* is the result of definitely planned work which is the consequence of a prior *service input* made with intent to create output; (2) that *money income* is the earning flowing from planned work as a consequence of a prior *money outlay* made with intent to generate income.

From the businessman's point of view, and hence the point of view of accounting theory, the key to this doctrine is in the word "intent." Service input and its money counterpart, cost outlay, are entered upon with the clear intention of establishing a relationship with subsequent service output and its money counterpart, income. That is to say, input has the objective of producing an effect on the economic condition of the enterprise. Hence cost outlays are more than mere cash disbursements or liabilities incurred. Outlays for cost express in homogeneous money price, the heterogeneous service input made in the effort to produce an acceptable service output. In a similar way revenue and earnings (incomes) are more than mere cash collections or accrued assets receivable. Incomes express in money price the fruition of enterprise efforts— the ripening harvest, as it were, from a prior planting carefully cultivated. This is quite a different condition from a mere speculative venturing, even though the outcome of the prior planting may be subject to unpredictable and uncontrollable risks.

Economic condition, then, is a relationship as financial condition is a relationship. Whereas the latter is a relationship of debt to debt paying capacity, the former is a relationship between income derived and the cost of producing it. For many purposes a knowledge of financial condition is important. But economic condition is a foundation to financial condition and to many other aspects of business. Whenever business managements or investors attempt to think in terms of causes, it is the details of economic condition which should receive major attention.

The clue to the concept "economic condition" is found in the term "net income"; and the explanation of net income is found in the conjunction of two elements: one is the acceptance of service output by customers *at a price;* the other is the preparation of the service output for customers *at a cost.*

Imagine a pair of shears in the hands of a tailor. The lower blade moves only forward on the table top but the upper blade also moves up and down in the cutting stroke. Net income, like the cloth under the tailor's hand, is shaped as by the interaction of the blades of a pair of shears—revenue as one, cost as the other. It is obvious that both blades are necessary to produce the result. But their action is not necessarily equal. One blade may rest passively on the table while the other blade moves actively up and down under pressure from the operator's fingers. The passive blade represents revenue—the element under little direct managerial control; the active blade represents costs—the element under considerable managerial control in the activity of producing net income.

Cost outlays are much more subject to the enterpriser's decisions and choices than is revenue; he controls the timing of his cost outlays and their apportioning among types; he selects the quantity and agrees to the buying price; by following his selections with expenditures or contracts, he induces a flow of service input. We may say then that the costs thus incurred express quantitatively the *causes* which actuate the inflow of services, or that the chosen input of services *causes* the outflow of cost expenditures. But whichever way the proposition is stated, the result is that costs represent "solidified" managerial choices made with specific intent.

The shears illustration clearly expresses the thought that net income is the result of a favorable or unfavorable *relation* between revenue and cost. But the relation changes more readily under the influence of costs than revenues; profit is likely to accompany low costs, and loss is likely to be associated with high costs. If "A" is a marginal producer, he is so because his costs are high in relation to the price the market is willing to pay; if "B" makes a good profit with a similar product in the same market, he does so because he has been able to get his costs low in relation to market price.

(*Accounting Review,* March, 1937)

12. Claims upon Income

Most of the accounting literature, except that dealing with bookkeeping and cost accounting, stresses the data in the balance sheet and the condition of solvency. Only in recent years has the basic character of the information in the income statement been given adequate prominence. Why is information about income so important?

It is not enough to answer that earning power is at once the blood stream of an enterprise and the basis of most judgments about the value of the enterprise itself. This is true. But the income statement gains much of its importance from the variety of interests reflected in its data, and from the fact that the interested parties can be, and at times are, in conflict.

If each of several conflicting interests were to produce an income statement from the original transactions of their common enterprise, would any one of the results be wholly acceptable to the other parties? Charges probably would be made in which self-interest tended to color the interpretation given to some of the transactions included, or tended to exclude transactions in order to modify the form and content of the presentation.

Under such conditions, independent auditors would have had to be invented even if commercial evolution by way of trial and error had not already anticipated the need. Since auditing was not invented to meet modern complexities, auditors today probably seldom realize that the independent status they have gained makes them in effect "moderators" among various interests represented in the different figures of the income statement.

Reduced to its barest essentials, an income statement is a calculation (1) of the revenue produced by the operations of an enterprise, and (2) of the way that the total has been divided among the claimants. Although the dividing of revenue is generally controlled by statute or contract, and although many claims are settled in advance of determining the gross revenue, it still is an economic fact that the revenue is shared. It is also a fact that a complex and unending struggle goes on with change in the sharing as its object.

The independent public accountant is not a party to these contracts nor is he a critic of their objectives. But his professional opinion supports the income statement in his report. Thus, willy-nilly, he becomes an interpreter, or moderator, or middleman—one who takes no sides but renders a professional opinion after a technical examination of relevant evidence, and in this way puts his judgment and competence at the disposal of all parties in the community of interests.

Part of the reason for the ascendancy of the income statement in late years is the fact that the balance sheet does not report upon the sharing of enterprise revenue. The balance sheet is reasonably adequate as the

principal statement under fairly simple conditions: when there are only
a few sharers of the revenue with power enough to push their interests,
i.e., when the primary parties at interest are proprietors or partners who
have ready access to profit and loss details. If government (for taxes),
workers (for wages), customers (for prices), lenders (for interest)—if all
these are considered to have claims upon the revenue of an enterprise,
a balance sheet does not furnish them with adequate information.

"Profit" once was considered the balancing figure to the assets, liabilities, and capital; later "surplus" took over that responsibility. In both
uses, the single figure was presumed sufficient for any reader of the balance sheet; the income statement was thought to contain confidential
information not suited to wide circulation, and anyway it consisted only
of "analytical details," being a supporting schedule that elaborated somewhat upon the really significant amount, the net change in proprietorship.

The inadequacy of the balance sheet to serve all purposes has contributed to the increased recognition of the usefulness of the income
statement. This recognition also leads us to see that assets are related
to revenue charges and to revenue even more closely than they are linked
to liabilities. In fact, if the legalistic term "assets" were to be dropped
from accounting, some brief substitute term would undoubtedly be
sought which would convey the idea that all assets are, in economic
effect, "deferred charges to future revenue."

(editorial, *Accounting Review*, October, 1944)

13. Interacting Forces

There is a very large community of interest behind every important income statement. In a very real sense the modern large corporation is an
unusually efficient co-operative society whose creative activities spread
wide benefits widely. The community thus associated in laying claim to
a sharing of the revenue produced includes: consumers who use the
products; workers who create and distribute the products; management
which supervises and plans productive activities; investors who supply
the savings needed to create production facilities and to pay many claimants in advance of the receipt of proceeds from sales; and government
which needs tax revenue from enterprise income in quantities varying
according to the scale of activities laid upon governmental agencies.

If the wishes of some interests prevailed, selling prices would be low;
the wishes of others would bring about high prices. Costs would be high
or low, profits great or small, taxes increased or decreased, if one element
or another were in a position to enforce selfish, and shortsighted, demands. No single view can prevail. A balancing of forces is necessary.
But the result is a state of equilibrium that is ever changing; each action
produces reactions which in turn produce further action.

High wages may force higher selling prices while creating increased buying power. Lowered prices increase buying power even more broadly than do high wages, but prices may fall so low as to put all costs under strong pressure. Substantial interest and dividend payments may be a socially inexpensive way of stimulating new industry, and through it to create wider employment; yet a necessary time lag in this accomplishment may conceal the real facts from those who press for an immediate showing of results. Incentives to management increase costs; but proper incentives are likely to increase inventiveness and planning, and these are factors which have the effect of reducing unit costs and lowering selling prices through increasing the efficiency of workers and equipment.

Balancing here cannot be pictured as being like the action of an apothecary's scale; rather it is the resultant of many complex, interacting forces, constantly changing, little or much, here or there, slow or quick. Sudden, large, concentrated changes may be tremendously disturbing to the whole enterprise structure. An enterprise could easily be taxed out of existence, with attendant losses of employment and tax collections; wages could be artificially forced to a height where customers could no longer pay the resulting product cost; sales prices could be forced down to a point where dividends were impossible, where employment could not be maintained, where governmental tax revenue was threatened.

Enterprise equilibrium is easily thrown into unbalance; the highest arts of business management are required to do well the simplest job of producing reasonable enterprise stability in the midst of ever-changing conditions. A condition of growing unbalance is hard for an untrained eye to read from a series of financial statements. For the person who wishes to try, the series of income statements is the best reading; for the people in the community of interests, or their competent representatives, that statement should be required reading.

The public accountant has an important moderator function to perform in this connection: he has the complex task of using his technical competence to fashion complex materials into a widely useful form that is ready for the uses of a mixed community of interests; he has the important social task of holding his independence in such high esteem that his report can be accepted by all parties at interest as factual in whatever degree that is possible, and unbiased in so far as conscious effort and special training can make it so.

A periodic determination of revenue and assignable cost, and of the resulting net income, by no means provides the only data necessary to an intelligent resolving of issues raised by conflicting economic interests. But income statements that have been examined and accepted by competent independent public accountants offer to all parties elements of trustworthiness that are difficult to duplicate elsewhere for data of similar importance.

(editorial, *Accounting Review*, October, 1944)

14. Creative Management

One should no doubt refer to "cause and effect" circumspectly in these days of science, for effects are usually considered to emerge out of a complex of antecedent conditions rather than from a specific cause. Yet it is difficult to think of the conditions antecedent to the appearance of earned net income and not try to see at least some distance into that complex background.

What lies back of the revenue which flows from the customer's acceptance of a product? As "causes" of demand, consumers' wants will probably stand first. But the wants behind demand are not wholly beyond the influence of an enterpriser's expenditures. Many managerial decisions are made with the definite intention of influencing demand. Improvements in old products, devising new products, forceful and truthful advertising, skillful styling and designing, attractive price-quality ratio—the enterpriser's cost expenditures for such as these cannot change human nature perhaps, but they can uncover latent wants and make effective many wants formerly unsatisfied. In this sense even an individual seller's costs can lead to the ultimate acceptance of that seller's output and to a consequent inflow of revenue. If outlays can "cause" a demand for specific services, they can be considered causally related to the revenues which flow from the services rendered.

Besides wants as the primary causes of demand, there is also the matter of consumer purchasing power. Wants are fulfilled only at a price. The price which will convert wants into purchases depends upon the intensity of the want and the ability to pay. Can the seller's expenditures influence these? Intensity of want can be influenced probably very little, but ability to pay can be influenced a great deal. For example, wherever ingenious policies and wise expenditures result in low costs and consequent low prices, the effect upon the customer's purchasing power is direct and beneficial. In that sense also, business expenditures can "cause" demand and lead to acceptance of the product.

But demand and even sale do not of themselves yield a profit; they can only offer a chance to profit. The opportunity to earn a profit appears with the customer's acceptance of the product, but profit realization to an important extent depends upon how successfully the costs have been kept below the revenues. This accomplishment is seldom accidental. To be sure, cost is partly the result of the state of the supply market at the time, but to a large extent costs are subject to the choices and the resourcefulness of the producers. Good buying, high worker efficiency, inventiveness—expenditures for these elements and many others, if made with reasonable foresight and clear intent, do have the planned result, namely, costs which are lower than the relevant revenue income.

Managerial policies are made effective through costs. Costs therefore are quantitative expressions for policies translated into action. Manage-

ment, having recognized wants to be satisfied and being desirous of contriving a supply to fill the need, can effectively express itself only in expenditures made or expenditures avoided. By acting in this way management succeeds or fails in its objective of providing a desired economic
service at a cost which will be less than the price set by marginal producers in a competitive market.

How can management know when and what to cease producing? Only
by learning to distinguish the successful from the unsuccessful attempts.
It has been said,[6] "It is only when past plans for production and past
costs have been accurately adjusted to the demand that exists when the
goods finished arrive at the consumer's market, that goods sell for prices
that agree with past costs of production" (including producers incentive
payments in the concept of cost). Since a manager cannot foretell the
future and therefore cannot at the moment judge the wisdom of his
present costs, he can become "accurately adjusted to the demand" only on
the basis of a comparison of his past plans, as partially expressed in his
prior costs, and present market demand, as partially expressed in his
present revenues.

An enterpriser's major function then is first to discover economic wants
which he believes he can be the means of satisfying; second, to choose the
necessary elements of service input and to direct the production and distribution of the service output accordingly. Market analysis, it is true,
may be able to indicate some elements of current economic wants in
quantitative terms. But the most important data for the guidance of
enterprise efforts are the cost of input and the revenue from output. These
data come only from accounting. Of the two kinds of data, cost is the
more useful to management because it is more directly under managerial
control and more expressive of causal factors in management's prior
planning.

Cost in business is the special province of cost accounting. It is in this
area that the most important elaboration of accounting techniques has
been devised. And it is in this area that is found the clearest conception
of cost as representing causal factors. Modern management is creative
management largely because accounting can aid men to measure causal
factors at their inception and record these quantities for review in the
light of subsequent events.

In the light of this analysis, the chief objectives of accounting may be
epitomized into three propositions: (1) to record details of revenue
income in such analytical form that the data will be useful in distinguishing the results of differing causes; (2) to record details of expense
outlay in such analytical form that the data will be of service in distinguishing the causes or differing results; (3) to marshal analytical detail
with such skill as to reflect the association of known results with relevant
causal factors in a useful and dependable degree.

[6] Garner and Hansen, *Principles of Economics*, p. 167.

It is obvious that business managers are not scientists and that business is not a science. Yet enterprises are successful for the reason that causative efforts generate fruitful results. And management plans its efforts with some knowledge of past accomplishments. Accounting is peculiarly suited to the function of providing management with useful data which aid in reviewing past efforts in the light of subsequent results. Accounting, without being a scientific instrumentality, does nevertheless provide to management something like the service which instruments for making highly refined measurements provide to scientists.

(*Accounting Review,* March, 1937)

15. A Balance Sheet Dilemma

Value has not always been one of the problems of accounting—if accounting shall be conceived as including bookkeeping. Bookkeeping is the record side of business and has had an organized existence as "double entry" since the Middle Ages. Until very recent years, few problems of valuation existed. Bookkeeping, being a record, dealt with what was, not with what might be, that is to say, with prices paid or prices received.

From early times there has also been auditing of some kind. Only recently has "valuation" been considered a problem of auditing. Early auditors were content to check the accuracy of records made in terms of the price of actual transactions. What circumstances can be found that tend to explain the change that took place?

One such circumstance is connected with the "trust period" in the United States centering about the year 1900. Consolidations were the order of the day accompanied by optimistic expectations of future profits from the economy of large-scale production. One result was overvalued assets and excessive stock issues. Occasionally the "water" of overvaluation was expressed in a goodwill account, but more often the properties taken over in the consolidation process were valued by the new directors at a figure arranged to cover the securities issued. Under these circumstances it is evident that financial statements "as per the books" could not be accepted at face value. Because of the "overvaluation" of the assets when brought on the new books of a merger, pressure falls upon the public auditor to present and certify to balance sheets which shall reflect "the true financial condition."

A second circumstance is strikingly similar, although having its own characteristic. In a subsequent generation it is found in rising prices which left the purchased assets, as recorded in the books, quite noticeably *undervalued* as a basis for other mergers, refinancing, etc. Again financial statements "according to the books" are unacceptable for credit and finance purposes. Then it was "undervaluation" which brought pressure upon the public accountant to present and certify to balance sheets which shall reflect "the true financial condition." Problems of goodwill had become problems of appreciation.

These circumstances explain in a measure why "valuation" looms so large as an accounting topic. So much attention was given in the profession to the auditing side of accountancy and so much importance was attached to statements for credit purposes, that *value* came to occupy the center of the stage.

But accounting was not ready, apparently, to go all the way with value balance sheets and make them wholly by periodic appraisals, that is, frankly and completely single-entry statements. Nor was accountancy quite ready, apparently, to go so far with value balance sheets as to conclude that profit is simply the difference in the present worth presented in two financial statements at different dates—because to do so would make appreciation surplus identical with earned surplus as a source of dividend declaration. And this does not seem wise.

Balance sheets by valuation, therefore, create serious problems of income determination, and the correct determination of net income and surplus profits available for dividends is still an important aspect of business, as important perhaps as credit and finance may be. Yet on the other hand, neither is accountancy able to hold to the purely cost or outlay balance sheets; to do so, it is thought, would destroy the presentation as "a statement of values," since this seems to be the *sine qua non* of credit-granting.

Here accounting is wrestling with a dilemma: a purely cost balance sheet is unacceptable, and a purely appraisal balance sheet is unacceptable. The result is a balance sheet which is often neither fish nor fowl, but containing not infrequently some items on an appraisal basis and some on a cost basis.

Resolving such a dilemma can be greatly aided by recognizing the inherent differences between the wishes of the users of financial statements and the limitations of accounting.

The businessman, the banker, and the investor may have many occasions to "evaluate" a property, or prospect, or market, or stock of goods, but accounting never has. Accounting has a record function, not a valuation function. In the process of his professional service, the auditor has many occasions to present financial statements to clients which shall aid them to "evaluate" one thing or other; but his statement is never really a statement of "values," for values are too momentary and too subjective to be clothed in these figures. The presentation must be a statement of prices—just what prices however is still a subject of debate, perhaps the most central subject of debate in modern accountancy.

If cost prices only are used, then bookkeeping logic and tradition are both satisfied, but not bankers contemplating extension of credit, not insurance companies contracting protection indemnities, not promoters planning mergers or refinancings with the attending sale of securities to the public. These interests, it seems, would prefer financial statements that show "values," meaning selling prices, replacement prices, or so-called "going value."

One cannot censure any of these parties for wanting such information; it is necessary to the formation of judgments prior to making commitments. But it is an open question whether such value figures are reasonably within the function of accounting and the capability of accountants.

From the standpoint of credit-granting alone, the function of accounting might seem to be to present a statement of the financial condition of the enterprise; and this of course would be largely a question of "valuing" balance sheet items as of conditions of the moment. "Financial condition" and "valuing" are terms which could hardly exclude making conscious allowance for outside conditions of the moment. If this conception of function should prevail, accounting statements would need to reflect inventory, not merely at cost or the lower of cost or market, but at current replacement prices, and need to report plant assets at appraised reproduction cost less accrued depreciation. Under this approach there would be little need for carefully kept accounting records of actual transactions. It would suffice to have records of physical units of goods and plant; these would be appraised when and as the dollar figures were needed for a statement of financial condition.

However, it is to be observed that accounting and auditing do not exist merely for the sake of providing information as a basis for credit-granting. There are other parties, particularly operating management, who have great need for accounting figures that reveal cost rather than value—costs as they enter the business, costs as they remain in the business, costs as they leave the business through sale or loss.

Under this conception of the service use of accounting, the balance sheet would consist of ledger balances of cost prices carried forward to subsequent periods. If credit-granting interests desired more information than this, such additional facts could be shown—in short, in parentheses, or in footnotes—as would enable the reader to "value" the inventory, the plant assets, or the whole enterprise for himself.

Accounting under these circumstances would become a matter of producing the most accurate statement possible of purely cost facts, supplemented by as broad a presentation as possible of collateral data which would be pertinent to different reader purposes. The auditor under these conditions would frankly and plainly separate the two unreconcilable elements, thus certifying to cost or cost-derived facts, but merely reporting, and perhaps interpreting, additional "value" figures that might serve certain readers' purposes.

(*Accounting Review*, September, 1929)

16. Recoverable Outlays

We know that the cost or purchase price of an article bought for resale is not necessarily a measure of its value—we have seen too many "marked-down sales" and too much unsalable stock on the shelves to be really deceived, although terms like "value," if loosely used, sometimes confuse the issue. We know that no buyer feels any compulsion to pay as much as an article has cost or more; he judges its worth to himself and either pays the asking or not accordingly.

It is true that we do not hesitate to use cost price in the accounting records, but this is not analogous to considering that figure as *value*. The cost price is an ascertained fact, an expenditure, a closed transaction; as such it calls for a "tentative" record so the fact will not escape us when in due time cost price becomes a pertinent factor in the calculation of profit. But what will happen next to the article itself, what its value will prove to be—this remains to be seen when actual exchange has taken place. The record is not intended to represent value, but rather to set forth a cost, an outlay, an item in suspense, so to speak. The situation is much the same with the cost of goods made rather than purchased complete. The record, such as a process inventory or finished goods inventory, is a record of recoverable outlay and not a record of values. Like goods purchased, the goods manufactured are, as it were, outlays held in suspense awaiting final disposition; they are a type of investment, nothing more. What they are *worth* will depend more on future circumstances than on past acts of production.

In the final analysis the value of goods for consumption depends basically upon the scarcity of the goods themselves and the relative urgency of the consumer's need for them. Past costs as such have very little influence; under pressure, very evidently differing prices will be asked and paid. But probable future costs will bulk large in the formation of present judgments. In the meantime, however, outlay cost is a definite quantity which acts as a record of temporary investment while real value (customer's esteem) is in the process of determination in the market.

Productive equipment is subject to similar reasoning. If buildings are built or acquired, their cost is recorded as the only monetary fact which we know to be a fact. What fixed assets are *worth* depends on other and less substantial considerations, such as the value the market places on the product flowing from those means of production; the probable volume of production in association with the presently expected prices the goods will bring.

Fluctuations in the repurchase price of goods held for resale of course call for corresponding changes in resale (offered) prices. The merchant who fails to mark up his sales prices as replacement prices increase is probably selling for less than a competitor who bought later; thus the former may lose a profit he might have had. If he fails to mark his prices down when the purchase market is falling, he will lose business to competitors who bought later than he did.

There can be little question therefore regarding such circumstances. But there must be serious doubt whether changes in purchase prices (after purchase) can properly be considered as affecting recorded costs (investments already made). Price fluctuations for replacements may suggest that consumers are now setting a higher value upon those goods and so will pay a higher price for them—or middlemen think consumers will do so. But until consumers take our goods—thus proving the existence of effective demand—there is no justification for a change in prior recorded costs.

There are two sides to value, the demand side and the supply side. The businessman must be always guessing at people's wants (demand). He must be always changing prices—not so high as to push consumers to seek substitutes or a competitor's offerings, not so low as to miss a possible profit. Information on the demand side is intangible, consisting of shrewd surmises and keen observation—"reading the market," "feeling the pulse of demand." This is the subjective side where the questions are such as these: what do people want; are tastes or fashions changing; has consumer purchasing power improved, and the like.

On the other hand, the businessman is constantly concerned with the supply side. For him this is tangible, concrete, and under his control. Here it is a question of directly determinable outlays, investments, processes, and perhaps a question (after the market has been tested a little) of cutting costs, lowering expenses, increasing turnover, speeding production.

Accounting can be of little or no service on the demand side, for accounting cannot deal with human wants, tastes, reactions. On the supply side, however, accounting can be of much service in keeping the businessman informed regarding the limits below which there will be no profit, regarding the points at which expenses might be reduced, and regarding the inner workings of his carefully proportioned investments. These however are all questions of cost or price—never questions of "value."

Cost is not value and is not entered in the accounts as such; cost is a "refusal price," the point at which profit or loss begins. The businessman's real interest in cost therefore is not in connection with setting prices or measuring value, but rather in the calculation of profits. On the basis of the profit (or loss) he withdraws his product from the market or adds a new one, thus influencing prices; or he cuts his costs, that is, he accepts the prices as determined elsewhere, yet continues to contribute his influence by keeping his supply on the market.

The businessman views society not in the broad sense as to ultimate causes as economists do, but as an individual bent upon finding a profit out of acting as an intermediary between demand and supply. In his contact with demand he must work in a practical way with such subjective elements as wants, tastes, etc. In his contact with supply the businessman deals with concrete units of goods, equipment, and services at definite contract prices. His success is conditioned as much by his choice of prices as by his choice of the kind of goods and number of units. Between these two—supply and demand—the businessman achieves his profit. According to his discernment and powers of observation in connection with demand, according to his skill in efficiently combining suitable materials and services in connection with supply, he profits well or poorly.

Accounting stands by to serve primarily in connection with the second phase of the businessman's activity—the supply or cost side. Its particular service lies, not in attempting to measure esteem (that is, value) but rather in the individualistic function of recording capitalistic investments and advances, and of weighing these against the returns flowing from them under the influence of management.

(Accounting Review, September, 1929)

17. The Cost Limit to Price

Accounting is concerned with *price,* however frequently the businessman may be concerned with *value.* The latter must of necessity estimate value, i.e., judge the importance which this or that object probably has in the mind of the buying public. And the buyer must also weigh alternatives and make choices, i.e., estimate values. This process is inescapably associated with all business and all consumption. But the accounting connected with this process is concerned only with the accomplished facts (price) that result from people's value judgments. Were accounting loosed from this anchor of established fact, it would be afloat on a sea of psychological judgments which, however inescapable in business and consumer actions, are beyond the power of accounting as such to express.

Much of the loose usage of the term "value" in accountancy may be due to a generally held view that value in business is "cost plus," that price equals cost plus profit. As a matter of fact however price less cost equals profit. The two expressions are by no means equivalent. Price is not a derived element; the reason is that profit is unknowable until exchange has occurred and therefore cannot be added, as a fact, in advance to cost. This is a difference between expectation and profit.

Actual price and real profit come into being at the same time when exchange takes place. Until that time the proper equation must be: offered price equals cost plus expected profit. In reality profit rather than price is the important unknown factor. After exchange has taken place, price is known, cost is already known, only profit remains to be computed, using the two known elements. Thus profit, not price, is the derivative. It is misleading therefore to think of the elements in the relationship as shown in the first equation.

In like manner there may be confusion of thought in the phrase "an article is worth what it costs." From the standpoint of a buyer this probably is not far from an acceptable statement if the transaction has been completed. But the phrase is more often used to refer to the stock of goods of a producer or seller. Here the phrase would rest upon a belief, consciously held or implied, that cost is the basis of value. But objects are not useful because they have cost productive effort; the effort is expended because the objects are considered useful. Goods are valuable not because they cost something; costs are incurred because goods will be valuable, or thought to be valuable. Hence cost is not the basis of value. If cost is to be justified as the basis for reporting an inventory of unsold goods, it must be by other reasons than that it expresses the value of the goods. As an expression of the *investment* in goods, cost is quite acceptable, but not as an expression of their value.

Another evidence of some misconception of the influence of cost in business is found whenever businessmen discuss unfair competition. Competitors offer unfair competition, it is said, when through ignorance of real costs they sell at prices which do not cover real costs. This is indeed serious competition and a fit subject for educational efforts by trade associations and others. But it is not, as is usually implied, an indication that prices are necessarily established by lowest cost-producers.

A producer who is ignorant of his real costs is practicing self-deception in regard to his profits, and this may lead him to be content—for a time —with less than reasonable price. But actual costs are none-the-less real though they are not recognized; real costs have to be covered in some way. It may be covered out of price, out of profits, or out of capital. Costs do not vanish; outsiders do not donate their goods and services; if price does not cover costs and leave a profit, then profit is cut into by the situation; and if the price is such that costs are not even met, then the goods and services acquired (costs) have been paid in part out of capital.

The ultimate consequence of a continuation of these circumstances is obvious—the producer who persists in his ignorance eliminates himself and releases the market from the menace of his acts. He is not a "low cost-producer" but a low profit-maker. He is a thorn in the side of the trade because he is content—knowingly or not—with less real profit than the others, and not because his costs are lower or because his "cost" plus profit, make lower prices.

The real nature of cost in relation to price is to furnish on the supply side the *limiting factor* to price—the point beyond which production cannot be maintained. One can sell a part of his total product consistently below real cost, provided other items carry enough profits to compensate; one can sell all of his products below real costs, provided the attempt is only temporary. But to sell all the products always below cost would soon exhaust the whole capital and thus eliminate the producer. His cost has been his limiting factor.

Cost is not, therefore, the basis of price by the addition of profit; it is the working limit of successive subtractions from "tentative price" in the process of finding the figure at which exchange will actually take place. One guesses what people will pay and guesses again if the first turns out badly, deducting something meanwhile from the first offer. Cost is the *warning point* in this process of successive repricing; it may be disregarded for a short time or for a few items, but ultimately its control is effective.

(Accounting Review, September, 1929)

18. Symbols of Reality

The balance sheet is fast losing its traditional characteristics as a summary of the balances of the real accounts after closing the nominal accounts in the ledger. The figures in the balance sheet no longer consist simply of *invested outlays* carried forward to a new fiscal period, although this aspect has been presented for a long time as an essential characteristic of the double-entry system. The balance sheet is coming to be considered as a statement of property valued at an amount equal to whatever securities are issued, or as a statement of "values" on which investors are entitled to earn a fair return.

In the light of these circumstances, some discussion of the economic nature of value and of the relation of value to accounting may be in order. Consideration should be given to value and price, for the failure clearly to distinguish these two concepts makes for confusion of thought today even as it did in the lifetime of Adam Smith and David Ricardo.

Fundamentally, value resides in someone's mind and is attributed to or read into an article, rather than residing inherently within it. Thus value is rooted in "desiredness," in the subjective importance of the thing in question, in its real or fancied usefulness.

Value varies with individuals and according to circumstances for the same individual; wants and tastes shift as one changes in age and condition; differential preference among men for the same things or for different things is the principal element which makes trading possible and keeps one man's gain from being another's loss, as once was thought to be the case. An article therefore can have more than one value at one time. In fact, it could conceivably have as many different values as there are individuals tentatively appraising it for themselves and as there are differing purposes actuating the individuals.

Assuredly value is a vague sort of a thing, subject to all the whims of mankind and turned by the least wind of altered circumstances. It is essentially psychological at base, and therefore is associated inseparably with demand. It always lies in the future—quite the contrary to the old idea that value was stored up labor of the past—it is always an appraisal of needs still to be experienced.

Whereas value is an estimate of what price might be, price itself is an established fact. Value is a subjective estimate of an article's relative importance; price however is a compromise between several such subjective estimates and is measured by the quantity of money for which the article is exchanged. Thus it takes two contending minds to make a price, just as it takes two to make a contract; a value however can exist in one mind alone, untouched by another. But there is no price in the economic sense except for closed transactions—exchanges. All else is estimate—tentative prices—price tags, so to speak. Bids and offers are not prices; they are tentative attempts to *find* a price, i.e., to find a common meeting ground of two valuations.

A seller's announcement (offered price) is not "value"; it is not even the seller's own "valuation." It is simply his attempt to read the minds of the whole body of purchasers. The merchant seeks to guess the strength of the demand and to set his figures accordingly; if sales do not follow, he knows the guess was wrong. He may then change the figures and try again, or he may attempt to influence demand in other ways—advertising and the like. If a sale is made, a price has appeared. The seller may never know whether or not he could have gotten more had he asked, for the buyer's valuation is within his own mind and not in the price he paid. The price of a closed transaction is usually as near as one can get to a definite expression of the buyer's valuation.

Thus bid and offer prices are a means of bringing about a meeting of wills and a resulting transfer of commodities; in a sense, prices (that is, words and figures) are mere signs and symbols representative of the reality which is in the mutually satisfactory exchange of commodities. And it is precisely in this capacity as symbol representations of realities that prices come into touch with accounting. Accounting, in all of its analyses of an infinite variety of transactions and in its records of innumerable financial occurrences, seeks to embody the realities of the moment in permanent figure representations—in symbols which lend themselves to arithmetical summarization and manipulation.

(*Accounting Review,* September, 1929)

19. Value-in-Use

Discussions regarding "value" and "valuation" are perennials in both accountancy and economics. Time and argument have brought some degree of agreement among economists concerning the primacy in economics of the problems of value. But among accountants there has not been a corresponding degree of agreement upon the issue of "value versus cost."

Cost was the only basis considered in early accounting because the function of bookkeeping did not extend beyond an accurate recording of the giving and receiving of goods, services, or money. If there was any process which might properly be called "accounting valuation," it was merely that of translating varied coinage into the common money of account, or of attaching to goods in barter a "price tag" expressed in terms of the local standard money of account. But this is not the modern connotation of the term.

Perhaps the most influential factor in bringing "valuation" into accounting thought was the stimulation given to auditing by the British companies acts of the middle nineteenth century. Corporations were largely owned by absentee stockholders and managed by elected directors having great powers of decision regarding enterprise finance and operation. Company creditors were still further removed from knowledge of company affairs than were the stockholders. Audits were prescribed by those Parliamentary acts apparently with the object, in the interest of these absentee parties, of bringing the actions of directors under independent scrutiny. Since stockholders and creditors of limited liability companies were protected only by the capital fund of the enterprise and the company's continuous business life, dependable reporting of accounting data became of greater importance than in the days when business enterprises were predominantly proprietorships or partnerships. This development of corporations and the attendant regulation thereof in the public interest—by means of accounting and auditing—were important forces in accentuating, if not creating, the accounting problems now suggested by the terms "accruals," "depreciation," "capital versus revenue expenditures."

Accrual accounting evolved to disassociate income from receipts and expense from disbursements. Revenue expenditures had to be distinguished from capital expenditures in order to permit long-lived assets to be treated differently in the accounts from the treatment accorded to expenses, for the latter made their whole contribution currently. Depreciation was the means of effecting a practical apportionment of fixed asset cost over a long life of productive usefulness.

This was accounting on a cost basis. The processes of estimating assets consumed (depreciation) and of determining income accrued and expenses deferred could hardly be properly called acts of valuation. They are better described as acts of apportioning original cost outlays into the necessary periods of revenue-earning operations. "Valuation" would refer to the subjective process of placing a market price of some kind on the objects in question, that is, of estimating their worth or usefulness. This is not the work of an accountant or the function of accounting. Yet accounting writers have used the term "valuation," loosely to be sure, but so frequently that readers of the literature get an impression unjustified by the facts that valuation is the central theme in accounting.

A part of the explanation of the confusing use of "value" and "valuation" in accounting is the seeming inability of the language to supply either a suitable word in place of "valuation" which would compactly express the processes of so adjusting receipts and disbursements that the record would disclose income and expense instead, or a word in place of "value" to express the arithmetic product of a number of physical units multiplied by a cost price per unit.[7]

Another part of the explanation, no doubt, is the failure of accountants to distinguish "value-in-exchange" and "value-in-use." That is not surprising, for accountants have seldom had much training in economics. Among economists this distinction has long been a familiar one.

Value has long been the central theme of economic philosophy. Much of the debate has been about such questions as, why do the same things have a different value for different people? Why does the value of an unchanged object vary from time to time? The clue was found in the concept of *utility*—"the power of giving satisfaction." Value, it was concluded, resides not so much in the object itself as in the idea of "satisfaction" which is held by the prospective users of the object.

Because the term "value" is thus deeply imbedded in economics as one of the chief elements in that increasingly popular philosophy, the connotations it carries from that field are likely to be the prevailing ones, and any concepts in conflict held elsewhere will be productive of confusion. The word "value" therefore should be cautiously used in accountancy or perhaps even abandoned.

What we discuss in accounting as "cost versus value" is in fact "value-in-use versus value-in-exchange." The former seems a natural material for accountants to treat, for the primary function of accounting is, as Professor W. A. Paton so well puts it, to record cost price as it enters an enterprise and to trace cost price through many intricate conversions until in the end it leaves the enterprise in one form or another. The latter term seems an unnatural material for accounting because value-in-exchange is essentially subjective and fleeting at best. It would seem therefore that accountants would have a direct responsibility for correctly disclosing value for use (original cost price) but very little responsibility for exhibiting as estimate of value for exchange (replacement or market prices).

(*Accounting Review*, September, 1935)

---

[7] One important economist explained value as a product of quantity (a measure of use value) times price (a measure of scarcity value) and contrasts this with the "purchasing power" meaning of value. John R. Commons, *Industrial Economics*, pp. 516-19.

20. Pressures for Valuations

The early choice of the balance sheet as the main statement tends to place finance above operations; and finance, in turn, looks upon value-in-exchange as basic. Why should the balance sheet (the statement which alone could give rise to questions of value for exchange purposes) have come to occupy first place in public accounting when the income statement (wherein value for exchange could not be at issue) would seem to be the natural summary of the chief data of a business enterprise? It is suggested that this preference may have arisen in British practice for the following reasons:

(1) The balance sheet included assets borrowed as well as assets invested and earned. Whereas the income statement reflected economic transactions only, the balance sheet showed the results of both financial and economic transactions.

(2) Most of the balance sheet items could be objectively verified. This afforded a convenient and tangible basis for the auditor's examination of the stewardship and fidelity of the directors as the stockholders expected him to do.

(3) The stockholders, being in effect outside of active management, were interested mainly in the amount of assets available for distribution (as profits) rather than in the details of the way current profits were being earned, as would be the case with insiders—active managers—who were responsible for results.

(4) It has been the basic theory of double-entry bookkeeping that the balancing item of "profit" in the balance sheet would be identical with the undivided portion of the accumulated sum of net profit items from the several profit and loss statements; hence the latter could safely be ignored by the auditor since the data were duplicated in the balance sheet.

In the beginning only original cost was used, but later a philosophy of conservatism dictated that original costs be occasionally modified by the auditor. The "cost-or-market" dictum is an example. It appears to have originated near the middle of the nineteenth century in connection with the development of commercial law in the German states. (Weiner, *Journal of Accountancy*, Vol. 48, p. 195; Hatfield, *Modern Accounting*, pp. 92, 102.) The rule was applied especially to the valuation of security investments held by banks but was also extended to include mercantile stocks of goods.

Depreciation is another example. Because the periodical amount was at best an argumentative estimate, businessmen often took advantage of that fact to make a "conservative valuation." The effect was, of course, to mix two different things: the amortization of original cost and the conservative reservation of past profits for future contingencies.

For the most part, this conservatism was the banker's or it was largely inspired by him. If it seemed to be the client's conservatism, he had the banker's loan in mind; if it seemed to be the auditor's conservatism, he but desired to anticipate the client's wish to satisfy the banker. Both client and auditor believed in the wisdom of conservatism, so they readily accepted the banker's view. The point is that, while the auditor was not clinging very hard to original costs, the seed of the idea was planted that value for exchange (sale or liquidation) and not value for use was the keynote of at least some parts of the balance sheet.

American income tax laws and regulations beginning in 1913 made the consistent use of original cost difficult in several ways. Depreciation was a large deduction in the calculation of taxes, and if the corporation could get "conservative" estimates accepted by the Bureau, the tax base would be smaller. And, further, as a purely expedient measure, it was made permissible under the law to restate the assets as of March, 1913, as a new depreciation base. A few years later the excess profits tax law presented a definition of "invested capital" as part of the computation of the profit which was to be exempt from the tax. One experienced observer writes of this period: "Many corporations restated their plant accounts in order to increase the surplus by restoring excessive depreciation or maintenance charges made according to the conservative ideas of accounting which were common before the war." (Stanley G. H. Fitch, *Journal of Accountancy,* July, 1935.)

It is obviously hard to cling to original costs when most counsel is against it. This was particularly the case from about 1924. "Permanently higher level of prices," said economists; "assets are to be judged by earning power, not cost," said investment bankers; "replacement costs can be used in the rate base," said the utility commissions; "the dividend base shall be the excess of aggregate assets over debt and stated capital," said various legislatures; "short of proven fraud directors have full legal authority to value assets as they see fit," said some courts. Then in 1931-33, an epidemic of asset write-downs followed closely upon the heels of the prior wave of write-ups, with the result of further unsettling the concept of usefulness of original cost.

There is then some basis for belief that original cost is not inviolate. The trend in recent opinion (i.e., in the 1930's) creates a strong impression that original cost has no standing whatever.[8]

There may be little prospect of value for exchange (purchase power) dropping entirely out of consideration. Nevertheless, accountants can advocate value for use (original cost) in season and out of season. If the views of spokesmen for the profession supported this approach, that fact would provide strong support for the almost defenseless individual practitioner wishing to convince his clients.

The profession could very well in a similar way support a rational and

---

[8] Twenty years later original cost is still under fire. But it is significant that a strong defending fire is appearing. (Comment added in 1954.)

realistic cost allocation theory of depreciation, that is, one which had as its sole objective the sensible amortization of past cost outlay—and turn a deaf ear to "value-shrinkage" depreciation—except to advocate surplus reserves to cover. This attitude would also lend support to the individual practitioner struggling to cling to original cost rather than "conservative values," "replacement values," "capitalization-of-earnings values," "insurable values," "security-for-loan values."

The individual would no doubt also welcome support for his view that capital stock account should uniformly be credited with the full consideration received from shares issued. He would welcome support in opposing the deliberate write-up and write-down of fixed assets under the influence of price-level changes. But his opinion is not asked by businessmen before the event. Even if he later ventured to assert that such valuations were not beyond criticism, he probably would face the counter-assertion that a simple merger or a newly formed corporation taking the property could establish the desired "value" beyond the accountants power to criticize.

(Accounting Review, September, 1935)

CAPITAL AND SURPLUS

1. Technical Terms

Accountants are familiar with the phrase "assets and liabilities"; perhaps occasionally someone wonders how the term arose. Another phrase once was widely used—"effects and debts." Was this the antecedent?

In 1761 an English author wrote that every trader who was in financial difficulty should "make out a general state of his effects, as well what he owes as what is due him, to deliver to his creditors when they assemble to examine his affairs in conformity with the second article of title eleven of the Ordinance of 1673." The advice was also given that merchants who could not pay their debts should file a petition "attaching two accounts which they shall sign and affirm to be true, the one of the value of their effects and the other of their debts."

These quotations, from Wyndham Beawes *The Merchants Directory* (2d ed., 1761) obviously refer to statements of assets and liabilities (if not to balance sheets derived from double-entry records) even though effects were to be reported in one "account" and debts in another.

An affirmation is also mentioned; it is of interest since it foreshadows certificates of professional auditors: "I, the underwritten, do certify to all whom it may concern, that the State here above of all my effects, as well debtors as creditors, contain the truth, and that I have not omitted anything, or made use of any person or names in it that are not my true and lawful creditors, in faith of which I have signed the present, the 29th day of May, 1750."

At another page the author wrote: ". . . he must also strike a balance for the greater ease of his creditors, that they may see with a cast of the eye the truth of his affairs and what they have to expect; and he must likewise put underneath the said State, an account of all losses that have happened to him . . . that he may justify his conduct to his creditors in case he has not effects sufficient to pay them their whole due, that they may have nothing to reproach him with."

Beawes also refers to the case of Miles *v.* Williams & ux. where this phrase occurs: "All those effects and debts which he could take in or turn into money." And again: "debts, effects and estate of the bankrupt." Reference is made to the statute 5, Geo. III, Section 1 for this sentence: "The Bankrupt is to discover to the commissioners upon oath such estate and effects as he may have."

Beawes undoubtedly drew upon French authors for many of his rules. He relied especially on Savary whose handbook on mercantile practice, in appropriate sections, expounded the French bankruptcy law of 1673.

Some phrases from the French author (6th ed., 1712) will illustrate how close the English was to the French terminology.

"Je soussigré certifie à tous qu'il appartiendra, que l'estat cy dessus de tous mes effets tant actifs que passifs, contient verité. . . ." [I the undersigned certify to all concerned, that the state of all my effects as well active as passive, comprise the truth. . . .]

The French author says "l'estat . . . de tous mes effets"; the English statute says "Estate and Effects." The French author says "l'estat de mes effets tant actifs que passifs"; the English author says "state of my effects, as well debtors as creditors," and also "as well what he owes as what is due him." The English court says "effects and debts," "debts, effects and estate." The French *estat* is thus translated "estate," or "state," meaning "statement"; *effets* is thus translated literally "effects," meaning properties, therefore assets.

In the quotations below the French use of *effets* is further varied. ". . . en cas qu'il ne se trouvant pas assez d'effets pour les payer entierment de leur du. . . ." [. . . in case that there cannot be found sufficient effects to pay (the creditors) entirely what is due them. . . .] "Avoir assez de bons e effets pour satisfaire ses creanciers." [To have sufficient of goods and effects to satisfy his creditors.] The French phrases *assez d'effets* and *assez de bons e effets* are faithfully rendered by Beawes as "has not *effects sufficient* to pay."

The modern word for "effects" (that is, properties) is "assets." Apparently the phrase "sufficient of effects" was shortened through long usage (or in translation) to the anglicized word "assets" (for *assez*). A literal re-translation of "assets" back into the original sense could use the term "sufficients" or "enoughs" to pay his debts.

Used as nouns, the adjectives "sufficient" and "enough" do not make clear sense to us whereas "effects" and "property" do. But "asset" was not now thought of as a direct translation of *assez*; it has become a true technical term and as such carries its own connotation—that of property available to pay debts. Later in business and accounting the term "assets" came to mean any property held by a business enterprise for use in its operation. Then, by extension, it was made to include any debit balance that was applicable to a future period under the accounting objective of trying to associate expense with revenue in the period when the expense made itself felt.

If anyone thinks of assets in the original meaning of the term, and lawyers often do, he may object to including under that heading any item which seems inappropriate for use in paying debts. But when one recalls that *assez* was a French adjective made over into a technical English noun, he ought not to object too much upon finding that "asset," once simply a legal term, has grown into a technical term in accounting as well and has a specific accounting meaning.

This is not the only case of an adjective evolving into a technical noun.

Another transformation that is clear to see involves the German terms for debit and credit in an account—*soll* and *haben*, literally "shall" and "have."

As bookkeeping developed in Italy, the principal verbs used in a sentence written to express a business transaction (especially a loan) came to be standardized in the Latin forms *debet dare* (shall give) and *debet habere* (shall have). When these terms were first brought over into Germany, they were translated literally as *soll geben* and *soll haben,* and these became the terms designating respectively the left and right side of an account. When German usage had completed its construction of double entry, the two basic technical names for the two sides of an account were not derived from the Latin roots such as are still clearly reflected in the English words debit and credit. From *soll geben,* the second word was dropped, leaving *soll* to mean "debit"; from *soll haben,* the first word was dropped, leaving *haben* to mean "credit."

Since technical terms are intended to express a limited meaning, their connotation from general usage cannot be relied on to furnish a clear clue to their technical significance. So it is with the term "asset." In accounting usage its technical meaning has developed beyond its meaning in law, where the term still retains most of the early coloring derived from *assez de effets.*

(editorial, *Accounting Review,* July, 1946)

2. Balance Sheet Headings

Most balance sheets of today are headed by the term "assets and liabilities." Others include "and capital" on the right side. There may be some opinion in favor of "assets and equities." But the logical appropriateness for corporations of "equities" in place of "liabilities and capital" has not yet overcome the desire to preserve the traditional emphasis on the dissimilarities between creditor and owner.

The heading has not always included three terms. Research has not been made that would indicate when the word "capital" was added to "assets and liabilities." Neither can a definite date be set for the beginning of the two-term heading, since a scattered early use could easily be the exception rather than the rule. However, the dates of some early usage may be interesting for the indication they may give of the persistence of earlier terminology.

In some cases the headings were simply Debtor, Creditor, or Dr., Cr. Thomas King used these terms in a textbook of 1717. Robert Hamilton (1797) wrote, "The Dr. of the Balance Sheet contains every kind of property belonging to you and every debt owing to you; and the Cr. contains every debt owing by you: therefore the difference of the sides will exhibit your nett estate" (p. 286). The Bank of France (reported in

Hunts Merchants Magazine) for 1841 and 1845 also used these simple headings. The London and Westminster Bank in 1851 spelled the headings out.

Incidentally Hamilton (p. 285) also said regarding inventory: "It is much more proper to value the goods on hand in conformity with current prices, than at prime cost; for the design of offering any value is to point out the gain or loss; and the gain is in reality obtained so soon as the prices rise, or the loss suffered as soon as they fall."

The East India Company is the basis of an article in the same magazine. In the company's accounts for 1733 the heading is "The Effects and Credits." It is noteworthy moreover that the article (1840) refers to the exclusion from company reports of forts and buildings abroad "because they were not assets . . . any further than they could be disposed of." Thus implying that the word "assets" was restricted to uses referring to items available for paying debts.

A number of authors of bookkeeping texts near the turn of the nineteenth century were using the word "effects." Robert Hamilton (1797) said a bankrupt was compelled to deliver "an account of his effects upon oath." Patrick Kelly (1803) referred to "my effects, both real and personal." William Jackson (1816) wrote that a merchant must keep accounts of his effects, his debts active and passive, and his losses and gains. James Maginnes (1817): "Take an inventory of your effects." Nicholas Harris (1842): "Inventory of my effects and debits."

Peter Duff (1848) reflected a small change in terminology. He spoke of making an opening entry of "effects and liabilities." In 1853 Thomas Jones in a textbook gave to a balance sheet the heading "Resources and Liabilities"; and in the body of his discussion (as pp. 119-20) he referred to "assets." But this last was not in a statement heading.

There is other evidence to indicate that the newer terminology was widely accepted about the middle of the nineteenth century. The same Thomas Jones, in an article in *Hunts Merchants Magazine* (forerunner of *Commercial and Financial Chronicle*), used the heading "Resources and Liabilities" in 1843. Bank statements published in that periodical for 1839, 1848, and 1850 also used this heading. Some banks preferred "Liabilities and Means" (Bank of New York, 1844), presumably intending "means" to be equivalent to the earlier term "effects"—cash being a *means* of discharging liabilities.

"Assets and Liabilities" was the heading used by banks in South Carolina in 1850. But the Bank of England used "Liabilities and Assets" in 1839, and the banks in Rhode Island (1840) followed the English usage. Published statistics of the banks of New Orleans (1842) had one column headed "assets."

Apparently banks were the first to use the term "assets" regularly in statement headings. Possibly this may have been because with them liquidity (debt-paying ability) was an important matter, as it was also in the law of bankruptcy and trusteeships. The use of "effects" and "resources" in ordinary bookkeeping may have reflected the authors' desire to avoid a foreign-sounding technical term, such as "assets." Certainly many authors stressed their intention to make the subject simple; this would be one way to try for that result.

(editorial, Accounting Review, July, 1946)

3. Assets and Surplus

One of the handicaps that accountants work under is a technical vocabulary made up for the most part of words in common use. Thus any reader of an accountant's words, by supplying his own connotation, may miss entirely the essential thought intended.

Some words create special difficulties because of long usage in a certain setting. For example, the word "asset" has so long been used with a legal connotation that accountants now are sometimes tempted to drop it as an accounting term. "Surplus" is another word that tends to mean different things to lawyers and to accountants. But abandoning terms that seem to contribute to misunderstandings would only shift the burden to substitute words. And these might serve no better; lacking as they must the rich connotations of the familiar terms, they perhaps could not serve so well.

Probably a more helpful approach would be to labor at gaining an understanding of the other person's connotation and at explaining our connotation to him. This would not be easy; and it might take a long time to complete the meeting of minds. Yet the attempt could be beneficial from the beginning for it would at once break down the thought that there could be any proprietary interest in a word.

It may be interesting therefore to take note of the origins of these two items, since current connotation often continues to express early meanings. If one may judge rightly from the examples quoted in historical dictionaries (such as Murray's) the word "surplus" has from the beginning been the more general and "assets" has been the more technical term.

Surplus (or surplusage) derives from the medieval Latin word *superplus,* a term which as early as the sixteenth century was sometimes rendered into English as "overplus" (Ympyn, 1547). Usually the sense that fits the early context of the word is that of simple excess or remainder, as surplus of yarn, of meat, of money, of faults, of population. Adam Smith (1776) wrote of an exchange of surplus pelts for blankets; Benke (1790) indicated that surplus produce forms the income of a landed proprietor; Jevons (1878) said the rent of better land will consist of the surplus of its produce over that of the poorest land.

The term is used in law as well as economics. An English statute of

1553 (7, Edw. VI, c. 1) says "deliver . . . the surplusage and overplus of the value . . ."; a later statute of 1670 (22, Charles II, c. 10) speaks of making a distribution of "the surplusage of the estate of any person dying inestate"; in 1827 the law of inheritance clearly states that surplus from the sale of land did not form part of the personal estate that could be passed by residuary bequest.

It is not surprising therefore that lawmakers writing statutes relating to business enterprises should before long use the term "surplus profits" in much the same manner that one would refer to surplus pigs. Presumably it did not occur to any one then to ask whether there were any other kinds of profits or to inquire, if some profits were surplus profits (i.e., excess), what the word "profits" meant without the adjective.

The word "assets" also got its legal significance very early. In the English law of estates (as in Lyttleton's *Tenures,* 1574) the word was spelled in the sixteenth century as at present, assets. In old French it was *assez* (enough). In earlier usage (late popular Latin), *ad satis* (to a sufficiency) was a frequent substitute for *sates* (enough) and had much the same connotation as was later given to *assez.*

The Anglo-French law phrase *aver assetz,* a term from the law of estates and executorship, is a significant transitional term carrying a Latin meaning over into English. Literally it says "to have sufficient"; but to make the meaning clear it needs to be rendered as "to have sufficient [effects to satisfy the testator's debts and legacies]."

In Blackstone's *Commentaries* (1768) the author points out that a deed by an ancestor was binding on an heir only in so far as the latter had inherited property "sufficient to answer the charge . . . which sufficient estate is in law called assets." (Vol. II, p. 244.)

By easy stages the meaning has passed from that of property sufficient to cover a testator's legacies, to that of the property applicable to the payment of the debts of a bankrupt, and thence to that of the property of a going concern available to creditors of the enterprise if they should seize it at that moment because of suspected insolvency.

These concepts of the meaning of "assets," having been long embedded in legal thinking, continue to the present time to tie the term subconsciously for many people to some issue of financial solvency. But accountants and businessmen must often use "assets" in a much broader sense than lawyers. The result often is a failure to understand each other. All concerned should realize that the term has a double meaning that is easily grasped. Assets are properties (and property rights) that are judged useful to the economic purposes of the owning enterprise, and were acquired by it to serve those purposes. At the same time various types of debt were incurred incidental to acquiring the needed working properties. And because of these debt contracts, assets must also be recognized as properties capable of being realized upon for meeting financial obligations.

For some purposes one concept will be the more important; but the other has its moments of importance too. For accounting use it is clear that the most basic idea of assets will be one related to economic purposes—because the primary service of accounts is rendered to an economic enterprise. Since the act of incurring liabilities is only incidental to economic productivity, the service of assets for paying debts is to accounting no more than a secondary meaning of the term.

From the dual meaning of assets, it follows that the balance sheet has a dual significance. It may be considered as a "solvency statement" presenting a contrasting of debts and the possible means of their discharge. And it may be considered as a "capital statement" wherein first emphasis is given to the productive left side rather than to the unproductive right side where the emphasis lies in the other case. Since the basic significance of financial statements in business relates them to the process of earning profits, it must be understood that the list of assets may very well include some items that would have little debt-paying power in the event of enterprise liquidation. But this use need not be misleading; it may reasonably be assumed that all users of the balance sheet will be well enough informed to be aware of the way the two concepts of assets limit each other.

(editorial, *Accounting Review,* July, 1946)

4. Surplus Terminology

If an example were sought from accounting to show that living language changes, the word "surplus" would be a good one to use. It was not originally a bookkeeping term, having come rather late into accounting from earlier use in law. Its antecedent in bookkeeping was "profit." But before the noun "surplus" became as prominent in accounting literature as is the noun "profit," it passed through a long chrysalid stage in law as an adjective in the phrase "surplus profits."

Why was a modifying adjective "surplus" added to the noun, "profits?" Why was the word "profits" later dropped from the phrase, leaving "surplus" to stand alone as a noun? Why were adjectives subsequently added to the new noun to produce the modern term "earned surplus?" Perhaps direct answers cannot be read from a few examples of changing usage; but it may be interesting to look at some samples nevertheless.

A sample of corporation charters granted by American state legislatures between 1822 and 1869 showed in most cases that no specific mention was made of the source from which dividends could be declared, presumably relying on the common law to control the matter. A few however specifically refer to "clear profits," "actual profits"; and few more say that profits available for dividends are determined by the directors "after setting aside a surplus fund." In New York a statute of 1825 declared it unlawful to make any dividend except from surplus profits. This statute was entitled "An act to prevent fraudulent bankruptcy by incorporated companies." The theory apparently was that a dividend not from profits would work a fraud on the creditors by conveying to shareholders an amount of property which should be kept to pay creditors.

An earlier example shows a similar lack of a sharp distinction between profit and surplus. The charter of the Bank of the United States (1790) provided that dividends could come only from profits and that the directors should lay before the stockholders a "statement of debts . . . and of the surplus profits if any after deducting losses." A bylaw provided that assenting directors would be personally liable "for the amount of the surplus so divided," if dividends exceeded the profit.

The clearest meaning in these various examples is that reflected in the phrases "clear profit," "actual profits." The intention plainly was to specify profits clear or net of expenses and losses, and to exclude from the dividend base unreal credits of every kind since these would not be "actual." These distinctions are more important now than they ever were; but modern terminology sometimes still fails to make them clear.

At about this same time charters and statutes also used the terms "surplus fund" and "surplus profits." "Surplus" in the first phrase is obviously connected with the idea of profit assets held back from dividends, presumably because the assets were needed for current operations or perhaps for future dividends. In the second phrase, the adjective "surplus" probably was intended to mean profits over and above expenses and losses, that is, profits not needed to cover revenue charges. In a sense, therefore, the phraseology seems aimed at correcting the same bad practices which presumably created the need for the phrases "clear profit," and "actual profit." This intention seems present, for example, in the charter of the Bank of the United States where deducting losses is specifically mentioned in the same clause that names profits as the dividend base. In the bylaw of the bank, surplus seems to be used as a noun, but actually it is still an adjective with the related noun "profits," being understood from the context without repetition.

There is a reference in *Hunts Merchants Magazine* to the report of the Liverpool and Manchester Railway of 1843, where it was said that the net profit (as the difference between receipts and expenses) was increased "by the addition of an undivided surplus." If all profits (except those specially earmarked) were customarily distributed, it would be quite natural to think of the dividend base (profit) as being augmented from an occasional carry-over from the past. We would now say it the other way—increase the prior surplus by the addition of current net profit.

In the same year the other usage was also reflected. In a statistical statement about the Eastern Railroad it was said that the old surplus reserve fund was a certain amount and that the surplus fund was increased a certain amount as a result of the year's operations. In 1845 it was said about the New York and Erie Railroad that its eastern division earned "a considerable surplus beyond the current expenses." The same magazine in 1847 said that the Reading Railway, after paying all expenses, had a surplus of net earnings of a certain amount. And of the South Carolina Railroad it was said that one item in the auditor's property statement was surplus income (probably meaning undivided profits).

In these examples the word surplus has been used to refer to (1) an undivided prior balance, (2) a reserve fund, (3) an excess of revenue above expenses, and (4) an income item in a property statement. Yet in spite of an apparent diversity of usage, the connotation never gets far away from that of profits, though the profits concerned may be those related to current expenses, to a prior carry-forward, or to the present dividend base. Thus the term "surplus" at about 1850 is not yet linked directly to assets; but the use of the phrase "surplus assets" is not far away in the future.

After the middle of the nineteenth century the term "surplus assets" appears in court cases, especially cases in Great Britain. In 1869 "whole surplus" was used in referring to assets of an enterprise in dissolution. Surplus assets, it was said, must be distributed pro rata.

In 1889 and in 1894 the courts referred to dividing the surplus after payment of liquidation expenses. In 1896 a court tried to link the two terms by saying that surplus assets means surplus profits (as a synonym?) and then explained that surplus assets are those remaining after payment of debts and recoupment of capital (New Transval Co., ch. 750, 1896).

According to this last concept, profit will be expressed by the assets remaining after an enterprise liquidates debts and capital. And since these profits stand in the form of assets, surplus assets are surplus profits. Presumably by transfer of meaning, the same identity of terms would carry over to a going concern. Thus surplus asset value (however derived) would become distributable as surplus profits. American financial practice in the 1920's often fell into this pit of false identity.

But the British courts were too alert to fall into that terminological trap. They have ruled as follows: In 1870 (Salisbury v. Metropolitan Railway, 22 L.T. 829), an unrealized increase in the value of land is not profit; in 1894 (Vernier v. the General and Commercial Investment Trust, 2 Ch. 239), an unrealized value decrease due to fluctuating prices of fixed assets is not loss; in 1899 (National Bank of Wales, 2 Ch. 629), a surplus upon the valuation of assets is not necessarily profit; in 1918 (Ammonia Soda Co., 1 Ch. 266), write-up of fixed assets could not create a surplus to meet a deficit from trading operations.

(editorial, Accounting Review, July, 1946)

5. Surplus, American Style

American courts have used the term "surplus" in various ways. A sample of seventy cases (one-third being dated between 1861 and 1889) shows the word used as an adjective (thirty-one cases), as a noun (twenty-three cases), and as a noun modified by an adjective (sixteen cases). There was some tendency for the use as an adjective to decrease as the years passed and for the use as a noun to increase. As an adjective the most frequent use had the form "surplus profits" with "surplus earnings" following closely. In a few instances, mostly early cases, "surplus fund" was referred to.

When "surplus" is used alone as a noun, the possibilities for confused meaning grow greater since the word seems to refer sometimes to profits, sometimes to assets. In Williams *v.* Western Union Telegraph Co. (93 N.Y. 162-1883) the court referred to surplus in a general sense as the excess of property over the limit defined by charter (i.e., authorized capital stock) but went on to say that in a strict legal sense surplus is always regarded as surplus profits. From the context of other cases it is clear that the word sometimes refers to assets and sometimes to profits.

It was perhaps not well understood until more recently that the word "profits" always carries within it a reference to "surplus assets," but that the phrase "surplus assets" does not always connote "profits." This relationship exists because "profit" has a meaning limited to asset gain realized from actual exchanges, whereas the phrase "surplus assets" may include a change in asset values by appraisal and without exchange, or may refer to liquidations which result in residual (surplus) assets.

It is confusing rather than helpful to use alternatives such as "surplus or net profit" as is sometimes done in statutes. Does this mean "surplus (that is, net) profit," or does it mean to allow a choice of either "surplus" (assets) or "net profit?" Other combinations are equally unclear: profits and surplus (current profits and prior surplus); earnings or surplus; surplus or undivided profit.

The noun surplus is sometimes modified in the law cases by an adjective; usually the accompanying word is such as undivided, undistributed, accumulated, or distributable. Later additional adjectives such as earned, paid-in, capital, appraisal are used. And as a result of attaching adjectives the intended meaning grows clearer, but not wholly clear. For "paid-in surplus" can refer only to assets (invested) and not at all to profits (earned); "earned surplus" can refer only to profits (earned) and not to assets (invested); "appraisal surplus" can refer neither to assets as they were invested nor to profits newly earned. The problem of clear terminology is still plainly present.

The use of no-par stock and the practice of appraising fixed assets some years ago combined to generate many of the modern problems of surplus terminology. But the roots of the problem reach far back of these current practices.

Perhaps in law "profits" became "surplus profits" out of an attempt to express the idea of "profits net of expenses and losses." Perhaps "surplus profits" was later compressed to "surplus" in order by indirection to leave paid-in surplus available for current distributions to stockholders. For example, the New York Assembly in 1881 (following a statute of 1825) made directors liable for dividends "except from surplus profits," and in 1924 changed the phrase to read "except from surplus." And perhaps the use of no-par stock, with its accompaniment of stated capital and paid-in surplus, produced (under the concept of unimpaired capital as the prevailing dividend test) such unpredictable uses of surplus accounts that the single term "surplus" needed to be replaced by "earned surplus," "appraisal surplus," "paid-in surplus."

The evolution of the use of "surplus" is a typical illustration of the need for a continuous scrutiny of technical terms. For they have a habit of accumulating different meanings, especially if they are words that also are in general use. Not definition and redefinition, but explanation of connotations is called for; not abandonment of useful terms, but alertness to new shades of meaning is indicated.

(editorial, *Accounting Review*, July, 1946)

6. An Overworked Term

Although the English language is the richest in number of available words, the important word "capital" is badly overworked. It is used to mean: assets originally contributed; a specified portion of the original consideration for shares issued; the total par of stock issued; the total assets segregated into one enterprise; the net worth as of a given date; the amount of property which must not be distributed as dividends. Moreover the context, especially in financial statements, does not help the reader very much to sense the meanings intended, although adjectives can help.

In its most frequent use the word has a legal connotation, as partner's capital, capital stock, etc. Their usage connects the word capital with the nondebt portion of the balance sheet right side and derives its significance mainly from legal concepts surrounding estates and insolvency.

The companion word assets has indications of similar legal origin. It apparently came out of the French word *asez* (enough). The term as used in France originally referred to the sufficiency of a deceased person's property to cover his debts and legacies. Apparently the principal consideration was the debt. They were thought of first; the property was secondary, being security back of the debts. Today it seems more natural to think first of the property that is being managed in the interest of the people who have contributed assets to the enterprise. The point of view taken when an enterprise is operating as a going concern and when it is insolvent is necessarily very different. The best terminology therefore would be one that would clearly indicate which of the two fundamental conditions was referred to.

Both "capital" and "asset" often contain a legal rather than an economic connotation. They are, therefore, poorly adapted to the real concept involved, for the subject matter of bookkeeping is basically economic and only incidentally legal.

Capital is also one of the basic terms of economics, but the point of view is quite different from that expressed in law. In economics capital refers to property. Economics looks at the left side of the balance sheet for capital; law sees capital as a part of the right side. Since a business enterprise is an economic entity before it is a legal entity, it is more logical to conceive of the balance sheet as the statement of an economic entity designed to reflect the properties and investments attached to that enterprise. An economic form of balance sheet then would be as follows:

Balance Sheet[1]

Properties	Investments

"Investments" include all items on the right side of the statement: accounts payable, bonds payable, capital stock, surplus, and reserves. If the statement is relabeled as follows,

Balance Sheet

Capital Forms	Capital Sources

the meaning which underlies "properties" and "investments" stands out more clearly.

One further statement will even more strongly emphasize the point here under consideration. This time "capital" appears in the heading; the whole balance sheet is but a "capital statement."

Capital Statement

Kinds (Classified)	Origins (Classified)

Bilanz

(Aktiva)	(Passiva)
Vermögen	*Kapital*

Here it is plainly suggested that investments (*Kapital*) are passive (*passiva*) and await the final results, while properties (*Vermögen*) are active (*aktiva*) in producing results.

These various "balance sheets" reveal the essential (economic) nature of capital. Capital is recognized as a single element even if it may be viewed from two sides, as one sees the "heads and tails" of a penny. The balance sheet is *all* capital (property). But its bilateral form enables the reader to see property (1) as it exists in fact, and (2) as it was invested by its contributors. In a sense, therefore, the balance sheet shows capital on the left side and capital again on the right.

---

[1] German balance sheet terminology is even more significant.

Obviously the same word ought not to be used in both sides of so important a document, as seems to be implied in the present practice. Accountants speak of capital assets (on the left side) and of capital stock (on the right). But it is only on the right side that the word "capital" is actually spelled out on the statement.

Should the attempt be made to drop the use of the word capital as an account name? Because accounting is so closely associated with economic enterprises, it would seem logical for it to develop a terminology upon an economic base. Capital might be a good place to start.

The essential nature of the elements which deserve the name of capital is economic. The names which label the kinds of capital existing in an enterprise are listed on the left side of the "capital statement." Nothing need be said of them here; for the most part (except the word "assets") the names are quite descriptive as they are. But the same cannot be said of the items on the right side.

No change is suggested in regard to debts; the names in use (accounts, notes payable, bonds, etc.) are already free from any confusing association with the term "capital." They form a class of "outside" equities contrasting with "inside" equities (capital stock, surplus, reserves, etc.). The outside sources of economic capital represent people or companies who advance property on contract for a short period of time and those who advance upon long-term contracts. These sources may obtain various forms of priority and security through the terms of the contracts themselves. But in addition, because of the limited liability of shareholders, those who advance (lend) property have a further protection from the loss-absorbing margin created by the "inside" suppliers of economic capital. This situation suggests that *margin* is a better key word than *capital* for this section of the statement. The classification along these lines would be as follows:

Capital Sources: (Equities)

(1) Outsiders:
Who advance property for short terms (debts)
Who advance property for long terms (bonds)

(2) Insiders:
Who contribute a margin (stock)
Who accumulate a margin (surplus)

Specific new account names for the latter section (old names in parentheses) could be:

Margin for Protection of Creditors (Capital Stock)
Margin for Fluctuation of Property Values (Capital Surplus)
Margin for Equalization of Dividends (Earned Surplus)
Margin for Specific Purposes (Surplus Reserves)

Accountants who still have a bookkeeper's liking for short account names might prefer:

> Creditor Margin
> Fluctuation Margin
> Dividend Margin
> Reserved Margin

or these:

> Dedicated Capital
> Returnable Capital
> Revaluation Capital
> Retained Earnings

Such a terminology would have an economic rather than a legal base. But its absorption into law is problematical. Lawyers have a distaste for new terms not tested in common law. And its acceptance in accountancy is unlikely until accountancy breaks the parental (law) apron strings and openly establishes the new alliance (economics) which has been implicit within it from its medieval beginning as double-entry book-keeping.[2]

In the ten years since W. A. Paton made use of the very logical term "equities" to head the right side of the balance sheet, there has been little disposition to adopt this word into the working vocabulary of accountants. The above suggested terms are here recorded in the interest of possible further discussions of basic concepts.

(Accounting Review, December, 1932)

7. Conflicting Ideas

The idea involved in the word "dividend" is related both to the concept of enterprise income (an aspect of earning power) and to the concept of enterprise solvency (an aspect of capital). Since the terms capital and income are by intention sharply distinct, this apparently alternative approach to the calculation of a dividend base bears within it the seeds of a conflict in ideas. If we think of dividends as being a certain kind of withdrawal of proprietary assets, another source of conflicting ideas appears through an unconscious neglect to distinguish sufficiently between a proprietorship and a corporation. Why has this come about?

When an issue is raised about excessive withdrawals, proprietorship law sharply stresses solvency rather than profit. A proprietor may ignore the distinction between his profit and his capital if he needs to withdraw assets, though surely it were wiser to learn from good records which element was affected by his decision. His creditor, however, is protected

---

[2] "One theory of the balance sheet rests upon the idea that the statement is a means of calculating [divisible] profits. This concept originated under influence of ideas which evolved in connection with the juristic development of corporations and which to this day cannot be shaken loose from their domination." Nichlisch, *Die Betriebswirtschaft,* p. 704.

in any event by the right to seize proprietary property whenever he can find it if that is necessary to pay the debt.

It is not customary to refer to proprietor's withdrawal of profit assets as a "dividend," for he is not dividing or sharing what is already his. We think of that term as applying exclusively to corporations. But it was not always thus. In the days of British parliamentary companies (East India Company, Hudson's Bay Company, etc.), the term used was "division" rather than "dividend." The distinction is significant. These companies at first operated as trading ventures, not as continuing enterprises. Merchants contributed their own goods to the "joint-stock pile," and when the voyagers returned the whole property (or its proceeds) was divided among these contributors. If the share then received (the "division") was larger than the amount invested, the person concerned had gained the difference. His profit was knowable only after the particular venture had been terminated.

This was not the case where proprietors were using Italian double-entry records. The peculiar essence of "enterprise accrual accounting," as this method could be called, probably dates several generations before the appearance of the first printed text in bookkeeping—Paciolo, 1494. That essence lay in two facts, (1) that by following its rules for record-making the proprietor accumulated his transaction facts as they occurred, and (2) that the resulting carefully organized records made it possible for him to calculate his accumulated profit at any time (via his income and expense accounts) without terminating his business, actually or hypothetically.

In this contrast of methodology we can see other germs of conflict of ideas about calculating the most significant figure resulting from transacting business. In one case inflowing income less outflowing cost of goods sold and expenses gives "profit." This method was associated with the idea that the enterprise was a continuing organization. If continuity rather than periodic termination was the central fact, then calculation of profit from the record rather than from final proceeds was a rational procedure. If the concern was cast in the mold of a terminable venture, rational procedure would suggest making the calculation only at termination. But an individual, comparing his return with his investment, would arrive at a figure that could properly be called "surplus" (or deficit) rather than "profit" (or loss).

The point of the contrast is this. The two calculated results seem identical. "Profit" seems to carry within it the idea of a remainder (a surplus), and "surplus," meaning an improved status, seems to speak of profit. Yet this identity is only superficial. It is important that we shall distinguish calculated results derived from data available only at termination of an enterprise and results derived from currently accumulating data in a continuing enterprise. The two terms profit and surplus can make that distinction. Yet in accounting we often fail to use them carefully for that purpose.

Dividend law, falling into the same error, sometimes contributes to unclear thinking. One rule may speak of profits, another of surplus, and a third of both in the phrase "surplus profits." Different courts in ruling upon comparable situations may speak in one instance of profit resulting from excess of income over expense as being the significant fact where a dividend is in question; in another case the significant fact may be stated as the excess of the value of the assets over the sum of liabilities and capital. One phrasing speaks of a calculated profit, another of a calculated surplus. Yet termination of enterprise is not a fact in either situation. Accountants feel that different methods of calculation should reflect a difference in circumstances; they reason that, if the circumstances are different, the results are not strictly identical even though the figures might be the same.

The fact of limited liability is also significant. Modern limited liability companies, with their continuity of life and operations, slowly evolved out of terminable joint-venture trading. "Dividends" evolved out of "divisions." By use of double entry a dividend base became knowable almost at will and long before liquidation could take place. Included with these changes was a conversion from agency accounting (shipmasters reporting to home merchants) to proprietary accounting (profit calculation without termination).

From the example set by continuing proprietary enterprises wherein limited liability was absent, the incorporated companies derived a particularly useful method of accounting. Actual trading activities however were little different from those followed in separate ventures except that continuity and limited liability became enterprise characteristics.

In some ways this combination was a fortunate one. By use of double-entry records an accounting figure for surplus was ascertainable in a balance sheet constructed from records, and an account-calculated profit figure was obtainable in a profit and loss statement constructed from records. Yet the mixing of differing background ideas and the continued and often indiscriminate use of the terms surplus and profit have had some unfortunate consequences, particularly in providing opportunities for confused thinking about the meaning of "dividend base" in corporation practice.

Company directors, being in a better position to have dependable knowledge of company affairs than other interested people, quite logically acquired personal liability for improper dividends. According to early statutes in Great Britain there were three kinds of improper dividends: (1) those not out of company profits (7, 8 Vic, 110, 1844), (2) those which reduce capital stock without authorization (8, 9 Vic, 16, 1845), (3) those declared when the company is insolvent (18, 19 Vic, 133, 1855).

These situations present three kinds of fraud. A dividend not from profit is contrary to the concept lying within the word "dividend." Investments are made so the company may hold assets (capital) with which to earn profits; only dividends tied into profits will preserve the distinction between the "tree" and its "fruit." Other dividends are fraudulent because by name they seem to recognize this important distinction whereas in reality they do not do so. A dividend which constitutes an unauthorized reduction of capital stock is a fraud because it is a false representation to the recipient shareholder that there have been commensurate profits. A dividend declared when the company is insolvent is a fraud on the shareholders from being a false representation of existing profit, and it is a fraud on the creditor from being a disbursement to shareholders of assets to which the creditor has a prior claim.

These three dividend texts can be made into two. The first of the above is a profits test; it asks the question: Are there profits enough? The other two are subtypes of an assets test; they ask the question: Are there assets enough? We are thus back to the conflicting ideas involved in the terms surplus and profit. If there are surplus assets (in excess of liabilities and capital stock), dividends are possible without director liability. If there are profits (excess of income over expense), dividends are possible without director liability. Does this not set the stage for confusion? Shall we look to balance sheet or income statement for the clue? What course should we follow if there is no exclusion from the dividend base (via statute or common law) of price-level change?

The effects of change in price level are very much in mind today. In this connection it is interesting to observe that the British courts a good many years ago clarified the statutory meaning of "profits" in two important particulars. The essence of one case in 1870 (Salisbury *vs.* Metropolitan Railway Company, 22 L.T. 839) was that price-level increases did not produce profit in a dividend sense. In the Vernier Case (2 Ch. 239, 1894) the ruling can be said to mean that price-level decrease did not produce loss in a dividend sense.

These ideas strike the reader as reasonable and logical interpretations of the basic idea lodged in the word "dividend." Whether or not the thought was in the judge's mind at the time, it is a noteworthy fact that these two decisions reflected sound economic reasoning. Adam Smith made the point a century or more earlier (1776) that gains are made only if goods "change masters." He could properly have extended the thought by adding that losses chargeable against profits should be directly recognized only if the goods changed masters under loss-producing conditions. But perhaps this contra point was assumed as a self-evident corollary. We now speak of realizing profit in much the same sense as the economist's old-fashioned phrase. If he had clearly placed his prestige behind the companion idea, we perhaps might now have less confusion of thought regarding the accounting treatment of losses, and perhaps fewer conflicting ideas about the dividend base.

(*Hermès*, Quebec, Spring, 1953)

8. The Trust Fund Doctrine

The ideas of "dividend base" expressed in American state statutes seem at first to be similar to those in British company law and thus would provide a similar background of corporate practice that would have an influence upon accounting ideas. But it is useful to search out differences, since knowledge of their whys help establish awareness of the intertwining of ideology from dividend law, corporation finance, and accounting theory.

Our ideas of dividend base are three in number: (1) no dividends except from profits (or surplus profits); (2) no dividend when the company is insolvent; (3) no dividend if company net assets are less than the liabilities and capital.

The first of these rules seems particularly similar to one of the British rules. However, the frequent use of the term "surplus profits" in our statutes indicates a dislike for relying on the word "profit" alone. Possibly this may have resulted from a belief among some legislators that the word profit standing alone might be constructed to authorize dividends out of current profits although a balance sheet deficit was present. Or it might be that the adjective "surplus" was often used in an attempt briefly to convey the thought that the dividend base was to be balance sheet surplus, i.e., prior undivided profits plus or minus the results of current period operations. It should be noted that capital gains and losses in the United States have long been considered adjuncts to operating results. Thus a capital loss entered direct to surplus would there meet current operating gains, the two together becoming the key figure of the net dividend base. A separation of capital loss and operating gain (leading to a dividend from the latter alone) could be considered in the United States as disregard for proper creditor protection.

In regard to the second rule, a dividend when the company was insolvent would create director liability, not because the action would be called director's fraud, as in England, but simply because creditor protection had been impaired by the director's disregard for the absentee creditor's interest.

The third rule is sometimes stated with "liabilities and capital" as the dividing line between dividend and no dividend. If the "value of the assets" is less than the sum of these two items, a declared dividend will make the directors liable. In later years under the statutes of no-par stock, many states have changed the older rule by making "liabilities and stated capital" the dividing line. The two ways of stating the rule give

very different results. This follows from the fact that by one wording
capital is impaired and dividends stopped when losses cut into contributed capital (though the company is still solvent), whereas by the other
rule "stated" capital is not considered impaired and dividends need not
be stopped until losses have first wiped out "paid-in" surplus as well as
operation-derived earned surplus.

Where British law rested director liability upon unauthorized return
of capital to stockholders, American law looks upon a dividend declared
when losses have impaired capital (or stated capital) as creating director
liability because the prior asset margin protecting creditors has been
decreased by director action. Although the distinction here is not great,
it is expressive of differing modes of thought. And it may be worthwhile
therefore to examine further the concept of creditor protection which
lies back of the American ideas.

A leading judicial decision in this connection was rendered in 1825
by the Supreme Court of the United States (Wood *vs*. Dummer, 13 Mason
308). Mr. Justice Storey said in part:

> "It appears to me very clear upon general principles as well as legislative
> intention that the capital stock of banks is to be deemed a pledge or trust fund
> for the payment of the debts contracted by the bank. . . . The individual stock-
> holders are not liable for the debts of the bank in their private capacities. The
> charter relieves them from personal responsibility, and substitutes the capital
> stock in its stead. . . . Bill holders and other creditors have first claims upon it;
> stockholders have no rights until all other creditors are satisfied. Their rights
> are not to the corporation stock, but to the residuum (assets) after all demands
> on it are paid."

Directors therefore were not charged with fraud for paying company
assets to stockholders before all creditors claims had been paid. Their
responsibility rested upon two conditions: (1) the stockholder's private
property could not be reached by the injured creditors; (2) the directors,
like trustees, had accepted with their office a responsibility for making
special effort to safeguard the rights of absentee interests. For more than
two generations, this "trust fund doctrine" dominated American legal
reasoning about director liability. Even after 1892 (Sanger *vs*. Upton)
when the fact was recognized that directors were not technically real
trustees, their responsibility was not plainly and directly placed upon
fraud as such. The doctrine of the Sanger case was that company debts
created an implied contract with creditors that owner capital would not
be withdrawn until creditor claims had been satisfied from the assets.
Here is "breach of contract" rather than "fraud." The sense of the latter
term is usually that of a planned financial injury, and this would not
apply to inadvertent injury or the result of mere negligence by directors.

Whichever line of legal reasoning may be followed, British or American, the intent is the same, that is, to charge directors with a special duty
to act in respect to shareholders with full regard for the priority of
creditor claims upon the assets of a limited liability company.

Why does this intent exist? Why is it reasonable that stockholders' limited liability should be accompanied by a personal liability assigned against directors?

In partial answer it may be noted that creditors of the company cannot, as with proprietorships, seek payment from a stockholder's private wealth. If they were deprived of this right without some kind of substitute, creditors would become increasingly hesitant to lend; their savings would not be made available for productive employment; society would stand to lose the fruits of the production omitted. Directors' liability therefore became a second line of defense, as it were, giving reassurance to absentee creditors. Their first line of defense was the loss-absorbing capacity of the capital stock account. If company management chooses the part of wisdom they will set up balance sheet reserves, or retain surplus in the business, to take the first shock of losses. These accounts would then constitute an antecedent line of defense in protection of absentee creditors. Reserves thus serve a variety of useful purposes: they put company earnings to work among the operating assets; they stabilize the dividend base by holding back some profits against the day of losses; they defend directors against some of the risks of illegal dividends; they constitute an added margin of protection for creditors and thus encourage saving and investing. The auditor therefore should be an informed critic of reported reserves.

It may seem that these matters concern company financial management rather than accounting as such, and that lawyers rather than accountants would be the people to advise concerning limitations within the concept of the dividend base. But it will be observed that the topic here under discussion is an area where law, accounting, finance, and management come into close contact. It may well be said that legal advice alone would seldom be sufficient aid to directors. They of course need to be informed as to statutory limits and common-law interpretations, and they turn to lawyers. But they also need to be reliably informed regarding the company's objectively determined earnings of past and present periods, and as to the dependability of the reported financial status of the moment. Indeed they need to know also a good deal about the forward plans of management, of probable future debt burdens, debt payments, etc. To serve all these needs information may be sought from lawyers, professional auditors, and internal accountants. Each of these parties while offering his particular service would be best equipped to serve with maximum effectiveness if his thinking was influenced by some knowledge of the service expected from other advisors. All parties at interest would be well advised to have some grasp of the possibilities for confused thought that lie in the terminology and background of dividends. Words and phrases and practices have a way of persisting in use all the while that the underlying ideas are changing. Clear thinking and wise acting may sometimes suffer as a consequence.

(*Hermès,* Quebec, Spring, 1953)

9. Subdivisions for Net Worth

In the late 1920's certain tendencies in corporation finance were much under discussion among both accountants and lawyers. The reference here is particularly to the consideration given by accountants to appreciation of property values and by lawyers to desirable reforms in corporation statutes. The accountants' debates resulted in a carefully considered definition of earned surplus by a committee of the American Institute of Accountants; the lawyers' discussions produced the Uniform Business Corporation Law.

Both of these innovations were distinctly progressive and beneficial. The accountants, by defining earned surplus, have indicated their approval of the subdivision of surplus into earned surplus and capital surplus; the lawyers, through section 25 of the Uniform Statute, have shown that they favored a required subdivision of surplus which will produce separate accounts for paid-in surplus, revaluation surplus, and surplus profits. And the lawyers, by their further recommendation in section 25 that cash dividends from revaluation surplus be prohibited, have shown full agreement with the accountants who have frequently expressed their conviction that revaluation surplus was not profit.[3] The uniform statute further provides that the stockholder shall be specifically notified of the nature of his dividend, if the latter is declared out of paid-in surplus.

These statutory provisions together with the prior discussions make it clear that accountants and lawyers still believe that the consideration given for shares of stock is an important indication of "capital," and that they still think of dividends as realized profits and not as capital returned. These pronouncements constitute definite steps of progress since they plainly attempt to correct certain distorted ideas about the nature of corporation capital and dividends. But a corresponding correction in terminology is not made.

When surplus is subdivided, all of its new parts should not carry over unchanged from the former connotation; the subdivisions are presumably set off because they are *different*. The new terminology, however, is found to be simply the old legal term "surplus" plus a qualifying adjective, "paid-in," or "revaluation," or "profits" as the case may be. Verbally this seems to preserve the *similarity* of the subdivisions; yet the restrictions laid upon both paid-in surplus and revaluation surplus indicate that these two "surpluses" are related to capital and not to

---

[3] Some economists have long held that "increase of value is not income." See Irving Fisher, *The Nature of Capital and Income*, 1906, p. 351. Later the author is more specific: ". . . the value of any capital is always and necessarily the capitalized or discounted value of the income expected from the capital. It follows that savings and appreciation in Capital Value are always capital, not income." *The Income Concept in the Light of Experience*, 1927, p. 8.

profit. The terminology therefore is inconsistent with the treatment required.

Upon further examination it will be noted that the accountants' and lawyers' ideas of the basic elements of the net worth section draw somewhat apart. From the discussion of earned surplus it appears that the accountant's idea may be represented as follows:

$$\text{Net Worth} \begin{cases} \text{Capital} \dots \dots \begin{cases} \text{Capital Stock} \\ \text{Capital Surplus} \end{cases} \\ \text{Surplus} \end{cases}$$

From the uniform statute the lawyer's idea appears to be:

$$\text{Net Worth} \begin{cases} \text{Capital} \\ \text{Surplus} \dots \dots \begin{cases} \text{Paid-in} \\ \text{Revaluation} \\ \text{Profits} \end{cases} \end{cases}$$

Evidently there are two concepts of surplus: (1) Surplus is realized and undivided profits (accountants' concept); (2) surplus is the excess of assets above debts and stock (lawyers' concept).

In most cases, before no-par stock and appreciation put in their appearance, these two aspects of surplus were essentially identical; thus a single name would suffice. But as soon as the two situations became different, the old name "surplus" became inadequate for both purposes. And it is doubtful whether the easy way out, merely prefixing an adjective, is a fully satisfactory alteration of usage.

If clearness of expression were to be the guide, the terminology used in the law might better have been somewhat as follows: Net worth consists of dedicated capital, returnable capital, revaluation capital, and retained earnings. This would contrast with the present terms: capital stock, paid-in surplus, revaluation surplus, surplus profits. The principal thing accomplished by such a change would be to indicate to the reader, by the account titles themselves, that the items were related to capital as such. Failure to make this distinction clear will leave the account titles inconsistent with the meaning of the accounts.

If common words are given a technical meaning not clear to non-technical readers, the communication in financial statements would apparently be directed exclusively to the technically informed. Most people will tend to associate the word surplus with profit, e.g., "surplus profit available for dividend." The new terms therefore could easily carry an unintended meaning to many readers; the terms paid-in surplus and revaluation surplus would seem to indicate only differing sources of divisible profits. However they do not intend to speak of sources of dividends. The uniform statute plainly shows this aspect by requiring that notifications be given of the nature of a distribution from paid-in surplus (since it is a return of invested capital), and by prohibiting cash dividends out of revaluation surplus. Stock dividends, being merely a diluting of the outstanding shares, are not prohibited and would not seem a distribution of profit.

It is clear therefore that the chosen account titles are inconsistent with the limitations expressed in account usage. If the word capital, with suitable adjectives, were consistently used in the net worth section of the balance sheet, this usage could have the effect of indicating by the terms themselves the separateness of earnings from appreciation and contributions from stockholders.

(Accounting Review, December, 1932)

10. The Meaning of Capital Stock

That part of an owner's property which was active in his business affairs was at first very probably recorded (if at all) in a simple personal account—a credit to some sort of "master's account" by the slave or agent who was responsible for attending to business affairs. From the agent's point of view he "owed" the master for the sum entrusted; the master saw only a sum of money working in his behalf. To the latter this would be his "principal sum" and as the adjective came to be used elliptically as a substantive it would be thought of as his "principal." If the term had in this form been attached to his account, the title might be expected to have become "master's principal." When we see that the old Latin root word for the adjective "principal" was *caput* (head) and that this word evolved into the medieval Latin *capitalis* and into the medieval Italian *cavedale,* and finally into the English *capital,* it is not hard to convince ourselves that "master's capital" or "John Jones, capital" probably grew out of such a past.

Shift the scene to the seventeenth century. The trading companies, such as the East India Company and others, developed a species of enlarged partnerships. Each participant contributed from his stock of goods. The united contributions constituted a stock of goods owned jointly by the participants, in other words, a "joint stock." By the middle of the seventeenth century "cash debitor to stock" was a typical opening entry. The stock account was representative of the economic capital held as assets by a joint-stock ownership.

Presently the several terms crept together. For example, an act of Parliament in 1697 regarding the Bank of England (889 W & M C.20) mentions "governor and company. . . ." At present the combined term "capital stock" is in constant use, but we seldom recognize the redundancy created. "Stock" originally referred to the goods possessed; "capital" referred to the proprietor's principal sum—his total of ownership. Not only are two apparently opposing concepts united in the phrase, but it has also been given a third meaning, that of a margin contributed by limited liability corporation shareholders for the protection of creditors. Moreover, we often drop the noun "stock"; then we use the adjective "capital" to mean such different things as (1) the assets, (2) proprietorship net worth, (3) the legal measure of the limit to corporation dividends.

Obviously broad possibilities exist here for confused thinking. But perhaps more important is the fact that never, until quite recently in the long development of accounting for business capital, have there been deviations from the concept that a capital account recorded the contribution of the proprietary interest.

Various factors in the United States have produced the new doctrine of "stated capital." The vogue for the corporate form for doing business was one factor. Others included an increased appetite, following the finance drives for World War I, for security investments, and the then current freedom from restraint in the characteristics given to no-par stock. Under this doctrine "capital stock" became a portion of the stockholders' creditor protection. The rest of the contribution ("paid-in surplus") was to remain under the unrestrained control of the stockholders and directors, almost as if it were earned surplus derived from operations.

This revolutionary departure from long-established practice should not be condemned on the ground that nothing new can be good. On the other hand, mere novelty should not recommend a practice on the ground that everything old is inadequate for modern conditions. The use of a new idea in practical affairs should not alone constitute a sufficient endorsement, nor should the existence of abuses constitute sufficient reason for the abolition of a practice which has inherent merit. But anything which is as revolutionary as the doctrine of stated value does call for thoughtful appraisal.

Several alternatives suggest themselves at once. We could go back to the traditional conception of capital stock as the whole contribution and thus be free of "stated value." We could abandon entirely the idea of a fixed sum, however determined, as a margin for creditors. The first would be equivalent to a repudiation of recent developments and would require restriction of many current practices. The second would be equivalent to accepting the revolution as progress and extending it to its logical sequel.

If we are to hold to the idea that capital stock represents the whole of the stockholder's contributions, it probably would not be necessary to abandon no-par stock entirely. No-par is much too useful to be legislated out of existence merely because it may be open to some abuse. No-par stock should be retained for the sake of its flexibility as an original issue, if for no other reason.

Restriction is needed, however, for stated capital in both original and subsequent issues. If the whole contribution concept is to prevail, the stated value concept must give way; the two are so antagonistic as to be irreconcilable. Therefore, any statute requiring the whole consideration for an issue of no-par stock to be credited to capital stock account must also prohibit stated value. This will necessitate allowing complete latitude in the price at which par stock is to be issued.

The use of any statutory minimum price for stock issues would also constitute a failure to recognize the fact that there is no relationship whatever between the number of shares and the value of the property. In a sense a statutory minimum price constitutes an equivalent of par value as well as an invitation to establish a "stated capital" by resolution of the directors. If a minimum price for stock issues is included in the laws in an attempt to protect the investor against fraudulent stocks, this sort of protection could more properly be attempted through so-called "blue-sky laws" which would classify shares as types of investments.

Another corollary to the fact that the number of owners cannot of itself affect the value of the property is complete freedom to increase or decrease the number of shares outstanding, by stock split-ups and recombinations, and openly to issue shares for intangibles and promoter's services. It would seem that such practices could not be highly objectionable, provided the interested public was given unmistakable notice of the facts.

In the case of subsequent issues of no-par stock under a statute requiring the whole consideration to be credited to capital stock account, there might be a question whether this would not constitute an impairment of the rights existing stockholders had in accumulated surplus as of that date. Since every share of common stock, new or old, has an interest in the net worth, it might be argued that part of the purchase price was paid for an interest in past surplus and therefore was not a proper credit to capital as such.

Yet a credit to paid-in surplus or to earned surplus of a part of a capital contribution would be still more objectionable. Hence the common sense thing to do would be to avoid hairsplitting and credit the whole consideration to capital. It may reasonably be assumed that the stockholders have voted on the question of the new issue and that they realize their action will be a dilution of existing equities, i.e., those held by themselves, the existing stockholders. If, knowing the facts from full disclosures, the stockholders assent to the diluting action, it must be presumed that they see compensating advantages to their company which lead them to be willing to admit new claimants for part of the existing surplus.

(Accounting Review, August, 1933)

11. Search for Flexibility

The appearance and acceptance of no-par stock seem to have changed the prior theory that capital stock account should always be credited with the stockholder's whole contribution. Although objections can be raised to this change, primarily on the ground that directors gain new powers to dispose of parts of the stockholder's contribution, it may none the less indicate a trend that may look like real progress. If this be true, it would be a mistake to attempt to defeat change merely to hold to the traditional practice.

Yet the issue may lie deeper than the traditional versus the progressive. Under the earlier practice corporation finance was principally called upon in the formation of a new grouping of capital—the creation of a corporation where none had existed. Under more recent conditions corporate finance activities have been much more commonly directed toward merging existing companies and to rearranging the capital structure of going concerns. The older problem was mainly one of assembling aggregates of limited liability capital under one management and issuing documentary evidences of those contributions. The newer problem is related to "values," i.e., to a growing consciousness that a corporation is being constantly "appraised" in the security markets, that its securities draw their value primarily from earning power, that assets are valuable only according to the earnings they produce. The modern problem of finance therefore is to try to maintain a reasonable degree of agreement between a naturally fluctuating element (value of assets) and a naturally rigid element (limited liability capital obligations). Hence we have the search for flexibility of capital which seems to be behind most of the capital financing problems of today.

These considerations suggest a capital flexibility for corporations that would approach the flexibility of proprietor's capital, provided the creditors of limited liability companies were given suitable protection since creditor protection is still necessary if business on credit is to continue unabated.

The minimum margin of protection has heretofore been a capital stock account representing either the whole contribution or a designated part of it. But in any event the capital has been a fixed sum. Obviously flexibility of capital and a fixed sum of capital are incompatible. So the question appears whether the creditors might not be given satisfactory protection without the use of a fixed sum of capital as a margin. If this were accomplished it should have the effect of making the capital structure more flexible so far as stock and surplus were concerned.

Assume the following legal restrictions upon corporate capital stock:

(1) In lieu of a fixed sum as a margin for creditors, the corporation shall pledge itself not to allow the relationship between the total indebtedness (including preferred stock) and the reasonable value of the total assets to fall below a percentage which the corporation's charter agrees to maintain.

(2) All preferred stock must have a par value expressing the liquida-

tion preference in assets, and is to be cumulative, callable, nonparticipating and preferred as to income (in order to exclude borderline cases which are closer to common stocks).

(3) All common stock of whatever class must be without par value and may be issued for any consideration satisfactory to the directors and stockholders.

(4) The creditors (including preferred stockholders) shall have the right to elect a certain number (minority) of directors annually.

(5) Upon the failure of the corporation to maintain the specified ratio of assets and indebtedness, the creditors (including preferred stockholders) shall immediately have the right to elect a majority of the directors.

(6) Insolvency and the usual seizure through the courts of assets specifically pledged would follow upon the failure to pay interest or principal on a bond when due, as at present.

If the assumed restrictions were in force the following would be some of the expected consequences:

(1) A plainer recognition of the principle that all suppliers of capital differ from one another only as to the terms of their capital contract and that the corporation should be managed so the interests of all parties would receive consideration.

(2) The creditors through their representatives on the board of directors would have a voice in the management and direct knowledge of current plans and policies. This representation, with the enforced maintenance of a definite ratio of assets and debt and the conditional right to control the policies, would be an effective substitute for a fixed sum margin and for the so-called trust fund doctrine of capital stock.

(3) With the creditors thus better protected than at present, common stock account and surplus could be made as flexible as an individual proprietor's capital account. The legal necessity for distinguishing between common stock and surplus would disappear; a single "net capital account" would suffice.

(4) The "net capital account" would be a true net worth account, a real indication of residual proprietorship, fluctuating as proprietorship investment fluctuated, subject to increase or decrease in the number of "participation certificates" as the holders saw fit and to such withdrawals or assessments as the directors, representing all suppliers of capital, should decide.

(5) Although subaccounts would be desirable for accounting purposes, a single net worth account could suffice. It would be credited with:

> Original contributions
> Profits earned
> Capital gains realized
> Appreciation write-ups

It would be debited with:

>Asset losses sustained
>Asset write-downs
>Dividends declared
>Reserves transferred to special accounts

In the past, creditors' margin was the whole sum contributed by stockholders. At present, the tendency is toward a director-designated portion of the contribution, apparently in a search for greater flexibility in treating and reporting proprietary capital. The proposals here outlined increase the protection of all classes of creditors, and at the same time increase the flexibility of capital accounting and management. On the surface that would seem to be a desirable accomplishment. It would of course be supported by an analytical breakdown of the heterogeneous contents of a "master account."

(Journal of Accountancy, August, 1933)

12. Profits Test for Dividends

There is a tendency for American statutory law to rest dividend declarations upon the existence of an excess of assets after excluding appraisal increases. This is accompanied by a tendency to drop the traditional common-law test of the existence of profits. The growing preference therefore seems to be for an indirect control over dividends by rules which say in effect: Maintain capital, then all excess assets (except from appraisals) may be disbursed as dividends. This type of rule creates the problem of defining the capital which is to be maintained. On the other hand, a direct approach to dividend control would favor a rule which would say in effect: No dividend disbursement may be made beyond the amount of the accumulated profits. The problem then would become one of defining profits for dividend purposes.

Presumably either method could be made to work satisfactorily, provided only that the respective definitions were comprehensive and their interpretations clear enough to furnish trustworthy controls in all instances. But recent changes in corporation statutes have not shown much tendency to produce an adequate definition of the capital fund to be maintained before dividends may be declared. Therefore it is fair to say that but little progress has been made under the assets test in the direction of adjusting statutory law to modern corporation problems beyond ruling out appreciation values.

Perhaps profits as a dividend base would be no easier than capital to define satisfactorily. Yet that approach has the better chance for ultimate success in use because the nature of profits is much better understood by most people and because the accounting technique of measuring profits is better developed than the technique of measuring capital.

The problem of calculating profits has been the central theme of accounting from its beginning, and all of the slowly accumulated knowledge of the subject bears directly or indirectly upon profits.

In an examination of the problems likely to be raised by the use of the profits test alternative, it may be difficult to distinguish sharply among transactions which seem to possess profit characteristics and those which may properly be taken into consideration in dividend declarations. And even if clear distinctions could be drawn, it may still be hard to decide where statutory control should stop and managerial policy begin. Yet difficult of solution or not, the problems need to be faced if good accounting, sound finance, and dividend law are to be interwoven into an intimate fabric of business control.

The first important question raising an issue between surplus and profits as the dividend base was the availability of appraisal surplus for cash dividend. By this time it is probably safe to say that the decision has been rendered in both accounting and law. Yet it should be noted that the basic issue was not whether capital was maintained or impaired by dividends out of appreciation surplus or whether assets should or should not be revalued, but whether the declaration was from realized or unrealized profits. The question was fundamentally one of distinguishing true profit from something which merely had the debit and credit characteristics of profit. Whenever men saw clearly that appreciation credits were not profits, they were convinced that such credits should not be considered in indicating the amount of assets which could be paid to stockholders as dividends.

The discussion of appraisal problems led accountants to favor the use on the balance sheet of an item named "earned surplus," and led lawyers to favor statutory exclusion of appraisal values from forming a basis for cash dividends. These two results are not true counterparts. The accountant advocates clear separation in the financial statements of earned and unearned surplus, or more strictly speaking, of realized and unrealized profits. His thought is to provide figures which can be a direct and positive aid to dividend policy. The lawyer, through statutes which permit any excess of assets not related to asset appraisals to be paid out as dividends, succeeds in providing only a negative guide.

It would not be difficult to exclude cash dividends based on appreciation and at the same time harmonize statutory law with both the preference in common law for a profits test and the accountant-businessman conception of dividend source. This could be accomplished by a statute in which the thought was that cash dividends could be declared only from current or accumulated profits determined according to the principles of good accounting to have been actually realized. Such a phrasing would crystallize in the statute the important and fundamental distinction between realized and unrealized profits as is already done in accounting.

Because statutory law is usually considered to be a codification of common law, it is difficult to understand why the common-law doctrine that dividends presuppose profits is not given more direct expression in recent statutes. If this had been done, that no-man's-land lying between accumulated realized profits and stated capital would be much less of a problem. If the area between stated capital as margin for creditor protection and earned surplus as the source of stockholder dividend were clearly defined in the statutes, it would seem to promise at least some relief from apparently interminable argument.

To be sure the use of the profits test is not without its difficulties. Yet, despite its obvious problems, it has a better chance than the assets test of clarifying dividend questions. The reason is that the theory and technique of measuring profits are better developed and the nature of profits better understood than the nature of a maintained capital fund.

If profits shall be the test, where shall the line be drawn in defining distributable profits, and who shall take the lead in fixing that line's location?

It is probably fair to say that accounting opinion led the way in favoring exclusion of unrealized appreciation from cash dividends. It probably is fair also to believe that representative accounting opinion favors disclosing clearly operating income separately from nonrecurring profit. It is not readily determinable whether professional accounting opinion would favor distinguishing these two types of gains for dividend purposes as well as for income tax calculations. But it may be noted that accountants probably would be inclined to agree with the rule of some of the newer statutes, such as in Illinois for example, that paid-in surplus may be returned to stockholders only if accompanied by clear notice of the peculiar nature of the distribution.

Will accountants take the lead in extending this practice as they did with the separation of appraisal surplus? Perhaps they can go beyond mere disclosures of varieties of surplus and urge in every suitable way that dividends be restricted to earned income rather than to earned surplus. Perhaps they can consistently advocate carrying all major capital value adjuncts to capital surplus, while confining all operating results to profit and loss surplus so that the two surplus accounts shall always mean just what their titles say.

Accounting literature dwells at length upon auditors' duty to disclose true financial position; little or nothing is said regarding any necessity for disclosing true earning power. Yet trustworthy knowledge concerning the latter is far more important to more people than information concerning probable ability to pay debts. And it is very doubtful whether earning power can be satisfactorily deduced from a study of even the better present-day certified balance sheets.

Accountants have long been familiar with the usual reserves and may be relied upon in an audit to satisfy themselves that reserves made necessary by creditors contracts and reserves which reflect the stated policies of the directors are properly expressed. But there is not much evidence that accountants have tried to work out a technique for making clear the distinction between income earned and income available for dividends, or the distinction between surplus realized (and therefore according to present legal ideas fully available if the directors choose) and surplus assets actually financially disbursable should a dividend declaration be made. In the service of the client however the auditor is under no compulsion to rest content when he has revealed the legal maximum which might be declared—if it could be disbursed.

If accountants will realize the limitations upon the effectiveness of their service which flow out of the belief that professional duty is satisfied when the auditor sees that the letter of a statute is not violated, and if accountants can be persuaded to accept some responsibility for fostering an extended acceptance of sound financial practices, the law may be expected to follow accounting leadership. Changes in the law are made to correct demonstrated bad practices or to codify established custom and good practices. Law follows rather than leads public opinion. And in such matters as these, experienced public accountants constitute the best sort of public opinion.

(*Accounting Review,* December, 1934)

13. Earned Versus Realized Income

It is usually presumed that the accountant's use of earned surplus is designed to reveal by contrast the existence of an occasional unrealized surplus. This would be the result only if "earned" and "realized" were synonymous terms. They often are used in this sense, but there is a distinction which these differing words draw very well. Consider this sentence: "He was a man who realized a fortune but did not earn it." Actual receipt and possession present only one aspect. In business, by the use of accounting, it is more important to know whether the things possessed are explained by services performed.

Consider operating income and capital gains. Both are realized increments to total assets. Yet only one is earned in the sense of being compensation for the active rendering of services; only one is useful as a measure of the power to produce a recurring return. Nothing is done actively to earn a capital gain. Ownership of the asset sold is enough to give the seller clear title to the asset received in exchange. Transfer of title is indeed the final act of realization. But there is a distinction between being claimant to the proceeds of a sale, and having earned a return by reason of services performed.

Perhaps this distinction between earned income and unearned profit, as well as the distinction between realized and unrealized profit should be given consideration in the law of dividends.

The issue of capital gains versus earned income has repeatedly been raised over a long period of time. The *Journal of Accountancy* in July, 1933, pointed out that the accountants consulted when the first American income tax laws were passed more than twenty years ago were in favor of the British plan of ignoring capital gains and losses. More recently, the Secretary of the Treasury in his 1921 report criticized the taxation of capital gains because men have a tendency, in order to avoid high taxes on the increases, to keep property which they would rather sell. In 1923, he expressed the opinion that it would be sounder policy not to recognize either capital gains or losses for income tax purposes, that being the plan followed by all other countries having income tax laws. In 1921, Robert Montgomery expressed his opinion (*Auditing Theory and Practice*, p. 321) to the effect that, while capital gains were legally available for dividends, they were less likely to create false impressions as to earning power if they were held as a contingent reserve for possible losses from other capital adjustments. Yet Congress has never yielded.

Perhaps the tax laws are not, as some may believe, a simple grasping for the utmost revenue or a gladly welcomed opportunity to "soak the rich." Perhaps there may be a real difference between the judicial—and therefore also legislative—conception of income and that held by businessmen and accountants.[4] The courts' view that excess assets (surplus) are the basis of dividends and that maintenance of capital is the primary consideration is consistent with the view that income consists of all "gains from whatever source derived." There is also a certain consistency in the apparent attitude of American courts in holding that capital losses must be made good before earnings are available for dividends. This would not follow if capital gains were held not to be income.

The other view is that capital gains are not income; that capital losses affect capital and not the availability of current or accumulated earnings; that dividends are more properly based upon earned income than upon balance sheet surplus. This is approximately the view expressed in British income tax practice and held by many American accountants.

If the difference in opinions is based upon different conceptions of the nature of income and dividends, then there is still a place for further discussions. Differences may grow less as mutual understanding increases.

Accountants are always greatly concerned that no bookkeeping usage or financial statement practice shall be permitted to create false impressions or work a deceit upon the reader. The advances made in accounting have largely been the result of a constantly increasing refinement of the disclosures which will reveal conditions and causes. Wherever accountants have found a complex account or term, their instinct for clarity has led

.

[4] Maurice E. Peloubet writes: "One of the principal causes of the unspeakable complexity of our tax laws is the endeavor to tax everything rather than to tax what is definitely recurring or ordinary income and limit the tax to that." *Journal of Accountancy*, September, 1934, p. 197.

them to seek to break it down into its constituent elements. It is this urge which placed accountants on record as favoring a separation of realized and unrealized profits both in financial statement practice and as a matter of law, and which may be relied upon in the end to bring increasing support for a similarly effective separation of operating income and capital gains.

The two terms themselves indicate the existence of distinctions. Operating income arises out of the regular activities of the enterprise—furnishing a service, buying and reselling a line of goods, or manufacturing and selling newly formed products. It is in the nature of a recurring return for services rendered, a sort of management wage. It is the net resultant of associating income increments (revenue) and income decrements (expense).

Capital gains and losses on the other hand are nonrecurring returns which arise from occasional, sporadic transactions in capital or liabilities. They occur outside of the regular fulfillment of the particular function of the enterprise. Their magnitude is much less subject to conscious control by managerial acts than are operating incomes; their very existence is conditioned by influences outside of the business. They reflect strongly the changing sweep of the business cycle and are for the most part fortuitous results. In fact capital gains, when they are not outright gifts, are simply realized value increments which in their unrealized state are subject to specific dividend restrictions both in law and account. Capital losses, when not purely the consequence of unpredictable physical disaster, are simply realized value decrements against which experienced and conservative judgment will have built up such reserves as may be possible.

Surely there is ample difference between realized value increments and service-earned income to warrant drawing both accounting and legal distinctions.

From a business point of view the sale of a capital asset is merely the conversion of a long-lived asset into some kind of short-lived asset which is judged more suitable to the existing circumstances. There is nothing to disburse to the stockholder except in liquidation of some of his investment. If a capital asset for replacement should cost less than the one displaced, some new liquid capital is made available for other uses; if replacement should cost more, additional liquid capital is locked up in a fixed asset.

If replacement is not in question, there has been an increase in liquid capital regardless of any profit or loss from the sale. The liquid asset may be used in any way that any working capital may be used. That is one side of the picture, a side often neglected from overstressing the purely legal fact that title to property has been passed. It does not necessarily follow that sale (passing of title) is the only criterion of the appearance of a distributable profit. That conclusion follows only where the concept of distributable profit fails to distinguish capital increment and earned income.

In both cases it is true that the enterprise is better off in terms of total assets than it was before the transaction. But there is a vast difference in the significance of the increase of assets in the two cases. It makes a difference to the management, the stockholders, the lender, to practically everyone concerned—except possibly the lawyer—whether the assets to be distributed arose as a capital asset increment or as an earned income. The permanence of the stockholders' investment, the security of the lenders' advances, the wisdom of the management's future policies, all are concerned in the clear disclosure of the full facts regarding the limitations of use under which the assets are held.

If these obviously different subelements of "profits" are to be recognized, they require only very simple changes in accounting practice. Entries in earned surplus would be restricted so that the contents of the account would harmonize with the thought behind the account title, i.e., here is the resting place of undistributed, past-earned, operating income. Present usage makes the same account title cover both earned income and capital gains. Capital gains and losses should receive separate treatment consistent with their own nature and be debited or credited to a capital valuation account (if desired, capital surplus or even paid-in surplus might be used). Thus used, a capital variations account would be in effect an adjunct to capital stock account, indicating by its credit balance a preponderance of accumulated capital increment, and by its debit balance a preponderance of accumulated capital decrement.

Accounting is now mature enough that it need be no longer afraid of the big bad wolf, "deficit account." That is merely a capital valuation account with a debit balance, and it may constitute the most enlightening item on the statement. A deficit should be required to be disclosed in at least one balance sheet. Indeed there is no fundamental reason why it may not be plainly carried in as many balance sheets as need be. Capital impairment is not something to hide. It is something to disclose, something to be overcome by subsequent income or by a reorganization of capital structure.

It would seem as easy in law as it is in accounting to recognize the fact that profit may have subelements. Corporation statutes could provide (1) that cash dividends may be declared only from current or accumulated net income as determined by the principles of good accounting to have been earned in operating the business, and (2) that paid-in surplus shall be given special treatment: (a) capital gains shall be carried into paid-in surplus, (b) any cash distribution chargeable to paid-in surplus shall constitute a return of capital to be called a "division" and all parties at interest must be notified that such distribution is not based upon regularly recurring income created by operations.

With this sort of practice established, there would be less pressure upon directors to protect earnings through covering deficits by revaluing assets.

(*Accounting Review,* December, 1934)

14. Income Available for Distribution

One of the issues raised by a proposal to rest dividend declarations upon profits rather than surplus is the question whether income earned and income financially available for distribution should be distinguished. The mere presence of surplus does not of itself justify dividends. Many changes may have been made in assets derived from profits that would render them unavailable for distribution or might make equivalent disbursement unwise.

The law's attitude has been that directors should have a free hand with assets so long as disbursements did not reduce the capital margin established for protection of creditors. Thus the law is content to set a bare minimum to directors' action on dividends. The layman would believe that the law might instead have placed a premium on the use of a standard of acceptable practice above a minimum. For if legal availability and financial availability were brought closer, the law would be in the position of fostering sound practices rather than leaving the way open for some unsound practices to be called legal.

The experience of recent years has made it plain that a simple showing of "surplus" on a balance sheet is often open to misinterpretation. Common understanding and general practices made such "surplus" seem to mean realized profits. Yet some companies found it possible to submerge unrealized profits in their surplus. After considerable agitation this situation is beginning to be remedied. But common understanding and general practice also consider surplus or even earned surplus to mean "the amount available for dividend if the directors decide to declare it." As a matter of fact, directors are under no such wide freedom and their financial statements are not of the highest type if they fail to disclose the real limitations involved.

Some of the most definite and inescapable restrictions upon the availability of surplus arise in the contracts made by the company with its security-holders. Bond indentures frequently provide that sinking fund reserves must be set up. Preferred stock contracts have been known to require that a certain amount of surplus shall exist before dividends may be paid on the common stock. These and numerous other contract clauses definitely restrict the availability of surplus no matter how completely it may consist of realized profits.

In addition to contractual restrictions, numerous restrictions are placed upon the financial availability of surplus by voluntary action of the directors for prudent administrative reasons. The usual surplus reserves for contingencies, extensions, capital losses, etc. are still "surplus available for distribution" as far as corporation law is concerned. In the balance sheet they are but outward and visible signs of the directors' intentions regarding surplus which otherwise would be unknown to most people. And since the directors' actions in regard to reserves can be rescinded, such reservations can be restored to surplus if desired. So too certain contractual reserves, like sinking fund reserves, could be returned to surplus when the object of the reservation had been attained.

But does the surplus account after such restorations represent surplus which is financially available? It may and it may not. And if such surplus could not be completely disbursed out of current assets, is not the reader deceived who looks to the surplus account for the clue to possible dividend disbursements?

Neither law nor accounting has yet succeeded by prescription or practice in making clear the financial limitations on dividend distribution which exist at the date of the balance sheet. Yet financial availability probably is the most significant single item of information buried in that statement. Not how much realized profits have accumulated but how much of the realized profits could be disbursed: that is the most pertinent question.

A reserve created out of earned surplus for plant extensions is returnable to earned surplus when the saved current assets have finally been converted into fixed assets. Yet it is plain that a large part of the earned surplus would be quite impossible for declaration as a cash dividend since the earned assets were no longer available for current disbursement. The statement would be nearer the truth if the reserve were closed into a nondistributable capital surplus, thus leaving earned surplus as a closer approximation to the concept, surplus earned and available for distribution.

The same question may arise regarding a sinking fund reserve after the related debt has been discharged. At that time the accounts show a plant paid for out of assets derived from earnings. The earned assets are locked up in plant, and as a result the same amount of what was once earned surplus is now undistributable surplus. This reserve, like the extension reserve, would be more properly transferred into a capital surplus, or perhaps be made the basis of a stock dividend.

Surplus may also be made unavailable for distribution without the use of contract reserves or voluntary reserves by merely converting the assets which it represents into nondisbursable forms. An enterprise cannot continue operations without maintaining a revolving fund of working capital. In fact that fund has a certain minimum which is as indispensable as productive plant. That much surplus at least is at all times financially unavailable for dividends.

If working capital is larger than current requirements dictate, then more surplus is locked up than otherwise would be the case, and less is financially available for dividends. If working capital is drained lower than normal, additional surplus may thus seem to be released for distribution, but at the risk of cramping operations if cash is disbursed for dividends that should be kept for current expenses and debt payments.

Funds could be released to cover dividend declarations by some restricting of inventory replacements. Surplus previously tied up in fixed assets becomes available cash to the extent that depreciation is recovered in collections from sales and not subsequently reinvested in fixed asset replacements.

As to surplus locked up in the minimum fund of working capital, a good accounting treatment, following the precedent of sinking fund and plant extension reserves, would be creation of a reserve for surplus invested in working capital. If this and other similar adjustments for availability were consistently carried through, earned surplus could be brought into close approximation to the concept of "earned surplus financially available for dividend declaration." If this concept were activated, the reporting of surplus would undergo another development comparable with that involved in separating realized and unrealized surplus, and in distinguishing earned and unearned surplus.

(*Accounting Review*, December, 1934)

15. The Assumption Beneath Dividend Tests

The profits base for dividends is the one which accords with the universal opinion of laymen regarding dividends, as well as the one which the common law would provide in the absence of a specific statute. The common-law view as expressed in the statutes uses a wide variety of terms such as profit, net profits, accumulated profits, profits earned in the business, profits actually earned and on hand, surplus profits arising from the business, net earnings, and actual net earnings.

But many of the states have gone beyond codifying the basic idea of the common law that "dividends presuppose profits." Two other tests have been set up: a solvency test and a capital impairment test. A corporation is insolvent if its assets aggregate less than its debts to creditors; capital is impaired if the assets aggregate less than the sum of the debts and the stock. In both of these situations use is made of the assets total to find whether or not an excess of assets exists. It is desirable therefore to give attention first to contrasting the net profits test and this excess assets test without raising the question at the moment of subordinate distinctions such as the insolvency test and the impairment test.

In a simple situation the assets test and the profits test would give identical results. This is clearly the case because goods sold will bring in more assets than are given up and the resulting increase in the assets account is exactly counterbalanced by the new increase in the profits account. It is in fact the primary function of the profits account to reflect and measure this change in the assets. In this way accounting is able to present the same quantity so it may be viewed from two angles.

But behind this seeming identity of increased assets and increased profit is an important underlying assumption which seems to have escaped many legislatures and courts. This assumption is that all assets, those just received as well as those just parted with, are expressed in original costs, that is, in terms of the prices at which they entered a business transaction as part of the legal consideration. So long as this assumption is true, the assets test and the profits test will give identical results, and one can measure the amount of distributable assets by choosing either of the two methods of computation. But as soon as this assumption is violated the two tests fall apart and cannot be used interchangeably. If the assets are increased by mere valuation, there is no more property to distribute than there was before; the property previously existing is only given a new price tag. The resulting situation is as lacking in real change as a stock split-up which merely alters the number of units in an otherwise unchanged capital stock account.

The fault of having two bases for dividends is that they may be considered identical when that is not the case. With two bases in existence, the way is opened for creating an excess of assets by revaluation and for paying dividends out of prior profits while allowing revaluation surplus to take the place of the profits withdrawn. The resulting balance sheet seems to show a large surplus still available for later dividends, for the ordinary person will assume that any surplus will of course represent undivided profits. The corporation may thus be accused of accomplishing a deception while seemingly following an allowable practice.

The presence, in the law of dividends, of two ways of determining the amount available for distribution is therefore confusing to say the least unless those two methods are never lacking in complete identity. And since that is too much to expect of any two methods, one method or the other should be dropped.

Many state statutes, apparently to make assurance doubly sure, have included more than one test for dividends. This, instead of giving added protection, has merely made confusion more possible. But corporation practices have been under fire of late, and during the last seven years a number of important revisions have been made in the corporation statutes. Here was an opportunity to clear away previous sources of confusion.

Did the revisions succeed in reducing the confusion?

In 1928, final approval was given by the American Bar Association to the Uniform Business Corporation Act which had been under consideration for some years with the object of pointing the way for the states to bring their corporation statutes into closer agreement. In the next several years thirteen states rewrote their corporation statutes, some following rather closely the lines indicated in the uniform act. The following summarizes the changes from the prior law of these states.

	Dropped	Retained	Added
Profits test	5	3	3
Capital Impairment test	0	4	7
Solvency test	5	3	3

If one looked at the full statutes, it would be clear that a confusing variety of dividend tests is still in existence in spite of the hopes for increased uniformity among the states. Change there was, but not in the direction of a swing towards the profits test. In fact there was a tendency to drop the profits test and the solvency test while adding the capital impairment test.

In the ninth draft (1924) of the Uniform Act, dividends were to be based on "surplus or profits arising out of the business," a phrasing found at that time in various state statutes. But in the tenth draft (1927) this phrasing disappeared. In section 24, paragraph III of the final report (1928) appears this statement among others:

No corporation shall pay dividends in cash or property except from the surplus of the aggregate of its assets over the aggregate of its liabilities, including in the latter the amount of its capital stock, after deducting from such aggregate of its assets the amount by which such aggregate was increased by unrealized appreciation of fixed assets.

Here the emphasis is placed upon excluding unrealized appreciation from the cash dividend base. But in the process of writing the section, profit was not mentioned as a dividend base. It would be interesting to know whether the profits test (which derives from the common law) was abandoned because it was difficult to define; because it was regarded as a counterpart of the capital impairment test (after appreciation surplus had been excepted); or because it was feared that a profits test would permit dividends to be paid from current profits even though the company was insolvent or its capital impaired.

A view of a sample of changes in dividend law made in the years immediately following the approval of the Uniform Business Corporation Act shows that the following tendencies appear:

(1) Appreciation surplus is being recognized as unavailable for cash dividends.

(2) Stated capital and paid-in surplus are given statutory authority as compared with the traditional practice of bringing the full consideration received into the capital stock account. (In some cases however paid-in surplus is being placed under some restraint.)

(3) The capital impairment test is being given preference over other tests.

In the few statutes where capital impairment is the sole test, the confusing assumption of an identity existing between a profits test and an assets test disappears, and that is perhaps beneficial as far as it goes. If more states follow that lead, the total benefit would be increased. But it would still remain an open question whether another resolution of confused identity—that of preferring the profit test alone—would not have greatly expanded the clarity of dividend law and at the same time brought law into closer harmony with the basic function of accounting, that is, the function of making an objective calculation and a clear disclosure of periodic net income.

(Accounting Review, June, 1934)

16. Solvency and Creditor Protection

An issue arises as between the profits test for dividends and the assets test. Recent statutes (in the 1930's) suggest a further drift toward the latter; yet much could be paid in favor of the former. What theory underlies the long use of a solvency test for dividends? Is such a test still justified? What problems may arise if a profits test should be used exclusively?

If a given statute excludes the profits test, confusion in thought is still possible until a further exclusion takes place which will also exclude either the solvency test or the capital impairment test.

The desire to give creditors special protection appears as early as 1570 (13 Eliz. c. 5) at which time one of the indications of fraud was stated to be the transfer of property while insolvent. The English Companies Act of 1855 placed dividends under this solvency test, and this undoubtedly exercised considerable influence on American legislation in those states which passed general incorporation laws at about that time.

At common law, insolvency was merely the inability to pay one's debts. This view was reflected in our national bankruptcy act of 1867 and in many state statutes as well as in the law of many foreign countries. The depression of 1873 revealed the harshness of this rule, however, and the National Bankruptcy Law of 1898 was designed to make bankruptcy depend upon a hopeless financial condition rather than upon a temporary embarrassment from the lack of working capital. Hence the concept of insolvency now expressed in many dividend statutes calls for a comparison of the aggregate of the person's assets with the aggregate of his debts.

But it is doubtful whether the creditors need this specific protection in the corporation statute because the disbursement of assets in payment of a dividend when the company is insolvent would constitute a fraud upon creditors and an act of bankruptcy regardless of the dividend statute. If the creditors are to be given rights of action against directors as well as against the stockholders receiving the assets, the authority could better be given in the bankruptcy laws than in the dividend laws.

The inclusion of a solvency test in the dividend law whether consciously or not, rests upon two theories: (1) that lenders and owners are essentially different and are antagonistic, and (2) that saved capital is timid or defenseless, needing much coaxing and protection to bring it into the hands of those who felt they could employ it to advantage. From this it follows that a distinct boundary between owner and lender should be erected so that the latter could know when he had become owner and the owner had become former-owner.

This is plainly the philosophy of an era of individual enterprise, but its doctrines are carried over almost unchanged into the modern era of corporations.

The era of proprietary enterprises seems definitely to be passing in this country. Here it is the custom for even the small enterprise to be cast into the mold of the corporation. Yet corporation law and accounting practice tend to continue to work within the mold established by the single enterprise where lenders and owners are regarded as distinct persons. The persistence in the law of the idea that lender and owner are different and the persistence in accountancy of the double title in the balance sheet, "liabilities and capital," reveal a resistance to change which implies an inability to adjust our ideas to real trends. If the corporation is to continue to be the predominating form of business enterprise, it would seem reasonable to bring our rules and practices, including those relating to dividends, into conformity.

When we look closely at the corporation we see a separate entity endowed by law with the powers of human beings except those associated with personality. The only contact it has with human beings is by contract. Its contracts are principally with book-creditors, bank-lenders, various types of bondholders, several classes of preferred stockholders, and additional classes of common stockholders. The contracts vary in details as to security pledged, voice in current management, priority in sharing the net revenue, priority in sharing assets under liquidation, and the like. Yet, various as these relations may be between outsiders and the corporation, all individuals in the former group are alike in being separate from the corporation itself, in being suppliers of economic capital and in having a claim against either assets or revenues, or both. In other words, the fundamental nature of corporations is such as to emphasize elements of likeness and thus to unite all supplies of capital into one category, rather than to stress elements of difference which in a proprietary enterprise naturally separate lenders and owners into two categories.

This distinction in the essence of a proprietorship and a corporation, if it is as basic as it seems to be, should also be reflected in the concept of insolvency. Should insolvency in corporations mean, as in proprietorships, that lenders shall replace owners in having full title to the property?

It may seem that financial difficulties within a proprietorship under earlier credit conditions would naturally lead to a procedure permitting the lender to take charge of the insolvent borrower's assets. But this procedure may not fit modern conditions. Who will buy the assets of a 10,000 mile railroad so that its creditors may be paid? Will complete transfer of title (control) from stockholders to bondholders provide better employers and managers than the dispossessed stockholders? The modern way out is to undertake a reorganization of the capital structure of the corporation in trouble, this being accomplished by mutual agreement among all suppliers of capital.

The relationship among creditors, stockholders, and their corporation may upon occasion need readjustment under existing circumstances. Dividend law however is not the place to set up regulations regarding corporate insolvency or financial reorganization. Better protection of creditors usually will emerge from reorganization. It is enough in dividend law merely to stop dividends when profits no longer exist than from liquidation. This protects creditors to some extent, but it is reorganization that protects them most. by offering them a voice in reconstituting the company on a basis from which the interests of all capital suppliers may come in for fair consideration. Modern creditors are risk-takers too.

With a solvency test being stressed in today's statutes, there continues to be an implication that accounting reports should be constructed in terms of asset values versus debts to creditors. And accountants continue to strive to comply, as far as conscience permits, though they realize that the bookkeeping basis of their art is not constructed to provide anything more than the objectively determined data called "historical cost," something that definitely is not "current value."

(*Accounting Review*, June, 1934)

17. Creditor Protection and Unimpaired Capital

It is a note of progress that most states and the Uniform Corporation Act use other tests for dividends than solvency. Dividend statutes are not the best places to set up regulations regarding solvency or financial reorganization.

If the assets test were simplified, the solvency part of that test could be dropped, leaving capital impairment alone to contest for preferment over the profits test. Capital impairment is still a test designed primarily to secure creditor protection in limited liability companies rather than a test to relate dividends to their natural source. There is a difference between saying that distributions must not be made out of capital and saying that distributions may be made only out of profits. Since the two tests are not interchangeable, it would seem that one must ultimately yield primacy to the other.

One thorough student of dividend law makes a clear-cut choice, when he says: "Dividend law will suffer from uncertainty and confusion until the theory that dividends are measured by the value of the assets is frankly abandoned." [5] This preference rests not only on the logic of the

[5] Joseph L. Weiner, "Theory of Anglo-American Dividend Law," *Columbia Law Review*, XXIX, No. 7, 1930—his concluding sentence.

situation but also on the social desirability of decreasing the possibilities of law-inspired confusion. It should be added that accountants, by their new tendency to lay increasing emphasis upon the primacy of the income statement over the balance sheet, are showing evidence of approaching the same point of view. If they have heretofore seemed to stress the balance sheet, it may have been in part because of their wish to conform to the established legal views of a legal matter.

One weakness of the assets test is that it usually leaves the basis of asset valuation undecided. Thus it creates the so-called accounting problem of "valuation." "Aggregate of the assets" is a favorite phrase in the statutes. Does that mean original cost, liquidation value, present replacement cost, appraised value, or reasonable value? The statutes leave a great deal to the directors' interpretation, subject perhaps in the end to review by the courts if anyone raises the question.

This basis for confusion and dispute has long been a part of corporation law. Recent enactments have only partly met the problem by making a specific exception for appreciation surplus and requiring such revaluation to be deducted in arriving at the "aggregate of assets." This eliminates cash dividends out of appreciation, but questions arising from other valuation bases are not answered.

Another weakness of the assets test is that strictly speaking it is a maintenance of capital test rather than a specific direction regarding dividends —a negative rather than a positive control. Its theory is: maintain the capital fund for creditor protection and all else may be paid out in dividends. But there may be an honest difference of opinion regarding just what capital should be maintained. Is it the stockholders' original contribution or a stated part thereof? Is it the equivalent of the original investment in assets at current replacement prices, or should it be an equivalent of investor purchasing power? It is easy to see that a broad basis for much dispute still remains.[6]

Some of the consequences of the doctrine of creditor protection in dividend law should be examined. For the more that dividends rest upon accounting reports of profits, the more important that calculation becomes to accountants since theirs is the major responsibility.

The creditor is presumably interested in his margin of security. In theory he has loaned at small risk because of a fund existing to absorb losses before they could reach his debt. Capital stock impaired therefore is a creditor margin impaired. What rights does the creditor acquire if his margin of protection should be impaired? The answer is: none (if the impairment originated in business losses) until the assets aggregate less than the debt, at which point the bankruptcy statute begins to run. The answer is also none if the original capital fund is reduced by stock-

[6] This issue was still very much alive twenty years later in 1955. It lies at the heart of the current debate about the impact of changing price levels upon accounting data and reports.

holder action which transfers stated capital to surplus. Only in case impairment arises from a dividend declaration does the creditor gain any
real rights. And there are those who doubt whether creditors derive any
real protection under the trust fund or holding-out doctrines. A real
legislative regard for the protection of the creditors' margin would attempt to give them some specific rights whenever the assets fell below
the original capital, or perhaps below the capital as it stood when they
made the loan.

The mirage of the impairment test as a creditor protection is made
still further evident in the freedom with which stated capital and paid-in
surplus may be manipulated to reduce the margin of protection below
that afforded by the full consideration received for the stock issued.

The merger of several corporations by exchange of shares raises the
problem of prior surpluses. Strictly speaking, the new shares are issued
for the total assets without distinction as to assets originally invested or
assets saved out of earned profits. But that would cause the new company
to begin business—as new companies usually do—without an accumulated
surplus out of which to pay immediate dividends. This however is not
as satisfactory as it is to begin with a surplus. So ways and means are
devised for juggling the shares exchanged so the desired result will
emerge. This situation produces what has been termed "the practical
necessity" for providing statutory authority for paid-in surplus in the
Uniform Business Corporation Act. Just what objection there could be
to recording acquired surplus as earned surplus is not clear, unless it is
due to an overstressing of the legal separateness of the identity of the
old and the new corporations.

Perhaps paid-in surplus could be accepted without much objection if
it were limited to the merger situation. However, when it unites with
no-par stock and opens the way to separating all consideration received
into arbitrary divisions of stated capital and paid-in surplus, then one
begins to doubt the advisability of accepting without question even the
apparently justifiable paid-in surplus resulting from a merger with an
exchange of shares. Once the door is opened to substituting a stated
value, as chosen by the directors or stockholders, for the full consideration as the basis of the capital stock account, the line is moved still farther
back which indicates the point at which capital is impaired by dividends
and creditors' rights are endangered.

Creditors have had little real protection from the trust fund doctrine
when capital stock represented the whole consideration for the shares;
they have much less if, say, half of that consideration is put in paid-in
surplus and thereby left payable at the directors' discretion. The obvious
preference which legislators show for a capital impairment test for
dividends suggests a tender regard for the creditors' security since the
theory of that test rests upon maintenance of the capital fund. Yet giving
direct statutory recognition to a stated capital which is deliberately less

than the full consideration seems to imply that a capital fund for creditor protection is now much less important than formerly was the case.

In fact the substitution of the profits test for the capital impairment test would protect the creditors as much as they are protected now and that without the need of any trust fund doctrine to help. A profits test would of course make directors personally liable for any other kind of dividend and that would be as much protection as the creditors now enjoy. They are not protected against a loss of capital in the course of business now nor would they under a profits test. If a block is to be placed in the way of paying dividends out of current profits in the face of a capital deficit, the place to deal with that is in the section relating to reduction of capital and not in the dividend section.

From all of the above considerations it would seem that the primary concern of dividend law has been and still is creditor protection. Throughout there seems to be a failure to recognize the fact that other parties may be even more concerned in the results of operations of a business than the creditors and that the interests of the former may not be satisfactorily met by describing divisible funds in terms of aggregate assets and the aggregate of debts and capital. For the management, for the holder of income bonds, for the owner of participating preferred stock, and for the government through its income tax administration, correct profit calculations are much more important than correct surplus accounts and balance sheets.

What could be more logical therefore than to rest dividend law upon the profits test which would serve all parties at interest equally well? After all, those who supply the capital for modern corporations are not to be classified, as was the case long ago for single enterprises, into creditors and owners each with a different legal status. They are all suppliers of capital, and they all are claimants against earnings and residual assets according to the terms of their respective contracts. They have more common than antagonistic interests.

(*Accounting Review*, June, 1934)

18. Background of Paid-in Surplus

It was a complex background out of which no-par stock, stated capital, and paid-in surplus emerged. One part of the social and industrial complex which lay back of this development was the conviction among businessmen, perhaps growing out of the experience of 1921, that financing through security issues was preferable to customary short-term financing through bank loans; another part was the greater familiarity on the part of a large number of people with securities in general as a result of war finance drives and liberty loan investments; still another part of the background was the apparent preference among corporate directors for capitalizing in various ways the economies (and profits) of technological progress when they might have advocated a sharing of these benefits with the great mass of consumers through voluntary price reductions, and with wage increases. During the long wave of prosperity before 1930, these conditions and opinions created a great appetite for securities. This constitutes the first element of the background; the second was the no-par stock movement.

Statutes permitting no-par stock were initiated for the purpose of avoiding the deceits which often had accompanied the issuance of shares with fixed par. No-par stock was essentially an effort to approach, in the corporation, the simple accounting logic of the proprietorship wherein the price of the contribution would be credited to the capital account. The idea was that the new stock would eliminate all need for artificial valuation of assets made to cover underwriting and similar costs of issuing stock. And sensibly used it probably could have accomplished that objective. But the unrestricted opportunity to interpret unadjudicated statutes for oneself made a strong appeal to a certain type of mind in the surrounding atmosphere of easy money. Consequently, there appeared a willingness in some people to search out loopholes in the laws and to stretch all technicalities beyond the spirit of the statute if necessary. This in a large measure prevented no-par stock from performing its full measure of service.

In the absence of new restraints accompanying the new type of stock, the individual was left free to choose the financial practices he would follow. This freedom fitted in particularly well with the philosophy of this inflation period—especially with the doctrine that recent earnings justified higher valuations for assets on the ground that the earnings were bound to continue in this "new era of permanently higher prices." The result was many appraisals, reorganizations, stock dividends, split-ups, mergers, new incorporations, holding companies, investment trusts, etc.

Out of this background came paid-in surplus and appreciation. The former was logical enough in connection with an excess payment in cases where new stock was issued which gave the new holders an interest in past surplus along with prior stockholders. But of course the excess price should have then been credited directly to earned surplus as a simple equalizing payment. It would be quite logical for merged companies to carry over into the new organization the same surplus accounts as existed before the change. The obvious intention would be to continue unbroken the dividend continuity, especially for preferred stock, which had previously been established. It would seem that this carry-over could still be properly called earned surplus. But the form rather than the substance seemed to control the ideas, and since a new corporation could not have earnings of its own at once upon organization, the total assets came to be regarded as the consideration for both a capital stock and a "paid-in" surplus on the new books.

This unfortunate following of form rather than substance, when linked up with no-par stock, produces the doctrine of stated value. This is actual retrogression, for stated value is a partial reversion to the idea of par value which no-par statutes were attempting to abandon. Stated value in fact was more than mere retrogression; it was a pernicious expedient as well. It fostered the doctrine that capital stock account could express any sum directors might designate as the margin for protection of creditors of a limited liability corporation. The older idea was that this account received the total consideration exchanged by stockholders for the stock issued. As a result of the new idea about capital stock, a part of stockholder contributions could be placed in surplus either at the time of incorporation or later. Such surplus would be held at the discretion of company directors. And let it be noted, such surplus would be very different in nature from that carried over from a prior earned surplus of mergered companies.

Appreciation write-up of assets likewise seemed to enjoy much support from surrounding conditions of the 1920's. Credit, it was argued, was extended to a company on the basis of values, not costs. That is to say, security issues could be justified according to the value of the properties regardless of the original cost of the assets—if prospective earnings promised a good return. And current earnings, it was thought, were entirely satisfactory and promising. On that reasoning a known amount of securities could be issued—an amount nicely calculated to absorb the anticipated earnings.

Furthermore, the thought ran, appraised asset values were obviously sound because replacement costs were now so much higher than formerly —were still mounting in fact. Finally the power of directors to value business property according to their own judgement was, short of demonstrable fraud, quite undisputed in law.

Join this kind of doctrine with the much discussed idea regarding the "necessity" to calculate depreciation on a high base in order to recover in sales adequate amounts to meet mounting replacement costs, and one can hardly escape becoming an advocate of asset write-up. As to the credit item accompanying a write-up, there seemed no logical place to dump it but in that familiar catchall, surplus. And there was no existing prohibition against such a disposal.

Here, in somewhat figurative language, is a picture of the way part of paid-in capital and appreciation credits found their way into surplus. And here too, because some people recognized the possibilities of deceit being made easier by such practice, is the basis for later reactions which brought in their wake changes in many state corporation statutes, especially in excluding appreciation surplus from cash dividends, and changes in accounting reports, especially those which classified surplus into revealing subtitled items.

(*Certified Public Accountant*, April, 1933)

19. Creditor Interest in Surplus

The basic theory of American dividend law has long been associated with the desirability of maintaining unimpaired the fund (capital stock) dedicated in an enterprise to the protection of the creditors of that limited liability corporation. The point is not often made however that corporation surplus likewise serves as a protective margin for creditors.

The creditor's first protective barrier is company surplus. This figure is not only an indicator to stockholders of a possible dividend source; it also indicates to the creditor the amount of property withdrawal or value shrinkage which may take place without capital impairment. Into this situation come recent changes in dividend law introducing no-par stock, stated capital and paid-in surplus, prohibition of cash dividends from appraisal surplus, etc. Involved here is a clash of old and new ideas; and in the midst of these developments there is the possibility that directors are being given greater powers than ever of modifying the margin that exists to protect creditors.

The older idea of protective margins included only capital stock. But that account was considered as expressing the whole of the stockholders' contribution taken at a fair value at the time it was made. The newer idea, one associated with no-par stock statutes, is that capital stock (creditors' protective barrier) is a designated sum and may be less than the stockholders' whole contribution (by the amount of "paid-in" surplus). Associated with the older concept was the idea that the original capital fund contribution should be kept intact, even to the extent of making good all existing capital impairment before declaring dividends. Under the newer concept directors, or directors and stockholders, seem to have gained a good deal of freedom to reduce the protective fund (capital stock) by either initial or subsequent assignment of some part of stockholder contribution to the status of (paid-in) surplus.

Whatever may be later debited to a surplus account of such an origin is in effect a debit against stockholder contribution. Hence, it is a debit against the creditor's second protective barrier, that is, against capital stock.

This defensive barrier is not now as substantial as it used to be in the days when losses that impaired capital stock were expected to be made good out of earnings before dividends were again resumed. Stated capital may not be cut into by dividends and that is some creditor protection. But assets frittered away in losses through bad management reduce creditor margin as well as dividend possibilities. Capital stock can be reduced by transfers to paid-in surplus. Then the latter can be used to absorb an asset write-down. If an existing earned surplus has been retained after the asset revaluation, there seems no restraint except that of the principles of sound finance, upon directors' action to declare dividends out of such earned surplus. Since creditors lack voting power, they are powerless to intervene in protection of the shrinking of their margin by director action.

It seems therefore that the new idea of the nature of capital favors stockholders by making it easy for management to absorb the effect of losses (into capital if desired) rather than having to restore the loss by saved future earnings before declaring subsequent dividends. Creditors however find that their second protective barrier has been reduced (capital impairment is thus put further off) and, if earned surplus survives an asset write-down to paid-in surplus, they find that their first protective barrier can be reduced by disbursements to stockholders.

The designation as capital stock of a sum less than the whole consideration and the practically unrestricted power freely to transfer amounts from stock to surplus, both indicate a distinct lowering of the points at which the creditors may, through the courts, become vocal in their own behalf. That being the case, it would seem but just that the creditors should in some way be given a voice earlier in their own interest.

To accomplish this, the creditors' rights might be extended by statute somewhat as follows: (1) any petition to the Secretary of State made for permission to reduce the amount of its capital stock, either as a partial liquidating distribution or as a transfer to some surplus or reserve account, shall be accompanied by a certificate that notice of the proposed reduction in capital stock has been mailed to the corporation's principal creditors and preferred stockholders fifteen days before the stockholders' meeting in which the action was voted; (2) when creditors who hold as much as 20 per cent of a corporation's total indebtedness and/or preferred stock conclude that an impairment of their margin of protection by dividends or losses is imminent, they may have an audit made for them by a Certified Public Accountant of their own selection to determine the facts.

Another and more positive method of providing creditors with an earlier voice in their own behalf would be to give them by statute the power to elect a majority of the directors whenever a Certified Public Accountant's balance sheet indicated that the designated capital fund had been reduced either (a) by dividends, (b) by losses, or (c) by transfer to surplus. If this power were given to creditors, the law should further provide that such voting control would cease and the creditor's directors would retire when a satisfactory rehabilitation or reorganization of the capital structure had been accomplished.

This latter proposal, it will be noted, gives the creditors a less complete control than they would have in a receivership, but could give them a temporary majority control earlier than usually would be the case. The thought behind this type of legal right is that an early co-operation between creditors and stockholders, especially during a severe depression, would probably result in increased salvage for all parties through a sensible reorganization.

Behind the first and milder suggestion is the thought that the creditors probably could find ways of influencing the action of the stockholders and directors if they, the creditors, had early knowledge of the full facts in the case. Perhaps a direct contact with management could be provided if the creditors and preferred stockholders had at all times the right to elect a minority of the directors. Their representatives would thus be acquainted with the company's policies and condition, and could speak for the creditors' point of view when changes were necessary or desirable.

Modern conditions require that a company be managed with all suppliers of capital in mind and not merely the holders of the common stock. In fact, the best managements are not unmindful of the interests of labor and the general public. What is needed is for managements which might tend to be laggard in some of these respects to be "helped" to a better point of view.

(*Certified Public Accountant*, April, 1933)

20. On Defining Earned Surplus

It would be difficult to settle upon a definition of earned surplus until surplus is itself first defined (for the former is but a portion of the latter) and until the nature and definition of profit or realized income have been described (for earned surplus is as inescapably associated with realized earnings as it is with surplus). Furthermore, it will be difficult to define either surplus or income until consideration has been given to the nature of corporate capital stock (for questions of surplus arise only in connection with corporations and the distinction there is one running between capital and income).

Is corporate capital stock any arbitrary figure stated in the charter or selected by the directors as an indication of the protective margin contributed by shareholders in lieu of unlimited liability? Or is it the whole of whatever property was paid in? Is profit, or net income, to be considered as the increment in the value of the whole of the property in a given length of time? Or is it the net proceeds which are the consequence of managerial skill in keeping the cost of producing the return somewhat below whatever gross return is afforded by market conditions? This is not the time or place to develop these important preliminary questions. But a sequence of definitions would undoubtedly add to the clearness of the thought expressed in the final definition. A good sequence of definitions would be: corporate capital stock, surplus, profit, and finally, earned surplus available for dividends.

In the definition of earned surplus as phrased by a committee of the American Institute of Public Accountants, the long parenthetical clause detracts greatly from the power of the definition to convey a clear-cut thought. If this alternative clause is held to be indispensable, it should follow the definition proper in a collateral sentence. In another collateral sentence a brief definition should be given to show the sense in which "profits, income, and gains" are used. It is also suggested that the verb "measures" be used in these definitions where possible in place of the verb "is"—this to indicate the fact that surplus is not a thing of itself but rather a certain aspect of assets.

Following this last idea, the committee's "collateral definitions" might be changed as follows: "Surplus in its broadest sense is *an adjunct to capital stock accounts designed to help measure* the total amount of the stockholders' equity . . . etc." "Paid in surplus *measures* the amount received . . . etc." "Revaluation surplus *measures* the appreciation . . . etc."

It is also suggested that the short paragraph about balance sheet captions be shown under the "standard practice" section of the report.

Having in mind the above comments, the following definition of earned surplus is offered as incorporating some of the points mentioned:

Earned Surplus is the quantitative representation or measure of that portion of the assets obtained from any type of realized income which has been retained in the business without being permanently dedicated as undistributable investment by a formal transfer to capital stock account.

In this definition, "quantitative representation" conveys the idea that surplus is itself an abstraction and is related to concrete things only by definition and usage—"that part of the assets" indicated that surplus is a function of assets and that *earned* surplus is only a part of a larger whole. The phrase "from any type of realized income" names the only possible source of earned surplus, yet states that source broadly enough to cover the profits and gains as named separately in the committee's definition (see terminology report in the *Journal of Accountancy,* July, 1922) for "income." The phrase "which has been retained in the business" further qualified "that part of the assets" since some of the income-produced assets may have been paid out as dividends, and takes the place of the phrase "from the date of incorporation" in the committee's definition. The phrase "without being permanently dedicated . . . etc." makes it clear that not all of the retained assets from income sources constitute the basis of earned surplus, since some assets may have been retained and thus made unavailable by stock dividend.

(*Accounting Review,* June, 1930)

21. Dividend Test for Strong Companies

It might be well if dividend law made a distinction between financially weak and financially strong corporations. Where, because of the nature of the business or by choice, a corporation uses borrowed capital sparingly, it would seem proper that it should have greater freedom to withdraw assets according to the wishes of the common stockholders than would be the case where a corporation, by the nature of its activities or by choice, operates on thinner ice by reason of a large proportion of "protected" capital obtained by borrowing at pledged rates of interest or preferred dividends.

Dividend statutes are designed to protect creditors; yet creditor protection does not, in fact, rest as much upon any stated sum of capital investment as upon the relative proportion which debts bear to assets. A company with a high ratio of assets to debts affords high protection to its creditors, and the stockholders therefore might well be accorded large discretion in the amount of asset withdrawals. A company with a low ratio of assets to debt affords low protection to its creditors, and its stockholders therefore might well be more severely restricted in the amount of their withdrawals.

Clearly it is the desire to afford creditors better protection which prompts legislation to lean upon a capital impairment test for dividends rather than upon an insolvency test. The latter test, if it stands alone, comes into play too late to afford real protection, whereas the former stops dividend withdrawals while there is still a margin (in the amount of invested capital) between the creditors and loss from company insolvency. It was no doubt the desire to increase creditor protection still further which prompted the clause in the North Carolina statute preventing dividends if the debts exceed two-thirds of the assets,[7] and the clause in the California statute to prevent dividends if the assets are less than one and one-fourth times the debts.[8]

Are the ratios there used adequate to afford a desirable increase in creditor protection beyond that provided by a capital impairment test?

The first question involved in considering the adequacy of a statutory ratio of assets to debt must be: What is comprehended in the two quantities to be compared? The principal issue in regard to "debt" is whether the aggregate should include preferred stocks.

The usual conception of preference shares is that they represent that part of ownership which has a superior status over some other part. If this is the case generally, they should not be included with debts in making the ratio calculation. But financial practice has produced so many preferred issues that rise above a simple ownership equity that they partake of most, if not all, of the characteristics of creditorship.

California, Illinois, Michigan, and Pennsylvania, by permitting dividends out of paid-in surplus to be declared only on preferred shares, give those shares almost the same protection as to continuity of dividends as is given to bonds for interest.

These examples serve to indicate that the distinctions between preferred shares and bonds are fading and to suggest that, in calculating the margin of protection for superior interests, these two sources of capital may be classed together.

•

[7] Sec. 1179, amended 1933.
[8] Sec. 348 b, amended 1933.

The principal issue in connection with the term "assets" is the particular method of valuation to be used. The California statute uses the phrase "taken at their fair present value." This presumably is something more than liquidation value for the latter term would mean that current assets would be greatly reduced and tangible fixed assets would have to be stated near scrap values. "Fair present value" on the other hand might be taken to mean appraised replacement value—obviously an impractical basis for deciding upon dividends each year—or it might mean original cost after allowing for a proper annual depreciation charge to operations and excluding any appraisal write-up of plant and land.

If this last meaning prevails, the definition of assets is close to that which would be approved by public accountants as an amount determined according to accepted accounting principles. If this is the meaning to be conveyed, statutory provisions would avoid the possible implications of seeming to mean annual appraisal, if the ratio clause in the law used some such phrase as ". . . that the assets of the corporation after such dividend distribution or withdrawal taken at a value *determined according to the accepted principles of accounting for going concerns* will at least be equal to one and one-half times its debts, liabilities and shares having a preference in dissolution."

The next question concerns the size of the ratio which would stop dividend withdrawals in time to provide adequate protection to security-holders who are not primary risk-takers.

A margin of 25 per cent seems low, especially if the assets have not been valued close to liquidation value for making the ratio calculation. If liquidation of the corporation is in fact imminent, it is too late for this type of dividend restriction to begin to apply. If the assets are on a basis above liquidation value, an asset margin of one fourth more than the debts is insufficient recognition of the probable shrinkage under adverse financial conditions.

Certain studies of published corporation financial statements, including both going concerns and companies approaching insolvency or reorganization, show that the ratio of assets to debts most often met is noticeably higher than 125 per cent.[9]

While these studies are out of date, it is unlikely that similar modal averages would now (i.e., 1938) vary significantly since the working assets and earning power of different types of industries have inherent characteristics which strongly influence the proportion of the various securities constituting their capital structure.

From two other studies[10] similar ratios have been computed for a large number of companies which either entered into a receivership, defaulted on bonds, or underwent a material financial readjustment. The studies

[9] Computed from Bulletins No. 27, 29, 32, 35, Bureau of Business Research, University of Illinois, Urbana.
[10] Bulletins No. 31 and 51, Bureau of Business Research, University of Illinois, Urbana.

examined various balance sheet ratios for a number of years prior to failure in an effort to learn which ratios gave earliest and most consistent indication of approaching financial difficulties. Some of the data incidental to this purpose permit the calculation of the proportionality between total assets and total debts.

This showing should be particularly interesting because withdrawal of assets for dividends becomes increasingly unwise and legal restrictions increasingly justifiable as a corporation approaches insolvency. Restrictions are too late when insolvency has become a fact.

On the whole the evidence here is similar to that for going concerns, with the added feature that the ratio grows noticeably smaller as the companies approach receivership. Six years before failure the ratio (excluding preferred stock) is close to two and one-half times; in several lines it is very nearly three times. In the last year before receivership or default the ratio is generally down to two times. When preferred stock is counted with debt, the sixth year before failure shows ratios varying between one and one-half times and one and three-fourths. In the last year, three cases show a little more than equality between assets and total obligations; three others show something less than one and one-half.

It would seem therefore that a statutory proportion of assets one and one-fourth times the debts would have placed a restriction upon asset withdrawals in only a few of these cases, and those only if balance sheet figures for assets were used and preferred stock was counted with bonds and current debts.

A statutory test (using balance sheet assets and counting preferred stock with debt) of two assets for one of debts would have stopped dividend withdrawals early in the six-year period for most of the companies that later failed. A test of one and one-half of assets for one of debts would have stopped withdrawals for many companies two years before failure, and for all companies in the last year.

If preferred stock is not included with debt, the statutory ratio would need to be higher. It would take a ratio of two and one-half or three to one to stop withdrawals as early as the fifth year; a ratio of two to one would stop dividends in the last year only in some cases.

It was suggested above that a statute which related dividend withdrawals to a ratio test would provide suitable creditor protection. If it were desired to distinguish further and thus encourage financially strong companies in contrast to weak companies, the statute could call upon accounting for additional co-operation by adding to the above the following clause: . . . provided that when the earnings of the current fiscal period before interest charges, determined according to acceptable principles of accounting, are less than equal to interest charges plus preferred dividends, no dividends on common stock may be declared even though the ratio of assets to debt is above the prescribed minimum.

(*Harvard Business Review,* Autumn, 1938)

IMPACT OF PRICE-LEVEL VARIATIONS

1. Variety in the Concept of Income

There must be a concept of income (or profit) bound up in the technology which we call accounting. This is true because the word accounting now carries the connotation of a technology resting on ancient Italian double-entry bookkeeping. And because the unique contribution of double entry (i.e., the integration of real and nominal accounts) was, and is, focused upon the computation of enterprise net income.

Accounting was gradually perceived to be a systematic and widely useful method of classifying concrete money facts. But it needs to be emphasized that later adaptations of this methodology to uses wherein accountability rather than profit is the objective do not change the fact that some concept of income is basic to this technology even under these circumstances. Adaptation meant that variety in the concept of income became inevitable with attendant possibilities for confusion.

In the sense of useful record-keeping, something akin to accounting was in use in England before double entry was known there. On the landed estates of the sixteenth century very elaborate accountability records were kept by separate operating departments—farm, kitchen, bakery, etc. Internal check between departments was fully developed; expenditures were budgeted in advance; the resulting records were carefully summarized and annually audited. The summaries (financial statements?) were in the form we know as "charge and discharge"—that is, reporting details which say: "I am accountable for . . ."; "I discharge my responsibility in these ways. . . ." Clearly this was not an acounting calculation of net income.

Commercial profit was of course not unknown in seventeenth century England, but it was not calculated for equal time periods. This was the day of the great trading companys—East Indies Company, Hudson's Bay Company and others. The trading voyages of the East Indies Company, for example, were joint ventures. The contributing members divided the proceeds from the sale of goods brought back from foreign lands. Profit could be calculated by each partner from comparing his own original costs and the final proceeds. This was profit in the true sense of the word rather than income. It was the result of liquidation; it measured the net of a closed venture, not a periodic calculation from continuing operations.

The calculations of accountability in the feudal estates were annual and the records were continuous, but the activities were not commercial. The calculations of an individual's profit upon liquidation of a trading venture were related to commerce, but were not based on continuing records. It was the Italians who, through many generations of evolution, succeeded in combining these two elements. Italian double-entry bookkeeping provided a continuing record of commercial transactions. This made it possible to make interim calculations of operating net income whenever desired. It does not change this characteristic of double entry that the accounts were seldom closed annually. The merchant could see the accumulating results at will by looking into the main accounts in his ledger.

The third idea of income is found in Italian double entry—that of a continuing, interrelated flow of revenue and expense associated with a continuing commercial enterprise under management. The records of the day included real accounts, particularly debts receivable and debts payable, and nominal accounts (goods, expense) that were closed into a profit and loss account and thence into capital accounts as at present. The origin of the balance sheet was a "balance account." Herein, particularly when the personnel of a partnership changed, were assembled by transfer entries the balances of the several real accounts remaining open after all nominal accounts and the profit and loss account had been closed.

Several aspects of Italian double entry should be noted because of their relevance to this third idea of income.

This method did not involve an appraisal calculation of net worth as of two different dates; it therefore did not reflect a concept of income as an appraised increment in property values. It used historical cost not for anyone's convenience but for the reason that cost represented money capital invested (risked) the measured money outcome of which, when compared with historical cost, would make it possible after the fact to judge the wisdom of having taken the prior investment risk.

The familiar sequence of entering transactions and closing the accounts was used from the fifteenth century. This sequence of methodology was closely related to the main contribution made by double entry.

The primary contribution was not that of securing equality of debit and credit in journal entry or in the trial balance. It lay in the integration of real and nominal accounts. It is this "invention" that makes it more rational than convenient to record the same transaction fact in two categories. It is integration between the two major groups of accounts that causes the capital statement and the income statement to tie into each other. The larger significance of this tight interrelationship is clear when we note that here, for the first time, was a method for systematically and continuously recording the interaction of capital on income and of income on capital, thus making it possible to observe the separateness and the interrelation of finance and operations. Obviously a very fundamental process had been devised. Its fundamentalness is more clearly visible now than at its beginning. For that early foundation still lies beneath modern accounting in a setting of complexity utterly inconceivable in an earlier day.

The next three hundred years showed little change in double entry itself. This was the time of its slow spread throughout the world. Gradually, and ultimately completely, double entry replaced accountability records (charge and discharge); and continuous (i.e., periodic) calculation of income replaced irregular calculations of the liquidation profit of terminable ventures.

Late in the eighteenth century a direct statement was made in Adam Smith's *Wealth of Nations* to the effect that profit could arise only if "goods changed masters." This idea we now call the realization principle; it seems as reasonable under the new name as under the old phraseology. By inference both expressions include the idea that unrealized value change does not generate profit or loss. Before realization, price change only hints that profit or loss may eventually materialize. This inference, so plainly lodged in the British economist's phrase of 1776, gained support in the English courts in 1870 and again in 1894 in cases which ruled in essence that price rise and fall did not affect profit available for dividends.

Another idea, developed in the early days of British railroads, involved a concept of profit radically different from the one now associated with the use of historical cost and the amortization of fixed assets. The traditional British double-section balance sheet originated at this time. It was accompanied by a replacement doctrine about the way to account for fixed assets. That is to say, maintenance cost and replacement items were charged against revenues; periodic amortization of original investments in fixed assets was not used.

Several reasons might account for these practices. Possibly engineers held the opinion that wear was not currently measurable. To economists loss from wear would not be considered as currently realized since goods did not change masters. The idea that fixed assets represented capital permanently sunk in the enterprise no doubt had a legalistic origin. By analogy a business enterprise would be considered similar to a landed estate. The law of estates and inheritances had long before established the concept of corpus and income—the one being the claim of the remainderman, the other measuring the interest of the life tenant. In order to do justice to the basic intention of the testator, the corpus had to be maintained intact. As a consequence, income to the life tenant could only be an excess of estate revenue beyond the amount necessary for maintenance of the physical corpus. On this basis, with a railroad considered analogous to a trusteed estate, it would be reasonable to treat fixed assets as "capital permanently sunk" (corpus) which would be as useful as ever if parts were replaced as needed. Until replacement was necessary, enterprise revenue, still under the analogy to estates, would be available for dividends after deduction had been made for actual operating expenses. In other words, fixed assets would not be considered to create operating expense merely by being in existence and use.

In all probability enterprise management also had its reasons in support of the prevalent concept of enterprise income (i.e., income calculated by replacement accounting rather than amortization accounting). Amortization could easily have seemed highly artificial and unrelated to operating expenses. Not a few people are still inclined to lay considerable stress on "out-of-pocket" expense and to look upon fixed asset cost amortized into expense as "mere bookkeeping." Furtehrmore, dividends for railroad stockholders were particularly hard to earn in the early days, even without amortization being treated as an expense long before replacement became necessary.

Such ideas could spell out justification of the then prevalent concept of cost and net income. Sometimes today the thought is advanced in the United States that the avoidance in England of the use of amortization of historical cost indicated a conscious intention in the accounting calculations to match current money prices for fixed asset expenses with revenue of similar purchasing power of the day. The idea could be an *ex post facto* rationalization of the known practice, since there is little in the literature of the time indicating that this kind of justification was then influential.

In view of the variety of concepts of income in Europe, it will not be surprising to find a variety in the United States as well.

Early in the nineteenth century corporations were chartered individually, each by a separate act of a state legislature. By the terms of some of these charters dividends were restricted to "clear profit," by others to "actual profit." Apparently these phrases would mean (1) profit clear of cost, expense, loss, or (2) profit actually realized, not mere anticipated profit.

Such meaning would still be quite understandable. Yet in 1825, when New York State passed the first general incorporation law, dividends were there limited to "surplus profit." Thus a third idea was introduced, and as always variety made for confusion. Did the new phrase mean excess of gross income over cost and expense? Profit after deducting reserves and appropriations for retained earnings? Dividends out of retained prior earnings plus or minus current operating net? In what way was the new phrase better than the other two?

A century later the New York statute had dropped the noun "profit" and made the adjective "surplus" into a noun. Dividends were to be from "surplus." In retrospect, the change seems to have been ill-advised; and its reason for being is not clear. Is it significant that the change was made in the booming days of the 1920's when revaluation of assets was of frequent occurrence? Did such appraisals produce a credit to "surplus?"

Was the balance of surplus, thus increased, available for cash dividend? Was this new dividend base introduced into the law at this time by accidental coincidence?

It is not necessary to search for answers; possibly there are no answers. But whatever the reason for the terminology, it did not survive for a century as did the term "surplus profit." Before many years, lawyers and accountants each in their own way showed that they favored limiting cash dividends unmistakably to "earned surplus." Thus, at long last in the 1930's, some of the variety of connotation lodged in the phrase "surplus profit" in the 1825 statute was to some extent clarified. The phraseology of the 1930's seems to intend to refer to profit rather than surplus, but in a way (by the adjective "earned") which tells (1) that appraisal credit is not included, (2) that both prior retained earnings and current net are available, and (3) that both the fruits of operating activities and the excess proceeds from sale of fixed assets are to be considered available for cash dividends.

Two points may be noted in connection with the last item above. It is in accord with the idea of taxable income expressed by statute and by the Supreme Court (income and gains from whatever source derived). Or perhaps it should be said that the over-all concept of realized gain as income has always been the view typically held in all sections of American opinion. In contrast, it is characteristic of British opinion to treat capital gains as distinct from operating gains.

Ideas about the concept of income are more sharply than ever under debate in America today because of the impact of a devalued currency and several years of sharply rising price levels. The issue concerns the choice between two ideas: (1) income is the spread between historical cost and revenue from current sales; (2) income is the spread between current cost prices and revenue from current sales prices.

Only brief consideration of this issue can be given here. A few comments may be in order, however, in the setting here provided of variety and change of concept over a long period of time.

The question is at base one of the connotation of the word "realize." Realization was clearly a feature of Italian double entry of the fifteenth century, since it made use of invested cost and not appraised valuations. It was also a feature of the thought in eighteenth century economics as shown by the phrase "goods must change masters." These ideas were generated by thinking about business enterprises. In later years however economic reasoning came to be focused strongly on the individual person and today upon society as a very large group of individual persons. A person and a society do not "realize income"; personal and social "well-being" is the keynote. A typical leading question of today asks "can a person's money income measure his state of well-being?" Since his cost of living is a critical factor in his well-being, his money income is significant to the individual primarily in terms of its purchasing power.

Social economists therefore are very much concerned with statistics which reflect the relationship between wage incomes and costs of living.

This interest is natural and understandable since men everywhere work in order to consume. And anyone desirous of improving the ratio of work to consumption will want to observe, and perhaps try to influence, that ratio. But thinking which is appropriate to an individual's well-being cannot be equally appropriate to a business enterprise. The analogy is not close enough to permit safe reasoning by analogy. The enterprise is an institution; it works to produce, not to consume. "Purchasing power" ratios are not there as significant as for individuals; purchasing is a relative small phase of productive enterprise. Since most of the property held is not kept for exchange, its value in terms of possible current selling price is not constantly an issue.

Because the enterprise is focused toward production, the chief question before its management is not whether physical capital is being maintained but whether the capital in hand is being effectively employed in production. Effective employment can only be judged after the fact. Hence it will always be necessary for those who decide to risk capital, in asset form or as cost or expense, to be able later to know the dollars previously invested (risked) in order to appraise the prior decisions when its fruits in dollars become known. "Purchasing power" accounting would not provide figures for prior invested costs which management could study. Management needs double-entry account data (historical cost) in order to make this backward appraisal of management decisions. If additional information is desired, it should be supplemental, that is, provided outside the framework of historical cost double entry.

The present debate therefore is one of concepts rather than of managerial objectives or record technology. Accounting has proved itself a very flexible instrument; it is able to incorporate a new methodology if the conceptual objectives are acceptable, that is, if new ideas do not negate the continuing usefulness of existing ideas and objectives.

There is good reason for believing that the spread between current replacement costs and current revenue is not net income to an enterprise. The reason is that *realized* price rise is one of the inseparable elements of the measured results of effective enterprise management.

Income calculations guided by the present generally accepted concepts are not unrealistic in fact or ideology. They may seem unrealistic however to one who does not know, or accept as rational, the basic ideas that underlie existing accounting methods. Perhaps that unwillingness to accept prevailing ideas as sound accounting may be due in part to a confusion of realism for an individual person and realism for a business enterprise under management. It could also be influenced by a belief that accounting, the pliable dutiful servant, should make calculations as desired.

People who know the inside picture of accounting ideology and see aspects of a profession in all applications of accounting will not be easily influenced to reason about an enterprise as if it were an individual person or to accept a doctrine of subservience on the part of professional accountants.

The current debate on income concepts is clearly part of a continuing process of examining into the inner structure of the ideology which has been a long time in the building. Debate is a road to progress. And whatever the outcome presently, progress will result, if not at that time, then later when and if the facts of debate, after trial, have to be revised. It was made evident above that something like trial and reversal appeared in connection with the concept of a proper dividend base. It could happen again.

Variety of concepts we have had and still have. It would be well for us to keep this fact in mind because variety will persist, and persisting will constitute a continuing basis for misunderstanding. To the extent that we are able to appraise rationally and fully the significant differences between concepts, we will be better able to exercise good judgement as individuals and perhaps now and then help to clarify the thinking of others.

(*New York Certified Public Accountant*, July, 1953)

2. Doctrine of Replacement Cost

The concept of profit usually considered as underlying enterprise accounting may be stated this way: *Profit* is the result of providing an outflow of economic services valued by the purchaser at a price higher than the cost of the input of economic factors required to produce the output.

This phrasing of the concept rests upon the following ideas:

(1) Receiving and giving (exchange) are basic to economic activities.

(2) The basic purpose of double entry is systematically to bring into comparison the money price of the things received and given by a specific enterprise.

(3) Enterprise accrual accounting is a refinement of double-entry techniques by means of which cost and revenue are periodically and sharply associated much as if cost represented enterprise effort and revenue represented results of effort.

(4) By referring to data from his accrual accounting an enterpriser is able to compare cost given (incurred) with revenue received (earned) and consequently is in a position to judge the satisfaction with which his services have been accepted and the skill with which he has kept his costs below the price the market would pay.

Thus it is evident that there has been an inner consistency in the traditional views of profit even though time has brought modifications and refinements. Business custom, reaching backward far down the centuries, has consistently made use of original, outlay costs as the basis of profit calculation. Five hundred years of bookkeeping practice reflect this theory of profit because bookkeeping employs the ideas of businessmen. In a similar way commercial law reflects the same business tradition; original cost is the basis of profit calculations under dividend laws and income tax laws.

But this philosophy has lately been challenged; another theory has been advanced, a replacement cost theory of profit. It may be briefly stated thus: Profit is measured by the margin between the revenue which sales transactions produce and the amount necessary to cover replacement costs of similar goods.

It would be interesting to search out the logic possessed by this concept which could make it prevail against the forces of experience-tested custom, and then to determine whether we should see in this theory the result of a passing reaction to disturbed economic conditions or a concept which is the next step in evolutionary development. But the time to work it out is not available. I must be content to speculate a little about the origin of these modifications of the customary profit concept.

The doctrine of replacement costs in accounting seems to have two sources of American origin. The first is in public-utility rate discussions where the problem of setting controlled selling prices at the proper level brings out many strong arguments, in periods of advancing prices, in favor of including the recapture of replacement prices as an element of the rate base. The second source of replacement doctrine is found in the point of view of promoters and investors who tend to judge balance sheet "values" by the yardstick of stock market capitalizations of prospective earnings.

It should be noted that both of these conditions constitute special cases which are peculiarly sensitive to price changes, one because close governmental control precludes the adoption of selling prices which would provide revenue to be stored up in times of plenty against the time of depression; the other because value judgments in connection with securities are based upon guesses of probable future business earnings.

It is difficult to see how we can justifiably follow special points of view in formulating a general concept.

Replacement cost doctrine also has a European source. There, a deliberate fiat money inflation after World War I made all common-sense rules ineffective, especially income tax laws. Of course an artificially generated competition in the raising of prices and getting rid of money would raise problems of pricing policy and problems of equitable taxes and conservative dividends. The managerial problems of inflation were terrific. But the conditions were artificial, temporary, and very unusual.

Should artificial, temporary, and unusual circumstances dictate the

formulation of a concept of profits which presumably would be expected
to have a general application?

In the background of these replacement doctrines there run waves of
war and postwar price fluctuations. These price movements were made
clear to our eyes by the newly developed statistical technique of index-
numbers, and only too plain to our experience by the artificialities of a
paper prosperity and later by the amount of unemployment in a very
real depression. The perspective of recent years is thus well suited to
creating the impression that swift and extensive changes in price levels
are becoming a normal condition.

Then this recently formed impression encounters the basic idea that
accounting is designed to avoid *mental* images of profit potential by
expressing profit in definite quantitative terms, using for this purpose
a technical methodology for recording and contrasting the bargained
prices of both the input of services received and the output of services
rendered. From the meeting of these two ideas—accounting as a record
of original prices, and widely fluctuating prices as a normal pattern—
there seems to have come the conviction that accounting for outlay cost
can no longer be considered a dependable guide for those who look to
accounts for essential information. And the conclusion then follows that
account-keeping or financial statement practice must be modified to suit
the new background.

These views seem to me to be based upon several fallacious assumptions: (1) the assumption that problems of income distribution (dividends, income tax, speculative security profits) are of more importance
than problems of the measurement of income generated by the creation
of new wealth or the rendering of acceptable services; (2) the assumption
that accounting has a more important obligation to supply data useful
in managerial pricing policy than it has in facilitating the comparison
of past input of services (costs) with past output of services (revenues);
(3) the assumption that accounts and statements are merely tabulations
of statistical data related to certain kinds of social income and as such
are open to any desired manipulations by statistical methodology, such
as weighting by index-numbers, reduction to averages, elimination of
seasonal variations, etc.; (4) the assumption that accounting records of
cost prices in the traditional manner will conceal from businessmen and
investors the significance of contemporary price changes; (5) the assumption that recent price fluctuations establish the pattern of the future. I
believe that these assumptions are erroneous and that a concept resting
upon unsound assumptions cannot be accepted as sound.

The primary and central problem of business, and hence of accounting and finance, will always be income. This problem has two subdivisions, one related to a methodology for computing the income created
and the other to a methodology for criticizing the economic reality of
the results. The first of these is obviously accounting, when accounting

is defined as a reasonable, realistic, convenient method of calculating profits by expressing quantitatively a great diversity of actual business transactions. The second is valuation, which may be defined as an interpretative procedure designed to subject accounting results and business policies to critical examination. I am of the opinion that valuation is not accounting.

The fundamental error of those who argue that profit calculation by the use of replacement costs is a function of accounting is that they confuse the two separate techniques of computing and of criticizing. If criticizing—evaluating—is consciously accepted as a separate function, there is practically no limit to the ways in which the available data may be made into homogeneous statistical series and subjected to interpretative manipulation like any other social statistics. For example, no one has made the suggestion, but it probably would be very easy to substitute the simple statistical study of real income (ratio of money income to price level) and real wages (ratio of money wages to cost of living) for the complicated technique of adjusting accounts by index-number of wholesale prices for the purpose of becoming conscious of the significance of price changes.

But it is basic to this freedom of statistical analysis of the results of business operations that the original data of business operations be recorded and reported first in the way in which they transpired, that is, in terms of bargained prices. This accounting is well prepared to do with a high degree of dependability while acting well within its function.[1]

(*Accounting Review*, March, 1936)

3. Appreciation from Reorganization

An enterprise which is merged with another has in effect been sold and thereby has lost its prior corporate identity.

Preliminary to a merger, the various interests concerned agree upon the terms under which the sold corporations will lose their identity and be absorbed into the new one. These preliminaries imply separate valuations by different groups of men with widely different self-interest; the final result of such separate valuations is a figure agreeable to all parties. Thus the transaction has, so to speak, "had the test of the market"; that is to say, it has felt the influence of conflicting self-interest.

A most important point here is that an exchange has actually taken

---

[1] Twenty years have passed since the above was written and more than twenty-five years since I expressed similar views in *Accounting Review*, September, 1929. Continued price inflation has greatly stimulated argumentation critical of continued use of historical cost. Although I have followed the recent literature closely, I still believe there is merit in a clear separation of "the techniques of computing and of criticizing."

place. After the transaction is completed the fact can never change that the specific price appeared. The valuation held in the mind of the buyer may soon prove to be very elusive; the valuation held in the mind of the seller, although apparently now plainly demonstrated, may have been much less than he might have realized if he had pushed the bargaining further, or the shares he received may turn out to be a bitter disappointment in the market. But whatever happens thereafter, a price marks a definite turning point or exchange. Value, however, is a most elusive element, so changeful indeed that men can hardly be sure they ever see its real countenance.

For the seller the figure finally determined upon may include an appreciation; for the buyer the same figure is a cost or outlay. The same figure is entered in the books of both parties. The justification for this is that the condition now expresses price rather than value. Value, being a subjective element, an opinion of probable worth, is inseparable from the individual who is doing the valuing. The seller had his opinion of the property, and the buyer had his. Each had his own idea as to the probable effect upon his own self-interest of consummating the proposed merger. The psychological valuation of each party forms the basis of the agreement price.

Thus it may be said that to all intents and purposes the price which finally results from their bargaining discussions is a mutually satisfactory figure-representation of the opinion (valuation) of each party at that moment. It cannot be said that the buyer has an artificially inflated figure in his record, for it has been determined by the same process by which any lawful price is determined; and it cannot be said that the seller has a fictitious profit in his books. Appreciation as such does not appear and would not be appropriate in the accounts.

But the case is different when a reorganization is involved. If the revaluation and refinancing are wholly within the existing organization, this may raise grave questions as to the reality of the figure readjustments. Here there is no meeting of different minds; no separate and independent valuations are derived as a result of give-and-take bargaining. In a word, there is nothing here to convert value (opinion) into cost (actual outlay price). The basis for entering appreciation on the books is in this case only the judgement of a single board of directors. Even if that judgment be supported by an engineering appraisal, the increase in value has not had the benefit of the test of the market; there has been no contest of separate self-interests.[2]

Appreciation under these circumstances is inescapably intangible. It is like capitalized goodwill which has been used as a device for making the property side of the balance sheet fit the predetermined securities

[2] If an engineering appraisal reveals an overdepreciated plant (price fluctuation excluded), the necessary adjustment is a result of past depreciation computations and not of "appreciation."

structure, which securities were those considered necessary to absorb the probable earnings. Appreciation, if it is represented by securities in the reorganized corporation, is in direct analogy with goodwill. Can inserted goodwill create an acceptable credit to surplus?

(*American Accountant*, July, 1930)

4. Credits from Appreciation

If assets are revalued as part of a purchase and sale or in connection with a corporate merger of actually independent bargaining parties, no account reflecting appreciation is needed. To the old company the result is like liquidation profit in representing additional assets for distribution to prior stockholders. To the other company the newly acquired assets are an investment carried at their cost measured in cash paid or securities issued. Surplus account would not be involved.

But suppose directors, in a unilateral action, revalue their company's assets and credit the increase to surplus. What will be the attitude of the independent certified public accountant?

The professional accountant is strongly impelled to maintain a sharp and unobscured separation of capital and profit. And a credit to surplus looks very much like profit. But profit should be that figure which indicates how much the assets have increased as the result of transactions. Capital should be that figure which indicates how much of the assets must be protected against distribution. Profit as here described would therefore be limited to net gains from operation transactions and gains from the sales of capital assets; capital would consist of contributed investment and unrealized appreciation surplus, if any. Surplus in the usual sense would not be involved. Perhaps "revaluation capital" would be a good account to use.

If this classification were fully acceptable to everyone concerned, the accountant could consistently accept the injection of appreciation into the assets even though it was not accompanied by an issue of stock in a refinancing operation or a sale of the concern. If this classification of surplus were accepted, it would plainly indicate the capital character of the increment to assets and make it permanently nondistributable just as capital is nondistributable except in the case of final liquidation. But there is important precedent which looks in another direction.

The English courts as early as 1866 in the case of Birney v. Ince Hall Coal Co. (35 L. J. Ch. 363) held that the surplus of gross receipts remaining after all liabilities (including contributed capital) had been deducted from the value of the assets would be the net profit divisible among the stockholders.

The United States Supreme Court in 1925 (Edwards v. Douglas, 269 U. S. 204) has said that surplus account represents the net assets in excess of all liabilities including capital stock, and that this surplus may be paid-in surplus, earned surplus, or it may represent "the increase in valuation of land and other assets made upon a revaluation of the company's fixed property."

From the language of these decisions it seems clear that here at least the judicial view is that surplus of every sort is available for dividends. The position of the court is quite understandable. A court is mainly interested in seeing that dividends do not impair the capital fund which was dedicated, so to speak, as a margin of protection to creditors in consideration for the limitation of liability of shareholders. Directors may not without personal liability declare dividends whch cut into this fund of capital, but any credit balance which is neither debt nor dedi-cated capital is subject to the directors' disposal. On the basis of this logic, the courts could hardly hold otherwise than that any type of sur-plus is legally available for dividend, for they are not concerned with the wisdom of the directors' judgment in regard to dividend or reserve policies. Because of this legal attitude, some directors and legal counsel, and no doubt some accountants, are inclined to argue that there is noth-ing to gain by the classification of surplus and the separation on the balance sheet of earned surplus and appreciation surplus.

What then is the relation of the certified public accountant to these conditions? What can he do in the face of the freedom with which direc-tors may value property which is basic to new stock issues, and in the face of the fact that the courts open the way for dividends out of any type of surplus?

Short of evident fraud, there is nothing to which the accountant can object in regard to the purchase and sale of a concern, or a merger. The appreciation is determined by the joint actions of both sides to the deal. Both parties are free agents, they make a valid agreement, and the closed transaction reveals the price. Whether either party, or both, was mistaken in his judgment is no part of the accountant's interest—manifest fraud or collusion aside. Even though identically the same men are concerned in the new corporation and the old, there is at least the legal form of a bargain between two independent parties, because the law recognizes each corporation as a separate entity.

In case the appreciation appears in connection with a revaluation of the assets and a reorganization of the capital structure (without a sale to outsiders), it would seem that the accountant's attitude here could very well be much the same as it is toward goodwill. That is to say, the accountant will be much interested in carefully scrutinizing the details of the changes. He will then decide for himself whether he cares to continue to be a party to the transaction. The law allows directors such a wide latitude in setting a business valuation upon property that the accountant has little power but persuasion with which to influence the figures used. If he continues his contact, he will be mainly concerned with seeing that the result of the transaction is not set forth in a manner likely to be considered misleading.

When appreciation is brought into the statement unaccompanied by a purchase and sale of the concern or by an issue of stock to cover, it is clear that some aspect of surplus will be involved. The accountant's impulse is then to show the surplus classified as to kind, for the guidance of the reader, and to try to persuade those concerned to hold any un-earned surplus as unavailable for dividends. Generally speaking, the ac-countant's attitude would probably be much the same as it is toward reserves; he can scrutinize the circumstances with care and try to con-vince the client that an open statement of the facts and a conservative policy are wisest. But beyond this he can only decide for himself whether he will continue or not to be a party to the report, and act accordingly.

(American Accountant, July, 1930)

5. A German View of Appreciation

The author of the book under review[3] surveys the growing tendency evidenced in German accounting literature to favor separate reporting for value change [appreciation?] and profits. Theory is strongly in favor of separation, law strongly opposes it, practice tries to steer a middle course.

These three fields form the basis of the author's outline. About 140 pages are used to present the attitude of writers on business economics upon the question; about 76 pages indicate the accounting practices which might be considered as having been influenced in some degree or another by the problem; and about 130 pages to set forth the con-cepts of income which have been written or interpreted into various tax statutes.

Part I is an extensive survey of the literature of business economics for evidence indicating the trend of opinion. In spite of differences re-garding details and methods by which value changes should be elimi-nated from the accounts, there is a general agreement in the need for separation. Profit (for which calculation is desired) is "the measure of the fulfillment of economic function and a signpost to the enterpriser's future actions." As thus defined, profit excludes value changes; the latter show the results of the mere possession of certain kinds of properties under changing outside conditions and not at all the effect of the en-terpriser's economic effort. Value changes, therefore, are related to capi-tal and not to profit, and should be reflected in a "valuation" account which would be an adjunct to the capital account.

Part II presents the various valuation practices of accounting. For the

[3] "Tendenzen Zur Aussonderung Von Vermoegenswertaenderungen . . . ," Heinrich Horn, Berlin, 1931.

most part these practices (sales price, original cost, cost or market) are based upon juristic consideration—mainly, the protection of creditor interests—and lead, not to the calculation of true (economic) profit, but to "conservative" financial valuations, that is to say, to an understatement of profit by waiting (when prices are going up) for actual realization to take place, and by an overstatement of losses by not waiting (when prices are falling) for actual realization to determine the final result.

While practice usually stresses the realization principle, it does not follow it consistently when conservatism is indicated. Yet by expressing a preference for realization, practice in effect excludes valuation changes from profit and thus indirectly supports the doctrine of a separate accounting.

Part III gives extended consideration to the German tax requirements under a succession of statutes, and dwells upon unequitable taxation (because of fluctuation gains) and upon errors in the amount of the true profit which are introduced through calculated depreciation on an original costs base.

It is evident in this book, as in other German works, that writers on accounting there have been led by experience in and after a period of tremendous inflation to regard the economic basis of accounting as more important than the legal base. They consistently turn to the economic function of the enterprise as a starting point and generally pass next to the economic concept of profit connected with the enterprise. On this foundation separation of value change (appreciation) and profit is a matter of direct logic. It does not matter that the methods of accurately separating the two may be difficult and argumentative, or that the juristic view is slow to look to economic considerations rather than to the interest of creditors. The author's philosophy is that matters of sound principle do not rest upon expediency; if sound principle prevails, adequate technical methodology will ultimately be developed. Nor does adequacy of managerial information depend upon juridical limitations; management is free, if it so desires, to refine its concepts and analyses beyond those which may be satisfactory for use in certain types of litigation.

(book review, *Accounting Review,* December, 1931)

6. Workability of Stable Prices

One of the keystones of the new federal administration's policy (i.e., in 1933-34) is to bring about a rise in prices, some say to the level of 1926. Presumably at some selected point the attempt will then be made to stabilize prices.

Under these circumstances a pertinent question would be whether a long plateau of stable prices would be desirable. We are not without experience in stable price levels. Most of the 1920's showed a plateau of average wholesale prices which was one of the wonders of a wondrous age. It was widely accepted as plain evidence that business had at last solved the riddle of economics and had brought supply and demand under control. The level price charts themselves were considered proof that the supply of goods was being quickly and properly adjusted to changing demand. If demand were running ahead, the price curve would have moved upward. But it stayed level. If supply had run ahead, the price curve would have fallen. But it stayed level.

This was in a large measure the basis for the then current belief in a New Era, a period of endless prosperity because business had learned skillfully to conform to economic law and keep an even keel. Stable price level was seen as an ideal accomplished.

But the dream was shattered. And now from the perspective of several years of enlightening depression, we look back upon the debacle and point to speculation as the big bad wolf that blew the house in. This naive explanation satisfies us as easily as did the New Era philosophy. We condemn speculation but see nothing wrong with the New Era of stable price levels which was so rudely interrupted and wish meanwhile that we could recapture a stable price level while all speculators were in jail or frightened into inactivity.

Therefore it seems that one of the New Deal policies is, in effect, a mere reaching out for the very conditions which characterize the New Era. And it raises the question of whether a new leveling of prices will prove any less a mirage than before.

Analyze speculation, the asserted cause of the depression. Behind it was an expectation of profit. The basis of the expected profit was the demonstrated profit of the immediate past. That past, the 1920's, was a period of stable wholesale prices. Whence came the profits under stable prices?

Since profit is always the difference between selling prices and costs, and since selling prices were "stabilized," there could be only one explanation—lower costs. Progress in the technical arts had reduced costs; skillful adjustment of supply to demand kept prices stable; the benefits accrued to the corporations in the form of profits. These profits were partly reinvested and partly distributed as attractive dividends which further stimulated competitive buying of profit-yielding shares. Then came the climax—October, 1929.

This is the picture of a former stable price level and some of its consequences. We have had little to assure us that the stabilization of prices will accomplish any less.

It was a fallacy during the New Era to assume that stable price level was the key to an economic millennium. And the same fallacy could rise up to plague the New Deal. It will always be fallacious to judge results by reviewing only a part of the causes. There are more factors at work in our economic life than supply and demand for goods at wholesale, and there are other important data besides average price levels.

Suppose that some "Supreme National Economic Council," with a wisdom born of hindsight cradled in, say, four years of depression, could have soberly considered the deliberate policy of a stable price level in the 'twenties. It is very doubtful whether they would have permitted it to become operative, for by hypothesis, they would have foreseen the results as we now know them. They would probably have worked for a flexible equilibrium among numerous factors instead of stability of wholesale prices. They would have urged that selling prices fall so consumption might continue to absorb production, that the hours of labor be shortened so men might be freer to consume, that profits be held in equilibrium between excessive dividends and overinvestment in new productive plants. Thus they might have had a chance to head off the debacle of 1929. A policy of stable prices with falling costs could never hope to avoid a crash.

It is not yet clear whether the new administration will progress to a stable price level without a possible repetition of the prior "inflation"; or presently produce "flexible equilibrium among numerous economic factors."

(radio talk, April, 1934)

7. Price of Purchasing Power

In its entirety accountancy may be considered as consisting of three distinct areas: recording, verifying, and interpreting. Or as the author (H. W. Sweeney, *Stabilized Accounting*, 1936) names them: bookkeeping, auditing, stabilizing. His book is concerned with the third area.

When and if rapid and extensive price-level changes occur in this country, a technique for interpreting some of their effects will deserve considerable attention. The author does not ask, but it is a fair question: what is the present status of the inflation-born techniques developed in European economic literature? Even periods of wild inflation pass or are brought under control. The most lasting element flaring out of the continental experiences of the 1920's is likely to be the quickening given to the consideration of the fundamentals of accounting theory.

Price has been traditionally the keynote of orthodox accounting: the record was always one of prices paid or received in the past or of prices to be received in the future. In this book, purchasing power becomes the major theme. In this substitution lies its chief contribution because, like the concept of real wages, it leads men to think below the surface; it is a source of complexity because the significance of a changing power to command other goods is much more difficult to grasp than the idea of the unchangeable cost of goods which results from an actual transaction: a case of the concrete versus the abstract.

Behind the newer philosophy lie much more abstruse economic phenomena than are involved in the simple economics of exchanges (actual transactions). If prices of goods and services rise, the purchasing power of money and debts falls. When goods are expressed in terms of money, we see varied price levels; when money is expressed in terms of goods, we see varied purchasing power. But a difference in accounting is to be noted; money and debts represent potential services, but goods in hand represent actual services in hand.

The distinction is important because goods in possession are not yet effective purchasing power; they become so only when offered in a market. But fixed assets, for example, are not held for marketing. Therefore they have real purchasing power only through the product they make possible or because they are to be abandoned as productive capital by one ownership and taken over by another ownership. Since the last case can hardly be considered apropos to a going concern and since accounting is especially designed for going concerns, it follows that, as far as fixed assets are concerned, exchange value (current price) has very little significance whereas use value (unamortized cost) is of highest importance. Statements, therefore, which purport to show "values" other than costs are purely hypothetical statements, that is, statements as they would be if something or other were to happen—if replacements were made at present prices, if old assets were sold in competition with new assets produced under different conditions, or the like.

Purchasing power is quite abstract until put to the test of being exercised. What looks like power now may tomorrow be very different; what looks like a power may in fact be a not-power for the want of a will to put it to the test of exchange. Suppose all business concerns expressed their fixed assets in terms of current general price levels (general purchasing power). The entire lack of reality here will be evident when we see these concerns in large numbers trying to exercise that power about the same time. So it seems that a theory which seems helpful in analyzing an individual situation may be quite untenable if applied to the whole situation.

Which, then, is the more difficult element to hold steadily before the mind, the significance of purchasing power in the abstract or the natural limitations of accounts in terms of actual prices as of specific dates?

If profit computation rather than display of values is the basic function of accounting (as the outlay cost view of accounting methodology maintains), then the most fundamental concept in accounting should be the concept of profit. This book proposes a new concept of profit but leaves to magazine articles much of the discussion in support of it. What proportionate benefit can be expected from an elaborate technique for computing profit according to a new concept of what profit is, when the new concept has not been well established or firmly linked to the methodology?

Is profit the margin between original outlay cost and actual sales price, as orthodoxy holds, or the margin between current market price (whether measured by specific replacement prices or by an index of general price levels) and actual sales price? Should not the basic concept of profit be centered upon the earning of a return from one's activity in rendering economic services, rather than upon the severability or nonseverability of the assets remaining after maintaining capital, either nominal capital, physical capital, or "real capital" as the author indicates?

The case of stabilized accounting would have been stronger if more emphasis had been given to a consistent synchronization of financial statements with both the upswing and downswing of price levels; if the author had offered his technique as an approach to the separation of losses or gains arising in scarcity fluctuations and losses and gains from managerial skill and executive efficiency; if the proposals were advanced as systematic alternatives to the impulsive write-up and write-down of assets as a means of altering costs in order to change calculated profits when changing conditions create a sort of mental panic.

While the reviewer may seem unduly critical of so important a pioneering work, and perhaps too obviously of a different school of thought, the fact remains that the book is much appreciated. Its value to students must be great even if it did no more than to reveal to them some of the problems which monetary manipulation and the resultant inflation for a time visited upon Europe. This is no time complacently to hold that "it can't happen here." But the author's contribution is more than a reflection of European thought, for his innovations so extend and refine the techniques developed abroad that he almost succeeds in converting them into a methodology.

Some of us may be skeptics from conservatism or from choice; but that does not preclude the possibility that some others may be definitely ahead of current opinion and possessed of a greater vision than most.

(book review, *Accounting Review*, September, 1936)

8. Interpretation

Back of a co-ordinated body of accounting principles will be found two significant underlying concepts, that of accounting function as a technical information service, that of accounting as a quasi-statistical methodology.

Beyond accounting as methodology and tested results as data, there lies interpretation. It would be no more appropriate for accountants to undertake the formulation of principles of interpretation (and call them principles of accounting) than for nonaccountants to urge the incorporation of interpretative methods into accounting methodology. Once the

data are as complete as we can make them and disclosed as clearly as
we can devise, the conclusions one draws from them are individual, depending much more upon the understanding and skill of the interpreter
than upon the accounting data under examination.

An approach to interpreting financial statements is found in the field
of investment analysis. But now and again financial interpretation is
presented as if it were a part of accounting, though accounting is essentially a reporting. For example, violently fluctuating price levels raise
a question of the comparability of prior items and recent items in accounts representing the same kind of goods but different cost prices. And
we are sometimes asked to consider index-number adjustments of financial statements as an aspect of accounting. Some people feel that financial
statements will be more intelligible if the significant items are expressed
as ratios and turnovers. And we are therefore asked to treat ratios as a
part of accounting.

Index-numbers and ratios however are no more than devices to aid
readers in comprehending the message which accounting statements contain. They should therefore be considered merely as adjuncts to accounting and not as a part of its procedure or under the control of its principles.

Certain practices have achieved acceptance in accounting which are
"foreign" to basic accounting theory since they are interpretations that
have been interpolated into account adjustments and thence into financial statements. Examples include allowances for bad debt losses and
cost-or-market pricing of unsold goods. These changes in accounts are
not at the moment of their use expressive of actual change in closed
transactions. Instead they are interpolated interpretation, one being
based upon statistical averages of past experience with sales on credit,
the other being based on no more than a fall in purchase price of similar goods outside the reporting enterprise.

These practices may be considered by some people as precedents for
inserting other interpretative figures into the accounting calculations of
periodic net income. And it may be unconvincing to answer the proposal
by explaining these practices as "conventions" accepted by long usage.
If pressed we may feel embarrassed by "inconsistency" in accounting,
that is, the failure to deal with all items on a single basis. And if accounting principles cannot be consistent, they cannot be brought into
a single, co-ordinated body of theory as a solid point of departure for
interpretation. I am not ready to concede that a single, co-ordinated body
of accounting theory is impossible of construction; it has not been fought
over long enough yet.

Such a body of theory need not seek to change an established practice
of reporting current assets at less than historical cost. Basic theory can
be consistent in holding that current assets, like other assets, are costs,
that is, bargained prices carried forward, but the application of basic

theory need not restrict the reporting of current assets to unamortized cost. It is only necessary that all who deal with financial statements shall be brought to understand that the figure for cost is historical and the figure for less than cost is interpretation. Properly to express this distinction as to inventory in the balance sheet and income statement, it is merely necessary to report and separately name cost, allowance, and less-than-cost remainder, rather than to state only the latter with a notation of "the lower of cost or market."

These considerations, I believe, explain that section of the American Accounting Association's "Tentative Statement of Accounting Principles" (1936) which, without being set up as one of the principles, suggests the underlying point of view of the whole: "A history of cost and cost amortization is a consistent record of actual occurrences measured according to an intelligible formula, and constitutes an essential starting point in financial interpretation. For this reason accounting is not a process of valuation but a methodology for the allocation of historical costs and revenues to the current and succeeding fiscal periods."

The emphasis given to historical cost throughout the "Tentative Statement" has raised the criticism of undue restriction upon the freedom of management to deal with changing conditions. It is said that because management is given great responsibility it should have wide authority to act upon its best judgment in discharging that responsibility. Corporation law, for example, places few restrictions upon asset revaluations, apportionment of share consideration, reacquisition of shares, determination and treatment of losses, restatement of capital, etc. Why should accounting principles create restrictions beyond those instituted by the law? The answer is, I think, that standards enforceable by public opinion should be above the minimum established by law in order to bring about prohibition or punishment if exceeded.

The critics feel that the emphasis on historical cost implies an unchanging reporting of that figure alone; such rigidity, it is said, would preclude adjustments of security structure to fit earnings and adjustment of asset values to fit security structure. But it will be noted that neither accounting principles, accounting practices, nor accounting public opinion can of themselves prevent management under the law from making any of these adjustments. Accounting can only make it evident that asset revaluations, restatements of capital, and other similar adjustments are departures from the objective base of verifiable bargained prices between actually independent parties; that once the connection with objective fact is severed, we are adrift in a sea of opinion and conjecture; that opinion may be anywhere between carefully canvassed facts and wishful thinking, and conjecture may be anywhere between that based upon cautious study of the long run and that based on passing fancy regarding the short run; that we cannot afford to break away at will from "an intelligible formula" for allocating costs and revenues in the calculation of profit without substituting some equally dependable guide, if it is accounting truth we seek.

The central question here is how far management can go in restating previous accounting facts (cost) by substituting uncorroborated personal opinion of values for amounts that have been objectively determined in actual transactions in the market. It is no doubt beyond the province of accounting principles to draw the lines separating (1) data from actual purchase and sale between really independent bargaining parties, (2) data from exchanges between legally separate, though centrally controlled, corporations, and (3) the restatement of accounting figures by management fiat.

Here are three ways in which the items in the financial statements may be derived. They cannot all be equally authoritative; if all of the methods are used in a given statement, the report can hardly be said to rest upon a consistent application of an intelligible formula.

Accounting principles are perhaps quite incapable of properly drawing distinctions between (1) a value tested by really independent bargaining, (2) a value legally established only by quasi-independent bargaining, and (3) a value not tested at all but resting at best upon some asserted analogy with certain collateral conditions outside of the enterprise. Although the function of accounting is to provide dependable, relevant information to interested parties (information which derives its force from being objective, verifiable, and accumulated according to intelligible, consistent theory), accounting can place no restriction upon management's decision to rest its chosen figures upon any chosen base, for management can disregard accounting standards. But accounting standards should have something to say about the way such information should be reported to the public so that the circumstances and responsibilities of the case may be clearly revealed to the reader.

(*Accounting Review*, September, 1938)

9. Wishful Thinking

History repeats itself—but with variations. The details and timing may change; yet elements of the prior pattern reappear. So it is with accounting. Income determination today presents problems which have plagued business and accounting before—specifically the problem of deciding how far reported net income may be brought under the influence of desires rather than facts.

Two generations ago a good deal of attention was given to the distinctions between capital expenditures and revenue expenditures. Businessmen sometimes may have charged capital items as expense and at other times charged expense items as assets. But these decisions were not necessarily entered upon with the intent to mold the figures of financial position and operating results closer to desire. No doubt the men concerned felt they had due provocation. An inescapable uncertainty was involved in getting new enterprises well under way; and it was advisable to be cautious whenever the basis for dividends and income taxes was under calculation. For resources that departed the enterprise either as dividends or taxes were gone for good.

Professional accountants of that day—just as today—were well aware that these ideas about income determination could be explained by pressure from conditions and from human nature. However, they were also aware of the possibility that managerial decisions could be biased, expedient, wishful, uninformed, or even fraudulent in intent. Accountants therefore developed rules by which income determinations could be critically tested. This was not done in a spirit of animosity; rather it expressed a truly scientific spirit. Professional accountants believed then, and still believe, that income determination should be factual as possible, that is, as far removed from whim as it can be. Yet, because they recognized the limitations of accounting, they never claimed that accounting was or could become a true science. It was clear to them however that, in the public interest, accounting had to produce something more than a willful presentation of wishful thinking.

There is a surprising vitality in the idea that desirable figures can be justified and rationalized if they can somehow be brought into the accounts. A generation ago, in the 1920's, wishful thinking again began to influence the figures. A belief seemed widely held (not without its appealing provocations) that accounting results would be molded closer to desire if depreciation expense debits could be modified to suit the economic winds that were blowing. The basic issue thus precipitated and long debated was whether income determination was acceptably or unacceptably modified as a result of newly appraised values attached to depreciating fixed assets.

Now in the 1940's, in still another generation, that belief has again come into focus; the economic winds of rising prices are again blowing strongly. This is the setting of one of today's problems. The problem itself presents several alternative ideas: (1) that the fixed assets be again appraised in line with current price trends so that depreciation expense and calculated net income will be modified accordingly; or (2) that surplus reserves be created to carry management's message that profit determinations and surplus accumulations are not the realistic bases for dividends and income taxes that they would be under more stable economic conditions; or (3) that reserves be created, with similar intentions, out of periodic net income before transfer to surplus; or (4) that so-called profit and loss reserves be created by clearly labeled charges which will unmistakably modify the calculated net income of the period, with this same purpose of clearly sounding a managerial warning.

The issue presents a choice among alternatives. Can theory be of any help in thinking through such an issue?

Perhaps theory can help, if we do not expect too much. Theory, you will agree, can be an aid to understanding, and understanding united with practical wisdom can carry us a long way toward a good choice. Perhaps it is too much to expect either theory or practice to be completely satisfactory alone. I am convinced that theory could not, for theory does not direct; when we use theory we do not seek to prescribe. We are only trying to analyze, to understand, to persuade. Theory therefore must consist of explanations, definitions, reasons, justifications, persuasions. And only sometimes of suppositions and hypotheses.

(*Illinois Certified Public Accountant*, March, 1948)

10. Depreciation and Price-Level Change

What do we need to understand about the problem of depreciation under a condition of rising price levels? There are at least three answers.

(1) We need to understand that although history often repeats itself, it seldom actually duplicates the past.

Looking back into the 1920's and 1930's, we find the striking features of the statistical picture to be the upward spiral of prices and the succeeding downward spiral. In the midst of the rise of the 1920's, the future of the 1930's was obscure. We are again in an upward spiral, and again the future is obscure. You may guess if you wish that the pattern will be very similar or very different. But it might be better merely to guess that later hindsight will again make us wish we had had better foresight.

When accountants think back they remember a wave of asset write-ups; they have not forgotten the justifications then advanced in support. They will also remember the wave of write-downs. And as they remember, I suspect they will see that the justifications for the write-ups were nullified by the justifications advanced in support of the succeeding reversal of prior asset adjustments.

Will the same price cycle be repeated? And the same accounting cycle? If businessmen, in order to validate the judgement they are duty bound to exercise, must get the assets appraised so their ideas about "protective depreciation" may be effectively expressed, I expect they will have appraisals made. Yet it is safe to assume that because of past experiences they would prefer not to go that far.

What can professional accountants do in this connection? They can appraise in retrospect the justifications (theory) that were once offered in support of write-ups and write-downs. They can appraise the new justifications soon to be offered and then seek to aid management in finding and following a sound policy. Management, if it will, can appraise the situation too and be ahead of the auditor when he comes. The auditor, I'm sure, would prefer management to take the initiative.

(2) We need to understand the impact of price-level changes on management.

The reasons that urge management to do something in the face of increasing economic uncertainty are likely to seem compelling. An understanding attitude is especially necessary since it is management that decides; the auditor can only persuade, acquiesce, qualify, or withdraw. It will help greatly if both parties understand the conditions and prospects, and if both believe that the solution of cyclical problems is largely a matter of good managerial policy, carefully directed toward operating under disturbing outside conditions. The solution does not lie in having a few new entries made in the accounts, thus presenting the auditors with an accomplished fact.

In the face of either rising or falling price levels it would seem wise to weigh outside evidence as carefully as possible and shape all managerial policies accordingly, whether they concern borrowing or lending, raising or lowering sales prices, constructing plant or refinancing, holding assets representing surplus or disbursing them in dividends. All this I believe management can do without appraising fixed assets; without creating misleading credits called revaluation surplus; without being under the necessity of later reversing the field with asset write-downs.

This weighing of outside evidence and this shaping of policy inevitably involve questions about values. And value, I submit, is not an accounting question. If it were, then accounting becomes simply a mirror to reflect regular appraisals. If that should come to pass, the primary factor would be obscured which it has always been the primary function of accounting to report; that function, in my opinion, is to report the investments made and the things that happened to them in the operation of a going concern. This means that costs, having once entered an enterprise (and no other amounts deserve accounting consideration), can be changed only in two ways: (1) by exit of that investment from the enterprise or (2) by manipulating the investment fact under a theory that the value not the investment cost of an item reflects its accounting significance.

If the second treatment is once entered upon, the primary fact of an investment made is thereby submerged; investment is therefore completely lost to sight as part of the base for financial decisions. Throwing away one half of the available facts can hardly be the most satisfactory basis for decisions. Most people need more facts, not less.

(3) We need to understand why novel ideas about depreciation-reporting are again being advanced.

The ideas are not conceived, I am sure, in a purely selfish or antisocial mood. In business as elsewhere men have a very human desire for stability and an attendant sense of security. It is wholly rational to be disturbed by departures from normal, and the impulse of all of us is to try to do something about it.

Businessmen are striving to achieve reasonable stability. They need a reasonably predictable near future so plans can be made intelligently. (Planning, let us notice, is a very important part of their social contribution.) The striving of the businessman is his way of making an effort to achieve; his achievement is the result accomplished by the effort. Thus present and prospective efforts and accomplishments, quite outside of accounts, are the basis for a multitude of managerial and investor decisions.

At that point accounting enters. Its basic task is to make possible the intelligible comparison of enterprise effort and enterprise accomplishment. Accounting does this by expressing effort as expense figures and accomplishment as income figures. But accounting is only an instrument. It does not make expense what it is, nor income what it is. Business effort generates expense, and business accomplishment generates income. Doing things to the figures that represent expense or income can only becloud a real understanding of the relation of effort and achievement. The object of financial statements is to give understanding of that relation.

The normal status of business operation, and hence of accounting, is one of relatively stable price levels, or one of slow and limited changes. Business thinking is thus cast in a mold of normality. When abnormality comes, we are disturbed; normal planning and judgement are clouded. We try to compensate by setting a new gauge of the normal. We may revalue the fixed assets or experiment with other ways of altering expense-income comparisons. We attempt to rationalize what we want by persuading ourselves that revaluation is the way to get in a position to buy higher-priced replacement units; that this is the way to re-establish a stable platform for business decisions. But is that true?

It may be argued variously that recasting assets and depreciation figures is an easy way to those ends, or a good way, or a poor way. Which belief (theory) is the most justified? A specific answer may not be important at the moment, but it is necessary to hold fast to these two ideas: (1) that the most information is the best base for decisions, and (2) that changing the records to new figures submerges the information already available in the form of old figures.

(Illinois Certified Public Accountant, March, 1948)

11. Limitations of Accounting

How far can the wind of current conditions be permitted to change the established facts of accounting record? Little, if at all. Shall we then bury our heads in the sand of recorded transactions so we can ignore the wind? That is not a reasonable alternative.

We can hold to the established facts of actual enterprise transactions as recorded in the accounts; we can hold fast to cost until the counter-pressure becomes irresistible. When that time comes—that is, the time of real full-tide inflation—no accounting record will be useful, not even if it had been remolded daily by any scheme men can devise, or if it were left wholly untouched in terms of transaction cost.

Professional accountants are in a position to use persuasion to bring management to accept and act on the idea that changing conditions and the approach of abnormal circumstances can be met by managerial policy without laying heavy hands on the ledger accounts. This is but to urge the use of dual vision: (1) to view ledger facts about investments in assets and services as evidence to be used in weighing achievement against the effort it has cost; (2) to view the current trends of prices outside of the ledger as evidence pointing toward future efforts, and future accomplishments, and therefore as data indispensable to forming plans against the future.

To get ready to pay higher prices for replacement items does not require fixed asset revaluations and the so-called "automatic recapture" of additional depreciation from customers. One can get ready by asking higher sales prices where the market permits; by lowering expenses to the extent of managerial ingenuity; by using modest dividends and adequate managerial reserves at times when calculated profits are high; by expanding capacity at strategic times of low costs.

Beyond this the profession could be of considerable service by explaining divergent ideas about the nature of profit. No one is closer to the problem of profits than public accountants. In times of little change people consider profit as income less outlay cost. In times of considerable change men seem to shift their beliefs. The theory of profit then leads many people to assert that profit measurement should be income less replacement cost. Such a shift in point of view no doubt occurs because it is human nature to prefer concepts close to current self-interest. Yet understandable as the second idea of profit may be, it fails completely to accord with the functions and limitations of accounting.

More people must somehow be brought to know the functions and realize the limitations of accounting. Accounting and accountants should not be expected—or allowed—to take over responsibilities that are management's. It is management that should weigh the accounting facts from the ledger in comparison with the evidence of present and prospective economic currents that have not yet introduced specific transactions into the given enterprise.

One of the limitations of accounting that should be made clear whenever possible has to do with such phrases as "unstable value of money," "fixed dollar base," etc.

It is sometimes said that accounting rests on a basic assumption that the money of account has a stable value. An accountant's statement about assumptions relative to money has only the intention of given a warning that accounting has only limited power to give expression to values. But that "assumption" may have become somewhat misunderstood. Some people, apparently because of their view of this "assumption," seem to believe that accounting rests on the sands of unreality. They are convinced that the value of money is not stable; for they see prices changing constantly. If price change is the fact and if accounting assumes price stability, it will be natural for a skeptic to ask: How then can the money figures reported by accounting mean anything dependable?

Accountants should be ready to explain that the relationship between accounting and money price is not one of assumption. There is in business and accounting a belief that money price can usefully represent diverse goods and services. Actually this service of money price is not a belief but a fact that is fully supported by experience. For money price does acceptably represent physical goods in our computations and our thinking. And that's all money price means in accounting.

There is also a belief that many business decisions for the near future can be dependably rested, in part, upon data established in the near past. This belief too is a fact; it is supported by experience which shows that the ratio between money and goods usually changes so slowly and moderately as to afford a dependable factual platform for decisions. There is no accounting assumption here; there are economic fact and managerial experience. When slow change becomes rapid, obviously the change in rate of change must be given attention in making business judgements, but not in accounting as such.

Accountants should therefore be ready to explain that the "money limitation" of accounting is one of fact rather than assumption, and that the disturbing assumptions are outside of accounting. For example, it is false to the function of accounting to let anyone assume that accounting is already a system, or can be made into a system, for keeping recorded transaction facts in tune with changing economic values.

Professional accountants could well be even more firmly opposed to spreading fixed asset revaluations on the books than their past writings have indicated. They could lend support to the use of managerially determined reserves and could aid in bringing the public to a better understanding of the intentions of such actions. There will be little objection from accountants to the creation of surplus reserves, the theory being that surplus allocation is management's decision.

(*Illinois Certified Public Accountant*, March, 1948)

12. Managerially Determined Charges

Under the pressure of rising prices, management may wish for a more forceful presentation in the income statement than depreciation based on historical cost of the assets. In attempting to implement that desire, the opinions of professional accountants may be found to be adverse.

Additional allotments to the usual account for depreciation reserve will be acceptable as an appropriation of net income of the period, or as an appropriation of surplus. But reporting in the income calculation an allotment higher than amortization of original cost will bring objections: lack of objectivity, beyond review and independent verification, distortion of the period's actual results, willful as to amount, etc. Yet the same type of objections could have been advanced in an earlier day—and probably were—against managerially determined allowance in the income calculation for doubtful debts and for straight-line depreciation of capital that was "permanently sunk" in fixed assets which would normally be fully maintained out of current revenue by repairs and replacements. Accounting and business practices have now advanced beyond that point. May it not lie in the future that other managerially determined charges will become similarly acceptable? At present management may not be generally trusted to exercise restrained and careful judgement in creating such cyclical charges. It will be argued that it would be better to wait and see how the cycle develops. It will be urged that the creation of surplus reserves or perhaps footnotes to the income statement will provide ample disclosure of managerial judgement of the probable impact that cyclical change of prices exerts upon the enterprise.

But can surplus reserves successfully provide statement readers with a clear and sharp reminder of the shadow that lies across the usual income statement—the shadow that appears whenever important price-level changes are in full swing?

Management is seeking ways to issue effective warnings, including warnings that dividends in certain amounts are not advisable. The most effective place to state that warning, some people believe, is the charges section of the income statement where the depreciation item appears. There is this to be said for that treatment: it does not present one-tenth of the fuzziness of disclosure that was inherent in the older procedure which included revaluation of assets and altered depreciation expense.

Management seeks to fly other warning signals—warnings that taxation, based on the usual figure presumed to represent unquestioned net income, may result in injustice in the sequel. For, during important price movements, a part of calculated profit presently proves, in retrospect, to have been more shadow than substance.

The essence of business judgement is to anticipate expected change and to take in sail before the storm comes close. Why can't we harness this vast accumulation of skill in judgement to the service of public policy? Why can't we make more use of judgement-determined figures?

These may seem farfetched ideas at this time. A full-scale inflation can't happen here, we say. Nevertheless it is worth noting that the problems of today would be the problems also of a terrific inflation—only they would be multiplied by a factor of 10,000 or 100,000, perhaps more. There is relatively little pressure now to attempt accounting and managerial solutions for today's inflation. There would be very great pressures in a real inflation. Isn't this the time then to oil up the machinery of cyclical defense? Later it may be too late to organize pilot-plant operations to learn cyclical analysis and policy.

My central thought as outlined here is that accounting has definite limits of function. Because that is true, information that accounting cannot effectively supply must be obtained by management for itself as a part of the basis of managerial policy. But accounting nevertheless has a great unused capacity for forceful, emphatic disclosure. The germ of a very useful idea may lie in managerially determined charges in the income statement. The boldly emphatic and eye-catching disclosures now made in a few income statements show a clear skepticism concerning the near term reality of present profit calculation—skepticism which would be even more healthy in a time of really high inflation. This technique of forceful disclosure, now so easily brought under criticism as a radical departure from custom, would probably be quickly rejected in a real inflation—for the reason, be it noted, that it was not nearly forceful enough. We would then soon be importuned to accept index-number adjustment of all transactions, accounts, and statements.

Would that treatment actually produce better disclosures? I doubt it. I doubt that any adjustment system could make a useful servant out of accounts under extreme inflation. I have no doubts about the usefulness at that time of simple original cost figures—they would be utterly useless. Do what you will, accounting will be helpless under extreme inflation.

What to do? We need not despair—yet. Until the extreme is much further along, all concerned should do their utmost to produce constructive ideas that may help—especially ideas that may help managerial provisions to become satisfactorily rational, conservative, realistic estimates, whereas they now may seem bound to be surcharged with wishful thinking, arbitrariness, even resentfulness.

(*Illinois Certified Public Accountant*, March, 1948)

13. Supplementary Charges

If management favors using supplementary depreciation charges in the income statement—a practice not yet sanctioned by presently accepted accounting principles—could the professional accountant state in his certificate the opinion that the practice was desirable in spite of lack of widespread sanction?

The answer to the above question would turn upon the showing of independence within the auditor's certificate. If he must qualify when he disagrees with some policy of the client, he would seem free, perhaps duty bound, also to qualify when, under his independent, professional judgement of the immediate situation and surrounding circumstances, he chooses not to conform to a practice favored by others.

It would probably be a healthy thing for professional accountants to take a position—even in a certificate—as to any generally preferred practice, providing that position was clearly reasonable and useful.

I think there often is merit in putting the prevailing thought of the day into contact with the idea that it may not be unreasonable sometimes to break a little with the past when good judgement dictates. But I do not see much evidence of that in individual ideas so far published in the literature stimulated by the impact of changing price levels. There may be "the germ of a useful idea" in the frank indication of supplementary depreciation charges in the income calculation.

Although supplementary charges would be a forceful disclosure of management's judgement of the current situation, I see difficulty involved in objectively reviewing such managerially determined charges. The public will need to be assured by the existence and use of effective auditing procedures as well as by certificate phrasing that the auditor's acceptance of the key figures in the income statement rests on more substantial foundations than managerial fiat.

(personal correspondence, spring, 1948)

14. Judgement-based Depreciation

Periodic accruals (used in the fullest sense of the words) have been a primary factor in raising fifteenth century record-keeping to the quasi-statistical technology we call accounting. Perhaps supplementary charges in inflation times are a recent phase of the long evolution of accrual accounting.

Every step of the development of accrual methods has been contested, sometimes by those who wanted to retain freedom to bend the figures closer to desire, sometimes by those who simply wanted the familiar ways left undisturbed. Yet the periodic determinations of accounting are superior today largely because evolution has continued. In time it may perhaps produce better ways for emphatically reporting the "facts of life" when business conditions are in a state of material change.

The problem of what constitutes good accounting treatment is complicated by a contest between two doctrines: (1) that experienced business judgment is the best basis for calculating periodic income since the task is quite beyond satisfactory treatment by formula; (2) that freedom to report periodic income according to experienced business judgment will tend to become, in too many cases, merely license to manipulate the results willfully and wishfully.

As a consequence of this contest, there is a tendency to place restraints on possible deceptive treatments and to restrict the freedom to follow the guidance of experience and judgment and the logic of the circumstances —this being accomplished by rules, regulations, formulas, whether created by the profession, in government bureaus, or through legislative action.

Perhaps this kind of result is inevitable in a trial-and-error democracy. Even so, we should try to find ways to lean the results more and more toward those resting upon judgment-directed freedom to act—all this, of course, without removing the bars against willful and arbitrary manipulation of accounting facts.

Thinking this way, one easily becomes skeptical about accounting "formulae." They soon come to be used as a substitute for a considered judgment under the circumstances. I think of the "cost-or-market" rule as having been at one time a practice that was quite suited to certain uses. It has outlived its usefulness largely because it became a formula and now is often applied with little consideration for its real nature or the surrounding circumstances. *Lifo* may become another special purpose formula stretched beyond its character, especially if applied to fixed assets. It is gaining extensive acceptance for inventories largely perhaps because it seems a defense mechanism ready to hand in a period of rising prices. It seems also to promise some relief from pressure for more wages, dividends, taxes. Increased withdrawals of this kind, business experience and business history tell us, are often not justifiable by the real facts considered over a reasonable period beyond an immediate condition of price inflation.

More realistic reporting might well emphasize experienced business judgment which realistically visualized forward conditions as well as the immediate present. Possibly stating an opinion in the certificate independently of presently accepted principles of depreciation accounting might be a way of forcefully presenting the results of a reasoned judgment of the way circumstances affect an individual case. This would avoid stating results under the direction of a formula.

Supplementary charges for depreciation derive from much the same kind of theory as allowance for doubtful receivables. There is no universal formula or dictum governing the latter; I see no need for one to govern the former. Both debits should of course be determined on the basis of the best facts available. The resulting determination of depreciation charges could be tested for reasonableness by a *Lifo* formula among other ways, if desired. But the best test is hindsight. Thereby subsequent review will provide a fresh look at prior decisions and a means of gradually learning—as we have done with doubtful receivables—to improve current judgment-determined debits.

There should be a road leading toward improved reporting and a further extension of the principles of accrual accounting. For accounting

makes some of its most important contributions by using accrual methods
to sharpen periodic income determination.[3]

(Journal of Accountancy, July, 1948)

15. Accounting and Inflation

Americans realize that they are in a period of creeping inflation, but
they seem at a loss to know what to do about it. Other countries have
experienced a similar dilemma, notably Germany and France after World
War I. Especially in Germany, a flood of literature appeared describing
what should be done to and by accounting. There is little evidence, however, that those recommended modifications of accounting helped to slow
the speed of inflation or helped the people to escape the ultimate consequences of an extended rise in prices.

This raises some questions for us. What reasons are there to lead us
to believe that fundamental modifications in our established methods of
enterprise accounting could do any better? Would changes in business
accounting help to reduce the continuing expansion of our circulating
medium? That development was systematically fostered initially some
twenty years ago under a get-us-out-of-depression psychology. Would
changes in accounting reduce the tendency for government bonds to
pile up in banks where they become a base for expansion of loans that
are purchasing power to individuals? Would changes in accounting help
to raise present low interest rates? Low rates in themselves encourage
borrowing and hence encourage further competition for goods and services, with the consequence of pushing prices ever higher.

I am as sympathetic as anyone to all reasonable attempts to make accounting data more serviceable. However, I do not care to see accountancy
charged with responsibility for mitigating a rising spiral of inflation.
Accounting is now being considered by some people as contributing to
the build-up of inflation; reform in accounting is being viewed as a possible means of leading us out of this economic danger.

Accounting methods cannot, in any reasonable sense, have been responsible for our inflation; and changed accounting methods cannot
reasonably be expected materially to affect the economic, financial,
psychological, and diplomatic conditions underlying our inflation. In
view of this situation, accountants may as well become reconciled to the
fact that they and their art very probably will be damned for neglect to

---

[3] (It might well have been added here even in 1948, that index-number adjustment of
the figure for depreciation expense would be just using another formula, easy of application and simple to review as to the calculation. Being a formula, its use does not
express experience-tested judgment, and it would have the undesirable effect of concealing the figure for depreciation based on historical cost. An openly dated supplementary charge would not have these faults.)

change, or damned for belated and ineffective change, as the case may be.

The thought appears now and then that there is no such thing as a principle of historical cost. In a certain verbal sense this is perhaps true; in a conceptual sense however there is a definite need for something which might bear the title "accounting for invested cost." There are no accounting principles in the dictionary sense of immutable laws. The laws of nature are not operative as such in accounting. The objectives and reasoned preferences of experienced men are the operative controlling factors in accounting.

The ideas embodied in the phrase "accounting for invested cost" may be difficult to formulate in a way that would spell out a principle; and these ideas may undergo evolutionary change. Yet these ideas still have a basic relation to all other aspects of the whole which we have come to call accountancy. For they touch the objectives, limitations, and preferences which make accountancy what it is.

What shall we say accountancy is? I suggest that it is a rational and widely useful discipline, distilled through many years of trial and committed at its base to aid enterprise managements in their need for a means of appraising in retrospect the wisdom of prior decisions which passed at once beyond recall.

We cannot afford to subtract the conceptual sense of the phrase "accounting for invested costs" from our discipline, or to allow it to be smothered by arguments born of a union of the exigencies of the contemporary scene and of a definitional approach to logic. Accountants need not feel on the defensive. Concepts are more significant than terminology, no matter how skillfully definitions may be entwined.

Ideas that effectively served the needs of the past, instead of having two strikes on them, may quite possibly be able to contrive also to serve the needs of the present. Accountancy may do this even though the complexities of today seem to some people to cry out for immediate solution through new methods. Immediate, hurry-up solutions have a way of turning sour after a while. Witness the asset write-ups of the 1920's. New methods which survive are not usually really new, being most often supplements that give added support to existing time-tested methods.

In essence the issue behind any discussion of the significance of invested cost will always involve the dilemma of cost versus value as the clue to accounting function. And always the discussion will fail to break the dilemma by defeating one side. In the 1920's and 1930's appraisal write-ups and write-downs expressed the same dilemma as that being faced today. The dilemma was not broken; the same accounting choice again is, cost or value. There are new overtones now, but they do not change anything basic. Perhaps some action may soon be agreed upon. But it cannot constitute a solution since the word dilemma means that a choice among alternatives is to be faced. Whatever the choice expressed in a solution, it is likely to be temporary in effect, unless complex circumstances other than the choice selected shall make recurrence of the old dilemma impossible.

Surely there is little probability of circumstances appearing that will permanently separate, or combine, cost and value. Some men will continue to know that they need value information to judge their future, and other men will continue to know that they need cost information in order to discharge their responsibilities. Cost and value must somehow continue to live together.

(Accounting Review, April, 1952)

16. Invested Cost

It is fair to say that the concept behind a term is more important than the words which clothe it. This must be so since a concept involves purposes and limitations, and these cannot be suitably reflected by a phrase of a few words. So perhaps it may add something to look briefly at certain terminology.

The adjective "historical" as applied to cost in accounts may seem inappropriate because it may convey the idea of an accounting usage that had merely the virtue of having survived. Survival is indeed a characteristic of the cost concept. But the concept survived because of its continued usefulness; its usefulness now does not flow from its age.

The adjective "original" applied to cost has apparently been considered to have lost general usefulness because it has been given a sharply particular meaning in the accounting requirements prescribed for some regulated industries. ("Cost to the first owner.")

A particularly significant phrase would seem to be "cost price," except that some people might think it could only refer to a unit price. The term "aggregate bargained price" might cancel out this deficiency, for each word in that phrase adds something definite to the intended meaning. "Invested cost" carries much the same basic idea as "bargained price," and perhaps is the most useful term in the list.

If properly understood, any of these phrases can be seen to touch some part of this concept which so many accountants consider an important aspect of their art. The words "historical" and "original" point one's thought to the fact that the data in accounts rest upon accomplished events. These terms therefore tend to negate any idea that account data speak of current or future values. "Price," in the two examples given, seems to point one's thought toward an agreement between independent parties. For an accounting use there is no reality in a price tag; that is no more than an invitation to buy; it speaks of a possibility to be made real only through a separate act by some person other than the writer of the price tag.

The word "invested," as attached to cost, carries to the mind the following thoughts: that the two parties concerned have negotiated a meeting of minds; that each party is satisfied the exchange will prove to his advantage; that now, for the first time in this situation, a figure in dollars has emerged which justifies a new entry in the accounting records of both parties.

"Invested cost" seems to embrace more of the concept involved here than any of the other terms alone. It comes closest to reminding the reader of the relation of accounting data to management's use. It does this in part because "invested cost" is a phrase that can speak of liabilities and income as well as of assets and expense. It must be clear that expressions such as "replacement costs," "income expectations," "fluctuation profits," etc. lack the concreteness attached to the term "invested cost."

(*Accounting Review,* April, 1952)

17. Service to Management

Accountants have shown reluctance at submerging the long-developed techniques related to double-entry accounts and historical cost. So they are sometimes charged with being unbending traditionalists. It is comforting, in this respect, to know that accountants seem to have plenty of company. A survey of opinion[4] revealed, as of three years ago, that a wide variety of people were opposed to changing corporation income reporting in order to reflect price-level fluctuations. Bankers were nine to one of this opinion; business executives and lawyers, three to one; controllers and government officials, two to one; accounting teachers, three to two; security analysts, seven to five.

But the sample was not all of one opinion. The loyal opposition, as the British say, was represented by economists and statisticians; these voted in a ratio of seven to four in favor of reflecting price change in the income statement.

The present disturbed condition of the world politically, economically, psychologically, is bound to have an impact upon accounting as on all aspects of our life. This impact could conceivably be received in silent acceptance; or it could be received with discussion, analysis, debate. All of us can be thankful that we can choose the second alternative.

The current impact of changing price levels has stimulated a spirited discussion of accounting ideas. I am sure that accountants welcome debate, even though they may feel, as I suspect many do, rather inadequately prepared by experience to enter publicly into it. Economists, however, are more accomplished in the arts of analytical and persuasive argumentation. Undoubtedly we could profit from their example. Accounting has always been concerned with doing; its present-day ramifications are such,

[4] *Journal of Accountancy,* November, 1948, p. 366.

it would seem, as to show that we are in need of other experience also, particularly experience in dealing analytically, persuasively, and verbally with controversial ideas.

Various ideas have been put forward in the name of making accounting more serviceable; but some of these seem to me capable, if adopted, of befogging some of the important services accounting has been rendering for a long time. Such a result would hardly be progress. On the other hand, it would indeed be progress to develop new techniques for making enlightening, supplementary, interpretive analyses of data already available in today's financial statements and in the accounts behind them. It would not be progress if index-number adjustments entered ledger accounts, no matter how the resulting accounts might be named; and it would not be progress if index-number adjusted items were substituted in statements for items now standing within the framework of the concept of objectively determined invested cost.

The various ideas of change are undoubtedly put forward with sincerity and in good faith. But do they derive from a clear appreciation of the fact that accounting renders primary as well as secondary services? Is it not the primary function of accounting to furnish to management data about past transactions (invested cost) so that management can benefit from the knowledge of past experience when considering the next future commitments?

Management must be able to review its prior efforts; and no better measure of these exists than invested cost. Cost, to management, is an investment, a calculated risk; management dare not lose sight of that investment as a risked cost; to do so will deprive them of the basis for judging, in retrospect, the wisdom of having entered upon that risk. And such a backward look at prior decisions, if it embraces objective data identifiable with prior decisions, can be a substantial factor when management faces decisions for the upcoming future. How else can we explain the development of standard cost and budgeted expense than that these are created to stimulate comparisons which rest upon invested costs?

Can it reasonably be considered a function of accounting superior to this one related to management, to say that accounting must furnish investors and lenders with data that have been already projected into the future, e.g., data as to replacement prices? Perhaps investors do wish to capitalize forecasted income in order to produce an arithmetical evaluation of the company's stock, and thus to be able to decide whether to buy or sell. Does it follow that nominal accounts and the income statement must furnish forecasted data? Replacement prices are forecasted prices until a given enterprise pays them in the market; then, for that enterprise, they become invested cost.

Take note of the fact that accounting, under the earlier name of double-entry bookkeeping, has developed out of the trial-and-error attempts of owner-operators of business enterprises to get data in aid of man-

agerial decisions of their day. The direct descendants of this conception
and of the practices it has sponsored are modern industrial or managerial
accounting, including cost accounting, standard cost methods, internal
control, internal auditing, controllership—these being ably supplemented
by break-even analysis, business budgets, statistics of general economic
conditions.

When we look about us, it seems clear that business management has
grown greatly in skill since the days of Paciolo and Columbus. I do not
presume to say grown great because of accounting. Yet it is beyond dispute that the data furnished to management by accounts over a great
many generations were data which we have come to call historical costs
(or invested costs) meaning data drawn from actual transactions of a
given enterprise acting in open bargaining exchanges with other people
or other enterprises.

Note that data of this kind have served business management well for
a very long time; that modernization has duly expanded the capacity of
accounting techniques to continue to discharge this function satisfactorily; that management does not attempt to make decisions solely on
the basis of account data; that management could not, and cannot, make
the most dependable judgments under guidance of nonaccount data
alone.

(*Accounting Review*, April, 1952)

18. Accounting and Economics

Suggestions for making basic changes in accounting methodology, in
spite of obvious sincerity, may not have included full recognition of the
obligation that accounting still has to serve management with historical
cost data; they may not have drawn upon a clear appreciation of the
real capability of management. Perhaps some people have had a feeling
of sympathy for management; perhaps they feel that managements face
vast complexities without being book-educated in the arts of comprehending and reacting rationally to the surges of a dynamic economy.

I believe that most American management is keenly aware of the trends
of the times. I doubt that this awareness could be substantially sharpened
by any amount of tinkering with accounting. On the other hand, there can
be little doubt that management, and the public that has contact with
financial statements, would welcome useful supplementary analyses of
the possible impact of economic conditions on the enterprise of their
interest.

Some people see so much unused usefulness in accounting data that they
tend to become evangelists for a new accountancy. They see so deeply
into the economic kind of realities and into economic methods of analysis

that they are carried away by a vision of a new accountancy that will incorporate these methods. Sometimes other people, similarly impressed with unused usefulness, tend to become apologists for accountancy as they know it.

Accountants are said to have a good deal of traditionalism in their convictions; and it is said that their ideas and methods of accounting are falling out of date. Critics see in accountancy a strong tendency to be conventional; it leans more upon ideas accepted by common consent as useful rather than on ideas justified and supported by closely defined terms and precisely worded arguments. Hence accountancy seems to some people to be necessarily shot through with expediency. Accountancy it is said is utilitarian; hence it should be open to change whenever a new group of potential users sees possible new uses.

One can grant the grains of truth in these complaints and ideals. Yet we must remind ourselves that accountancy is a practical art. Practicality therefore must bulk large in accountants' choice of ideas and methods. This is not equivalent to saying its reigning forces are expediency, convenience, tradition; practicality does not rest on these. Rather accounting as a practical art carries the flavor of "practicable," that is, satisfactory in the light of experience and of capacity for use, satisfactory in the light of methods that are attainable and of ideas that are acceptable to many users.

If one has been strongly nurtured in theory, practicality probably seems to take second place to the greater value of new and stimulating ideas. To one strongly influenced through close contact with active accomplishment, theory often seems only a source of ideas to be judged and, perhaps, tried.

The ideology of accountancy has grown up out of experience in using its methods. Its accepted theory therefore has a practical slant which is sharply conditioned by a commitment of accountancy to serve the management of individual business enterprises. Perhaps it is not too much to say, merely by way to completing the thought, that the ideology of economics grew out of observing people living and working as units in society. Being basically a philosophy, economics is naturally concerned with logically related ideas and with thoughts about attaining a better society.

Does it not seem that these two disciplines, though they do have something for each other, are nevertheless in actual contact only at a few points? If economic philosophy had to become as practical as accountancy has always had to be, ways would have to be invented for applying its ideas effectively, which is to say, ways of getting people to apply good economic reasoning to their decisions. If accountancy were to aspire to become as theoretical as economics, it would have to sacrifice a good deal of its present essence—objectivity—and be willing to extend its methodology to embrace forecasting the future.

Wherein is the gain, for economics or for accounting, supposing either or both of these extensions of disciplines could be accomplished?

I may perhaps express an opinion; but it will only apply to one of these extensions. A great disservice to a great many people could emerge if accountants attempted to produce data in financial statements which for a given enterprise would be essentially subjective projections into an unknown future—these data being offered in exchange for the progress already achieved in making accounting data as to the past dependably objective.

In working to produce objective, verifiable data, accountants have been particularly aware of certain duties that rest upon management. Management is duty bound to invest (buy) enterprise assets at the most advantageous available price and to disinvest (sell) at the most advantageous available price. That is a fundamental part of the working of our system of free enterprise. The system stands to suffer in some degree, and management surely is handicapped, if responsible executives cannot judge in retrospect the outcome of their prior commitments. A classified record of transactions stated in terms of invested costs (prior commitments) would seem an essential element for this use.

As a consequence, accounting has an obligation to record and report historical or invested cost, not as a convention or a tradition, but as a service necessity. Along with this duty there rides another: an accounting duty to guard the integrity of its data against internal modifications, if those modifications seem likely to undermine objectivity and reviewability.

An example of such modifications would be the injection of data such as replacement prices; these are still wholly outside the prior decisions and the recorded experience of that enterprise: reserves, yes; collateral interpretations as space permits, yes; but not adjustments which may obscure the reading of management's activities as expressed in the recorded, invested, contractual costs of that particular enterprise.

Facts outside of an enterprise, such as replacement prices, do have significance to management, but they can hardly be considered facts suitable for use in ledger accounts. Until the enterprise has itself bought at a new price, its prior purchase cost should remain an unchanged statistical and historical fact. It is historical because it happened; it is statistical in the sense that another price substituted will undermine the statistical integrity of the category involved.

(*Accounting Review*, April, 1952)

19. Interpretative Progress

Some excerpts from two books with which I have been identified are quoted in an article by George O. May (*Accounting Review*, October,

1952) and may, in the view of some readers, seem to constitute negation in my own words of the position I took in the article to which Mr. May refers (*Accounting Review*, April, 1952). I am inclined to let the arguments there presented speak for themselves in favor of holding to invested cost figures within the accounts and financial statements. But I would like to try to illuminate the thinking behind the excerpts.

"Accounting is relative and progressive. . . ." If that paragraph were today rewritten it would still, I think, be persuasive but perhaps in need of some expansion of the term "progressive." Accounting should indeed be progressive; it clearly has shown that tendency in the marked development of its industrial and managerial uses.

A similarly far-reaching progressive development has been slow to appear in auditing. Still less has accounting shown a full measure of progressive development of its interpretative aspects, i.e., in the collateral work of making the results of technical accounting processes understood by more and more people. Perhaps index-number adjustments are intended to constitute an advance in the latter area. And few indeed will take exception to this or any other interpretative endeavor, provided the effort does not meanwhile emasculate the well-known and still very useful data which emerge from the normal accounting process.

It would hardly be progress if its price were the submerging of accounting's basic information (which I prefer to call "invested cost") or the yielding of anything on the objectivity issue. It is not likely to prove to be progress merely to develop new and wider areas of data to be brought within the framework of double entry, following ever further the lead in this respect of fund accounting and standard cost accounts. There must be limits to accounting adaptability as there are limitations in the significance of invested cost. A permanent cleavage between balance sheet and income statement (between objectivity determined real and nominal accounts) cannot properly be called progress. Yet this result seems in the making if the reporting of price-level effects is not definitely restricted to supplementary analyses.

Modern cost accounting shows the possibilities within double-entry techniques for becoming a better administrative instrument. That status was not achieved by force of the fact that costing data were presently tabulated "in double" within the framework of the trial balance. On the contrary, cost accounting, by the nature of its data and techniques, brought a distinct gain to bookkeeping in giving it additional administrative usefulness. Cost data, on the other hand, became more dependably factual because they had been set into the midst of a pre-existing integration of the real and nominal accounts. As a consequence product costs, manufacturing expenses, and net income of manufacturing enterprises were firmly tied in with assets that were visible and cash that could be counted. In other words, cost data changed from being statistical data by becoming accounting data.

It is worthy of note that index-adjusted figures, recorded in ledger accounts and presented in the financial statements, would gradually reverse this process and cause accounting data to be considered more and more as merely statistical data. Yet this change would have been made under the name of increasing the facilities of accounting for rendering useful service and perhaps on the basis of a conceived analogy with cost accounting. The analogy is clearly faulty because there is a vast difference between the objectivity of incurred costs and the artificiality of figures derived from application of an index series.

It would indeed be an extension of accounting as an administrative instrument if supplementary analyses of the impact of price-level change were prepared and presented in close physical association with the customary financial statements.

Undoubtedly accounting "faces a challenge" at a time when price movements become severe. If the challenge is met by action in the field of collateral interpretation, accounting-trained men may be able to make a contribution to public understanding of the dangers that monetary inflation holds for all of us, rather than leaving that action entirely to others. Other people will as a matter of course have their own reactions to price-level rises. Part of the challenge to accountants will be in the opportunity opened up for them to inform themselves in statistical methodology sufficiently to be able to use the interpretive techniques of index series in connection with interpretative techniques of accounting.

If accountants expand interpretative efforts in this manner, they may be able to render outstanding service because they will then be equipped to act intelligently in two analytical fields—in accounting as such and in statistics as applied to interpretation of account-derived data. The alternatives to preparing for this service are: (1) incorporate in accounting the effects of statistical formulas furnished by others according to their conceptions of appropriateness to their own interests, or (2) leave the task of interpreting accounting data wholly to others. Alternative (1), as I believe, would be highly inadvisable; alternative (2) is perhaps the easy way and may appeal to those who tend to construe "accountancy" as primarily the service of professional auditing. Yet there may well be a justifiable hesitance to decline to take some part in the processes used by those whose training and objectives point their work toward the study of nationwide data as bases for making national economic policy. But to take some part does not necessitate making over our own peculiar techniques in order to do so.

The organized compiling of statistics of national income is not, and cannot become, an application of accounting techniques; and surely accountants will not aspire to remake enterprise accrual accounting into a statistical methodology—to the detriment of the objectives of accounting as such—so that economists interested in national income data may have figures deriving from business activities precast in a pattern to fit their ideological needs. The price for this accommodation would be, I think, too high to ask accountants to pay—the price of undermining the present public understanding of accounting figures which would follow if invested cost were submerged by the use in accounts of index-number adjustments of invested cost.

Some question has been raised of a possible reluctance to break with tradition. Most people probably will be inclined to favor tradition for practices they like and to be critical of tradition in regard to practices they dislike. This is, of course, one of the paths of progress. Yet a proposal for making over ledger account figures (such as invested cost that is amortized into depreciation expense) through application of index-numbers is not objectionable because it is a "break with tradition." It is objectionable because accounting then becomes a mixture of two very different techniques. This surely is unwise, particularly since it would involve an uncritical acceptance of formulas prepared by nonaccountants for nonaccounting uses. But more important, the use of such adjustments for enterprise income calculations means the abandonment of the essence of accounting technology—the close integration of real and nominal accounts and of financial and operating data. This is surely unwise for it invites the ultimate transformation of accounts into unintegrated statistical categories.

It is true that accounting practice has never forsaken the use of value here and there. That refers to "a tradition carried forward." Cost reported in the accounts is also "a tradition carried forward." There will therefore be an unending clash of the idea of value and the idea of cost. Yet the significant fact of a history is not that one or both of these cases have historical roots. It is rather in the fact that evolutionary development has brought refinements in the techniques of enterprise accrual accounting and that this has steadily rendered less necessary a resort to valuations in order to obtain a suitable knowledge base for business decisions.

We can all agree with A. Lowes Dickinson (as of 1904) that while accountants "look more and more to cost, they cannot ignore value." Yet we may well add, after some fifty years of time for further consideration, that value, being subjective and ever changing, can best be considered as information which from the nature of the case should be supplementary to a clear, objective reporting of invested costs. These costs have been committed to the enterprise's planned activities and need to be later knowable when the dollar results of the planned activities must be compared with the dollars invested and risked in the planning.

Accounting serves two very different and very important groups—management and investors—one of which represents the money market (capital and debt); the other represents the creative market (cost and revenue). One group is basically concerned with making value judgments, with deciding to invest or disinvest. The other is committed to making judgments to produce or not produce, to produce this or that, now or later. Until one group or the other gives up its natural concern for cost or value as the case may be, accounting must strive to serve both. It will take constant effort to do this satisfactorily while never deserting one for the other. It may be an effort for some to accept the idea that certifying financial statements for use in the money market is not necessarily a superior service to that involved in preparing accounting data for use in the productive activities of individual business enterprises. This two-way problem of accounting will be very greatly complicated if it also becomes a responsibility of accounting to produce figures ready-made for use in the statistics of national income as an aid to governmental economic planning. The two-way problem can be met by accountants however if their responsibilities are clearly reported upon separately. Financial statements firmly resting upon objectively determined, invested cost would report on data of particular significance to operating management. Collateral, supplementary, interpretative data, using index-numbers among other devices, would constitute the accountant's contribution to all parties interested in "purified" accounting data for incorporation in statistical presentations.

(Accounting Review, January, 1953)

20. Disposable Income

Towards the end of the double decade of 1933-53, the event of most significance to accounting theory and practice undoubtedly has been the debate on the realism or unrealism of the usual accounting calculation of periodic income when business enterprises are operating under the impact of considerable change in price levels.

Because the nation's economy is not much changed and the accounting debate is continuing, we cannot now see this event in as good perspective as is possible with events under earlier conditions. Interpretative generalizations are therefore more difficult to form. This is particularly true because the ideas and methods currently debated have not yet been considered under the psychological impact of falling prices. Indeed, there is very little tendency even to discuss these problems under a hypothesis of falling prices.

An observer of ideas favored in the 1920's and those well received in the 1950's will be struck by a certain degree of similarity between the present apparent attitude toward possible future price levels and the doctrine of a permanently high level of prices that was current during most of the 1920's. It was believed some thirty years ago that federal reserve management of the volume of available credit would put an end to wide swings between prosperity and depression. Is history about to repeat itself with new materials and new management? One kind of "managed" currency, begun a generation ago, did not succeed in its great function. Will today's kind of "managed" currency succeed any better? And will a failure be comparably devastating? Such questions might possibly be answerable when we can look back on the present from the vantage point of 1973. In 1953 we can only try to understand the situation as it is today in the light of recent background ideas and events.

The debate on the nature of accounting income is part of the current picture, but it is not as new as one might think. It is a vigorously renewed consideration of ideas that have been mildly contending in economic literature on one hand and in accounting literature on the other for a long time. The basic differences among income concepts today were well known yesterday.

Writers on economic theory usually take the point of view of a person. To an individual the significant figure in his affairs is the amount of his disposable income. Writers on accounting take the point of view of an impersonal business enterprise under management. For interpreting enterprise activities and results, the most significant aspect of account data is the amount of earnings that appear as a result of the supervised activities, not the disposable amount.

Enterprise accounting is centered upon periodically computing the fruits of enterprise. However important ultimately, the question is quite secondary in the functioning of enterprise accrual accounting, whether or not the full calculated earnings should be considered (wisely) disposable. If the earnings of an individual worker were viewed in a similar manner, he would have to include in his concept, deductions for social security and income tax withheld. It is human nature perhaps for the individual to think otherwise; to him the wages are his net disposable amount because he or his wife has control over this much spending. But it is likewise human nature for enterprise management to treat the gross amount paid to an individual for his services as deductions in calculating enterprise net earnings. This is so because that latter figure, not disposable proceeds, best expresses the success or failure of management planning.

The fundamental question that has recently been under debate, therefore, is whether enterprise accounting should be reconstructed to fit the personalized, disposable income concept of economics.

An answer seems to be slowly emerging in accounting literature. It is that supplementary data should be regularly furnished with the financial statements in order to show, or enable one to calculate, separately the effect of price-level change on important accounting figures.[5] This in

.

[5] The *Journal of Accountancy* for November, 1952, indicates editorially that statements on behalf of the American Institute of Accountants, the American Accounting Association, the Business Study Group, and the Institute of Chartered Accountants in England and Wales came to substantially the same conclusions with regard to supplementary disclosures and the continued use of historical cost.

effect indicates that accountants, while recognizing the distinctions between the concept of income in economics and in accountancy, are not convinced that one concept should be substituted for the other.

This review of the situation as of the moment might well be supplemented by a brief indication of important surrounding ideas and conditions that have inspired the debate.

The assertion is often met in one phraseology or another that income statement results are unrealistic because the usage of accountancy (historical cost) fails to report separately the effects of changing price levels and of managerial decisions. It may be noted that this failure, if failure it is, runs throughout more than five centuries of the use of double-entry bookkeeping. This long life does not of itself justify continuing the usage. But the fact raises the question of why the ideology is under such sharp criticism just now. The peculiarities of enterprise accrual accounting have been noted and occasionally mildly questioned before, but never so sharply as at present. The reasons then must be sought more in the circumstances of recent conditions than in the function of accounting.

In part the criticism is a reaction to the pressure of high taxation in association with other conditions. It is inescapable that income taxes should generate discussion of income and its computation. As the tax presses, discussion is stimulated. Criticisms of the burden of taxation probably express an unconscious reaction against its causes—war costs, preparation to resist aggression, high governmental spending, asserted waste at home and abroad, etc.

Theoretically, income tax is a forced sharing of enterprise net income. Actually, like all taxation, the tax becomes a part of the cost of doing business. Yet tax costs are under less control of managerial decisions than other costs. Moreover, this forced sharing of the proceeds of enterprise ignores, in its rules of calculation, the idea of disposable income. As a result, when the disposable income concept is urged upon accounting these days, it is no doubt partly with the thought that the earned income concept applied in taxation produces unfair results. Unfair, that is, in the sense of tending to force management to turn to the money market for funds to finance high-cost replacements and/or expansion of plant, rather than depend largely on proceeds from earnings and from depreciation reserves.

From this analysis it would seem that criticism is not directed at accounting in its ordinary use but is more expressive of concern about a type of rigidity in the rules of taxation. If that is the case, it would be reasonable to expect less resentment at even higher dollar taxes if the calculation rules gave reasonable recognition of the need for, and the economy of, untaxed, reinvested income. A measure of that recognition has now been given the home owner who sells and buys another home. If the rules of tax calculation were realistically adjusted, the charge that accounting is at fault would be much softened.

(Accounting Forum, May, 1953)

21. Back of the Income Debate

The debate on the impact of price-level change upon the accounting calculation of enterprise net income has no doubt been in part stimulated by a complex area of contemporary ideas and actions which stirred fears of vast changes in the American way of life. Some people even spoke of "creeping socialism." [6]

Only two aspects of this atmosphere of change can be touched here, and these but briefly. The sudden abandonment of the gold standard by the American Congress in 1933 impressed many people as a step towards a managed currency far greater and more uncertain in its effects than that entered upon a generation earlier through formation of the Federal Reserve System. The new motivation was indeed humanitarian—that of changing the trend of prices and public confidence from depression toward renewed prosperity. And the action no doubt had effect, although there is evidence that the bottom had already been reached by the summer of 1932. Yet the ultimate repercussion, some twenty years later after a long period of "reflation" plus hot and cold wars, has been a mounting fear that a self-induced but uncontrollable inflation was not an impossibility.

One form of expression of that particular fear is the debate on income calculation. If a certain amount of "management" of the currency, plus a war, can produce the degree of price inflation shown in published statistical data, it is inescapable that many people will wonder where further monetary management plus vast expenditures in preparation against possible worldwide aggression will take price levels and income taxes which ignore the economic aspect of asset replacements. In thinking along this line some people recognize that such a drift is a dangerous one; they then seek counteracting ideas. Disclosure in accounting statements of inflationary drift is one such counteridea that will call the reader's attention forcefully to the fact.

Other aspects of the situation seemed to foreshadow continued increase in governmental use of accounting figures in making national policy decisions. Views have appeared to the effect that, if the figures for enterprise income were the usual ones from accounting statements, the figures might be considered deceptive when used as part of national income statistics. And if, as seemed likely, decisions for governmental action to influence economic activities would in the future be guided by these national income statistics, it would seem that the statistics used ought to make it possible for policy-makers to see the effect of price-level changes separately from the effect of a totality of other factors.

Economists and statisticians, being concerned with these matters, are clear in their opinion that adjusted accounting figures would automatically make for better national income statistics. Most of the literature

[6] Compare: Herbert Hoover, *The Great Depression*, pages VII, 40, 329-32, 335-36.

arising from the debate on income has been in explanation of the economic concept of income and of the statistical distortions expected to result from failure to correct these data by removing the effects of price-level change. The accountant's contribution to this literature has been explanations of the objectives of accounting (strongly oriented toward enterprise management) and the technical peculiarities of accounting (periodic data objectively derived from enterprise actual transactions). These aspects of accounting indicate concisely the characteristic service rendered by accounting and the area of damage to that service which seemed likely to emerge from direct change in basic accounting methodology.

The present stage of an accountant consensus, as a result of the literature so far developed, has been indicated above. The beliefs among accountants in favor of preserving enterprise use of historical cost and of providing supplementary disclosures of data pertinent to the given enterprise and price-level change are reasonable results of careful consideration of many aspects of an important matter. And research on methodology for adequate disclosure is continuing.

The significance of the results emerging from these circumstances deserves brief comment. For more than twenty years much thought has been given to income in relation to accounting theory and practice. The problems of accounting income posed in the 'thirties and the 'fifties were different; yet the later discussions have been clearly an extension of that earlier sharpening of a realization of the importance of income in general and of accounting calculations of enterprise income in particular.

It is evident also in recent literature that accounting and statistics are recognized as different quantitative techniques which cannot be merged without loss to both. Index-number adjustment made to remove from data the influence of price-level change is a statistical technique. If it were used for directly changing specific invested costs as recorded in ledger accounts into "adjusted" costs, the results could well be considered to reflect a perversion of accounting function. On the other side, it is doubtful if the statistics of national wealth and income, as suggested, can be classified and marshaled by methods that correspond to double-entry technology. The reason is that the recognition of debts between accounting entities is part of the integration of real and nominal accounts in enterprise accounting. Statistics of wealth and income for the national economy as a whole must eliminate debts as being canceling offsets. And since national wealth can only be known by count and calculation, as if by inventory, and since much of it is not related to production of income, the details of wealth cannot be integrated with the details of national income production for interim periods of time as is necessitated by double-entry technique.

Introducing dual categories into the accumulation of national income statistics does not reach into the essential characteristic of enterprise accrual accounting. The phrase "system of national income accounting" therefore should not be understood to imply incorporation into statistical methodology of the basic elements of business accounting. This is not to say that the operating subsections of government cannot usefully adapt many of the features of commercial accounting to their management problems. Considerable progress has already been made in recent years in this direction, and more is in prospect. But that development is not "national income accounting."

The final interpretative comment can be put in the form of several questions. Are the effects upon an enterprise of its managerial decisions and its price-level changes really separable? If accounting figures, objectively derived out of actual business transactions, are in fact modified through the application of index-numbers of average national commodity prices, can the resulting net figures assuredly express the effect of managerial effort any better than a hypothetical percentage applied to the accounting figure for net income in order to break it down by kinds of causation? Can statistical arithmetic dependably replace the skill and judgment of experienced businessmen in penetrating beneath account symbols in order to grasp the economic, financial, and managerial realities involved in enterprise activities?

It is a very appropriate supplement to this presentation to quote from a famous economist a paragraph which compactly reflects his conceptions of the services and limitations of financial statements:

"It is pedantic . . . to treat profit statements as if their significance depended wholly upon their adequacy. To take that view would be to misconceive the role that profit statements play in modern life. They are made primarily as guides to future action. However difficult the task and uncertain the result, every businessman who wishes to plan intelligently must make periodic attempts to ascertain whether his past policies have been successful, where they have left him at the moment, and what his prospects seem to be. Perfect accuracy is not attainable, but for working purposes it is not required—a fair approximation serves most practical needs. Anyone who wishes to get some insight into modern economic life must accept this situation as it is." [7]

(*Accounting Forum*, May, 1953)

22. As to Index-Numbers

The objectivity of the most carefully prepared index of prices is far from equal to the objectivity of the basic data at present entered into ledger accounts. In statistics the data under manipulation are necessarily derived from sampling or from antecedent computation. In accounting the basic data are intensely original. They are neither samples nor averages; they

[7] From "The Problem of Measuring Profits," Wesley C. Mitchell's introduction to *Industrial Profits in the United States*, by Ralph C. Epstein and F. M. Clark, National Bureau of Economic Research, 1935.

speak specific amounts mutually agreed upon by the parties to actual exchange transactions.

Comparable dependability of the message conveyed by data of such differing origins is also affected by the amount and kind of processing normally given to the data, and by the available techniques of verifying the data in their original forms and their final forms. As between systems of index-numbers used to modify other data and the carefully integrated classification of original data which we call double entry, there is a wide difference in the kind and intention of both the manipulative processes and the verification procedures.

Index-numbers represent masses of data compressed into averages; account data are sums by addition or remainders by subtraction. This is a significant distinction. Moreover, reworking the data subsequent to the initial marshaling processes involves very different types of modifications in statistics and in accounting. The formula for and content of index series, for example, are sometimes changed to include new items in the average, to readjust the weighting of the items used, to refer the percentage calculations to a different base year, etc. Accounting year-end adjustments as between nominal and real accounts have effects on the data that do not even loosely parallel the effects of these statistical modifications.

Year-end modifications of the original data collected in accounts may seem arbitrary to nonaccountants. Yet apportionments between balance sheet for next year and income statement for this year, especially such advance estimates as fixed asset amortization and bad debt allowances, are subject to verification and testing far beyond a retracing of the steps of recording and computing. Most estimates, certainly those for bad debts and depreciation charges, are later validated by subsequent events within the enterprise. Debts remaining still uncollected after an interval are a means of putting to test the prior advance estimate of expected bad debt losses. From assets actually retired or sold intact we presently are able to test the validity of prior assumptions as to probable length of useful life, and thus to test the validity of prior depreciation charges recorded in the accounts.

Without the possibility of such subsequent validation by enterprise events, we probably would have been forced by accounting good judgment to use voluntary surplus reserves rather than direct charges against current revenue. And thus one of the outstanding developments in modern enterprise accrual accounting would not have occurred. If other developments capable of contributing in a similar manner to the sharpening of the periodic calculation of enterprise net income shall appear, they will undoubtedly be welcomed by accountants and businessmen. But it is very doubtful whether index-number modification of account data based on invested cost could "contribute in a similar manner," for the reason, among others, that suitable subsequent validation is by no means assumed.

It can be granted that income calculation by the use of invested cost does not produce figures acceptable to all parties as unambiguous. But depreciation charges determined through adjustments by an index series will produce no less ambiguous results. And for comparative purposes the latter would be much more ambiguous, especially when, as recently, the index series used had been altered for reasons of statistical policy. Perhaps invested cost is not as completely objective as may sometimes be claimed—if the claims are a little extravagant. Yet an asserted equal or superior objectivity of index series or of index-adjusted accounting data has even less actual objectivity than invested cost criticized.

Present-day accounting for all its discoverable flaws is a tried and proven technology as it stands. Some may say this is also true of index-numbers. And that too in a measure can be true, even though the time period of its testing under practical use has been very short in comparison. But another point also needs to be made. Index-number adjustment of data constitutes a technique for manipulating economic statistics interpretatively in an attempt to enable the marshaled data to lead the observer's mind deeper than the surface indications of the raw data. This service is indeed a valuable one. Yet it by no means follows that this technique is a suitable one to be injected into accounting as part of its technology.

Any analytical technique, including index-number adjustment, can with full propriety be applied by any suitably trained person to any available data, including data produced by established accounting procedures. Such collateral use, however, would not submerge the message which many people want to read out of present-day financial statements. Nor would such collateral interpretative use of statistical techniques constitute a making over of the pre-existing and still useful technique of enterprise accrual accounting.

It is very doubtful that American industrial society would be well served by accounting made over into a statistics-collecting device in order that its data shall be a ready-made mass to be directly incorporated into statistical data for use in policy-making decisions at the national level. Our industrial society cannot afford to lose, or see seriously damaged, its most vital source of the information (account data) so important to managerial decisions at the individual business enterprise level.

Let us by all means be as co-operative as possible in understanding and in aiding the laudable objective of improving the art of statistical analysis. By developments in this area, theoretical economics may make good an element long lacking, that is, a practical and quantitative technique in aid of sound economic decisions. But the co-operation of accountants in this evolution surely should not be rendered at the price of converting our present mild drift away from strict historical cost into a reporting of "values" manipulated out of historical cost through application of an index series.

If that price were paid, the result would be disintegration of the integration of balance sheet and income statements of real and nominal accounts. This far we must not drift.

If inflation continues to grow, we may have to do the logical thing, as some countries have done, and produce a statutory requirement for revaluation of all assets and liabilities—and in that manner change the charge for depreciation expense. However, I do not see good reasons for accountants voluntarily to compromise their art by accepting index-number adjustments into the ledger on the assumption that this legislative step will not or should not be taken. When our type of inflation subsides, the debate on modifying accounting methodology will die a natural death. If by that time we shall have already fundamentally changed the structure of accounting ideology and chosen to neglect the use of supplementary reporting, we shall then, and not without considerable loss of prestige, need to undo the change previously made.

(Illinois Certified Public Accountant, March, 1955)

23. Prestige for Historical Cost

We do not need to make an attempt to support the use of historical cost in income determination by linking it with double entry for the prestige it might thus acquire. The significant fact is just the reverse. The prices men paid and received in their business transactions were costs in the sense of original or paid costs before there was a systematic technique for organizing those known facts into significant categories. Historical cost enjoys prestige therefore not from a history of centuries of association with double entry but from the fact that it has been a natural cost, that is, a prior figure representation of a known fact awaiting recording and association with other known facts. Prestige in fact flows in the other direction. The prestige so long enjoyed by double entry and now plainly evidenced by its very wide acceptance and increasingly effective service has come in a large measure from the fact that it usefully and dependably classified established, reviewable, quantitative facts of great interest to a given enterprise's owners and/or managers.

For much the same reason it is clear that double entry is not merely a technique like algebra wherein equations play such an important role. The derived rule that parallel equal amounts will produce equal dual totals may seem to be a algebraic explanation of the way equal debits and credits in transactions produce equality in the trial balance summary of transaction effects. But this would be a very superficial explanation of enterprise accrual accounting, if we may use a phrase which avoids the bias likely to be inherent in the familiar term "double entry."

Trial balance equilibrium is a simple, incidental consequence of a deeper characteristic of the technology which was at first called "the method of Venice," or in other countries "records according to the Italian method." None of the older terms have ever suggested the real heart of the technique; none of them is appropriate today. The descriptive phrase "enterprise accrual accounting" not only fits into the present, it also aptly epitomizes the essence of bookkeeping in Paciolo's day.

The real contribution that was evolved in practical use by Paciolo's antecedents was integration of real and nominal accounts rather than an equilibrium of summarized account balances. It is the power of integrating financial position (capital) and earning power (income) that has been the foundation of the prestige of accounting throughout its centuries of use. To destroy this integration and the associated interlocked interdependence of balance sheet and income statement would be to sacrifice a most valuable technology for one lacking this characteristic. This could hardly be called progress.

If a new ideology generated by the impact of rising price levels and certain economic doctrines shall succeed in pressing index-number adjusted figures into ledger accounts (as in cost accounting we now insert standard cost figures) the result would be to destroy the essential integration just mentioned, while maintaining an apparent equilibrium in the trial balance that is more artificial than natural.

A failure to understand this basic characteristic of accounting or assessing it as mere algebraic equilibrium could easily result in placing in the wrong place the limitations inherent in accounting.

The limitation often asserted is that accounting is unrealistic in its calculation of net income because it does not exclude from that figure the effect of changing price levels. Actually the limitations within accounting are those associated with the fact that while each of its accounts are quasi-statistical categories, its scheme of categories lacks the flexibility and diversity of the categories that statisticians like to create.

But note this fact. In achieving a regrettable limitation from the point of view of statistics and economics, accounting achieves a desirable limitation peculiar to its type of information service.

If we permit ourselves to become confused as to these two kinds of limitation, we will be lending ourselves to actions which will tend to drive a divorcing wedge between balance sheet and income statement, between capital report and income report. Such a result would quickly progress from statements to ledger accounts. Having thus sacrificed mutually integrated data and estimates tied to subsequent validation by specific later events, we could presently find ourselves to all intents and purposes statisticians though still called accountants. For the useful restraints imposed by limitative accounting methods to accounting objectives would have been so loosened that the statement once called "balance sheet" would become an appraisal statement of property values compared with known liabilities; and the statement once considered as reporting enterprise income would become a calculation of economic income through application of some index series. Perhaps it is long association with accounting theory that makes me cold to such a prospect. Study of the origins and changes of accounting ideas and methods is responsible, I am sure, for my belief that the wrong decision now could bring disastrous results in the long-run usefulness of accounting techniques. Supplementary disclosures of index-number adjusted figures would, of course, be an interpretative action that would not interfere with continuing to report in the basic statements the data resulting from the characteristic integration of real and nominal accounts which continue to record basic data in terms of prices actually bargained between independent parties—the so-called historical cost.

Historical cost, after all, only means "prior invested money price." By using this sort of basic record all parties at interest are better able to see, after the fact, the measure of prior decisions. If that backward look is denied them, as by the substitution of external current events not active within the enterprise, the essential function of accounting will have been negated and its outstanding characteristic will have been perverted.

Income and financial position are indeed affected by outside events. But this influence is exerted through the effect outside events have upon management's current decisions. Present circumstances cannot have previously affected prior decisions. A pig farmer's decision to sell tomorrow may be influenced by the total dollars received yesterday by a neighbor for his pigs. But the events across the road do not constitute an established fact for our farmer's accounts. The distinction there is the one which runs between "influence" and "measure." If I were management, I would not want my accountants to weigh the influence of events in order to convert influence into account measurement (not even lower of cost or market). If I were auditor, I would be skeptical of imputed values, of forecasts paraded as facts; useful as these may be in aid of management decisions, they would be too subjective to warrant support by inference in an audit certificate.

(*Illinois Certified Public Accountant,* March, 1955)

24. Modifications as Disclosures

Consistency within a remodeled accounting method probably would wither under the impact of falling prices, for the surrounding condition would then present a very different picture than that seen under rising prices. If index adjustments were avoided under falling prices, accounting would be open to outside belief that it can blow hot or cold as users wish the figures to suggest. Generations of accountants have labored to change older accounting usages which might lead to similar beliefs.

Today we sometimes find the thought variously expressed or implied that accounting unrealism is leading businessmen into errors of judgement based on accounting figures in historical costs. I doubt that businessmen commit the economic error of buying and selling in ignorance of price trends. No modification of accounting method will assuredly lead them out of policy error.

If in answer accountants lend strong support to index-number adjustments under rising prices, they must be prepared strongly to urge application of index-numbers during falling prices also. But if price levels fall, the accountant's strong desire for consistency will hardly be enough to preserve in business a prior practice of adjusting historical cost figures by the application of an index series.

There is little in the published literature to convince the reader that a revised account-reporting of periodic income would be permitted to continue to function under falling price levels. It is debatable whether the idea of year-to-year consistency now lodged in the auditor's published opinion would be strong enough sanction assuredly to bring about the continued use of index adjustment of accounts if we entered a period of sharply falling price levels. It may also be doubted that accountants and businessmen will be inclined to commit their policies to the presumption of an unending upward spiral of prices.

When and if the use of index-numbers becomes an accepted basis for entries in ledger accounts or for producing figures in substitution of invested costs in the financial statements, that action might perhaps call forth the rather harsh word "manipulation" because of the costs thus concealed or submerged. It would raise a question of adequate disclosure. And the doctrine of full disclosure as now practiced is one of the great contributions of American accountancy to our modern industrial capitalistic society. If invested cost and cost amortization are clearly disclosed, an informal addition of collateral interpretative data such as index-adjusted figures would not merely avoid a charge of submerging significant cost data, but would in fact constitute a distinct forward step in expanding accounting disclosure.

Use of supplementary disclosures of index adjustments for elements in the income calculation should, in the readers interest, include indication of the index series used or recommended. This would help anyone concerned to make parallel adjustment computations for balance sheet figures if he desired. Not even the advocates of adjusting income statement figures have proposed the consistent, parallel adjustment of the related balance sheet. Nor have they said very much in justification of such ignoring of the tight interrelation of these two major financial reports.

Modification of the income statement is usually proposed as a contribution to reader understanding. That would imply an improvement in disclosure. Yet the extensive remodeling proposed, although perhaps in line with the highly polished theoretical ideas of a relatively small number of people, would produce a report much less understandable to a very much larger number of people, including many investors and businessmen. The heart of the problem is one of choosing between contributing to the understanding of the few or the many. Unless, of course, we are ingenious enough to be able to contribute substantially to both at the same time. It is doubtful whether even great ingenuity could get up that mountain on one horse.

Perhaps we face in accounting the same kind of problem as others face in getting the many to understand, as the few already do, the concept and significance of money wages versus real wages. In their own interest many may need understanding of this distinction. But to achieve that understanding, it would not help them to receive some new form of wage payments in lieu of wages paid in legal tender dollars.

In a similar way a great many users of financial statements probably are in more need of better understanding of the distinction between and the interrelation of the money income and the economic income of a business enterprise than they are in need of a new type of income report. Partly through an effect of income taxation these people are slowly achieving an improved understanding of the elements involved in the present method of calculating periodic net income. If we succeed in making present methods more understandable by building more interpretation on that growing foundation, appreciation and acceptance of the service accounting already renders will continue to expand.

(personal correspondence, spring, 1951)

25. Making Technology Understandable

Study of economics will reveal among other things the distinctions between price and value, income and purchasing power, money wages and real wages, speculative returns and wages of management, along with other examples of an apparent kinship between basically different ideas. It is not inconceivable that these glimpses into the intricacies of ideology may sometimes condition the student to doubt the understandability of the financial statements he may see. After adding a modest study of accounting processes, he may come to believe that his knowledge of economics enables him to see possibilities of reader misunderstanding. For it would occur to our hypothetical student that ordinary people will not be able to see, as he does, through and behind the statement figures into the economic realities which he considers accounting so incompletely portrays.

As a result of such a thought sequence it would be but a short step to a further belief, namely, that a great many people could benefit from his kind of understanding of the nature of money as an economic engine and as one factor in price, of the significance of fluctuating price levels and changing purchasing power of the national currency, as well as other concepts which underlie economic life, and consequently stand behind the figures of accounting reports.

Our student will have observed that the income statement, because it customarily expresses costs incurred in prior years, does not reflect current costs throughout. His study of economics will also have prepared him to recognize the fact that, under customary accounting ideology, the net result of an income statement calculation will consist of a mixture of profit attributable to a rise in prices since the goods or assets were purchased, and profit attributable to the skill of management in avoiding or reducing risk, in buying wisely and selling persuasively, etc.

It would be clear to our hypothetical student that other readers of accounting statements may fail to take into consideration the fact that accounting does not produce a disclosure of these separate kinds of profit causation. Their inescapable failure, it would also seem clear, could only leave these unfortunate people badly informed as to the realities of the enterprise whose statements were in their hands. Since the many users of financial reports—the "economic illiterates" for whom his sympathies have been aroused—cannot or will not educate themselves in economic analysis, or go to college to have it done to them, the only way to go to their aid is to reform accounting ideology so that accounting presentations of income calculations shall be more realistic. Being "realistic" in this situation would mean that the final net figure in the income statement should not include profit attributable to price rise.

Our hypothetical student might conceivably rationalize his idea of the problem facing users of accounting reports into a pressing need for reconstructive accounting ideology. And, from his study of statistical methodology, he may think he sees a method for implementing the needed reform. He will know that index series have been used in statistical operations to eliminate the effect of seasonal change of price data in order to isolate in the remainder the price change attributable to "cyclical movements." Since accounting costs are basically price data, they could be similarly modified by this technique in order to present all income statement items in terms of current price equivalents. As a result, profit from price fluctuation, the "unrealistic" element in the usual income statement would be excluded from the final net figure. And as a result of this result, typical users of this modified form of accounting report would be considered informed of the facts he should know.

The above rationalization may seem farfetched and therefore unconvincing. Yet, regardless of the way they may have arrived at their conclusion, a considerable number of people apparently believe that readers of financial statements are being misled and need a revamped calculation of net income to correct this threat to their financial good judgment.

Let us examine this idea. An important aspect of reader use of accounting reports which is not included above needs consideration.

There are a great many users who, whether or not they realize the complex character of enterprise net income, have achieved a satisfactory understanding of the significance to themselves of this important accounting figure, along with a useful understanding of the interrelation of computed net income to the various elements reported to them in the associated balance sheet. The proposed modification of income statement figures is generally advocated by people who seem to feel no compulsion in their ideas to keep these two reports closely integrated. A willingness to see double-entry techniques abandoned altogether seems implicit in this attitude. Yet integration of these two statements is an outward symbol of the principal contribution "invented" into double-entry records, namely, the tight integration of data about financial condition (real accounts) and data about the economic results (nominal accounts) of the use of the property and debt which together tell of financial solvency.

Robert H. Montgomery once wrote of "The Curse of Balancing." And at times the effort to bring assets, liabilities, and capital into balance for the report's equilibrium does seem somewhat overdone. But the alternative of no balancing would be disastrous. For example, complete disregard for integration of nominal and real accounts (balancing being only a result of this integration) would soon bring all cost accounting computations outside of the validating contact they now have with cash and other balance sheet items. We would then have retrogressed several generations back to the days before job costing was brought into the framework of the financial trial balance.

It may be argued that index adjustments are not complex; that it would be easy to educate report-users into an adequate understanding of their intention if not into the technicalities of their use; that users are in need of some kind of education in realistically appraising the income statement.

It may well be, however, that changing accounting ideology while leaving the income statement to present an apparently unchanged face, would not accomplish the educating said to be needed. A very considerable handicap would exist in the fact that users of financial statements are habituated to the present bases of reporting. Those habits would have to be unlearned—a not inconsiderable task. Teachers are well aware of the extreme difficulty of eliminating previously well-learned ideology; the older the individual, the greater the difficulty. One would conclude that the expected result of modifying the statement would be confusion rather than clarification—attempted re-education to the contrary notwithstanding.

Helping more people to read the message in financial statements with more understanding is hardly best approached by introducing a basic change in what most users already understand in a useful degree. Completely new users of financial statements might possibly learn to read adjusted figures with some understanding since they would have nothing to unlearn. But we cannot hope to wash out of the brains of present users the old understanding of the present accounting ideology, however strongly we may be convinced it would be for their own good. Theoretical benefit would fail for quite practical reasons.

No one would be tempted to try to make a textbook in economics more understandable to sophomores by introducing many footnotes in various foreign languages. A good deal of the modern literature of economics may seem to oldsters almost to be written in a foreign language. For economics has been rapidly developing additional technical vocabulary useful for making new distinctions that seem currently important to its technologists. This new enrichment of terminology accompanies new ramifications in objectives and methodology. Yet communication meant for specialists is not equally serviceable when aimed at, or met by, laymen. This fact could prove an additional handicap to reader understanding of index-adjusted figures—unless, to be sure, it is assumed that readers would be completely satisfied upon being assured they need not try to understand since their interests had been carefully considered in choosing the methodology.

Has accounting been drifting towards an increasingly technical vocabulary? The rephrasing of numerous items in today's financial statements suggests an awareness that such drifting may be a fact. Our usual technical terms often are words in general use. And accountants in their own way are technicians; hence improving their techniques brings a need for better vocabulary to communicate sharp distinctions in ideas to each other. Yet the results of accountants' work, even more than that of economists, must be presented to a large and nontechnical public. We are trying to help that public by reducing the technicalities of our presentations to them. It could not help the readers if technicalities were increased, particularly if some of them were drawn from aspects of economic technology.

Accounts, as inanimate categories designed to receive and report data, are open to any degree of breakdown and renaming of the constituent parts. This is the way accounting data have been progressively refined over many generations. As evolution continues it becomes increasingly necessary that change be entered upon carefully and advisedly so that more and more technology will not find its way into accounting reports where the result would be decreased opportunity for the essential message to reach the reader's understanding. The limiting factor to modification of accounting ideology is not rigidity in account categories or in accountants' thought processes; the limit is partly at least in the readers' preparation to understand the message presented, however skillful the presentation.

Critics of accounting "unrealism" could carry more conviction if they showed more evidence of appreciating the fact that accounting, although in itself much more than bookkeeping, is inescapably committed to the integration of real and nominal accounts, this being the very essence of double-entry bookkeeping. Instead of shrugging off the accountant's idea of having a duty to be convincingly objective in admitting data to his scheme of accounts, the arguments of advocates of accounting change might come with better grace if they showed that they recognized in the strong desire of accountants for data derived from clearly objective, verifiable evidence a reaching toward one of the attributes of scientific method.

(personal correspondence, spring, 1951)

26. Toward Understanding Accountancy

I have read with interest Professor R. J. Chambers' plea for "a theory of accounting" (*Australian Accountant,* September-October, 1955) and wish him well with the project, in the event that he should elect to continue to develop his theme at length. Since it clearly would be an attempt to explain accountancy to nonaccountants, it might prove to be a real contribution to better understanding on the part of many people. Since economists try to explain their doctrines to accountants and others who will listen, any intelligible explanation of accountancy to economists should be encouraged.

Professor Chambers refers to some writing of mine, so perhaps I might undertake to set deduction and induction in contrast, since he follows the one approach and I the other.

There are, in my view, two roads leading toward understanding accountancy. One could well be that envisaged in Professor Chambers' outline—when the blueprint of the road has been fully converted and the way opened for travel. This road of deduction could be an instructive and rather pleasurable route. The other, I fear, must be a longer and harder way—one which some people, perhaps many people, would not wish to take the time to travel. This would be the road of full-scale, technical preparation in the arts of this complex technology—the road of experience, whether experience is vicarious through the literature of accounting practices or by personal contacts in the field. Do we not learn of chemistry best in the laboratory (that is, by experience) rather than by lecture, definition, and description? The analogy seems to indicate that experience of two kinds is the true basis for learning to think in a technical subject matter.

A useful supplement to this second approach—one which would provide additional and enlightening understanding of accounting technology —could be found in some parallel study of accounting history. This could provide a view of the way, and of the reasons, that accountancy over a long period of development outgrew its early garments of routine recording and, with almost magical adaptability, became the language which makes modern business comprehensible. Granted, this collateral study would be hard to come by because the literature of such history is still sparse. Yet I commend the effort, for acquaintance with the origin of accounting and its ways of growing can be very convincing in demonstrating that its basic ideas have proved to be very basic indeed, though they appeared and grew without benefit from deductive logic.

I can be understandingly sympathetic with economists who, for uses appropriate to their section of social science, would like to see accountancy reconstructed more closely to their desires. I can commend their ingenuity in adopting some surface aspects of double entry in setting up their "social accounts" in order better to study the course of a national economy. But I cannot generate any sympathy for collateral proposals (and Professor Chambers' outline seems to lead inevitably into a justification of price-level adjustments) which, by injecting index-number adjusted figures into the double-entry process, in business accounting, would confuse more users of enterprise accounting data than it could possibly enlighten. Let me add at once that no similar objection would lie against supplementary data of whatever type which would be considered interpretatively useful.

The thought can be developed a little further by means of a few questions: Who would make use of modified historical cost figures—practitioners or theorists? What do practitioners say? Through association committees, professional accountants in Great Britain and the United States have declined to recommend change in accounting technology.[8] A conclusion emerging from an extensive survey of the practice and beliefs of security analysts (Horngen in *Accounting Review,* October, 1955) is stated in these words ". . . the most startling discovery in this investigation has been the united stand of security analysts against 'tampering' with conventional financial statements by application of price-level adjustments."

These two groups of technicians, we may be sure, do not undertake to speak for their clientele—enterprise managements and security-investors. But who could believe they would take a stand far from an attitude acceptable to these important interests? Especially when the voice of practical experience supports the stand and when a common sense compromise is available. This compromise proposes use of supplementary presentations of the effects of price-level change. The idea has the support of two research agencies having no clients: the study group on business income sponsored by the American Institute of Certified Public Accountants, and committees of the American Accounting Association.

If the modification of accounting in the form proposed has been rejected by practical men in accounting and by security analysts—men whose views probably accord with the attitude of businessmen having

.

[8] In 1948 and again in 1958, the American Institute of Certified Public Accountants queried 150 important business people on the desirability of modifying recorded costs by index adjustment. In both texts, opinion was generally negative.

managerial responsibilities and of investment bankers—then who remains as the principal beneficiaries? Would it be labor? Testimony of labor spokesmen seems in the negative. ("Corporate Profits Hearings," Washington, D.C., 1948, pp. 430, 443, 460.)

Is modification advocated for the benefit of isolated, individual investors who do not look to analysts for interpretation of financial statement data? Until evidence in negation is presented, the thought will persist that advocacy for such limited use is purely theoretical, that is, along the line of a belief that such investors ought to study financial statements related to the securities they buy. But practical men will continue to believe that the casual investor will not be led to change his habit by the availability of financial statements which will seem more incomprehensible than the conventional ones he does not now use.

Do we, by a process of elimination, come to the question whether modification is being advocated primarily in the belief that it would benefit "social accounting?" Is this belief accompanied by conviction that this benefit would be so widespread as to accrue to all members of society? Surely that would involve assumptions of such proportions that practical men would thereby be made extremely skeptical. It is fallacious to assume that data from "social accounts" (including elements of adjusted historical cost figures from enterprise accounting) would, under use by economic advisors to people concerned with central governmental policy, accrue inevitably to the benefit of all society. Unless, of course, "central governmental policy" is the kind necessitated by a full commitment to a managed economy. I take it that procedures which may seem to contemplate such an outcome in the United States will be considered objectionable because there is little support for a managed economy here.

If the principal remaining usefulness of adjusted accounting figures is that of supplying highly technical economic data for incidental interpretative study by anyone interested, it would seem that analytical tables supplementary to the usual financial statements would prove fully ample.

If the significance of the statistics derived from "social accounts" and the methods of compiling them are considered useful elements in helping college students to develop their reasoning powers, there can be no objection to such use, providing, as I fear has sometimes been done, the material is not converted into covered propaganda in favor of a managed economy.

Surely these would be relatively minor uses for modified account figures. And the question at once appears whether such limited uses, others having been rejected, are important enough to negate the considered judgments of the technical groups mentioned, and to justify risking the creation of much confusion on the part of the largest groups of users of financial statements.

If a systematic statement of accounting objectives along the lines of Professor Chambers' outline would help economists to understand the meat of accountancy—without making them advocates of changes in its established techniques—some such scheme of deductive logic might prove very helpful to people whose reasoning is more philosophical rather than practical.

I confess, however, to being skeptical of the same scheme's usefulness as part of preparation for professional accounting (public or private), or as an introduction provided in college for future businessmen to the "language of business." This language of business grew to its present stature and broad usefulness quite without aid from a "logical system of thought." No doubt this language can and will continue its growth by the same means—that is, by practical experience under use, by trial and error followed by intelligent retrial.

This is the central theme of the monograph, *Structure of Accounting Theory,* from which Professor Chambers quoted some sentences.

The element which has been given too little attention in accounting literature has seemed to me to be the objectives which control what we do in accounting action. Understanding of accounting can, I believe, be greatly furthered by a careful consideration of the interrelation of objectives and the technical means of reaching those ends. Accounting actions were made visible and useful long before men sought to show that their actions were rational as well as convenient or customary. Accounting theory began when teachers began to justify accounting action to their students. The justifications necessarily dealt with the objectives and intentions back of the actions under study.

It is significant that the element which emerged from this line of evolution was not a "theory of accounting" built from a central idea outward toward the details of a technology. Rather the result was "a body of theory," an interweaving of beliefs, convictions, and explanations, as these gradually developed, and are still developing, out of experience with the practical use of accounting. This is the aspect of theory which awaits an organized presentation.

Precisely because this kind of antecedent development has been taking place along the road of particular experiences (induction) it now seems possible that the whole of accounting actions and beliefs might at last be regrouped into an integrated pattern. Not a pattern in substitute for the one that has been developed out of practical experience, but a supplementary pattern, a deductive arrangement of related ideas, which could convincingly show how accountancy has within it a certain amount of heretofore unobserved logic.

We can hope this would add to the prestige of accountancy and widen understanding acceptance. But surely it would not be wise to cast the teaching of a technology into such a theoretical framework; or to believe that a scheme of progressive logic, moving through a sequential series of assumptions and justifications toward specific technical actions, could of itself justify the submerging of data which express enterprise invested cost, and this merely in order to present to all readers the current price equivalents of data (invested cost) which are already so expressive of prior managerial decision and action.

Current price-level data can indeed be helpful to well-considered decisions. Yet they cannot possibly be an acceptable substitute for an indication of our prior actions. It is not we who have acted in regard to these current equivalents; these arise from the action of people outside of our enterprise entity. The data therefore lack the first qualification for entering our accounts—relevance to our entity by reason of action in and for our business entity.

(Australian Accountant, February, 1956)

27. Choice Among Alternatives

Ideas are mobile units, in some respects not unlike freight cars in a marshaling yard. Every switchman and every builder of verbal models knows that the units may be marshaled into a train by starting at either end. The switchman, however, works under certain restrictions: someone else has brought the units into the yard; hence he has no choice of the units to be included; his objective is set for him—place the units in a sequence which will facilitate dropping each at the proper station with a minimum of train switching.

The verbal builder, however, chains ideas into idea-models with a relatively free hand: he can choose the units to be included, selecting among alternative ideas the ones he thinks most desirable; his arrangement of units is also of his own choosing; his objective is a simple one— that of choosing and arranging idea units in a manner convincing to himself and persuasive to his readers that by his sequence of thought (or assumption) another idea (conclusion) has been given creditable support.

The fact of the matter is that there are two ways of thinking of accounting theory.

One way is to consider the theory as the many explanations, reasons, justifications which will help us understand why accountancy (technology and profession) is what it is. Judging by some of the recent literature, the other way is to aim at constructing one, all-embracing theory of accounting. This "model" would be a tightly reasoned argument arranged to justify ever wider applications of accounting to new situations.

There has been far too little demonstration in the literature of the first way of thinking of accounting theory. One result is widespread belief, particularly among nonaccountants, that accountancy is more conventional than rational, more traditional than progressive; and that it is for the most part a loose collection of useful arts without a philosophy to cement the separate parts into an integrated whole.

Yet, whenever we are able to examine the long-developing ideology which has inevitably been associated with the practical use of accounting, the conviction grows that accountancy is both rational and progressive, and that its parts are being welded into an integrated whole by the actions and choices of men close to the uses of the technology.

The other view of accounting theory is being reflected particularly in some of the items in the literature which suggest in one way or another that "economic engineering" (control of the economy?) needs better data for its use than that supplied about enterprise net income by the usual process of accounting. Sometimes this view appears in the form of advocating the injection into accounting processes of cost figures as adjusted by application of a price index series. Again, it may appear closely associated with a plea for the formulation of "a theory" of accounting.

Clearly the latter concept is quite different from the former. For theory, as explanations, reasons, justifications, does not contemplate producing "a" theory, that is, a didactical arrangement of ideas which persuasively presents a series of compact propositions, beginning with a broad, distant premise (assumptions?) and emerging at a predetermined point with a more-or-less predetermined conclusion.

Because these two approaches to accounting theory are quite different, it may be of interest to examine the possibilities for choosing assumptions suitable for supporting differing conclusions.

The view has been expressed [9] that it is possible to frame a theory of accounting without reference to the practice of accounting. "Since the fundamental premise for a theory lies outside of the field of accounting proper . . . the following propositions therefore seem necessary" (as a basis for the theory). The author continues with these four propositions:

(a) Certain organized activities are carried out by entities which exist by the will or with the cooperation of contributing parties.

(b) These entities are managed rationally, i.e., with a view to meeting the demands of the contributing parties efficiently.

(c) Statements in monetary terms of transactions and relationships of the entity are one means of facilitating rational management.

(d) The derivation of such statements is a service function.

Considered in connection with the author's development of this thesis, these stated premises from outside of accounting technology seem to be derived or to be derivable from a sequence of implied alternative choices which can perhaps be formulated as follows:

(1) We may choose to assume either that the various kinds of enterprise which can use accounting data are basically alike in important particulars, or that it is their differences which are significant and controlling.

(2) We may choose to assume either that intentional actions by enter-

---

[9] For example, "Blueprint for a Theory of Accounting," by Professor R. J. Chambers (University of Sydney), *Accounting Research* (London), January, 1955.

prise management are likely to be significantly rational, or that they are likely, by neglect of reasoning, to be largely intuitive and imitative.

(3) We may choose to assume that accounting symbols, being units of local currency, should be considered either as representing a stable value of money, or as representing an unstable value of money.

(4) We may choose to assume either that the preparation of account data and financial statements, as a service function of a service instrumentality, can be carried on according to established custom and tradition, or that preparation can be carried on in whatever manner may be appropriate to providing the kind of data the users will need.

The author seems to believe that the alternatives here stated last are the significant ones. The resulting sequence of choices is brought to a focus which, it turns out, gives support for a certain conclusion about presumed accounting deficiencies.

(1) Differences between modern entities are significant and controlling. (Therefore the entities need account data suited to the peculiarities of each?)

(2) Actions by entity management are likely to be intuitive or imitative. (Therefore entity management needs assistance toward rational bases for decisions?)

(3) Account symbols should be considered as representing an unstable value of money. (Therefore a change in accounting technology is needed? That is, a change is needed to prevent the misleading intermingling therein of the effects on net income of price-level change—an external condition—and on managerial judgment—an internal condition.)

(4) Accounting is a service technology. (Therefore its service should be such as will provide whatever the kind of data users need?)

Standing alone without the parenthetical clauses, each of these chosen alternatives could strike a responsive chord in the minds of many practitioners; for each assumption is perhaps not so much "from outside accounting" as might be imagined.

Consider each item by itself. In system work the accountant cuts the cloth to fit, and he usually is skeptical about uniform accounting systems.

The independent public accountant knows, perhaps better than most people, how often managerial decisions have been intuitive—that is, self-centered, short-sighted, wishful thinking. Is it too much to say that professional accountants have persisted throughout the past one hundred years in their efforts to reduce the tendency of some people to try to make inanimate account data show what the human being wished to see?

Accountants, along with nearly all of the population, have been aware of changing price levels. In the view of all these noneconomists, changing prices tell us of unstable value of goods and services rather than of unstable value of money. It is not convincing to hear it said that these people mistakenly assume a stable value of money. The man who has goods while wanting money, and the man with money wanting goods, will each appraise the two economic elements in relation to his wishes. He may or may not note that the "value" of each is the reciprocal of the other. Businessmen and accountants, most people in fact, choose to make their decisions by thinking of the goods aspect; the remaining few believe better decisions would result from thinking of the money aspect of the reciprocal.

Professional accountants have long struggled with the problems of providing data needed by managements and investors. As a result of an extensive accumulation of experience, accountants have come to several relevant conclusions: that men often want, and need, data which are not within the function of accounting to supply or practitioners to certify; that it should lie within the province of people specially trained and experienced in accounting to set the limits of their technology in the matter of supplying all information a client might find useful; that the professional accountant should confine his professional work to dealing with objectively derived and convincingly verifiable data which have been collected and marshaled by well-known procedures from evidence of actual business transactions; that there can be no objection to any desired amount of collateral, interpretative use of properly derived account data, including such devices as averages, ratios, trends, and projections.

Although the importance of each of the alternatives chosen will not be strongly disputed by practical accountants, it does not follow that all aspects would be endorsed, or that the sum of the several subconclusions as indicated would be considered as leading to a generalization convincing to most accountants.

The principal generalization drawn by the original author from such a chain of assumptions is, in effect, that account data prepared under guidance of his four propositions would "incorporate features which economists have found it useful to adopt in studies of business behavior and social problems." Specifically, this refers to account figures modified by application of a statistical index of price-level change.

This generalization could be considered to be justified as the logical consequence of this selected choice of assumptions.

Additional support would be afforded by the following propositions:

(1) "Social accounts" (presenting the national economy in tables of interrelated figures) can usefully serve an "entity" which is quite different from other account-using entities; these social accounts need business income figures as adjusted for price-level change.

(2) Decisions of importance rest upon data descriptive of the entity we call "the national economy," and these decisions can be more soundly rational for that entity if business income figures are expressed in economic fashion.

(3) Accounting symbols (money price of transactions) need to be cleared of the effect of price-level change before being used in economic

analysis. This adjustment is desirable in order to measure separately the effect of the totality of business decisions.

(4) Accounting as a service technology should serve this entity (central government?) as well as other entities.

It will be observed that this series of propositions tends to support the stated generalization. However, suppose we start with a different tentative generalization. Could we rationalize it into a conclusion by assembling several individually persuasive propositions?

In order to try this procedure, let us take the following as the tentative generalization—an opposite of the one above—and try to support it by a chain of assumptions based upon the unused parts of the several alternatives outlined previously. It will make the issue clearer if the assumptions are called up in reverse order.

Tentative Generalization: Business accounting should not be distorted out of its natural limitations by the injection into this technology of revenue charges which have been modified by application of an index series of price-level change. *Corollary:* Supplementary interpretative disclosures of price change effects would effectively serve all users without constituting distortion of established technology.

Of the several alternative choices of premises, consider the following:

(4) It will support the tentative generalization if we can justify the assumption that the preparation of accounting data and enterprise financial statements can best be carried on according to established accounting technology.

(3) It will support the tentative generalization if we can justify the assumption that, in using money price of enterprise transactions as quantitative symbols of measurable activities, we need only think of the symbols as representing goods and services considered relevant to this enterprise.

(2) It will support the tentative generalization if we can justify the assumption that actions by enterprise management today are likely to be significantly rational.

(1) It will support the tentative generalization if we can justify the assumption that various kinds of entities which can use account data are basically alike in important particulars—especially in these features which are in tune with the central and controlling characteristic of accounting.

Assumption 4 above may seem merely to reflect blind adherence to old ideas and neglect of new ideas. Yet the fact is that the known course of accountancy's modern development clearly indicates a willingness of the part of businessmen and accountants to extend the services of accounting and to improve its techniques.

Older ideas have been abandoned or modified to meet new situations. The American voluntary audit for credit purposes was a deviation from the British statutory audit of company directors' stewardship. New ideas, if deemed relevant to accounting and well within its limitations, have been supported by accountants: standard costs in factories, accounts for appropriations and commitments in fund accounting, the *Lifo* formula, for example.

The acceptance of these ideas and their introduction into the accounting framework, surely must weaken any belief that accounting techniques are so rigid as to be beyond change. Change there has been, but always it has been kept within certain limits. Imputed interest as a cost has been rejected because, since it does not arise in an objective transaction of this enterprise, its use would inject unilateral, hypothetical figures not tied to bilateral, bargained transactions.

The thought at once arises that standard costs also are hypothetical figures. The answer is that standard costs, and even *Lifo*, are firmly tied to enterprise actualities in a way not seen in the case of imputed interest and index-modified revenue charges. *Lifo* is based on actual exchange-priced transactions of this enterprise; accounts for variations from standard cost tie the latter to invested costs. Fixed asset depreciation is not properly determined by managerial fiat as may be convenient. Depreciation changes can be denied admission to the status of a cost only at the risk of making very misleading disclosures of the real situation as to enterprise net income.

In accepting changes into accounting technology, ideals are in control: the most truthful accounts, statements which provide full disclosures. It is the objective of accountants to attain and hold these ideals as closely as possible. It is to this end that the integrity of the framework of systematic methodology is maintained, that is, so that the data from this methodology, and the appropriateness of system operation, can be critically reviewed as to relevance to the enterprise in question and as to factual accuracy.

Assumption 3 emphasizes two points: money prices are symbols of non-monetary realities; the realities in question are goods and services and contractual obligations which are clearly relevant to the given enterprise. Enterprise action deals with these realities; the service capacity of goods must be considered before the financial, the money side, can have meaning. Goods and services are acquired in an effort to attract customers, that is, to serve the public. The price tags of these diverse efforts are significant; but not so much from expressing purchasing power of money as from rendering diverse efforts homogeneous and quantitative—this so that these efforts in due time may be brought into arithmetical relationship with achieved results which have also been rendered quantitative by agreed exchange-priced transactions.

The use of money prices other than those associated with transactions of this enterprise would clearly introduce irrelevant data into the record, thus injecting an unethical element of misrepresentation. Moreover, systematically restricting the source of account data to transactions of this enterprise also has the desirable effect of making verification more feasible.

The price of the goods purchased is a natural fact with which business-men must of necessity consciously concern themselves; the causal factors back of that price are not. Supply and demand for goods and services is a causal factor which is a direct consequence of the mass of individual economic actions. Statistics tending to reflect change in these elements provide helpful information for management use, yet do not in them-selves modify accounting procedures.

Another important causal factor is the available supply of money and credit. And this is subject to planned controls exercised by statutory au-thorities. It is beyond the function and power of businessmen as indi-viduals—though within the authority and power of the Federal Reserve Board—to determine over-all fiscal policy, and thus affect the price level.

Under these conditions, how would knowledge of "changing value of money" as money help the businessman? One man's study of current fiscal policy is not likely to increase his ability effectively to serve his clientele; his study of the prices of goods would.

To pose businessmen and accountants with a necessary choice between considering money units as representing a stable or an unstable value of money is equivalent to implying that each man of them should con-sciously act in the interest of the economy as a whole. Would not they then be forced to neglect their primary responsibilities to their own constituencies when they consciously tried to share in the control of the national fund of money and credit in order that price fluctuations for the whole economy should be suitably influenced?

For businessmen, data of the changing prices of goods and services are significant; for current policy-makers, data of the changing purchasing power of money are significant, since these people are charged with tak-ing action to influence the nation's business. Is it not, therefore, largely a confusing exercise of semantics to make it seem that businessmen and accountants have a responsibility to act with conscious choice as to whether the "value of money" is stable or unstable?

Assumption 2 makes the point that enterprise management today is much more rational than intuitive. The latter kind of management pre-sumably would not use data indicative of larger-than-local conditions; thus the significance of changing average price levels would be missed. Is this the reason his accounting should be changed, so that the larger scene will be inescapably spread before his mind?

No doubt there are many men making business and investment deci-sions who do not research their way into decisive action. Yet many of them, perhaps most, are able to manage with satisfaction to their stock-holders, employees, customers, bankers, tax collectors, and themselves.

May there not be an important element in successful enterprise management which theorists without administrative experience or responsibility could easily overlook, or too sharply discount? Good business judgment is a vital factor in management; and it cannot be satisfactorily compressed into a phrase, "always act to maximize the profit."

Judgment is an element which does not lend itself to definition; formal education is at most an uncertain factor in the creation of good judgment. Judgment grows best as it feeds upon responsible, rather than vicarious, experience. The raw materials of experience are the details and peculiarities of a particular enterprise, of its customer clientele, of its material and labor markets. Then follows knowledge, in the same pattern, of the industry concerned. This is a long way from study of the economy as a whole, perhaps so far away that most businessmen cannot indulge in broad studies and still meet the duties of the day at the office. Yet, this doing first things first seems to have proved satisfactory throughout the centuries. Men apparently were able to develop good judgment before statistical methodology and economic doctrine were available to guide them. There is little evidence that, as a class, they did not manage "rationally." By what other road have we come to the present stage of industrial development?

There is plenty of evidence of the use of techniques of rational management. The modern development of controllership, forecasting, market surveys, personnel testing, all of these, though nonaccounting, indicate growth of rational management by use of devices designed to sharpen and broaden judgment based on experience.

Accounting as it is can well be called the oldest technical aid to rational management. Over the centuries it has been reporting, after the fact, on the status and effectiveness of prior managerial decisions. This highly useful reporting continues today without having felt a need for departure from the use of accounts which consistently stated past efforts as measured in terms of exchange-priced transactions. Nor is there convincing evidence that any significant portion of the total mass of business and investment decisions based on such account data was anything but rational. Disturbing instances of bankruptcies and losses by security-holders have usually been related to neglect of account data, outright fraud, or to conditions unavoidable through a knowledge of accounting data.

In fact, the astonishing accomplishments of modern business seem of themselves to be the strongest argument in support of the tentative generalization posed above. Since accounting technology in its usual form has served during this period, and has steadily grown under those conditions, it is only reasonable to believe it has served well as an instrument in aid of this achievement. If this is true, it would also seem reasonable to believe that the natural limitations of accounting technology have not stood in the way of its ability effectively to provide its kind of service under new and different conditions. Where these limitations have been reached, supplementary techniques have been constructed and have demonstrated in use their ability to contribute as expected.

Business does indeed need rational management. The need has long been recognized. How else explain the advances made in managerial techniques and skills? It is noteworthy that the present degree of rational management has been achieved without damage to any of the earlier instruments used in aid of rational business judgments. Nonaccounting techniques, by acting within their own function, supplement rather than change the natural limitations inherent in accounting.

This kind of useful approach has again been proposed as a satisfactory way of augmenting the information service of accounting: specifically, a supplementary, quasi-statistical statement presenting a calculated effort to separate the effect of changing price levels upon revenue changes and net income, and to suggest in the resulting residual figures the effect of managerial decision as such. This arrangement will leave account and financial statement technology unchanged. It would seem also to offer the kind of special information which special interests have indicated would be particularly useful to them. Yet the literature critical of accounting "realism" shows few signs that this solution is satisfactory to the critics. Can it be that an urge to effect a reform in accounting technology is more persuasive than securing the specified data? If published reports are slow to include a supplementary income calculation, that could no doubt be changed by request of the people qualified to present the views of the principal users of accounting data, such as business management and investment counsel.

Assumption 1 entertains the idea that similarities among enterprises using accounting data are of controlling significances.

Here is a case of important similarities existing among relatively less important differences. Because this is so, it is similarities not differences which make accounting an appropriate technology in individual applications. Like other technologies, accounting cannot be all things to all men. Accounting lacks universality, and accountants will not be persuaded otherwise by assertions that it ought to be rested upon principles of universal truth. It is doubtful, for example, whether applying the word "accounting" to the recording system used in totalitarian countries does anything to make accounting universal in fact. It will not be a record system dedicated to the truthful analysis of exchange-priced transactions and presentation of the distinction between, and interrelations of, capital (real accounts) and income (nominal accounts).

Other systems for producing managerially useful data can no doubt be constructed, and may suffice for this purpose. But these would need to include certain definite characteristics and limitations to be in fact what the word "accounting" has come to mean to us. A useful arrangement of data is being used under the name of "social accounts." The use of the adjective here makes it clear that a distinguishing adjective might well be used elsewhere, as in "business accounting." Somewhat the same kind of misunderstanding could arise from overgeneralization of the word "democracy."

It may be complimentary to use the word "accounting" in noncharacteristic applications. But it will trouble many accounting technicians to see efforts made to introduce modifications into their technology in order that the resulting data shall be more suitable for direct use in certain noncharacteristic situations.

The distinctions here considered are illustrated by two types of accounting adaptations. Many features of business accounting, particularly those facilitating internal control, are rapidly being put into use in various operating divisions of the federal government. In sharp contrast is the adoption of certain surface features of account classifications to form statistical tables given the name "social accounts."

The first adaptation will make its contribution by increasing operating efficiency; the second adaptation is expected to make its contribution by promoting analytical study of change among several segments of the whole national economy. The first adaptation takes accounting as it is and, as is done in fund accounting, uses all account classifications except those dealing directly with dedicated capital and profit; the second adaptation appears to furnish the primary impulse toward advocating the idea that throughout business accounting the invested cost figures (risked capital) should be modified by application of a price index series.

This proposed modification contains an overemphasis on an economic idea (purchasing power) in association with a tendency to believe, erroneously I think, in the validity of the assumption that accounting, because it is a service technology, should be able, and accountants should be willing, to modify its technical features as may seem useful to any type of entity. Accounting has registered, in use, a marvelous adaptability. But close examination of its many differing forms will show there are limits beyond which adaptation may become emasculation.

The existence in practical use of variations *from* the original Italian scheme of business records (adaptation) should not be considered indicative that variation *of* accounting (basic modification) will be easily sold to its technicians.

Accounting is indeed a service technology, but since accounting cannot offer a universal service to all types of entities, one of the basic premises needed for "a theory of accounting" seems not to support a conclusion in favor of modifications by application of index-numbers. So, too, the other basic premises come into question as to their place in a chain of reasoning leading to the same conclusion.

The flexibility of the several semantic arts—of assembling chosen alternatives, of adducing reasons in support, of chaining assumptions into a sequence—has been suggested in this presentation. The conclusion of

the experiment can perhaps be put this way: different switchmen probably would organize a train of freight cars very much alike; different
builders of verbal models, having differing conclusions in mind, probably would construct differing chains of reasoning.

(*Accounting Review*, July, 1956)

28. Economists and Accountants

Accounting and economics have been closely interrelated longer than
most people may realize.

Double-entry bookkeeping—the continuing backbone of accounting—
was fully developed in its essential features by the end of the fifteenth
century. Its procedure made a systematic record of enterprise capital
employed productively under the guidance of management, and a record
of income generated by management's use of the invested assets. Clearly
double entry, a very long time ago, was the record side of economic action—records of investing, of buying, selling, judging, risking, records
related to servicing the economic wants of customers.

Businessmen in those early days knew that capital, productively employed, could reproduce itself and generate income. They knew, too, that
income saved became new capital. Through long trial and error men
converted mere memoranda of debts into a recording methodology which
translated these naturally related economic phenomena into integrated,
quantitative measurements of capital and income.

This integration was accomplished in the record by means of interrelated accounts for assets and accounts for expense-income. These two
major classes of accounts were called about a century ago by a German
writer "accounts of remainders" and "accounts of results." We call them
by the much less informative terms of "real and nominal accounts."

The early literature dealt only with methodology. Textbooks included
nothing we could call theory. It fell to eighteenth century economists,
apparently without conscious intentions, to supply a theory framework
for double-entry bookkeeping by their writings about capital and income.
Capital they considered a stock of goods productively employed; income
as wealth created over a period of time by the employment of this capital.
Hence, capital is like a fruit tree; income is like the tree's fruit. The
income (fruit) may be consumed or as seed invested to replenish or expand the orchard.

With twentieth century perspective we can see that fifteenth century
businessmen were reacting in very practical ways to the inherent nature
of the economic factors we call capital and income. We can see that
eighteenth century economists were describing in words the inherent economic nature of capital and income. Centuries apart both businessmen
and economists were dealing with the same social phenomena—particu-

larly with the productivity of capital under independent enterprise management, and with the profit motive as an incentive to capital risk and managerial efficiency. The world is still benefiting from this wedding of accounting practice and economic explanation.

From this background it would seem that the ideas of economists and accountants should be in close agreement. Yet such is not the case in some important particulars. Because this is so, it would be in the public interest if these two parties came to understand each other more fully. The need for this mutual understanding has been given some attention on the side of accounting instruction. Accounting majors in these days study economics as well as accountancy. And the higher they go in academic work, the more economics they take.

This curricula requirement is a natural result because educators perceived two things about accountancy: (1) that accounting translates economic actions, particularly actions affecting business enterprises, into quantitative terms suitable for classifying relevant enterprise events into interpretative categories; (2) that the recording methodology compresses the economic decisions and experiences of enterprise management in a manner which makes the data particularly useful for back reference and guidance toward the future decisions.

This useful service began some 500 years ago with the appearance of double-entry bookkeeping. While that methodology may seem to a casual observer to be little more than clerical work, the fact is the practical procedures there introduced were so basic that they could be satisfactorily continued in use for centuries and in modern times could prove surprisingly adaptable to highly complicated new situations.

Although economic action has always been taking place, economics as we understand the term is a newer discipline. During most of its development as a field of knowledge, economics has been philosophical in approach—that is, it leaned towards reasoning along historical and theoretical lines concerning the way people make a living and react to their economic surroundings. It is only in relatively recent years that refinements and broadening have made statistical methodology into an instrument for producing quantitative measurements suitable for economic reasoning.

Students who major in economics usually include some study of statistical methodology. But that other quantitative discipline, accountancy, is seldom a part of the program. I have often wondered why, since accounting is very significantly related to the firm and its management, and that section of theory, microeconomics, is closely concerned with studying "the firm."

Accounting shows some of the aspects of statistical methodology, but does not go so far as to include time series. Accounting classifies data about economic acts, but only for those transactions which directly involve a given enterprise. Perhaps this subject is not often accepted by students of economics because accounting instruction is still organized strongly along time-consuming lines and with continued emphasis on technical procedures as such. Or perhaps it is because accounting data, being created for individual business enterprises, do not suitably express economic data for the nation as a whole. This last would seem a not unreasonable surmise since economists from the time of Adam Smith's *Wealth of Nations* have been accustomed to concern themselves with a society as a body of individuals.

For example, considerable interest is now developing in what is called "social accounting." This is a statistical approach to an extensive organizing of data dealing with nationwide economic activities. These statistics are desired so that governmental policies may be formed which may help prevent imbalance between segments of the economy.

This ideology is compactly expressed by a recent writer in these words: "An essential preliminary to the formation of consistent [governmental] policies is a catalogue of information about receipts and payments throughout the national economy. . . . The most appropriate way to set out this information is in the form of a system of accounts." [10]

It may be noted in passing that enterprise accounting has progressed a long way beyond reporting on receipts and payments. Perhaps it is not too much to say that this change is one of the major refinements of accounting technology, and thus makes of accounting a more effective aid to the decisions of managers and investors.

In contrast to the interest economists have in society and the individual people who make up society, accounting has seldom sought to serve individuals separate from a business enterprise and has never aspired to attempt to classify economic action for the whole of a nation. These are inherent differences, and both parties would do well always to bear them in mind.

Differences in the thinking by economists and accountants about account data have become clearer in recent years in connection with a still continuing discussion of the statistics of national income as part of "social accounts." It is understandable that new clarity now should be appearing; the viewpoints of the two groups are being more clearly brought out by discussion.

Economists have become increasingly concerned about events which affect the nation's well-being. This interest seems to have been associated with a marked increase in conditions which conspired to give emphasis to the power of central government to become a factor in the national economy.

When decisions of vast economic importance are to be taken within central government, they should of course rest as much as possible on dependable economic statistics. In no other way can men's minds com-

---

[10] Gilbert Walker in Chapter 9 of *The Accounting Field*, Donald Cousins, ed., London, 1954.

prehend the complex issues and screen out emotional reactions. Economic statisticians, eager to improve nationwide statistics, have become dissatisfied with those data which derive from enterprise accounts.

The essence of their corrective proposal lies in the idea that statistics of national income would be improved if the cost figures used by business in computing enterprise income were modified. The modifier would be a series of index-numbers representing the fluctuations registered by changing wholesale price levels. The index would be used to multiply invested dollars into so-called current equivalent dollars.

The theory back of the proposal is that such an adjustment would eliminate from the accounting figure of profit the effect of rising price levels. Accounting net income without such an adjustment has been called "unrealistic." It is said that this kind of modification would convert accounting net income into a "realistic" figure.

Most accountants, however, are still unconvinced by this asserted distinction between realistic and unrealistic. But it may be of interest, therefore, to take a brief look at some of the ideas which keep economists and accountants from more ready agreement in the matter of calculated net income.

For example, economists and accountants have quite different basic ideas of income. As long as this situation exists, the parties will be likely to differ as to the realism of accounting calculations that use dollars of invested cost. Yet this fact need not stand in the way of increased mutual understanding.

Economists view income as a complex of several ideas of which three are mentioned here:

(1) Income is wealth which the owner can disburse over a period of time and be as well off at the end as at the beginning. Here is a strong leaning toward analogy to personal well-being. Presumably, by this concept, a business enterprise—a social institution—could have no "earnings" unless it were as well off in value of assets at the end as at the beginning of a period. The influence of price-level changes and of the price of asset replacements would under these ideas seem inescapably involved in the calculation of current well-being.

Such reasoning seems to be appropriate in regard to the well-being of a person. But is it equally suitable to reasoning about an impersonal, economic institution such as a business enterprise?

(2) A second idea of interest here is that economists consider the current value of a business enterprise to be measurable by capitalizing the expected earnings of that company.

Note that such a valuation as of two dates could be considered as providing one kind of measurement of improved financial condition. Note also that "valuation" under this concept would need to make use of *expected* earnings—this because "value" is a future-looking word, whereas "cost" is a backward-looking word. Accountants find expected earnings

unacceptable for most accounting uses. The reason is found in an unwillingness to cut loose their thinking and their service from the provable
objectivity of accounts kept and financial statements made in terms of
costs actually incurred by this enterprise before the current date.

This position has been given recent support by two prominent accountants, G. O. May and J. L. Dohr, in these words:

"Since 1941 it has been more and more widely recognized that books
of account and balance sheets disclose the amounts that have been invested—not the value of what exists. The most natural substitute for
book value would therefore seem to be book investment." [11] A more extended analysis of reasons in favor of adherence to invested cost has been
made by Professor W. A. Terrill under the title "Cost Basis—Accounting's Samson's Tresses." [12]

(3) Economists believe that the real income of an enterprise is made
visible only after corrections of accounting net income have been made
to eliminate the effect of "changed value of money"; that is, the effect of
changing price levels. The idea inherent in the first phrase also prompts
an assertion that accountants assume that money has a stable value
although fluctuating price levels show how unstable the money unit
really is.

It is too large a problem to undertake here to analyze the question
whether the value of goods or the value of money is the unstable factor.
Perhaps the dollar sign that is shown or implied before each item in
financial statements is responsible for some confusion of thought. Some
people may think it symbolizes value; others think of cost.

Does the symbol of a crossed S ($) in this country or a crossed L (£)
in England mean that the accompanying digits speak of a quantity of
value, or of an agreed-upon price? The symbol alone does not differentiate. At the moment of exchange of an item the digits may express both
value and cost. Later the same digits for the same item can only express
cost. A transaction of today is an accomplished fact. The price agreed
may seem to measure value as of that moment, but that "value" may soon
change—for example, if customers show no interest in the merchant's
new purchase. But the merchant's cost price does not change for that
reason. If the merchandise is unsalable, his loss is measured by the invested cost, not by the customer's current valuation of the item. If this
is true for a loss, can the calculation of profit from sale be logically rested
on any other figure than invested cost?

Accountants are quite aware that the primary goal of their technology
is measurement of enterprise income. They realize that any person's judgment of the value of an enterprise is conditioned by his knowledge of at
least two matters of quantitative fact which present different problems of
measurement:

[11] *Journal of Accountancy*, April, 1955.
[12] N.A.C.A. Bulletin, April, 1955.

1. Profits earned by the enterprise under management.
2. Possible unearned value increments behind the enterprise.

Accountants believe that only fact number one can be measured by use of accounting. As to the second factor, they consider measurement of such increments to be beyond the reach of accounting techniques. The reason for this view is the belief that unearned increments are largely the result of the effect of general economic conditions upon personal opinions as to value in general. Hence, nonaccountants using nonaccounting methods would be the best people to attempt such an appraisal of subjective opinion.

We have been viewing economists' concept of income and now should look more closely at the concept held by accountants. It starts from the idea that enterprise assets may derive from three sources: (1) from lenders, in exchange for debt pledges; (2) from proprietors, in exchange for ownership certificates; (3) from customers, in exchange for services rendered by this enterprise.

Only such assets as are derived from customers can normally qualify as being associated with enterprise net income or earnings, and then only if the asset newly received from a customer shall consist of these two measurable parts: (a) one part that reimburses the enterprise for the cost it has invested in the items sold and in service expenses; (b) one part that affords compensation for enterprise risk, for use of capital, for management skill exercised on behalf of the enterprise.

It is an important function of accounting to measure these two parts. In case the excess of sales price over purchase cost (goods and expense) is zero, the accounting evidence shows that customers have been unwilling to pay a price sufficient to include any compensation for the enterprise factors mentioned. The message to management is plain: somewhere policies and decisions and actions have been out of line with conditions that prevail. If sales price fails even to reimburse purchase cost, the message is the same with additional emphasis.

In further analysis of accounting ideology, we may take note of two other underlying beliefs: (1) Belief that enterprise compensation is not directly separable into distinct rewards for risk, for use of capital, for managerial skill, and for a residual amount due to the effect of external economic movements, such as price-level changes.

The reason for this view? It is that economic causes are too intermingled to be untangled for separate measurement by accounting technology.

(2) Belief that income cannot arise directly from new investments or borrowings, or by action of owners in creating an item in their accounts called "goodwill," or by owner action in repricing assets already possessed.

The reason for this view? It is that no service has been rendered by this enterprise in connection with these purely financial actions.

A corollary to this reasoning is seen in this other belief: while economic change, present or prospective, may affect people's opinion regarding the value of an enterprise or of some of its products or of its securities, yet such opinion is subjective and outside of the reviewable facts within the enterprise in question. For this reason, such opinion cannot logically change the existing ledger account pattern of objective facts which will indicate the knowable structure of the enterprise.

Economists and accountants work within differing disciplines. And ideas suitable to one probably will seldom be directly suitable to the other without change in connotation. Nevertheless, debate about concepts of income, as one example, is a healthy development since discussion can lead to better mutual understanding between fields that are inescapably in constant contact.

Perhaps full identity of concepts and purposes is not necessary. It seems doubtful if extensive modification of such a serviceable technology as accounting would necessarily be in the public interest. Whatever corrective force might lie within accounting figures for income after adjustment by index-numbers, that force would be powerless materially to counteract the ideological, financial, political, and emotional pressures which create and maintain so much dilution of the currency as to produce continuing rise of price levels—the same rising price levels which accountancy and business management are being admonished to change merely by modifying their accounting processes.

When they understand the concern which prompts economists to wish for different enterprise account data, accountants can take appropriate steps outside of the customary boundaries of accounting theory and method as already proposed. Supplementary data will prove even more usable by economists than would altered financial statements. And the proven serviceability of usual financial statements to many other people will be left undisturbed.

The discussion that has lately been in progress about the impact of price-level change upon accounting and the middle-ground result which seems to be emerging (supplementary statements) is an example of the kind of social service that can flow from better mutual understanding following upon careful analysis and friendly debate. Data supplementary to the use of financial statements no doubt would be acceptable to economists. And it would be clearly within the accountant's concept of full disclosure. "Full disclosure," in the view of accountants, "corresponds in economic affairs," as Professor Cannon puts it, "to the institutions of free press and free speech in political affairs." [13]

It probably is of minor importance who makes up the supplementary presentation. Accountants might well make the schedule as an adjunct to the usual financial statements—providing (1) they need not certify to it,

---

[13] *Journal of Accountancy,* March, 1955.

and (2) that they will equip themselves with an adequate understanding of the needs and of methodology of economic statistics—an understanding that will carry beyond the arithmetical computations of applying a designated index series to certain key figures involved in the usual calculation of net income.

If accountants do not provide this collateral and interpretative information, economists will compute their own adjusted figures as well as may be. They probably would prefer not to undertake this task for they would readily see the need for extending their knowledge of accounting ideology, if not its methodology.

It would not be helpful if both parties avoid responsibility by taking an attitude of "let the other fellow do it." Professor John T. Wheeler has given us two sentences which seem particularly appropriate here. "Accountants have been too quick to label economics as impractical and of no use to them. Economists have been too apt to regard accounting as a useless business ritual which had no application to their field." [14]

It is not impossible that both parties are in error. Some economic theorizing—perhaps a good deal of it—is not very useful to accountants and businessmen. Perhaps economists could extend the area that could be useful, i.e., "economics of the firm." To these people, some brief acquaintance with accounting procedure may indeed leave an impression that it is ritual, i.e., strictly according to custom, convention or formulas. Could not accounting writers make other material available to students and economists? It would make good a present deficiency in accounting literature. Can we not see in the criticisms of economists a need for clear, logical, verbal explanations of and justifications for accounting concepts and ideology?

(Illinois Certified Public Accountant, summer, 1956)

29. Accounting Dynamics

Mr. F. Sewell Bray, of London, has published a new book of his lectures, entitled *The Interpretation of Accounts,* which illuminates the area of his particular research interest.

First thoughts upon reading the work: The title of the book points to an aspect of accounting that is often neglected. The interpretative, analytical, informative potential inherent in capital-income accounting has not been explored very far. In accounting education these interpretative possibilities are seldom examined beyond a course in financial statement analysis. Yet, from indications in some enterprises of staff positions labeled "analyst," it is safe to presume that data buried in account categories are in some companies closely examined for informative inter-

[14] Chapter 2, *Handbook of Modern Accounting Theory,* 1955, Morton Backer, ed.

relations of significance to management. A need exists for a literature in the interpretation of accounts to supplement the substantial literature of accounting technology and professional auditing. Perhaps this volume will be an item of this kind.

Now as to the book itself. The author is both an accountant and an economist; his Chapter 10 is titled "Auditing Theory," and Chapter 9, "The Nature and Purpose of Direct Taxation." His strong interest in social accounts is reflected in Chapter 11, "A Formal Review of Social Accounting." Chapter 2 is titled "The Formal Principles of Public Company Accounting." Since 1944 he has been author or coauthor of nine books on various aspects of accounting. The two latest of these are reports on research made while serving as Stamp-Martin Professor of Accounting.

The volume under review is published for the research committee of the Society of Incorporated Accountants, and carries a foreword by Bertram Nelson, president of the society. A first view of the objective of the book comes in this foreword. "The whole purpose of Professor Bray's book is to suggest that three view points (about the purposes of accounts) can be reconciled. . . ." The three divergent views are those of enterprise management, those indicated in the companies acts and tax legislation, and those of ". . . economists, who have discovered the merits of accounting technique as a method of analysis."

The chapters consist of eleven research lectures given between 1953 and 1955, for the most part before meetings of accountants. Other settings include student groups, economics and statistical societies, and the British Institute of Management. About one half of the book (110 pages) is given over to four chapters titled "Accounting Dynamics." These present in considerable detail the author's present theme. Other lectures deal with some of the same materials, adapted to the particular audience then present. Sometimes the lectures seem designed to show to accountants the concepts of economists, others to show economists and statisticians something of the potentials of accounting technology.

Accounting dynamics, the author points out, ". . . can and should be looked upon as part of the general interpretation of accountants. . . . Our primary purpose then is to consider those forms of differential accounts which promote business adaptability to change" (p. 41). "The essential task of accounting dynamics is the isolation and magnification of changes in accounting aggregates in order that we may study the changing economic pattern of an accounting entity (p. 53). In the accompanying context he speaks of "those who engage in expectation accounting." This is for accounting a new term perhaps, but not a new idea. The practice of industrial budgeting from its beginning a generation ago has dealt with "expectations"; the same could be said about standard cost. The phrase, however, very effectively indicates the direction of the author's interest.

American readers should be mindful of British use of the phrase "in the accounts." Usually the context will show that the reference is to some form of reporting accounting data—financial statements or schedules, we usually say. References to price-level adjustments "in the accounts" are more likely to mean "in the statements" than in the ledger categories.

The author gives little space to ratio analysis of financial statements—the most familiar approach to interpretation of account data. His emphasis is elsewhere. "We are principally concerned with accounting change." "Change, when it occurs, demands recognition and adaptability." "We are trying to analyze what is really happening behind those aggregate figures which appear in accounts, in order that we may bring about a wider use of the figures passing through the hands of accountants" (p. 62-63).

The approach he adapts to analysis of changes reflected by business enterprise data has some kinship to funds statement computations. He writes of "Sources, Earmarkings and Utilization of Funds" (p. 37), "Capital Change" (pp. 65, 161). Chapter 8, "Capital Changes," gives detailed attention to this analytical presentation. Section 1 of that schedule is called "Savings and Asset Formation," and includes on one side, "retained income," "earmarked income," "provision for depreciation" (cost allocation and price change adjustment are shown separately), "inventory price change adjustment," and a balance, "excess asset formation." On the other side: net expenditures of fixed assets, change in deferred expenditures, change in total inventories.

Other analytical sections are titled "Gains and Losses," "Long-term Financial Changes," "Working Capital Changes," "Tax Adjustments and Change in Provisions." The last section is "Summary Account of Capital Changes," and includes, among others on the left, a final item, "Asset Value Adjustment," on the right, "Capital Value Adjustment." For each side three money columns are provided: Indicated or Expected Standards of Change, Actual Changes, Differences (p. 171). Here, as elsewhere in the book, a good deal of explanatory text accompanies the schedules.

In the details of the sections (except for items of adjustment for price change) the similarity to familiar accounting presentations is close. "The dynamic functioning of the entity became observable by analyzing changes in the relationships among the details of the schedule." "The bi-lateral functions of capital change" are disclosed in the summary account. This summary (p. 173) is arranged to show that "the positives and negatives [e.g., excess asset formation versus excess saving; increase versus decrease in working capital, etc.] will always counterbalance to give a zero total. Some of the terminology and arrangement here seem designed more to make interpretation of capital changes understandable to economists than to accountants and management.

Numerous writers in the *Accounting Review* have evidenced dissatisfaction with the service that could be rendered by the usual funds statement. Professor Bray seems to have felt the same analytical deficiency and, drawing upon the approach used in social accounts, to have sought to show how to increase the analytical information to be made available.

Most of the material in the four chapters on accounting dynamics is used to present and explain an arrangement, in statement form, of enterprise operating data. Pro-forma statements, "a permissible minimum," are presented early (pp. 35-38); in Chapters 4 and 5 (pp. 72-74 and 100-104) a detailed "Product Operating Account" is set up to permit comparing changes between the results of two periods.

The first section sets goods and outside services acquired for production ("input") in contrast with sales and change in inventory ("output") thus producing a debit balance forward of net output, i.e., "value added." The second section deducts from "value added," the sum of various operative and auxiliary labor costs, and selling and distribution salaries, thus producing a debit balance forward of "variable margin." The third section, the most detailed of all, comes to a remainder of "operating income" often deducting from "variable margin" certain costs (goods, services, labor) which do not vary with output, e.g., standing overheads, administrative and management costs, imputed or actual rents, depreciation of operating assets.

Here again some aspects of the arrangement and titles suggest a concern for making account data more understandable for economists' use in their own analytical computations. For example, the "value added" figure can easily be associated with external statistical data (census). The term "capital formation" probably will carry a broader connotation for economists than for management. The mention of imputed rent and the placement of depreciation charges in the calculation also seem directed more toward economic analysts than managerial analysts of production cost factors. The previously mentioned inclusion of price change adjustments for depreciation and inventories also tends to adapt the presentation to economists' use, particularly that involved in setting up schedules for social accounts.

In order best to serve this purpose, however, disclosures of this kind would need to be universally adopted and used in business. Manifestly this change would take a long time to bring about. Usually statutory provisions and established customs do not yield readily to the persuasiveness of new ideas or to the logic of changing conditions. It is not clear from information available here whether or not an earlier apparent hesitation on the part of British businessmen at publishing details of their operations has materially changed. It could be that the usual public disclosures of present-day operating details are considered by some observers still to be relatively incomplete and in need of voluntary expansion.

Last thoughts: The arts of interpreting account data do indeed need development. Since the early days of cyclical analysis, the ability of economists to extract significance from accumulated factual data has continued to grow. The development of "social accounts" is a more recent example. The research and analytical thinking back of the papers in this volume and beneath the author's other publications has been a worthy endeavor. Yet to this reviewer, because of his own bias, no doubt, it seems likely that the over-all influence of the best research and the most persuasive presentations in this area will show up in economics more clearly and sooner than in law, taxation, accounting, or business.

This is not to say that businessmen, administrative accountants, and professional accountants are opposed to new analytical techniques. They have co-operated very well in the development of accounting to its present state of high usefulness. And they could obviously learn much from analytical economics. Nevertheless, they undoubtedly will be slow to accept modified procedures which could cloud the reviewability of the recorded financial fact of prior business decisions. Some of these data surely would be smothered if into ledger accounts were injected extraneous adjustments which would cause the modified figures to reflect results *as if* the enterprise had taken action it had not yet taken.

Professor Bray's book does not argue for injecting price-level change into the ledger, though other writers in their fervor for an economic type of realism make it difficult to avoid the conclusion that they consider this kind of reform appropriate, and that they look at reaction against it as little more than mere traditionalism. As an accountant, this author will be well aware that more is involved than "traditionalism." One element likely to stand large in the mind of accountants would be suggested by the question: Would negative adjustments upon a downswing of prices be equally acceptable if the positive adjustments which make up the present pattern of thought were now generally accepted?

In the service of informed enterprise management, calculated estimates of the impact of price-level change could prove very useful indeed. So too could other types of economic analysis. And perhaps the time is close at hand when trained economic analysts should be on the staff of large business concerns. But to get these useful interpretative benefits, it is not necessary extensively to "reform" accounting technology itself.

Professor Bray writes as a realist well aware of both the accounting and economic point of view. As a realist, he does not reach for new accounting technology. At most his presentation stresses the thought that operating statements might well become more flexible, more revealing, more useful than merely to continue serving as a formal adjunct to audited balance sheets. It is clear he has in mind the needs of management as well as those of economic analysts. And perhaps he would agree that no persuasive reason stands in the way of making effective use of collateral interpretative information in the event that reporting price adjustment effects in the formal financial statements also comes to be considered objectionable.

Viewed in that light, the contribution of this book could be said to lie in the care and understanding the author shows in striving to make accounting ideas more understandable to economists, and the ideas of economic analysts more understandable to accountants and businessmen and others who usually have not had formal training in economics.

Accounting needs a body of logical theory to support and explain the objectives and limitations of its technical services. And it is clear that a good many ideas useful in the structure of accounting theory can be found in the literature of microeconomics. It seems less certain that accounting theory could benefit as much from ideas out of macroeconomics where the methodology of social accounts has been derived partly out of accounting.

On the other hand, philosophical economics also has needs, particularly those related to techniques for bringing its reasoning powers to fruitful use in practical affairs. Econometrics and social accounts are instruments serving this need.

Because these needs exist, and because social economics and enterprise accounting are inescapably different disciplines, the research activities of this author and other thoughtful students should continue. Because economists and accountants will continue to think in different ways, it is well that some people try to improve mutual understanding between these groups. Out of understanding, each party may appropriately adapt ideas from the other with no thought of advocating modification of one discipline in order to satisfy the theory of the other.

It is fitting that the organized profession of public accounting should support such research and exchange of ideas; and it is particularly appropriate that a man who can see both economics and accounting should take up the task of moderator. Perhaps college classes in economics and accounting theory will in the long run prove to be the most important training ground for greater mutual understanding. Your reviewer strongly hopes that other dedicated teachers will appear who have had training in economics and accounting, and if possible, practical experience in contact with business.

It will be through research, writing, and exchange of ideas that the most satisfactory progress will come. The important thing after all is not whether index-adjusted value or historical cost is theoretically the more significant. Both have a useful function. The thing which does matter to the future of accounting and enterprise management is whether and to what extent the interpretative modifications by application of price series indexes of data out of business accounts will be set in analytical contrast with the recorded experience of exchange-priced transactions of the enterprise concerned—thus to help stimulate sound next decisions by its management. It is perhaps not too much to say that steadily improved decisions in business could conceivably contribute as much to society as would governmental policy rested upon analysis of social accounts for the nation.

(*Accounting Review*, January, 1958)

ACCOUNTING PRINCIPLES

1. Authority or Logic

Quid est veritas? Definitions alone cannot completely explain an abstract term like truth. We need standards by which to judge degrees of truth; we need principles to help us to perceive varying degrees of departure from truth.

Shall we say conformity with the pronouncements of authority is conformity with truth? There are various types of authority. Some derive their principal strength from power to enforce their pronouncements.

Accounting principles can hardly derive from the authority of statutory law and judicial decisions. The one is concerned with rules of conduct which inflict punishments for the violation of stated maximums and minimums. The other is the result of the effort to see justice done under the specific circumstances involved. Neither is intent upon establishing general principles or desirable standards for accounting. In fact, law is upon occasion inclined to look to accounting knowledge for guidance.

Another kind of authority draws its strength primarily from an established prestige which persuades men that a given pronouncement is a well-considered and reasonable suggestion.

The customs and conventions of accounting are embodied in a literature prepared by men of maturity and experience. Their testimony carries weight; we honor pronouncements based upon age and experience. But times and conditions change. The pronouncements in the literature may be only the expression of a familiar tradition or of experience that has not faced all the varied present-day problems or their equivalent.

Men speak of a consensus of authoritative opinion, of generally accepted practices. But the same men may give little consideration to devising a means of collecting those opinions which can safely be considered authoritative; and they may offer no suggestions for striking an average or for reconciling conflicting views. They seldom seem to realize that such a survey would have to be repeated periodically to be useful.

These are some of the weaknesses in an appeal to authority as a test of truth. But the method has an element of strength. An individual may be perfectly satisfied with his own opinion; yet he will be well advised to seek the views of others before making an important decision. Though there may be disagreement in council, there is also wisdom.

Perhaps the test of truth lies in logical relationships.

Instead of looking for principles in pronouncements of what is customary or accepted, some may hold that a man's own rational good sense is the best guide. Or, if he hesitates to trust common sense that much, resort may be had to syllogistic analysis. This type of analysis will permit conclusions to be deduced from perceiving relationships between obviously true propositions and the question at issue, or it will put principles to the test of being logically linked to premises that are themselves clearly acceptable.

But this approach also has its weaknesses. It is often extremely difficult in a field like accounting to establish satisfactory relationships between the several ideas under analysis. Too often one must rely upon intuitive insight; frequently significant distinctions are overlooked. In addition, the conclusion of a syllogism is not necessarily true; it can be a valid conclusion by the rules of logic and still be untrue because the antecedent premises are not true. Assumptions, postulates, and axioms may be useful starting points, but they do not necessarily represent truth.

Yet here too there is an element of strength. From an examination of the logic of various propositions we come to a realization that truth is not absolute but relative. Thinking is likely to be much improved when it raises the question of what idea underlies a proposition or what idea must be previously assumed before a given statement may be accepted. Logic introduces into thinking a desirable element of caution, of looking beneath the surface. It also encourages the effort to arrange ideas into a tight organization for their better understanding. The mere introduction of order into ideas already possessed may easily lead directly to the perception of new ideas.

Perhaps the test of truth lies in agreement with natural laws.

Science has made rapid strides by discovering the laws which govern natural forces. Painstaking observations and countless controlled experiments have provided an ever-widening comprehension of the limits within which nature operates. Knowledge of these limits has established boundary lines beyond which the application of natural forces may not be pressed without a penalty accruing. It is of tremendous significance, for example, to the steamship designer that the resistance of water to the passage of a ship increases as the square of the speed; it is of additional significance, however, that the power necessary to overcome resistance increases as the cube of the speed. Truth here is action within the natural limits; falsity is attempted action outside the limits.

Perhaps there are laws of economics and of business. Success may be explained as resulting from action within the limits set by those laws, failure as penalty for violations of those laws. As we study business successes and failures we think that we do catch glimpses of truth and falsity, of the limiting boundaries which confine our action. If those boundaries can be expressed as formulas or laws, those expressions become principles of business, and, indirectly, principles of accounting. However, but little success has attended the efforts to formulate those laws. We do not know how to predict either business success or failure to an acceptable degree; the chain of causation is too complex and changing, the power of experimentation too weak. Human psychology is baffling; it is generally unpredictable, except in the mass and over the long run alone, and few enterprises contact sufficient masses for management to be able to place much reliance on averages and the statistical laws of large numbers.

Yet there is strength here in the midst of weakness. We can learn much from science to help make accounting more useful in presenting the truth. We learn that objectively determined facts are more likely to approach the truth than uncorroborated personal opinion; that it is better to bring our ideas into conformity with facts than to try to force the facts to agree with our ideas; that an impersonal attitude toward facts can only be achieved by consciously guarding against the unconscious pull of wish.

For example, calculated profit is now much less subject to the personal opinion of interested parties than it ever was. Profit is not "what I say it is," much as I might wish so to believe. Already it is an impersonal calculation based largely upon objectively determined, verifiable facts. The time may come when the word "largely" will be inappropriate in the above sentence. When it does, the calculation will be a closer approximation to truth than is now possible. That time can be hastened by increasing the proportion of objectively determined, verifiable facts available for use in accounting, and by decreasing the reliance upon belief, wish, opinion.

The determination of accounting standards and the formulation of accounting knowledge into co-ordinated principles has an important part to play in this evolution. Its part is important because principles and standards are important aids in the recognition of truth and the separation of nontruth.

(*Journal of Accountancy*, April, 1939)

2. An Organized Body of Knowledge

Accounting methodology came before accounting theory. Bookkeeping had a long development as a records-method serving the day-to-day needs of business even before teachers of the art did any more than describe existing practices. When rules of thumb in teaching bookkeeping were superseded by reasoning transactions into appropriate accounts, then it was plain that theory was being put to use.

Other circumstances exerted an influence upon the development of useful theory. But it was the auditor who gave theory its modern significance. He found expenditures loosely supervised; thus the way was open for concealment or fraud, and scrutiny of details by an independent third party was made difficult, if not impossible. He therefore developed the theory that accounting facts should be supported by documentary evidence and validated by the authorizations of responsible parties. His examinations often revealed a misleading treatment of validated facts and he elaborated his ideas of proper treatment, i.e., accounting theory. In this he probably was not altogether an independent innovator; the profession was new, and the force of the management's views was strong. Not all of the growing body of theory was thoroughly rationalized out of basic principles; some of it no doubt was a justification of what seemed at the time the best practice. In any event much of the theory was before long embedded in custom.

Accounting theory, since it has grown largely out of accounting practice, may seem to serve principally as a means of explaining and illuminating what is done in accounting. But theory has a further obligation, that of strengthening practice by subjecting customs to analysis and testing their justification by finding the relation of customary ideas to basic concepts and purposes.

It may be too much to say that theory's analysis of accounting ideas is a guide to truth; such a statement seems to imply that whatever is theoretical is true and much that is practical is not necessarily true. This is not an acceptable generalization however. But theory can be helpful in the search for truth whether truth is concealed by dishonesty, bias, or ignorance. Because truth is relative, not absolute, any knowledge that is of assistance in judging degrees of truth will be useful knowledge. A knowledge of accounting theory falls in this category.

The desire to make the revealing of truth a major objective marks the public accountant as a man who is striving for high professional ideals. Yet attainment of truth as an objective is not easy. The will to illuminate the truth may be defeated by an imperfect recognition of falsity, or it may be made ineffective by an inadequately developed technique of reporting. Or the will to truth may be rendered impotent by the lack of power to insist that technology be permitted to reveal the recognition of truth.

The ideal of making every financial statement tell the truth requires something more than a desire that it shall do so. The desire must be suitably implemented; it must have adequate backing. Behind the wish there must be, (1) *power*, that is to say, sufficient independence and courage to be able to insist upon truth in financial statements; (2) *skill*, that is to say, sufficient technical competence to be able to convey truth to another mind; (3) *knowledge*, that is to say, sufficiently well-developed standards and principles to enable the auditor to separate business judgment from wishful thinking, and objectively determined facts from biased opinion. How the requisite power and skill may be attained need not be considered here in a discussion of theory. Although these two factors are no less important than the third, the ways of attaining them are easier to perceive than are the ways of recognizing truth by the aid of theory based on knowledge.

There are various ways of perceiving that which shall be considered truth. The customs and conventions of accounting may not have kept pace with the requirements imposed by new conditions, and a consensus with regard to what shall be the accepted practices is difficult to obtain. Logic is helpful to clear thinking, but it tests validity, not truth. Science reveals the laws of nature and describes the limits within which natural forces operate. Similar laws and measurable limits have not yet been found governing business. We may still hold to the basic idea that accounting statements should express the truth. But in the above tests for truth we do not find much guidance to the recognition of accounting truth.

There is another avenue of approach, however. Perhaps the philosophical view of the nature of truth may provide some useful ideas.

In science it is the function of thinking and research to collect experience and give it organization and unification. Organization and unification alone give experience a meaning: a new object or idea acquires meaning to the extent that it fits into our previous organization of objects or ideas. J. A. Nicholson (*An Introductory Course in Philosophy*) illustrates this thought with an example. A peasant who saw a steam engine for the first time had difficulty in fitting the new object into his mental organization of objects; he was sure there must be a horse inside to make it work.

The advancement of science has been founded upon two factors, (1) close, detailed examination of experience in clearly marked areas, and (2) constant striving to perfect an increasingly complex organization of that experience. Yet that organization of knowledge always seems imperfect to the scientist; absolute truth still escapes. The more complete, the more accurate, the more subdivided into categories that the organization of an area of knowledge becomes, the closer we come to truth in that area.

Truth then is an ideal, as goodness and beauty are ideals. It is the striving for the ideal, not the attainment, that generates most understanding and progress; every closer approximation is a source of satisfaction and a reward.

Professor Nicholson asks: "If truth is an ideal, what do we mean when we say that a particular judgment is true?" He answers:

It can only mean that the judgment fits into the organization of facts that we have already accomplished. A statement is false, on the other hand, when it cannot be fitted into such an organization. On this view of truth, knowledge and opinion differ only in degree. The scientist is said to have knowledge only because he has organized the facts of his particular field far more comprehensively: he has moved a stage nearer the ideal than the laymen. But no knowledge is absolute. There are degrees of truth; and the degree is to be determined by the comprehensiveness of the organization into which a particular judgment enters as an organic element.

If we carry this conception over to the field of accounting, the basis by which to judge various accounting situations or propositions should be a close-knit organization of our present stock of accounting ideas. We have a large enough stock to start with; it has been accumulating for a long time, but the organization has never been very thoroughly put together.

An improved organization of accounting ideas into an integrated whole can be accomplished. It will never be perfect; it must be free to grow as change comes and as understanding deepens. No body of knowledge was well organized in its early stages. Yet merely trying to improve the organization reveals blank spots that need filling and debatable areas which are not sufficiently analyzed.

But of this we can be sure: "An idea that forms part of a logically coherent system . . . is more likely to be true than an idea that has not yet entered into such a system."

What Nicholson calls "a logically coherent system," might also be called "a coherent body of doctrine," "a consistent system of theory," "a group of interrelated concepts and principles," "a set of standards by which to judge variations."

The approach to such a body of doctrine must give weight to the meaning inherent in "logical," "coherent," "consistent," "interrelated." Such a body of accounting theory may in some part seem unpractical and unrealistic, yet not be without usefulness. A coherent body of accounting theory can afford a basis for distinguishing between necessary or useful variations from accepted practices, and unnecessary or deceptive variations. It can help to free the public accountant for really important critical appraisals of the practices he meets. It can help him to guide management toward well-considered judgements, toward suspended judgement until the facts are fully examined, toward impartial weighing of factors and responsibilities—in a word, toward a scientific attitude.

(*Journal of Accountancy*, April, 1939)

3. Questions of Terminology

Among the comments of friendly critics of *An Introduction to Corporate Accounting Standards,* some relate to the terms they used. I feel sure they will welcome my attempt to clarify some of the points they have raised.

Q. Why avoid the word "principles" and use the word "standards?" Is the word "rules" synonymous with either "principles" or "standards?" Is a "principle" inherent in the nature of the situation to which it applies; is a "standard" established by authority; is a "rule" the outgrowth of general acceptance?

A. The terms are not synonymous; each has its work to do. A rule tells how some action is to be taken. Principles touch more closely the question of why the rules are what they are. Where some important aspect of accounting theory is crystallized into a sentence, the result probably states a principle. But rules and principles do not solve the problem of concisely stating accounting ideas. I think we need standards as well because a standard is expected to provide a basis for comparing the relative desirability of several lines of action.

Perhaps the distinctions can be more clearly made by examples. *Rule:* Divide the first cost of plant by the number of years of useful life to get the periodic charge for depreciation. *Principle:* In order that the cost of producing periodic revenue shall be completely revealed, the contribution made by plant must be recognized by the periodic amortization of plant cost into expense. *Standard:* Amortize historical cost into expense in proportion to production, and reserve separately for expected obsolescence. *Acceptable variation from standard:* Amortize historical cost over the expected useful life of the asset by combining depreciation and obsolescence. *Unacceptable variation from standard:* Occasionally revalue plant assets according to price-level changes and then amortize into expense.

The most useful features of the concept of accounting standards are, (1) it definitely recognizes the existence of exceptions; (2) it tries to indicate a sequence of preference among alternatives; (3) it clearly marks certain treatments as undesirable.

Q. Are standards to be unchanging like the axioms of geometry or are they susceptible to constant change and improvement? Would standards be changeable from year to year as financial expediency warranted? Would everyone be freer to set his own "standards" than to establish his own "principles?"

A. Just what shall be stated as a standard, what shall be considered an acceptable variation from standard, and what shall be treated as an unacceptable variation from standard, should not be decided by each individual for himself. Every man would then be a law unto himself, and a selfish or short-run point of view might too often prevail. On the other hand, I doubt if standards can be "established" solely by authority. Rules can be so established; but standards can only be stated or phrased. Acceptance—that is, establishment—comes from usage. If standards are stated by competent bodies, after full and fair consideration of the issues, they will carry more weight with those who use them than if they were otherwise derived. But if a so-called standard seems to derive its acceptance mainly from some power which prescribes conformity, then we are dealing only with a rule even though it is otherwise named.

Finding the idea which needs formulation as a standard is itself difficult. But phrasing the thought and the variations from it is even more difficult. There will usually be less disagreement about the idea than about the phrasing, and often it will be a major problem to unite rational accounting theory and customary accounting practice. But these difficulties only indicate the presence of a long task which calls for time and persistence.

Possibly this is not only a long-time task but an unending one. Since standards are not unchanging like the axioms of geometry, a given standard is clearly susceptible to improvement in the light of later experience. There would be no acceptable basis for year-to-year change, however, especially if the only reason was that of financial expediency.

(Accounting Review, December, 1941)

Rules are authoritarian in nature; they seem to dictate conformity with indicated procedure. But business conditions are so varied, and managerial judgment plays such an important role in business success that enough rules could not be constructed to anticipate all situations; and it is obviously impossible to reduce the accounting of an enterprise to a few rules.

The term "standards," however, carries a connotation different from that of "rules." While rules are made to afford a basis for conformity, standards are chosen as points of departure, when and if departure is necessary and clearly justifiable. "Standards," therefore, would not rigidly confine practices, but serve as guideposts to truth, honesty, and fair dealing in accounting reports. To serve their purpose most effectively, such standards would be expressive of the deliberately chosen policies of the highest types of businessmen; they, therefore, would be acceptable by business concerns generally as guides to good accounting practices and adequate financial statements.

The term "principles" does not carry this connotation of adequate flexibility. Perhaps that is why some men say there are no real accounting principles, or so few of them that they constitute overgeneralizations which are unlikely to be helpful in practical affairs.

What accounting textbook writers are prone to call "principles" have nothing in common with the physical laws of nature; nor are they comparable to the accumulated precedents of the common law which rest upon evidence and testimony in court wherein the pros and cons have been fully argued and carefully weighed in arriving at a judgment; nor are they akin to the unwritten laws of social customs which derive their force merely from unthinking acquiescence.

On the whole, therefore, I am inclined to hold to the conception of a standard, for a standard directs a high but attainable level of action without precluding justifiable variations.

The phrase "justifiable variations" should not be construed as merely another term for managerial decision to depart from a recognized accounting standard.

Since it is obvious that business management is not a science, it is to be expected that managerial decisions based on judgment will frequently be put to test; and since accounting is not a science, it may be said that accounts and financial statements reflect many of the judgments made by management. Hence, if accounting standards are to be helpful to management, pronouncements regarding standards should give as many indications as possible of the basis for good managerial judgment. That is, where alternative treatments of a situation are available, the discussion accompanying a statement of accounting standards should indicate the considerations involved in making a choice; where law permits something less than wisdom would dictate, accounting standards should propose that normal action should be above the minimum.

It will be understood that once an accounting standard is properly stated it becomes a guide, not a control. Departure from standard will always be possible, but the burden of justification falls on the one who advocates a variation. Acceptable reasons for departure must, of course, be something more than the desire of an individual or the convenience of management. A sounder basis should be sought than timely expediency, vague conservatism, or persuasiveness to investors.

(Journal of Accountancy, August, 1938)

4. Guides Toward Good Judgment

Management deserves a more constructive guidance toward good judgment than mere advice, such as: avoid arbitrary or fictional values; state real values as nearly as possible. Can accountants, out of their accumulated experience, offer no suggestions of ways for increasing the impartial judgment that should be characteristic of good management? Would it not be more helpful, for example, to suggest ways and means for approaching a case of exercising good judgment regarding real values versus fictitious values, rather than being content to advise acceptance of one and rejection of the other type of value?

Management may, upon occasion, be led more by wish than objective judgment to postpone to a more propitious moment recognition of needed adjustments; management may persuade itself, or be pressed from outside, to throw capital losses against paid-in surplus, while capital gains are consistently passed to current income; management for various reasons may be led to influence the calculation of net income, through depreciation, by writing fixed asset values now up, now down. If a flat declaration is made in a given case that managerial discretion has been exercised, is that sufficient to satisfy the auditor that objective judgment and not wish is the base of the action in question?

It is not necessary to suspect management's motives in order to raise questions about, let us say, the acceptability of a given treatment of losses. Management may have been innocently misled by a false theory that it has the power to stabilize earning calculations by accounting adjustments. But the fact is that figure calculations do not make profit or avoid loss; accounting can only reveal profits and disclose loss. Reality lies behind the figures, not in them. It has come to be almost universally understood that ignoring depreciation in the accounts does not prevent plant wear and tear. Does writing up fixed assets actually increase the cost of using the assets, and does writing them down decrease the burden of owning assets that were bought at high price levels?

It is not generally acknowledged that a belated recognition of obsolescence expresses a diminution of assets even if the amount is charged against some kind of surplus. Is not the income statement the recognized means of conveying information to the reader about asset diminutions? Why should loss diminutions have a status different from that given to expense diminutions?

There would seem to be opportunity in these situations for useful suggestions toward good judgment. Difficulties would of course face the organized profession in any attempt to offer such suggestions or to make pronouncements upon accounting principles. An auditor is in no position to demand corporate practices above a statutory minimum, or unaided to change the direction of management's accounting decisions in particular situations. It is only natural that opinion within the profession would be against both a rigid codification of accounting rules and a statement of principles which would be no more than a rehearsal of minimum accounting practices now current.

While the reaction to the problem is understandable, some of it may rest upon erroneous premises. A pronouncement of accounting standards above the minimum would be no more embarrassing than a minimum statement, and no more enforceable by the accountant as an individual. But the backing which an authoritative statement of high accounting standards would give to individuals could be invaluable in helping them to secure a gradual advance in corporation accounting practices. It could give courage and strength, also, to those who hope to see state corporation laws further improved.

The use of the conception of "standards" instead of "principles" would carry with it the thought of stating standards as points of departure, while making plain the necessity for clear justification for any variations from the standard. Obviously this would be quite the reverse of a rigid codification of accounting rules, and it would emphasize the quasi-judicial nature of the public accountant's consideration of the reasons given him in individual cases in support of departures from the standard.

Because the auditor must act as an independent critic of the maintenance of high standards of corporation accounting, it is entirely logical that the combined experience of the profession should be drawn upon in the framing of standards, especially in the direction of making clear in the context ways and means by which management may be assured that its accounting decisions will rest upon intelligent and impartial judgment.

A clear and concise statement of accounting standards emanating from the profession and supported by its organizations would undoubtedly be welcomed by corporation management as well as public accountants, just as the several statements on recognized audit procedure have been welcomed. The latter were accepted as explanation to the business public generally of the basis upon which would rest a certificate that was un-qualified as to the scope of the examination. The former would undoubt-edly be accepted as a message to the business public of the basis upon which a certificate would rest that was unqualified as to the auditor's opinion. Qualifications in the certificate then would become indications that the standard scope of investigation had been limited or that the company's accounting or reporting methods were not consistently in reasonable agreement with recognized standards.

The public looks to the profession for leadership and initiative in these matters. The day is past when public accountants were regarded merely as experts in unraveling tangled accounts, or as detectives bur-rowing in figures to put the finger on a dishonest clerk. A truly profes-sional status is being achieved, and the public is coming to expect of the professional accountant not only technical skill, but high ideals, firm convictions, and a broad conception of public service.

The profession could well afford to assume this high type of unselfish leadership. We need no longer fear that anything we say will be used against us; initiative will no longer bring the accusation that public ac-countants are but fostering a self-seeking monopoly. The public ac-countant owes a clear duty of professional skill and judgment to his client; but he also has an obligation to the public, to the legion of pres-ent and prospective absentee investors: an obligation of judicial disin-terestedness, of independent views, of strong convictions on fair play.

The principal reason accountancy is rapidly gaining a real professional status is that the public is more than ever before convinced that public accountants stand for these ideals; their technical capabilities may even be considered somewhat secondary to a high sense of moral obligation.

(*Journal of Accountancy*, August, 1938)

5. Conventions and Rules

Most discussions concerned with accounting conventions, rules, and principles tend to emphasize their differences. Yet there are important similarities in the concepts labeled by these three terms.

The three ideas all stem from accounting actions, actions that are responses to recognized needs. The three concepts achieved recognition as useful accounting ideas by processes of induction. That is to say, con-ventions, rules, and principles were generalized into words out of satis-factory experiences (actions) in meeting accounting needs. Because of common origins and similar objectives in the ideas behind these three terms, they are more closely related than might seem to be the case if the words themselves or their usual dictionary definitions were examined.

As a consequence of this close relationship, it should be possible to start with any of these three forms of expression and move to any of the others by a suitable change in phraseology. Furthermore, if this degree of relation is found to exist, there should be in that fact a good basis for believing that a co-ordinated body of basic accounting doctrine is reasonably possible of statement.

Let us consider an example. It is a convention of bookkeeping that its classification categories (accounts) have two sides—left, right; or debit, credit. This may be considered a convention because (1) this arrangement is not indispensable since another could be equally satisfactory, and (2) this usage is now accepted as satisfactory without much questioning as to whether the customary form is necessary or not, best or not. This convention as to accounts, whether or not it is always physically reflected in the columns of the record, is an established fact of accounting and a fact that makes a significant contribution to the complete articulation of accounts one with another.

This aspect of accounting could be stated as a fact, that is, as a convention established by usage. For example, "Every ledger account is a dual category, a form which long experience has shown to be particularly appropriate to the needs of accounting records."

With a slight change in phraseology, this statement of an accounting convention can be made into an accounting directive or instruction, or requirement. "Design and use every ledger account in a manner that will make each one serve as a dual category, one aspect being called debit, the other called credit." Such a sentence would not be a suitable beginning for a text in bookkeeping or a treatise on system design. But it will illustrate the distinction here observed between a convention and a directive. The latter issues an order, as it were; the former states a recognized fact.

Neither of the above forms of expression is here considered equivalent to a rule. The concept of a rule might well be considerably broader, broad enough, that is, to include the statement of a directive plus its justifying reason or a clearly implied reason. Thus conceived, the above convention becomes, upon suitable modification of phrasing, this rule: "Make each account serve as a dual category because dynamic balances [those that are modified by either positive or negative changes] are more informative than is a simple total."

We may now note some of the characteristics of a directive and of a rule. The directive, lacking a stated reason, says in effect: do it this way; this is our office practice; under certain circumstances this is the preferred method; it is justification enough that this procedure is generally accepted, etc. A fully stated rule of action should include, or be clearly linked to, a justifying reason. The additional usefulness of such a statement, under many circumstances, will be obvious. A simple directive is enough in field practice to start an experienced assistant on the next task. The most useful assistant will know a good reason for the task assigned as well as how to carry out the directive; and unpleasant results can follow from routines carried out in a routine way, without interest in or knowledge of at least some of the "whys" of the task.

When inexperience is present, rules as here considered will be more appropriate than directives as to method alone. This thought applies with particular force to textbooks. The principal distinction between teaching bookkeeping as a clerical procedure to be remembered, and teaching elementary accounting at the college level so it will be understood, is likely to flow from the relative amounts of how and why in the two methods of presentation. Perhaps this observation should be extended to cover all accounting courses and all learning by doing.

(New York Certified Public Accountant, August, 1950)

6. Rule and Principle

The terms conventions, rules, and principles have at base more similarities than differences in connotation. As a result, by variation of phraseology, the idea behind any one of the terms could be made to reflect one of the other terms. If conventions derived from experience— tested accounting action—can be rephrased to read as an accounting rule, can a rule be reworded so it will state an accounting principle? Before trying this conversion, let us look at some of the characteristics of a principle.

Scientists are concerned with understanding the forces of nature and in putting those forces to work. Their approach is experimental. The tested and retested formulas that result are often stated in the form of a mathematical equation. This is possible because the scientist has succeeded in learning the way antecedent factors and associated results are related and how they vary together. An equation from science compactly expresses relationship. It is a form of stating a principle. Scientists wishing to produce certain results find that the way has been opened by prior formulas, for therein it was shown that prior results followed upon certain combinations of factors.

Perhaps we can find a clue here to the chief characteristic of a principle: a principle must express a significant relationship.

Can some accounting rules (a directive plus its reason) furnish the clue for the formulation of some accounting principles? Can we detect "significant relationships" running between a directed accounting action and the reason for desiring that action? Would it be useful if the "significant relationship" expressed by an accounting principle was usually the kind of relationship which exists between a desirable accounting end and a suitable accounting means to that end?

It may be agreed for example that one desirable end (in designing a system of accounts) has long been that of getting as much information into one category as possible, without at the same time clouding the sharpness of the classification. The means to that end was developed rather early in the evolution of double entry. Early experience with personal accounts showed that the record was less confusing when the plus aspects of account A were written together on one page and the minus elements were written together on the opposite page. From that development came our bilateral form of ledger account; it collects items relevant to a single kind, yet separates the items as being positive or negative in their effect. One category thus supplies three kinds of related data: total debits, total credits, net difference (plus or minus) between the totals.

In the above statement of an accounting rule we can see an idea that could be considered an end or aim of bookkeeping. It is desirable that each account category shall furnish a maximum of classified information. In the same rule is a clue to a suitable means to that end. It would be useful to segregate the positive and negative factors in each account in a way that would facilitate the frequent calculation of a dynamic remainder or running balance. These two ideas, already expressed in the form of a rule, can be restated in the form of a principle in these words:

Dynamic Balances. By making each account a dual instead of a single category, accounting is able to operate its system of classification (bookkeeping) as a scheme of dynamic balances which will be modified by both positive and negative changes.

This form of expression states first a means suitable to achieving the end indicated and then in careful phraseology states an end or objective or intention of accounting. Here are two important ideas characteristic of accounting—ideas which have evolved from trial and error in use. By a certain kind of linking of the two ideas in one sentence, a further idea is made evident. For a fact of usage is there set into a significant relationship with a conscious intention, that is, into the relationship running between a desirable end and a suitable means to that end. Perhaps this example may serve to indicate how two accounting ideas cast in the form of an accounting principle lead us to recognize a third idea, that of a useful, significant relationship. By producing, in effect, a third idea out of two, a principle makes a similar contribution to that made by an account, where a debit total considered along with a credit total produces a third element, an amount measuring net change.

Incidentally, the balance of an account is not always enough for the analyst to know; by itself it usually cannot give any clue to the forces which worked a net change in its amount. He therefore will often need to know whether debit changes or credit changes (or what proportion of one to the other) explain the change in the balance.

In a somewhat similar way, recognition that a significant relationship links two accounting ideas may often lead us to make highly useful inquiries about its constituent parts—inquiries whether the end is in fact as clearly desirable as it seems; whether the specific means indicated is in fact as suitable as could be devised.

A few other general comments may be appropriate. It will be clear that the phraseology used in a given verbalization of a principle may vary between different authors while still expressing a significant relationship between important accounting ideas. And it is inescapable, even desirable, that the linkage of two ideas should be subject to debate as to their relationship. The adjectives "desirable" as to ends, and "suitable" as to means should be carefully examined while studying the interrelation of means and ends.

Questions of what is good and not so good will have to be faced when thinking of "desirable" and "suitable." It may be in this area of trying to be consciously rational that the major usefulness may lie of attempting to formulate accounting principles. Perhaps the process of achieving or improving statements deserving designation as a principle may be more rewarding than the achievement itself. Perhaps the usefulness of a stated principle may most often be found in trying to test it in use as an aid to clear thinking.

(*New York Certified Public Accountant*, August, 1950)

7. Theory and Principles

As a basis for describing a principle before constructing one, we need to think first of the idea behind the word theory. If we view the term broadly (that is, not confining it to "a theory") theory can be properly called a body of doctrine. It is an area of beliefs, explanations, justifications related to an area of practice. Its elements are descriptions, definitions, arguments, inferences, explanations, reasons—and principles.

Using a broad concept of the nature of theory in this way is an advantage because it helps to make the point that theory could conceivably exist without principles; the other elements when well integrated would still be theory (a body of doctrine). Principles may well be called "fundamental truths." But not all principles are derived from experimentation, as in science. Some principles can be compressed out of an existing body of theory relating to an area of practice. Even these principles, we should perhaps add, are empirically derived since ultimately they root back in practice—and customary practice derives from the results of trial and error (that is, experience, if not experiment).

In science a theory may be based upon a principle which is verifiable by experiment. But in nonscientific subjects like accounting it probably is better to think of a principle as a fundamental truth of theory crystallized into a carefully phrased sentence. This idea has a counterpart in science. For "principle" thus defined it somewhat comparable to an explanation (theory) which scientists compress into an equation. Such equations do more than reflect the results of experimentation; they show that significant relationships exist between the elements concerned. Fundamentally the equation is a highly compact explanation—therefore a sort of headline in the theory area involved.

Auditing principles (and all principles related to accounting) can be like that—compact, fundamental truths formulated out of auditing theory and cast into phraseology designed to show a significant relationship between two accounting ideas.

If an auditing principle is somewhat like an equation, what will the equated elements be? Part of the answer is that our principle will seldom consist of equated elements; the relationship in accounting is seldom that of equality. A clue to the kind of relationship most suitable to formulating accounting principles is found in the paraphrased quotation given by J. F. Blair[1] from the writings of the philosopher John Dewey (about a "clear idea of ends") and in Mr. Blair's very quotable statement, "It is uniformity of purpose we are seeking, not uniformity of practice— that is, uniformity of ends, not of means."

It seems likely that an accounting literature with improved teachability might grow up when debate about accounting theory (aims, objectives, definitions, principles) has provided an improved structural framework. Thus theory would come to justify in action the phrase in Mr. Blair's definition of theory as "a plan that exists in the mind." The mental plan (theory) is what it is because practice in meeting its accounting problems has placed a foundation under theory. But theory makes a contribution in turn. It can make practice more and more rational, that is less and less "under the control of customs and traditions that have not been examined in the light of immediate conditions"—as John Dewey's phrase puts it in the quotation given by Mr. Blair.

Even students can be introduced to some of the roads to good judgment although most of that art will have to be sought along the road of experience. One way to push students in this direction is to face them with the problem of choosing among means having variable suitability for a stated objective.

(*Journal of Accountancy*, April, 1947)

8. Phrasing an Audit Principle

An emphasis upon purposes, ends, aims, objectives, intentions has long been an element in good teaching in accounting as elsewhere. The discussion of accounting principles in recent years now leads to another thought: perhaps in giving verbal expression to our principles we should incorporate clearly perceived accounting aims in the formulations. There

[1] *Journal of Accountancy*, February, 1947.

are many existing rules, but seldom does the statement of a rule go far enough to include aims and objectives.

Perhaps the following phrases about auditing ends can be useful for formulating a few auditing principles.

(1 a) To allay doubts as to the factual creditability (figure accuracy) of the data in financial statements.

(2 a) To support (or question) the dependability of account classifications in the financial statements and the reliability of the basis thus made available for interpreting the data disclosed.

(3 a) To substantiate the representations which management makes in the financial statement.

There are of course other aims of the auditor besides these; and there may be other ways of phrasing the above objectives. But the samples are at least characteristic since they point to the auditor's duty to satisfy himself regarding (1) the figures, (2) the classifications, and (3) the policies involved.

And discussion of ends at once suggests considering parallel means. This pairing of desirable ends and suitable means to those ends can be very useful in formulating important accounting truths. To accompany each of the three aims given above, parallel ways and means may be phrased as follows.

(1 b) Test the transaction sources and amounts by appropriate audit procedures.

(2 b) Critically examine the structure of the accounting system and the way it is actually operated.

(3 b) Find suitable corroborative evidence and appraise the accounting policies currently in effect.

These ends and means when suitably paired present certain significant relationships which can readily be accepted as expressing fundamental auditing truths (principles). In the restatement below, phrasing is changed somewhat to produce better sentences.

(1) The possibility of error, misrepresentation, fraud in the accounts leaves the statistical creditability (figure accuracy) of the financial statements open to doubt unless the transaction sources and amounts have been tested by appropriate audit procedures.

(2) A critical examination by qualified persons of the structural mechanisms of an accounting system and of the way it is actually operated, supports (or questions) the dependability of the account classification in the financial statements and the reliability of the basis thus made available for interpreting the data disclosed.

(3) The independent external auditor seeks to substantiate the representations made by management in the accounts and statements by finding suitable corroborative evidence and by appraising the accounting policies currently in effect.

No doubt there are other high-level principles of auditing; certainly there are many subaims, objectives, purposes of lower rank. The literature of auditing should make these clear as well as the usual procedures. In that connection emphasis ought to be given to the meaning of the adjective in the phrase "desirable ends." Aims and ends are not only various but graded as well; some are more important than others. Professional men can greatly enrich the technical literature by drawing on their experience and judgement to discuss (1) the ranking in importance of various auditing objectives, major and minor, (2) the clues that suggest the relative desirability or necessity of specific audit aims, (3) the kind of circumstances that might temporarily shift the ranking of subordinate aims.

The means of attaining auditing objectives are much better described in the literature than the objectives themselves. Resourcefulness and ingenuity in developing ways and means have long been characteristic of professional accountants. Frequently, however, texts on procedures and techniques have not been very well organized for teaching or for learning. Probably students would benefit as much from learning to think auditors' thoughts as from study of descriptions in a set sequence of what an auditor does.

The adjective "desirable" was stressed above in connection with "ends"; the adjective in the phrase "suitable means" also needs emphasis. The means available to use under specific circumstances usually exist in more variety than could be effectively used at the time. Choosing certain means out of many because of a particular suitability probably calls for more professional good judgment and practical wisdom than did the original devising of the way and means transmitted to the present.

It is in part this capacity for appropriately accommodating techniques to circumstances that makes the professional accountant a professional. It also is a professional's responsibility to know a wide range of possible ends and objectives and to sense gradations of desirability among them— again according to the circumstances at hand and with full regard for the welfare of all parties at interest.

It is clear that desirable ends and means suitable to those ends are important aspects of auditing, as of all accounting. If then a pairing of ends and means will express a fundamental truth (because together the two elements reveal a relationship that is significant to auditing) there emerges a highly useful instrument in aid of better understanding. It is indeed deserving of the name and status of "principle of auditing." And the usefulness of a principle will be enhanced if it is recognized as compressing a good deal of theory into a few words. For principles necessarily are tight generalizations—headlines as it were which cannot themselves tell the whole story. Alone principles are inadequate; but as central parts of a body of doctrine (theory) they can serve a very useful purpose.

(*Journal of Accountancy*, April, 1947)

9. On Logical Inferences

There is a growing movement, in the interest of clear thinking and orderly practice, toward the formulation of concise propositions regarding accounting. In this process some test is needed by which to know whether a given proposition does in fact present an accounting principle. In this connection it has been said [2] that the principles of accounting "are characterized by their coercive or compelling quality because inherent in accounting principles are business laws which must be obeyed if in the long run the enterprise is to survive."

For present purposes we may pass over the question whether the "compelling quality" lies in accounting principles, business principles, or economic principles, and from another angle look at the problem of putting an asserted accounting principle to test. If there is some question about demonstrating the coercive power of accounting principles, perhaps this may be tested by analyzing the way those principles, being in the nature of conclusions, can be tied into acceptable premises which lead to the conclusion (principle) under examination.

Fundamental truths of accounting (principles) may either be generalized out of practical experience, or deduced from stated premises which are accepted as true in themselves or demonstrated as true by convincing argument.

In the one case the propositions are considered as truths because experienced men agree that out of various possibilities these are the most desirable, the most descriptive of what seems best. In the other case the propositions are considered as truths because they follow, by logical analysis, from prior propositions which are obviously true. When both methods yield similar results, we may feel sure we have obtained an expression of fundamental truth.

Behind propositions of the first class are the habitual actions and customs of businessmen and accountants. Out of their experiences generalizations emerge which epitomize the soundest practices from among many instances.

Behind propositions of the second class are statements of ideas or theories offered as truths which, when accepted as premises, form the bases for drawing logical inferences regarding further truths.

The two processes of generalizing from experience and inferring from premises work hand in hand. Convictions derived inductively from the particulars of experience may form the premises from which to derive, deductively, additional convictions; and conclusions reasonably inferred from acceptable truths may become the expression of accepted standards of practice.

It is particularly important, however, that these two reasoning processes be in one's consciousness side by side because the weakness of the one is tested by the other. Faulty judgment may often be forestalled by putting the propositions involved to the test of their logical relation to

[2] Gilbert R. Byrne, *Journal of Accountancy*, November, 1937.

antecedent premises and assumptions. On the other hand a skillfully arranged chain of deductive inference may lead to a conclusion which will not work well under existing limiting conditions. We say the conclusion is impractical, inexpedient, unconservative, etc. But a realization of the logic of the circumstances need not be useless even then, for it will have increased our care in weighing the reasons for doing otherwise than logic and consistency might seem to dictate.

The study of the significance of propositions generalized into principles, and the use of rules of logic to test for consistent interrelations will bring other propositions to light—propositions which must be previously accepted as true (premises) before the conclusions (principles) can be considered wholly valid. This sort of analysis can lead to a re-examination of the phrasing in which our judgements have been rendered into words, with the result that our fundamental truths will be recast into different forms until we are satisfied that the basic thought is clearly and unmistakably expressed. Such analysis also carried us backward, so to speak, from principles to premises, and from premises to assumptions—those axioms or postulates which express truths so self-evident as to exclude doubt.

Further examination of the assumptions thus revealed may disclose that they are unwarranted; this may then shake our whole structure of ideas. Or it may show us in ways we never suspected that our structure of principles and practices rests upon slender foundations. Again we may be led to debate the fundamental assumptions and thus re-explore the purposes and objectives of accounts and accountants, and to attain a new realization of the limitations inherent in our ideas and activities.

Lest this approach be thought highly abstract and unprofitable, let it be remembered that good practices and sound principles are supplementary rather than contradictory. Principles will tend to stress consistency of related ideas and clear statement of thought; practices will always be strongly influenced by the great diversity of the conditions under which applications of accounting principles must be made. The best results in writing and practicing accounting are most likely to follow upon the combination of a thorough understanding of sound, consistent theory, and a skilled judgment in weighing the necessities for practical deviations.

The primary mechanism for attaining a knowledge of what is true in accounting may therefore become the integration of induction and deduction in the study of accounting—the correlation of practice and theory. This is the approach to science, for knowledge originates in experience but it develops from reflection. Theory does not extend the boundaries of experience, but it does widen and deepen reflection about past and future experience.

(*Accounting Review*, March, 1938)

10. Accounting Syllogisms

There are several ways of arranging propositions in order to examine this logical interdependence. For the purpose of illustrating a way to test accounting propositions, consider the hypothetical syllogism. This consists of (1) a major premise which expresses a condition (the antecedent) and a result (the consequence), (2) a minor premise which either affirms the antecedent or denies the consequent, and (3) a conclusion which is a logical inference if the minor premise truly affirms the antecedent or truly denies the consequent.

An Example

Major Premise: (Antecedent) If verifiable events like bargained prices constitute the best objective evidence available of the reality of transaction values, (consequent) then revenue from actual sales marks a valid realization of profit or loss.

Minor Premise: (Affirming the antecedent) The best objective evidence that new value has entered an enterprise is found in verifiable events such as actual sales.

Conclusion: (The consequent is true) Therefore revenue from actual sale marks a valid realization of profit or loss.

The usual approach to an explanation of "realization" is through the law of sales—legal title has passed; the property received in exchange is our asset. Yet, for the above syllogism, analysis may be even more convincing than the law, since it clearly sets forth the propositions that must be accepted or demonstrated before the conclusion regarding the particular accounting practice will follow. Careful statement of the propositions is also made necessary by this method for it is desired that the underlying assumptions be revealed and scrutinized. If a premise rests on an unacceptable assumption, it cannot be considered true and a conclusion seeming to be derived from it cannot be a valid inference.

The accounting ideas briefly outlined above may well be restated, with accompanying arguments, in a more complete demonstration of this method.

Realization

Assumption: (a) That the business enterprise in whose service accounting makes its principal contribution is a going concern; (b) and that figures representing bargained prices can symbolize revenue and cost realities.

These assumptions are necessary to the premise because without going concerns the periodical tests of interim profits which so occupy accounting would be unnecessary, and because accounting could not then carry out its major function of expressing objective reality in symbols (figures). It is beyond the power of accounting to express subjective reality such as the enjoyment of satisfactions.

Major Premise: (Antecedent) If verifiable events like bargained prices constitute the best objective evidence of the reality of new value, (consequent) then revenue from actual sales marks the realization of profit (or loss).

If the antecedent is accepted, the consequent follows because the bargained prices of actual sales are verifiable events. But can the antecedent be accepted? An affirmative minor premise is needed which says that it can.

Minor Premise: Verifiable events do constitute the best objective evidence of the reality of new values.

Argument: Business results (revenue) are what we receive for what we give (output). Why test the results? Because reality of profit is not assuredly present at all times. If total liquidation of the enterprise were completed, perhaps this would be sufficient to confirm the profit or benefit. But interim judgments cannot await the ultimate; we must have some basis for testing the reality of profit now. No indecisive test—unchecked personal opinions of values, unrestrained optimistic hope of profit—could be accepted as a dependable basis for important decisions such as making investments, declaration of dividends, petition in bankruptcy. Only decisive tests which rest upon verifiable facts are satisfactory.

Bargained prices in actual sales meet these conditions, for they reflect the combined, but independent, judgments of a willing buyer and a willing seller regarding the value involved at the moment in the transaction. When two individuals each directed by self-interest reach an agreement, the judgment of the one substantiates the judgment of the other; this eliminates the bias which might exist in an uncorroborated opinion.

Conclusion: Revenue from actual sales marks the realization of profit or (loss).

Cost and Revenue

Assumptions: (a) That business enterprises are distinct economic entities regardless of their legal form; and (b) that economic entities (business enterprises) are subject to managerial control.

These assumptions must be previously accepted or the premise to follow cannot be accepted, for without these assumptions (1) there would be no basis by which accounting could separate certain economic facts (those applicable to an enterprise) from all facts; (2) accounting would be unable to record economic facts in the same manner for individuals, proprietorships, and corporations; and (3) without management (or its distant authority, investors) there would be little or no use for such facts as accounting might attempt to record.

Major Premise: (Antecedent) If the facts most essential for the formation of sound managerial policies for a business enterprise are periodic, matched costs and revenues, (consequent) then periodic costs and their related revenues are the most important data for accounts to produce.

If the antecedent is true, the consequent seems to follow, for accounting is a fact-recording instrument for economic (business) enterprises, and as such must deal with facts of importance to the enterprise.

Minor Premise: (Affirming the antecedent) Periodic, matched costs and revenues are highly essential facts for enterprise management to know.

Argument: People have diversified wants of vast extent capable of being satisfied if suitable use values are but contrived. To contrive these use values, capital and labor are combined into business enterprises. The people responsible for the effective operation of these enterprises need to have (1) a quantitative measure of the investments made (risked) in preparing to render economic service (this would be dollars of cost) and (2) a quantitative measure of the reception which users accord that service (this would be dollars of revenue).

The reason that operators need these facts is that management has to make many choices and decisions which directly affect the contriving of needed use values. Management therefore needs a means of translating heterogeneous economic transactions into homogeneous data. With this translation accomplished management will then be able to compare and visualize the summarized actions taken in order to render service and the summarized quantitative acceptance of the service by customers. The money prices involved in actual, bargained exchanges have been shown throughout a long period of use to be an exceptional means of rendering transactions homogeneous and therefore quantitatively comparable. Faulty though bargained prices may be in expressing "value," no better means of securing dependable figures about enterprise efforts and accomplishments have been devised.

If this argument is convincing that management needs objective facts as a basis for its judgments, and that bargained prices constitute the most dependable available measurements of essential enterprise facts, then the minor premise will be acceptable, thus successfully affirming the antecedent. Hence the conclusion inherent in the consequent is valid.

Conclusion: Periodic costs and their related revenues are the most important data for accounts to produce.

Historical Cost

Assumption: That freedom of managerial choices under open competition are characteristic of our economic life. If this underlying assumption is not acceptable, the following premise falls. The reason: Careful measurement and prior record of managerial choice (costs) are less useful where choices are not dictated by the pressure of competition in ideas, goods, and services.

Major Premise: (Antecedent) If the aggregate costs incurred to secure the service input of a business enterprise constitute the most important quantitative measures of managerial choices made with intent of affecting revenue, (consequent) then the cost recognized in accounting and recorded in the accounts should be outlay price (historical cost).

The consequent follows from the antecedent because "cost recognized in accounting" is equivalent to "quantitative measures of managerial choices." The minor premise affirms the truth of this antecedent.

Minor Premise: In responding costs incurred do constitute important measures of management's prior choices and decisions.

Argument: In responding to changing conditions and to competition, management makes many choices among various useful elements, and these decisions cause costs to be incurred as the chosen goods and services are contracted or received. Subsequent clear judgments regarding the effectiveness of these choices must rest upon some dependable quantitative recorded expression of these decisions. Otherwise prior choices could not be usefully compared with later results.

Conclusion: The only cost recognized in accounting for record purposes should be outlay price, that is to say, historical cost.

Other syllogisms could be arranged from the many established ideas of accounting. They would be unlikely to indicate that very many such ideas were invalid. Yet such analysis, like the samples above, might do a good deal to strengthen accepted ideas, particularly from the fact that well-considered arguments in support of carefully phrased propositions (premises) would have to be prepared.

(Accounting Review, March, 1938)

11. Premises as Objectives

Professor Leo A. Schmidt has given us in the *Journal of Accountancy* for November, 1949 an excellent sample of deductive logic as applied to accounting. I hope he will write a book on accounting logic sometime. It would not only be stimulating, but there he would have space to deal also with the inductive side, and an opportunity to present an extended analysis of whatever in accounting seems illogical or limiting. This is a good road to a realistic appraisal of the solid foundation of logic that lies, often unrecognized, beneath the best practices, and of the justifications offered in support of those spots of illogic that have gained general acceptance.

Professor Schmidt's major premises could also be called high-level generalizations about accounting; in a very real sense they express accounting objectives. In a book there would be space to present other accounting objectives (duties?). For example, there is a duty (which might be made into a major premise) to maintain the integrity of objective accounting data against dilution by events outside an enterprise. In other words, it is a necessary objective of accounting to operate within the limitations of double-entry accounts and a trial balance in equilibrium, and to produce financial statements that result only from the objective data accumulated by this instrumentality.

With more space the author could also warn us that very broad generalizations, such as many major premises will be, may seem to constitute an invitation, as it were, for readers to use isolated generalizations out of their logical context. For example, his premise 2, rephrased ("accounting must guide management in its two great missions, to preserve property and to make profits") could easily become a basis for someone to contend that management could expect accounting to introduce into its processes whatever data management might consider useful. And, it may be noted, accounting technology is flexible enough to do just that if "can do" were the only consideration.

And his premise 3, "as between any two methods of accounting, that method is correct which tends to lead to the more desirable social-economic results," if used out of its context, might seem to be offering to convert double-entry account data, while still within the framework of the trial balance, into such social-economic data as may seem useful to people who are not accountants. Can that be done and still preserve the basic integrity of accounting data, that is, objectively derived original cost data?

(Journal of Accountancy, March, 1950)

12. Induction and Deduction

The article by Gordon W. Stead (*Accounting Review,* October, 1948) is an interesting analysis of accounting ideology. At the top of the author's chart of idea interrelations stands "integrity." It is the author's intention to show how the successive aspects of doctrine (principles, canons, standards, rules) derive from this one "fundamental concept," it being his view that this dependency is "the direction of causation."

It will be no detraction from his constructive contribution to the development of the concept of an integrated body of accounting thought to try here for a supplementary pattern—one leaning toward a line of discussion he avoids when he chooses to show that rules of conduct derive from immutable principles.

In this supplementary pattern it will be the view that principles have been slowly distilled out of actions. This view would help to express the idea that accounting rules, having first been the fruits of tentative actions, grew in significance until they became guides to predetermined actions. As these accounting actions grew increasingly diverse and complex, so did the attendant rules, customs, practices. As this diversity falls under more and more critical consideration, it becomes increasingly advisable to decide whether there are elements of order, sequence, interrelation within the mass.

Accounting has been developed for the most part inductively out of particulars. After the particulars of experience have produced a mass of rules, the major problem of subject matter becomes one of organizing the accumulated doctrine (expressed in rules, procedures, etc.) into a cohesive body of knowledge. Knowledge will be recognized as cohesive if its details can be set into a clarifying order from which it will be plain that important relations can be chained downward (deductively) from a top concept, although the various aspects of doctrine may have originated in rules about particulars. This is to say that accounting thought can profitably be explored along both the roads of induction and of deduction.

A graphic pattern to help express the inductive approach could take the form of a pyramid standing on a broad base and sloping sharply to a peak representing the top objective of accountancy. The broader sections below the top and above the base would stand for antecedent objectives which, growing out of actions represented by the base, gradually build up to one focal objective capable of justifying all lower objectives and their related actions.

This pattern would attempt to deal with objectives of the art, not objectives of the artist, that is, with accountancy rather than accountants. Mr. Stead's view seems to focus on the latter. In putting "integrity" at the top he points (1) to integrity as the element that distinguishes the accountant from the bookkeeper, (2) to the umpire function of the accountant and to his reporter function, (3) to the accountant's ethical duty to acquit himself with integrity.

Obviously it is useful to consider the human side since accountancy, like a corporation, cannot operate without human aid. Yet, just as it is helpful to think of and deal with a corporation as if it had existence and capacity separate from its human adjuncts, so it seems likely to be helpful to think of accounting objectives separately from the people who developed that art through the long past and those who keep the instrumentality functioning today. This should prove helpful since accounting is useful because it is a way of thinking and of preparing to think; as such it becomes a vehicle for expressing men's intentions converted into actions. A man will more quickly learn to use a vehicle—put it under his will and control—if he first learns the characteristics built into it. Only thereafter does he understand the mechanism well enough to apply it most usefully to his needs.

In our pattern a broad foundation extends beyond the edges of the base of the pyramid proper. This represents the multitude of particulars within a business enterprise—actions, instances, documents, transactions involving properties, promises, rights, in a wide variety of kinds and amounts and intentions. These are the particulars of business activities. These are also the particulars which must be molded by the purposes and actions of accounting so that accountancy may become the primary information service of business.

Accounting is action; it is doing; accounting action works with the transaction mass which expresses in detail the breadth and depth of enterprise action. There are six types of accounting action, and the types stand in a clearly perceivable sequence.

Areas of Accounting Action:

1. pricing business transactions
2. analyzing transactions into debits and credits
3. posting debits and credits into ledger accounts
4. making periodic adjusting and closing entries
5. preparing financial statements
6. auditing financial statements

These "areas of accounting action" may be considered as the large bottom section in the pyramid figure. But it should not be overlooked that within these areas the building blocks are set in a discernible sequence. Is the sequence inherent and significant, or accidental and artificial? The former idea seems more plausible because in the sequence can be seen an orderly progressing of actions toward some still unstated objective or purpose. Can accounting processes (actions reaching toward goals) be related to accounting objectives (intentions that motivate actions)? Such a relationship should be discoverable; accounting actions do not just happen. Actions are purposeful; they are nothing if they are so random as to be futile. Actions become intelligible primarily through their objectives.

(*Accounting Review*, July, 1949)

13. Interrelation of Objectives

The broad base of a pattern for arranging accounting objectives in a graded series to form a pyramid would represent several kinds of accounting action. The next higher section should represent the objectives which justify the actions represented in the section below.

Intermediate Objectives

1. to reduce objects and events to price data
2. to transform price data into account data
3. to compress the mass of account data by using quasi-statistical means (categories)
4. to reassign, as between time periods, the data previously classified into accounts only as to qualitative characteristics
5. to organize periodic data into interpretative summary report statements

6. to examine into the adequacy of the disclosures made by accounting report statements

We build the pyramid upward by adding another, and smaller, section near the top. Here we try to express as antecedent objectives the reasons justifying the objectives in the section below, in the way that the objectives therein justified the actions classified in the lowest section. The sharp peak will represent a further compression of "whys"—an objective that is analyzed out of the whole structure below the peak.

Antecedent Objectives

1. to represent greatly diversified economic events and objects (transactions) in a manner that will permit them to be marshaled into a variety of useful calculations

2. to prepare economic data to enter a particular pattern of quasi-statistical classification (double-entry accounts)

3. to substitute a small number of general categories (accounts) for a multitude of particular events (transactions)

4. to substitute segments of time (fiscal periods) for an unbroken flow of events and for the simple summaries by kinds initially accomplished by accounts

5. to communicate compactly and understandably the compressed mass of enterprise events

6. to create confidence in the dependability of the reported accounting data

What objective stands at the peak? Can the whole pattern of accounting actions and objectives be the complex of a single purpose? Can the variously stated objectives be compressed into one so that each separate objective can be recognized as a partial fulfillment of the one major purpose?

A tentative formulation is suggested here: The top objective of accounting is to aid a person to understand a business enterprise by means of data.

Audited financial statements (item 6) are an aid to understanding an enterprise to a degree beyond that supplied by unaudited financial statements (item 5). Data made more comparable by being carefully classified into fiscal periods (item 4) are beyond question thereby made an important aid to an understanding of the significance of the flow of enterprise events. The compressing of a large number of like instances into one total, such as is accomplished by every ledger account, is an indispensable aid (item 3). Besides compressing a mass of data, accounts produce a sharp classification of data according to closely defined transaction qualities (item 2). None of this aid could be effectively accomplished unless the first step (item 1) in the sequence is taken first. For as long as events and objects are knowable only in their heterogeneous characteristics they will lack the homogeneity necessary to permit them to be marshaled into informative categories and remarshaled into understandable communication reports.

Another phrasing of the top objective might be arranged to incorporate the essence of the subordinate objectives: In order to achieve its chief objective of helping the people concerned to understand a business enterprise, accountancy must classify its data without misrepresentation, compress them without distortion, report them without concealment.

This second phrasing may seem to say more than the first statement and for some uses may therefore be preferable. But the briefer first statement seems more appropriate as the outcome of a pattern which attempts to connect the systematic features of accounting actions with a comparably systematic plan of related accounting objectives.

After the pattern of objectives and actions is known, it is possible to chain one's thinking upward through various levels of justifications. And if desired, it is also possible to trace the effects of the top objective downward through several strata of subobjectives until its influence on rules and actions is perceived. Rules and actions may then be seen to express the application or accomplishment of objectives derived out of prior needs. Only in this sense do rules "derive" from antecedent principles.

In a field like accountancy the word "immutable" is too strong an adjective to be attached to its principles. The principle of nature expressed by formulas to calculate the action of the force of gravity is indeed immutable. But no principle of accounting can have that quality. For us, principles can only be man-made expressions of man-made relationships; and these are not likely to be immutable, however significant and useful those statements of perceived relationships may be.

(Accounting Review, July, 1949)

14. Working Concept of a Principle

Accounting conventions, rules, and principles are more closely related in accounting usage than general definitions by dictionaries of these three words would lead us to suspect. If the ideas involved in these terms can be shown to be closely related in fact, the way would be opened to form a working concept of an accounting principle. It would be a concept for joining ideas from accounting theory with actions from practice. Such a union would give support to the belief that accounting principles are derived inductively out of accounting actions designed to serve accounting objectives.

A highly significant accounting action is made evident in the purposeful arrangement of the data presented in financial statements. The action is significant because it intends to add to the reader's grasp of the message embodied in the figures.

In the early days double-entry figures stayed in the ledger. When ledger figures were first separated from the ledger, they were presented as faithful copies of the respective accounts—balance account, profit and loss account.

Gradually the judgment of accounts led them to make these summaries of ledger facts more useful. Action (practice) implementing that intention introduced interpretative organization into the statements—group totals and remainders, contrasting of related items, descriptive terminology, etc.

These are action facts from practice. It is but natural that by precept and example the accountant should transmit the accepted practice to the novice. If need be this instruction could be epitomized into a simply phrased directive, perhaps such as this: "When you prepare financial statements organize the data into significant group totals, subgroups, and contrasting remainders, and label all of the items with descriptive names or phrases."

Such an instruction would compress recognized practice into a few words; yet no indication would be given of the justifying reason back of the action. This could easily be done; we need only add another clause to the instruction. This phrasing would suffice: "because an interpretative grouping of reported data increases reader understanding."

One may say the reason is so obvious as to be unnecessary. Yet it is obvious only to the initiated. To the layman for example it is by no means obvious that accountants have consciously chosen as one of their objectives the aim of using careful arrangements to make financial statements more understandable. Yet the primary purpose of keeping statements has always been to make a business enterprise more understandable.

If we bring together the above directive and its associated reason for being, the result becomes a full statement of an accounting rule. When well-known accounting actions have been clearly tied to appropriate justifying reasons, the way has been opened for converting one form of expression (a rule) into another (a principle). Where this is acceptably done the line of derivation of that principle leads straight back to experience-tested action. Thence that principle is an inductive generalization. And the form of expression should be one by which a desirable accounting objective is related to a suitable means of attaining that objective.

By applying these ideas to the rule derived above, the following phrasing indicates a conversion of the rule into a principle of interpretative grouping. "Financial statements present organized accounting data in group totals, subgroups, and contrasting remainders as a means of increasing the reader's understanding of enterprise activities."

Whenever we see suggestions or examples of new arrangements of the data in financial statements, or even entirely new types of statements, we are looking at an application of this principle. If we should happen to be the person working up new arrangements of data, we need to keep clearly in mind the objective that is compactly indicated in the principle. It is not an easy accomplishment, this attempt to help an unknown reader, for we cannot be sure we know just the kind of presentation that will appeal to his mind informatively. Hence decision in the phrasing of this principle cannot of itself produce increasingly understandable financial statements. It could perhaps stimulate further experimentation in arrangements in the hope that reader reactions may gradually furnish clues of what is helpful, what is not.

(New York Certified Public Accountants, November, 1950)

15. Provisional and Inconclusive

Of induction in accounting this may be said. Rules derive from experience, not from rationalization. But rules should be more than directives to action; actions need to be consciously associated with reasons and justifications. Objectives should be knowable; they should be attainable by recognized ways and means.

Does this sort of relationship exist between accounting ideas and accounting actions? Consider an illustration: "Give recognition to the fact that enterprise financial statements are necessarily somewhat provisional and inconclusive."

The action thus directed is one of recognizing a fact or condition which experience has shown impinges upon accounting. Accountants habitually react to the fact that one of the inescapable limitations of accounts is this: The figures recorded therein cannot be other than somewhat provisional so long as the data pertain to a going concern. They react for the most part by declining to say or do anything which would indicate that they consider any element of accounting data as an absolute. No item can be an absolute because, as the term "going concern" indicates, finality in a business enterprise comes into the picture only when the concern's assets are wholly realized and applied in liquidation of debts and ownership claims, and because future events, while they cannot alter the quantitative fact of a prior investment or expense incurred, may nevertheless modify the current significance of certain figures.

Accountants realize that the relative significance of figures objectively determined today will be interpretatively viewed later and in the light of subsequent events by the persons interested. This is to be expected. People habitually view previously determined facts in this way and formulate their own opinions. This they do without asserting or thinking that prior facts are misleading because they do not bear current price tags.

In the above paragraphs we find reasons which explain the action directive. If the directive is linked to a concise phrasing of its justification, we shall have fully stated an accounting rule. The following clause should therefore be annexed to the first statement above. ". . . because the effect of future events may modify the seeming finality which some people may read into the figures in financial statements."

It is not difficult for the layman to be overly impressed by the fact that a balance sheet presents figures to the last penny and shows assets and equities equal to the penny. This may seem to tell of microscopic accuracy. The informed reader knows that the reporting of pennies is merely an aid to checking the arithmetic of the clerical processes of bookkeeping. Pennies are so small in proportion to the dollar amounts that they cannot carry quantitative significance or constitute proof of minute accuracy. On the other hand some readers of financial statements may be so conscious of the vast surrounding atmosphere of events, past, present, and future, that they are skeptical of any financial statement which does not reflect a similar conciousness on the part of those responsible for the figures reported.

These extremes serve to illustrate the range of the problems involved in trying to make accounting communications communicative. This is not the place to walk through the gate thus opened before us. It is appropriate however to restate the phrasing of the above formulation of a rule. The following restatement, it is believed, will more directly suggest an accounting principle. "Unless financial statements are recognized as somewhat provisional and reconclusive, the seeming finality which some people may read into the reported dollars and cents figures may obscure the fact that future events can modify the significance of the figures while the figures remained facts in themselves."

The most important phrase in this principle probably is "significance of the figures." These are words which point to the fact that inconclusiveness does not flow from frailties within the original data (historical cost) or from rigidities in recording methods. The reported figures have been objectively determined, painstakingly classified, and thoroughly reviewed. The figures taken together may, for example, indicate at the moment a certain margin above insolvency. Yet a small cloud now on the horizon of business conditions may indicate a change in the direction of the economic winds which may soon change the solvency picture of this enterprise.

Figures in financial statements must be recognized as quantitative symbols of what has already transpired in the enterprise. They cannot reasonably be asked to pretend to anything more. If the reader imagines that they should, or can, vary with the shifting winds of changing conditions—especially as to changing price levels—he is letting his own wishes render fruitless the efforts of accountants to communicate useful ideas about the past of a given enterprise.

We can see here at the same time the usefulness and the inescapable incompleteness of a verbal statement of an accounting principle.

By linking an accounting objective with a practical means of attaining

that aim, we are made aware of an important relationship within accounting. Consequently we are just that much more alert to the close-knit
structure of accounting elements. Yet we need also to be aware of the
necessary incompleteness of a single principle. It is incomplete from being
isolated from companion principles. And it is incomplete from being a
highly compressed phrasing of ideas which could be, and must be, very
considerably expanded and intertwined with other accounting ideas.

Apparently this is an inevitable dilemma of a complex technology.

(New York Certified Public Accountants, November, 1950)

16. The Stable Money Assumption

Businessmen and accountants are sometimes charged with lack of realism
in financial statements because they prefer to hold to the use of invested
cost. The charge usually includes the statement that these parties erroneously assume that the monetary unit has a stability it does not possess.
It also asserts that this assumption lies at the heart of a subtle deception
buried in financial statements, especially in the income report. Because
adherence to historical cost rests upon a mere assumption, the critics
imply that a change in practice would be easily justified since old assumptions can readily be replaced with newer and better ones.

Suggestion of changes away from invested cost deserves careful examination for the reason that its adoption into accounting practice would
produce substantial alterations in present-day accounting principles.
While practices and preferences may be readily modified to meet new
conditions, it seems wiser to move much slower in matters of principle,
for real principles are so closely knit together that destruction of one
may begin to unravel the whole.

To say someone merely assumes that the dollar has a stable value implies he does not realize how money and goods are tied together, goods
being the purchase price of money and money the purchase price of
goods. Accountants and businessmen may not be economists, but they
do not need any special kind of education to know and allow for this
relationship. They do not assume stability; they know that neither money
nor goods have stable values or unchanging prices.

Like all citizens, accountants have assumed that the statutory features
of our money system were firmly established. This long-held assumption
has proved to be erroneous. In 1933, as part of the effort to move the
nation out of depression, gold was devalued about 30 per cent and government bonds were once more **made** part of the base for paper money,
thus taking the place formerly held by promissory notes resulting from
commercial loans made by banks. The basic assumption of a stable
monetary system (not stable purchasing power) was thus disrupted. The
then current political theory considered maintenance of full employment

of first importance, even if the soundness of the monetary system had to be risked in the process. The shock of devaluation was great, whatever the justification of the moment. And since the fact of devaluation (and the resulting impulse toward "reflation") continued long after depression had passed, the initial shock persisted and was soon accompanied by a fear that subsequent devaluation could come easier from the precedent of the first and from again substantially raising the debt limit.

The effects of these policies and actions, as intended, had a definite influence on price levels; and sharply rising price levels presently generated questions regarding the accounting methods of calculating enterprise profits. This questioning included the renewal of a not unfamiliar charge that accountants and businessmen based their accounts on a false assumption. When the "money unit assumption" was first advanced, it was already an established idea which underlaid all men's ideas and thus had to be part of the explanation of the nature of accountancy. More recently the idea has been made to seem a weakness of accounting alone.

This spot of history shows that accounting is part of the fabric of its times and hence will be better understood if its contacts with other idea areas are known. However, the main point to make here is that the flaw in accounting, if any, was not of accounting origin; hence it becomes questionable whether modification of accounting methods could remove the flaw.

It may sometimes be thought that accountants are insensitive to the causes of price-level change, or that their preference for the use of invested costs demonstrates a blindness to the influence of rising sales prices upon enterprise profit. Accountants would be blind indeed if their contacts with business failed to make them fully aware that sales prices and purchase prices will fluctuate with different timing and range.

Accountants however do have an assumption. It is not that the value of the dollar is stable; it is not that managerial action is wholly responsible for the calculated amount of enterprise net profit. Accountants know that profit results from the interactions of management decision and economic change. Their assumption is that an attempted separate calculation of the two causative forces is unwarranted. They can well believe that no suitable methodology is available for convincingly making such separate calculations. The application of index-numbers to invested cost may be thought to effect a true separation measurement of the two causes. Yet the results thus "separated" probably would not be much more factual than those from a judgment-directed dividing of the final net profit figure into two parts estimated to reflect respectively the contribution of management and the effect of price change.

Another thought might be added. Regardless of the method used to try to calculate separately the effect of these two factors, it may well be a fact that management decisions, by skillfully adjusting enterprise policy and action to changing conditions, are themselves more largely responsible than is usually thought for attaching price rise profits to their enterprise and for avoiding contact with many price fall losses. Without being seers, managers nevertheless have to make thoughtful appraisals of the trend of events. Without being bound by the past, they nevertheless draw heavily upon their prior experience with successful and unsuccessful policies as measured in their historical cost data.[3]

A unit of account, it is said, is the dollar of prior price contract bargaining only by force of tradition. Since this is only a usage of convenience (a postulate), the dollar price of current outside bargaining could be easily substituted (a new postulate). Yet the use of bargained cost dollars for accounting purposes may well be considered much more than a generally accepted convenience. If the idea and the practice are more deeply rooted than in the surface soil of convenience, they will probably be harder to change than by a proposed new postulate as to new usefulness. The deep-rooted idea would then have to be overthrown and the new idea thoroughly sold as a substitute. Overthrowing may not be easy.

Regardless of when and how historical cost came into accounting use, it is a fact that accounts evolved out of the needs of operating management (owners in the early days) for information regarding their own past business actions. These actions, at the time of execution, could not have been expressed quantitatively and uniformly except in terms of the money price of the bargains made. Even barter was reduced to money equivalents for the record. These money figures in accounts proved very useful for subsequently understanding and reviewing the past when thinking of the future. The same basic usefulness still lies within the power of account figures or invested cost. If these accounts are prevented from speaking of measured prior commitments, this basis for later acting with actual knowledge of many past judgements may be lost to management with a consequent added risk of unwise decisions.

It may also be difficult to accept the argument that any kind of "objectivity" is suitably objectivity. An index-number series from government sources is, to be sure, well beyond personal manipulation by the ultimate users. Yet such averages can hardly be forced into universal use; bargained dollars (invested cost) are already in universal use and are deeply embedded in personal psychology and fundamental law. Any index is not only complex of determination (and therefore difficult of verification), but it also rests upon a changeable formula of calculation. It does not alter this weakness to say that change in the formula is not willful or arbitrary. If it were changed for any reason, its results lose

[3] "In living, man proceeds by comparing today with yesterday, and projects plans for tomorrow by a study of the movement [trend] thus indicated in conjunction with study of the conditions of the environment now existing." John Dewey, *Human Nature and Conduct*, cited at p. 453 in the *Social Philosophers*, New York, 1947.

comparability with the past in the same way that accounts in past dollars are charged with poor comparability.[4]

The objectivity of historical or invested cost however is not the result of a formula or of a traditional convention. This kind of objectivity comes quite naturally out of day-to-day business activities and the interplay of self-interest among independent parties. The resulting figures are unmistakeable, unshakeable, and they are widely understood by all sorts of people and supported by legal sanctions resting upon the same characteristics just indicated.

As an historical fact there undoubtedly has been some drifting away from strict adherence to invested cost in accounting. A question of more importance is whether further drifting might not undermine, rather than enlarge, the service accounting is able to render.

Will successive and progressive departures from cost decisively weaken the power of accountancy and accountants to maintain and extend high standards of accounting objectivity? If a weakening of objectivity should develop, would it mean that financial statement figures could then be made more nearly what persons at interest wished them to be?

Accounting restraints that help minimize wishful, willful figures take the form of pressure from accountants for practices which conform to generally accepted accounting principles. The principles most likely to be useful in restraining undue departures from good accounting practices may very well be principles which disclose the close-knit logic which is present in the interrelation of desirable ends and suitable means for achieving those ends. These would be useful for this purpose because good objectives (desirable aims) will be more persuasive than customary preferences.

Two principles are presented here for examination in the light of recent suggestions stimulated by the rising price levels characteristic of the 1940's and 1950's. They can be stated as follows: (1) accounting transactions derive their homogeneity . . . in part from the use of prices in terms of one money system, and in part from the relevance of transactions to a given enterprise and to its objectives; (2) transactions committed to the accounting record which have not been determined by the bargaining of independent parties in contact with the given enterprise . . . may make a report deceptive for lack of objective determination of all the raw data.

The objectives or ends indicated in these two principles are (1) to assure that the data entering the accounts of an enterprise are homogeneous and (2) to assure that data entering accounts shall have been objectively determined. Both aims are necessary ones: the first, in order

.

[4] One index series (Warren & Pearson) shows a change in general price level from 99 (1914) to 95 (1932), or an increase of measured purchasing power of about 4 per cent. Another series (Snyder) shows a change from 100 (1914) to 132 (1932), or a decrease in measured purchasing power of about 24 per cent.

that the assembled figures may be freely used in arithmetical combinations; the second, in order that those same figures shall be dependably
verifiable by people who are strangers to the transactions.

Together the two principles state the essence of invested cost usage
in accounting. This basis can therefore be considered under challenge if
the means of attaining the ends stated in these principles are questioned.
The means referred to are (1) figures stated in terms of one money system, (2) prices resulting from the bargaining of independent parties in
contact with this enterprise. These ideas are questioned if the continued
accounting usefulness of the money price of enterprise closed transactions
is doubted, and if, in place of the money price of our own prior transactions, the suggested substitution is the price of transactions entered
into by people not in contact with our enterprise (current dollars or
replacement price equivalents).

Such questioning of established accounting ideas would assert that the
units (as dollars) to be used in expressing transactions and accounts must
be appropriate and self-evident; that the unit traditionally used (contracted dollars of prior transactions) has never been more than an assumption or generally accepted convention; that assumptions or conventions of appropriateness can be changed by general consent because an
assumption or convention is an idea arbitrarily accepted to be true as
a basis for reasoning or action, but not yet proved true.

In specific application, these assertions do not propose the accounting
use in the United States of a system of money other than dollar currency.
The criticism is that the *meaning* of "dollar" changes, and consequently
any 1930 dollars still lodged in an account, cannot mean the same thing
as dollars of 1950. The reasoning is that all prices have become markedly
higher and the current purchasing power significance of old dollars of
invested cost has become correspondingly less. This argument in effect
challenges the homogeneity of an account having both 1930 and 1950
dollars in it and implies that accounting, by persisting in recording only
invested cost dollars, operates upon a mere assumption that all account
dollars are alike in significance, or that fluctuations in purchasing power
of money are without significance.

Challenge is also given to the necessity for basing accounts only on
transactions relevant to and actually entered upon by this enterprise.
Other bases of objectivity are suggested as also satisfactory. Outside transactions of other people (expressing the price they paid) are stated to be
"objectively determined prices" since they have been bargained by the
parties concerned. And even if these individual prices are often difficult
to learn, a government-constructed index of general prices is proposed as
a useful substitute, being, it is said, clearly objective from having been
determined by departments of the federal government beyond the bias
of accountant and business-users.

These ideas may challenge both the above principles, and yet may not be able to overthrow them. This is likely for the reason that homogeneity of the data in an account, as accounts are now kept, is true homogeneity because the nature or quality of the items classified under that head, and not the value of the money amount, will be the key to the items' presence in that account. Overthrow is unlikely also because objectivity of accounting data is not merely a matter of verifiable figuring. The data must also be clearly and demonstrably revelant to the given enterprise as such. It is not enough that a transaction shall have taken place; the only one deserving recognition in our account is one executed by us in our own interest and in contact with outside parties.

(*New York Certified Public Accountant,* January, 1954)

17. Cohesion or Disintegration

There is a wide and growing awareness that skills in interpreting the data available in double-entry accounts and in correlating them with other data have not kept pace with improvements in accounting technology or with the analytical procedures of auditing. The root sources of most of the recent criticisms of accounting reach back into this fact. If accountants would develop their ability to interpret (i.e., render the meaning clear) as well as they have over the years increased their powers of analysis (i.e., penetrating beneath the surface of facts), many people who have to make important decisions in this complex world might be greatly helped in the discharge of their responsibilities. And it is not unreasonable to expect that the same increase in interpretative skill may also succeed in making accounting data (and through it, the business enterprise) somewhat more understandable to many people whose responsibilities, though proportionately smaller, are nonetheless important to themselves.

There is far less mystery about accounting figures than laymen seem prone to believe; and there are more limitations than is realized by some people who seem to feel they know a good deal about accounting and businesses and society. It may not be necessary to revolutionize accounting ideology in order to increase the usefulness of its technology. It would be revolutionary if index-number adjustment figures were to be incorporated into accounting methodology. It would be a complete answer to criticisms, which have called up this revolutionary suggestion, if accountants developed collateral interpretative skills and techniques. And perhaps more important, this line of development could be an important aid in preserving the cohesion that molds accounting ideas into an integrated system of thinking. It could have this result because it would tend to discourage the efforts some people seem to be making to press irrelevant effects into the accounts of enterprises which have not yet been a party to transactions at current prices. There seems to be an urge to get replacement prices into the accounts in place of invested cost, although the one is closely relevant to the given enterprise because it has been a participant, while the other is an irrelevant effect because the enterprise has not been a participant.

It may be useful to approach a consideration of the effect of pressing index-number adjustments into ledger accounts if we attempt to formulate a principle of accounting (as one item in an integrated body of accounting ideas) and then take note of the probable effect of excluding that principle from serving as one guide among others to rational accounting actions. Let us call the following item "principle of irrelevant effects."

If fluctuations in price levels are ignored as a basis for changing directly the statistical effects of transactions previously entered in the account . . . omission would tend to avoid the introduction of irrelevant and confusing modifications in the objective measurement of enterprise efforts and accomplishments.

In the growing literature from the debate on the significance of price inflation and replacement prices in relation to accounting methods and financial statements, many suggestions appear which perhaps can be usefully appraised if placed in contact with the above formulated accounting principle. This may at the same time afford an opportunity for scrutinizing the principle itself.

It is possible to cull a number of stimulating criticisms out of recent accounting literature. Some of these follow: that financial statements neither show the reader the effect of fluctuating price levels nor attempt to eliminate such effect from calculated net income; that all costs in the income statement are not stated in terms of comparable dollars (e.g., wages and depreciation) in spite of the fact that related revenues always reflect current prices; that the use of current purchasing power dollar equivalents throughout the income statement would produce an increase in the significance of that statement.

The principle of irrelevant effects is directly challenged by such ideas since under that principle these ideas would be denied admission into double-entry accounting.

The introduction of replacement prices or index-number adjustments into the structure of accounting would introduce confusion rather than clarification. This modification would be adopted by some companies and rejected by others unless, in some unimaginable fashion, it could be prescribed for all enterprise. Furthermore, a voluntary extension of the use of these ideas to apply also under falling price levels would scarcely take place. If it did, confusion would be compounded since the lower index-numbers very probably would often produce smaller expense deductions from revenue than the actual invested, out-of-pocket cost of the expense item.

The use of index-number adjustments to represent replacement prices would introduce data into the ledger accounts that were irrelevant to the enterprise. We should therefore examine the significance of "irrelevant."

A useful and compact form of stating important accounting ideas can be made by linking each of the desirable accounting ends and objectives with suitable and relevant ways and means, thus forming a verbalized principle. Upon examination, every accounting principle would be found tied back into fundamental ideas which cannot be divorced from accounting.

One of the groundwork ideas which constitute the underpinning for accounting is the entity concept. It may be stated this way: for accounting purposes a business enterprise is treated as a distinct economic entity or operating unit regardless of its legal status as proprietorship, partnership, corporation. The business enterprise is a unit for production or service specialization; for selective investment at the saver's discretion; for managerial control decisions; and for serving as a framework for assembling data of importance to management and investors.

This means that events occurring outside the ownership and management boundaries of a given enterprise are distinctly different from events within. Inside facts are real in being clearly relevant to us; outside facts are often important to know, but for our accounting they are unreal in being another person's transactions not directly affecting us.

A companion concept of importance leads us to organize accounting ideas and actions so they will focus upon a going concern rather than on an enterprise being dissolved. Dissolution of some kind will come eventually, whether by voluntary retirement or involuntary winding up because of bankruptcy; but that condition is not in constant contemplation; hence it is not a suitable statement of underlying fact (premise) for accounting ideology.

A business enterprise is in fact an operating unit all of its life; it is in liquidation only at death. At rare intervals it approaches death by liquidation, but does not die. By reorganization and scaling down of debts, the enterprise can often escape the final climax. Where an enterprise is in process of winding up its affairs, it is inevitable that we view its assets as *values,* since the question at that time is "What could the assets bring at sale?"

Many people feel tempted to ask the same question about a going concern. But if accounting attempts in answer to provide values in the financial statements, it would seem to do so on the assumption that dissolution was under consideration. If this were not the fact, the use of the balance sheet to express selling or liquidating values would be very inappropriate, particularly because, unless dissolution was in view, the fixed assets would not be for sale. If the producing assets were to be sold, the ability to produce (and survive) would be lost.

Here are facts, not assumptions. Consequently, accounting figures, not merely traditionally but with complete logic, reflect cost dollars and not value dollars. Cost as here used is sometimes called purchase price, invested cost, historical, or original cost; perhaps as "bargained exchanges expressed in money prices of that moment."

Each of the two concepts here briefly described present a clash of ideas: as to "entity"—whether accounting should work only with data internal to an enterprise or should give expression to events outside the given enterprise; as to "going concern"—whether enterprise accounting should use cost as the basis for its financial reports or should incorporate value figures (current price equivalents) as financial statement data. If the above principle be unacceptable, that choice would then indicate the choices to be made in the alternative interpretations of these two basic concepts regarding the business enterprise for whom accounts are to be kept. Will accountants wish to make this reinterpretation of basic concepts?

The thought might be added that price-level changes should not be permitted to produce modifications in the account record because this action would disastrously disrupt the integration between enterprise real and nominal accounts—a relationship which may well be considered the most distinctive and significant aspect of enterprise accounting. Already some tendency appears in the literature to argue for replacement figures ("current dollars") in the income statement and to ignore any collateral effect upon the balance sheet. This may mean that some people, thinking of accounting data as just more statistical data, fail to see that this integration between accounts and between financial statements is an important feature of accounting. Even accountants argue these days that the income statement is more important for more uses than the balance sheet; yet few of them would agree to carry this thought so far as to divorce the two statements completely by neglecting their integration.

If index adjustments (values) were introduced in substitution for invested costs in both statements, some "contra account" such as capital adjustment account would have to be brought into the balance sheet to absorb the contra effect of enlarging the asset figures. Since such a "balancing account" could not be considered creditor claim, stockholder contribution, or retained earnings, it would not only be a highly abstract and confusing item, but it would also indicate that integration between the statements was quite artificial. Acceptance by accountants of such a "reconciliation account" would seem to suggest that they too were willing to believe that close and logical integration between the two statements, and between real and nominal accounts, was of decreasing significance. For this reason acceptance of a contra account seems doubtful as against support for the principle.

The essence of the matter becomes clearer when we look at a possible extreme development wherein no attempt whatever is made to dovetail the two leading financial statements. Each then becomes an independent presentation. In place of the balance sheet there could be a statement of appraised property values. It would not necessarily be presented in association with the separate statement of the sources of the properties, i.e., from creditors, stockholders, reinvested profits. Thus there would be no balance sheet as such. The income statement, being entirely separate, might then be stated in terms of values according to any index-number system desired or required; or it might be stated in terms of expense based on invested cost, while the property statement was made in terms of appraised values or by use of an index-number series different from that used for the income statement.

The final result: Accounting, having lost its most essential integrating characteristic, would become purely statistical and completely utilitarian; its principles, losing their conceptional cohesion, would fall apart and drift into neglect. The force of accounting logic would be lost; it would then come close to being possible for accounting to be all things to all men, available to support whatever views it seemed expedient for men to hold. If the new doctrines about the impact of price-level rise are to be accepted and accounting correspondingly modified, the price of gaining the asserted benefits for some uses would likely be disintegration of the cohesion between present-day accounting ideas.

(Illinois Certified Public Accountant, March, 1954)

PART THREE *On the Profession*

QUALIFICATION TESTING

1. Types of Auditing Questions

Nearly 2,500 questions were propounded in the auditing section of the CPA examinations from 1896 to 1941. Dividing this period into two nearly equal lengths (1896-1919, 1920-41) shows certain types of changes to have taken place.

	early	later
Questions on audit procedure	44%	35%
Questions on audit theory	21%	25%
Questions on nonaudit topics	35%	40%

Some of the increase in nonaudit questions may have been due to the fact that the American Institute did not include separate examinations in accounting theory.

When the questions on audit procedure are classified by types and ranked as to frequency of use a comparative view is obtained of certain areas of concentration. Before 1910, "outline audit program" and "how verify cash" were the essence of 74 out of 101 questions. The remainder dealt with "instructions to client" and "verification of expense and income." Between 1930 and 1941 question types fell into more nearly equal groups. Three topics were represented in 15, 16, or 17 instances: verification under named conditions, verification of inventory, tax matters. Three other topics were summarized into 13 or 14 instances each: verification of expense and income, verification of cash, audit of estates.

Emphasis has shifted from complete audit programs to verification procedures appropriate to specified sections of an audit.

In the area of audit theory questions there is considerable similarity between the subperiods as to important topics but some variation in ranking of the topics emphasized. The top three topics included 49 questions in 1896-1909 and 91 in 1930-41. "Evaluation of evidence" was ranked first in the earlier period and second in the later period. "Application of principles among alternatives" was third and first in the early and the late periods respectively. Questions dealing with the nature of auditing were in first place early; in the later period "extent of auditor's duty" was in third place.

There was a slight increase in the later years in the use of nonaudit questions. Top ranking went to "capital or revenue expenditures" in the early examinations and to display of facts in accounting statements in the later tests. "Asset valuation" was second (early) and sixth (late). "Accounting systems" was fifth (early) and second (late).

These condensed summaries are not of themselves conclusive; yet they are indicative of the direction of change.

Broad general questions on the nature and purpose of auditing are of late being replaced by questions that are more pointed and specific. It is to be hoped, however, that attempts to test the candidate's powers of generalization will not be entirely abandoned.

Earlier auditing examinations made frequent use of questions on the theory of accounts. The trend has been away from this type of question and toward theory as it involves accounting statements. Probably many situations which formerly constituted test materials have become elementary and commonplace and thus have now lost much of their former usefulness for examinations. But the same fundamental theory problems remain—problems of clear classification, of good account names, of adequate segregating of account content. Only the setting has changed; we now think of items in statements more often than we do of accounts in the ledger.

There is a tendency to decrease the number of questions that seem to expect a picture of auditing as a process of checking details and verifying accounts, and to increase questions which view the auditor as a professional man whose qualifications and services have a known social significance. Questions which relate strictly to audit routines and procedural aspects tend to decrease. There is a tendency toward increase in questions that give the candidate an opportunity to indicate his realization: that accounting statements provide important data for use in forming social, managerial, and investment policies; that the auditor is expected to make a critical evaluation of methods found and of the treatment of the facts; that he must be able to decide upon variations in the extent of his procedures according to the circumstances and to choose wisely among alternatives without subservience; that his service extends beyond the mere verification of accounting figures into keen judgments regarding the organization and efficiency of the client's staff for providing adequate internal safeguards.

Auditing literature in the past has been largely descriptive of procedures. Is it not advisable that we write deeper into the subject than that? Where is the material that can stir the novice with glimpses of the heights of professional service? If we have literature that can help students to lift up their eyes, examiners can ask questions that will help indicate which candidates are best qualified by temperament and vision, as well as by technical skills, to enter upon the high responsibilities of practicing a profession.

Only a small number of questions touch upon the audit report. Since rendering a report is the focus of much that the auditor does, a need for questions on report construction or on problems dealing with some item in a report would seem to be clearly indicated. It is something of an art to express facts and comments clearly in a text. Since it is a necessary art, and, as we are constantly being reminded, one in which novices are usually deficient, questions of this kind might prove a desirable stimulus as well as a test. It will no doubt be granted that examination questions have a definite influence upon the selection of educational materials.

The subject matter of the examinations is undoubtedly changing as conditions change. That is to be expected. But it still is an open question whether the changes have been in proportion to professional developments. If too many questions are colored by recent events, the test may be unreasonably severe, even unfair, for young candidates. On the other hand, if too few questions touch on present conditions, the test may be inadequate from the point of view of the welfare of the profession. The same kind of dilemma must be faced in the re-use of earlier questions. Certain areas of subject matter need to be tested in nearly every examination; other areas in some sort of cycle of intervals.

The tendency over nearly half a century for auditing examination questions to change has been small in comparison with the changes that might have been made without getting unduly ahead of the text literature. Does this slowness to change produce examinations that give due weight to the increasing social importance of the auditor's work? Are the questions designed, in part, to test intellectual fitness to grow in professional responsibility?

(*Accounting Review*, October, 1943)

2. Testing Professional Fitness

Can auditing examinations test professional fitness? How far can they be expected to furnish clues to such fitness without becoming too lengthy, too unfair, too hampering to the growth of the profession?

Other evidences of fitness are also sought: age that reflects reasonable maturity; testimonies in support of good character; formal education in accounting and related subject matter; practical experience in accounting. These approaches are significant and useful, but could they properly be considered sufficient if associated with an inadequate audit examination and an assumption that field experience will provide that test of fitness?

CPA examinations as a whole still follow closely the original pattern established in 1896 and now are apparently firmly fixed by a long succession of similar statutes. Only a few states have added new examination papers to the familiar list. More often newer subject matter has been pushed into one or the other traditional papers—if space permitted—or passed over altogether. Is it reasonable that the examination in auditing —the heart of the profession—should continue indefinitely to be assigned no more time than that for commercial law?

The auditing examinations between 1896 and April, 1941 reflect a considerable dilution by extraneous questions. Out of 2,338 questions, 874 did not deal with auditing as such. Nearly one-half (48 per cent) of these dealt with statement presentation. These are matters of concern to the auditor, to be sure, but they do not test auditing knowledge. Sometimes questions on cost accounting are also found here. Does this signify that "auditing" is expanding to include "cost inspection?" Are professional public accountants being retained to make cost audits? They might well be asked to do this; they now review internal control and pass judgment on internal auditing. If cost questions appear in the audit examination, they presumably should refer to audit aspects.

Audit examination questions in the sample are heavily weighted toward the balance sheet. The small proportion of questions touching upon income, cost, expense, and revenue is noticeable. Is scrutiny of income determination actually a mere 10 per cent of the external auditor's responsibility? Is 80 per cent of the audit aspect of balance sheets still centered in working capital position? The questions of the generation before 1941 seem to suggest affirmative answers. The reasons supporting the usage are not disclosed; presumably examiners have had justifying reasons.

What preparation, knowledge, aptitude, or fitness are auditing questions designed to test? In order to try to formulate some opinion on the matter, a small sample of CPA questions was analyzed along this line. Those included were the audit papers for New York examinations, October, 1941; April, 1942; and Institute for November, 1941; May 1942. Here was a sample of 54 questions. About 46 per cent were on audit procedure; 13 per cent were on audit theory; 41 per cent were nonaudit questions. This distribution conforms closely to that shown in the larger sample extending back to 1896.

What kind of testing were the candidates subjected to in this compact sample?

Character of test

(1) Test memory of typical textbook propositions	12
(2) Test judgment in simple situations (explain choice among alternatives)	11
(3) Test judgment in complex situations (include discussion, give reasons, etc.)	8
(4) Describe simple procedures	7
(5) Justify simple procedures	6
(6) Test memory of many instances	5
(7) Describe complex procedures	4
(8) Justify complex procedures	1
Total questions	54

This ranking of question types shows several interesting things. There is a certain concentration in the first three classes—thirty-one out of fifty-four questions. Of the thirty-one, there are nineteen which are tests of judgment and twelve which test the memory. Of the same thirty-one top-ranking questions, nineteen are so framed as to be nonauditing questions and therefore could be just as properly used in an examination in accounting theory. All of the descriptive questions (Items 4 and 7) come from questions that can be classified as auditing procedure.

Opinions will differ regarding the most desirable ranking of these types of tests. But certain observations may be worthwhile. Memory tests of textbook material probably should not regularly and persistently rank first. They should rank high in the list, however, because a great deal that is useful can be learned from books with much economy of time. Testing judgment in simple situations should rank high—perhaps first, most of the time. Capacity for exercising judgment is a most important professional attribute and some clue to its existence in the individual can be found from even simple situations if they are skillfully presented. The third item in the list may be higher than it should be most of the time. Overemphasis on this type of question could easily make an examination devastating. Items 4 and 5 probably call for ranking below the middle. Many people would consider Item 6 the least significant type of test. Items 7 and 8 are here lower in the list than their usefulness for testing purposes would suggest. More questions of this type could well be used.

Two other opinions may be added. About one-sixth of the fifty-four questions dealt with matters that have received rather recent emphasis (punch-card accounting, responsibility for details of inventory and receivables, United States tax notes, surplus adjustments, certificate details, etc.). It would be easy, in a given examination or in a series of consecutive examinations, to stress recent past events unduly. One need not believe that six out of fifty-four is "undue stress," in order to make this point; nor is it necessary to set specific limits to the phrase "recent past." On the other hand, because considerable emphasis is already indicated as being placed on textbook propositions, some attention to recent events of importance is advisable for proper balance.

The other point is that carefully considered phrasing of questions can convert many nonauditing questions into questions clearly suitable for an auditing examination. Many nonauditing questions deal with a transaction or with the treatment of an item in the statements. These could be framed either as something for the candidate to do (accounting) or as a situation already accomplished and now under critical scrutiny (auditing). Again, questions which require the candidate to make a choice can be made a much more effective test of his judgment by asking for his reasons as well.

Some questions should present dilemmas and choices. In practice the auditor has to deliberate and decide, and not infrequently he has to justify his action. Some questions should require the exercise of ingenuity and resourcefulness in framing an answer. These are important qualities in an auditor and are worth trying to find in the candidate, even though examination questions cannot reveal them very conclusively.

Some questions should be specifically designed to give the candidate an opportunity to express himself in clear, forceful language if he can. He is expected to be able to do so in practice. Is there any substantial basis for the obvious avoidance of an occasional "essay type" of question? This issue will face anyone who reviews a small or a large number of examinations.

All critics of the preparation of candidates say that young men in the profession usually seem unable to express themselves clearly. Would it not put a well-advised pressure upon students and teachers if the professional examinations frequently asked a question designed to lead the candidate to organize a few ideas in good readable English? No doubt answers would be harder to grade with one point allowed for this and half a point for that according to a prearranged "model" solution. Yet grading of essay answers is successfully accomplished in many college courses every month. If the grading of CPA examination answers should be something more than looking for deviations in calculated results, the other type of grading can be used there also and with benefit. It would not take a great deal of judgment to classify the answers to an "essay" question from two hundred candidates into five categories of graded excellence.

The impression persists that too many questions are little more than memory tests or such as call mainly for descriptive answers. Are these as good a test of latent professional qualities as questions that stimulate answers involving judgment? Could not more questions be suitably framed to reveal the candidate's resourcefulness, or to lead to a demonstration of ability to choose among alternatives without seeming to overstress this kind of test? These are matters of professional importance at least equal to the ability to construct a bank reconciliation schedule.

Of course any examiner could pose enough questions of professional judgment to floor all candidates if he did not remember that both his experience and maturity of mind are beyond those of the candidates. Some questions give the impression of premeditated difficulty or of specialized subject matter beyond the knowledge of all but a few. Such questions do more to hamper recruiting for the profession than they accomplish in raising the standards of admission. The profession is already handicapped in recruiting by seasonal activities and large turnover of staff. Public accountants are not always able to get the best young men available. Young men do not want special favors or easy examinations; they want regular employment, steady progress, and examinations suited to their knowledge and prospects.

We are most unfortunate in being forced to get along with a type of examination that tests all candidates at a single level and admits to the test only those who have already practiced the things they are to be tested in to see whether they may practice them. It would be much more in line with the dignities of a profession to require a preliminary examination or to prescribe substantial preliminary technical education in which the school tests could take the place of a formal preliminary professional examination. Then the professional examination for license to practice could become a real test of technical competence at a high level. As matters stand, nothing but compromise examinations can result. Any other kind at present would either admit numerous insufficiently qualified individuals or set the bars so high as to do untold damage to the growth of the profession. A planned evolution would seem to be indicated.

The problem of modifying the auditing examination is in a large measure the problem of using accounting theory effectively in professional testing. Whether clearly recognized or not, theory of some kind underlies and gives support to all practices and procedures. Behind the practical treatment of accounts, theory will probably be something less than pure idealism and something more than the idea that tradition is the most acceptable guide. But surely everything that is done in accounting is done for some reason or other. In those reasons lie the explanations of the treatment; the explanations express the theories that are inseparable from the practices.

Behind the practical procedures of auditing also, there must be theory of some sort. Auditing involves a critical examination of the client's accounting treatment of the facts. Audit procedure is a way of putting the auditor's knowledge of theory—what the treatment might be under the circumstances—into contact with the accounts as they are. If he does not know accounting theory, statement theory, auditing theory, how can the auditor be effectively critical? How can we thoroughly test professional candidates if the use of theory questions is neglected?

It seems clear that theory is a natural part of both the problem examination and the auditing examination. It is equally clear that the original pattern of CPA examinations has already been modified with benefit in developing comprehensive tests under the title "accounting theory and practice," which extend over two long half days, the two parts usually being graded together as one examination. From this I draw the idea of continuing and extending this type of modification, since it has already proved beneficial. The next step might be to develop another comprehensive test under the title "auditing theory and procedure," to consist of two half-day parts to be graded together. The questions could include much of the area of accounting theory; skillful wording of questions could relate the matter clearly to the auditor's duty, judgment, or knowledge background and make the questions specific and objective. Questions should regularly be set to include ethics broadly considered, moral responsibilities of professional men, and other similar topics, in addition to auditing techniques and statement theory.

The examination in accounting theory and practice has come to be a real test of analytical power and skill in marshaling data—important professional matters indeed. An examination in auditing theory and procedure could be made a comparable test of professional attitudes and auditing techniques. These too are important matters.

One could go even further with this arrangement. It should not be difficult to get acquiescence (1) to subdividing a three-day examination into two separate sections of one and one-half days each, and (2) to making a passing grade in section A examination plus a certain amount of experience in public accounting a prerequisite for admission to section B. Section A, with an educational requirement but no experience requirement for admission, could include two half-day examinations in accounting theory and practice separated by a half-day examination in commercial law as it is now constructed. Section B, with an educational requirement (that is, a passing grade in section A) and an experience requirement (such as three years of satisfactory public accounting experience), could include two half-day examinations in auditing theory and procedure separated by a half-day examination in administrative law and finance.

Thus section B would become an examination in professional matters and reach a somewhat higher plane than section A where the questions would deal more generally with accounting practices and technical skills. The outcome could very well be a definite elevation of professional standards without making the examinations baffling to the properly prepared. Harder questions would merely eliminate candidates and would not necessarily raise the average level of ability in the profession or inspire better academic preparation for entering the profession.

The elevation of standards would come from two causes: (1) the educational preparation as a prerequisite to section A and an academic point of view (especially at the postgraduate level) conditioned in part to the functioning of section B in the CPA examination; (2) the separate testing for knowledge and attitudes directly characteristic of the professional man in this field.

(*Accounting Review*, October, 1943)

3. Notes for a CPA Law

Revision of a CPA law of long standing is an action not to be taken in haste—or too long delayed. Since work upon proposed legislation regarding the Illinois CPA laws of 1903 and 1927 is underway in committee, it may foster constructive discussion to give consideration to the following ideas among others.

(1) In order to hold himself out to the public as a *Certified* Public Accountant and to certify to the financial statements of a business having

more than $500,000 capital, the practitioner must (a) be of good moral character, (b) must be over twenty-one years of age, (c) must have passed a technical examination, (d) must be registered with the state as being in public practice.

2. The technical examination will be given on the same date in two separate sections:

section a—Auditing, accounting theory, commercial law, one-half day each.

section b—Practical accounting problems, two days, being four half-day sessions.

3. Admission to the two examinations would be based upon differing requirements.

a. To enter the first examination (auditing, accounting theory, commercial law) the candidate must satisfy one of the following conditions:

(1) six years of public accounting experience for himself or with a firm of professional accountants, or

(2) four years of public accounting experience and two years of college or equivalent, or

(3) two years of public accounting experience and a bachelor's degree, or

(4) a bachelor's degree in commerce from a recognized college including a major in accountancy equivalent to at least one-fourth of the total credits required for the degree

b. To enter the second examination (practical accounting problems) the candidate must satisfy one of the following conditions:

(1) prior passing grades in the first examination and one year of additional public accounting experience after having passed the first series of examination.

(2) a master's degree from a recognized college, including a major in accountancy equivalent to at least three-fourths of the total credits required for the degree. The certificate and the license to practice for candidates successful under this section will be withheld pending completion of one year of experience in public accounting.

Significance of Such Provisions

(1) The way is open for the PA with six years' public experience to take both examinations without a high school education. It is possibly advantageous to join with this for the first year an oral examination and consideration of type of experience for present PA's who had either (a) passed a written PA examination or (b) been in public practice with not less than five clients for three years prior to being registered as a PA.

(2) The way is never completely closed for a person to prepare for the CPA examination by practical experience (six years) and private study. The PA group would in time become an avenue of preparation for public recognition for those who could not obtain the necessary formal schooling.

(3) A premium would be put upon definite educational preparation of a broad and technical character as is fitting for a real profession.

(4) The plan conforms to the trend in legislation already established in several states and gives recognition to conditions now inherent in most CPA applications in Illinois. A study made in 1937 of Illinois applications showed that 82 per cent of the cases in the period 1925-34 had more than two years of college and that most of the successful candidates had two or three years of experience.

(5) Separation of the examination into two parts would simplify the work of examining and improve the candidates' preparation by reducing the strain of sitting for all subjects at one time.

(personal correspondence, spring, 1939)

4. Examination Functions

I have been looking over the examination for May, 1943. Since I have at times expressed opinions about examination deficiencies—and may have to do so again—I perhaps can pass on, without committing you as an examiner, the favorable impression the latest have made.

In the accounting papers the committee has presented three clearly marked areas of testing, with little or no overlapping: (1) to show how well the candidate can work his way through masses of related data and marshal the facts understandably; (2) to show how well he is oriented in the usual procedures to be followed in reaching and expressing a professional opinion about financial statements, and in the duties, responsibilities and limitations of a professional accountant; (3) to show how well he can think rationally, how clearly he can explain the whys of given treatments, how convincingly he can argue the choice of alternatives, and how correctly he can express his ideas in written English.

The candidate's reactions in these areas of testing afford a good basis for judging his intellectual fitness to be recognized in the profession. The present papers are noteworthy for the care with which the areas of testing have been kept distinct. As a result, if a candidate is deficient, his defects can be located in definite professional areas. This basis for examiner judgment is obviously superior to the mere accumulation of marks for correct solutions according to pattern solutions.

More specifically about the theory paper: The questions are well chosen and clearly stated. They tend strongly to deal with relatively current materials. This can be overdone, with the result of rapidly exhausting the available topics, and handicapping the candidate who has not been able to keep up to date on all new materials. Some pressure of this sort is a very good thing—it forces people to read currently and to realize that education is not all from college textbooks or one's own current audit experiences. Too much reliance on the recent may not give a fair view of the candidate's real understanding of theory.

Enough of the questions ask "why," say "discuss," or use other phrases to bring forth a few paragraphs of connected discourse, so that some opinion may be reached of the candidate's power of verbal expression. Continued pressure of this sort will have more effect in stimulating attention to ability to write clearly than all the complaining that public accountants could do in a decade.

Objective-minded accountants perhaps distrust their own grading of such answers. But it is no harder than judging a good letter written by another or a paragraph in a report. In the University we face this problem constantly and often meet it in this way: Grade only one question at a time. Make at least two trips through all papers on that question, first a quick scanning of the answer and a sorting of all papers into a few piles according to first impressions (excellent, poor, and probably two categories in between), and second, a careful reading of the papers in each pile with possible reclassification in mind and a reasonably consistent standard of quality (of answer *and* of writing) within each class. Being satisfied to that point, give all papers in one class the same, or nearly the same, grade on the question. After grading each question thus, re-sort one candidate's answers into his paper and recapitulate all questions to get the grade on his paper as a whole.

By 1946 (1896 plus 50) the examinations will, I hope, have outgrown their short pants and old-fashioned pattern to become—not a zoot suit of ultramodernism—but a well-tailored, well-fitted outfit that looks the part.

(personal correspondence, summer, 1943)

5. Admission to the Profession

Recent suggestions of useful provisions for consideration of state societies planning new CPA legislation reflects progressive leadership on the part of the Institute. Emphasis is given to procedures that look toward licensing public accountants and restricting public practice to them. Professional discipline is more directly described than is the case in present CPA laws. Ways are indicated for strengthening the educational basis of admission to the profession. It is suggested that the amount of practical experience required of examination applicants should be decreased as the amount of his formal and technical education increases.

A useful principle is expressed by these ideas. It is this: practical experience is more important as preparation for public practice than as a way of preparing for written technical examinations. Under this principle applicants who meet the stated requirements of technical education and graduation from college shall be entitled to be examined in theory, auditing, and law without having had prior practical experience. The examinations in accounting practice, however, would be open to these persons only after two years of accounting experience. No permit to practice would be issued without prior experience.

Thus the certificate, being based upon a technical examination, becomes evidence that the holder has demonstrated a satisfactory standard of knowledge. And the permit, resting in effect upon other qualifications, tends to become evidence that the applicant has satisfactory practical experience and maturity to constitute a basis for professional good judgment, and satisfactory character to form a basis for professional integrity. Breach of any of these three professional qualities—knowledge, judgment, character—justifies disciplinary action as outlined in the statute and as provided by the common law dealing with professional negligence. A permit to practice, therefore, is a necessary part of the pattern of public recognition of the profession and public control in the general interest.

Some may feel that the law proposed would be stronger, and more in line with the regulations governing other professions, if the experience requirement (comparable to medical internship) could be fulfilled if desired after passing all parts of the CPA examination.

This view may rest in part upon the thought that a requirement calling primarily for maturity and experience as the principal basis for admission to a test of knowledge might upon occasion serve as a means of holding down a desirable growth in the number of people in practice. But it should be noted that if there is no restraint by licensing, any number of people can engage in public practice regardless of what hurdles are set up for becoming a CPA. And the opinion may not be unfounded that the public will learn the usefulness of expert accounting services more rapidly from the existence of many qualified and authorized practitioners than from the practice of a sharply smaller number. Unless adequate growth in the profession occurs, the demand for expert services is very likely to outrun the number of practitioners so far that the public interest may not be well served.

In plain terms, this country could use qualified public accountants in greater numbers than current net increases are likely to produce. How else explain the persistent growth of self-styled experts? Is it not a fact that in 1913-15 one important consideration, among others, tending to prevent Federal Reserve Board rules from prescribing certification of statements in support of commercial paper for rediscount was the lack of enough qualified public accountants to do the work?

In comments by the Institute's committee it was pointed out that the provision for admitting to parts of the examination without prior experience candidates with a stated preparation should be regarded as optional. It should be optional in the sense that omission of this provision need not affect the decision to use other sections of the suggestion. However, it would be unfortunate if the comment should be construed as expressing a belief that such omission was generally desirable.

The possibility of separating practical accounting from the rest of the CPA examination, in the case of persons who have had adequate technical instruction in college, is a most constructive and progressive feature. It introduces in a very sensible way an American application of the idea of an intermediate and a final examination. Such a separation might perhaps benefit the applicant somewhat by dividing his prior preparation. But even greater benefit would come to the profession as a whole and to the public from the encouragement thus given to otherwise capable men who find a single, hard examination exhausting, to say the least.

(editorial, *Accounting Review*, October, 1945)

6. Candidate Preparation

Not infrequently 50 to 60 per cent of the candidates in a given CPA examination pass one or more papers in business law, accounting theory, and auditing, whereas 8 to 12 per cent pass in practical problems. These diverse results generate doubts and questioning. As might be expected, most of the doubts have two sides: the tests are too long—the candidates have not learned to work rapidly and effectively; the problems are made too hard by concealing or omitting essential information—the candidates have not learned to penetrate to the important aspects within an array of facts; the grading is too strict and "exclusionistic"—the candidates imagine that demonstration of a superficial knowledge should be sufficient.

No matter on which side of the fence one stands, these doubts, though common enough, do not get at the heart of the matter. The basic fact is that the sitters and the tests are not tuned to each other. This is a two-edged fact: most sitters are inadequately prepared for some parts but adequately prepared for others—admission to the examination or to part of it is not based upon reasonable evidence of a probable adequate preparation. In other words, candidates of all gradations of preparation and aptitude are mixed together for the same tests.

Most teachers would rebel at trying to test sophomores in accountancy and graduate students in accountancy by the same examination. If parts of the examination put the latter to a test, most sophomores would be bound to fail; if some parts are adopted to that group, these items would not be a real test for the graduate students. If both groups are forced into the same test, is the poor showing the fault of prior preparation? Or does the reason lie in the regulations which force us to attempt to do the unreasonable?

If some CPA papers are textbook subjects, as is sometimes said, they probably could be segregated and administered under regulations suited to the nature of the tests. If some papers are for testing candidates at the senior accountant level, these too could be administered separately under regulations suited to the nature of the tests.

If the CPA examination is not to remain frozen irrevocably in the mold of 1896, the allotment of topics covered should be extensively recast in harmony with modern conditions. If the examination topics named in the statute are beyond change because of the rigidity of statutory law, there would seem to be nothing to prevent giving the topics at examination time in any grouping that was desired, and nothing to prevent setting a suitable time interval between certain parts. Most statutes no doubt are already flexible enough to permit two days, or four days if necessary, to be devoted to screening tests in auditing, law, and theory; they probably are flexible enough to permit the board to suggest supplementary, voluntary aptitude tests also, if desired; they probably are flexible enough to permit exclusion of candidates from selected parts of the examination until a year has elapsed since passing the other parts, and until satisfactory practical experience is accumulated, if the latter had not been obtained earlier.

There is a great deal of flexibility in the present laws if it is sought out. No doubt all the usual topics could be given on two different levels, thus constituting two stages in giving professional qualifying tests. Some part of the "textbook, intermediate" examinations could very well consist of practical problems at a lower level than those used in the "final." Some of the "senior testing" could with reason include questions in auditing, law, and theory of a more advanced type than would be satisfactory in the "intermediate" test.

(editorial, Accounting Review, January, 1945)

7. Experience and Education

The fact that a few years of practical experience are held to be the principal test for admission to the CPA examination is likely to create a curiosity regarding the implied definition of the word "satisfactory." If the term is variously or vaguely used, the public may come to question whether experience, in actual cases, will be in fact experience that is broad enough to be really educational.

People may wonder what there is in a few years of accounting experience to educate a man for a technical accounting examination. Could three years of work, mostly with mechanical details as a junior assistant, do much to build up competence for solving CPA problems? Have the staff members with whom an applicant has worked for three years made a conscious effort to teach their art to the novice?

It surely cannot be that the mere passage of time in certain surroundings constitutes satisfactory experience for admission to an examination.

If a limited experience is made the principal basis for admission to a knowledge test, and if that experience does not of itself contribute reasonably to that knowledge, there is a serious inconsistency somewhere in many CPA laws.

Professor John Dewey points out that "no experience is educative that does not tend both to knowledge of more facts and entertaining of more ideas and to a better, a more orderly arrangement of them." The last phrase suggests what probably is the greatest weakness of learning by doing the day's work: the accumulation of facts and ideas does not follow an orderly pattern suitable to the act of learning.

If a limited experience is required not because of its educational features, is it then required as a protection to the public, as a hospital internship is required subsequent to a college degree in medicine? But without a requirement of prior accounting education, this required experience in accounting comes presumably at the beginning of accounting knowledge. How then can it protect the public?

Many times the importance of impressing the public that the public accountant deserves a real professional status is overlooked. Published and maintained standards of admission, especially in regard to educational preparation, become known to the public. To attorneys, judges, government officials, and members of the staffs of governmental agencies, among others, these standards offer evidence of an acceptable basis for professional status. Required experience cannot accomplish these results to the same degree.

An individual public accountant could earn a reputation for technical competence without statutory support. But statutory recognition is a tremendous aid to the creation of a body of men of tested skills. An individual public accountant can earn a high technical reputation regardless of his formal education. But statutory standards of education for admission are an immense aid to the growth of public confidence in the services of members of the profession. In all probability, as the profession prospers, so will the capable individual prosper.

Educational requirements for admission to CPA examinations in the early years were generally in harmony with the requirement (graduation from a four-year high school) that was the rule for the older professions of the day. It is of profound significance to accountancy that this comparability no longer exists. Accountancy has been left behind. And this has happened in a period marked by greatly increased social usefulness of accountancy and by new responsibilities for independent public accountants.

This condition may make thoughtful people wonder whether public accounting is going to miss the bus by not being ready for the trip.

Teachers are not alone in advocating higher education requirements in CPA laws. But they apparently form the only group which is generally agreed on the point. In taking that stand they are not actuated by motives

of personal advantage any more than practicing accountants are in clinging persistently to experience as the principal standard for admission of
their employees and others to the examination.

Teachers and practitioners both know that the issue is the welfare of
the profession, and that the broad public acceptance of public accounting
as a profession is involved. Fundamentally there should be only one possible area of disagreement—the speed with which the higher standards
should spread.

A slow approach has been evident for some years as the states adopted
regulations permitting candidates to substitute college education for part
of the required practical experience. Schoolmen recognize this as progress,
slow as it may be. They believe, however, and not without reason, that
the significance of education is greatly misunderstood when a college degree can be substituted for only one of five years of required experience,
or when the experience requirement is upped from three years to five so
that a college degree can upon occasion be substituted for two years of
practice.

Why not speed the recognition of the principle of giving credit for a
college education by turning the formula around? The basic requirement
for admission to the CPA examination could be a college degree with a
major in accountancy. The privilege then should attach of substituting a
given amount of practical experience if a degree had been earned in some
other field than accountancy, and of substituting still more practical experience if a person had no college experience of any kind. In addition,
and to protect the public, a requirement could be added that a person
successful in the CPA examination but lacking in minimum experience
would wait for certification until satisfactory experience had been accumulated.

(editorial, *Accounting Review,* January, 1945)

8. Examination Statistics

It is not easy to compile enlightening statistics of the results of CPA examinations. The simplest ratios are not always revealing; for example,
the ratio of certificates granted to total number of candidates sitting
usually seems discouragingly low. It is of interest, however, to note the
analysis of the results of ten Illinois examinations (May, 1939, to November, 1943) prepared by Professor Hale L. Newcomer and published in
the *Bulletin* of the Illinois Society for September, 1944. The essential
facts from that analysis, plus some additional details, are given here to
show that the elements of real significance often lie beneath the surface.

In ten examinations, 2,564 people (85 per cent of a total of 3,006) sat
for all parts, and 442 (15 per cent) sat for one or two parts as re-examination for a prior "condition" in some subjects. This latter percentage

calculated for each examination (but not in date order) gives the following: 22, 18, 17, 15, 14, 12, 12, 11, 9.

From the ten examinations, 536 certificates issued. Of this number, 252 (47 per cent) were a result of successful completion of all parts at one sitting; 284 (53 per cent) were a result of passing off a prior condition. Calculated for separate examinations (not in date order), the latter percentage shows the following: 74, 72, 71, 63, 60, 48, 44, 40, 39, 29.

Of 2,564 candidates sitting for all parts, 490 (19 per cent) were conditioned in one or two subjects under the board's rules and were therefore entitled to one re-examination in the subjects failed. A breakdown of the figure 490 shows that 284 candidates (58 per cent) later passed re-examination, that 158 (32 per cent) failed re-examination, and that 48 (10 per cent) had not been re-examined. Of the 490 conditioned, 442 sat for re-examination; of those re-examined, 284 (64 per cent) passed. Calculated by separate examinations this last percentage shows the following: 86, 76, 72, 66, 65, 62, 61, 56, 56, 46. (Note: The percentages at this point are not too reliable because the number re-examined in this period from a condition in the prior period is not known.)

Calculated on the basis of the 3,006 candidates sitting, 1,980 (66 per cent) failed (1,822, or 61 per cent, failing all parts; 158, or 5 per cent, failed in re-examination); 536 (17 per cent) passed (252, or 8 per cent passing all parts; 284 or 9 per cent, passing re-examination). The percentages here must remain incomplete because 4 per cent of the total were conditioned and some of this number are also in the 284 who passed re-examination.

Judging from these results, re-examination after a condition in some subjects seems to be a rough sort of final examination following what for a number of people was in effect an intermediate examination. How then would the above results appear if considered as the returns from an intermediate and a final examination?

Those passing all parts can be assumed to have passed those parts which might have been serving as an intermediate, or screening, examination. They numbered 252. The candidates who were conditioned can also be assumed to have passed the parts being used as a screening examination. They numbered 490. Together these produce a total of 742 for the ten examinations, or about 25 per cent of the 3,006 sitting.

If these figures resulted from tests set up as screening examinations, presumably based primarily on textbook materials, the results would seem low indeed. In college practice no examination having such results would be considered as suited to the students allowed to take it. Or perhaps 75 per cent of the students were not prepared. In either case some modification would be necessary, probably a better selection of those having a reasonable presumption of suitable preparation, and also a searching reorientation of the examination materials so that they would unquestionably constitute a fair test of the preparation deemed suitable.

If the above results follow in the main from inadequate preparation, as examiners often contend, certain questions may be asked. Should we continue to admit the unprepared and let a very high percentage of initial failures convince the overambitious that they are not prepared? Should we seek ways and means of improving the preparation of those deserving to sit by doing a better job of teaching accounting in the classroom and in the field? Should we set up new standards of admission to the examination (separate from standards for admission to public practice) in order to screen those poorly prepared for whatever reason from taking even an intermediate examination until they had qualified in some suitable manner? Should each CPA examination be offered in two sections, one consisting of tests redesigned to harmonize reasonably well with adequate candidate preparation, thus passing a normal 50 per cent to 60 per cent?

(editorial, Accounting Review, January, 1945)

9. Intermediate Examinations

Consideration might well be given to the thought that admission to the profession of public accounting should rest upon a graded series of qualifying tests. The intention would be to test progressively the knowledge of professional aspirants.

At least a high school education has now come to be generally required for admission to the CPA examination. Hence there is no need for a "preliminary" examination in this general subject matter. An examination interposed between high school graduation and the CPA examination would therefore be in the nature of an "intermediate" examination on the way toward professional status, or it could be considered as an "admission" examination preceding the CPA test.

In order to implement this approach the CPA laws should require: (1) graduation with a degree from a college program that included among other subjects at least twenty semester hours of accountancy and twelve of closely allied subjects (such as economics, finance, business administration, commercial law, etc.), and (2) a grade average in that program which was, in the opinion of the authorities of the college in question, at least 25 per cent above the minimum required for graduation.

Two substitutes should be made available for applicants who could not meet this standard. The first substitute could be a degree with a similar grade average in a program that did not include accountancy and commerce courses, provided that such general education had later been supplemented by at least thirty-two semester hours of courses of college grade in accountancy and closely allied subjects as above. The second substitute could be a "CPA Admission Examination" for those who could not satisfy the second educational standard or its first substitute.

Admission to this qualifying examination would be extended: (1) to those who had more than two years of college work but less than the amount required for a bachelor's degree; (2) to those whose grade average was lower than the standard stated above in the second educational hurdle; (3) to those whose bachelor's degree in general subjects had not been supplemented by enough accredited courses in accountancy and allied subjects to qualify them under the first substitute above; and (4) to those who had less than two years of college work, provided these applicants had had six years of business experience.

When psychological tests of aptitude for professional public accounting work have reached a satisfactory stage of development, they might also be given at this point to furnish supplementary evidence of desirable qualifications.

This CPA admission examination would preferably be a three-day session using about six different papers on subject matter generally included in the junior and senior years of a college of commerce or school of business which offers an accounting major. As an example of possible subdivision, the examination might require three-hour papers in the following subjects:

(1) general and cost accounting

(2) auditing and income tax

(3) commercial law

(4) business administration (financial management, production management, marketing management)

(5) finance (money, credit and banking; public finance; taxation)

(6) economics (general economic theory)

Such examinations should be nationwide and perhaps would best be given on the same date at a number of universities. The questions should be prepared by a joint committee consisting of several members of the American Institute of Accountants and several members of the American Accounting Association, representing the accounting teachers. The grading of the papers probably should be entrusted to college commerce teachers in local committees integrated with the CPA examining boards of several states.

(editorial, *Accounting Review*, October, 1943)

10. Planned Examinations

If "admission" examinations were in use which tested applicants on accounting and related subjects at the level of juniors and seniors in a college of commerce, the CPA examination itself could become a "final" examination set on a still higher level as a further testing of professional qualifications.

There should be two avenues of entrance to this examination: (1) either a college degree including substantial studies in accountancy, or satisfactory grade in a "CPA admission examination"; or (2) ten years of satisfactory public accounting experience as attested either by letters of assurance of satisfactory service in the offices of certified public accountants and/or by letters of assurance of satisfactory service from ten clients of an applicant who had been in public practice on his own account.

In organization of subject matter this professional examination should break with the precedents of half a century of CPA examinations. Its questions and problems should be grouped along functional lines. This would amount to the subdivision of testing materials into numerous topical papers. Each topic would soon come to be recognized (1) as testing a specific area of accounting knowledge, (2) as providing an opportunity to demonstrate specific types of technical skills, or (3) as giving occasion for expressing personal judgments on professional matters.

The following topics are offered to indicate the possibilities of using this method of exploring a candidate's preparation. An examination extending over three days could provide possibly six sessions of four hours each. A dozen testing areas are listed below. To include them all and to give each one equal weight would limit the time to two hours for writing each paper. Probably that time would usually be sufficient. But enough flexibility should be permitted in constructing the examination to permit three-hour papers and one-hour papers to be given at times in certain topics. Some topics could occasionally be omitted, provided this practice was not repeated in such a manner as to change the general pattern of the test.

TOPICAL AREAS FOR TESTING

Systems and Administrative Accounting
Problems of Income Taxation
Theory Aspects of Income Determination
Valuation Theory and Application
Requirements of Regulatory Bodies
Financial Statement Preparation
Verification Procedures
Alternative Practices in Accounting and Auditing
Standards of Internal Control and Audit
Analytical Techniques and Interpretive Problems
Professional Ideals and Responsibilities
Technical Writing

By wishful thinking in this way we can see how things might look if we took a fresh start. Examiners have certain definable objectives; traditional ways are not necessarily best ways of meeting the objectives. Examinations are not satisfactory if they are designed and graded mainly for "knocking off" many candidates. They are made up satisfactorily only when their content over a period of time epitomizes the knowledge and skills that actually form an essential part of the work of professional accountants. If installment liquidation of partnership affairs, for example, is today an infinitesimal part of professional accountants' practice, it is difficult to justify long problems on that subject in present-day examinations. On the other hand, if a part of nearly every day's work consists of technical writing wherein words and phrases have to be carefully weighed, it is highly illogical not to test the candidate in this skill.

In a sense this outline is another approach to the idea of a *planned examination*. It carries the implications that the starting point for professional examinations is not the years of experience of the applicant or the ingenuity of the examiner in baffling the candidate. The starting point for preparing examinations is a broad and comprehensive view of the qualities and knowledge a professional man should possess, and a lively realization of the current status of educational development. The examination should be consciously designed to test the candidates accordingly. The ideal is not how difficult, but how revealing, the test will be.

One may be led to wonder, amid the pressures arising in the present, whether the profession might not be better off today if in the past twenty years about 20 per cent more men had passed through the CPA examination to enrich their demonstrated foundation of knowledge and skill through subsequent experience. Wherein would the profession have suffered if this had been done? One may wonder, too, whether continued testing along established lines, and at the established rates of mortality, may not react unfavorably upon the profession in the next twenty years when the social responsibilities of public accountants will have greatly increased.

If professional examinations have to serve not only as a technical test but as a screening test as well, the proportion of failures is sure to be high, and many men of promise are likely to be lost whom other methods might have salvaged. A good deal of "screening" should precede the professional tests rather than constitute a part of them. And there should be a high degree of correlation between professional examinations and professional education—each one influencing the other, each one being conducted with conscious consideration of the other.

(*Accounting Review*, October, 1943)

11. Selective Screening

Scattered along the avenues of entrance into professional public accounting are a number of hurdles which test the aspirant's fitness to serve the public in that capacity. This is so, not because a spirit of monopolistic exclusiveness actuates men already in public practice, but because the longer that public practice exists, the greater becomes the conviction that public interest requires ever higher qualifications in accounting practitioners. Hence the hurdles along the way.

One of the most important qualifications for public practice is aptitude. Yet very little is known about the content of the term. Is it not time that some study be given to the questions of what aptitudes to look for, how to recognize signs of latent aptitude, how to distinguish real from pseudo-aptitudes?

Teachers would like to know some of the answers so that they can advise students as the opportunity arises. They can hardly deny graduation to a man who demonstrates knowledge and understanding because they think some personal trait indicates lack of aptitude. But they could advise him. Practitioners would like to see some indicators of aptitude so that they could recruit new members of their staffs more confidently. Those who aspire to the profession, perhaps more than any others, would like to learn something about their own aptitudes.

One of the hurdles along the road is a college education. It is of interest to note that this particular hurdle has appeared naturally and with little or no legislative pressure. Only one state at this time requires graduation from college for admission to the CPA examination. Yet in a recent period of seven months almost three-fourths of 466 new members and associates admitted to the American Institute of Accountants were college graduates. This hurdle is principally a test of survival, of capacity for intellectual growth, of ability to learn. The CPA examination, on the other hand, is designed to sample the content of the candidate's technical knowledge, however that knowledge may have been acquired.

Practical experience is another hurdle. This one is deliberately placed in the path, but the reason is not the one usually presumed. It is not because working experience is now considered a preferred way of gaining knowledge, but because the public interest requires that the public practitioner have more than knowledge. This hurdle subjects the aspirant to a test of ability to work with people and under direction, of ability to orient his knowledge effectively to a situation at hand, of ability to learn from observation without getting lost in the deep forest of a multitude of facts.

None of these tests would be adequate alone. Together they are reassuring; but they are not final. A man may be a college graduate and a CPA of considerable experience, and still be unsuited in temperament, personality, and other qualities for public practice—that is, a man with good training, but without aptitude. All along the road there is need for some kind of practical, dependable aptitude tests.

Could tests be devised that might help a man to decide whether he could probably benefit in college from a study of more than the usual introductory course in general accounting, that might help him to decide at the end of his college work whether he should prepare for the CPA examination, that might help employers to decide whether to provide the individual with the needed experience and guidance in furtherance of his preparation for serving the public as a professional accountant? If such tests could be constructed, they would be useful in many ways. If aptitude tests can be devised to help distinguish a man who is best qualified to become a pilot of an airplane from one best qualified to become an air navigator, surely tests could be constructed that would detect latent capability suitable for the work of a public accountant.

Professional men probably "know what they like" in the way that many people react to music. But it would help all concerned if they could more closely identify the desired qualities. It would be even more helpful if teachers and practitioners, with the aid of experienced psychologists, could produce a method of identifying certain personal qualities in objective ways, so that college records of classroom results could be supplemented with additional information, although not as part of graduating requirements, and so that personnel records in accountants' offices might contain data beyond the vital statistics of the individual, a transcript of his college record, and the vague impressions of personality that come out of an interview.

A number of tests could perhaps be devised and tried on experienced accountants in an experimental way. Those tests that seemed most revealing could then be subjected to further observation by using them experimentally with young men recently accepted for professional work and still under training and scrutiny, and by using them experimentally upon college students who wish to major in accountancy and may later be further observed in class and office.

On the other hand, it may be impossible to obtain any agreement as to the aptitudes desired. Elaborate tests would hardly be warranted if the qualifications were simply to be "good at figures," or if the employer were content with his own appraisal of an applicant's personality, once he knew his scholastic rating in college. Or it may be impossible to detect by psychological tests the aptitudes which underlie the capacity to grow professionally.

But if it could be done! If we could learn enough about aptitudes, is it not very probable that we could learn how aptitudes could be improved by teaching and training? Or is aptitude something that cannot be changed by any means? Many people would like to know.

(editorial, *Accounting Review*, July, 1943)

12. Usefulness of Aptitude Tests

A committee on selection of personnel was established by the American Institute of Accountants in 1943. It is clear that vocational counseling and recruiting in the profession would work best if it rested upon factual evidence of the individual's capabilities. The committee is developing a relevant project which has three stated purposes: (1) "To define the mental and personal qualities which make for success in professional accounting"; (2) "To develop in collaboration with educational institutions, a procedure whereby promising young men may be discovered and guided toward the profession and their progress appraised at regular intervals"; (3) "To establish a battery of tests and supplementary techniques for use in evaluating the qualities which are important for professional accountants."

This type of examination technique may prove so fruitful and dependable that its use may in time be expanded beyond its association with educational counseling and recruiting of staff personnel. Some part of it, for example, might be found to be a reliable pre-examination indicator that an applicant was ready to sit in the CPA examination with a reasonable expectation of success. Then it might be useful as a voluntary adjunct to the usual technical state examinations. If this status is acceptable, it could become a part of the Institute's service to state boards of examiners.

The candidate's score would be significant collateral data for the board, the employer, and the person himself. Possibly it might gradually evolve to the point where it could be adopted by state boards as part of their admission rules, in somewhat the same way that technical education is now gradually becoming part of the admission rules.

The wide use of these national vocational tests, besides providing directly useful data to applicant and employer, could become a means for drawing the schools and the profession toward improved mutual understanding. In the profession there are pressing problems involving recruiting of competent personnel, raising standards of professional service to the public, securing public recognition of the professional aspects of public accounting. In the colleges of commerce there is the ever-present problem of adequately preparing students for careers which the students themselves have not yet chosen.

Public accounting is not so well known that, as with medicine and law, students will make an early choice of that field for their career. Since students are undecided, it is part of the teacher's logical function impartially to help students make a decision. This testing service could be of considerable service here.

But the profession must take the lead in selling itself to the public for service and to prospective employees for careers—and then make good on both counts. The profession cannot expect all the best students to be channeled in one direction; and it should not expect all who major in accounting to be aiming at public practice. Many students plan to enter private accounting, and many others recognize accounting courses as providing good education for the managerial positions in business they are seeking.

The realization will grow that the study of accounting can prove highly useful in the education of lawyers and economists, among others. It would speed the day of this realization if accounting teachers would give effect, in concrete ways, to the fact that for mature students in fields like law and economics whose study of accounting is at best a minor matter, the usual slow approach to accounting through bookkeeping techniques is entirely inappropriate.

But the schoolmen's dilemmas are not ended when students choose to major in accounting. There is a duty running both to the individual and to the profession of educating these accounting majors broadly rather than narrowly. It is a major educational problem—and professional men should lend a hand in the solution—to unite satisfactorily a suitable general education and a suitable technical education. A good many, perhaps most, university departments are under criticism these days as fostering a program which is suitable only for a person who has chosen that particular field as his particular specialization. This being the case, men in the profession should not expect too much specialization in the colleges. But they would be wise to ask that their recruits should have had some instruction in accounting.

These vocational tests may not be of much help to this school problem of how much specialization is too much. But when ample data accumulate from the results of the tests, it should be somewhat easier to see how to improve the quality of whatever amount of technical education is decided upon.

Data from these tests can be expected to help the profession in making some of its choices as well as the schoolmen in making theirs. Educational alternatives already are under consideration.

The profession may ultimately choose to fill most of its staff needs by using people with a good deal of general education, expecting technical education to be accumulated in the field and privately outside of office hours. Some people are now inclined to think highly of this approach.

The profession may ultimately choose to lend organized support to the idea of purely professional accounting schools. These might rest on a base of four years or two years or no years of general college education, and may include little or no adequate contact with subject matter that is often considered closely allied to accountancy, such as economics, finance, management, and business law.

Or the profession may come to a middle-of-the-road conclusion that the best is a combined program that thoroughly mixes throughout four college years general education, commercial education, and accounting education.

All these programs will be tried. Differing philosophies of education will be in competition. Each school and each graduate will be convinced his way is the best. How can sound conclusions be reached? Shall dependence be given to personal reactions, or shall factual aids be called upon to help produce a good long-range judgment of the alternative?

It is here that the accumulating data from these vocational tests may prove unexpectedly helpful. Already available are published curricula reflecting differing educational policies; and there are the transcripts of individual records reflecting a single person's program content and college grades. These data alone are hardly a satisfactory gauge of either the individual or the school. The test scores, by individuals and by schools, would add significantly to the means of judging both.

When all accumulated data have been studied in connection with a sound plan for a graded rating of professional success, it might ultimately appear that the future of an individual was reasonably well foreshadowed by (1) educational content, (2) scholarship standing in college, (3) vocational test results, when this evidence was interpretatively combined with an adequate appraisal of personality factors.

(Accounting Review, October, 1946)

13. Testing for Mental Qualities

In any program of testing for aptitudes appropriate for professional accountants it will be desirable to see clues to answers to the question: How well are the mental qualities of the individual oriented toward the work of an accountant? Such a question would usually test the applicant regarding "linguistic" ability. It does not deal, as might be supposed, with foreign languages or extemporaneous speaking, but rather with simple word-power and comprehension—with the ability to differentiate meanings, to call up useful associated ideas. It also puts him to test regarding "quantitative ability." This is not so much speed in arithmetic as power to perceive interconnection of ideas and relationships that are expressed in numbers.

Everyone whose work is above a purely routine level needs some linguistic ability and some quantitative ability. And tests of this sort therefore have a broad and general usefulness. But for prospective accountants they have special significance when cast in forms clearly relevant to an accountant's life and work.

The accountant needs some linguistic ability because often he must follow fairly complex discussions intelligently, and because he must forcefully clothe his ideas in words to reach another's understanding. Yet verbal language is not the accountant's medium of expression in the sense that it is for the poet or novelist. His medium is figures rather than words. More than that, figures constitute the principal material he must work with before he undertakes to convey his ideas to other people. Hence for the accountant figures are both a material to be understood and a medium for bringing understanding to others. Most of his energies, in study and in practice, are devoted to penetrating the meaning embedded in an organized mass of figures, and in translating that meaning to others' minds through compactly rearranged masses of figures. That is why a purely theoretical study of accounting ideas cannot alone constitute accounting education. Incidentally, that is also the reason why economic statistics and investment analysis are such good collateral studies for accounting students.

A good deal of planning throughout the whole educational system is directed toward developing verbal and quantitative abilities in the students. And since the cumulative benefit to the student is measurable, it should be assessed both for his own use, for the school, and for the subsequent employer.

It will be clear that the schools can use these materials to advantage. As an aid in counseling they should be distinctly worth while. Students would benefit in that they would be helped to fit in better; and the schools should benefit from the students' improvement. Most students entering college are undecided regarding their future career. Hence most schools of business stress instruction in widely useful general business subjects and give relatively less emphasis to specialization. These tests of mental qualities should be useful in helping students to an early choice among whatever fields of study the college of commerce may offer.

But this benefit may not be without its price in administrative difficulties to overcome. The class periods needed may present a problem for some of the advanced or achievement tests. Perhaps equivalent time in larger groups outside of class could be substituted. But even that raises questions. Would voluntary attendance introduce a bias into the sample by failing to reveal the adequacies or inadequacies in ability of the absentees? If accounting orientation tests are required of all students, would conflicts develop from other departments wanting their own testing programs? Would required attendance for an orientation test be criticized as duplicating existing testing programs, such as freshman placement tests? Perhaps these difficulties may not arise in most situations, or they will disappear after a reasonable amount of local adjustment.

The Institute's project for selection of personnel will touch accountancy itself in a series of "achievement tests," some of which will soon be available at cost to schools and public accountants.

These tests are designed for use at three levels.

I. At the end of the student's first year of the study of accountancy. Using accounting subject matter and standardized, objective, multiple-choice questions, Level I achievement test will enable the student to demonstrate his group of fundamental accounting ideas. For convenience of administration, selections of the material will be prepared in separate booklets of a length suitable for the typical classroom period of forty-five or fifty minutes.

II. (a) At the end of the major sequence in accounting, that is, at or near the time of graduation of college seniors with a major in accounting. (b) At the time of employment on the staff of a public accountant. The material in the Level II achievement test is more advanced and professional in character than that in Test I and will require more time to write. It, like the Level I test, will be available in sectional booklets and will use multiple-choice questions rather than the CPA type of problems.

For both of these achievement tests, national norms will eventually be determined for use as a bench mark in gauging the scores made by individuals or groups. Norms for Level II tests will be separately established for college seniors, junior staff assistants, semisenior assistants and senior accountants.

III. At the expiration of about four years on the staff of a public accountant. The Level III achievement test is planned to be used at about the time the staff man should be ready for the CPA examination. It might, therefore, have added usefulness as a "pre-CPA indicator."

(Accounting Review, October, 1946)

PROFESSIONAL RESPONSIBILITIES

1. Technology and Profession

Is public accounting a business? By what tests? If it is a technology, by what tests? What tests would indicate that it is a profession? Each view deserves a hearing.

Here are some suggestions. Perhaps a clue may be found in the type and extent of educational preparation considered necessary in the three fields. Special preparation might seem to apply, in ascending order, to a business, a technology, a profession. A clue may appear in the kind and degree of public recognition that the public welfare is in some way involved. Public recognition (by setting standards, restricting activities, etc.) might seem to apply in ascending order to a business, a technology, a profession.

Another clue may be seen in the attitude which persons directly concerned have toward their status and their responsibilities. The following small sample of the views of leaders in public accounting during recent years may be of interest in this connection.

"Whether he likes it or not, the professional public accountant frequently is required to appraise the activities, the transactions of others, and say what he thinks, let the chips fall where they may!" "Once a public accountant's independence is impaired . . . his usefulness as an interpreter among conflicting interests is at an end." "We must be no more subject to influence by governmental authority than by the desires of management." "The work of the public accountant is widely recognized as being heavily weighted with public interest . . . our value to the economy and our great postwar opportunity for service lies in our ability to serve as impartial interpreters of the financial results of corporate operations." "The largest part of the function of an accountant is discharge of obligations to a public with whom he never comes into contact, often against pressure from people who are able to affect his interests quite extensively." "In all the world there is no ethical requirement quite like that placed on the public accountant. He must be the judge of his employer in the interest of people he does not know, and he must take no profit from knowledge that comes to him in his confidential capacity."

The views quoted show that leaders in public accounting are keenly aware of the public interest involved in a profession. They are speaking, it may safely be assumed, not as individuals, but in an effort to make articulate the unspoken convictions of their colleagues. One does not become a member of a profession by thinking himself so; nor does group assertion of professional status create the condition asserted. But if consciousness of professional characteristics is not in the minds of the practitioners, there is no profession, legislation to the contrary notwithstanding.

It is reassuring to see such clear reflections of professional consciousness. The public accountant has a high social function to perform as well as a direct obligation to serve the client. He is not a public accountant merely in offering his services to the public generally; nor because he has qualified by passing examinations and being publicly proclaimed, as it were. He is a public accountant because his work for clients often has a public aspect beyond the client. He must be independent or he is not "public" in this sense; he must be judicially minded or he is poorly equipped to discharge his public function; he must do his work under disciplined self-control or he may fail to meet his responsibilities in a satisfactory manner.

Over the years a wide array of professional techniques have been devised that are as useful in carrying out the auditor's high social function as they are in serving the client. His social responsibilities have lately been enlarged and accepted. His position as an intermediary is not new, a creation of modern responsibilities. Centuries ago his prototype stood between the nobleman and the bailiffs who managed the estate; today he is ready to "stand between" whenever his technical competence and independent status make his experience or judgment useful.

When a public accountant finally accepts a large corporation's income statement, he may not be fully conscious of the intricate and extensive community of interest behind the figures. But he is keenly alive to the necessity for a thoroughly dependable, understandable presentation, and he is prepared to see that the statement is just that. He is interpreter-moderator by profession, not by employment.

(editorial, *Accounting Review,* October, 1944)

2. Responsibility for Education

A degree is an academic ranking or station granted by action of an educational body. This has never been characteristic of the CPA certificate. In New York the law is administered by the central educational authority of the state; in Illinois the law is administered by the state university. But in neither case has "CPA" been considered to symbolize an academic degree.

A license is an authorization to do particular acts not permitted to all. This term is closer to the idea inherent in the CPA certificate. A certified public accountant is a public accountant who has been vouched for as having met certain qualifications. But because "particular acts" permitted to CPA's alone have not been given much legislative recognition, the certificate is generally something less than a full license. This may be because accounting is still in evolution—gradually growing toward a type of public service that will be widely recognized as deserving: (1) restriction of practice in the public interest and (2) restriction of entrance to those having an adequate educational preparation.

In the field of medicine the two elements are clearly separated: practice is restricted to those qualifying under the statute; authorization to practice, through a separate action, rests upon an educational base—a university medical degree plus hospital experience. But that kind of professional status was not quickly achieved. Neither will full professional status be quickly achieved for public accounting. But many times there will be ways of aiding the trend in the desired direction.

In the first period of the profession's development in the United States, the initial difficulty to be overcome was that of getting any kind of statutory recognition whatever. The next task was to spread that recognition throughout all states and territories. We took what recognition we could get. It was little enough: a right to the exclusive use of a distinctive title. It was not a degree following upon an educational program; it was not a license to engage in restricted activities. It was only a statutory toe hold.

After some years, perhaps a generation, the first period began to fade into the second. A few states began to recognize that restriction was in fact in the public interest and not a monopolistic dodge, as state legislatures were often persuaded was the case. Under restriction the public ultimately would be served only by certified public accountants. Strangely enough, that idea was not well supported by CPA's themselves. But some progress toward the inevitable was made nevertheless.

Another feature of the second period of evolution was the gradual adoption of the device of accepting college education in partial satisfaction of the usual practical experience requirement. It was a sort of back-door approach to the outright requirement of higher education for admission to the examination, or a way of avoiding a forthright acceptance of the idea of a "preliminary examination."

Rules granting conditional re-examination have come to have somewhat the same effect as an "intermediate" examination. Probably this development constitutes a tacit admission that the profession might be suffocated for want of sufficient new blood if the certificates continued to go only to those who, without being otherwise forced into adequate preparation, could succeed in passing all parts of a long and stiff examination at one sitting.

This second period therefore is characterized by the formulation of various kinds of rules which attempt to satisfy the growing belief that the public interest clearly requires restriction of practice to those shown to be specially qualified to serve, and the belief that formal education should be accepted as the principal first step toward qualifying for the profession.

This is the stage of our evolution we are in at present. The length of the period can easily be stretched out a generation or more into the future if inertia holds many sections of the profession immobile. On the other hand, a good start has been made; the pattern for development is known. If energetically followed up, the start can easily bring the profession to its third period without unusual delay.

In the third period there would be wide public acceptance of the professional standards that were so tentatively viewed in the second period. And there would be clear-cut statutory recognition of the ideas which as rules had proved their worth in earlier experience. As a result, standards of admission to examination and to public practice would be properly differentiated; standards of testing at various levels of preparation would be carefully devised and followed; quality of service to the public would be on an upward spiral; and the demand for accountant services would exceed anything we can imagine now.

(editorial, Accounting Review, January, 1945)

3. Aid for Small Practitioners

It has been said that "accounting has developed from a service department to become a social force." Implicit in this thought is the idea that public accountants are aware they must accept new obligations to society as their technology becomes a social force. They have clearly accepted the duty to bring qualified people into the profession. The support given to university education in the subject and to the work of providing suitable technical examinations and of fostering effective legislation is a part of this activity. So too, is the stress now placed upon selective recruiting and the development of a program of personnel testing.

It is also a social obligation, as well as sound firm policy, to aid staff people to attain full competence. To this end some firms provide special training for beginners and diversify the experience as an aid to their professional growth. Much more could be accomplished in this area if staff educational activities were as systematically developed for seniors and as widely used as is staff training for beginners.

Is there not another social obligation—that of helping qualified men who wish to establish a small independent practice? These small firms, located for the most part in the smaller business communities, would often prove to be missionaries for good accounting in business. That would be good for the profession as a whole. They would perform much-needed services in their communities. That would be good for the communities individually and collectively. Does the man with a small practice and only a few assistants get as much help as he deserves from the state and national accounting organizations? How could the man who wishes to practice in his own name be given a helpful hand without doing violence to professional ethics?

Questions like these were put to several certified public accountants practicing in smaller towns. Their suggestions and a few ideas of the writer are combined to form the outline of the paragraphs that follow.

Local businessmen outside the larger industrial cities realize only vaguely how a public accountant can help them. Could they not be informed in a suitable manner of the services professional accountants offer? Perhaps this might be done effectively through articles in trade journals. This would enable the authors to give a definite trade slant to the described services of accountants. Brief case histories (identities concealed) of the way external accountants had proved helpful would be a very useful kind of material. Reprints could be made available to small firms in a position to serve local clients in the same line as the trade journal. Such articles should make it a point to explain the preparation and testing a public accountant must undertake, and outline the professional and statutory discipline under which he does his work.

Such aids as these would seem to be within the power and spirit of the American Institute of Accountants.

The state societies could do even more. Through suitable committees they could publish the names and addresses of qualified (registered-certified) local accountants available to serve a group of neighboring counties. They could survey their state for communities whose probable accounting needs were provided for inadequately.

Committees could supply occasional accountant speakers before local service clubs, or provide speech outlines for local accountants to build upon; they could make reading recommendations on matters likely to be of concern in local practice, make known the names of men or firms having specialized experience, and invite local practitioners to avail themselves of an opportunity to consult with these men regarding appropriate local problems.

There are various barriers between public accountants and certified public accountants. Some of these could be removed in the public interest. There are distinctions between them that cannot be bridged merely by goodwill; and the public should be well informed of the statutory qualifications demonstrated by one and not by the other. Yet, as regulatory legislation spreads and both groups are licensed to practice, they both will come to understand that their basic interests are not antagonistic; that they very seldom are in actual competition; that useful needed services are performed by men who do not have certificates. It would be better for all parties, and for the community, if these practitioners became better acquainted.

Why not grant licensed but uncertified public accountants guest memberships in the state society? Why not aid in the formation of "county chapters," so that licensed practitioners, whether certified or not, would be encouraged to meet occasionally in friendship to exchange experiences? Several neighboring counties could be grouped for this purpose so that the number of people attending would not be too small. These "chapters" could also become the site of occasional joint meetings with the state society of certified public accountants. Men with local practices would learn much from those having broader experience, and men from the larger firms would find most local practitioners to be men of sound professional ideals and considerable competence. Perhaps several useful joint committees could be formed through which interim contact could be maintained. It is not impossible that aid and advice would encourage many to prepare for the CPA examination who otherwise would not make the effort.

Professional men naturally have a strong constructive imagination. If they put their mind to the problem in the state societies, more and better ideas would no doubt emerge than have been suggested here.

Can the large firms help to vitalize professional accounting further by lending aid and encouragement to the development of local services? Several things could be tried; some of them might prove very constructive.

If a staff man thinks he would like to develop an independent local practice his first questions will probably include these: Do I have the necessary qualifications? Where is there a promising location? How do I go about getting a foothold?

Members of the firm could canvass questions like these in advance and formulate a planned approach to helping the man who indicates that he wants a local practice. The qualifications, they could point out, probably would include ease in making friends with strangers, since creating a good impression is probably more important in meeting one's own prospective clients than it is in beginning a new assignment already contracted by the firm. A willingness to perform small services cheerfully and well will be desirable; those frequently develop into more substantial engagements. In some ways a young attorney has an advantage; he can expect to pick up numerous small fees; but small-fee work is not yet customary in public accounting. There are not very many full-program audits in most smaller communities. But when the businessmen there gain confidence in the local professional accountant they will furnish more small engagements than a staff man familiar with large engagements would expect. Incidentally, it may be found that most local attorneys and bankers would prefer that the income tax returns their clients now bring them should be prepared by competent accountants.

Where to locate is certain to be a problem. It need not be in virgin territory that has no accountant servicing it, provided the potential need is greater than the available service. But in any event a location will not be easy to choose. Experienced partners should be able to suggest survey procedures for their man to try. Volume of general business by localities, figures on industrial production, bank clearings, taxable property, post office receipts, etc. might furnish some initial clues. As the field is narrowed, vacation visits to several possible locations should prove helpful. A study of the local telephone book would reveal the available public accounting services, and might often afford a quick insight into the diversity of local enterprises.

Are there any further ways in which the firm could help after these preliminaries have been settled? It would seem that there are. For example, the partners could hold open the possibility of a return to the staff within a certain time limit in case the venture turned sour. They could underwrite a living-expense loan to be drawn upon during the man's first year alone, when, as, and if needed, to be repaid from early fees. They could sometimes induce a few smaller clients to transfer their accounts to the new practitioner; they could refer requests from new local clients to local practitioners; they often might be able to use the new man as a local representative of the firm; they could encourage the local man to consult the firm on technical matters, program advice, and the like during his early years of practice on his own account.

Assistance of this kind would be invaluable to the new practitioner. It would make him a friend and booster for life; and it would make a real contribution in expanding the services of accounting.

If it will help to keep America a strong and democratic republic to assist tenant farmers of demonstrated ability to become the owners of farms, and to assist capable mechanics and others of suitable experience to start their own small businesses, then it would seem to be a public service in more ways than one for the organized profession to offer concrete and practical help to qualified individuals desiring to establish a small accounting practice.

(editorial, *Accounting Review*, April, 1946)

4. Gradations of Qualities

Scattered through the literature are numerous discussions of the qualifications deemed important in independent public accountants. Yet in no one place have these qualities been outlined in terms of the different levels of public accountant employment. In building an expanding organization, a firm necessarily faces many problems in selecting members of the staff. As a firm grows, the analogy tends to weaken between a public accountant and one who, like a physician, renders personal service direct.

As the accountant's staff increases, a better analogy is the medical corps of an army in the field: gradation of responsibility becomes necessary; recognition of variations in abilities is essential; establishment of lines of consultation and control is unavoidable. A principal and an assistant can do only a limited amount of work; a staff of juniors, seniors, and partners can do much more.

Later it will be advisable, as the firm grows, to insert other ranks in the sequence, such as semisenior after junior, and manager between senior and partner. Gradations above senior rating may be further indicated by the terms supervisor, manager, principal, junior partner, resident partner, senior partner, consulting partner.

A generalized description of occupational levels can become a means of showing staff men what lies ahead of them professionally as to expected qualities. Such descriptions would clearly imply that advancement is by merit; that no one expects to reach a higher rating without having fully met the responsibilities of the next preceding rank; that step-by-step progress can be a strong educational force; that planned self-development is a vital supplement to an accumulation of experience; that much of the preparation for facing future responsibilities comes from use of off-duty time.

It is to be noted that the different levels of accounting work are not in fact so sharply defined as the following outline might seem to suggest. The work at any one level blends at the borders with the work below and above. And various personal qualities usually extend well beyond the work levels where they are first mentioned. Men in the lower ratings would be expected to show in some degree the rudiments of many of the qualities which, when matured and polished, are important to men in the higher ranks.

Junior Assistant. The qualities desired in a junior assistant are only partly related to his immediate duties. They are also foundations for future occupational growth. The best assistant will have a good attitude towards his work; will be energetic, industrious, and conscientious in his assigned tasks. He will need to be patient with masses of details and somewhat of a perfectionist in his striving for correctness. He needs stamina for long working hours in season. There is particular need for holding in confidence information coming to his attention. A strong elemental curiosity is desirable—a wish to understand the reasons for his tasks. But if he is overassertive or too opinionated he will stand in his own light and perhaps cast a shadow on the firm as well. Highly important is a dependable capacity to grow, that is, to grasp instructions, to remember procedures, to apply technical knowledge to the situations at hand, to learn when to make decisions on his own and when to ask advice.

Semisenior. He needs further development of the qualities listed for junior assistant, as well as new ones related to his present and prospective responsibilities. He will be expected to show increasing capacity for intelligently grasping instructions and for asking advice when needed but not where it is within his competence to decide. His deepening insight into the usefulness, or limitations, of specific auditing techniques will give him an increasing pride of craftsmanship..

There is need also for further developing the audit type of curiosity begun as a junior. This requires alertness of mind and a suitable power of imagination. Personality also becomes increasingly important; the semisenior must be able to work effectively under varying conditions and with different kinds of people. Since he sometimes supervises the work of others, qualities of friendly leadership must appear. And since he is now beginning to write reports of his work, he needs to develop his ability to express facts and ideas in concise, understandable language.

Senior or In-charge Accountant. In addition to and in extension of qualities related to lower ranks, he needs in general a greater resourcefulness and more initiative. Even more than others, he is alert to differences in the conditions met, to alternative ways of getting things done, to individual capabilities among members of his immediate staff. A well-developed constructive imagination will be a valuable asset in sensing points of weakness in accounting systems and office organizations which might have openings for fraud and mismanagement.

Since the senior accountant deals directly with important members of the client's organizations, he must be able to demonstrate to persons outside his own firm that he is independent in his professional viewpoint. This is not to say that he can with propriety display a sense of superiority. Rather his will be an attitude of unwillingness to be influenced by the conditions or the people he meets unless he is also thoroughly satisfied by the supporting facts.

He should be supported in his independent views by a sure knowledge of accountancy and a wide experience with professional techniques. For something more than self-assurance is wanted. There is need for ready adaptability to new conditions and for self-confidence in weighing evidence with a healthy skepticism and an open mind. Yet all this should be tempered by an ability to consider calmly the reasoning of others and to join the recognition of unusual situations with a willingness to discuss them with his own superiors before making commitments.

Manager or Supervisor. His technical qualities are similar to those for a senior, but he will approach his work largely from an executive's standpoint. It is important, for example, that he shall have strong analytical ability and a retentive memory because as a manager he may move among several concurrent engagements.

Even more than the senior accountant he has need of the personality and the character to deal understandingly with people—clients, clients' staff, professional associates. He will need maturity and varied experience to be able to review intelligently the judgments of men under him as well as the work accomplished. It goes without saying that he exercises considerable authority, but it will be equally obvious that he should exercise authority with tactful consideration for the views of others. It is quite possible to express dissent without giving offense. He will find that suggestions can be made and followed up without "pulling his rank," as the army phrase has it.

Partner or Principal. The distinguishing qualities of a partner are those which clearly point toward leadership. This includes, along with high technical abilities, a capacity for stimulating men to conceive useful ideas. It also involves a faculty for stating a point of view effectively and forcefully to an executive or to a group of people. A partner has need for a certain quality of persuasiveness: he often has to deal with moot questions; he may undertake to reconcile conflicting interests; he may wish, within the limits of professional ethics, to describe the values of professional services. In a word, the partner or principal must have mature judgment and be broadly resourceful, not only in overcoming difficult technical circumstances, but in meeting human problems as well, not the least of which is the task of creating staff morale and building an enthusiastic organization.

(*Journal of Accountancy*, December, 1944)

5. Growing into Responsibilities

As is the case in any organized society, the work of public accounting falls into various occupational levels. These serve not only as aids in subdividing the work but also as means of fitting the assignments to the capabilities and experience of the personnel. Naturally different occupational levels reflect appropriate differences in responsibilities as well as differences in activities.

A part of the functioning of a planned gradation in occupational levels therefore is educational; work assignments are graded in part according to varying degrees of difficulty and to the prior experience of the person assigned. Gradually an individual's field education brings him into contact with the basic aspects of all sections of an audit program. His instructions are educational as to the method and his responsibility therein; his contact with the same audit area in different enterprises is educational in regard to individual differences; and his rotation into various sections of the audit is educational from gradually presenting audit programs as a whole consisting of recognizable parts, subject to considerable variation as occasion may require.

The staff man will wish to execute his assignment in a satisfactory manner, i.e., learn to follow instructions intelligently; and he will find it to his advantage to observe the way each assignment contributes factually to the audit report and certificate. Gradually he comes to a full understanding of the tight interrelation between preparation for bearing larger responsibilities and ability satisfactory to execute additional responsibility when the opportunity comes. Preparation should therefore be conscious and continuous so that growth in responsibilities may be progressive and fruitful.

Junior Assistant. He need have no prior experience in public accounting in order to make a beginning. But he should have a foundation; it should be either reasonably broad and diversified experience in bookkeeping, or a good general and technical education at the college level. If the first alternative is to be effective, a concurrent supplementary program of study will be necessary.

In recent years there has been a definite trend toward recruiting for the profession persons who have had a college education. It has been found that college work sifts out a great many of those who have a low capacity for growth, and that graduates of good scholarship usually advance rapidly in responsibilities. This is to be expected. It reflects the increasingly technical aspects of the work and the broadening of the relation of accounting to finance and business, and to society.

After appointment to a staff position, the college graduate, no less than the nongraduate, faces the need for study. It may be in part informal self-development; but it should be persistent and relevant. He comes to realize that "commencement" was just what the dictionary says.

Semisenior. In addition to the preparation outlined for junior assistants, the semisenior will have had two to four years (probably longer if formal education has not been adequate) of satisfactory public accounting as a junior or an equivalent in business. As a result he will have a reasonable acquaintance with general audit procedures proportionate to his growing responsibilities. Even though he may be a college graduate, he will be advised to continue studying. After having made a thorough study or review of the literature of auditing while mastering his duties as a junior, he will find it is now time to supplement his practical work by preparing himself to take the CPA examination.

Often it seems that men who make the most progress do so largely by using out-of-office time to prepare for future responsibilities. It is hardly necessary to add that all staff members should be continually giving thought, and study as well, to the qualities expected in higher ranks.

Senior. Preparation for senior status and responsibility is long and hard. Sometimes it is without intermediate designation as semisenior. By the time they reach senior grade, most men will have passed the CPA examination and will have had a number of years of satisfactory public accounting experience.

It is very desirable for a senior accountant to be a college graduate. The importance of a broad rather than a brief and specialized education, or no formal education at all, now becomes increasingly clear. An extensive knowledge of accounting theory and of the state of current accounting opinions is a great advantage. And acquaintance with the basic literature of economics, finance, business administration, and business law often proves very helpful.

Some of this preparation is made available to college students majoring in accountancy; consequently a considerable part of it is studied long before direct application becomes possible. But much knowledge that is currently important is knowledge that becomes available only currently. Keeping up to date therefore becomes a part of current professional life.

Manager. Preparation usually is but little different from that of a well-prepared senior. With few exceptions he is a CPA. Probably he is a college graduate, although some men with proper experience and temperament may reach this level, and higher, without that background. A considerable term of service as senior in differing types of engagements is usually necessary to produce the desired breadth of knowledge and maturity of judgment. To the extent that personality can be consciously influenced, it should be deliberately fostered.

Partner. As to preparation: there is no school for partners, but partners are forever studying; they write no examinations, but they are constantly being tested. Preparation for partnership is all that has been outlined above for the other ranks—multiplied by two and continued on to the end.

Junior Assistant. Although his assignments are varied, his initial responsibilities are necessarily limited since he is presumably lacking in previous similar experience. In this respect his work is like that of the nurse or laboratory technician who collects data that serve as the basis for a physician's opinion, or that of a law clerk who makes extracts of analogous cases for the use of his principal. Yet his work is important, for it furnishes an essential part of the basis for his supervisor's professional opinion. The junior is expected to draw up typical analyses and schedules of accounting information, the preparation of which requires even in the beginner the exercise of skill, care, and no little judgment. In addition he does other assigned work, such as checking samples of footings, postings, extensions, and vouchers. These initial responsibilities are broadened rapidly, however, as the junior acquires sound judgment in deciding upon the significance of the transactions touched by his work and as he develops an alertness to notice and report upon unusual items or circumstances. He is making progress.

Semisenior. His growing responsibilities are an expansion of those of a junior. This means that his work now will often be that of carrying out designated sections of an audit according to the usual methods and with only general supervision from a senior accountant. It becomes increasingly important now to see clearly the interrelationships of the organic parts of an audit program so that the significance of his own assignments will be understood. Sometimes he may direct the work of several junior assistants; he may also execute simple and repetitious types of engagements alone. Such work well done is in itself part of the preparation for advancement.

Senior Accountant. In addition to those associated with lower ranks, his growing responsibilities involve conducting any or all phases of an audit engagement, subject only to a minimum of supervision as to initial planning and subsequent review. To him falls the duty of assigning assistants of varying experience and of directing their work on designated tasks. The men working under him expect to receive a large measure of their training from their contact with his experience. He can train them well or negligently. He must co-ordinate schedules of financial information drawn up by other people; and he will be expected to prepare a draft audit report that is well designed to cover all accounting phases of the engagement.

After sufficient experience, the senior accountant may become somewhat of a specialist in auditing certain lines of business, in tax matters, or perhaps in system and budget work.

Manager. Much of his responsibility takes the form of reviewing the work of other persons. In many cases he will supervise the progress of several concurrent engagements of moderate size, or oversee several sections of a large engagement. He will review the working papers already passed upon by senior accountants, critically examine drafts of reports, and pass judgment on the adequacy of the auditing procedures used and on the acceptability of the accounting practices found. This often calls for a well-developed ability to transcend detail and see the larger issues. In addition, there is a responsibility to the organization to train members of the staff for future growth as well as for adequate discharge of current duties.

If, for a time, on the way to the status of a junior partner, the manager were in charge of a branch office, he would often meet clients initially and again after the report was rendered, as well as keep in touch with the work in progress. In such a situation he would have considerable latitude in arranging his office organization and making his staff assignments so long as he acted within the boundaries of the policies and principles of the firm. Members of the firm, moreover, would always be available for advice or for help in making the hardest decisions.

Partner. It is an important responsibility of a partner to keep the firm's relations with clients upon a satisfactory basis. The fact that he discharges other responsibilities well will often prove a distinct aid in dealing with clients. For example, it is a partner's constant preoccupation to maintain high standards of professional service and ethical conduct throughout his entire staff and practice. Staff selection and staff training require much careful thought. These are some of the ways of developing the firm's capacity for the effective service that means satisfied clients.

An honest pride of profession carries weight also; and so does the sincere wish to be helpful within professional limits. This means in part that well-balanced, unprejudiced consideration must be given to the welfare of all parties at interest in every engagement, but especially in consultations about matters of accounting policy. It hardly need be added that participation and leadership in professional and business organizations are expected of partners.

The above outline is no doubt inadequate in many ways. Perhaps too little is said about formal, technical education as a basis for entry into professional service and for facilitating advancement; too little may have been said about the amount and variety of knowledge needed at the higher levels, or about the kind and quality of technical skills that have to be acquired. It must be quite evident that the necessity for developing good judgment has been mentioned without accompanying suggestions of how the developing can be fostered.

Even if the outline may seem inadequate, it may perhaps still underlay the thought that formal, technical education for a career in accountancy should not be technical alone. The start in technical education was made long ago; it aimed to provide a better basis for professional growth than field experience alone. For greatest growth and greatest service, educational preparation needs to be more than technical. It must help the future professional man understand people, social organization, industrial and monetary economics, and many other nonaccounting aspects of life today. Public accounting not only operates within an atmosphere of economic and social conditions; it also is rapidly coming to be an important instrument in service of the welfare of society.

(Journal of Accountancy, December, 1944)

6. Types of Professional Men

The soldier, the clergyman, the attorney, and the physician are considered professional men. They are experts in their respective fields of training and offer expert service to other people. Yet in many cases it is difficult to draw a line through their activities and to say that here ends the work of an amateur and there begins the service of a professional. That is also true for accountants.

It is customary to speak of an officer in the armed forces as being "in the service," meaning in the service of his country. If the professions could be characterized by one word it would be this word "service." It is the purpose of the profession of arms to defend the country, the people, the institutions, the chosen way of life. To carry out this purpose the military forces must be ready and able to take definite action if the citizens through their government decide that the national welfare requires it. An officer does not conduct active military operations because he wants to do so; he acts because his public needs that service. All action before that time is training and preparation.

To be a professional requires extensive technical knowledge and skill. In a field in which the necessary knowledge is easy to obtain and the desired skills are easy to acquire, a profession is not likely to develop. The profession of arms is not that kind of field. Becoming a professional soldier therefore is in a large measure a matter of education, training, and temperament. There is a vast military literature, and most countries have a number of specialized military schools. By classroom work the professional expands his technical knowledge of the arts of war and his understanding of people. By field exercises he develops skill in planning the details of military action and in dealing understandingly with people.

In addition the military officer must be possessed of a high sense of duty; he puts the welfare of his men first, and the people before the army; he is loyal to the cause and to his superiors; he has a strong sense of what is right or necessary; confidential information is safe with him.

Many of these characteristics apply also to the professional accountant.

The purpose of religion is to inspire people to right living, to high accomplishments, and to an understanding of matters of the spirit. Clergymen are the professionals in this field. Others may devote themselves to the religious life, but that does not make them professionals. If the keyword of the soldier is security, the keyword of the clergy is morality. The task of the latter is to fight for morality in the group and in society at large, with a primary interest always in the individual. Public welfare is his great concern even though he works through individuals. By leading individuals toward high standards of right living, he strengthens society and improves human relationships.

Like the soldier, the minister of religion has need for technical knowledge and special skills. Preparation is long; the subject matter is difficult. Human beings are infinitely more complex than any conceivable machine, and the motives of their actions are often obscure. It is seldom easy to apply technical religious knowledge skillfully and with good judgment. Explaining the ways of the spirit, the nature of the soul, the duty of man, the futility of sin, are difficult tasks indeed—tasks that call for education and training suited only to a professional. Here too is a vast literature to be understood and interpreted. Technical education is very necessary—education in psychology and in human personality, human nature, human problems. And training—training in public speaking and in written discourse, in meeting people easily, and in sensing the spiritual or emotional needs of people, together with practice in ministering to those needs.

It goes without saying that the clergyman will be tolerant toward others' views and wholly trustworthy of confidences, as befits a professional man. Accountants can do no less.

Medicine has long been recognized as a profession. The public welfare aspect of good health is readily understood. The need to relieve suffering and to repair bodily damage cannot be argued; nor can the necessity for eradicating the sources of poor health. The physician's keyword is health —health of the individual, the group, the public.

He is a specialist in public service without being a public servant. He is a professional as opposed to the amateur who indulges in self-diagnosis and self-medication without adequate technical knowledge.

Here again mere technical preparation alone does not make a man into a professional. He must also have a clear sense of dedication, of service, of duty regardless of self. The physician is self-effacing and sympathetic. He derives keen satisfaction, as professional men always do, from the assistance he is able to render.

Yet carrying on his task takes more than a desire to serve; the physician must be capable as well as willing. He must be a technician, and possessed of wide knowledge and deep understanding. He too deals with immensely complicated situations; just how complicated the layman cannot possibly understand. His education is long and exacting; the literature is vast, and great areas of knowledge are being constantly widened. We marvel that men can organize such vast and diverse materials into understandable sequences.

Professional accountants can find many similarities in their own work.

Justice, as the keyword of the attorney and the judge, takes its place along with security, morality, and health. These men are professionals also. They are professionals in spite of the fact that many of their kind of activities can be and often are performed by other people. They are professionals, not by their own declaration but because organized society desires justice—the fair and evenhanded balancing of the facts, of the rights, the duties, the powers, and the intentions of the parties to litigation. Because it is the purpose of law to provide orderly conditions for living, for resolving disputes, for correcting frauds, for deciding upon the punishment for wrongdoing; because trained professionals are needed to execute the will of the people through the operation of government and the administration of justice, there is a group of professional men concerned with justice and order.

To serve society in these particulars the attorney and the judge, like other professional men, have need for a fine sense of duty. The welfare of the people in general, as well as that of individuals, is involved. These men strive to exercise an impersonal, unbiased restraint upon unfair actions or criminal acts. To serve their purposes and to perform their duties these men require a technical knowledge of the many fields of law and a deep understanding of legal situations and problems, of legal principles and precedents. It also requires technical skill in finding the applicable law, in organizing persuasive arguments, and in delivering them effectively in writing or in speech. In a word, the individual must have education and training, two important aspects in every profession, especially where the volume in materials is great and where complex situations are numerous.

Professional accounting also rests upon the same factors.

(New York Certified Public Accountant, April, 1952)

7. Characteristics of a Profession

A profession starts as an occupation. By slow stages it advances to the point where it is widely accepted as being a profession. Most of the early steps are unplanned; change at first is individual and largely accidental. Only at long last do men enter upon activities and policies conscious of possible professional import.

Primitive witch doctors and blood-letting barbers could not lay a planned foundation for a profession. Today one of the strong convictions of the physician and the surgeon is that they must not only serve well at the moment, but also seek to improve the foundations on which their profession will rest in the future.

A similar contrast of individual self-interest and the ideal of serving others professionally could be drawn between tribal chiefs settling local disputes personally, and statesmen drawing up a constitution for a nation or a group of nations, to the end that an unborn multitude may live at peace under conditions of impersonal justice.

The scribes of ancient Egypt, recording and classifying taxes received and disbursed in kind, were following an occupation of recording. Certified public accountants of today, attesting to the credibility of complex financial statements so that men may rely with additional confidence on the accounting representations of other men, are practicing a profession.

It has been said that the engineer is "the pioneer in the professionalization of industry." It might also be said that the public accountant is a pioneer in advancing the professionalization of business management. Because of this similarity in their fields, the thoughts of engineers upon the subject of professions will be of particular interest to accountants. An eminent engineer has written an excellent and compact statement of the attributes of a profession.[1] A part of his address is the following:

What marks off the life of an individual as professional?

First, I think we may say that it is a *type of activity* which is marked by high individual responsibility and which deals with problems on a distinctly intellectual plane.

Second, we may say that it is a *motive of service,* as distinct from profit.

Third, is the *motive of self-expression,* which implies a joy and pride in one's work and a self-imposed standard of workmanship—one's best.

Fourth, is a *conscious recognition of social duty* to be accomplished, among other means, by guarding the standards and ideals of one's profession and advancing it in public understanding and esteem, by sharing advances in professional knowledge, and by rendering gratuitous public service, in addition to that for ordinary compensation, as a return to society for special advantages of education and status.

Next, what are the attributes of a group of persons which mark off their corporate life as professional in character?

·

[1] "The Second Mile," by William E. Wickenden, President of Case School of Applied Science, an address before the Engineering Institute of Canada (*The Engineering Journal,* March, 1941).

I think we may place first a *body of knowledge and of art* (science and skill) held as a common possession and to be extended by united effort.

Next we may place *an educational process* of distinctive aims and standards, in ordering which the professional group has a recognized responsibility.

Third in order is *a standard of qualifications,* based on character, training, and competency, for admission to the professional group.

Next follows *a standard of conduct* based on courtesy, honor, and ethics, to guide the practitioner in his relations with clients, colleagues, and the public.

Fifth, I would place a more or less formal *recognition of status* by one's colleagues or by the state, as a basis of good standing.

And finally *an organization* of the professional group based on common interest and social duty, rather than economic monopoly.

From this it is evident that professional accountancy and professional engineering are in many respects very much alike. Both rest upon thorough education and develop best through combining study and experience; both have many service aspects that affect the public interest; both are evolving toward full public recognition as a profession.

A high sense of individual responsibility and of duty to guard professional ideals marks a personal virtue that is clearly recognized by public accountants. Every public accountant who takes pride in work well done and who is more strongly actuated by motives of service than desire for gain, is reflecting the personal virtues so frequently evident in professional men that they have come to be considered professional attributes.

The professional characteristics that are attributed to a group can be classified into two categories. The first is recognition of professional status. This covers not only the informal public recognition shown by a demand for the services of experts and the recognition that is associated with membership in an organization, but also the varying degrees of formal recognition indicated by statutory enactments. The second characteristic is preparation for professional service. This category covers the four other group attributes mentioned by Dr. Wickenden. It is noteworthy that each of the four gives the professional something to learn: to learn to use and extend a particular body of knowledge; to learn to exercise due influence upon the aims and standards of the applicable educational processes; to learn to acquire the training, competency, and character that are a necessary basis for being accepted into the professional group; to learn to live according to high standards of personal conduct.

These are some of the tests by which people have come to judge a man or a group to be professional. A most convincing evidence of professional growth is the steady improvement and extension of professional characteristics. A profession must come about by evolution; it cannot be created by fiat or fancy. The earlier stages of the development of a profession therefore do not clearly reflect the professional attributes that later appear so characteristic.

So important is professional education and training for accountants as well as engineers that another paragraph from Dr. Wickenden is quoted here.

Engineering schools ought to be less alike, less standardized by imitation. The men who are to lead the profession will need longer training, and one that is both broadly humanistic and more profoundly scientific. Great numbers of workers in technology could do well with a more extensive type of training. For every *one* who should receive post-graduate training possibly *four* would find the present course sufficient, and *ten* would find an intensive two-year course more suitable. The science of economy needs to be more strongly emphasized at all levels. A science of human work needs to be created and systematically taught.

The engineer's job will be so varied, and will change so fast, and his tools will so increase in variety and refinement with the advance of science, that no engineer can hope to get a once-and-for-all education in advance. We must expect to re-educate engineers at intervals throughout their careers. The most important development of all may come in after-college education.

By education and examination a profession undertakes to "guarantee at least minimum standards of competency." In return, the public protects that profession from the incompetent judgment and adverse effects of the unqualified by giving professional men a special status by law. "Professional status is therefore an implied contract to serve society, over and beyond all duty to client or employer, in consideration of the privileges and protection that society extends to the professional."

All CPA legislation is a form of recognition of the existence of an area of special technical knowledge that can be used in the public interest and that can be tested by state examinations. These statutes are an acknowledgement that public welfare is involved in the practice of public accounting. In addition federal legislation which regulates security issues and stock exchanges now requires accounting investigations to be made by independent public accountants in connection with proposed distributions of securities. Thus the possession of special technical knowledge is coming to be linked more and more with the opportunities for public practice.

Education has been considered for a long time to be an essential element of preparation for professional practice. Yet formal technical education in accounting has had to make its own way with little or no aid from legislation until recently. In other words, effective recognition that the public interest required that education for public accounting should be technical and adequate was slow in coming. The teaching of technical accounting (beyond instruction in bookkeeping) was begun by men who were practicing accountants. Much of their teaching materials were derived from CPA examination questions. A knowledge of accounting problems and techniques is obviously basic to professional competence. But a broader education than technique alone is essential as a foundation to broad, full-fledged professional service in the public interest. Sometimes accounting instruction still lacks such co-ordination with instruction in business administration and economics as would benefit the long-run interests of the profession.

Independence has long been considered by accountants as a basic characteristic of a public practitioner. But until recent years independence has been given very little direct legislative support in America; and discussions of independence more often than not have seemed to imply that its importance had somehow been questioned or that its efficacy was in doubt. Seldom until recently has independence been treated analytically from the point of view of the reasons why it is in the public interest, or with the intent to explore the question of how far accountants can succeed without outside support in preserving their independent status.

From this brief survey it is clear that at least three elements must be present before a man's activities can properly be called professional: (1) special knowledge and appropriate skill, (2) public recognition of an inherent public interest, (3) moral and economic independence. Accountancy is no exception. These fundamentals apply here as in other professional activities.

Occupations do not become professions by definitions, statutes, or assertions. Professions are what they are because their practitioners render services that are professional in character and in the public interest. "Public welfare" is the keynote whether spelled out or not. It is the pathway to public recognition; it is the reason that education must develop a special body of knowledge, and that practitioners must use it. "Public welfare" explains many things: independence, self-imposed high standards of craftsmanship, ethics, and discipline, and the consciousness of a social responsibility that all professional men possess.

(New York Certified Public Accountant, April, 1952)

8. Auditor Independence

The nineteenth century statutes by which the British sought to control joint-stock companies for the better protection of investors plainly show that Englishmen of that time had a very clear idea of the nature of a corporation and of the proper relation of directors to stockholders. The company was merely a mechanism for drawing scattered capital together and putting it to work, the stockholders were investors who pooled their savings for a common objective, the directors were elected representatives ("stewards") of the stockholders and were charged with the direct responsibility of managing the investment for the investors' benefit. But a knowledge of human nature and the existence of an historical background which included the stockjobbing period immediately preceding 1720, combined to lead the British to frame their corporation statutes in such a manner as to provide the stockholders with other representatives who were to "test the stewardship" as it were of the managing representatives. At first the critic was an auditing committee of stockholders, later an independent professional auditor.

The developments of the past few years in our own country have raised questions similar to those which must have agitated Englishmen several generations ago. Can elected directors and hired managers of corporations touched with a public interest because of the extent of the company's operations, the number of employees or investors, or the character of the service rendered—can such men chosen by one group of investors be depended upon to manage the corporation with a balanced consideration for the best interests of all concerned? Can a way be provided for independent third parties to review the acts and proposals of the managing representatives in a critical manner and with the interests of both present and prospective investors in mind?

British and American experiences dictate a negative answer to the first question in enough cases to show that the problem of securing a responsible management is not a negligible one. The British precedent of the auditor-critic suggests an affirmative answer to the second problem and thereby raises the additional question of whether the English plan of electing auditors in the stockholders' meeting should be adopted in this country or some other plan devised to improve investor protection.

The first reply to the last question probably would be that Englishmen are not altogether satisfied with their own system. In spite of election of the auditor by the stockholders, we are led to believe that the goodwill of the directors is important, that the selection of the auditor practically always rests with the directors in the final analysis, that the courts have so circumscribed the auditors' duties as to make the stockholders' protection rather formal, and that "until auditors are insured a much greater degree of independence than they at present possess, it is hardly to be expected that they can be an effective safeguard against waste of shareholders' funds in company administration." (See *Financial Democracy*, Miller and Campbell, Chapter 4.)

The second reply to the question of transplanting the British system is that conditions peculiar to the United States would seem to make election of the auditor by the stockholders even less satisfactory here. Getting stockholders out to meetings is everywhere a problem, but the impression persists that it is particularly difficult in this country.

Most of our security-holders act alike in spite of differences in the terms of their contracts: bondholders by agreement have no vote for directors and policies; stockholders neglect to exercise their prerogative and thus voluntarily place themselves in the same category as bondholders as far as management control is concerned. Stockholders do not seem to feel ownership responsibilities; and they are quite likely to look to the market for the clue to the value of their holdings rather than to financial statements. This has a tendency to make many directors more market-conscious than the art of good management would dictate.

In addition to the other things, we have devised a very extended array of securities contracts with numerous and complex diversities. This vast expansion in the types of credit instruments has greatly diluted the sense of ownership. The situation is no longer one of the simple pooling of capital in a joint stock by individuals receiving a very similar interest in the enterprise. The diversity of securities makes for diversity of interests; and diversity, abetted by complexity of the contract, opens the way to a possible subtle undermining of the prior rights of senior securities by new issues.

The situation therefore calls for an American plan to fit American conditions.

The only American plan so far developed aims at investor protection through the application of the provisions of the Federal Securities Act and the Securities Exchange Act, supplemented by regulations issued by the Securities and Exchange Commission.

It is desirable to raise the question whether the possibilities have been fully canvassed for investor protection by a more effective use of experienced public accountants. The work of our public accountants has now been given a statutory recognition it never had before. But that is only a tardy recognition of just a part of the service which they are competent to perform. Here is a body of men, estimated to be approximately 14,000 in number,[2] who by education, experience, and ideals of service are unusually well qualified to fulfill in America the spirit of the early British theory of the corporation auditor: an independent and expert critic of the stewardship of the directors, acting in the interest of all investors.

Public accounting is faced with certain weaknesses which are probably inherent in the present scheme of things.

(1) Auditors are engaged by the same officers or directors whose activities are to be examined.

(2) Auditors may be dropped and others substituted at the pleasure of the officers or directors; and the deposed auditor has no recourse even though he may suspect that attempts to mislead investors are contemplated.

(3) Auditors have no power effectively to criticize directors' valuations or financial proposals even though the equity of some prior stock is being weakened. When their powers of persuasion are exhausted auditors have but little choice between acquiescing and resigning.

(4) Auditors may be subjected to subtle pressure in many ways: the scope of their examination may be restricted more than is wise, the time allowed may be arbitrarily limited at the psychological moment, their reports may be suppressed and their recommendations disregarded.

These situations, even when they do not create definite open issues, can do much to undermine the auditor's feeling of independence and

[2] 31,500 as of April, 1958.

prevent his convictions from showing teeth. Unconsciously he may seek ways of meeting concrete situations without realizing that, while constituting technical "disclosure," his phrases may nevertheless fail to carry the necessary message to the reader. He may perhaps qualify his certificate. But that device very likely gives the average reader the impression that the auditor was merely dodging responsibility, or it fails utterly because of its cautious phrasing to accomplish its purpose of putting the investor "on notice."

This is no indictment of public accountants; no other equal group of men in contact with affairs will assay a higher average of disinterestedness and impartiality. Certified public accountants have made an enviable record of high-minded, expert service and many individuals have repeatedly demonstrated that they set their convictions above fees. Yet the fact remains that the conditions under which they perform their critical and quasi-judicial function constitute a definite culture medium in which the germs of professional weakness can and sometimes do grow. The principal issue here raised is whether a practical way can be found to reduce these handicaps upon a real professional independence and to utilize an increase of auditor independence for the public good.

(Journal of Accountancy, April, 1935)

9. Technical Competence, Plus

It is not unusual for accounting teachers to stress knowledge as an important aspect of preparation for a career in professional accounting. And it is perhaps understandable that sometimes they may not show full appreciation of the existence of other factors besides technical competence. Are colleges presumed to confine their operations within the functions of handing on accumulated knowledge and testing students for retention?

Accounting practitioners, on the other hand, often emphasize the fact that qualities other than technical competence contribute greatly to successful professional service. Perhaps they sometimes give the impression that personal factors are more important than technical preparation.

It is not easy for each group to grasp the point of view of the other. Yet, it is important to the profession and to the public that this be done.

Bruce Bliven (*Men Who Make the Future*) tells of a study made by Dr. Catherine Cox Miles of the life history of three hundred famous people. She sought evidence of early signs of high intelligence and of quality traits that were common to the whole group. She found the following characteristics to be typical: physically active, mentally alert, cool-tempered, kind, modest, persistent, conscientious, trustworthy. Out of such ingredients, the people in this sample of society had fashioned lives which later marked them as famous people.

Are these characteristics the signs of high intelligence? Probably not. But they do constitute some of the elements that make for success in any field of endeavor. Are these characteristics teachable? Accounting teachers would like to read some discussions of that question. Are these characteristics recognizable, measurable? Accounting practitioners would like to read some discussions of that question. They would like members of their staff to have qualities like these.

We should all like to know that the incoming members of the profession came from the best homes and had the best natural abilities and the highest type of personality. We should be happy to learn that college graduates with the best general education, the highest scholastic standing, and the finest technical training were all trying to come into our field of work. So would business, government, and the other professions.

Wishing for the unattainable ideal might sometimes lead us toward a sort of inferiority complex: colleges of commerce may seem to get the students who are poorly prepared; graduates with the highest scholarship may seem to be going into other lines of endeavor than public accounting; people do not seem interested in developing schools that will specialize in training people specifically to enter the profession of public accounting.

If public accounting cannot have all of the best students, it can surely have a fair share of them—provided students who are good prospects are not frightened away by the long list of virtues and capacities desired.

It is clear that preparing persons for professional accounting is the joint responsibility of teachers and practitioners. There is the duty of sifting those who have reached their highest level; and there is the duty of developing those who show further capacities. The colleges can do some of this, but they cannot do it all. Part of the sifting of professional qualities and technical competence must be done within active units of the profession. Both there and in the schools, the basis of the sifting should be definitely known and carefully fitted to the conditions. The colleges cannot be solely responsible for the complete development of those qualities that are teachable. They should do much of it; but a great deal of education must be supplied in one way or another after the individual leaves school and while he is in the midst of his daily work. Programs of staff training within the firm afford one approach; after-hours study provides another.

The profession is in need of more thinking and writing on these problems. The development of the individual should be an unending process up to the highest level he is capable of reaching. And that process should be planned and organized from beginning to end. It is true that one can learn to swim merely by jumping off a bridge, but there are better ways. And there is more involved in developing a profession than merely devising tests to exclude people from it. Neither teachers nor practitioners can effectively do the whole job either of sifting individuals who have reached their limit or of developing individuals who have extra capacity. But both groups could benefit from thoughtful analyses of the qualities desired of individuals and from constructive suggestions as to how this quality and that ability can be detected and fostered.

What are some of these desired qualities?

Scattered through the literature of accountancy where the characteristics of a professional accountant are discussed is mention of numerous qualities that seem to be related through the fact that they touch the personal conduct of an individual in some way. Some of these are simple and obvious, such as good habits of speech and dress, well-groomed appearance; others are more complex, such as readiness at all times to maintain one's professional independence, ability to sense the full implication of the rules of professional ethics, willingness to set the example in all aspects of conduct. Between these types are numerous qualities briefly compacted into phrases like these: dependable and vigilant in duties; intellectually honest even in the face of a dilemma; unsusceptible to outside influence; possessed of ample moral stamina; inclined toward moderation in all things.

The qualities of personality are numerous in the literature. Many of them are suggested by a word or two: tact, patience, poise, self-possession, persuasiveness, flexibility, due reticence, punctuality, courtesy, good humor, high spirits, friendly dignity, conversational reserve. Other items in the list use more words to express the essential idea: ability to get along with people, to get one's self liked, to hold fast to the right way without being dogmatic and assertive; capacity for securing respect for one's opinions, for impressing another with the values of professional services, for bringing about recognition of professional skill and judgment, for criticizing without giving offense.

The ideas that seem to deal with qualities of mentality are variously expressed. Here we find alertness, thoroughness, perseverance, concentration. Stress is often placed on imagination—reasonable, vivid, constructive, restrained imagination. Mention is made of a fund of common sense, of ready response to experience, of power to comprehend quickly and visualize clearly. Abilities of various sorts are included: to distinguish differences sharply, to see logical interactions, to draw careful inferences, to think clearly and correctly.

Certain qualities desired in professional accountants seem more related to aptitude than to the other categories.

Are the following characteristics proper ones to ascribe to an aptitude for accounting: pride in craftsmanship; ability to write clearly and concisely; capacity for presenting dry facts interestingly; speed and accuracy in arithmetic; facility and interest in the use of figures; facility in figure analysis and figure interpretation; enjoyment in untangling problem materials; analytical ability in dealing with one complication at a time out of many; analytical ability that is resourceful in the face of massed detail or inadequate data; ability to deal with analytical details without confusion or panic; good judgment in weighing evidence and interpreting facts; good judgment in the technique of using language and figures expressively; ability to use words within their real meaning, to separate near synonyms, to state the full truth tactfully; good selective judgment in the midst of many possible procedures; ability to choose wisely and well among a variety of acceptable ways; awareness of the interrelations and ramifications of business activities?

It would seem that the CPA examination can only be part of the evidence of professional promise.

(editorial, *Accounting Review,* January, 1944)

10. Trained Powers of Observation

Some laymen probably tend to conceive of the public accountant as a "checker-upper" of bookkeeping details. And no doubt there are "tick-mark practitioners" whose work might seem to support that view. On the other hand, some laymen seem to believe that the public accountant carries his verification activities to such a point that his signature on a balance sheet practically guarantees that no fraud has been concealed beneath the figures.

Businessmen of substantial experience are better informed and expect more in one case and less in the other than these extremes. They know that the best service the independent public accountant can render his client is sometimes not too closely related to verification at all.

On this point M. C. Conick, president of the Pennsylvania Institute of Certified Public Accountants, in *The Spokesman* (November, 1944) includes these ideas about the talents of a practicing public accountant: "His trained powers of observation to discern quickly and accurately accounting problems dealing not with generalities but with specifics, such as purchasing, pay roll, inventories, personnel, sales, financing, reorganizations, federal and state tax effects, requirements of the stock exchanges and public regulatory bodies, and others." "His training and experience to devise or improve accounting methods and systems and to prescribe procedures for a more effective and sounder internal accounting control for enterprises, regardless of variety, size, or complexity." "His training and experience to verify accounts independently."

A good deal of the usual classroom work in the upper division of college deals with CPA examination problems, either directly as published or remade in varying degrees of topical difficulty. Can this kind of educational experience serve to develop the strong powers of observation which Mr. Conick places first in importance? Formal education cannot expect to replace entirely the educational aspects of practical experience. But are we doing all we can to develop the powers the practitioner needs?

Second in his list is devising and improving systems. Does a single course in accounting systems—the limit of the usual offering—provide enough preparation in this direction? It may be that systems should be to accounting education what anatomy is to medical education. If more instruction in "accounting anatomy" is proposed, what is to be excluded from the present four-year program? First answers probably would include a proposed five-year program, or a highly specialized professional college, instead of replacing anything. But these possibilities may be so far away from realization, and for so many reasons, that we are thrown back upon the necessity for giving further study and experiment to the improvement of the typical four-year program. When that has been reasonably well done, perhaps most of the educational problems that remain could be satisfactorily met by the development of staff schools for men who are clearly committed to the profession and already experienced in it.

These considerations raise still other questions about the teaching of accounting. Are the students in accounting classes trained by their work into good habits of clear thinking? Is their curiosity developed into a wish to explore accounting details and understand its imponderables? Do they grow to like searching about within something that is puzzling? Does their activity produce a feeling for orderliness and appropriate organization of facts? What parts in their instruction are designed to generate the power to discriminate sensibly between alternatives, and to judge relevancy, adequacy, significance, right and wrong? What is done, by clear intent, to condition their minds for future growth from experience, to exercise their minds in constructive imagination and fertility of suggestions?

Most of these, perhaps all, should be goals in teaching accounting. Clearly this approach would be more desirable than that of mildly hoping that the students will catch the idea finally.

(editorial, *Accounting Review*, April, 1945)

11. Technical Monographs

Some items in the Institute's "Refresher Course" promise to supplement the usual auditing text material in a very useful manner. The list of topics to receive separate treatment under the title "Auditing Procedure" includes: changing concepts and procedures; new auditing techniques; audit programs and working papers; receivables, inventories. These items seem to show that the discussion will be aimed above the junior assistant. There is a place for that kind of help to staff men. It is a commendable venture in collecting, organizing, and sharing a rich accumulation of technical experience. And as such it will be a direct aid to the development of technical good judgment in the staff.

But why stop with five brief monographs dealing with auditing? This should be only a beginning. Inventories and receivables have come in for extensive and detailed consideration in recent years. There is evidently a great deal more to inventory treatment than can be adequately covered in a few rules and some generalized procedures; and there is far more variety in the conditions which surround the verification of receivables than most college texts reveal. These items in the refresher courses are reassuring, because they undoubtedly will show that professional accounting is more technical than college graduates realize, and because the organized effort now getting under way in this research venture may itself grow into a vital contribution of even broader scope.

Perhaps it will not be long before these few monographs on auditing are supplemented by others which will provide a full exposition of additional areas of auditing experience. Is there not a good deal that could be said about techniques of confirmation, techniques of vouching, techniques for reconciliations, and the like? Though such technical literature would not be prepared for the general public, many sections of the public would come to know about it; and perhaps it would help to modify the layman's notion that auditing is only "holler and tick."

If this venture in technical literature is worth while it may be even more worth while later on to expand the outline. It would be wholly reasonable to re-examine the technical patterns of auditing at intervals of a few years and revise the related monograph series as needed, thus keeping the ideas expressed in print close up to the firing line of experience.

(editorial, *Accounting Review*, July, 1945)

12. Auditing Progress

Teachers who feel that textbook literature of auditing has not kept pace with the needs of the time may take heart. Some public accountants are thinking much the same thing about practice. The chairman of the Institute committee on auditing procedure has something to say along the line in a recent article in the *Journal of Accountancy*.

In that article Paul Grady estimates that textbooks in auditing usually give seven-eighths of the space to balance sheet accounts and one-eighth to accounts directly concerned with income and expense. Auditing procedures in the field for the most part also reflect a similar "unbalance." In other words, clear recognition seems not to be given in auditing to the increased significance of the income statement, although the matter has been given considerable attention in connection with financial statements and accounting principles. He favors a program that would give additional emphasis to a comprehensive review of operations and to a careful study of the business factors that lie behind the records.

It has become increasingly clear that a shift is taking place in the focus of accounting attention; the tendency now is to lean away from "balance-sheet valuation" and toward "income determination." The change seems a desirable one under the conditions that face this generation of accountants. A similar focus could therefore very appropriately be reflected in audit procedure.

Such a development need not bring about any neglect of balance sheet accounts. For revenue and expense elements are still welded to assets and liabilities; and the ultimate convincing test of the satisfactoriness of operations still lies in the current assets. But the interconnection of assets and revenues is as significant as the relation of liabilities to assets. Auditing procedure seems to neglect this fact. Educational materials, Mr. Grady points out, could help to speed the change-over by the simple device of rearranging the presentation of auditing procedures. ". . . receivables would be dealt with immediately following and in direct relation to comments on the examination of sales and revenues; inventories, property accounts, and prepaid and deferred items would be similarly related to costs and expenses. This arrangement would correspond more closely with the chronological order in which the auditing work should be done."

Another statement of high significance deals with the need for practitioners on every occupational level to be continuously and consciously aware of their objectives. "Considerable improvement in both literature and practice would also result from an increased emphasis on the objectives of each phase of the examination. Each person working on an examination must continuously keep in mind just what he is seeking to prove, and must understand the relation of his particular work to those objectives."

Students too often come to look upon their course as a means of fixing in mind a traditional sequence of auditing procedures. That approach perhaps has some usefulness. But if the impression is made on the student that auditing is just a routine to be followed, the work performed being ticked off the list and forgotten, he is poorly prepared to enter intelligently into his period of "internship" in a public accountant's office. Is the first study of auditing too early for the student to learn that procedures are what they are because of their objectives; that methods may vary according to the circumstances while holding to the same objectives; that even the novice is expected to be continually thinking of how things should be in comparison with the way he finds them?

Not many schools offering work for an accounting major give an advanced course in auditing. Consequently, the usual text is a compact survey of all phases of an audit. There is no time to present variable procedures or to give a full discussion of the separate phases of making an examination. The result is that the educational presentation of a single course lays down but a thin foundation of professional technology.

The fact is that little or no organized literature on auditing technique exists beyond that designed for a first course. Presumably any further technical preparation is expected to be obtained merely from observation in the field. That is one way to learn; in some respects it is the best way. But it unquestionably is a slow way, since an educational variety of experience is not easily provided or obtained. Technical literature serves as a time-saver. If it is available in sufficient quantity and of well-graded quality, it is a valuable supplemental diet to accompany the intake of experience. It is more than just another growth factor; it also aids in the assimilation of experience itself.

(editorial, Accounting Review, July, 1945)

13. Constructive Criticism

A dramatic critic makes an occupation of criticism. The public accountant is also a critic, not very dramatic, it is true, but he does take a critical view of whatever he examines. Is there anything in the first occupation to help us understand the critic's function in the second?

A dramatic critic need not be an actor or a dramatist to be a good judge of drama and acting. Assuredly he must understand both in the abstract in order to react intelligently to either in the concrete. He relies strongly upon an intimate knowledge of the drama of the past; he has developed a sensitiveness to the good and not so good in the dramatic arts. He has cultivated a deep appreciation of human nature. He will set a high value on skill as a reporter as well as on impartiality of judgment.

Understanding and sensitiveness of appropriate kinds are also basic to an auditor's critical function. The term "valuer" is not suitable for an auditor; it seems to make him responsible for knowing use values and probable sales values beyond the powers of one man. Perhaps "valuationist" is better. Wherever choices have to be made, relative "value judgments" will be involved. Whoever chooses deliberately among relative situations, judging some to be better and some to be worse than others, can be called "valuationist" in contrast to "valuer."

Necessarily a valuationist needs to be something of a critic, that is, a practical judge of good and bad. And a wise critic will be careful to exercise his talent only within a limited field in which he had acquired special knowledge. Some valuationists will be critics of the truthfulness with which dramatists and actors portray human nature in action. Other valuationists, such as auditors, are essentially critics of statistical truth in accounts and adequate disclosures in financial statements.

Because accounts are fundamentally statistical categories, each one should be so defined as to aid in the accumulation of statistically truthful data. Because accounting processes are used primarily to get the transaction events of an enterprise classified and reclassified into these statistical categories, the accounting system should be so designed and operated as to accomplish a proper classification and summarized disclosure of enterprise events and the effect of managerial decisions.

Because accounts and accounting processes are sometimes poorly designed or faultily operated, it is part of the auditor's function to act as a critic of the statistical truth underlying the financial statements. He is greatly concerned to judge whether the accounting system is such that the analysis of transactions and the making of records have a good chance of producing dependable data in the financial statements. And one of his important responsibilities is to form an opinion regarding the reliability of the data actually produced by the use of the system in a given fiscal period.

In his appraisal of an accounting system, the auditor is a valuationist judging critically the good and bad features, that is, the features of the system that make it well suited or poorly suited as a mechanism for producing truthful statistical classes of accounting facts. In his appraisal of the results of operating the accounting statistical mechanism, the auditor is again a valuationist, this time judging critically the good and bad features (1) of the interpretations given to events by the men using the classification and reclassification processes of accounting, and (2) of the financial statements as an adequate and effective means of disclosing compactly yet intelligibly the financial position of the enterprise and the results of the period's operations.

It is easy to be critical; one need only select a few pet ideas and find fault with all ideas that are different. But to be a discerning critic, to develop a faculty for constructive criticism, that is difficult indeed. Yet this is one of the qualities of a good auditor; and a great many practitioners deserve that rating. It is doubtful whether a faculty for constructive criticism is inherent. It is more likely to be strong in some men, or weak in others, according to the amount of thoughtful study and painstaking observation given to cultivating it. For it is study and observation that foster a real understanding of accounting theory and practice; and understanding is the *sine qua non* of a discerning critic.

The customs, conventions, and traditions of accounting, together with an acquired skill in their use, make up accounting practice. However, practice is not static—once learned, forever appropriate. Practice is variable according to the circumstances—not as pure expediency but according to a trained mind's conceptions of varying suitability. An understanding of variability among conditions and of the possibilities for variations in practice are necessary parts of the basis for discriminating between degrees of good and bad practices.

The reasons, explanation, and pro-and-con arguments of accounting constitute accounting theory. And theory as well as practice shows many variations. For explanations may range from good to bad; and reasons may be utterly convincing or completely irrelevant, or may show many intermediate gradations. An understanding of differences in quality between reasons is fully as important in an auditor as is an understanding of the possibility for varying the practice to fit the circumstances.

Since an auditor must in the nature of the case be a valuationist, he should be conscious of his duty to discriminate and to judge, and he should seek to learn the basis of good judgment and clear discrimination. For these qualities do not come into existence automatically even with the passing years of experience.

There is a statement pertinent to this point in a recent report (*General Education in a Free Society* by a Harvard University Committee): "Discrimination among values involves choice. The ability to discriminate in choosing covers not only awareness of different kinds of values but of their relations, including a sense of relative importance and of the mutual dependence of means and ends."

The need for exercising good judgement is often stressed in the writings of accountants. Yet the elements in the concept of good, as these relate to the act of judging, are seldom analyzed. And seldom does an accounting teacher deem it useful to draw the attention of his students to the need for an awareness of relations between different areas of choice and between differing means to a chosen end. Surely some attempts to teach the elements of discrimination are justifiable in college classes; the whole burden should not rest upon field experience alone.

(editorial, *Accounting Review*, April, 1946)

14. Statistical Truth

A statistical category labeled "Horses" and an indicated quantity of 100 convey a definite mental picture to the reader. However, if inspection of the corral showed 90 horses and 10 mules we would rightly doubt the statistical truth of the category as reported.

Several possible explanations of this misleading report of a statistical fact might be found. Perhaps the classification category was poorly named —the intention having been to report the number of "equine draft animals." Perhaps the purpose of the classification was not clearly perceived in the beginning. Perhaps the intention was to count horses, but the person reporting did not realize that there is a difference between horses and mules.

It is easy to see possibilities for statistical untruth in this simple example. But it is not easy to see the same possibilities in traditional accounting categories. Yet statistical untruth may also creep into these by way of the same kind of faults: misleading class name; inadequate definition or understanding of class limits; introduction of data irrelevant to the intended class.

For example, consider "cost of goods sold." The use of an inventory priced at market that is lower than cost will throw a "loss" into the "cost of goods sold" figure—a shrinkage that in fact is not at all associated statistically with the goods that have actually been sold by this enterprise. One or more of the elements of statistical truth are lacking in the reported figure.

Again, depreciation expense charged to manufactured product, if the rate includes allowance for probable obsolescence of machinery or product, will burden the cost-of-goods-sold category with debit dollars which cannot in the nature of the case have influenced the creation of that specific product. Factors outside the given enterprise do suggest that better machinery is available; but that availability is irrelevant to the manufactured cost of product derived from the use of equipment already in the enterprise. And idle equipment cannot convert its creative power (measured by investment cost) into product it does not work on.

To force product, and hence the cost of sales, to include a cost-loading for irrelevant factors is comparable with classifying mules as horses. And as sergeant Smith of the mulized artillery would say, "Don't fool yourself brother."

If expediency is a controlling factor, that easier road will sometimes be chosen. But the expediency does not change the statistical untruth of the category and its figures. If the amount involved is so immaterial as not to change the cost of sales significantly, then price shrinkage does not deserve consideration in the balance sheet item of inventory.

It might be said that the facts are unavailable to make possible a proper calculation of obsolescence separate from wear. The same idea prevailed long ago about estimating wear and estimated probable bad debt loss. Here the argument of unavailability is no longer regarded as valid. The reason: in spite of predicted difficulties experiment and experience with advanced estimates have shown that statistical accounting results are brought closer to the truth by use of estimates than by their neglect. Are all aspects of obsolescence so unpredictable that no estimates could prove acceptable? Would it not be an informative refinement of the statistical truthfulness of accounts to report separately the amortization of original cost and the presumed (estimated) approach of obsolescence? If a sharp concept of costs that will express contributions made to the appearance of product is desirable, surely an effort is justifiable to exclude the disappearance of cost (obsolescence) which cannot realistically be considered to increase the usefulness of product.

(editorial, *Accounting Review*, April, 1946)

15. Vocabulary of Auditing

The most significant words in the auditor's vocabulary are his verbs. They tell what auditors do and thereby acquire some measure of technical significance, that is, they reflect professional responsibilities (ends and aims) and technical procedures (ways and means). Rudolf Flesch (*The Art of Plain Talk*) makes this comment: ". . . the lack of well used verbs is the main trouble with modern English writing."

In order to inquire into different shades of verb meaning a varied sample of auditing literature was examined in the amount of approximately 1,700 pages. The most notable feature of the quantitative analysis is the fact that there was a high concentration upon a few verbs. In the sample some 475 verbs were used 6,500 times. Yet 85 per cent of the words (400 verbs used less than 20 times) account for 23 per cent (1,500) of the 6,500 uses. The top 14 words (those having been used more than 10 times) appear approximately 2,700 times.

Thus 3 per cent of the words make up 40 per cent of the uses. The 5 words (1 per cent) above 200 uses cover about 1,400 uses (20 per cent). The single word with the highest frequency (532 uses) accounted for about 8 per cent of the total.

Auditing Verb	Frequency of Use
examine	532
verify	249
determine	229
ascertain	208
test	206
review	178
check	173
compare	172
investigate	142
consider	138
obtain	137
inquire	121
inspect	105
prepare	103

It is possible to get a small clue to the direction of change in verb usage. Because R. H. Montgomery's *Auditing Theory and Practice* appeared as the first edition in 1912 and as the sixth in 1940, it is possible to make a vocabulary comparison at an interval of twenty-eight years. Some of the change may of course represent individual taste in the use of words. But almost certainly many of the differences will reflect change of ideas in the profession.

Between the editions of 1912 and 1940 there was little change in the number of different verbs used—a decrease of about 10 per cent. There were some differences, however, in the list of high-ranking verbs.

ORDER OF VERB PREFERENCES

1912	1940
1. ascertain	examine
2. verify	ascertain
3. audit	compare
4. examine	review
5. test	investigate
6. certify	test

Some words were demoted. Ascertain moved from first to second; test, from fifth to sixth; verify, from second to twenty-third place; audit, from third to twenty-sixth; certify, from sixth to fifty-sixth. Other words were promoted, so to speak. Examine was advanced from fourth place to first; compare, from thirteenth to third; investigate, from twelfth to fifth; review, which was so seldom used in the 1912 edition as not to enter the count, came up to fourth place. Several other verbs that were not prominent as of 1912 received more attention later, that is, were used 20 or more times in the 1940 edition. These included: confirm, substantiate, analyze, scrutinize, disclose.

The changes in the verbs preferred are informative. The words used less frequently in recent practice, such as audit, verify, certify, have been of a kind that was easily misunderstood by the public. They seem to carry a strong suggestion of conclusiveness, of incontrovertible fact, of categorical conviction. But these qualities cannot in the nature of the case attach to the accountant's exhibits or to the auditor's professional opinion. On the other hand, some words such as examine, compare, investigate, review have come into more frequent use, and not without justification, for the connotation of these verbs is much closer than the others to the real nature of auditing.

The importance of certain words to the profession suggests that they not only need definition but study for overtones, for varied uses, for relation to suitable companion words. The word examine is at the top of the list. There are many ways "to examine"; any one of the senses may be used upon occasion. The physician's deft fingers *felt* the arm for signs of a broken bone. The judge himself examined the witness, *listening* intently to the responses. The engineer, examining the gun part with calipers, *saw* that the tolerance limits were not exceeded. In examining a sample of tea, the expert took a sip of the brew to *taste* the flavor. The hunting dog examined the path until his inquiring nose *scented* a trail. How does an auditor "examine?"

Although English is a language consisting of a very large vocabulary, many words have acquired several meanings. Whenever a certain term is adopted into professional usage, it is advisable to establish its professional connotation in comparison with its more general sense. *Examine* is such a word in its accounting use. Obviously it does not there connotate use of the senses of smell, taste, or touch. Auditors listen (to answers of their questions), and they see (documents and accounts). But as a technical term of auditing, "examine" means more than physical hearing and seeing. Do text-writers take pains to make clear the mental side of the auditor's actions of examining by seeing and listening?

(*New York Certified Public Accountant*, October, 1947)

16. Words of Action

Frequency of use is not necessarily a clue to the relative significance of the verbs used in the literature of auditing. Qualitative factors are perhaps more significant. It will be helpful in appraising the quality of audit words to examine a classification of about 500 verbs.

Since verbs are words of action, it would be natural that some would relate to technical ways and means and others to professional ends and aims. Clearly there will be more means of attaining recognized ends than there are ends to be attained. Yet the perception of an interrelation of suitable means and desirable ends is very important to a professional. For audit actions (use of specific procedures) are not taken for their own sake. Most of them are preparatory in the sense that they enable the auditors to take sequential action directly related to the aims involved in his professional duties and objectives.

The activity pattern revealed by audit verbs consists of a center and a surrounding area. The center is formed by a relatively small number of verbs—those which say something about duties, objectives, purposes, aims, and ends. Typical verbs are *understand, report, recommend.* A much larger number of words of action fall outside this center; they say something about techniques, methods, procedures, ways, and means. Typical verbs are *examine, inquire, authenticate.*

As to verbs indicative of ends and aims: The auditor has a duty to the public, a duty to the client, a duty to his profession.

His duty to the public, and hence part of his aims, is implicit in such verbs as *report, state, comment, disclose, certify, qualify, express an opinion.* The meaning of these terms may be compacted in this way: Part of the auditor's duty is to reveal the full, relevant facts with an expert's feeling for their significance as objectively determined facts, and with a professional man's regard for factual dependability.

His duty to the profession, or perhaps it is better to say to his professional conscience, is partly expressed by his use of such verbs as *detect, discover, uncover* such things as fraud, error, misrepresentation, distortion, ignorance. A great many of his techniques are focused upon these aims. Besides the above moral duty he has an intellectual duty to understand, judge, decide. To be able to discharge the duty of understanding he must first *recognize, select, exercise care, distinguish, discriminate, interpret.* To be able to discharge the duty of judging he must first *verify, substantiate, corroborate, establish,* in other words he must *satisfy himself.*

The auditor's duty to his client is broader than that of examining and reporting. Some of the verbs in this area of the pattern connote learning something from the client and members of his staff. These are *confer, consult, co-operate, discuss.* Others reflect a duty to teach client and staff: *advise, counsel, influence, instruct, educate.* This teaching function draws other verbs around it to express differences in aims and in emphasis. Some are mild—*notify, inform, suggest;* others are strong words—*criticize, condemn.* Between these extremes are certain more suitable words: *approve, commend, recommend, advocate, persuade, urge, convince.* This last group is particularly descriptive of the way a professional accountant prefers to influence his client. As a whole, the group of words mean: lead the client toward a better control over his affairs.

In moving to influence the client, the auditor follows the road of persuasion. But when his moral or intellectual duty is involved, stronger verbs come into play. In the processes of uncovering and of judging he may find it necessary to *refuse, restrict, decline, refrain, limit;* and he may have to *demand, insist, ignore, object, disagree.* These are strong words; most of them express a clear dissent. The public accountant therefore is not all fair words and persuasion; when he has to put his foot down, you may hear the floor boards creak. But not from stamping and ranting. If there is any creaking it is from steady pressure calmly maintained. These verbs are associated with his duties to the profession, and they mean as a group: to understand what is, in the light of what ought to be.

In this attempt to see a pattern in the verbs of auditing, a central area of 55 words is found in which certain groups of verbs express various auditing aims and duties. Three groups are identified.

(1) Duty to *reveal* the full relevant facts with an expert's feeling for their significance as facts and a professional man's regard for factual dependability (7 verbs)

(2) Duty to *lead* the client toward a better control of his affairs (21 verbs)

(3) The aim of *understanding* what is, in the light of what ought to be (27 verbs)

Probably this showing as to aims and duty is in general accord with the opinion of most informed observers. It surely is the central purpose of auditors to understand, to reveal, and to lead. And it is to be expected that the verbs which express technical actions will be found, upon classification, to suggest the varied ways and means by which the auditor gains his understanding and does his revealing and leading.

Before the auditor can discharge with assurance the numerous responsibilities suggested above, he will need to employ many special techniques of investigation in order to gain full and clear insight into the client's accounting methods and results. Some of the corresponding verbs of ways and means have a rather general connotation; others present various aspects of specific techniques.

Associated with and related to verbs indicative of ends and aims are verbs such as the following which refer to audit ways and means.

At the top of the list are a number of words carrying the general sense of *find out.* Here are *ascertain, explore, investigate, determine, acquaint self, familiarize self, seek, search, trace, study.* These terms imply that the auditor finds out by doing something himself. Others indicate that he finds out through a technique of making contacts with people. Here are *ask, inquire, interrogate, question, interview, request, require, solicit, elicit*. A few more have a similar general meaning but are not readily classified in either of these two groups: *secure, procure, obtain, gain access, account for.*

There are other techniques of ascertaining besides that of "asking"; there are also those which center about "see." Here are directive verbs such as *see, observe, notice, watch, read, consider, scrutinize, examine.* With slightly different connotations are certain limiting verbs, such as *review, sample, survey, scan,* which suggest restricting the volume of detailed "looking." But there is more to an auditor's looking than merely seeing; he learns much that is significant by contrasting this with that. Hence the following verbs expressive of contrast are also important in his work: *check, recheck, compare, audit.*

A good deal of auditing action is inspired by the question: Is the showing authentic? It is entirely natural therefore that a number of technical verbs should suggest appropriate actions. The verb *authenticate* typifies the group generally; with it should go *identify, support, vouch.* Some of the others, such as *confirm, circularize, communicate, correspond,* mean getting facts by writing rather than by speaking. Others indicate actions somewhat related to arithmetic: *count, foot, figure, estimate, compute, calculate, average, approximate.* The list of verbs related to authenticate would not be complete without certain other terms of important technical significance in auditing methods. These are *analyze, reconcile, agree, correlate, prove, test.*

The above grouping of technical verbs is of course leading up to those involved in "reporting." But some others are to be noted first which are closely related, but preliminary to, reporting itself.

One group of verbs connect the auditor's work rather directly with the accounting necessity for sharply distinguishing data affecting different fiscal periods. Here are included *adjust, change, correct, reclassify, add, deduct, eliminate;* and words more directly related to periodicity, such as *accrue, defer, accumulate, amortize, apportion, allocate, capitalize.*

Another group of words immediately preceding those dealing with reporting express the general idea of organizing the materials for use in preparing a report. These verbs are *list, copy, record, compile, tabulate, schedule, separate, segregate, consolidate, classify, marshal.*

Finally the verbs that apply to the report: The auditor will *write, draft, prepare, sign* the report; then he will *issue, supply, render* and *submit* the report. Within the report he will *embody, incorporate, present, provide, reveal, display, exhibit,* appropriate details and summaries. In the text, he will *explain, amplify, elaborate, describe, refer to, point out, mention, justify, emphasize, summarize, outline, footnote.*

This qualitative analysis has presented 170 verbs (out of nearly 500) words tabulated as being the ones that have the most meaning in auditing. Nearly one-third (55) lie in the center of the pattern and relate to professional aims and duties. The remaining 115 words are related to various techniques dealing with the ways and means by which the public accountant does the technical work that enables him to discharge his duties as auditor.

Can the verbs of most significance be sifted out of the mass? For some purposes the most significant words are those relative to duty to the public (*disclose, express an opinion*), duty to the client (*consult, advise*), duty to the profession (*judge, satisfy self*). Verbs like those explain the profession and activate the professional. For the man in the field, however, and for the student, the most useful verbs refer to professional techniques, the ways of doing what needs to be done. Thus to find out one must *ask, observe, review, compare, study;* in order to authenticate one must *vouch, confirm, compute, reconcile;* to report one must *reveal, explain, qualify.*

If we boil down the kettle of verbs still further perhaps the sample might come down to this as an expression of the essence of auditing.

Ascertain by *examining* in order to *report.*

This sentence, like most broad generalizations, is so compact that it needs some expansion to be meaningful. Ascertain what? The facts. Examine what? The evidence. Report what? An opinion. Thus broadened the three essentials became:

Ascertain the relevant facts and the accounting treatment given them in the enterprise.

Examine and evaluate the evidence supporting both the originating transactions and the subsequent periodic treatment.

Report a considered professional opinion of the disclosures prepared by the client for interested parties.

If it is desired to bring the vocabulary of audit action to the sharp point of a single verb of highest significance, this could very appropriately be *satisfy himself.* The auditor is under heavy obligation to satisfy himself of the accounting truth of what he has examined. There would be little point in merely going through the motions of using technical procedures.

The auditor is concerned with factual truth. He must satisfy himself that the transactions happened as shown and that other relevant transactions are not omitted. The way to go about satisfying himself in this connection is to make intelligent, skilled use of appropriate professional techniques. To do all this requires a satisfactory present knowledge of accepted practices, both those in auditing and those in business.

The auditor is also concerned with statistical truth. He must satisfy himself (1) that classification of accounting data into categories (accounts) has been according to the nature of the transaction and its relevance to

the given enterprise, and (2) that reclassification of data in making assignments to fiscal periods has been made objectively and with good
judgement. The basis of satisfaction in this connection is knowledge of
the theory and function of specific accounts and of the principles of
proper determination and presentation of enterprise periodic net income.

In undertaking to satisfy himself the auditor puts his knowledge of
what is good up against what he finds. Hence he must have (1) a prior
knowledge of the good and the bad in accounting and in audit procedure
and (2) a present skill in making appropriate selections from his stock of
audit techniques and good judgment in applying them intelligently to
the situation at hand.

It can be concluded therefore that auditing is more than checking;
it is research for the emphasis is upon finding out and upon thinking
how to find out. In auditing it is more important for a junior assistant
to think what he is looking for than it is that he quickly and mechanically can compare sales invoice carbons with figures in the sales book
(see the Ultra Mares case). Even a junior assistant has to satisfy himself,
hence he and all concerned with auditing must have some questions in
mind to satisfy.

(*New York Certified Public Accountant,* October, 1947)

17. Techniques and Standards

The article by Samuel J. Broad (*Journal of Accountancy,* November,
1941) implies that a forthcoming publication on "Auditing Standards"
will replace the pamphlet, "Verification of Financial Statements."

The latter, and its predecessor pamphlets, have no doubt served a useful
purpose during the past twenty-five years in presenting a compact, minimum program for the engagement that is often called a balance sheet
audit. But when one notes the very small amount of change made in the
several editions of the outline, the thought comes to mind that perhaps
the time is at hand when the whole matter might well be restudied. A
statement of auditing standards might therefore be welcomed at this
time if it proves to be something more than verification of financial
statements re-edited. Yet, to serve the present purposes as I see them,
something more is needed than the material presented in Mr. Broad's
article.

The one important innovation in the 1936 pamphlet was Section I.
This together with three pages of Section II constitutes a mild approach
to "auditing theory." The first few sections of Mr. Broad's article have
much the same flavor. These materials might well be combined—even
elaborated. There really is such a thing as auditing theory; and too little
has been said about it up to date.

Most of the pamphlet, "Verification of Financial Statements" (about

32 pages of it) deals with auditing procedure. It lists 152 items which presumably are *musts* for an examination of a small or moderate-sized company. Mr. Broad has compressed this total into twenty-seven standards. Nineteen items about receivables become two standards; twenty-four items about inventory become four standards; ninety items about assets become nineteen standards; fifty items about liabilities, capital, and surplus become seven standards.

In some ways this compression is a distinct improvement over the long list of detailed procedures. The twenty-seven standards are, in my opinion, excellent generalizations about the auditor's principal responsibilities. But in some respects they are nevertheless inadequate. If the list of 152 items of procedure is an inadequate, compressed description of a typical audit, this list of 27 auditing standards is by itself an inadequate basis for good professional judgment. Yet the committee on auditing procedure could do the profession a great service by showing those who are professionally interested how good judgment may be cultivated and showing the general public that professional accountants actually have a basis for the exercise of professional judgment even though laymen may have thought sometimes that auditors merely agreed with whatever the business executives decided. If the committee's publications were to become educational in intent rather than directive, this kind of misconception might be materially decreased.

To be more fully adequate for present-day needs the material on auditing standards should be expanded in two directions from the twenty-seven items as a nucleus—in the direction of theory and of technique.

Let me illustrate by the use of a metaphor: an audit is like the pressure of the two handles of a nutcracker upon a walnut. The walnut is the engagement; the nut meat that is extracted is the professional opinion; the two handles are, respectively, knowledge of accounting theory and knowledge of verification technique. It is the pressure of these two fields of knowledge applied to the facts in a particular engagement which enables the auditor to render a professional opinion.

In the light of this metaphor an audit might be defined as a process of forming a considered professional opinion regarding the financial statements of an enterprise by means of a critical examination of relevant accounting evidence. We may well stress the phrase "critical examination"; this would be an examination of what is in the light of what should be. To determine what is, we need the services of a knowledge of verification technique; to determine whether the given treatment is acceptable, we need the services of a knowledge of accounting theory.

The reference in the present-day audit report to the *fact* that the examination was made in accordance with generally accepted auditing standards implies a knowledge on the part of the auditor of verification techniques. And the reference in the report to the *opinion* that financial statements are in conformity with generally accepted accounting principles implies a knowledge on the part of the auditor of accounting theory.

It is to be hoped therefore that the plans of the committee extend far enough so that the outcome will be much more than a compressed revision of "Verification of Financial Statements." The pamphlet might be continued as it is, or it might be allowed to run out of print. But a better plan would be to unite these procedures suitably with auditing standards and to join with the two certain additional factors of theory and technique thus to form a complete reorientation of the essentials of auditing. If this is successfully done, the result will not only provide a compact statement of minimum standards to support the assertion in the auditor's report, but an indication as well of the road to the art of forming good judgment.

Good judgment is not to be achieved through remembered rules, but rather from an ability to make wise choices among alternatives. Nor is good judgment likely to follow upon the dogmatic application of theory to the facts; it is more likely to originate in a sense of gradation among ideas as to soundness and usefulness. And again judgment cannot safely be sought merely in the use of traditional procedures; it is necessary also that the auditor have a sharp perception of variations under different conditions. To my way of thinking standards are much more important items of knowledge than rules, procedures, or conventions. And the principal reason they should be considered very important is that wherever we deal with standards we must be ready to face alternatives, gradations, variations, departures. When this can be done successfully we can say that professional good judgment is possible of intentional achievement.

(*Journal of Accountancy*, August, 1942)

18. Application of Standards

It is not enough that members of the profession should have laid before them a compact statement of auditing standards—the theory headlines, so to speak, of auditing. Those seeking guidance from standards could benefit greatly if suggestions were also available regarding the art of applying the standards to situations.

Let us take receivables as an illustration. In the 1936 pamphlet "Verification of Financial Statements" there are nineteen items of procedure touching receivables. In the article by Samuel J. Broad (*Journal of Accountancy*, November, 1941) receivables are the subject of two of the several standards presented. Perhaps between two standards and nineteen procedures relative to the audit of receivables there is room for presenting to the members of the profession something useful about theory underlying receivables and about audit techniques which are called upon in using specific audit procedures. By "verification techniques" I mean ways of putting the auditor's mind into contact with the client's records, and ways of testing what is against what should be. By theory I mean the reasons for using this or that technique, the explanations of why one alternative treatment in the accounts stands ahead of another; and I mean the justifications for accepting, criticizing, or rejecting a treatment found in the accounts.

Such a presentation to the members could not be as compact as a statement of standards or a list of the usual procedures. Each subarea of the audit would need to be presented separately and preferably under three sections in each area. As to receivables I visualize these three sections.

(1) *Auditing Standards for Receivables.* These would be compact statements of the auditor's duty in regard to receivables in much the same language as used by Mr. Broad in his article.

(2) *Accounting Theory Underlying Receivables.* Here would be given compact statements of the basis of correct accounting treatment, perhaps with a few references to the literature where useful elaborations could be found.

(3) *Techniques for Verifying Receivables.* Listed here would be brief reminders of the principal methods that auditors have found useful in making their study of receivables and indications of alternatives that are frequently met. Where appropriate, references to the literature would be useful.

Without attempting to be at all complete, I give below a few items for each section to illustrate the idea under discussion.

Auditing Standards for Receivables

(a) The system under which the receivables are maintained should be reviewed to the extent necessary to judge by the adequacy of internal control the extent to which certain verification techniques should be applied.

(b) The accounts and records relating to receivables should be examined or analyzed to the extent deemed necessary.

(c) Whenever practicable and reasonable, confirmation of receivables should be made by direct communication with debtors, the method and extent thereof to be determined by the circumstances.

Mr. Broad's wording is closely followed with two exceptions. That part of his item 9 dealing with the amount expected to be realized is here separated and used in the theory section; an additional standard is added in regard to reviewing the system of internal control.

Accounting Theory Underlying Receivables

1. It is possible from an adequate examination of the records of receivables to reach a conclusion that the accounts represent real receivables and to form an opinion as to the approximate amount the collection of receivables may be expected to produce in due course.

2. The total of receivables which will ultimately prove uncollectible can be dependably determined in advance on a basis of statistics and experience so as to permit estimated bad debts to be expressed currently as a debit in the income statement.

3. The use of the balance sheet to disclose current financial position requires that sharp distinctions be drawn between certain account classes; hence the

following definitions are necessary. (Here suitably define such terms as trade debtors, current assets, affiliates, and others that are appropriate.)

These statements of applicable theory indicate ideas which must be accepted unless some part of the accounting and auditing of receivables is to become untenable. Such statements of theory as these are of course not limited in application to receivables. They have considerable usefulness elsewhere as well and in a complete presentation would be repeated in other context as needed.

Techniques for Verifying Receivables

Applicable to standard (a)—system review:
technique of inspection

1. Inspect the organization and procedure of handling receivables, thoroughly in the first engagement for the client or the senior in charge, sufficiently to note changes in a repeat engagement.
2. Inspect the execution of the established procedures sufficiently to be assured that they are being effectively employed.

Applicable to standard (b)—content of accounts:
techniques of account analysis

1. Study the composition of customer's balances as classified in the aging schedule. Size of selection depends on number of accounts, amount of typical balance, adequacy of internal control.
2. Compare details of notes receivable with schedule; trace into the accounts the cash for notes maturing after close of period and therefore not seen; judge the value of collateral if any.
3. Study the enterprise's bad debt experience of the past in comparison with present reserve; judge adequacy of the provisions made.
4. Observe the separation of nontrade debtors, consignments, etc. and check the agreement between subsidiary ledgers and controlling accounts.

Technique of personal inquiry

1. Inquire of responsible authority regarding the status of past due receivables, accounts or notes written off, accounts hypothecated, and notes discounted.

Applicable to standard (c)—confirmation:
technique of confirmation

1. Personally send out the monthly statements to the client's customers, with return envelope addressed to the auditor.
2. As circumstances dictate ask, (a) return to auditor if incorrect or (b) return to auditor with indication of correct or incorrect. (Might add suggestions of how to choose between these alternatives.)
3. Communicate with the attorney or bank regarding notes out for collection or recently discounted.
4. Alternatives:
   If there are no complication factors—
   (a) Circularize all customers when the receivables consist of a small number of large accounts or constitute a high percentage of the total current assets.
   (b) Circularize a suitable sample when the receivables typically show small balances and a low maximum amount in any one account.

If complicating factors are present—
(a) Devise suitable substitute methods.
   (See "Case Studies in Auditing Accounts Receivable," Maurice H.
   Stans, *Institute Papers*, 1941.)

In this illustration reference has been made to four verification techniques: Inspection, account analysis, personal inquiry, confirmation. There are other techniques of more usefulness elsewhere than in the verification of receivables. Arithmetic techniques (adding, subtracting, multiplying, posting) are not important here. Vouching techniques (examination of related authenticated documents) are more important in connection with the verification of cash, accounts payable, capital expenditures, etc. Their use in connection with receivables seldom need go beyond examination of promissory notes in the files and recent sales invoices. This last item is not included in "Verification of Financial Statements" as part of the procedure in regard to receivables. But it might well have been. Omission of that examination was a significant element in producing the Ultra Mares case.

Perhaps there is also a technique of scrutiny, a technique of ratio study, and a technique of marshaling data. No doubt there are other "gradations of circumstances," other "series of alternatives," other variations from standard, besides those here suggested. If that is the case the Institute's committee could make an important contribution to professional development by thoroughly studying each technique, each variation, and describing the finer points of the skillful use of them. Such materials would not only help to produce good auditing technicians, but they would also go a long way toward improving average individual good judgment and resourcefulness.

To do what has been described above for receivables would require more space than was given to this subject in either the procedures of the 1936 pamphlet or the standards in the 1941 outline. To do the same sort of thing for the other aspects of an audit might seem to require a series of pamphlets on auditing standards rather than one. And why not? We have thought so long about the "musts" of audit procedure that we have failed to explain the "alternatives." A minimum audit program has apparently done little to create public confidence in the profession. A periodic assertion of the necessity that we feel for freedom to exercise professional judgment is not likely to impress very many people. But authoritative literature might do so, if it plainly showed that the choices made by auditors were not accidental or willful or biased, but deliberate and reasoned, and if it made clear by its details and its depth that auditors have sound bases for their professional judgment.

I favor an expanded program for the committee on auditing procedure. It is not enough to pass from lists of procedures to a small group of standards and case studies, and then stop. The task is not completed at that point. A thorough study is needed of each technique and of related theory in order to broaden the point of view of the publications. I do not like to think of accounting organizations as issuing pronouncements. They can make a greater contribution I think when through research and publication they analyze and explain—that is, when they aim to educate.

Material dealing with auditing standards can be widely educational. We think at once of students, teachers, staff assistants. But I make so bold as to suggest that there are others who will welcome educational materials, including professional accountants and their clients, governmental officials, and the public generally.

(*Journal of Accountancy*, August, 1942)

19. Classification of Surplus

In an increasing number of published corporation reports, income and earned surplus are being presented in a single statement. The reasons behind the practice are persuasive, and the trend might well be encouraged.

It was recognized some time ago that general surplus was becoming so mixed in content as to be no longer identified with undivided realized profits. This condition had the effect of precipitating a controversy as to whether surplus should be subdivided or regarded as an indivisible "excess" of assets over liabilities and capital stock. That controversy has now been settled, I think; both the Institute's "definition of earned surplus" and various changes in the corporation laws of a number of states have contributed to the present well-defined practice of separately stating appraisal surplus, paid-in surplus, and earned surplus in the financial reports.

But neither the Institute's committee nor the state statutes have given a clear indication of transactions that may properly be debited to the various surplus accounts. Obviously the measurement of the amount of assets that may be withdrawn by action of the directors is open to a great deal of confusion so long as debiting and crediting these accounts is not subject to some standard.

It seems inappropriate for details of accounting procedure to be enacted into statutes, and it will take a long time for all of the newer issues to be settled by court interpretations of existing corporation statutes. Under these conditions a clear duty devolves upon accountants to exercise leadership in resolving the issues in a satisfactory manner. Certain steps have been taken in this direction.

One of these is the extensive use that has been made of a surplus statement when classification of surplus alone seemed to produce an inadequate disclosure. This, in many instances, was a distinct improvement, since the number and variety of adjustments to surplus were often such that the net change in the surplus balance in consecutive balance sheets could not possibly convey the necessary information. But a surplus statement may not be entirely satisfactory. It may combine in one statement such diverse elements as adjustments to appraisal surplus, to paid-in surplus, and to earned surplus; and, even if limited to earned surplus, it may become a conglomerate of capital gains and losses, corrections of past income calculations, equity remnants, accumulated undivided profits of the past, current net income, reserve appropriations and releases, and dividend declarations. This is not informative.

Another step in the direction of clarifying practices touching net worth, one possibly taken because of the confusing aspects of typical surplus analysis statements, was the statement by an Institute committee of certain broad principles including the following: (1) "Unrealized profit should not be credited to income account of the corporation either directly, or indirectly through the medium of charging against unrealized profits amounts which ordinarily fall to be charged against income accounts; (2) Capital surplus, however created, should not be used to relieve the income account of the current or future years of charges which would otherwise fall to be charged thereagainst."

Clearly these sentences are intended to offer guidance, so far as broad statements can, to the proper treatment of certain types of transactions which may seem open to disposition in one of a variety of optional ways. The point is that some charges that have been made to capital surplus are of doubtful propriety. Even if there were no statutory prescriptions to this effect, appraisal surplus and paid-in surplus should not receive charges or credits which ought to be made in current income or earned surplus.

Both of these actions, one a growth of practice, the other carefully considered opinions of an Institute committee, deal with a possible confusion of thought regarding the treatment of certain transactions affecting net worth. These progressive steps might well be followed by others that will still further clarify practice.

The integration of income and earned surplus into one statement is one of these further steps; a statement of the implications of the two broad principles given above is another. Some suggestions are here offered on the latter point.

Accountants might well agree that certain typical items should be charged against capital surplus, the implication being that items not mentioned should be associated with current income or earned surplus. An opinion of this sort, if authoritatively supported, would reflect the treatment that accountants felt was proper in view of the purposes and uses of accounting reports, even though some other treatment might be permissible under the statutes of a given state.

Debits to *revaluation surplus* are acceptable for the following:

(1) Transfers to stated capital because of stock dividends.

(2) Fixed assets previously written up, now written down (not to exceed the amount of the original write-up credited to revaluation surplus).

(3) Intangibles originally brought into the accounts by a credit to revaluation surplus, now written off. (If necessary, create paid-in surplus by a reduction of stated capital.)

(4) Loss from sale of reacquired shares or from retirement of reacquired shares purchased at a price above stated capital per share. (*Query:* Should this last debit be limited to the pro rata portion of paid-in surplus applicable to these shares and the excess charged to earned surplus as a distribution of profits?)

(5) Deficit from earned surplus account after including the operating results of the current period. (If necessary, create paid-in surplus by a reduction of stated capital.)

(6) Cash dividends (other than clearly liquidating distributions) only when specifically permitted by the controlling state statute and then only for the purpose of protecting the continuity of preferred dividends during a temporary failure of current income to cover.

Although the above may be an inadequate consideration of the treatment of capital surplus it may be sufficient to point out some specific aspects of the question of whether items relevant to either appraisal surplus or paid-in surplus should be carefully excluded from any form of statement of earned surplus.

(*Journal of Accountancy,* January, 1940)

20. Equity Transactions and Income

It is a significant fact that assets are the focus of much of management's attention within an enterprise and of much interest on the part of parties outside the enterprise. In a very real sense men are "asset-minded," and for that reason accounting practices are strongly oriented toward assets. Other data than assets as such seem supplementary to and analytical of assets.

From the above it might seem to be sufficient to report only the assets held now against those held a year ago. Much could be learned from such a report. The quantity change in each kind of asset would be clearly evident, and the increase or decrease in total could be easily read. Some people might be content with such reporting. Others of a more inquiring turn of mind would wonder how much of the apparent changes were due to investment added or withdrawn by stockholders and creditors, how much was due to appraisal write-up or write-down of prior asset figures, and how much was trustworthily attributable to management's active administration of the assets in the atmosphere of current business conditions.

Assets and changes therein are indeed matters of high interest to the parties concerned. Yet a reporting of assets alone would be inadequate for many users because the reporting would not distinguish the results flowing from different causes.

Each asset account in spite of careful classification by type arises out of a variety of antecedents. The person with an inquiring turn of mind will want supplementary tables of figures which will help him to isolate and judge the different kinds of asset changes. He will wish to view the assets in the light of the diverse interests of the various parties who have contractual rights in them, and he will like to have the means of viewing the assets in a manner designed to give him some insight into the effectiveness with which the assets have been acquired, manipulated, and exchanged under the direction of management.

One of these supplementary tables would consist of a list of the present equity accounts and those of a year earlier (obviously these are the items on the right side of ordinary balance sheets). A comparison of these equity figures would reveal: (1) the (net) change in assets due to investments and withdrawals by creditors and stockholders, or to appraisal revaluations, and (2) significant alterations in the elements of the equity structure and changes in the relation of various equity items to the total.

Another supplementary analysis would explain all other asset changes. This one would set in contrast, (1) a report of efforts (expressed in costs, expenses, and losses) made in the expectation of inducing a net inflow of new assets, and (2) a report of the accomplishments (expressed in gains, incomes, and revenues) achieved by managerial activities in the setting of current business conditions.

This is but another way of saying: Assets and their ramifications constitute the central interest of all parties concerned in a corporation.

The equities sides of two balance sheets are in effect supplementary analyses which by comparison will reveal those asset changes which are involved in the administration of equities.

The income statement is, or should be, a supplementary analysis of the remaining asset changes—those involved in the management's efforts to use the assets effectively.

By the tradition of double-entry bookkeeping the balance sheet is given primary place, and the income statement is considered as a subordinate analysis of the noninvestment changes in proprietorship. It becomes evident that: (1) balance sheets alone are inadequate reports; (2) assets are a jumble of items derived from a mixture of equity transactions and economic transactions; and (3) the recent emphasis on the income statement is a natural result of perceiving the fact that therein lies the clue to enterprise value and managerial efficiency because it reports on operating transactions.

Such an explanation does not of itself bring about any alteration in the form of the usual statement. But it does show that under some conditions the content of the income statement may be something less than the theory of financial statements indicates that it ought to be.

The income statement is not in accord with the theory of financial statements:

(1) When it includes elements which are related to capital surplus in any of its forms.

(2) When it includes some of the results of equity transactions that are entered upon for their financial effects but produce net balances which have a surface similarity, as debits and credits, to losses and gains.

(3) Where it neglects to reflect all transactions in asset utilization, i.e., those entered upon for their productive effect.

(4) When it reflects an overemphasis upon recurring earnings to the exclusion of nonrecurring losses and gains.

(5) When no provision is made for including corrections of prior calculations of net profit.

When the reverse of these propositions is true, the income statement comes more closely into harmony with the essential theory of financial statement function. It is brought into closer accord with theory whenever capital surplus adjustments are excluded from earned surplus, and whenever income and earned surplus are integrated into a single report.

(Journal of Accountancy, January, 1940)

21. Clean Surplus, Pro and Con

If income and earned surplus are integrated into a single statement analytical of all nonfinancial changes in the assets between two balance sheet dates, the item "earned surplus" in a given balance sheet will change from that item in the prior balance sheet only by the net of dividends declared therefrom and additions coming from the current combined income and surplus statement.

There are several reasons in favor of this type of presentation. This arrangement would tend to highlight the estimate character of the income calculation. Too many people regard the final figure in an income statement as a fully established, indisputable fact and unlikely to need later corrective reporting. The truth is that the only complete measurement of enterprise profit or loss would be one obtained by considering as a unit the concern's life history from inception to termination. The next best thing to this impractical and long-delayed terminal report is a series of periodic reports, the summation of which will closely approximate the ultimate, terminable result.

Since we cannot do without periodic reports and wish them, in summary total, to approach the ultimate terminable result of the enterprise, all data from operations (whether classified as affecting a period's net income or the earned surplus of the moment) should be reported together and be viewed together.

This view would carry with it the idea of placing in the income calculation rather than in the earned surplus section all items in the nature of later corrections to prior expense and revenue estimates. This connotation, it is said, might be construed as unfavorable reflections upon well-intentioned management although estimate errors are unavoidable. The answer is (1) that no one can reasonably expect management to be clairvoyant; (2) that errors which later are seen to have been avoidable by exercise of better foresight or different reasonable policies, should be disclosed as a matter of useful information to management and in fairness to investors who are inescapably concerned with management's efficiency.

Another argument is that the association of net income calculation and earned surplus data would compromise the comparability of the operating results of successive fiscal periods, and distort the reporting of recurring income and expense by adding in nonrecurring and unusual items. The answer is that properly organized statements will still be as comparable in their details as are present income statements.

As to "distortion," that is something which depends on the point of view. The doctrine of distortion of the final figure usually assumes smooth regularity to be the natural phenomenon. Yet there is just as much justification for considering irregularity of the final figure as normal, in which case "smoothed regularity" would be the distortion.

The doctrine also assumes, erroneously I think, that the final figure will be the only significant amount and that it will, because of its position alone, become the multiplier when a reader undertakes to capitalize net income as a test of enterprise value. I think that to take such a position is to underrate the intelligence of the user in interpreting the statement subhead "nonrecurring." More errors of judgment would probably rest upon neglect to note the significance of nonrecurring items than from possible inadvertent overemphasis in considering them.

"Distortion," as usually thought of, is no doubt an outgrowth of the processes of accruing and deferring. So much progress has been made in accruing expense before disbursement and in deferring costs after disbursement that this quasi-scientific refinement of accounting should be preserved and extended. Perhaps it is this thought that gives rise to the notion that incorporation of nonrecurring items within the structure of the income statement will negate all of the good work that has gone into the skillful building of accruals and deferments into accounting. I am not disturbed by that fear. Whenever regularity can be detected and the amounts measured by dependably objective methods, it should be recognized in accounting procedure, for the effect is that the remaining irregular occurrences will thus be revealed and isolated for study.

The unattainable ideal is that all irregular occurrences will be eliminated through the complete perfection of the accrual system. But the fact that this is clearly unattainable should not be warrant either for excluding occurrences from the accrual system when dependable estimates can be made, or for extending the idea of the system so far that in some respects the effect is merely arbitrarily to smooth out irregularities that are inescapably irregular. Too many of the items often found as adjustments of surplus are objectionable on this very ground—their lump-sum disposition into surplus has the effect of leveling past, and perhaps future, calculations of earned income. Such items should come to the eye of the reader as he examines the statement of earned income.

Another objection to the combined statement is that its use will lead to ignoring the distinction between capital losses and operating losses (and gains). The answer is that too much has been made of their distinctions—they are distinct in some particulars—while their elements of similarity have been ignored. It is their likeness as similar aspects of asset changes which logically brings them into contact within the combined statement; their distinctions can still be revealed in the organization details of the statement. Thus nothing is lost and another advantage is gained.

It should perhaps be added that the more carefully one examines so-called capital gains and capital losses, the more evident it becomes that all losses and gains decrease or increase economic capital (assets) and are therefore equally entitled to be called "capital" losses or gains. No doubt the terminology was intended to isolate liquidation and reorganization adjustments of business. But the argument and the procedure are both poorly adapted to the reporting of a going concern. It is difficult to see how a going concern can suffer partial liquidation losses without concurrent cancellation of that much current or saved prior profit, or how a going concern can, merely by resolution, reorganize its financial structure to absorb a large loss of assets, and still carry the prior earned surplus forward undisturbed.

This brief study of the theory and practice of income statement formation seems to lend emphasis to the thought that there is need for (1) a thorough examination of the possibilities of an integrated income and earned surplus statement to assure the separation of adjustments to earned surplus and those to capital surplus, and (2) a re-examination of the sectioning of the statement in the interest of a more informative organization of the data.

The fundamental proposition is this: The content and organization of the major statement accompanying the balance sheet should be such as to constitute an informative analysis of the efforts of management to employ the capital of the enterprise in an effective manner. If this is an acceptable statement of purpose, it follows that the earned surplus and income statements must be combined in some way so that "management efforts" may be reported in one coherent statement for the study of investors.

The art of full and clear reporting admittedly presents many difficulties. But the alternative to facing and overcoming some of the difficulties is to leave in practice such a wide diversity of treatment for apparently similar items as to give the impression to some readers who compare corporation reports that corporations can treat various items about as they choose and still be within the range of someone's views of what are "accepted principles of accounting."

(Journal of Accountancy, January, 1940)

22. Standards or Standardize

The use of the word "Standards" in accounting (as in the title of the monograph, *An Introduction to Corporate Accounting Standards*) should not be interpreted as being related to standardization of methods, regimentation of opinions, or outside control over enterprise accounting practices.

The time is rapidly passing when corporations affected with a public interest can expect to enjoy complete freedom to be as peculiar in their accounts as their officers might wish. But regimented standardization is not the alternative. A better approach would be the formulation of definite standards for corporate accounting for the guidance of all concerned.

The public has at times been suspicious of the trustworthiness of corporation financial statements. May that not have been largely due to a belief that corporate officers had unlimited freedom to deal with their accounts as they wished and that the independent auditor had unlimited freedom to acquiesce if he wished to do so? Such a belief may be quite unfounded, as I think it is. But if the belief is strong enough, it may lead us into ill-advised experiments in procedure standardization.

Probably the public could readily be induced to give its confidence to standardized accounts designed and regulated from outside the enterprise. But that confidence would be misplaced. First, because standardization from outside, by transferring responsibility to a central few, would put a damper upon the initiative of thousands in the further development of accounting ideas and methods. Second, because there are other and better ways of improving public confidence in accounts and in accountants.

If the accounting decisions of corporation officers and the accounting judgments of professional auditors are founded upon high standards of accounting purpose and method, as already they are in the majority of instances, then the public could have this fact as a basis for confidence that corporation accounting and public auditing was neither subject to untrustworthy individualism nor as flexible to expedience as a willow switch.

The opportunity for public confidence to rest on such a basis could exist only if the standards upon which accounting judgments rest were themselves clearly established and widely made known. Accountants need to be in a greater degree of agreement than they are now upon the elements which lie at the foundation of their decisions and upon the methods by which they strive to arrive at good judgments.

There are other reasons why the formulation of accounting standards or accounting principles ought to receive extensive consideration.

1. Most accounting literature stresses procedures although this often is presented under the title of principles.

2. Accounting writing shows a tendency to accept judicial dicta as basic accounting ideas.

3. There seems at times to be a wide divergence in practice between the maximum and the minimum treatments of apparently similar situations.

4. It seems tacitly agreed that critical examination of financial policy should be excluded from the duties of the independent auditor although such examination could often be very fruitful.

Some may think that the phrase "accounting standards" is used as a synonym for "accounting principles." The word "standard" in this connection is a substitute, not a synonym. The word "principle" is full of meaning for us and ought not to be abandoned. An accounting principle is a crystallization from careful theorizing, a distillation from accumulated experience. It says something important about some aspect of accounting; it says this not as a law or a rule or a convention, but rather as a verbalization of concepts, an attempt at formulating previously inarticulate thoughts.

But the use of the word principle should not be permitted to carry the full breadth of meaning that is inherent in it. When the use of the word seems to lean toward the quality of universality, it becomes too broad to be useful in accounting, suggesting too much the idea of a law of nature. When its use seems to lean toward becoming in effect a synonym for the word "rule," then its meaning is too superficial, too like directing an action by no stronger force than authority to say "do it thus and so."

The word "convention" is sometimes used. It effectively avoids the sense of universality that seems sometimes to reside in the word "principle." But it avoids that sense rather too effectively. The phrase "an accounting convention" leans too strongly toward complete informality. It sounds too much like the word "conventional," like something which was once useful but now is merely traditional. Sleeve buttons on a coat, for example. It makes one think of the symbolic conventions of Egyptian art which were a mask for an inability to be realistic. It seems to imply that variation from a given convention would be merely "unconventional"; not something that is wrong or ill-advised but something that "just isn't done."

(Journal of Accountancy, July, 1941)

23. Point of Departure

The strongest reason for using the phrase "accounting standards" is that it includes the idea of possible variations from standard. Both "principle" and "rule" fail to imply that graded alternatives exist; they both seem to suggest that they rest on some middle ground, some compromise between better and worse. The word "standard" on the other hand carries with it the thought of a point of departure, a first preference. It seems clearly to recognize the possibility of a graded series of variations starting from a standard and grading down through—

> Necessary variations from standard.
> Acceptable variations from standard.
> Questionable variations from standard.
> Rejected variations from standard.

Accounting standards, in this sense of a preferred treatment and point of departure, are inherent in the nature of business enterprise and in the related purpose of accounting. Recognition of accounting variations is vital. Businessmen know that conditions vary; they think actions should be variable according to the circumstances. But their public accountant is ever fearful that he may be charged, when supporting such ideas, with desiring each to be a law unto himself, with the sky as the limit. Accountants need the protection of known standards; they need to be permitted, and helped, to explain such variation from standard as may be adopted; they need to be freed from automatic action dictated by oversimplified rules; they need to be helped to learn to weigh the reasons for and against varying from standard, thereby to develop good judgment in their own right and a means of defending that judgment to reasonable men.

When and if such a basis of accounting action is achieved within a business enterprise, it would seem to follow that accounting decisions would then be made that were satisfactory to well-informed auditors and capable of clear explanation to other interested parties. Here too is a basis upon which could be erected a structure of public confidence in accounting methods and results.

A brief consideration of inventory as an illustration of the idea of accounting standards may be in order. The accounting treatment of inventory is receiving a good deal of attention just now and notable progress is being made in uncovering the ramifications of the topic. But we may ask: Why is there an inventory problem? It only indicates a manifestation of the problem to say that we are becoming increasingly conscious of the fact that "inventory" is not simply one thing but a complex variety of things. There is a problem here that requires the thoughtful consideration of many people because inventory rules have not kept pace with changes in the ideas of what an inventory is and why it exists.

We may think that all are agreed upon the idea of what an inventory is until we explore the matter. We may unconsciously assume that our own idea has been the one that prevailed from the beginning until we examine the older ideas.

Several hundred years ago the concept of inventory seems to have been that of a listing and an appraisal of all property owned. Such a list served two purposes: (1) As the basis for entries opening a set of double-entry books when no prior record was available, and (2) as the basis for determining solvency at a time when very stringent laws penalized a fraudulent bankrupt.

Gradually the concept of inventory changed to that of goods for sale. In the eighteenth century it was a "stock of goods"; in the twentieth century it became "raw materials and finished goods." With the rise of short-term credit and an increasing use of bank loans, the inventory came to be regarded as a current asset that was only a step or two away from being cash available to repay current loans. The rule (lower of cost or market) that was begun much earlier, and for other reasons, was later accepted as expressing this liquidity theory of inventory.

Later developments, first cost accounting and the perpetual inventory and subsequently the shift of accounting emphasis from the balance sheet to the income statement, tended to weaken the earlier concepts. Now the inventory came to be considered by many people as a means of producing revenue, and hence as an element whose primary function was to become a factor in some calculation of net income, present or future. According to this view inventory was an account rather than a list of property or store of physical goods.

If the inventory is an important factor in the income calculation, then the pricing technique used in totaling a list of items should be one which is appropriate to that purpose. Since the inventory is primarily an account it, like all accounts, is to be treated with a systematic regard for the statistical characteristics of its debits and credits. Because it is an account it is a fit subject for verification procedures consistent with similar procedures for other important accounts. Let us explore this thought further.

The essential accounting aspect of inventory is that an inventory is first of all an account—a record of in and out, as is the case of every account. Inventory balance should be determined by accounting subtraction and thus provide a figure to be reported in the financial statements just as the cash account provides its balance. It follows that listing and pricing physical quantities merely provide a simple means of testing the accuracy of the account balance rather than a means of calculating that balance directly outside the account. Counting cash and reconciling the bank have the same testing purpose in connection with the cash account.

Evidently the word "inventory" can mean different things to different people. As a factor in merchandising or warehousing, inventory is an assortment of physical goods; as a factor in short-term credit or solvency, it is a group of values that are in the process of becoming cash; as a factor in the periodic calculation of net profit, it is an account—a category of certain unamortized outlay costs; as a factor in auditing, it is a list of goods that is made up and priced in order to afford a testing of an account balance. Only the last two of these ideas of what an inventory is can readily be called an accounting idea or an auditing idea. The basis of rules for the accounting treatment of inventory should be sought here. When this is done it will be observed that there is no place for the old rule of thumb, "the lower of cost or market." That rule may still have some relation to the granting of short-term credit and to tests of solvency in that it expresses a weak sort of automatic conservatism; the rule may still have some usefulness for pointing out to merchandising officers that in determining sales price policy conscious attention should be given to price trends in the current and prospective market. But in itself the "convention" has never been appropriate as a rule of account-keeping and of the calculation of operating profits.

If the old rule is appropriate only in special situations and is not very close to the heart of accounting, then it should be abandoned as a rule of accounting and something else set up as a guide to the accounting treatment of inventory. That "something else" could be an accounting standard with variations or exceptions plainly stated. Here is a trial statement of an inventory standard:

Inventory Standard

In the usual situation, the preferred basis for pricing goods entering an inventory account is the delivered invoice price or production cost; the preferred basis for pricing withdrawals from an inventory account is the earliest prices still represented by items on hand; the preferred basis for pricing a listing of items on hand as a means of testing the account balance carried forward to the next period is the invoice price of the latest items acquired to the extent that the purchased quantities are still on hand.

There are several reasons for favoring this kind of a standard over the rule of the lower of cost or market.

(a) Being set up as a standard this statement clearly predicates the existence of exceptions, something the old rule does not do. The old rule is too simple to cover modern complex conditions; its use can make an inventory figure in the financial statement seem to be an accounting fact although it is only an opinion regarding "value."

(b) The standard as stated fits many more of the present-day typical situations than the old rule does because cost accounting and perpetual inventories are characteristic in an industrial society.

(c) The standard expresses better than the rule the elements common to all types of inventory: *existence* (the price base is *our* transactions, not transactions in the market between parties outside our enterprise), *purpose* (conversion or sale, excluding equipment items as the early uses of inventory did not do), *measurement* (acquisition prices or production costs of our transactions are the only established facts suitable for our record), *movement* (inflow and outflow is typically first-in, first-out whether the units are identifiable or not).

(d) The old rule contains no suggestion that consideration should be given to the probable near future trend of prices up or down. Because of this factor the rule's vaunted conservatism may prove to be pretty weak tea. The most significant fact about a given inventory as a source of cash available to liquidate debt may be the trend of prices after the statement's closing date or after the date of audit.

There are several reasons for considering a standard plus variations from standard as providing a superior basis for deciding the accounting treatment to be accorded inventories.

> a. An inventory standard will be a better aid than a rule, such as the lower of cost or market, in distinguishing different kinds of situations which too often are merged as if they called for exactly the same accounting treatment.

The following practices need to be sharply differentiated; they do not call for the same treatment: (a) Eliminating inventory items from the records because the goods were not found on hand or were judged to be unsalable, (b) making prudent provision in the light of all the available evidence for anticipated shrinkage in or disappearance of profit margins, (c) changing the listing prices of inventory items in the process of calculating the total inventory figure. Change of listing prices is not a suitable way of making provision for possible loss; certainly it is not a way for eliminating unsalable items.

> b. An inventory standard will be a better guide to accounting action than a rule of thumb in both the usual situation and the exceptional situation.

A rule is a guide to action only in one of two directions: either the situation in question falls within the rule or it falls outside of its control. This fails to provide clear direction to the treatment to be given in situations that are related but dissimilar. A standard on the other hand covers the usual or most typical situations, and the associated variations cover necessary and acceptable modifications. Indication is also given, by briefly listing questionable or rejected variations, of the limitations of acceptability that are inherent in the particular standard.

c. An inventory standard will be a better basis for forming good judgments than will the customary inventory rule.

There is a little judgment involved in applying a rule; that is why it is a rule. And little training in forming good judgment is derived from merely applying rules. On the other hand judgment is involved in selecting the point in a graded sequence of ideas which is most appropriate to the situation in question. Such a graded sequence of accounting ideas is provided when the following steps have been taken: (a) State concisely the method best adapted to the accounting treatment of the usual situation in a given area of accounting problems. (b) Analyze the conditions surrounding other situations in the same area which are similar but with differences. Clearly recognize the need for making a limited number of exceptions to the treatment directed by the standard. Plainly indicate the reasons supporting the acceptability of certain variations in treatment. (c) Show that variations are acceptable only within limits. Grade the variations of treatment downward from the fully acceptable, as the justifications for a departure from standard becomes harder to make, until the unjustifiable, and therefore rejected, variations are reached.

(*Journal of Accountancy*, July, 1941)

24. Variations from Standard

One of the most persuasive reasons for using the term "standard" in accounting is the fact that the word clearly predicates the possibility of varying from the preferred way. Since variability is more characteristic of business events than uniformity, a single rule cannot apply equally well in all situations. Since variability is likely to fall into a graded series, variations in applying a standard should be visualized as a gradation in departure from standard.

Variations from a standard or preferred way of treating inventory in the accounts, for example, could therefore be recognized as falling into a graded sequence, perhaps described as necessary variation, acceptable variation, questionable variation, rejected variation.

A. *Necessary Variations*

1. If inventory items are either unsalable, unusable, completely obsolete, lost, destroyed or stolen, their cost should be passed to profit and loss when the fact is recognized.
2. If actual purchase price or production cost is unascertainable for inventory items, a reasonable approximation of that figure is acceptable, and disclosure of the fact is necessary.

From one point of view variation 1 might be considered descriptive of a type of withdrawal. But since it does represent typical occurrences, it is better to think of the situation described as a necessary variation from standard even though such incidents may appear with some regularity. In some situations such as those where exchanges of securities or exchanges of securities for properties have taken place and in barter transactions generally, the purchase price or production cost may be unknown. Obviously the inventory standard cannot be applied because the necessary knowledge of the facts is lacking. There is no alternative here except to determine a reasonable approximation of a cost figure (variation 2) and use that to express the item when it enters the inventory account, while it remains in the account balance, and when it is withdrawn.

B. *Acceptable Variations*

3. If actual purchase price or production cost for inventory items is not reasonably ascertainable, the following are acceptable approximations provided that disclosure of the pricing base is made:
   a. Average unit prices of purchases actually made, provided that variations in these prices are not so extreme as to destroy the representativeness of an average
   b. Standard costs, provided that the operation of the system makes for frequent revision of standard cost figures as conditions change
   c. Sales price less estimated marketing costs, provided that conditions prevailing in the industry tend to synchronize cost prices and selling prices
4. If convincing evidence is at hand (evidence of partial damage to inventory items, of probable obsolescence, of over-stocked supply in a glutted market, of sales prices fallen below cost of prior purchases) which indicates that actual cost probably will not be recovered, adequate provision should be made for the anticipated loss by a separate charge in profit and loss and a credit to inventory reserve for disclosure as a deduction on the balance sheet.
5. If the principal evidence depended upon to indicate that actual cost probably will not be recovered is actual or prospective decline in replacement price or reproduction cost, it is an adequate financial disclosure to state the estimated lower figure for inventory in parentheses in the balance sheet along with the cost figure, the latter being the one used in the cost of sales section of the income statement.

In some situations actual cost is not reasonably ascertainable although theoretically it could be calculated. Such variations in conditions justify variation from standard. In some instances convincing evidence may suggest that original cost probably will not be recovered. Use of the standard then might prove misleading to readers of the balance sheet. Hence variation from standard is acceptable to the extent of supplementing the balance sheet item for inventory, shown at cost, by deducting a reserve for possible inventory shrinkage determined as to amount in the light of all available evidence. Because decline in replacement price alone can hardly be considered convincing evidence of probable loss, that provision against that prospect should be made in the profit and loss calculation. The reader is amply advised of the fact by a figure shown in parentheses in the balance sheet.

C. *Questionable Variations*

Certain treatments have at times been given to inventories which in the writer's opinion are not justified by the purposes of inventory accounting. These may be classified as questionable variations from the standard. Such treatments might be abandoned except in so far as the peculiar facts involved may be considered significant in connection with the use of one of the necessary or acceptable variations from standard set forth above.

6. It is a questionable variation from inventory standards to assume that unit prices in the inventory sheets should be changed if the current price in the purchase market is lower than the original price paid for the items listed.

Several reasons supporting this view are briefly stated below.

a. The rule of the lower of cost or market is an oversimplified guide to the treatment of inventories. Under complex modern conditions what is needed is not so much the guidance of a rule of thumb as guidance toward good judgment in treating inventories appropriately according to the basic purposes of accounting.

b. The origins of the rule of cost or market suggest that the rule is more related to a banker's judgment of the liquidity of loan collateral than to the usual accounting use of inventory as an important factor in the calculation of realized net profits.

c. The existence of tax regulations which at present tend to lend support to the use of the cost-or-market rule, should not prevent accountants from advocating better methods. Such regulations might even be a reason for advocating a different basis for the accounting treatment of inventories, since better methods in practical use will ultimately influence tax regulations in the same direction.

7. It is a questionable variation from standard to assume that incidental peculiarities in an industry constitute unusual conditions of such a nature as would negative the use of a first-in, first-out basis for recording the addition and withdrawal of inventory units.

There are several reasons for restricting the theory of inventory additions and withdrawals to that which recognizes the inherent reasonableness of first-in, first-out.

a. If inventory units are in fact indistinguishable, one assumption as to the order of actual withdrawal would seem as good as another. In the last-in, first-out method and the base stock method we merely choose that assumption which best suits some assumed special purpose. We could just as well have chosen that assumption which most closely harmonizes with the actual conditions of physical withdrawals found in most business situations.

b. The extension of the method of base stock, or last-in first-out, to businesses wherein even the justification of unidentifiable units is absent, serves to indicate that the method is not so much a reflection of an asserted basic peculiarity of a particular line of industry as it is a method of accomplishing indirectly, and in the guise of an inventory peculiarity, certain objectives that are not clearly put in the foreground, and which may run counter to the essential purpose of accounting to reveal fluctuations when fluctuations there are.

c. By impounding very old prices in the balance sheet figure for inventory certain methods accomplish a *leveling* of the calculated periodic net income derived from actual transactions. Yet accounting should be considered as a means of *revealing* whatever fluctuations of periodic net income there may be either as the result of economic conditions or of managerial activities. Separation in the accounts of the effect of managerial action and of economic change is impossible even if it were conceded as desirable.

Any procedure which smooths out the effect of transactions and states the inventory figure in the balance sheet markedly below the cost invested in that asset is an undesirable adjunct to accounting calculations. This "leveling" of net income may indeed afford indirect relief from the effect of a lack of tax authorization to average several years results. But a desire for a fair basis of reasonable taxation is not a suitable starting point for the determination of those accounting rules that touch upon the calculation of periodic net income.

It is possible by accounting treatment to seem to overstress the complete and final validity of periodic figures; it is also possible by accounting treatment to understress the significance of fluctuations in the periodic figures. To err in either direction is to misapply accounting as an instrument of measurement.

Rejected Variations

It is an unacceptable variation from inventory standards to price unsold goods at (selling) prices higher than the cost invested in the inventory items.

This proposition is a familiar one in accounting and needs no extended list of reasons in support. Usually it is supported because the use of selling prices for inventory purposes would introduce an unearned profit into the accounts. An even more convincing reason is that cost prices must be used in order to show the reader whether original cost was recovered through sale of the goods, partially lost by selling below cost, or abandoned in advance of sale through profit and loss charges that anticipated future loss.

The superiority of standard over rule as a guide to the accounting treatment of inventories has been outlined above. This can be reinforced by viewing the weakness involved in attempting to rest the treatment of inventories upon a single, overgeneralized rule. In applying the cost-or-market rule, how would the pricing of the list of inventory items be different under the various conditions indicated below? Would a rule of thumb be dependably useful if a number of these differing conditions applied to different items in the same list?

(1) Market is already below cost.

(2) Market is falling but not yet below cost.

(3) Prospects are rather clear that market will soon fall still further below cost than it is now.

(4) Sales prices have not followed the movement of prices in the purchase market.

(5) Sales prices are clearly leading purchase prices in the decline.

(6) Market prices are drifting close to cost but strong indications are present that soon they are likely to turn upward.

(7) Product obsolescence is not yet evident but it nevertheless seems imminent.

Can such variables be given due effect in the treatment of a corporation's inventory if the staff accountants merely use the cost-or-market rule which they expect the auditors presently to insist upon? If the independent auditor insists upon stating the balance sheet figure at cost or market regardless of the company's pricing of material requisitions for cost accounting use, what good explanation can be given for the lack of agreement between the inventory ledger total and the balance sheet figure for inventory? If the auditing of inventory prices consists of nothing more than the application of the cost-or-market rule, what must the informed public think, under some of the market conditions listed above, of auditing as an exercise of professional judgments?

Surely better ways must exist of exercising professional judgment than by the routine application of an outmoded rule of thumb.

(Journal of Accountancy, July, 1941)

25. Inventory Conservatism

After the publication of the American Accounting Association's monograph, *An Introduction to Corporate Accounting Standards,* a number of readers raised questions regarding the meaning at certain places in the text. A sample of these which dealt with inventory accounting were answered as indicated below.

Q. If the rule of cost or market is repudiated, is that not equivalent to repudiating the principle of conservatism?

A. At best conservatism is a creditor's rule based on the theory that a prospective borrower may understate his obligations and overstate his assets. A banker who was not conservative would get few deposits to lend to other people. But the surveyor employed to mark the boundary of certain property is not expected to be conservative, only accurate.

It will be an advantage to accountancy if accountants will think of themselves as technicians in certain kinds of measurements. They can do this with advantage even though all of their measurements fall short of being as perfect as one could wish. The engineer never forgets, no matter how delicate his micrometer may be, that his work is correct only within limits.

Repudiation of the cost-or-market rule rests more upon doubts regarding the theories that underlie it than upon its relation or lack of relation to conservatism. Here are the underlying theories: (1) that a conservative view is reflected by overstating the cost of goods sold through lowering the prices of inventory items; (2) that a fall in repurchase prices is adequate evidence that a loss will result when sales will have finally been made; (3) that adjustments of inventory must be made through individual items rather than against the aggregate; (4) that probable losses should be anticipated by a profit and loss charge before a loss has taken place.

There is something to be said for some of these theories if taken separately. But viewed as a whole, as they must be with reference to this inventory rule, they produce a foundation that is not convincing.

Q. Is it sufficient to regard conservatism as something for parentheses or for interpretation, rather than a principle of accounting itself?

A. A careful appraisal of the monograph as a whole will be unlikely to leave the typical reader with a conviction that the authors have such a passion for great theoretical precision that it leads them to favor sacrificing reasonable prudence.

Accounting is measurement, and precision must be characteristic of measurement. Ideal precision is not attainable in accounting any more than in engineering. There are degrees of precision. Honing the cylinders of an inexpensive motor to a clearance of .015 inch does not set the standard or precision for a pursuit plane's motor. A greater degree of precision can be accomplished in accounting than that obtained from a rule of thumb like cost or market. Accounting will always lack complete precision; but its precision of measurement can always be improved.

The facts of business are not more complex than the facts of engineering. Why then do we hear so much about a conservative accountant and so little about a conservative engineer? Is it because the engineer is understood to be able to work within varying degrees of precision, but the accountant is assumed to work always within the precision of $.01? If a bridge engineer does undertake to lean toward conservatism, it will be by means of a safety factor added after his calculations have been made of the stresses to be expected. He does not try to calculate stresses "conservatively."

There is a way of giving accounting expression to conservatism, but the best way is not through repricing items in the inventory list.

Q. Do the authors oppose the proposition that expenditures originally regarded as costs should be recognized as losses and immediately written off or made the subject of a reserve when it appears that the original cost will prove not recoverable?

A. The problem is not whether cost may remain too long as the asset. Rather, when is original cost to be considered proven as not recoverable? The evidence supporting nonrecoverability will be varied; sometimes it may be irrefutable, again, only convincing or suggestive; or it may only vaguely hint at a possibility. The disposal of asset cost should rest upon a consideration of all the available evidence and upon a close judgment of the quality of that evidence.

The question mentions two alternatives, writing off and creating a reserve. The alternatives are not identical. Repricing inventory sheets is not the same thing as "writing off" since the debit will be classified differently. A reserve created by a debit to profit and loss is not the same as a write-off since its basis is different. There is even a place for a simple parenthesis informing the reader of the balance sheet of a price fact in addition to the original cost of the inventory. In fact, if there is no evidence to support an inventory adjustment except a decline in repurchase prices, such a parenthesis is a clear disclosure.

Q. Why does not the same reasoning that supports reduction of inventory for damaged or obsolete goods also support a write-off because of a fall in prices?

A. Damage and obsolescence is acceptable as a reason for adjusting the inventory not because inventory is "less valuable" but because an irrevocable loss has occurred. Price decline for goods we have not bought does not create for us an irrevocable loss. Price fall may be a warning of losses to come; but so long as a given price trend is reversible, as it always is, the loss in goods on hand is not yet very convincing.

An asserted permanent reduction in value from price fall is also unconvincing. The only permanent aspect of market price movements is that of change. When goods have been sold for less than their cost we are convincingly faced with an accomplished fact. Short of that stage we are dealing only with probabilities or possibilities. In accounting we cannot always wait for the accomplished fact; the accountant, like the physician, must at times work with probabilities. But we should work with them in a different manner than with accomplished facts. To write down inventory in the same way for goods that have been destroyed by water and goods for which duplicates could be obtained at a lower price, is not a very good demonstration of refinement in technique. Instead of this sounding like unimportant hairsplitting, I hope it may sound like an invitation for accountants to demonstrate to a critical public that accounting can refine its techniques.

(*Accounting Review*, December, 1941)

26. Early Uses of a Rule

Several surveys for the late 1930's[3] show that the rule "lower of cost or market" is still widely used although the percentage of companies using it seems from the separate samples to be declining somewhat. But a rule

[3] N.A.C.A. *Bulletin*, March, 1937; National Industrial Conference Board *Report*, February, 1938; *Journal of Accountancy*, October, 1940.

may be widely useful in business without having the character necessary to make it a fundamental proposition of accounting. If we wish to search out the character of this rule; if we would like to determine whether it is a convenient and expedient rule of thumb or a basic accounting idea, we might begin by looking up its ancestry.

The information is not available to enable us to find the rule's real origin or to trace step by step the way it came to receive the acclaim these surveys seem to show. Yet enough material is at hand to indicate that it is a result of the mingling of two bloodlines: expediency and convenience. It is this mixed ancestry which accounts for the notion that taking an inventory is a process of evaluation rather than a process of cost pricing.

Let us go back about five and a half centuries. If long-established precedent is enough to justify a rule, the rule should stand; cases are known as early as the beginning of the fifteenth century wherein goods in inventory were priced below their purchase cost.

A German scholar writing of the manuscript records of an Italian businessman, Francesco di Marco,[4] pointed out that an estate costing 366 fl. in 1393 was valued in an inventory of 1412 at 240 fl. "because the vineyard had been spoiled." He also showed that this man's furniture and utensils were valued by appraisers in 1408 at less than cost because "the items had deteriorated." These cases we would now say reflected damage and depreciation. But there is more. A stock of almonds bought for trade in 1406 at a cost of 60 fl. appeared still unsold in a later inventory at 50 fl. Beneath the item was this notation: "We have entered the 10 fl. in the debit of goods profit account as damage (loss) because we no longer value them as above since they have fallen in price."

It is doubtful that these changes were made in the inventories merely for the satisfaction of producing an accurate profit calculation and a conservative statement of assets. It is very probable that there was present some compelling force other than a high resolve to record only the truth.

In another place we find a clue to the probable reason for the practice of taking up every possible loss. The same author[5] points out that the tax burden in Italian cities early in the fifteenth century was very heavy. Sometimes several levies of $\frac{1}{2}$ per cent would be made in a single year besides several forced loans of 1 per cent. These taxes were calculated on the amount of the citizen's property less certain deductions. In one example for the year 1427, the tax was assessed on a citizen's lands, investments, and business capital, less an amount for debts payable, dwelling houses, etc. The author further points out that the amount of lands and investments could be determined by tax officials with considerable exact-

---

[4] Balduin Penndorf, *Luca Pacioli*, introduction pp. 36-37.
[5] Balduin Penndorf, "The Relation of Taxation to the History of the Balance Sheet," *Accounting Review*, September, 1930, p. 247.

ness and that therefore "endeavors to pay the lowest possible amount in taxes could be made only with reference to business capital."

Penndorf does not give the details of any method for stating business capital at a minimum. But recognizing every possible loss, even price change, would have that effect. He does indicate however that some merchants kept two sets of records and that others retired from business rather than produce their accounts. In fact the tax burden was so heavy, and tax evasion so widespread by 1458 that Italian taxation methods had to be revised.

There was therefore a good deal of incentive in the situation to bring men to seek plausible reasons for reducing the asset figures. Damage, deterioration, lower current prices could furnish such plausible explanations.

"Cost or market" is often spoken of as a general rule of accounting. But it is to be noted that tax expediency was no more than a special condition. As such it could produce only a special rule covering special circumstances. There is no basis in tax expediency for either a general rule of account-keeping or a general rule of reporting the results of double-entry bookkeeping.

Let us come a little further down to date, down to about the time Columbus discovered America. Paciolo published the first printed text on bookkeeping in 1494. He begins his discussion with a long description of what we would now call an opening entry. He advises the merchant who desires to begin keeping systematic accounts to prepare a statement (*bilancio*) "of whatever he has in this world, personal property or real estate." Then he goes on to say that precious stones should be included "according to current prices"; for silver articles he mentions, "giving each thing its customary price." In addition to leaving us in doubt as to what price he really means here he adds this disconcerting advice: "Make the prices higher rather than lower . . . so that you can make a larger profit."

Apparently "valuing" one's possessions at a high figure was thought to influence the price at which they could be sold. The idea sounds very modern. Some people, I fear, still believe that a high purchase cost is a basis for a high selling price. These people are as mistaken as Paciolo was. But it is more important for the present purpose to note that this discussion of inventory treatment was about an opening entry. Probably the assumption was that the merchant had no prior records of original costs and must therefore give the items their price. In such a situation some kind of "valuing" was inescapable if a set of books was to be opened at all. Until adequate records could make possible some other way of finding the data from which to construct an opening entry, valuing was the only method available.

In the absence of dependable records this approach must still be used. Until systematic records came into use, *valuing* the inventory was no doubt the usual case and as such was a proper base for the inventory rules which Paciolo mentions. After records are in use, however, *costing* the inventory from the records should become the usual case and valuing the inventory the exception. The center of any rule should be the typical case, not the exceptional one. At the present time a complete lack of price records or purchase invoices is so infrequent that this situation can only be a basis for an exception to a rule. The rule itself should be that pricing an inventory is basically a costing problem.

Two other items are of interest here. One of Paciolo's followers, Pietra, writing in 1586 about bookkeeping for a monastery, offers the advice in his chapter 13 that a value should be given to things harvested and things manufactured, but this value should be lower than current prices "so that the proceeds will not fall below this value in case of sale." Does this not advise pricing the inventory so there will always be a profit upon sale?

About a hundred years later (1682, 1690) an English writer, Monteage, deals with livestock inventories. In one example, cows are priced in a later inventory at the same price as in the opening entry. In another example, cows are priced higher than the opening price apparently because of recent higher-priced purchases. Sheep are priced as in the opening entry; lambs unsold are priced at about 25 per cent below the sales price received for their brothers. Both a bull and a ram are priced slightly below the opening figure. Another illustration is a horses account bearing two credit entries, one an inventory priced at less than the opening figure—the other is a transfer to loss and gain, where the item is labeled "for their use and impairing."

In these situations, besides being confused with depreciation, the inventories again deal with special cases. Harvested crops and the natural increase in farm animals must be priced in some expedient way if they are to enter into statement calculations as they undoubtedly should. But it may be doubted if these situations today represent typical conditions under which inventories are used.

Since the use of the cost-or-market rule rests partly upon situations where actual prices are lacking, it would seem to be a special rule of very limited significance. Such conditions no longer provide the predominate occasions for taking inventory.

(Accounting Review, June, 1941)

27. Inventory Pricing Abroad

A part of the background for the present-day rule "lower of cost or market" is the fact of its use in seventeenth century France and in nineteenth century Germany.

In France, under an ordinance promulgated by Louis XIV in 1673, merchants and bankers were required to keep a journal of their transactions for reference in case of dispute. They were also to have the book authenticated by the signature of a public official. In addition, as Professor Howard points out,[6] they were required every two years to make a statement (*inventaire*) of all their fixed and movable properties and their debts receivable and payable. The French law at this point used words that are almost identical with those used by Paciolo in writing about the opening entry. That early writer's instructions about opening entries were thus reflected in European law regarding periodic financial reports. And our own courts seem to consider that the inventory, and the balance sheet, still involve a valuation problem. They too are emphasizing the occasional situation, that is, the situation existing when solvency or the dividend base is in question. Yet, the usual situation is one involving the calculation of profits at the end of a fiscal period rather than solvency.

Jacques Savary, the principal author of the ordinance of 1673, published a book in 1675 entitled "Le Parfait Negociant" (*The Complete Tradesman*). In this he explained the statute and described current business practices. Among other things, he made some observations on the treatment of merchandise for inventory purposes. The reader is vaguely advised to take care not to estimate merchandise at more than it is worth. If the merchandise is newly purchased, he goes on to say, "and if one judges that it has not decreased in price at the factory . . . it should be put in at the current price."

The author's meaning here is not clear. He was speaking of newly purchased items and the phrase "current price" could mean the actual price recently paid. Did the phrase mean that the latest invoice price was to be applied to all units still unsold although some were bought at other prices? Is it possible that the author meant the words "current price" to mean merely "book price as already recorded," hence the actual cost price? If an item were not newly purchased, would its own cost price be used or the "current price" of similar items not yet bought? We begin to wish we could call up Savary's ghost and cross question him. His answers might also throw some light on Paciolo's use of the phrase, "current price."

But Savary's next comments seem clear enough. If the merchandise has begun to deteriorate or go out of style, he says, reduce the price considerably. He adds that you should reduce the item in the inventory accordingly if you can now get similar units at the factory for 5 per cent less.

Savary's advice to price the inventory pessimistically does not seem aimed at tax avoidance. Nor was there any hint that the statement was prepared for credit purposes. And it is doubtful if a man of Savary's

[6] Stanley E. Howard, "Public Rules for Private Accounting in France, 1673 and 1807," *Accounting Review,* June, 1932.

penetration would advocate these adjustments on the theory that current replacement prices were more nearly "true" than original purchase prices.

The explanation may perhaps follow other lines. The French ordinance, it will be noted, was quite general in its phrasing. It seems intended as a means of preventing falsification. The records required were to be available for use in court as evidence, but only in cases where the issues concerned rights in succession, dissolution of partnership, business failure, or property held in common by parties to a marriage contract. In these situations cost of inventory items, even if known, would not be material to the legal issues involved. Perhaps such legal problems furnished the principal occasion in seventeenth century France for taking inventory. But they do not do so now in America.

Additional evidence is available to show that questions of business solvency probably were the basis of the inventory practices fostered by the French law. The ordinance of 1673 became the basis for a part of the Napoleonic Code of 1807. In the section dealing with books of account, four items dealt with bookkeeping rules such as authentication, making an inventory of all property, etc., and six items dealt with the use of the records in case of litigation.

Professor Howard in the article previously mentioned has pointed out that French legal commentators have explained the relation of these rules to bankruptcy. Under the ordinance of 1673, the authenticated records would show the condition of the merchant's business at the time he became bankrupt and the antecedent conditions as well. The records would thus contribute a factual basis for a fair settlement with the creditors. If a merchant did not keep authenticated records, his bankruptcy was considered fraudulent and he was subject to the death penalty. This severity was altered in the code of 1807, but the essential use of the records in case of bankruptcy was kept in the law. By this later code, bankruptcy was fraudulent under several conditions, namely, if the merchant kept no records, if he concealed the records, or if the records did not correctly show his financial position. The penalty for fraudulent bankruptcy at that time became a period at forced labor.

Legal regulations affecting inventories in France are thus related to frauds suffered by creditors at the hands of a bankrupt.

Legal regulations affecting inventories appeared in Germany a little later, but here they were in connection with frauds suffered by stockholders at the hands of corporation promoters. The German Commercial Code of 1897 provided, among other things, that securities and merchandise which have a price-quoting market should be valued in the balance sheet at the lower of cost or market, and that other property should be entered at cost of purchase or cost of production.[7] This law of 1897 was a

[7] Joseph L. Weiner, "Balance Sheet Valuation in German Law," *Journal of Accountancy,* September, 1929.

revision of the Commercial Code of 1884. The latter was the outcome of an investigation into the causes of a wave of promotion and stock speculation which began in 1870 and came to an abrupt and disastrous climax in 1873. Much of the blame was placed on prior laws. It was found that promoters and their attorneys had interpreted a phrase of the law of 1861 as permitting the use of probable sales price in stating balance sheet assets. This enabled them to publish very attractive balance sheets and to sell vast quantities of stock on the surpluses shown.

Admittedly the code of 1861 was loosely phrased. The original draft of 1857 had proposed cost or market. But that wording was rejected as too specific and too restricting. "True value" was suggested but this was finally replaced by the phrase which went into the law: "The value which ought to be ascribed (to the item) at the date as of which the inventory and balance sheet are being drawn up." The vagueness thus deliberately written into the law was deliberately seized upon some years later to work a fraud upon security buyers.

It is easy to understand that the people would want such a law changed. It is easy to understand how a German court in 1873 was led to say that the figures in the balance sheet should not rest solely on willful individual judgment and pure surmise. It is understandable also how the lawmakers, in going back over the earlier discussions, should turn again to the idea which had at first seemed too specific. Vagueness in 1861 had exacted its price; in 1884, it seemed desirable to be specific. The amended rule then written into the law was worded peculiarly, but it was essentially the lower of cost or market. (Sec. 261 quoted in Weiner's article, p. 199.) As far as the effect of the law was concerned, it could as well have been cost alone. The reasons are unclear which prompted the Prussian representatives to make the original suggestion of cost or market to the conference in 1857. Probably they were merely following leads from the Napoleonic Code of 1807 and Savary's *Complete Tradesman* of 1675. Savary's book appeared in German translation the next year.

Both the French code and the German code were clearly designed in part to deal with inventory pricing. In both cases, however, it was with the intent of narrowing the opportunities for fraud. That is indeed a proper functioning of society's legal machinery; and lawmakers are justified in using devices that appeal to them as appropriate. However, it does not follow that accountants should give the resulting rule of law the status of a general rule of accounting. Unless accounting is considered to be a legal instrumentality, this use of inventory pricing could hardly be expected to produce an accounting rule. All that we have in the law is a special rule applicable to special circumstances.

In retrospect then we find convenience and expediency playing the major role in the early appearances of the cost-or-market rule. Sometimes, as in France and Germany, the rule was associated with the desire of lawmakers to narrow the opportunities for fraud. Sometimes, as in Italy, the rule seems associated with the hope of reducing the effect of a heavy tax. Surely fraudulent insolvency and tax expediency are not the predominant situations out of which a general accounting rule should grow. If these two cases represent infrequent and exceptional situations, they can only produce a special rule, that is, a rule which at best constitutes merely an exception to a more general rule.

Agricultural inventories, opening entries, and a few other situations also call for inventories on a noncost basis. But these situations no longer predominate. An inventory rule based upon them can no longer be called a general rule, even if once it could. It now would not cover a large enough portion of the cases calling for an inventory rule to make the idea a general rule.

If we must have a cost-or-market rule for special situations, or if we must have a rule about valuing inventory items when cost is unknowable, those rules should be made unmistakably secondary to the primary rule of inventories, and that rule should be that inventories should generally be priced at cost on a first-in, first-out basis. Such a rule does not come out of a single-entry conception of financial statements; and only a rule such as indicated can show that the balance of a goods account (inventory) has the same account characteristics as the balance of a cash account.

(*Accounting Review*, June, 1941)

28. Research Attitude of Mind

The trend of the discussion of inventory pricing seems to be toward a gradual resolution of some of the problems of inventory theory, thus clearing the way for changes in financial statement practice in this connection. However, only a beginning has been made in securing a change; most accountants still hesitate to advocate the use of inventory valuation reserves in place of the traditional cost-or-market rule. Yet the road to this modernization has been clearly opened by the reasoning that a deduction reported in both the balance sheet and the income statement could hardly be considered objectionable if the accountant believed the information significant and the method informative.[8]

If this permissive treatment became widely accepted and generally used, the outcome could be viewed with satisfaction for two reasons. The reporting of inventories will then have been brought up to the same level of informative disclosure that has long been customary for accounts receivable and for fixed assets. The sole justification for these deducted reserves is better disclosure of enterprise information to the reader of both financial statements. In years to come students will probably wonder why inventory had been reported as a single net figure for so many years

.

[8] "Inventory Reserves," Carman G. Blough, in *Illinois Certified Public Accountant*, March, 1948.

after the technique of reporting deducted reserves had been applied to other important assets.

The second reason for satisfaction will be that accounting logic would then replace a rule that came to be little more than a traditional habit of thought about inventory pricing.[9] The reserve method is logical for a simple and convincing reason. The accounting purpose of financial statements is to aid the reader to understand a given business enterprise. The objective of professional accountants in this connection is to see that disclosures are made which further that purpose. They have accomplished that objective in reporting receivable and fixed assets; they could with reason accept the logical relation of informative disclosure and valuation reserves in connection with inventory also.

It is not stressed often that most accounting methods are at once utilitarian and logical. This is an important element of strength. Without having a logical (rational and reasonable) relationship to accounting objectives, a given practice is only utilitarian and can drift into an easy expediency. But nearly all accounting methods are logical as well as useful. The cost-or-market rule is the outstanding example of an exception. Accounting needs the union of the logical and the useful. An improved disclosure of inventory data therefore would remove a spot of illogic that has been in financial statements as long as inventory has been reported at a net figure because of price changes.

Such modernization of inventory treatment would be a sign of further professional maturity; it will show that professional men will not hold interminably to a traditional idea or formula, and that they will recognize the way changed conditions can outrun older practices. It is a commendable trait to be disinclined to abandon easily a time-tested idea. But professional men are also strong in common-sense realism, for they know that after a case is made for a new usage, continued resistance to change can become the equivalent of retrogression.

Are the problems of inventory pricing all solved if inventory valuation reserves are clearly disclosed in the balance sheet and the income statement? Even if this reporting method is acceptable, a problem still remains since the calculation of the reserve has yet to be fully explored. There still is a question about the effective similarity or difference between (a) physical deterioration (loss, damage, depreciation of goods) (b) market deterioration (shifting demand, obsolescent goods, substitute products), (c) price-level changes (fluctuations in the volume of money, managed currency).

All three causes are mingled whenever inventories are shown at net figures. Will all three continue to be mingled in the calculation of the reserve deduction? Will this produce the best disclosure, or do some

[9] "If one accounting method is more logical and more useful than another, it should be generally adopted, though it fly in the face of tradition." From an editorial in the *Journal of Accountancy*, April, 1948.

causes suggest direct inventory adjustments while others seem better treated by a reserve?

(a) If goods are known to be lost, stolen, destroyed, should these be written off by credits direct to inventory, or should they be the basis for a reserve? (b) If goods are somewhat damaged or shopworn, and if the resulting market deterioration (customer opinion) makes recovery of invested cost problematical, should an amount be written off or reserved? (c) If price-level changes have occurred outside of the enterprise's own transactions, should the treatment call for write-off or reserve?

The first situation does not raise an accounting problem. The loss is objectively and positively determined; no part of the investment is recoverable; direct write-off is as appropriate as that for a debt known to be uncollectible.

As to the other two situations, there may be unsettled doubts. Are the two situations alike? If market deterioration and outside price changes are alike they should produce the same accounting treatment; if they are unlike they probably should receive different treatment in order to reflect that unlikeness in the accounting statements.

They are alike in the fact that marketing experience and judgment are needed to appraise the significance of each.

They are unlike in two particulars: (1) in the fact that market deterioration (salability) is judged from a study of goods now in enterprise possession and from the reactions of enterprise customers to the goods possessed. Here the inventory problem is a matter of repricing, of marking the goods to move them even if less profit, or no profit results—of releasing prior investment for profitable reinvestment in more promising kinds of goods. That however is not the same problem as posed by price-level change.

And they are unlike (2) in the fact that price fall is judged from a study of events outside of the enterprise. Although outside price data are sometimes definite and obtainable—and therefore seem clearly objective—judgments resting on this basis are in fact less realistic than are judgments on the apparently less objective basis of observed deterioration of goods. For in most cases outside prices ("the market") are not easily determined by trustworthy samples, especially since the goods now on our shelf may not be replaced at all, other goods with better prospects being preferred. Furthermore there is a large difference in "responsiveness" as between changes in sales prices and changes in purchase prices for different lines and at different times. If sales prices are not responsive to purchase market changes, the reasonableness of attributing an immediate loss to present inventory is thin indeed. As a third point, judging inventory by outside price changes tends to make a formula of market price ("the lower of cost or market applies item by item"). And the use of a formula tends to generate a habitual or routine action, that is, a treatment according to rule rather than under the guidance of a real analysis of the variables in the given situation.

It appears therefore that in some ways it might be a more useful disclosure to the reader of financial statements if price-level change were the only cause he would be expected to read into a deducted inventory reserve. The reader of course would have to be directed by accepted practices to know that all other causes operating on inventory pricing would produce direct adjustments before the amount entered the accounting statements. His understanding of management's message in the two financial statements would be improved by thus linking these inventory valuation reserve disclosures solely to the fact of fluctuating outside prices.

The deterrent to adding this restriction to the proposed modernization of inventory accounting by the use of valuation reserves would be a theory that change in outside price level was a symptom of market deterioration (salability) just as much as were observed customer reactions (not buying the offered goods). If this theory stands, it would link the two causes closely enough to justify using both in determining the deduction reserve; or if both are used in determining the reserve, this theory is the one underlying the action. The preferred solution of the reserve calculation problem ought to give primary consideration to reader understanding, including if necessary a campaign of reader education regarding the purpose that public accountants have in adopting a certain preferred method of calculation.

Professional men could increase their prestige by maintaining a research attitude of mind. Each client's inventory is a research problem for the independent auditor, one that is unlikely to be well solved by any kind of stock formula. Price responsiveness is always an individual situation; the factual bases of the judgment of the client's marketing executive regarding the marketing situation, present and prospective, should be appraised; the client's established policy of repricing to move goods and to release unproductive investment should be examined. All of these are essential parts of the basis for the professional accountant's opinion regarding inventory disclosures. A decreased reliance on a formula, coupled with a spirit of investigation consciously brought into the field by high-level staff men, is likely to prove more satisfactory than the same cost spread over more man-hours devoted to figure checking in an inventory by less experienced men.

A research attitude of mind probably already influences many public accountants in many situations. And as they look for new outlets to express this attitude, the study of inventories could well be accepted as another such situation, with the result of further improving accounting statement disclosures.

Perhaps the research approach may also help to clarify the concepts underlying such phrases as "useful cost," "normal profit," for in a sense these terms are like another formula. Useful for what? What is normal? Several answers are possible and some of them may indicate why the phrases are rather vague for use in accounting.

"Useful cost" might seem to refer to the usefulness that inventory items have for buyers. Would falling sales prices then be presumed to indicate decreased buyer interest, competition with alternative goods, a change in the buyers' type of operations, his decreased purchasing power thus passed on? Or the phrase could refer to usefulness of inventory for the seller as a means of attracting buyers and revenue. The offering prices attached to inventories are bids for customers. If the bids are not accepted by customers, the profit possibilities to the holder would begin to evaporate. This would result in a successive lowering of offering price until the goods were moved, perhaps with unquestioned losses. This action is "pricing," a phase of selling; it is not accounting action, a phase of objective profit calculation. No amount of accounting adjustments or price tag changes can "make" an investment into a profit or a loss. We only use accounting to calculate as best we can a result already present in the nonaccounting situation.

Inventory is useful to the holder in two ways: (1) as physical goods to attract customers and thus to derive revenue, and (2) as a measured amount of investment, the cost figures of which are useful primarily because they must be known before any calculation of merchandise profit or loss can be made. Inventories, as physical goods, have no usefulness for accounting; inventories have accounting usefulness only in terms of investment dollars, that is, only as costs representing an effort to produce revenue.

The cost-or-market rule directs that investment figures be modified so, it is said, they will thereafter represent "useful cost." Is that kind of "usefulness" an unbiased view? Is it not a "manipulated" use, a way of trying to show merchandising results—"normal profit"—by changing some book figures? If we are doubtful about the salability of goods because of suspected deterioration or obsolescence, why not use the technique now applied to doubtful accounts receivable and transfer the suspect inventory items to "doubtful goods" account? This in effect is just what a deducted inventory reserve would indicate, without the bookkeeping formality of segregation in the ledger. No doctrines of "useful costs" or "normal profit" are needed. The suggested accounting action is a simple earmarking of suspect items to await a decisive turn of events.

When deterioration or obsolescence are demonstrably present and the loss is complete and positive, the items need not wait in the status of "doubtful goods." When only an outside price-level change is involved the situation is different, for the investment adventured is still adventured, the outcome is still uncertain. At the moment, loss is pure hypothesis; it represents a theory or belief resting not on the goods possessed but on outside information about goods not possessed, goods which may never be bought. Loss which, in reality is only surmise, is under the old pricing rule treated as an indisputable fact. Surely surmise is a cue for indicating suspended judgment, that is, for using a deducted reserve rather than direct write-off.

The reserve treatment is therefore essential for price-level changes at least. In deciding whether estimated physical damage and marketing deterioration should join price change in the reserve, the principal factors to be weighed against each other are the expediency of joining the two versus the essential dissimilarity of the two causes.

(*New York Certified Public Accountant,* November, 1948)

29. From Liquidity to Earning Power

The double decade between 1933 and 1953 includes at the beginning of the period an event of major significance, namely, a new emphasis was given to the income statement. Some consideration of the conditions surrounding this development will give point to the view that professional accountants are keenly sensitive to the social significance of their work.

In the early 1930's a definite shift appeared from the familiar emphasis upon liquidity position as reflected in the balance sheet to a new emphasis on the figures reflecting enterprise earning power. This elevation of the income statement to a position of increased recognition was no doubt influenced by two interrelated aspects of the times: (1) the growing tendency in business of that day to shift a good deal of financing away from short-term bank loans and into the stock market through sale of equity securities, and (2) a rising criticism of many of the financial practices that had been observed during the booming 1920's.

The first of these aspects of the times has a long background. Short-term bank loans, made direct to the businessman on one-name paper, had gradually become general financial practice after the 1870's. This usage was related to the desire of the seller, in those postwar days of greenback money, to get cash quickly from the buyer. In order to encourage this action, the seller offered such a substantial deduction for cash (as 2 per cent for cash within ten days) that the buyer could well afford to borrow at the going rate of interest on a short-term loan from a local bank where he was personally known. It was expected that sale of most of the goods purchased would furnish the funds to pay off the note by the time it fell due.

Within a generation this financial method had grown to such an extent that many bankers could no longer personally know all their borrowers. Presently bankers came to rely in some degree upon the borrower's balance sheet for some of the clues to the probable safety of the loan. When the statement looked doubtful, or after a banker had had a few bad experiences with untruthful borrowers, he would require that a borrower employ a public accountant to examine his books and financial statements. Auditors who were called upon for such services developed the "balance sheet audit," an adaptation to American conditions of more extensive audit procedures inherited, as it were, from the practices of British chartered accountants. The certified balance sheet that resulted bore the name of an independent expert and thus gave dependable assurance to the banker as to the reliability of the representations indicated by the figures.

After the turn of the century a great deal of "commercial paper"—businessmen's promissory notes—was found to be in existence at all times; its record of collectibility was found to be very good. These facts became significant to banking. After long study by commissions of experts and legislative committees, the Congress created the Federal Reserve System and thus decreed in 1915 that paper money issued by banks should be secured in part by deposits of good current commercial promissory notes arising in the usual course of business. The theory was that expanding business activities created at the same time an increased supply of commercial paper and new demands for more paper money. When business activities contracted, one expected result would be a decrease in commercial paper outstanding along with a decline in the need for money. These ideas provided a basis for the new banking laws.

The use of short-term bank loans continued and grew; and so did the demand for audited, certified balance sheets. But in the winter of 1920-21 an abrupt, postwar fall in commodity prices gave the nation's monetary system and the prevailing financial practice of business a severe shock. Many borrowers, in the habit of renewing the bank loans they had made primarily in connection with inventory, were hard pressed at this time when renewal was refused and new loans were hard to get. Bankers had become alarmed at the sharp fall in prices and feared the effect on bank liquidity of losses that would come if businessmen had to sell high-priced inventory at sharply lowered prices and as a result could not pay their debts.

The price crisis proved relatively short lived, but the effect of the bad impression that lenders' actions had made on borrowers left the latter more than willing to use other methods of finance whenever they could do so. An alternative was not long in appearing. Business conditions were fundamentally sound and when the pressure on high-priced inventory relaxed, business activities quickly bounded upward. Soon high optimism replaced temporary gloom. The stock market, reflecting the times, boomed as never before. Shares from new issues or from reorganizations were absorbed so eagerly that this market became the chief source for business funds.

This type of financial activity, in contrast to that associated with bank loans, shifted men's attention from liquidity to earning power, from balance sheet to income statement. Interest in the income statement—the only place where earning power was revealed—was increased because plans for mergers, recapitalizations, new flotations, etc. rested upon earning power as the chief clue to the productive value of assets and to the ceiling amounts for proposed security issues.

The important usefulness of the figures for earnings had long been recognized in financial planning and long had been taught in classes on finance and investment. But not in a generation had actual financial reorganizations been so much in evidence. Now, in the twenties, security financing forcefully brought the great significance of earning power figures to the attention of professional accountants, among others. Accounting literature in the early 'thirties clearly reflected the fact; net income was called the most important figure coming out of the accounts.

It may be of interest to note parenthetically that nominal accounts are the unique characteristic of double entry and constitute the outstanding accounting contribution made by the Italians who in the fifteenth century helped business record-keeping to evolve into a thoroughly integrated technology. It is the integration of nominal with real accounts that makes it possible for us to measure quantitatively the interactions of financial actions and productive activities. Actually, the results obtainable by enterprise managers from their nominal accounts have been of utmost significance to them from the days of Columbus, the explorer and Paciolo, the accounting teacher. The importance of data on income and expense is not at all new.

The second aspect of the times that directed new attention to financial statements was criticism of financial practices current in the 'twenties. Whereas the change from bank loans to security issues gave rise in accounting literature to analysis of existing ideas about the significance of enterprise income and the structure of the income statement, the reaction to boomday financial practices and to the price collapse in 1929 brought into being an auditor's certificate which tied his opinion to "generally accepted accounting principles consistently applied." What events lay back of that result?

After a quick recovery from the low prices of 1920-21, a bounding spirit of optimism arose throughout the nation and grew rapidly from feeding upon its own success. Employment increased, business was active, prices on the stock market were rising, and nothing seemed likely to check them. Presently, a rationalization of the continuing period of prosperity began to form in men's minds. It was noted that the index of wholesale prices persisted in showing an almost horizontal trend. Since prices reflect the interaction of supply and demand, the conclusion was logical that American businessmen, without consultations or private agreements, were succeeding by voluntary and individual actions in keeping supply so effectively adjusted to demand that stable commodity price levels resulted. It was then an easy step for practical men to come to believe that they had solved the principal riddle of economies, i.e., how to achieve an equilibrium of supply and demand. If this had been achieved—the statistical charts seemed to confirm it—prices could be expected to remain relatively stable, and men could turn to other problems. This kind of vaguely perceived rationalization of surrounding economic conditions was strongly strengthened when some economic theorists advanced the view that the nation was on a plateau of permanently higher prices. Somehow it did not then seem significantly inconsistent that stock prices were rapidly rising while commodity prices remained stable.

The existing spirit of optimism and a certain amount of speculative fever flowing out of profitable activities also helped to make these ideas seem convincing. Yet some people had doubts and reservations. Among them were some discerning minds in finance (for example, Ripley in his book *Wall Street and Main Street*) and not a few professional accountants. The technical literature in the 'twenties reflected a tendency to put financial statements of the day under increasingly sharp scrutiny. Ripley was categorical and outspoken in his criticism of the current looseness which seemed to characterize financial practices and reporting. Public accountants were less outspoken; many of them believed that their professional responsibility did not extend to criticizing the financial transactions of clients. Yet their writings indicate a feeling of dissatisfaction with financial statements.

Then came the crash. Stock prices tumbled, slowed, and tumbled more and more swiftly. The bottom was made in 1932 [10] in the midst of a hot political campaign. The collapse was foreshadowed by significant movements in world prices for basic commodities. Few people gave heed to the signs; few pointed to the inconsistencies of "equilibrium" at home and price disequilibrium abroad. Recovery might have made early progress except for the bitterness of the election fight at that time and the fears as to the extent and direction of reforms that seemed imminent. The final element that turned America away from possible quick recovery from depression was the financial collapse of several European governments.

Questionable financial practices there may have been in America in the 'twenties, and some misleading financial reporting. And these needed correction. But presently the talk of federal regulation of security trading and of possible standardization of financial statements—perhaps even to the extent of prescribed bookkeeping methods—was alarming to professional accountants and members of the stock exchange alike. As a result the New York Stock Exchange and the American Institute of Accountants appointed committees to join in the study of the problems of financial reporting. If the rules of the exchange and the pressure of accountants' views might foster suitable reforms in financial reporting of

[10] A great deal of factual material and much careful analysis of contributing factors and of efforts to halt the movement are given in *The Great Depression,* the third volume of the memoirs of Herbert Hoover, 1952.

the future, the criticisms of questionable practices of the past would have had beneficial effect. This joint committee studied the problems for several years and in 1934 published their exchange of correspondence. The point of particular interest here lies in the fact that one outcome of the study was the formulation of a type of auditor opinion (certificate), the wording of which made specific reference to "generally accepted accounting principles consistently applied."

The sequence of events sketched above had an important impact upon accounting theory as well as practice. As to practice, the new wording placed the auditor's professional opinion squarely in line with the best ideas of good accounting (those generally accepted) rather than leaving the reader to believe that one man's opinion was intended to stand alone. The omission of the phrase "fairly present the true financial condition . . ." relieved the auditor from using words—such as "certify" and "true"—which might be construed by some laymen as a guarantee of full truth in the statement and a complete absence of skillfully concealed error in the accounts. It cannot be doubted that the status and service of the professional accountant was much more clearly indicated to the investing public by this change. This outcome, therefore, is an indication that beneficial results can emerge from study of criticisms.

As to the impact of events upon accounting theory, it is clear that the new wording of the auditor's opinion directed attention as never before to accounting principles. Authors of textbooks had earlier made frequent use in titles and chapter heads of the term "accounting principles." But they seldom attempted to guide the student in distinguishing controlling principles (theory) from preferred procedures (practice). Such separation now assumed new importance. The published correspondence itself took the lead by stating five carefully formulated accounting principles, the most important of which emphasized the distinction between items appropriate for recording in surplus and those related to income.[11]

The publication of only five principles seemed to invite the formulation of other important principles. Members of the American Accounting Association, being for the most part teachers of accounting, conceived the idea of attempting to compact a considerable area of accounting theory into principles—headlines as it were of the reasoning that supported the best accounting practices. In 1936 a committee of the Association published a short statement presenting twenty principles. Later committees over the years, after restudying the problem, continued to support the essence of the earlier report. That essence can perhaps be compressed as saying: (1) that the objective basis of account figures (those derived from

·

[11] A collateral discussion presently developed that is characterized by the phrases "combined income and surplus statement" and "clean surplus doctrine." The appearance of this usage suggests that some earlier and perhaps questionable practices included the use of surplus to absorb some adjustments which in that location had the effect of modifying reported net income.

the use of historical cost) makes any figures that do not reflect historical cost seem less desirable, and (2) that, since the most significant single figure periodically derived from accounts is net income, the focus of accounting theory should be directed toward securing the best matching of periodic revenue and relevant applicable cost and expense in computing that figure.

The approach of the American Institute of Accountants to principles has been different. In the late 'thirties research was made an important Institute activity. To implement that objective, two continuing committees were set up, one to consider problems relating to generally accepted principles, the other to problems of auditing procedure and standards. Presently a director of research and a special staff were provided. Out of the work of these divisions many bulletins have appeared since 1939, each reflecting careful analysis and the considered judgment of experienced practitioners concerning a single problem arising out of current practice. As a result, there is slowly accumulating a considerable volume of dependable guidance in the solution of many problems met in professional practice. The bulletins constitute, in a way, the common law of accounting practice and include clear-cut statements of committee preference with the supporting reasoning being indicated. If there is dissent within the committee, the individual member's views are compactly presented also.

Judging by the general lack of criticism from the membership at large, the reasoned preferences of these committees may well be considered as having been accepted by the profession. This acceptance, coupled with appropriate use, gives the principles and practices a validity which could not be expected in pronouncements, directives, or regulations from whatever body they might come.

From time to time groups of these bulletins have been compacted to summarize their interrelations. The essence of the thought emerging from these committees thus becomes a gradual unfolding of the guiding philosophy (theory) of professional practice. This core of theory (reasoned beliefs), it should be noted, is being distilled by discussion out of particular instances from professional experience.

The approach to principles adopted by the American Accounting Association, in contrast, leans toward distilling out of existing literature the theory essence that has already found expression. These two ways of improving theory clearly supplement each other in spite of apparent differences here and there. If conflicting views shall appear, as in a few instances has been the case, that fact in itself is reassuring since the ultimate result is bound to be better understanding by all parties, and perhaps a gradual meeting of minds on the issues.

Several studies have appeared in the literature undertaking to compare the ideas emerging over almost two decades from these two methods. The result: Ideas seem not far apart in most matters. This degree of informal consensus is reassuring as to the future of the profession and education for the profession. It is reassuring as to the future because these studies are so revealing of the past and the present. They show to the thoughtful reader the way earlier ideas stand up under analysis and under testing by new conditions. They show that practices, earlier and current, are neither purely personal, wholly arbitrary, nor merely traditional. For practices are shown to rest on reasons that are convincing to reasonable men. Those reasons are theory, whether they emerge from practitioner or teacher.

(Accounting Forum, May, 1953)

PART FOUR *On Accounting Education*

EDUCATIONAL THEORY FOR ACCOUNTANCY

1. Educational Growth

Accounting practitioners and teachers, by combining forces, have pushed educational preparation into higher planes than could have been visualized two generations ago. Few other countries have placed such a foundation beneath accounting; many of them also seem not to have had much faith in the benefits of compulsory basic education for all.

American beliefs favoring widespread education have been justified by many results which seem clearly to have been influenced by that policy. Among these are: maturity in our democratic form of government; steady growth in the will of the people to work to that end; vast developments in science and industrialization; multiplication of available areas of higher education and the wide use voluntarily made of them.

College education for careers in business came earlier than college preparation for accounting careers. The Wharton School, in the University of Pennsylvania, was a pioneer in 1881. The University of Chicago followed in 1898. After 1900, other universities began to build curriculums in business education in which the study of accounting played a part, in some cases through day classes, in other by evening classes.

One type of instruction sought to take the point of view of business management and teach the uses of accounting. A typical approach included the study of accounting systems and the adaptability of double-entry bookkeeping to different kinds of enterprise. Another teacher would prefer to pass by bookkeeping as such in order to introduce students at once to financial statements as aids in making managerial decisions.

After the turn of the century, technical education for public accounting came into the universities, first in New York University (in 1900) and soon thereafter in the Universities of Pennsylvania, Illinois, and Northwestern. Such courses of study were a direct outgrowth of the new CPA laws; New York's law came in 1896 and Pennsylvania's in 1899. In Illinois, after unsuccessful attempts in 1897 and 1899, the first law was passed in 1903. Courses in business had been instituted at Urbana in 1902, and for a few years the accounting course was given as a companion to the study of corporation finance.

Strictly professional courses were begun in 1907 at Northwestern's evening school then backed by a group of public accountants as sponsors. This program, like that at New York University, included intensive non-degree courses taught by practicing accountants and was intended to help candidates prepare for CPA examinations. Except for problems and questions from prior examinations, little technical literature was available at that time except British textbooks. Robert H. Montgomery's *Auditing, Theory and Practice* (1912) was the first substantial American auditing text.

Soon after Northwestern's venture got under way, day class instruction at Urbana was enlarged and given some orientation towards the CPA examination in a setting of appropriate collateral work in nonaccounting subjects.

In the matter of educational preparation the universities even at that early date were moving ahead of the provisions in the CPA laws. Before 1905, three of the seven CPA laws contained no educational requirement, and four prescribed a high school education or the equivalent. In 1913, eleven of thirty states had no educational requirement, while nineteen named the high school.

From the vantage point of nearly half a century later these educational requirements seem modest indeed. Yet is was a fact at the time that this hurdle stood in the way of many men who wished to take the examination; some of these already had considerable prior experience in public accounting. Much of the early pressure for certificates by waiver rooted in the high school requirement.

By the middle 1920's there were CPA statutes in forty-nine states and territories, of which forty-six required a high school education for admission to the examination. Although statutory pressure for higher education was still lacking, accounting education had continued to expand at the university level. The details are easily seen in almost any series of university catalogues. The significant aspect of this advance however is not in the expansion of faculty or of course offerings. Rather it is to be found partly in the merger of the two earlier and separate objectives of accounting education (preparation for business, preparation for public accounting) and partly in curriculum integration of accounting with important collateral subject matter, that is, a wide range of courses now grouped under such broad titles as "business administration" and "general education." The latter covered subjects often described as cultural, disciplinary, citizenship training.

This development viewed in perspective seems significant because it turned away from a simple objective of coaching for a technical examination, and toward a complex objective of developing minds capable of reacting rationally and effectively to the responsibilities of professional men whose way of serving society was by improving the usefulness of accounting and by attesting to the dependability of reported data.

To the informed observer of the current scene in the 1950's it will no doubt be clear that the prestige of accountancy today and its growing usefulness is in part a result of continued high aims of university education, aims whose fulfillment are being demonstrated in the constructive developments fostered by men who have benefited from these educational opportunities. It is perhaps not too much to say that public accounting justifies itself primarily because of the value dependable financial statements have for facilitating the flow of capital into socially desirable productive uses. The noteworthy expansion in the same half century of administrative accounting is not explained by any contribution it may seem to make to higher enterprise profit, but by the fact that good administrative accounting helps good management to make its own kind of social contribution in competition with poor management.

Accounting education at the university level has beyond doubt been a strong contributor to the advance of accounting use and prestige. And not a little of its contribution has come about through training teachers of business subjects in general and of accounting in particular. For teaching is an art and a philosophy in its own right. University classes turn out two products: better-prepared students and better-prepared teachers. The one prepared to learn much from the daily work of his career; the other prepared to reach beyond the mere transmitting of accumulated knowledge and methodology—important as that function will always be—by striving to use his teaching materials to train receptive minds to be ready to work and grow in the midst of ever-changing patterns.

This kind of contribution is not to be measured by number of students or university budgets. The measure should be sought in the later constructive accomplishments of the students. So many accounting students have flowed into the profession, public and administrative, and so much progress is evident that one cannot reasonably doubt that a relationship exists.

(*Illinois Certified Public Accountant*, June, 1953)

2. In the Course of Fifty Years

It was 1903 when an Illinois CPA law became a reality. For some time after that date those states which set up any educational requirement at all for admission to the examination specified only a high school education or equivalent. Many had no such provision in the statute until later years.

After a start in 1913 most states presently permitted substitution of college education for part of the required practical experience. Later a few began requiring a college degree including instruction in accounting. On the whole, however, formal education in accountancy was well ahead of statutory requirements. That is as it should be; it would be unreasonable to require more educational preparation than was available. Over the years progress in accounting education has continued to march ahead of statutory requirements. It is a particularly significant fact in this connection that many successful CPA candidates have for some years been people with college preparation. And this result, it should be noted, has come out of voluntary action on the part of the universities and the students, for even now the states that require college preparation are still few in number. There is evidence that well-planned accounting curriculums attract many of the best students in the colleges of commerce. Perhaps that is part of the explanation of the improved statistics of examination success, that plus better courses, better texts, better teachers, better examinations.

Space does not permit comparisons of curriculum content over a fifty-year period. Moreover, these matters have often been considered by committees of the American Accounting Association and by individual public accountants in articles for accounting periodicals. We are well aware of the major fact that would be made evident in such a comparison. The expansion and improvement of accounting course offerings were parallel to similar developments in companion subject matter related to business education, particularly such as enterprise economics, business finance, money and credit, statistical methodology, enterprise management, business law, business and technical writing. These being the facts, the major problem of curriculum-building for accounting students became one of maintaining good proportion in the subject matter of the recommended study programs. To prescribe more and more accounting technology, with attendant reduction in the amounts of business education and general education would inevitably tend to weaken the best functioning of professional preparation. It is understandable therefore that good balance between different subject matter became characteristic of most programs.

A particularly significant phase of expanding accounting education appeared about half way through the fifty-year period. This was the initiation of graduate work in accountancy. Such an expansion was educationally better than overspecialization in undergraduate accounting courses. Important nonaccounting aspects of education need not then be squeezed out of the earlier program. Standards of accomplishment and progress can be increased when few or no undergraduates are in the courses. And in addition, clear gain is derived from the maturing effect that flows from consideration of conflicting ideas and from increased personal responsibility for self-directed activities. This last benefit, plus valuable experience with written expression, is noticeably increased if a master's thesis is required.

These are not hypothetical benefits of graduate education but real ones recognized by discerning employers and reflected in salary and advancement.

Because teacher-training has become of increasing concern, programs have been developed in recent years leading to a Ph.D. degree with a strong emphasis upon accounting. In some schools these programs include accounting and other subjects for the written preliminary examination in a ratio approximating 1 to 3; in a few the ratio is nearer 3 to 1. Often this advanced study is associated in time with initial teaching experience. Thesis work usually is strongly emphasized; one third of the minimum program beyond the bachelor's degree is devoted to research and the writing of a resulting dissertation on some accounting topic.

The thesis requirement, and the oral examination based on that manuscript, long ago proved a wise one in other departments and it seems to be repeating in accountancy. Teachers recognize their obligation to contribute to the literature and know that experience in written expression helps them later to prepare textbooks that are understandable, teachable and suitable for transmitting to students the most useful distillations from the rich experiences of practicing accountants and the fruits of research scholarship. The research that precedes writing provides an opportunity to get a taste of research and introduces the candidate to the feel of making a contribution. It may be a contribution from critically sifting the important from the incidental, from sorting pros and cons into a synthesis of ideas, from revealing some threads of continuity in the history of accounting or some interrelations between accountancy and other areas. It is an exciting experience as well as a useful one.

In a concluding appraisal of fifty years of formal education for accounting in Illinois as a part of a larger whole, it perhaps should be said that this state is representative of general progress. Illinois has not been, nor desired to be, unique. If successes here may have been stimulating in other states, good ideas elsewhere have been equally stimulating here.

Early in the half century men in accounting work were largely self-taught. They learned to think in the field. Native talent energetically applied brought success in accord with the times. There is no reason for us now to feel superior. Men are still self-taught; formal education is merely assembled vicarious experience convincingly arranged. The individual himself does the work of learning. The classroom teacher and the text are only parts of the apparatus in aid of learning. The student teaches himself by putting to use whatever talent he has for understanding, absorbing, remembering, selecting, applying the ideas and methods transmitted to him.

In the period of fifty years, only the locale of learning has changed. In the present setting new and helpful apparatus has been devised and made widely available. As a result much time is saved for the learner, time that can be devoted to widening and deepening his preparation.

It should make us humble today to consider how firm are the foundations laid down fifty, forty, and thirty years ago by men with much less formal education than is common now. They must have been strongly possessed by their occupation; deeply sensitive to its obligations and consciously dedicated to its advancement. Technical courses cannot of themselves do much to build that spirit into successive generations. Well-prepared teachers, enthusiastic for their subject and realistic as to its social significance and its limitations in use, can and should supply some of the fire which cannot come alone from exercises in problem-solving.

The classroom teacher of accountancy is part of a system of activity dedicated to compressing experience, to widening of horizons, to stimulating rational thinking. But he can communicate a spark of enthusiasm only as a person dealing with people. The signs are plentiful in professional activities that accounting teachers throughout the half century have been successful in these functions. Practitioners today are just as dedicated as the pioneers. There has been in recent years a noticeable acceleration of accounting progress. Possibly a larger proportion of accountants than earlier are now keenly aware of the public welfare aspects of their work and of the interactions between accountancy and society.

The widening and deepening of accounting education and the increase in the number of accountants in service are of course partly results of national growth. Yet it should be noted that the use of old and new accounting techniques played an important part in that growth by contributing to better managerial and investor judgment.

Perhaps the greatest usefulness of increased formal education for accounting service is that it puts men more in tune with their times, and thus facilitates effective use of whatever talent, skill, knowledge they may have developed. If that kind of service of higher education is to run into the future, the significance of continued improvement needs to be kept high in our consciousness, and ever on the conscience, of both practitioners and teachers. For they have become indispensable to each other. One of the finest aspects of this long association in the past has been the fact that each group has been eager to co-operate, yet unwilling to seem to dictate.

(Illinois Certified Public Accountant, June, 1953)

3. Instruments of Educational Purpose

Education serves several general purposes which go a long way toward explaining the increasing popularity of all grades of formal education.

The first of these is to pass on the experience of those who go before to those who follow. Something within us urges that we save our successors as many steps as possible and as many rough spots as we can. It is that something which prompts the parents to deny themselves in order to give their children a better education than they themselves had. And it must be, I think, the same kind of urge which prompts men to write textbooks. Very few college professors make money from their textbooks, and the long labor of writing is not endured in the expectation of winning undying fame.

The second major purpose of formal education is to train minds to function smoothly and rationally. We must watch our terms here. Modern psychology is all against the doctrine of "training the mind"; the mind, it is said, is not a muscle to be so strengthened by one exercise as to function strongly in others. That is to say, we should not study mathematics to get training in accountancy; we are told to seek training in the field in which we wish our ability to increase. Yet we know that a man cannot grow intellectually as he should on a diet of mathematics alone—or on accountancy either, for that matter. Accountancy students may study mathematics because there may be occasions where the rules and methods and ideas of mathematics will prove helpful. Yet I believe that we can also benefit generally from such studies. In studying many different subjects we do learn a great deal about the "technique of learning"—about how to find answers, and how to fix important facts in mind, and how to pick out from the chaff the grains of principles. Much of the advantage of a diversified education lies in training us to do just these things in diverse fields.

Now if the purpose of education is to pass on accumulated experience and to train the mind to function smoothly, there must be some instruments or devices to aid the accomplishment of those purposes.

The first device made use of in formal education is the printed page, that is to say, books, magazines, libraries—reading in all that that implies. Say what you will about the shortcomings of "book larnin' " it is nevertheless indispensable—indispensable, that is, if one is to benefit within the space of a few years by a contact with a wide range of transmitted experience. Students therefore are purposely confronted with very wide ranges of ideas so they may gain in background and perspective; so they may gain a wide experience vicariously through other eyes and in a minimum of time. For after all, education is only another expression for experience. It is as much an educative process to work beside a master until you are proficient enough to become a journeyman, as it is to read the master's written ideas from a book. But the former method is slower. Classroom and book education are in no way offered in substitution for experience in the field; rather, it is merely in preparation for that stage of growth. This is particularly true of education in accountancy.

It is obviously impossible to reproduce in the classroom the actual conditions of practical experience. Yet some of the same effect can be secured from the use of problems. Problems, I believe, constitute the second device of education. We may not be able to train the mind with one kind of work to do all other kinds better, that is, to transfer training from one field to another, but the mind can most certainly be trained on any subject matter to function smoother. What the student gets from working problems is the experience of facing difficulties and of being forced to think the kind of thoughts that the man in the field has to think. Such training will prove beneficial later when the student himself is in the field. For the very reason that he has burned the midnight oil over many problems, he is better able in practice to apply his knowledge of theory and good professional practices to the difficult situations that he meets later. Those difficult situations are to him just new problems, and having learned something of the technique of marshaling facts and attacking problems, he applies himself to the solution of the problem in hand with vigor and efficiency.

The third device of education is the instructor. It might seem that anyone possessing books and problems could make himself acquainted with the accumulated experience of his chosen field and could train his own mind by the use of the problems without the intervention of other people. That can be done; it often has been done; and all honor to him who has won his way by such means. But anyone who has followed that path will know that the price is high and the wastage large.

What the instructor tries to do is to keep down the wastage of discouragement, short vision, and poor study techniques. In other words, teaching is a process of supplying encouragement, vision, and method. The instructor is able to correlate for the student many things which would otherwise seem unrelated. Because of his wider reading and his contact with actual practice, the teacher can illustrate and illuminate any book the student may study. Because he knows the processes of learning ideas and the methods of trying to work out solutions, he is able to criticize the student's attempts to learn, and to guide the learner's plastic judgments toward better reasoning. He teaches self-criticism and the "feel" of clear thinking more than the remembering of subject matter.

The functions of education then are the passing on of accumulated experience and the training of the mind to work smoothly and clearly; the three principal devices employed in furthering these purposes are books, problems, and teachers. These devices are employed in schools of all grades from the primary classes up to universities; and everywhere they are focused upon the same task. When universities give classes in accounting, they aim at these same purposes of education and employ these same devices. There is nothing mysterious about the teaching machinery of a university nor about the process of getting a college education; the machinery has just been described in brief, and the process for the student is just a species of work. The work is highly selective in its materials and strongly energized toward accomplishment, but it is just plain work, popular magazines and cartoons to the contrary notwithstanding.

(Certified Public Accountant, December, 1927)

4. Education as Experience

When we think of preparation for a career in accountancy, two elements come to mind which are written into most CPA laws, namely, experience and education. Usually "experience" is thought of narrowly as practical accounting work; and "education" as consisting of general rather than technical studies.

Are there two different ways of learning, by practice and by study? Do they suggest that accounting be learned by practice in an office and other matters learned by study in school? Can undirected study supplement accounting office work in a satisfactory manner, and can simulated practice be a satisfactory supplement to teacher-directed study in school? Are alternative approaches to the profession implied in the two prerequisites? Are experience and education merely variations of one approach because all education is a complex made up of different experiences and all experience is educational in effect?

At the center of any kind of education there is always the idea of a learner learning. Learning is an activity directed at gaining experience. Experience may be gained in two ways, personally and vicariously. Personal experience may be obtained by simple trial and error. Often personal experience is obtained from observation. The observer learns to duplicate what another does in his presence. To gain experience vicariously however is to act on a different level. Here learning makes use of generalized experiences. These are broken down into simulated experience and codified experience. In the first class are problems and experiments which offer concise substitutes for larger real actions but which are nonetheless typical of actual life. Codified experience is the compressed results of many isolated trials. This produces generalizations, principles, theories, and explanations.

Along with the learner learning there is usually a teacher teaching. Teaching is an activity directed at facilitating learning; it may be informal or formal. The most informal and unconscious teaching is that which is purely co-operative. Two bear cubs busily cuffing and clawing at each other are teaching each other useful arts for bears. The junior assistant is learning informally when he is co-operating with the senior in calling over vouchers, and when the older man shows the younger how to prepare a schedule that is needed at the moment.

Formal teaching is in some respects on a higher plain. Here a planned gradation of problems and experiments is designed to assist the learner to make rapid progress along predetermined lines. Also included in formal teaching is a careful selection of generalizations and principles which will help the learner to understand his hypothetical exercises and to see their interrelation.

It is the function of the teacher, therefore, first to act as a guide through a maize familiar to him but obscure to the learner, and second, to act as a planner to select and arrange accumulated experience so that the learning process will be speeded, broadened, and deepened. Teaching also has a responsibility for improving motivation when necessary. Natural ability to work now for a dimly perceived future seems to vary greatly among individual learners. Hence part of the service the teacher should perform is to supplement self-motivation. He is also called upon to develop as best he can his students' varying capacities to absorb teaching materials.

But learning and not teaching is the focus of education. The important thing is that the learner shall absorb experience. Teaching cannot inject knowledge; it can only facilitate absorption and direct the acquiring of skills. Obviously learning and teaching may be combined in varying proportions. Personal experience and informal teaching are usually related. Much education is of the type where a minimum of systematically organized material and outside help is combined with a maximum of self-motivated natural capacity to learn. Vicarious learning and formal teaching usually go together. They do not offer a substitute for personal experience but a quicker journey over a larger territory.

Fundamentally education is experience. Getting an education is getting experience. Providing an education is a matter of selecting experiences out of a vast store and adapting them to the time available and to the capacity of the learner. A good education will be one in which teaching and learning have worked together so effectively that, regardless of the proportion of one to the other, the individual concerned will not only be able to act but also to understand; not only to understand but also to act. If the "whys" are neglected, the learning process will produce only a limited ability to deal with new situations even though teaching has been concrete and objective. If the "hows" are neglected, the experience obtained will be so abstract as to be of small real usefulness.

Education for a career in accountancy, then, as in all education, has the objective of preparing individuals to act in certain ways with understanding. It, too, is a union of teaching and learning, combined in differing proportions. No single combination is the best under all circumstances. Almost any avenue of accounting education is capable of yielding good results under suitable conditions.

A complete education will take more time than a more-or-less incomplete education. An incomplete education can be accomplished with a minimum of formal teaching; a more complete preparation usually leans heavily upon the vicarious processes of learning. The amount of organized teaching and outside motivation that is necessary also varies according to the degree of completeness planned for the educational preparation. Some people must get what they can in a limited time at low cost, whereas others can extend the time with less regard for total cost. No one would expect the two types of preparation to be equally productive. The capabilities of men of large latent capacities can be developed with less teaching in less time than is necessary for men with lower native ability.

Such reasons as these help to explain the existence of variety in educational programs for accountancy.

(*Accounting Review*, July, 1942)

5. Capacity to Learn

Two interrelated factors exercise predominating influence upon the structure of accounting education: (1) the degree of emphasis given to the formal study of accountancy in comparison with other subjects and (2) the time students can spend on formal education. The first factor is conditioned by different theories of how best to prepare for a professional career. The second is conditioned by the students' capacity to learn.

Little can be said about making available different types of programs of professional education which will offer clear and direct variations according to students' capacity to learn. About all that is being done is to see that the subject matter of a given program and the requirements for admission and completion are interrelated, and to develop teaching methods that will take into consideration the students' maturity, experience, and previous educational record. Within these limits a variety of useful programs would be possible, but they would be only loosely adapted to specific levels of capacity.

Little basis exists as yet for definite statements that such and such amount of preparation of this and that kind is necessary for a successful career in professional accounting. There are various theories on the subject, but no one theory is likely to predominate until we have assembled and studied much more experience than is now available. An attempt should be made, however, to learn what practitioners think of the results of different types of preparation programs. Every sort of combination of factors can produce and has produced successful practitioners. Yet out of wide variety there must be some combinations which seem to work better than others.

About the time factor, something more definite can be said at this time. When a maximum of useful preparation is desired in a minimum of time, there will be a tendency to stress accounting techniques alone, thus putting business education aside as secondary and abandoning general education above the high school. Obviously educational facilities are needed that meet these conditions. Two groups would be served. First are those who have had general education or business education in sufficient measure but have later decided to add a knowledge of accountancy. They need supplementary education either in conjunction with working experience in accounting or in anticipation of it. Then there are those who, for reasons of cost or lack of opportunity, have had little or no formal education along general lines or in business. They may decide that some education in accounting techniques will give them a start in a field where personal experience may satisfactorily extend their training.

Intensely specialized programs of study undoubtedly have a place. Classes after working hours and correspondence courses often serve a very useful purpose in this connection. But intensive specialization works under very definite limitations. If used to supplement prior general education some disadvantage may appear because prior and present subject matter are not likely to be well interwoven. Generally speaking the best time to study the elementary aspects of one subject is at the time other elementary subjects are also in progress. Various conditions may interfere with a complete adoption of such a program but that does not, I think, negate the proposition as good educational theory. When specialization in technique stands very much alone it cannot be expected to lay down a very deep foundation for a career. In fact, it is perhaps better described as providing only an introduction to an opportunity to try to build a career mainly upon personal experience. That avenue has been successfully followed many times.

Has everything been done that can be done to orient a relatively short program of intensive study of accounting techniques to the particular function it is to perform and to adjust it to the particular needs of definite types of individuals? An off-hand answer is difficult. Perhaps thoroughgoing educational research would provide a basis for considering the question. But it would seem clear that a given program could not adequately serve widely different individuals.

Educational programs might also be studied under an assumption that for analytical purposes the time factor could be ignored. Attention could then be given to the problem of program content regardless of the time it might seem to call for in actual use. A complete education for a career in professional accounting would necessarily be extensive; probably it should run longer than four years. It should be inclusive, that is, cover an adequate general education and a thorough business education in addition to an extensive education in accountancy as such. The method should be one that used a judicious combination of vicarious experience (texts and problems) and personal experience (staff school and accounting employment).

Certain prerequisites would be necessary: (1) for best results students would need to make an early choice of the field and have the necessary time, money, and ability to benefit from an extended preparation; (2) suitable educational programs should be available or be organized; (3) extensive co-operation would need to be given by professional firms by means of interim employment, transition schools, and continuation of staff education beyond the CPA certificate. Such a list of prerequisites may seem discouraging; but there is nothing impossible in it. The most difficult to overcome is the first item. Many men decide early upon a career in medicine, law, or religion. Many could do so in accountancy as well.

(Accounting Review, July, 1942)

6. Learning to Learn

"Since one of the important requisites for success in after life is a willingness and ability to do one's job, and since the student's first job is academic efficiency, we need to stress (the technique of) scholarship more than we do. . . ." ("National Interfraternity Conference Yearbook," 1946.)

A student's primary problem is one of learning to learn. And educational programs should be so graduated that they automatically build up one's ability to learn. At each succeeding level the materials presented may be chosen on the assumption that the art of learning has already progressed to a point where this material will be understandable.

It may well be added that the student probably will find in later years that his absorption of the techniques of learning is proving to be as valuable as any particular subject matter studied; often it could prove even more valuable, especially if his work finally takes him into unfamiliar subject matter.

The study of accounting includes many educational benefits outside of the technicalities learned. These should be persistently pointed out to students. Take powers of analysis, for example; accounting is particularly fitted to develop these powers in its students. Teachers must see that instruction is recognized as serving this objective among others.

The student can use accountancy to help develop his powers of analysis because:

(1) he learns to convert actions into data and data into action

(2) he learns to use classification of data to compress the mass and thus increase its informative content

(3) he learns to be sensitive to good and poor in the definition of categories, and to possible irrelevance in the assignment of data to categories

(4) he learns to be aware that interrelations are everywhere, and everywhere are significant

(5) he learns that gradations exist in the significance of all kinds of facts and interrelations

(6) he learns that clearly perceived objectives should exercise control over actions

Surely there are educational benefits whether one uses accounting as such in later life or not. Having developed his powers of analysis by applying his mind to the study of accountancy, he can carry these techniques over into whatever work he may undertake.

The doctrine of learning to learn is an important idea for the teacher as well as the student. Perhaps one reason some students decide to teach is that they have learned to see into the learning process and believe they would like to help others to use the teacher's chosen subject matter as an instrument for learning to learn—or we could say, for learning the technique of continuing to develop one's capabilities. The teacher finds many opportunities to teach learning while the students think he is merely teaching accounting.

It is also worthy of note that improvements in text and teaching have included a definite broadening of the presentation. There is almost as much business management, business finance, business law, business economics in modern texts in accountancy, if we include more than first-year texts, as used to be needed to make up one third of a commerce curriculum.

Here an erroneous impression may derive from the language used. To the casual reader of accounting literature, the language is not clearly that of management, finance, law, or economics. The reason is that the language of accountancy is a composite of the other four plus a vocabulary originating in clerical bookkeeping. The well-prepared teacher of accounting knows this; he has had not a little educating in all of these fields. An important part of his classroom function is to open the doors to neighboring rooms for his students, to prepare his students to integrate these subjects when and where they meet them in their curriculum. The teacher who does that is making a contribution to the students' development far beyond any he could make by merely "hearing recitations."

An accounting teacher is poorly prepared for his assignment who is not prepared to make integrations of this sort. A teacher, well educated in the necessary composite of materials, who fails to integrate for his students, may be overspecialized and perhaps uninformed of his true functions as an accounting teacher at the university level. It seems clear, therefore, that well-taught accountancy can make a positive contribution to the education of all who, by entering a college of commerce, indicate an intention to study business, and this whether they entered to prepare for employment and advancement in business concerns, to prepare to establish and manage their own enterprises, or to prepare for public service as accounting teacher, certified public accountant, civil servant, or attorney-at-law. (Pre-law students often prepare in a college of commerce; a number of law schools have brought accounting instruction into their program.)

The doctrine of learning to learn played a part in developing the accountancy program at the University of Illinois where the decision was made in 1913 to place the first course in the freshman year and require it of all commerce students.

That action clearly rested upon sound educational reasoning. Since accounting subject matter was concrete and objective, it would be at once educationally useful and within the grasp of students during their transition from the high school to the college level of learning and labor. Part of its usefulness lay in the fact that, better than many other subjects, it offered a compact, preliminary introduction to business to the many students who, for one reason or another, would drop out of college before they had progressed very far.

The same student pattern still persists, and the same reason continues therefore for giving accounting in the freshman year. Another part of its educational usefulness is found in the fact that the subject matter of accountancy makes possible an orderly advance from the simple to the more complex. (Learning to learn.) Because students learn that accounting actions were always taken for clearly understandable reasons, the study of accounting seems to include elements of general educational benefit (learning to think). Furthermore, a foundation is laid for the better understanding of a variety of courses that come later in the curriculum in other subject matter and hence provides present preparation for later exercise in learning to think.

I am convinced that these educational aspects of accountancy are as useful for today and tomorrow as they were yesterday.

(Collegiate News, May, 1951)

7. Developing Capacity

Colleges of commerce, no less than colleges of liberal arts, strive to develop the capacities of their students. Accounting teachers therefore will be interested to note that many of the capabilities they try to detect and mature in students who select that subject as a major are also in the list of abilities which a liberal arts program undertakes to foster.

Dean William Glasgow Bowling of Washington University, St. Louis, concisely states the case as follows:

In the liberal-arts studies there is an interrelation of the cultural and the utilitarian. It is possible that in the past we may not have given enough attention to those values which are utilitarian and practical from some unfounded fear that such an assertion would be treason within the academic castle.

A college of liberal arts has always been and must continue to be the friend of the imagination; it has always been and must continue to be the guardian of the humanistic desire to know. A liberal education teaches one how to live. Yet a liberal education also provides opportunities for the developing of capacities useful in a time of emergency and helpful in the making of a living.

Among these capacities are the following: a capacity for clear and concise expression; a capacity to extract the correct meaning from what we read; a capacity for accurate mathematical computations; the capacity to use with a sense of workmanship some of the principal tools and techniques of the arts and sciences; a capacity to differentiate between facts and personal opinions and to organize and interpret such facts and personal opinions logically and coherently; a capacity for judgment; a capacity to locate easily and to use wisely the best sources of information for particular fields; a capacity to complete with some degree of success or distinction tasks which may, at the time, seem uninteresting and laborious; and the capacity to live with others sympathetically and understandingly and to work with them cooperatively and justly.

Nine capacities are listed. A person who has these in good measure could succeed in any one of many activities. It is not important where he gets them developed; it is important that the developing of his capacities shall have been a conscious objective of his education.

Some of the nine do not get as much consideration in an accounting curriculum as they would in a full program in liberal arts. The last one in the list is of this kind. Probably this capacity grows more from class-room contacts and campus activities than from subject matter studied and discussed. Another is ability to find sources of information. Not much time is given by accounting students to practice in this art. In later life this lack may occasionally prove something of a handicap; yet in total the handicap probably would not be serious because an accountant seldom has to do research of the sort implied. Of course, classroom training in library resources might be useful to him as discipline.

Almost any training with a disciplinary focus would be helpful to the prospective accountant—a great deal of his work in later life will have that connotation for him. That fact will be taken into consideration by accounting teachers in framing their educational curriculum and forming the content of many of the courses. Even so, the student's internship years after graduation may seem to contain more laborious and uninteresting detail than he had imagined possible. Some who manage to evade the efforts of teachers to develop a capacity for completing disagreeable tasks do not survive the early years in practice. It is perhaps just as well, for they probably could not be happy in the higher levels of accounting activity.

A capacity for accurate mathematical computation must also stand high in the list for accounting students. But it is doubtful whether this ability is fostered only by courses in college algebra, analytical geometry, trigonometry, or calculus. These may have some value if there is plenty of time in the accounting curriculum; but the value will have to come from the discipline received rather than from knowledge as such. If such courses train a man to hold his mind resolutely to work full of complex and uninteresting details, they may be useful for prospective accountants. But if other work has the same kind of disciplinary effects, it should serve this educational purpose equally well, and perhaps contain directly useful content as well.

We value very highly a capacity for judgment, and recognize that this is extremely hard to develop from texts and classes. Accounting courses lay great stress on solving problems, choosing among alternatives, recognizing misleading practices. But most of us continue to believe that these efforts seldom succeed in developing judgment except where it had some pre-existing natural basis.

There is no need to consider each of the listed capacities in turn; but they all deserve the consideration of accounting teachers. Some of the abilities probably can be developed better in liberal arts courses and by arts-trained teachers. Some of the capacities can no doubt be stimulated by suitable materials and capable teachers in almost any curriculum setting. Almost certainly some capacities could best be developed for accounting majors by the use of materials particularly relevant to the work of accountants, presented by teachers trained in that field.

It seems reasonable to conclude that educational programs for accountancy should continue partly cultural, partly technical. How the partition should be accomplished is the real question. When that is settled, much of the strain of curriculum-building will have vanished.

In the meantime many problems will remain. Since the curriculum will often be a mixed one, with a limited time available for liberal arts courses, one of the continuing problems is to find courses which are neither overgeneralized survey outlines nor masses of detailed materials that seem to be assembled for students who are beginning a long specialization in that particular department.

(editorial, *Accounting Review*, July, 1954)

8. Mathematics

In one outline of desirable qualities in a junior accountant (*Connecticut CPA*, January, 1944), mathematics is given a prominent place along with clear and grammatical English. The junior should have "Soundness of mathematical thought in analysis and solution of problems. Accuracy in performing mathematical processes. Ability to perform ordinary mathematical processes without mechanical aids. Form and arrangement of mathematical solutions."

Other writers in the past have frequently mentioned "mathematical ability" as highly desirable in a public accountant. And the question immediately comes to mind: Does this mean "inherent ability for mathematical work" or "education in that subject?" Does it mean knowledge of the language and methods of higher mathematics (college algebra, analytical geometry, calculus, actuarial computations) or proficiency and skill in the usual processes of arithmetic?

Arithmetic might well be called a technique that is basic in accountancy, but skill therein does not necessarily mark a man as being promising staff material. Higher mathematics as such is seldom actually employed in day-to-day accounting work as it is in a great deal of engineering. It seems then that some skill in arithmetic would be more useful to an accountant than knowledge of higher mathematics.

What many writers no doubt have in mind is not knowledge or skill, but rather some ability or talent or aptitude which they describe as "mathematical." The main usefulness of the study of higher mathematics for prospective accountants therefore would be in the development that this work might give to certain desired mental qualities. We shall put aside the possible collateral question of whether the study of mathematics can create a desired mental ability, or merely develop the abilities that are present, if any. The main question is whether higher mathematics is a necessary part of the education of an accountant. If that kind of knowledge is necessary in his work, it should be in the educational program of the accountant, as it is in that of the engineer and the scientist.

If the accountant needs a certain type of ability, but little or no mathematical knowledge, it is an open question whether the study of mathematics is the best way to attain that ability. If some other approach will develop the desired ability and at the same time give the student certain knowledge that will also be directly useful in his future work, it is clearly an advantage to follow this course, even if to do so means foregoing the discipline which is part of the study of mathematics.

It may well be that the idea which accountants and teachers really have in mind when they refer to "mathematical ability" is better described as "analytical ability." In some fields, such as engineering and physics, analytical ability—since there it must deal extensively with observations, refined measurements and predictions—must embrace the techniques of higher mathematics; in these fields, mathematics becomes in part the language in which thought is clothed. Analytical ability is very necessary in accountancy also. But it does not follow that it must rest on the same techniques as in the sciences. It is doubtful for example whether we could maintain that the language for expressing accounting thought is mathematical in the sense that the statement is true of the sciences.

If the qualities desired in an accountant were reduced to the bare minimum for professional survival, they probably would be: technical accounting knowledge and analytical ability. And if the needed analytical ability can be developed at the same time that progress is being made in acquiring the necessary technical knowledge, the economy of the combination will be plainly evident.

This thought should not need much elaboration; it is a matter of common knowledge that many public accountants of unquestioned analytical ability did not train on higher mathematics. It probably is significant also that statistics of student failures in accountancy often show close similarities to those of failures in college mathematics courses. Most teachers can recall several experiences tending to show that few students in engineering who were unsuccessful because of mathematics succeed in accountancy after changing colleges.

Probably very few teachers of mathematics would subscribe to the theory that prior training in accountancy would tend to make better mathematics students. Why should accounting teachers subscribe to the reverse? The fact is that the same quality of mind is indicated for both fields rather than that one is a feeder to the other. If the faculty for analysis, whatever that may consist of, is deficient, the person may reasonably be expected to experience difficulty in any field of study and activity in which that quality is important.

(editorial, *Accounting Review*, April, 1944)

9. Analytical Ability

Adequate technical knowledge of accountancy must of course be suitably supplemented by a semitechnical knowledge of business law, corporation finance, and certain aspects of economics. In each of these subjects there are problem areas of practice, where interest is centered upon customary methods and typical situations, and there are problem areas of theory, where the pros and cons of alternatives are debated.

But technical knowledge alone affords poor equipment for rendering professional service; among other needed factors is technical ability—something above and beyond knowledge as such. In accounting this may properly be called "analytical ability." There are other factors which can contribute measurably to professional success; but it is not too much to say that these, unaided by a faculty for analysis, would not prove very adequate.

If analytical ability is of high importance to a public accountant, some explanation of the meaning of the phrase is in order. These notes are a hazard in that direction.

Analytical ability is a complex concept which cannot be clearly described in a definition. A better approach is to examine some of its many constituent parts. From one point of view it consists of a faculty for arranging facts understandingly plus a faculty for understanding the facts as arranged.

A faculty for comprehending accounting facts (transaction data expressed in terms of money) is itself a complex of a number of abilities, some of which are: to hold in mind a complex changing pattern, to see scattered parts as integral parts of a whole, to find threads of continuity in successive details.

A faculty for associating accounting facts is likewise a complex of a number of abilities, some of which are: to see relative proportions quickly among figures, to sense the meaning of proportions among figures, to relate figures to ideas, actions, policies, effects, to judge which elements are the most significant.

From one point of view, then, analytical ability includes two faculties —the ability to *comprehend* and the ability to *associate,* and the two support one another. Part of the ability to comprehend (understand) comes from ability to associate (arrange), and vice versa. But that is not all. In order to do the comprehending and understanding that lies within accounting, in order to be able to grasp what is significant among many facts, it is necessary to have or to develop what might be called "figure memory," except that this term might seem to emphasize the memorizing of digits, which would be absurd.

Perhaps the concept necessary here is one that is better called "associative memory"—an ability to hold many facts and complex relations in mind at the same time that one is searching through them for the really significant. This is one approach at least to "grasping what is significant." Furthermore, in order to see through and behind figures to ideas and possibilities, it is necessary to have or to develop what might be called "penetrative imagination," a phrase to suggest that accounting imagination need not be identified too closely with the creative imagination associated with an artist, a poet, or a composer.

(editorial, *Accounting Review*, April, 1944)

10. Techniques of Analysis

In order to use his analytical ability in accounting, a person needs to have facility in manipulating figures and communicating ideas by this means. The accountant must have the ability to use figures fluently as a medium of thought and this ability in turn rests upon skill in three simple techniques: easy and accurate performance of arithmetical processes, legibility in writing and correctness in reading figures, concise and interpretive tabulation of figures.

Without this basis, the manipulation of figures which is so much a part of all accounting action, would be done only under considerable strain and without much confidence. Without appropriate skills, analytical ability would function at best under handicap.

If a facility in the use of figures is an underlying basis for analytical ability in accountancy, a facility for communicating accounting ideas is a necessary means for projecting the results of analysis beyond the accountant himself to other parties at interest. Unless the significance detected by analytical ability is clearly and convincingly revealed, the effort made is not justified. This ability to communicate, like the other ability here analyzed, rests upon certain simple techniques: combining words and figures expressively, writing English concisely, clearly, and correctly, stating the full truth tactfully.

Analytical ability, when associated with a wide knowledge of accountancy, should produce technical competence. This last is undoubtedly the primary basis of professional service; but the professional accountant, like any other professional man, needs more than technical competence. The other qualities needed are not under consideration here. But as a reminder that they exist, these may be named; physical capacity for concentrated work; capacity for continuing to grow with experience; a personality for friendliness and leadership; pride in professional craftsmanship; resourceful adaptability; and common sense—a term so admirably explained in Webster's *Dictionary of Synonyms* that this is quoted: ". . . a native capacity for seeing things as they are and without illusion or emotional bias, for making practical choices or decisions that are sane, prudent, fair, reasonable, and that comment themselves to the normal, or average good mind."

(editorial, *Accounting Review*, April, 1944)

DIAGRAM OF ANALYTICAL ABILITY AND ANALYTICAL TECHNIQUES

- See scattered parts as an integral whole
- Techniques of writing clear, concise, correct English
- Techniques of using words and figures expressively
- Techniques of stating the full truth tactfully
- Judge which elements are most significant
- Find threads of continuity among successive details
- Facility in communicating ideas
- Relate figures to ideas, actions, policies, effects
- Ability to comprehend
- Analytical ability
- Ability to associate
- Deal with complications one at a time
- Facility in manipulating figures
- Sense the meaning of proportions among figures
- Hold in mind a complex changing pattern
- Techniques of arithmetical processes
- Techniques of writing and reading figures
- Techniques of interpretive tabulation
- See relative proportions quickly among figures

11. Words and Figures

When professional accountants say that college graduates coming into their employment are commonly weak in English, they do not mean a deficiency in the ability to appreciate good literature. And when they say that the graduates are weak in mathematics, they do not mean the calculus or the method of least squares. They merely believe that it is a distinct advantage in the profession to be able to express one's self clearly in the mother tongue and to be able to deal with figures arithmetically.

If an accountant expresses a preference for graduates from a liberal arts program, may it not be that he believes graduates from a commerce program have often neglected these two fundamentals while studying other things?

Perhaps the colleges of commerce have placed too much faith in a few special courses such as freshman rhetoric and business letter-writing. It is doubtful that these are enough to give one a real facility in the use of language. More such courses in the curriculum would help, but the accounting major gets too little opportunity to practice the use of the English language outside of his rhetoric classes.

In contrast, a liberal arts course requires of the student a great deal of reading. Much of it puts him in contact with good writing. Foreign language is also required. One of the advantages of work in a foreign language is the enforced contact with the mechanics of language structure. In addition, in many courses frequent papers and reports are expected which give further practice in the use of language.

This raises some questions about the usual commerce curriculum for an accounting major. Is the major in accountancy doing so much work in marshaling quantitative data that too little time is left to practice expressing thoughts verbally? May it not be that CPA laws and CPA examiners through concentration on "factual" data—figure problems— have set a pattern of thought tending to neglect verbal problems? Is judging the answers to the essay type of examination question, if used in moderation, actually difficult for a mature and experienced account-ant?

As for weakness in arithmetic, do the graduates of colleges of com-merce, even after a good deal of figure work in accounting courses, go into offices with any real facility in handling figures? Do courses in an-alytical geometry, college algebra, trigonometry, calculus, actuarial math-ematics, give the student a real facility in dealing with figures, or do they only give practice in certain kinds of thought processes which are seldom directly useful in working professional accounting problems?

Perhaps higher mathematics should be studied for its disciplinary value rather than as knowledge for use. It does have the effect of reducing the number of those who go on toward graduation. But, so too do the ac-counting courses. There is another question: How much of the service of colleges lies in sifting and screening for the accounting profession those with capacity to learn quickly and ability to grow in powers of intensive thinking; and how much lies in transmitting knowledge and skill?

No doubt it is mere tradition that arithmetic is usually considered as "below the college level." If work in economic principles, sociology, and the like can be adapted to high school use, it seems equally reasonable to assume that "figure techniques" could be developed into a useful and disciplinary course on the college level. No doubt, college teachers of statistics, engineering, and finance, as well as teachers of accounting, have often wished for their students a better foundation in arithmetical processes. Some bold spirit may one day startle us by developing a graded sequential course in "Computations." Then we will be astonished to discover how well the basic processes of computation blend into the commercial use of figures, the statistical use of figures, and thence onward into the abstractions and short cuts of higher mathematics.

Life and labor in this day put a premium on ability to deal with words and figures. Colleges, no less than the lower schools, are charged with the duty of trying to develop these powers, among others, to the limits of the students' capacity. We have no false modesty about giving college students elementary instruction in the use of words. Why are we so different about helping them to learn to use figures?

The student heading toward a career in accounting needs thorough training in both words and figures—up to a certain point. The short cuts of higher mathematics are like poetic language—designed for special uses above the plane of ordinary use. The scientist and the engineer have need for advanced training in figures; the orator, the preacher, and the actor need special training in words. The accountant's work does not ascend to that level in either words or figures; his education, therefore, need not extend so far, but he needs more than he usually gets at present.

Public accountants get some of their most important supplies from educational institutions. Schools are a source of supply; practitioners are the customers. Many producers do not manufacture to order, but they do take careful note of the goods in demand and those that are not. The clues to their production thus come indirectly from the customers. The customer usually votes his preferences by making choices.

Public accountants, as customers of the colleges supplying graduates, are much like other customers: They know what they like; they are not sure just why; they hesitate to make suggestions for improvement. Manufacturers often try to learn to serve better by stirring customers to analyze the basis of their choices. Accounting teachers could do likewise.

On the other hand, practitioners have a direct and vital interest in the matter. They could with benefit take the initiative in exploring their own views about the characteristics desired of young men entering the profession. They could safely leave to professional teachers the task of deciding the means of helping students to acquire those characteristics.

Professional accountants have often said they like a new man to have a pleasing personality, to be able to use the English language with reasonable skill, and to have a capacity for dealing effectively with masses of figures. Are there no other suggestions? If the profession will be satisfied with these characteristics alone teachers will know how to respond. But just now teachers doubt that these traits are enough; and they are not entirely confident that their own ideas of what else should be in the list of objectives are as useful as they might be.

(editorial, Accounting Review, April, 1943)

12. The Whys of How

"In the undergraduate curriculum the stress seems to be placed upon the 'how' rather than upon the 'why'—upon doing rather than thinking. This is the attitude of the student and it appears that it is too generally that of the teacher. However, the responsibility for this attitude does not rest upon them alone. Practitioners have encouraged this approach to the matter, perhaps they originated it."

The writer of the above (Norman E. Webster, *Journal of Accountancy*, November, 1944) is a professional accountant and would no doubt be reluctant to extend his thought to cover the responsibility of teachers. For a teacher, it is easy to make just that point.

Teachers probably emphasize the hows of accounting because they believe it their duty to transmit knowledge of traditional procedures and because they want to use teaching materials that are concrete rather than abstract. Both of these are good ideas about teaching, but they are not very satisfactory if they stand too much alone. There is also a duty, perhaps the most important of all, to help students learn to think. It is difficult to accomplish this by holding closely to descriptions of established procedures. That approach would tend to put a premium on simple remembering and leave the student unaware that the future will often call upon him to resolve novel situations satisfactorily which were not described in his texts. For that reason among others something more than the how of traditional procedures is needed to make teaching effective. It is the why of things done that makes the most lasting impression and does most to generate a capacity to face new problems.

In thus placing due emphasis on the whys, it is not necessary to abandon the concrete and become confusingly abstract. Concrete situations and needs can be used as a base—a concrete foundation—for thinking about whys. The reasoning involved will then lose its color of abstraction, and the reasons given will become relevant, significant, explanatory. Theory (reasons, explanations), if it is related to definite situations, purposes, objectives, is not likely to seem abstract to anyone. And a treatment given to a situation, when rendered with understanding of its surroundings, objectives, reasons, can be a reasonable one even if it is customary and generally accepted.

Thus good teaching will not need to give less of the *how* to make room for more of the *why*. It will need only to see to it, in discussing concrete situations, that these are adequately clothed with good reasons (theory). If time presses we can then recall that the doctrine knowing a lot about a little is probably sounder than knowing a little about a lot. In most teaching some of the familiar topics could well be omitted and others enlighteningly amplified.

(editorial, Accounting Review, April, 1945)

13. Raising the Sights

Teachers are likely to discharge their professional obligations best if they set their sights high. They cannot hope to completely prepare students to be accountants. Their function is to prepare students to become accountants. "Capacity to become" is more valuable than drill in what now is. In line with this thought is another: accounting students need to be aimed toward more understanding and breadth, and less toward skills and techniques.

Are accounting students generally encouraged to read discussions of big issues; to examine conflicts between ideas within accounting and with ideas in neighboring fields? Isn't college a place for stretching one's intellectual tissues; for stirring the imagination with possibilities not yet devised into procedures; for exercising faculties of judgment under circumstances where the penalty for mistake is still small?

General students may elect a course in the history of economic theory; others may include in their program such items as aspects constitutional law, principles of jurisprudence, fundamental concepts of mathematics, philosophy of science. Students who major in economics, history, political science, mathematics, science, are offered options like these. Such courses are mind-stretchers. There are no comparable offerings for students majoring in accountancy. They only exercise their minds over minutiae. That of course is an important exercise because accounting inescapably involves a multitude of details. But accountants in real life are often concerned far beyond the details. Should not prospective accountants in school be led to lift their eyes some of the time toward distant horizons? If it is valuable to study the why as well as the how of specific procedures, it should be valuable to study, for example, the social purposes served by accountancy as well as the public accountant's contractual obligations.

It should be distinctly educational if students were to consider the way income would be expressed ideally if all difficulties of measuring cost and revenue were overcome. Those difficulties could then be given separate study with adequate perspective. Students, whatever their ultimate line of accounting service, would be benefited if they had a good understanding of the way cost accounting and administrative accounting have been evolving in close harmony with modern industrial needs. Compared to the cost of accounting of today, financial accounting is indeed "crude, timid, hidebound, and unimaginative," as one author puts it.

If we understood better how industrial accounting got where it stands, we probably could work more intelligently at the task of helping financial accounting and professional auditing to catch up. It is significant that industrial accounting has not been functioning within the confines of a pattern set in 1896 or earlier. Industrial accountants have not been circumscribed in action by holding to narrow views regarding both their function and the opportunities for extending their services. They have not hesitated to invent alternatives and vigorously argue their merits. Nor have they been fearful of boldly experimenting toward large, known objectives.

Outside of cost and administrative accounting most technical education is, in one way or another, focused upon the CPA examination. Even outside of review courses, CPA materials greatly influence the teaching content; this effect often extends into postgraduate courses. These can be useful teaching materials, especially if they teach one to think rather than merely learn to do. That is to say, there is no need to solve examples of every type of prior CPA problems in order to learn how to think through accounting situations. Have these teaching materials been carefully arranged in a sequential order so they will stair-step the approach to analytical thinking? Or are they being presented topically, with easy items given late in the program as well as early?

(editorial, *Accounting Review*, April, 1945)

14. Removing the Mysteries

One of the best contributions an accounting teacher can make to his students' progress is a skillful supplementing of the text at many points. This can be especially helpful for the novice and for the moment, if it translates accounting technicalities into nontechnical language and if it indoctrinates the student early with ideas about the larger objectives of the important features of accounting methods. The intention would be to divest the subject of its "mysteries" as soon as possible. If this is done, the necessary study of technology can later proceed with better understanding.

Accounting seems to some people to be a mysterious technology that is expected to produce scientific results. That idea is faulty. Accounting is not really mysterious and its results are not scientific in the general sense of the term. It is just a special way of organizing data about a business enterprise. These data are not significant because they are put into records. Significance derives from the fact that diverse enterprise events have been converted into enterprise data by the use of accounting ideas and methods.

Accounts are a technical feature of accounting and are closely related to the data-dealing functions of accounting. But there is no mystery about them. They are simply categories into which enterprise transaction data are to be classified. Accounts therefore perform the usual statistical service of all categories, that of compressing a mass of data into more easily comprehensible summary figures. The mass of transaction data, thus statistically compacted by accounting means, is for the first time made intelligible for use in accounting reports.

There is little that is mysterious in the report of the economic activities of an enterprise, the income statement. Behind this report lie two important concepts: that the category "expense" is a broader idea than cash "ex-spended"; that the category "income" is a broader idea than cash in-coming. It is for this reason that it is advisable to think of expense as representing "enterprise efforts" and of income as representing "enterprise accomplishments." By this means most of the "mystery" of nominal accounts and the income statement may be dispelled.

There is little that is mysterious in the other important accounting report—the capital statement of an enterprise. The traditional term "balance sheet" seems to say something significant but actually does not. Merely thinking of this report as a "capital statement" will avoid much straining to grasp the report's function from reading its traditional title. Together the two basic statements are then seen to deal with the two basic aspects of business—capital and income.

Behind this second report lies the subconcept of assets as kinds of capital working—that is, capital working for those who have invested in the enterprise; capital working for and with labor employed in the enterprise; capital working for governments which draw tax revenue from the enterprise; capital working for consumers of the products or services flowing from the enterprise.

Reported alongside of assets are the many items assembled on the right side of the statement. These represent sources of capital; they tell of capital waiting rather than of capital working. Some of the "mystery" of this statement disappears when we accept the parallel presentation as merely a convenient way of placing items side by side for easier visual comparison. More of the "mystery" evaporates as soon as we decline to think of the right-side items exclusively as liabilities and proprietorship. It is more enlightening to think of these items (notes payable, taxes and wages accrued, bonds and stocks outstanding, profits reinvested in the business) as sources of capital quietly awaiting a future outcome from use. Since together they express an aspect of capital (the "waiting" of various people who have claims against the capital at work and for its fruits) these items in total will inevitably refer to the same "capital" that is reported from another point of view on the other side of the statement —the point of view of capital as service potentialities.

It is another peculiarity of accounting that an account is not a single category. Yet the fact that every account is a dual category need not make accounts mysterious. An account category is designed to assemble related likes and opposites under one head. This treatment of data adds to the usefulness of the assembled facts. For it makes it easy at any time to ascertain three things: (1) a total of positive factors in the category, (2) a total of related negative factors, (3) the excess of either one over the other.

This scheme of statistical classification is particularly useful for recording data in a way that will reflect the effect of changes upon the balance of the account, while at the same time compressing a mass of transaction detail into fewer figures.

It will be noted that a dual category also makes it easy, when needed, to classify negative factors before the corresponding positive factors appear, and equally easy to show a long-lived factor slowly giving up its usefulness as time passes. Rather than being a mysterious feature of accounting, this method of using dual classifications makes the changes that take place in enterprise data all the more understandable because the accounts are thereby linked closely together.

Accounts would be purely statistical categories except for the fact that their two-sided arrangement permits them to be interrelated in ways that make them accounting categories—that is, categories which, in the record, dovetail the economic transactions with the financial transactions.

When economic transactions occur, the events are treated as data that work a change in economic accounts (expense or income) and also a change in financial accounts (assets or equities). When financial transactions occur (such as borrowing, lending, investing, disinvesting) the events, as data, affect financial accounts only. As a result of this integration, it is possible to produce two reports of high significance—an income report and a capital report—which mutually support (prove, test) each other. When the earning activities and the capital status of an enterprise can be clearly read from reported data, a unique way is opened for gaining a very helpful understanding of the enterprise concerned.

Where we view accounting without traditional and technical terminology, and see it in terms of functions and objectives, all sense of mystery tends to evaporate. Its technicalities then can be recognized as utilitarian rather than mysteriously significant.

(unpublished manuscript, about 1950)

15. Social Service from Accountancy

Accounting may be said to possess three principal use values: (1) as a foundation for practicing public accounting professionally, (2) as an in-

ternal information service for business management, and (3) as a way of
learning disciplined thinking about dealing with data. The first two uses
are well known; the third use value is the sort usually attributed to
mathematics and statistics. Yet accounting can serve some of the same
disciplinary purposes and at the same time inform the student concretely
about origins of some of the most important kinds of social statistics—
those derived from account data. It is part of the teacher's duty to make
this service clear.

Business activities are such a prominent part of modern life that an
elementary understanding of them by many people becomes important.
For example, business enterprises generate a very large amount of government revenue. It is even more significant to note that business "is the
paymaster of us all." Accounting is an excellent approach to understanding that paymaster and that generator of tax revenue. For business is the
primary source of wages of workers, wages of capital, and wages of management. Division of labor, use of machine power, and mass distribution
of products have created vast areas of employment at wages. By including, along with human employment, an intricate system of employing
the savings of all kinds of people, business enterprises become real co-
operative institutions, some of them on a grand scale.

Another section of this adventure in co-operation involves the development and use of skilled managerial planning. The final link in the
circle of co-operation appears at the point where goods and services flow
to consumers—people who are in the picture also in their capacities as
workers and savers.

It is evident from the existence of these interrelations that the activities of business enterprises will be very complex and technical in many
respects. It is this technical complexity of business that permits a quasi-
statistical discipline such as accounting to render its service of making
a business enterprise understandable to a wide range of interested parties.

Accounting can render this service, not because it uses records, but because its primary data illuminate so well the focal area of enterprise
activities. This is the active area represented by data showing the degree
of enterprise accomplishment in furnishing wanted goods and services
(in accounting, expressed as enterprise income); and the data significant
of the success of enterprise efforts to produce its supply of goods and
services at a cost below the sum the user can and will pay (in accounting,
expressed as enterprise expense).

Accounting thus makes an important contribution to the preservation
and advancement of productive enterprise through the informative comparisons it makes possible between efforts made (expense) and the results
achieved (income). This kind of comparison is particularly useful because it keeps management constantly informed of the way the enterprise
is or is not living within its income, and this in turn directs attention to
the study of external conditions affecting possible income and to the study
of internal conditions affecting necessary expense.

Living within one's income is no easier in a business enterprise than in a family. Yet the service rendered society by managerial skill in this respect is often misunderstood. For all parties touched by business activities benefit from management's exercise of managerial skills: skills in judging soundly among alternatives; skills in the resourceful devising of ways and means; and skills in the use of experience in appraising conditions.

It is noteworthy that the cue which calls up a manifestation of managerial skill often comes from expense and income data out of the enterprise accounts; and it is significant that the same data viewed after the fact, can act as a meter registering the results of prior managerial decisions. Accounting has a clear social use value here which may escape the student if the instructor does not see that it does not happen.

By dealing with concrete situations and specific procedures, the study of accounting can contribute a good deal to the students' grasp of enterprise activities, thus laying a useful foundation for later courses in other subject matter. This may prove to be a social service through deepening the understanding of many students. By dealing extensively with problems of converting actions into data and of classifying data into highly informative categories, the study of accounting fosters a respect for facts and a sensitiveness to classification truth versus classification untruth. By dealing with data for classification and compression, it puts students in touch with some very useful aspects of logic. Not by examples of syllogistic logic, it is true, but by making clear the consequences (distortions) that flow from illogical classification and inappropriately defined or poorly named categories.

Fully as generally useful as the above is the understanding which accounting can give of the way that known objectives exercise control over actions taken in regard to data accumulation and use. Accounting has general use value also because of the awareness it gives of interrelations. Account data are full of interrelations; in fact, making data interrelations understandable is an important duty of accounting.

These facts clearly show that accounting in its modern manifestations is far from being the simple clerical routine usually meant by the term "bookkeeping."

By working with data where perceiving interrelations is highly important, one acquires an awareness that significant interrelations exist everywhere; an awareness of the existence of variations or gradations in the significance of all kinds of facts; an awareness of the limitations that attach to the conclusiveness of even factual evidence.

Use values such as these have been recognized as lying in the study of accounting. Because of this, there has been a widespread acceptance of the subject matter as useful for study outside of a purely occupational framework.

(Accounting Review, April, 1950; July, 1950)

EDUCATIONAL METHOD

1. Early Accounting Literature

One of the chief instruments of education is the printed page. For four and a half centuries this kind of instrument has been used to give men some knowledge of the techniques of keeping and using accounting information. In that length of time an extensive technical literature has appeared. Generation after generation has contributed its share and always with an awareness of the needs of the day.

There was a long incubation period extending from about the year 1200 to perhaps 1500, or a little before. During this time the bookkeeping side of accounting was evolving by use into the organized methodology of double entry. Only manuscript books were available then; of these we know very little. But there is no need to doubt that after printing was invented the early printed textbooks closely followed the available manuscript texts wherein the prevailing practices were described.

After 1500 came another long period of slow development; perhaps this interval could be called four hundred years of adolescent growth. From our later perspective accounting before 1900 seems relatively immature in many of its aspects. The literature had by that time gained stature primarily in auditing. Continuing the figure of speech, accounting literature was like a young man emerging from adolescence—tall for its age but in many respects not yet showing the breadth and strength of young manhood.

The first printed book on accounting appeared in 1494—a contemporary of Christopher Columbus. Written by a monk named Paciolo, it was not the inspiration of a happy moment bringing into existence something not yet known, but rather a teacher's exposition of existing business records as kept "according to the method of Venice." The practices he described existed in trade before he wrote them down. He describes them in almost infinite detail, but gave us no theory. There is nothing to indicate to us the thoughts of those minds which finally "realized that the transactions of business in their entirety form a homogeneous whole which is capable of being marshalled into the framework of a system." (Brown, *History of Accounting and Accountants*.)

Paciolo wrote at a most opportune time. The invention of printing was allied with an awakening thirst for learning. The knowledge of record system at that time possessed by a relatively small number of Italian merchants, could not have remained local to one country for long under those conditions.

At the end of the fifteenth century the adolescent period of accounting literature begins with Paciolo's book on mathematics, geometry, and bookkeeping.

A very large part of this middle period—some three hundred and eighty years in fact—was characterized by the spread of Italian book-keeping through simple translation or plain imitation and occasionally through outright verbatim pirating. Generally the new books added such illustrations and transactions as the author's experience dictated; before long they were written in dialogue form with the accounts personified and entries thereto explained as if all of them involved debts created and debts discharged.

As an illustration of the impulse given by Paciolo to accounting litera-ture, it may be interesting at this point to list the names of the leading writers of the one hundred and forty years immediately following him. Paciolo (Italy, 1494); Manzoni (Italy, 1534); Schweiker (Germany, 1541); Ympyn (Holland, 1543); Oldcastle (England, 1543); Peele (England, 1554); Pietra (Italy, 1586); Petri (Holland, 1588); Mellis (England, 1588); Stevin (Holland, 1605); Wolff (Germany, 1610); Dafforne (England, 1636). Truly a remarkable showing even if it represented a large percentage of translation and copying.

Improvements came very slowly. The writers almost uniformly failed to expand the germs of logical analysis underlying the Italian method and therefore did not explain clearly wherein the entries were a record of conclusions reached by reasoning. Rather was the tendency the reverse, for very soon the explanations became mere precise rules, yardsticks to be applied unthinkingly to transactions as they arose. Apparently the search was for some touchstone which would make the translation of business activities into concise records an extremely simple matter.

Yet enshrouded as it was with the formalism imposed by dry-bone rules, the accounting of the day was fully adequate to its task because the transaction of business consisted of simple trading and transactions in banker's credits. When commercial supremacy passed to Holland the same accounting methods were still sufficient because the character of commerce was unchanged although far outreaching the older trade routes in extent. Nor did the subsequent seizure of commercial supremacy by England change these conditions.

Commerce was everywhere alike. Even the development of the East Indies Company and other great trading companies in the seventeenth century brought little change. All of the large enterprises of the day were engaged in trading and consequently lacked the complexities necessary to call forth fundamental changes in the simple merchandise accounting then in use.

Such was the condition of the literature until the period of adolescence had nearly run its course. Nearly three hundred of the four hundred years of this period had passed before the invention of power machinery ushered in the Industrial Revolution and the factory system. And for most of the remaining hundred years manufacturing was carried on only upon a very small scale. There were still no pressing needs which might call forth new developments in accounting; yet the germ of future developments lay hidden in the factory system nevertheless.

That germ bore fruit in the form of accounting literature in 1887 when Garcke and Fells published their *Factory Accounts*—the beginning of cost accounting texts. The book undoubtedly filled a need, for it rapidly went through numerous editions. Not until 1899 did it have a serious competitor. In that year Arnold published his *Complete Cost Keeper*.

But factory accounting was not alone as a representative of the new lines of thought being directed toward accounting. The professional auditor had come into some prominence and the multiplicity of his responsibilities were duly recorded by Pixley in *Duties of Auditors* (1881). In 1892 Dicksee added a volume on *Auditing* in which he presented an exposition of the existing practices of the profession.

With these writings the period of the young manhood of accounting literature is begun and that of adolescence ended. There is no particular significance in the year 1900, but it is a date convenient to remember as the beginning of the present period and one which is closely associated with the transition from small to large enterprises.

About this time it becomes plainly evident that attention is no longer to be confined to the purely recording aspects of accounting. The writers of the dozen years prior to 1900 (Dicksee, Pixley, *et al.*) show this unmistakably. They were the pioneers who first recognized the new educational needs and who, accordingly, wrote not of bookkeeping but of accounting. In the annals of accounting literature they deserve to rank with Paciolo because, not content with imitation, they followed his example and struck out into new paths.

(AAUIA, *Proceedings*, IX, No. 2, December, 1925)

2. Twenty-five Years Ago

The first decade of the twentieth century saw a healthy growth of the list of accounting books which were quite generally along the lines marked out by the pioneers a few years earlier. Mention of the principal publications of this period will bring to mind many individuals who should be highly honored; they were the teachers of us all.

The consideration of theory and problems, apart from that included in auditing texts, appeared in Lisle's *Accounting Theory and Practice* (1900) and Dicksee's *Advance Accounting* (1903). In 1905 Montgomery brought out an American edition of Dicksee's *Auditing*. There was a growing difference in practice here and abroad, but the latter author's *Advanced Accounting*, together with Lisle, continued for some time to supply the American students' needs for theory. The appearance in New York of

Spragae's *Philosophy of Accounts* (1907), Hatfield's *Modern Accounting* (1909), and Nicholson's *Factory Organization and Costs* (1909) may be said to mark the real beginning of American contributions.

It is difficult to express our debt to these and other writers of the period, for they widened the horizon of accounting greatly by the breadth of their vision. We may be sure they realized that the growing profession had urgent need of the written word—of digested practical experience formulated into principles and problems, and the accumulated wisdom of generations of practitioners. They saw that education by precept and example alone was too slow and inefficient to be an effective means of passing on the wealth of knowledge already available and so much needed for continued progress. They saw the need, and the responses, forming as they do the foundations for subsequent publications, have left their indelible imprint upon the profession.

Two decades from 1900 bring accounting literature down to the present writing. Most of the later years of this period loom large in our eyes; we have been part of it and we no doubt are biased by our nearness. But bias cannot explain away certain characteristics of the period—characteristics which increased the impulse to write in the field of accounting. It has been a period marked by great combinations of capital under corporate management; by far-reaching banking reform, and on the whole by conditions of general prosperity. There has been increased governmental regulation of public-utility companies, cost-plus contracts in war time, and a federal income tax statute. By way of response, these conditions have caused an increasing interest in accounting generally. They have been accompanied by a very rapid growth of collegiate instruction in accounting, and compared to the past, a tremendous output of books on accounting.

If this period should prove to be a milestone in the production of accounting literature, it will not be because men wrote for the sake of authorship, but because the books were a manifestation of the continued efforts of many men to help make better-trained accountants. The necessities of trade of this period can be read between the lines in the characterization of the prior decade. They call in no mistakable terms for better accounting and for more people trained in accounting. And the response is at hand; accounting and accounting literature have grown in answer to the needs of this period.

The literature itself takes on a new aspect. Whereas the books of the prior ten years were quite generally combinations complete in themselves of both theory and practice, there is now a noticeable tendency toward a separate consideration of these two phases and toward a development of special applications of accounting.

Without attempting an exhaustive catalog, the mention of a few recent publications will serve to indicate the direction of this tendency. Among those dealing with special classes of business at length are, *Practical Ac-*

counting for the General Contractor (Grant), *Bituminous Coal Mine Accounting* (Reed), *Brokerage Accounts* (Todman), *Municipal Accounting* (Eggleston), *Real Estate Accounting* (Mucklaw). Such books are a necessary part of the process of building the practice of public accounting into a profession. And it is to be hoped that the effort to expand this side of the literature will continue. While the principles of accounting are universally applicable, the framework through which they are applied varies considerably in the several lines of business.

There is also an apparent tendency to give separate consideration to the theory and to the practice side of accounting. A few examples from among the recent books will illustrate this fact also. Cole's *Fundamental of Accounting*, Paton's *Accounting Theory*, and Ficker's *Shop Expense* are examples of works which take the theory point of view. On the other hand, Jackson's *Audit Working Papers*, Bell's *Accounting Reports*, McKinsey's *Budgetary Control*, and Bliss' *Management Through Accounts* present various aspects of current practices without intending to consider accounting theory as such. All of these developments are full of significance to the accounting profession. But they are for the most part too recent to warrant an attempt to weigh the importance of their contributions.

(AAUIA, *Proceedings,* IX, No. 2, December, 1925)

3. Enriching the Literature

A vast field for accounting literature is waiting to be developed. Three possibilities are suggested here.

There is the matter of a more complete correlation with other subjects. Economics, for example, has a great deal to offer. Too much attention has been given to the thought that the two subjects are only distantly related because economics deals with society and accounting with the individual. Too little thought is given to the fact that economic laws at work act only through individuals and their judgments. The business judgments of individuals are largely based upon knowledge drawn from their prior accounts. The resulting business decisions are recorded in present accounts.

Statistics also might well be brought into closer relation to accounting. The full utilization of the data so painstakingly collected and classified by accounting is not to be achieved until they are worked over into statistics by the methods already developed for handling masses of facts and for extracting the utmost of their significance. It is no longer sufficient to rest content with the comparison of this month's accounts with those of last month or the corresponding month last year. As individual enterprises increase their span of business life, the wealth of statistical data preserved in their accounts increases in proportion and as it increases, becomes more valuable as a guide to future action.

Suppose conditions do constantly change. They are constantly recurring also. Subjecting the data for a period of years to the methods of statistical analysis can show in what manner and in what degree conditions are recurring.

It will enrich accounting literature, too, if future writers will draw upon the experience of other countries. No doubt the busy practitioner has no time to read accounting publications in a foreign language, to say nothing of setting out to learn the language in order to be able to read more widely. But some writers there should be able to make available to us the writing that others are doing. Reviews of foreign publications in accounting would be the least that could be done; translation of worthwhile books would be of far greater value. Some of the world's clearest thinkers and most patient researchers do not write in English. Their contributions are a closed book to most of us. It was not simply the work done within the close confines of one nation that made the practice of medicine a learned profession. The literature of accounting must grow by accretion as well as by accumulation. It can draw upon other sources of experience besides the accounting publications of other countries. Law is an example: tax rulings, commission rulings, cases at common law.

The literature, if it is to grow properly, must in part result from research. Observation, meditation, and personal experience alone cannot produce a great technical literature. Through necessity, tax rulings are being carefully digested and are being given effect in practice. But there is a wealth of material in the court reports that is unutilized as it might be for accounting. We may often disagree with the findings, for the courts follow the precedents of the law as they see them and not the tenets of accounting. But accounting literature can show few parallels to the forceful logic and cogent reasoning of the better law cases. Yet the ultimate conclusions to be drawn from accounts derive their validity from the logic of the argument and of the presentation. The literature of accounting is losing something by not drawing more upon law.

Then again we unthinkingly neglect to acknowledge our debtedness to the law courts for classifying issues and concepts which are fundamental to business and accounting. One might venture the assertion, at least until it is refuted by further research, that the development of the principles of accounting has been more closely related to the reasoning accompanying judicial decisions than to any other single source. And it is conceivable that writers in accounting might find assistance and guidance by reverting to original sources. It would take laborious research perhaps, but by way of analogy, we may note that this single factor of laborious research has done more than all else to bring the biological and natural sciences to their present state of perfection. Research is not without its rewards.

The third direction in which accounting literature might profitably expand is in the production of close studies of special topics. If a book on depreciation is worth while, or on goodwill, or on consolidated statements, perhaps one on inventories would be also, or on surplus, or reserves. Perhaps there is not material enough for a book upon accounts receivable, but there ought to be. Again, there is a parallel in science. The microscope will reveal material enough for a book upon the anatomy of a tiny insect. Perhaps accounts receivable, if subjected to similar examination, would reveal unsuspected details in appreciable quantities.

If there is a new spirit at work in the production of accounting literature, it is the spirit of science. But even as such it is still responsive to the necessities of trade which have always prompted the writings about accounting in the past. The need of the moment is keen analysis, for business was never more complex in its interrelationships, and wise co-ordination for effective administrative control was never more difficult; indirectly the response to this need is the accounting literature which we see developing before us and which is far too inadequately outlined herein.

To meet the need in business for keen analysis and wise co-ordination, the spirit of science is at work directing the impulse to question, to search, and to analyze. With that spirit active in business, accounting could not fulfill its mission as the handmaiden of commerce without exhibiting the same symptoms and exerting itself to the utmost to be of some assistance in welding the whole of business into a science.

(AAUIA, *Proceedings,* IX, No. 2, December, 1925)

4. Approaches to Elementary Accounting

During the long evolution of accounting, teaching processes have undergone an evolution of their own. The early texts used what has come to be called a "journal approach." The student learned almost at once to journalize transactions. Usually the basis of his analysis was in simple rules of thumb, such as, "debit what is received; credit what is given." The teaching process therefore was a simple one. The student was in effect led in the footsteps of a bookkeeper and shown, by many illustrative transactions, the sequence of the latter's operations. Teaching was by precept and example.

Later, perhaps by the middle of the nineteenth century, attention was directed to ledger accounts as a preliminary to analyzing transactions into debits and credits. The groundwork of instruction consisted of explaining the purpose of the usual accounts together with their respective plus and minus characteristics. These were the pigeonholes into which the student was to sort the facts originating in transactions. With these matters well in mind the student was prepared to make journal entries and otherwise follow the established sequence of bookkeeping operations. This was a "ledger approach."

Still later, possibly in the second decade of the twentieth century, teachers and text-writers began to favor a "balance sheet approach." Herein the first explanations to the beginner were pushed still further forward, beginning with the purposes and end results rather than with the first operation of translating or classifying transaction data.

The usefulness of accounting results were outlined; and the relation of simple financial statements to management was explained. With this foundation established, transactions could be viewed as incidents which altered in varying degrees the prior status of the enterprise. On this basis also, ledger accounts could logically be considered before journal entries. They could be described as convenient technical devices for collecting the "changes" which transactions produced in the prior financial statements. Journalizing followed. It could be taught as a process of thinking transaction data into subsequent financial statements by formulating journal entries which were to be posted into ledger accounts, there to rest until statement time came again.

This approach to understanding bookkeeping methodology was pedagogically very different from the earlier ones. It was in fact a complete reversal of the sequence of presenting bookkeeping technique to the learner. It began with the end results and explained bookkeeping backward as it were. It brought up exercises in traditional methods only after a need for a carefully organized procedure had been developed in the student's mind.

Clearly teachers were thinking of "economy of learning," and hoping that bookkeeping would now impress the beginner as a necessary and rational procedure for teaching definite, useful goals rather than seeming to be a traditional clerical routine to be remembered "as is" by virtue of repeatedly writing up examples like the text illustrations.

(*Accounting Review,* March, 1931)

5. Value of the Balance Sheet Approach

Its principal value lies in the fact that here for the first time an effort is being made to teach the elements of accounting from the student's point of view. If the modern philosophy of education means anything, it is that teaching should be a method of securing a gradual mental development in the student rather than a method of guiding the young person's hand through new processes. The older methods of teaching bookkeeping do not reach far in that direction. They were very little different from the ordinary method of teaching the plumber's trade to an apprentice. It was as if someone were constantly saying to the student: This is the way it is done, do as I do.

The first point in favor of the balance sheet approach is that it follows the best doctrines of the art of teaching. It recognizes from the very first that we are dealing with beginners and that we are aiming at the beginner's mind rather than his hands. It sets up an ideal of teaching how to think rather than merely how to do.

No doubt there are those who will say that it were wiser to learn to do some of the things in bookkeeping first and then to proceed with some of the "whys." I cannot entirely agree, although it is clearly impossible to teach advanced accounting theory from the very beginning. Even though the immediate aim of the first course is to teach the student how "to keep books," he will learn to do the task quicker and do it better if he has been introduced to his first work in the subject in such a manner that he can understand a reason for all that he is called upon to do.

It is not difficult, if we begin properly, to get the student to see very early that accounting merely attempts to represent in figures the changes that are constantly taking place in an enterprise because of the transaction of business. Unless the first course in bookkeeping is long deferred the beginner knows very little when he enters the subject about what is involved in the transaction of business. It is, therefore, a large part of the task in the first course to teach him what is done in business. The balance sheet approach is a valuable aid in developing accounting in this manner because it deals with business first and with accounting as an adjunct. It teaches accounting for what it is—an instrumentality of management. It forestalls the impression that record-keeping may be an end in itself.

Students can be easily led to see that information about the business which is worth while to the management cannot be had unless the changes that occur are systematically recorded; nor is it difficult to show them that experience has developed certain systematic procedures in connection with recording business facts which may as well be followed.

When the time comes therefore for expanding the list of accounts and the mechanism for recording facts, the student is prepared for it by this approach. If he has not already felt the need for a more detailed classification of expense, it will not take ten sentences to expand the concepts of business he has already formed so the need will be quickly perceived. If in the beginning business has been shown as a whole, that whole can easily be expanded from the first simple unit without confusion or change in basic concepts.

This principle, now finding a place in accounting through the balance sheet approach, is not new. It is the principle that learning is easiest and most effective when we work from the whole to the parts rather than from the parts to the whole. That principle is applied in art: rough outlines are first; details are later filled in. The architect does not conceive of his building brick by brick, beam by beam. The dramatist conceives of a theme and builds in the parts by "wholes" first; he gets to the sentences his characters will speak only when his "approach" is nearly complete.

Here is a great, broad principle of learning. If one hopes to reach into the understanding he must build up aims, purposes, and needs in the mind of the student; if one is to develop the ability of the student to recall and apply what is learned, he must build upon the association of ideas, and the association of ideas works best when founded upon a whole expanded into its parts.

(AAUIA, Proceedings, VII, No. 1, April, 1923)

6. Limitations in the Balance Sheet Approach

While there is much to be said in favor of the balance sheet approach, we must not be unaware of its limitations for general and widespread adoption. We must realize throughout that the presentations are essentially theoretical; and that the foundations are laid in economic arguments which the student must be prepared to receive. To be sure there are many places where students in beginning accounting come to that subject with a good foundation in economics. But it is doubtful whether the balance sheet approach is as yet fully serviceable where it is the practice to introduce beginners to the subject before they have had a thorough course in economic principles. For the maturer minds there is no doubt at all about the appeal of this presentation, but to students, let us say of college freshman grade or below, the preliminary explanations will very likely be too philosophical.

There may also be a temptation, when using this approach as a foundation, to proceed too quickly into higher theory. For the best training in accountancy this is a mistake. Full and proper instruction in accounting cannot be divorced from practice with typical ledgers. Without some measure of the grinding routine such as makes up the bulk of record-keeping, there will be little concrete background which can later be built upon while gaining further experience. It will be much more difficult for the student later to develop a full realization of what accounting involves, if he has no classroom experience in bookkeeping routine, and it will be much harder for him later to visualize his field problems in their proper setting.

We should not be unmindful of the fact that not everyone seeking a course in accounting desires or needs a training in techniques. For those seeking a cultural sideline, as for example the graduate student in economics, it is not difficult to justify the omission of most, if not all, of the so-called practice work. Perhaps a good deal of this might also be omitted from the curriculum of students who are aiming at the purely administrative side of business. For managers, bankers, et al., need not be concerned particularly with the technique of accumulating the business data which come to them for interpretation. However, for all others, it is a mistake to slight the practice work.

We shall need to have the balance sheet approach worked over somewhat and brought into harmony with practice sets for the classroom before we can freely claim the widest adaptability for this method. When this development sequence (i.e., the balance sheet approach) is used in the classroom, it is or should be followed by a considerable period of seasoning in the routine of keeping records. I have great expectations for the increased recognition of the value to teachers and students of the balance sheet approach. But it ought not to be reserved for those maturer individuals who by work in economics or other subject are already prepared to make the most of its clear-cut logic. Its value as a teaching method ought to urge us as rapidly as may be to make it available to the humblest beginner. I have such confidence in its essential soundness that I believe it will be serviceable wherever bookkeeping is taught, provided only that it be made available in a form suited to the class of students concerned.

The limitations of the balance sheet approach, therefore, may be summed up in this statement: Its serviceability will be limited only by our ingenuity in adjusting the style and the rapidity of presentation to particular groups of students. The book which proves to be the most excellent text for the junior or senior in college does not necessarily prove effective with the freshman, or grades below the college. But on the whole the encouraging characteristics of the method considerably outweigh the discouraging characteristics. I have great hope for its future, and among them is the expectation that the time will come when the older sequence of topics will be out of date as the daybook is today.

(AAUIA, *Proceedings*, VII, No. 1, April, 1923)

7. Past, Present, Future

If we think of the little that history has to tell us about the development of accounting, it will be clear that we are now witnessing an important development in our subject.

Accounting has developed in four periods, the earliest being characterized by mere unorganized, detached memoranda used by individuals simply to aid their memory. Then followed a period of attempts at organized record-keeping. This period culminated in the publication in 1494 of the first bookkeeping text, wherein record-keeping is shown to have reached a fully organized stage.

There was then a third long period in which bookkeeping was merely an art laden with formulas and rules handed down from generation to generation with very little addition. Perhaps that was to be expected if we consider the state of commerce and industry during those centuries. For when we find the factory system fully established and competition severe, we find also the development of cost accounting and the expansion of accounting mechanisms to meet this new need. I have no doubt that we should have seen some similar development one hundred years earlier had the need been then present.

Outside of this development of cost accounting near the end of the third period, neither the recording of financial facts nor the teaching thereof shows any great progress until the fourth and present period begins. The first signs of growth were in the books by practitioners wherein professional experiences were reduced to problem form and the practices of accounting were described. We hope the literature will continue to be enriched by such contributions; but we need more than this alone. We need more because classroom experience shows that students must be trained to think and to talk and to reason as well as to gain a familiarity with the practices of modern usage. In response to this need, additions are now being made to the literature in which there is a strong leaning toward a philosophical explanation—a building up of principles upon a strictly logical basis. For this phase of the growth of accounting we are indebted mostly to university teachers whose training in economics has made them keen analysts.

The balance sheet approach is a large part of this. Its whole attitude is philosophical. It answers the need for a logical development of subject matter, a rational and sequential explanation of each new step, an interweaving of ideas—in a word a real method of thinking. Accountancy is therefore ready to be placed upon a par with science, mathematics, and law as an exercise useful for securing mental development and increased mental power.

There will be times, if indeed it is not upon us now, when accountancy may well be regarded as a valuable cultural subject. A man of true culture has a wide understanding of life, a deep appreciation of man's aspirations and accomplishments, and a mental vigor fostered by the power to concentrate and to draw inferences logically. Literature, history, and mathematics have long been the framework of the so-called cultural subjects. It may not seem too presumptuous to place modern accountancy beside mathematics in this category.

This is perhaps the most significant aspect of the balance sheet approach. If the beginning work in accountancy rests upon reason rather than rule, and if it proceeds by logical steps, we may expect to see a superstructure of advanced accountancy raised upon that foundation which will be a closely knit philosophy uniting with aspects of finance, economics, law and organization into a united discipline. And that is as it should be. When the structure is completed—and to the degree it is completed—there will be no need for veiled apologies to the old reliables by this newcomer to the curriculum for the cultural values offered by it.

(AAUIA, *Proceedings*, VII, No. 1, April, 1923)

8. A Cost Approach

Elementary instruction in bookkeeping from Paciolo's day to the present has been built on trading transactions. Modern recording requirements are becoming increasingly complex, yet the essential pattern of book-keeping instruction has changed but little. It does not take much familiarity with the recording procedures used in cost accounting to bring realization that its sequences are more logical than those associated with trade as such. Would it be easier for beginning students to grasp the thought processes of bookkeeping if *conversion* rather than *exchange,* manufacturing rather than merchandising, was adopted as the focus of elementary instruction? What would such an approach be like? Surely we should not attempt to teach cost accounting as such at this point.

The basic appeal of the idea of taking a fresh point of view is that it would make it possible to show beginners that the work of accounting is to make transaction records in such a manner as to trace the conversions taking place in the capital invested in an enterprise from its entry into the business until the items final disappearance in one form or another from that enterprise.

Factory management is much interested in classified transaction data about their company. We explain this first. There are the principal "pigeonholes" (accounts) into which by bookkeeping methods the facts about transactions are sorted and summarized. Explain why management wants this kind of classified information. Explain each account in this connection. Explain accounts showing acquisition of labor, materials, and factory expense services as being on the same basis, that is, as investments (assets) awaiting conversion into product. Explain liability and capital accounts as sources of capital, and asset accounts as kinds of capital. Do not attempt explanation of operating conversions until later.

The next step is explanation of the peculiarities of an account. Explain columnar separation of items that increase and those that decrease the class of facts indicated by the account title. Pass over the peculiarity that some accounts are increased on the left, others on the right. Memorize this feature for each account studied. Explain modern meaning of debit and credit as adjective (debit means left side), as verb (to debit means to place on left side of an account), as noun (a debit is an item that should be placed on left side, whether plus or minus, of an account).

Then follows analysis of transactions preparatory to entering into proper accounts. Simplest practice at this time is direct entry into the accounts affected. The mental operations are these: What accounts are affected? Which side of each account? How expressed in terms of debit and credit? The inevitable equality and oppositeness of the elements for each transaction will need stressing. Relate this to the fact some account debits are plus, others minus.

We are not to use a sales account. In its place use a process that is unorthodox yet one which should help make transaction analysis easier to understand. Data for each sales transaction should include the facts necessary to see its constituent parts: a debit to customer, credits to labor, material, expense services (for amounts converted into the product now sold), and credit proprietor's account for the excess as profit. The origin of the information supplied may be explained as shop records which are not now under consideration. This recording of a sale involves a transfer to a customer of a part of the several prior investments made for productive uses. The balances in the operating accounts are investment remainders awaiting similar transfers when they are later converted into product that is sold, or later determined to have been lost without producing a sale.

Discuss "general expense services" in contrast with "factory expense services." Illustrate the subdivision of the former into "selling expense" and "administrative expense." Show that these expenditures are "investments in services" in much the same way that productive labor is an investment. In making sales entries at this time show also a credit to selling and administrative expense as indicating a *recovery* of a part of these "investments" along with a recovery of the part of the investment in material, labor, and factory expense.

After an intensive drill in these matters, introduce a variation of the previous methods of entry. That is, sales entries now are to be made in two parts: (a) debit customer, and credit sales; (b) debit cost of sales, and credit labor, credit materials, and credit factory expense. As a method of finding profit *in total* practice closing costs of sales and sales directly to profit and loss account without journal entry. Include the profit and loss account and the old-fashioned *balance account* in the ledger. This is to be the basis later of the financial statements.

Up to this point the student has been introduced to a minimum of technicalities. The plan uses factory accounts because there is a natural relationship or flow of values between them. It is easy to get the student to understand the technique of inter-account transfers by using accounts like these which lead to natural summaries. This will pave the way for later teaching the technical method of closing. By using the profit and loss account and the balance account the way is prepared for a later introduction of financial statements.

By keeping books of original entry out of the picture the procedure is very much simplified for the beginner. Journalizing, closing, etc. are nothing more than economies in making records after we understand what we are trying to accomplish; they are not an aid in understanding the essential procedure of classifying debits and credits, or an aid in making the classifying debits and credits, or an aid in making the classified records reflect the actual conversions in a quasi-statistical manner. This understanding of account function should precede exercise in bookkeeping methodology.

At this time the finished goods account should be introduced. Consider the problem of what to transfer to the debit of this account in order to record the actual conversions of material, labor, and services into finished product. Should we credit a portion of selling administrative expense and the proprietor's withdrawals, and transfer these also to finished goods? This gives the opportunity to discuss the basic philosophy of cost of production as "the proper inventoriable figure," and the necessity for a separate treatment of nonfactory expense as well for profit withdrawals.

Selling and administrative expenses having been distinguished from production costs, the next step is to show the treatment of the former. By means of problems, practice closing the accounts through new summary accounts (i.e., a "manufacturing" account and a "distribution and management" account). This prepares the way for the later introduction of the manufacturing statement and the trading and profit and loss statement.

At this time abandon direct ledger entries and introduce the journal as a convenient record of the debits and credits resulting from transaction analyses. Use for the most part previous exercises so that there will be no new problems of analysis at this time, except, perhaps, the problems of framing journal entries in proper form and of posting them with care.

This study should be based on simple process-manufacturing requiring periodical transfers of values according to quantity. Amounts should be even; there must be no problem of unabsorbed balances. Inventories will readily be recognized as the balances of certain accounts.

I would confidently expect a distinct gain in "teachability" to appear from this approach, growing first out of its logical development, and second out of the thorough drilling in the thoughtful analysis of transactions, which is made necessary by withholding the journal for some time. The things sought in this approach are simple: (1) an understanding of the logic of bookkeeping reasoning; (2) an acquaintance with the peculiar way of recording financial facts; and (3) the peculiar way of reflecting changes in physical production by corresponding figure adjustments in the record (i.e., internal transfers between accounts, closing, etc.).

In these few, and to the experienced bookkeeper, simple things, lies the mystery of double-entry bookkeeping. Our main task as teachers is to get these things over to the beginner regardless of the way bookkeeping was first practiced in the Middle Ages, and regardless (in the first part of the course) of the sequence now followed by the commercial bookkeeper in actual business. The task in the beginning is not one of teaching *procedure*, but of teaching *a way of thinking* about business transactions.

(*Accounting Review*, March, 1931)

9. Direction of Improvement

It is reasonable to expect that the educational doctrines which yesterday made accountancy into a suitable university subject could tomorrow continue to justify accounting instruction at all university levels. Yet accounting teachers will always have to face doubts, questioning, criticism—their own and that of others. Education for business has traveled a long road full of this kind of hills and valleys on the way to recognition as a university field; no subject in the commerce curriculum had a harder time to gain full acceptance than accountancy. Early criticisms intimated that "clerical methodologies" could hardly be considered suitable for university classes. Here and there the conception will probably continue for a long time that accounting must necessarily be clerical bookkeeping spread thinly over a number of courses. Such is the momentum—or is it inertia—of early misconceptions.

In the meantime, and despite criticism, accounting has grown into an effective instrument for rendering almost indispensable service to men who are concerned with the techniques of good business management. At the same time accounting knowledge and experience have demonstrated the ability to furnish the materials for fashioning a new profession. These developments in turn tend to generate further doubts and questionings on the part of some people.

The idea is sometimes met that accounting instruction has now become narrowly technical, being directed from beginning courses to graduate years, toward CPA examinations and professional auditing. This condition is more apparent on the surface than real at the heart. The criticism is generated more by impressions derived from the language used by accounting writers and teachers than by the fact that the subject matter is actually highly specialized, which it is not. We must therefore learn to write understandably about the broader aspects of accountancy and to supplement our teaching of necessary technology with a constant linking of these matters with the larger objectives that may not be so clearly reflected in the details.

We know that change is not only needed but that it does take place. A great deal of progressive development has taken place between the time of questioning the fitness of "bookkeeping" as a university subject and the time of questioning whether accounting instruction was becoming narrowly technical. These developments of the past have a continuing significance for the future. Thirty-five years ago the courses in elementary accounting in most schools dealt with clerical bookkeeping—a multitude of purchase invoices, pseudo paper money, imitation bank checks, etc. That approach could not survive in a university atmosphere. The instincts of college teachers led them to favor problem textbooks to stimulate practice in thinking in place of practice sets to provide exercise in bookkeeping routines.

The above example illustrates the direction taken early in improving accounting instruction at the college level, and the basic reason for the change. Developments of the same trend, and for the same reasons, have been continuous to the present time. The direction and amount of improvement that has taken place will be reassuring to anyone who compares the teachability of today's texts with those of thirty years ago. It is doubtful that equally sound developments would have emerged if they had been pushed through at high speed. Just as a boy needs time to become a man, and a man needs time to build his career, so do improvements in accounting instruction need time to seed and grow in the midst of the daily round of teaching duties.

A great amount of change has taken place in elementary textbooks in accounting. To have stood still in this respect, we can now see, would have stifled educational progress. Elementary texts—and others as well—will always need improvement. Conditions change, new needs arise, teachers learn how to teach better. Yet the fundamental reasons for accounting instruction in colleges of commerce remain the same. In colleges not definitely oriented toward commerce and business, and an industrial society, there is less reason for including instruction in accountancy. Nevertheless some instruction in that subject is widely offered in smaller colleges having a liberal education intention. And accountancy is finding a place too in law schools. These developments indicate that many people do not consider accounting a pure technique without nontechnical (cultural) values.

Improvement in method is not entertained for the sake of change but with the hope that it will result in better prepared students. In many ways a college is like a factory producing for a market. Our product, like theirs, is not produced according to buyer specifications; like the factory, the college must judge the appropriateness of its processes very largely, not by what the processors themselves might like, but by the reaction of markets to their products. We have heretofore experienced a very favorable market reaction to our accounting graduates. As long as that continues to be the case, we may feel sure that our attempts to keep improving our processes are successful.

Accounting instruction everywhere has developed under conditions of an expanding demand for people with that kind of college training. This aspect of the matter has been out of educators' hands; there has been no forced draft in the universities to attempt to create a market demand. The product of accounting instruction has gradually sold itself, just as the potentialities for service lodged in accounting and accountants have gradually sold themselves in use to the public concerned.

We should view the fine reception accorded our product by the market in a spirit of humbleness; inflated pride of accomplishment would be uncalled for. But we need not blink the fact that college faculties through the years, having sensed this growing market demand, have continuously planned ways and means of converting its raw materials into product that could be rated in that market as having useful and desired qualities. It should be a continuous objective into the future to keep our fingers on the pulse of this market and our eyes open for increased teachability in our subject matter. A companion objective would be to stand calmly realistic in appraising possible innovations. It would be unrealistic to fear change and resist all change, or to push vigorously for far-reaching change, or for change hurriedly instituted. In this factory analogy the product and the processes would be under constant scrutiny and selective improvement; the market would react unfavorably to the results of any other procedure.

When a factory has accomplished some leadership in its product, the management is naturally concerned, when change is under consideration, to decide whether that position will be preserved, improved, or damaged. And let us note that this attitude will not be simply a reflection of the selfish view of a satisfied producer; it will in a large measure be the view of a producer who has a very real urge to contribute to the social good that can flow from better quality product supplied to his market.

It seems clear that accounting instruction at the college level need not be, as it may seem to some observers, an example of overspecialization or a reflection of narrow educational objectives. Actually the social aspect of accounting service, rather than being a purely vocational intention, has been and still is the ultimate factor determining the best type of accounting instruction. Teachers trained by diversified education rather than by overspecialization are able to perceive this truth in many settings. And it is not unreasonable to expect that they will be able to apply it with skill in class, in what they write, and in considering improvements in instructional programs.

(*Collegiate News*, May, 1951)

10. As to a Fifth Year

A fifth year at college is not based upon the philosophy that, if four years are a good thing, a little more of the same would be a little better. Indeed much of the value of postgraduate work lies in the fact that it distinctly is not "more of the same thing."

If we are to characterize graduate work in a few words, we should refer to two points: first, that it does a great deal to ripen the student's judgment, and second, that it broadens his views within his specialty far beyond the effect of anything he has had in his undergraduate years. This result is the consequence of two elements; selectivity and method.

Postgraduate students have gone through a long process of natural selection. Most students who begin university work do not survive to obtain a degree; some cannot afford the cost, some find that they do not like the rigorous intellectual work, and some are dropped by the authorities for poor scholarship. Of course not all continue who are best equipped to receive further education, but this is certain: those who do go on and who successfully complete a postgraduate program have been well equipped for the accomplishment by their previous training and intellectual energy. They must have been, for the new pace is swift and the requirements high. One may get a bachelor's degree with a so-called "gentleman's grade" of C, but it takes very few C grades in graduate work to put one out of the running.

The other element which does so much to explain graduate work is the difference in methods of both study and teaching. The student is older, or at least more mature whatever his years; often he has been out of college a while. Then again he is never on the football squad or the staff of the student daily paper. Although he may be teaching part time, he is giving a full head of steam to his courses.

There are also certain subtle differences in his environment which conspire to ripen and broaden him. The classes are smaller; there is a closer contact between student and professor and a freer exchange of views. The professor is not occupied with pushing the students to do a reasonable amount of work, but with directing their steps through the maze of material at hand. For when a man once begins to realize the vastness of the available stores of knowledge which could be of benefit to him, and when he begins to see the marvelous interplay between different fields of knowledge, he may easily dissipate his energies along interesting, but for his purpose unimportant, bypaths. Since he may drink too deeply at some one spring, he needs the influence of a steadying guide.

Such an environment is well calculated to set a man upon his own feet where he can stand, as in later life, unpropped by a textbook. And after he has weighed and evaluated the views of many authorities rather than depending upon a single one, he has indeed established a broad foundation for later good judgment and for independent thinking.

Some thoughts may be added regarding the study program itself. It is not necessary here to frame a full curriculum, but two aspects of a fifth year deserve consideration because, in undergraduate work they usually are not often called upon to develop the student's growth. I refer to a thought-stimulating study of theory and a substantial amount of exercise in finding ideas to write about and in writing about them clearly and effectively.

The theory work will be something more than the details of the anatomy of ledger accounts and financial statements; rather it should attempt to reach back to basic concepts and fundamental doctrines—to the underlying philosophy, if you please. There is much more to accounting theory than merely the distinction between capital and revenue expenditures, and the equality of debit and credit. The student should be brought to realize that the principles of good accounting rest upon sound logic and that they are not just dogmatic assertions about customary practices. And he should also be brought to realize at this time the closeness of the bond between accounting theory and other subjects, such as business finance and business law, etc.

The universities are not unmindful of the need for training their accounting students to express themselves. In addition to the usual courses in theme writing and business letters given to all commerce students, the requirements in the postgraduate division include a thesis—a long, serious piece of investigation and writing to which the student gives about one-fourth of his time. The training which this undertaking gives in collecting information in the master's year, in organizing it coherently, and in expressing the material in clear, forceful language is obviously invaluable to the man who looks forward to a lifetime spent in trying to make facts and ideas clear to other people through accounting reports.

The writing of a thesis affords some training in expressing ideas in words, but the accountant must also use another medium—figures. He needs training not only in expressing ideas in words but in arranging figures in statements and other tabulations so they may tell a story to whoever shall read. More than that, he will write better audit reports if he has had some training in verbalizing figures. Figures constitute the language of the accountant's art, but too often he seems unconscious of the fact that not all readers are as figure-minded as he. The student needs to be awakened to this fact and trained toward a high capacity for converting or translating figures into meaning which will carry over to another mind. The accountant must be able to press his mind back of ink marks into ideas and underlying conditions; and he must be able to take his reader along. So a part of the young accountant's training should include report writing, the technique of interpreting figures, as well as the experience of writing a fairly long thesis.

With these three elements thoroughly covered, a part of this first postgraduate year should be devoted to a choice of collateral subjects, among which there may be advanced courses in corporation finance, investment analysis, economic statistics, management problems and policies, and the like. Usually it is recommended that some nonaccounting subject be included in the program because of the better perspective it will give of business administration in general. Even here in the graduate year we are not unmindful of the danger of treading a narrow path in gaining an education; high specialization will come naturally enough in due time in practice. Yet it will be observed that the further the student goes, the more attention, proportionately, he should give to his specialty.

Universities seldom consider themselves polytechnical institutions—trade schools to train one to a dollars-and-cents livelihood for tomorrow. Their focus is rather ten and twenty years hence; they aim at laying foundations. The individual must erect the structure himself—carve out his own career. Within their means the universities do their work well, but attendance therein and a degree gained constitute no guarantee. After all, the university is just what the accountant's office is: *opportunity*.

(*Certified Public Accountant*, December, 1927)

11. Aiming Beyond the Examination

A difficult problem underlies postgraduate offerings in accountancy. The major problem is how to provide advanced education in accounting that will be well suited to the needs of students with diverse undergraduate preparation; students with an intention toward professional accounting and others with industrial accounting objectives; students who know early and those who decide late that they will aim at a career of teaching accounting.

Perhaps experience so far has not produced a formulated answer to these difficulties. Tentative answers can be sought in each case of program-building with an individual. It should be a tailor-made program, as closely fitted to his intentions and prior preparation as possible. For example, rules about minimum work for a degree do not afford a good guide if prior preparation in the subject matter is itself at a minimum. The student's self-interest should make that fact plain to him; for presumably he seeks a certain advance in knowledge, not merely a year in residence. If he does not want to add suitably to his prior preparation (in order to benefit the more by the courses he will take), he should be content to take courses without being a candidate for a degree.

We cannot of course hope to bring all candidates for an advanced degree up to the same level of content and accomplishment. But we should feel a duty to those who make a good preparation for the degree awarded, to see that others should not get that degree on the basis of markedly inferior program content. Although some undergraduate courses may carry graduate credit, not many such should be accepted as part of the advanced preparation. While it is possible to waive the writing of a master's thesis, those cases should be few and rest on more reason than the student's wish to take courses instead. Most students do not realize the educational values of research and writing. This is especially true for accounting students since they have had fewer term papers to prepare than most students in liberal arts programs. Yet accountants have more need to be understandably articulate than students realize.

To the student fresh from a course in solving CPA problems, the graduate work may seem loaded with theory. This is true, and by intention. Graduate work should be aimed beyond the CPA examination. Yet candidates may expect to benefit indirectly by any deepening of their understanding of their subject. The student who has benefited well from some thirty undergraduate hours in accountancy can soon make himself ready to take the CPA examination. His graduate work should be forward-looking, not CPA cramming. A good way to study beyond the CPA is to dig deeply into theory. When properly viewed, accounting theory does not deserve the scorn some practitioners seem to give it. For theory is largely a consideration of the explanations, justifications, objectives, aims, why's and why-not's of actions and ideas that are customary in practice or are proposed as desirable conventions.

Study of theory does not make men impractical theorists in their field contacts with a client's accounts. On the contrary, it makes them alert and quick to question what they see; it gives them an added ability to grow with experience as the food. It adds another story to their educational structure; an upper story that is supported by the structure beneath, consisting as it does of an acquaintance with a wide variety of situations in which accounting is of service, and of extensive classroom practice in analyzing complex data into information problem solutions.

The man who has had good training in problem-solving and marshaling of facts as an undergraduate, and good training as part of his graduate work in reasoning from actions back to objectives (then appraising both the suitability of the actions and the desirability of the objectives) will be doubly prepared for a career in accountancy.

(*Collegiate News*, May, 1951)

12. Broader Teacher-Training

A clear need exists for accounting matters to receive thoughtful, disinterested, critical analyses of the kind that is natural for a Ph.D. candidate's research. The subject matter is full of questions warranting deliberative consideration; accountancy teachers and their students can benefit from this sort of preparation and from the course work which accompanies it.

Full-time concentration on accounting subject matter during graduate work should not be permitted. Substantial minor work in allied fields should always be required, perhaps even in the master's year. Since the teaching of accounting is more than the teaching of a particular technology, overspecialization for the Ph.D. degree is inadvisable. Very appropriate collateral subjects are available in economics, management, etc.

However, a strong dilution of the advanced study of accounting obtained by advising or requiring extensive contacts with other fields would be detrimental rather than beneficial to this program of teacher-training. Extensive contacts are not as necessary as it might seem; the reason is that it is or should be a natural and customary feature in many of advanced courses continually to show accounting in contact with economics, finance, management, government, law, etc. Teachers in accounting will have had work in these collateral fields, and it is to be expected that they will illuminate accounting from that experience. The nature and service of accounting is such that, even in elementary courses, it can introduce students to many collateral aspects of business. Accounting nature and service is the same at the graduate level; the graduate teacher therefore

is able to do and must do some co-ordinating and contrasting of accounting ideas with ideas from neighboring fields.

A comprehensive accounting examination could well be part of the
preliminary examination for a Ph.D. degree in accountancy. Here the
examining committee of the faculty would feel free to ask questions,
written and oral, of the candidate about any area or aspect of accounting.
In this approach the CPA type of data-marshaling problem probably
should be passed over since, presumably, the candidate has already had
a rigorous course in CPA problems.

Where it has been tried, the comprehensive examination in accountancy
has been considered more satisfactory than separate examinations in the
subject matter of separate graduate accounting courses and has not placed
on the candidate undue burdens of special preparations or nervous strain.
The practice is worthy of wider use in spite of possible future difficulties.
A comprehensive examination may some time become difficult to construct
within reasonable limits. Perhaps an increasing number of students will
wish to follow a Ph.D. program even though their master's work was
entered upon late in their college career. As a result, their preparation
may not be comparable to that received by students, with whom they
will be in competition, who have studied the subject longer and at higher
levels for a master's degree. Some candidates therefore may need more
than the minimum calendar time to prepare themselves as well as their
contemporaries will be. Some of that preparation may be through undergraduate courses taken without credit towards a graduate degree; some
by taking extra graduate courses; some perhaps by self-preparation, visiting classes, etc.

It probably has been said off the campus that bookkeeping cannot be
successfully spread so thin as to reach up to a Ph.D. degree. The neglected
fact is that accountancy is much more than bookkeeping. It is even more
than a new and growing profession, with all that word connotes. Accountancy is also an intellectual discipline; it is a language that expresses
economic action; its data are of growing significance to people charged
with large responsibilities. These are some reasons for being sure that accountancy is a fit subject for Ph.D. study.

(Collegiate News, May, 1951)

13. Effects of Graduate Work

In deciding to give graduate work in accountancy the chief problem may
well be that of deciding whether (1) to grant graduate credit for completing existing advanced undergraduate courses to people having a bachelor's
degree; (2) to provide further courses for exercise in solving CPA problems and CPA questions on theory, auditing, and law; or (3) to arrange
new courses the prerequisite for which would be adequate undergraduate

preparation in the usual accounting subject matter for an accounting major in a college of commerce.

If the latter choice is selected it probably would be for the reason that the time had come in that school to undertake to broaden and deepen the student's understanding rather than offer him more drill in putting together answers to CPA questions.

In making such a choice we are not without precedents. Postgraduate work in medicine is based upon prior study of medicine; postgraduate work in pure science only follows upon undergraduate work in science. The beneficial results of sequential education in these fields are constantly before us. It is plausible to believe that graduate work in accountancy should also be truly sequential in order to make the largest possible contributions to the advanced students' career.

If the courses in accounting beyond the bachelor's degree are not aimed toward the CPA examination, what will they be like? A student may believe they could only be more of the same, but harder problems. Such belief assumes that the measure of advanced work is always its greater difficulty. The fact is, however, that the real essence of a graduate course is in its difference, not its difficulty, although it must be added that the graduate school is no place for the mediocre student or the one who is satisfied to get along by the easiest road.

What then is graduate work like? What will it do for the typical student?

It will release him from extra-curricular activities and thereby liberate an immense amount of energy for application to scholastic activities. It will ripen and mature the individual's judgment beyond anything he has had as an undergraduate. Everything conspires to this end; he has but few class meetings to attend, and classes are smaller, freer exchange of views, closer contact with mature teachers, general discussions rather than text assignment and recitation—all of these characteristics of the usual graduate class tend to set a man on his own feet where he must stand unpropped by a textbook. Graduate work will broaden a man within his specialty. The views of one author are seldom accepted without question. Rather it is expected that many authorities will be canvassed and that differing views will be weighed and evaluated. That is distinctly broadening. A case can be cited in which a graduate student in accounting read 3,500 pages in a one-semester graduate course. That was of course unusual —and not at all prescribed—but it indicates that the way is opened for individual work.

What is graduate work in accounting expected to do for one?

In the first place, graduate work may be expected to increase the power of clear thinking by aiding the student to see his subject as a whole. For example, the study of advanced accounting theory need not be merely a matter of examining in detail the anatomy of ledger accounts and the arrangement of figures in financial statements, but rather it should be an attempt to reach back to basic concepts and fundamental doctrines. The class is brought in contact with the best literature of accounting, and is led in discussions down into the underlying philosophy and basic logic of the subject. The theme of the course is that the principles of good accounting rest upon sound reasons and are not mere dogmatic assertions about customary practices. In searching out the ultimate reasons for the most acceptable practices, the student is encouraged to look for help into commercial law, accounting history, and advanced economics, as well as into a wide range of standard accounting works.

A thorough study of "systems" may supplement the study of theory in helping the student to see his subject in the large. A valuable part of this phase of the work would lie in the comparative study of a large number of uniform systems as to origin, method of preparation, date of adoption by the trade organization, methods used in getting members to adopt, purpose served by a uniform system, etc. Here also special attention is given to specific types of business which have system peculiarities, such as professional, charitable, religious, service, extractive, financial, as well as trading and manufacturing.

In the second place, graduate work in accounting may be expected to give the student an added facility in expression. He is helped very greatly in this respect by the work he does upon a thesis. Approximately one-fourth of the student's time in his first year of graduate study should be devoted to the production of a serious piece of writing. The training which this undertaking gives in collecting information, in organizing it coherently, and in expressing the material in clear, forceful language is obviously invaluable to the man who, either in practice or in teaching, must look forward to a lifetime of trying to make facts and ideas clear to other people.

A course in accounting reports would direct the student's attention further toward the art of expression, but in a slightly different direction. He is given a training in verbalizing and interpreting figures. The accountant above all men needs capacity in this direction. Figures constitute the language of his art but not everyone can convert figures and tables into meaning which carries over to another mind. Therefore the accountant must not only have a high capacity for dealing with figure representations of things and ideas, but he must be able to see ideas and underlying conditions beneath the figures and to help his reader to do likewise.

Graduate work in accounting, then, will increase one's power of clear thinking and expand one's ability to express himself. And, if the choice of courses be well advised, it will also give the student a better perspective for business administration in general. It is possible, even advisable, to give part of the time to such collateral, nonaccounting work as corporation finance, economic statistics, factory management, and the like. Because the connection between accounting and business is so close, each program should include something of this sort along with accounting.

Anyone who has developed a love for accounting by his study contact with it—a mere interest is not enough—and has demonstrated an ability to maintain reasonable high scholastic standards, can profitably follow the subject beyond the bachelor's degree. If he does follow it up, he will very likely say in the end, as many have said before him, that one year of graduate study has been worth several years of undergraduate study. He may not stop to analyze the reasons this seems true. But it would not be difficult to realize that the effect was in part due to the benefit from a firm foundation of prior undergraduate study of accountancy, plus the greater freedom to reach down into deeper aspects of the subject on the student's own initiative.

(pamphlet, Conference on Graduate Work, Urbana,
Illinois, May, 1927)

14. Thesis Research

The accounting student who has a thesis to prepare should give some thought to what research is as well as to the selection of a suitable topic. It may be of interest therefore to note some of the characteristics of research and to indicate some areas out of many in which research topics might be found.

Research is thinking. Thinking involves persistent consideration of evidence and a careful choosing of the relevant and excluding of the irrelevant. It calls upon powers of distinguishing difference and observing similarities. The material must be recognized as suitable or unsuitable for the purpose. The training secured in doing a piece of research is a training in exercising judgement and discrimination. Any exercise of this kind is beneficial.

Judging the relevance of material is related to the matter of finding the implications of a problem, of tearing it down and finding in it the issues that may be crying out, so to speak, for settlement and consideration. In studying the usefulness of a problem as a research project we have to search for a pattern. It is better to see the pattern early in order to be able to reject unnecessary ideas. The pattern should not be preconceived and rigid, since it must be changed as the research develops. Architects do not try to get a complete pattern at the start. An architect enjoys marking up white paper in order to find the right pattern. He makes many experimental patterns and then changes them after critical inspection until he is fully satisfied.

Research is also hunting—hunting for a problem that calls for examination and hunting for material about that problem. Students who have to prepare a thesis must seek a problem; we cannot wait for an inspiration. How can we put ourselves in the presence of problems? How can we put ourselves in the way of relevant ideas after we have found a problem or an area of research? The answer is reading—especially reading current technical literature.

We cannot afford to overlook textbooks or any other part of the literature on our subject, although textbooks are not prepared for the purpose of presenting experimental or controversial subjects. We must try to find all the ideas that are related to the problem chosen. A valuable faculty to develop is to learn to compress a discussion. In the process of hunting for ideas, compressing or generalizing is a valuable aid.

Dissecting is another valuable aid. This develops critical faculties. We question the author's presentation; we try to sense unanswered problems, problems which he has not attacked but with which we may attempt to deal. We try to define the terms he has used, or restate his essential ideas in our words, and then define the terms we have used. We ask ourselves about his generalization or about our own: "What would be the consequences of this particular idea?" Let us assume that it is perfectly true, what then? Is the idea relevant to our problem? What is the origin of the idea? Perhaps conditions have changed or ideas have changed, and the terminology has not changed.

Practice in the association of ideas helps us to make new combinations. New combinations will present a new pattern. In research today, after so many people have been searching for so long, it is difficult to be startlingly original. But give your mind a chance to receive many ideas. Some of them may associate themselves together, and when they do, they may present a different pattern. Then find out how new it is and what might be involved.

Ask questions while reading. How adequate is this? How complete is it? How does one practice or principle tie in with another? It is surprising how many theses have evolved from an idea so short that it could be expressed in the words of a single sentence.

Accounting history invites research. The history of the accounting profession has not been written, and the methods by which gradual improvements have been made in accounting practices and financial statements have not been analyzed. Education has not been studied, nor has the development of educational methods and the gradual change that is taking place in textbooks designed for various levels of instruction. The history of professional legislation has not been compiled. What kind of legislation has succeeded, and what kind has failed?

The history of auditing technology could be studied; it has undoubtedly undergone an evolution. The same can be said for the history of cost accounting and the history of administrative use of accounting and the history of the ideas of accounting theory.

What part of law touches corporations and accounting? Is the law sound? Is it too restrictive? Is it not restrictive enough? Is it hampering to business? Is it failing to make use of accounting principles?

Is there a fundamental difference between the ideas of courts and accountants with regard to accounting? Are there new developments in the field? If so, why are they taking place? In what direction is the trend of development? Where does accounting end and finance begin? What use is accounting in regard to interpretation, in regard to policies? We can see that accounting has some responsibility in regard to all these problems. Why?

What is the relationship of accounting to corporation financial practice, income tax practice, corporation dividend law, and corporation managerial practice? Does accounting fail to meet the needs in each of these areas? Wherein does each area fail to comply with present ideas of good accounting?

(Accounting Forum, March, 1939)

15. Educational Objectives

Some people like to indicate educational objectives by pointing to certain intentions: that of polishing a young mind into keenness, that of developing competent judgment, that of stimulating a power to discriminate between degrees of importance. Yet it must be granted that unadorned keenness, whether natural or created, may become merely a faculty devoted to criticism; or it may indicate a mind particularly receptive to "keen" ideas, whether imported or domestic. Many employers, out of their experience with college graduates, would readily trade the best of keen edges for modest amounts of interested co-operation and effort.

Competent judgment at age twenty-two can at best be no more than a seedling planted in college days; it develops into something more than personal opinion only over the years. Much the same can be said about recognizing degrees of importance. That power grows from whatever it feeds upon. It grows slowly; it moves from one food to another; it must be able to serve a currently useful purpose by learning from a current intake of problems requiring choices. One cannot say, except within the framework of his own opinion, that study of political history better than study of managerial economics, will build power to see degrees of importance among ideas.

It is not clear in what respect more mental discipline is found in study of college algebra than in study of elementary accounting. Personal observation suggests that about as many students fail in one as in the other. This would seem to be a significant fact even though no one would think that this fact also proved equivalence of disciplinary value in the two subjects.

If a student is likely to derive generally similar educational benefits from any line of study that is successfully carried through under effective teachers, then it needs to be said that the principal gain from one choice over another flows from relative suitability for a chosen objective. This suitability is likely to consist for the most part in establishing contact with a special vocabulary and in the use of problems oriented somewhat to the particular objective. These are basic materials for any education; the results can be a "well-rounded education" from their use in any reasonable setting; yet this phrase has generally been attached to education that is not considered vocational. The thought will not down that a very high percentage of enrollees in most colleges of liberal arts are preparing for one or for alternative lines of later work; their intention therefore is as much vocational as that found in colleges of commerce.

The idea that a liberal education, by being well rounded is particularly suited to preparing future leaders, may express a splendid ideal. But may it not, in application, have the unfortunate effect of helping many students drift into a belief that by mere attendance they are acquiring a mission of leadership? Ability to lead and a sense of mission are very different qualities. The American experience with leaders has been such as to lead us to believe that seldom can we see that they have been clearly prepared for such service by their education.

There is a distinction between spending college years in "learning to live" and in "learning to make a living." We can be sure that a great many Americans deeply believe in the over-all benefits, for the one person and for the nation, which stem from having learned to pull on our own oar. This is but a reflection of the same ideology as that which prompts the vast majority of students to study with some line of work in mind. Leadership is probably more effectively prepared for by work experience than by study; the first is direct experience, the second can only be vicarious experience.

CPA statutes and administrative regulations in many states are now setting up educational requirements higher than graduation from high school. To some observers, the type of regulation that specifies prior credit in commerce courses, including accounting, may seem to exclude graduates of liberal arts colleges from employment and advancement in public accounting.

It must be clear, however, that even a required college degree would not be "a college degree in accountancy." And a thirty-hour specification of subject matter does not amount to a high degree of specialization in accountancy. People with an arts degree can, and many do, find various ways of getting supplementary college credits in that much business education. If those opportunities should prove to be unavailable to a large number of people, it would be entirely justifiable for a movement to be started in support of establishing "preliminary examinations" in statutory subject matter above the high school level. The absence of such a movement at this time may be significant.

It is certain that neither committees in the profession nor those in the state legislatures have sought to exclude people who chose to attend a liberal arts college or who decided after graduation to enter upon a career in accounting. However, one who shifts his objectives may reasonably expect to face some handicaps as a result. The important point is that for accountancy the handicap can usually be overcome, granted a reasonable amount of perseverance.

The motive back of this movement for increased educational requirements for CPA's is not exclusion but protection—protection for the public, not for the practitioner.

A stiff examination associated with stated educational qualifications sometimes generates a belief that insiders do not wish to see the group expand. Such a thought may only mean that the individual holding it has been unwilling to prepare properly for entering the profession. "Preparing to enter the profession" does not express the same idea as "admission to the examinations." The first idea is the basis of the rules for the second.

Men now in the accounting profession are more sensitive than other people to the ever-present need to see that steps are taken to protect the public against unqualified practitioners. It is easy to misconstrue their examination requirements. Yet the fact is that these rules derive from a strong sense of social responsibility. One may well add that this protection motive is supplemented by a growing conviction among professional accountants, as employers and supervisors, that special knowledge, not just mental keenness, is the basic element of technical competence.

(*Illinois Certified Public Accountant*, December, 1951)

16. Technical or Liberal Education

General education, sometimes called liberal education, and technical education with accounting and business as the technology, are not mutually exclusive or in the least antagonistic. Some individuals, from choice, may get too much of one, too little of the other. They are the losers in some ways and so is society. Some educators strongly favor segregating general education into the first two years of college and then require this program for admission to a choice among an assortment of "professional" specialities in the two years of the "upper division." Others favor carrying the separation to the extent of four years, with all professional or vocational education postponed into the post-bachelor years.

It would seem that an assumption is at work here: that liberal education and vocational education are incompatible, that mixing the two will confuse the students. Yet mixed programs have proved entirely satisfactory to the consumers—students and their subsequent employers. There is no evidence that an undue proportion of the students of mixed programs are weak in self-reliance or in accomplishment in their line of work. They appear to be as good citizens as any. It can be said that they reflect the results of a well-rounded education, even though the individuals are graduates of colleges of commerce or business administration, where a mixture of general and technical education is standard practice.

A typical program of a graduate of a member school in the American Association of Collegiate Schools of Business is usually an example of excellent economy in allocating subject matter over four years of study. Usually the student is between the ages of eighteen to twenty-two; approximately 50 per cent of his study time is given to materials that can very appropriately be called general education and 50 per cent to business and closely allied subjects—bread and butter subjects.

A CPA examination requirement of thirty semester hours in accounting and business subjects is actually good advice for prospective professional accountants, even though stated in the form of statutory law. And getting a college degree including some accounting is also good advice even though written into a statute. Obviously, in neither case is there an implication that college courses will of themselves be preparation enough to assure passing the examination, or to make a man a professional.

One of the justifications sometimes advanced in support of liberal education is its asserted tendency to develop in the student a sense of social responsibility. Here, as often is the case in broad generalizations compressed into a phrase, the reader is left to make his own interpretations.

The idea of social responsibility is most useful when it is made to carry the thought that individuals should strive to be less than naturally selfish, and given to more friendly consideration of human relationship than is usual among men. In this connotation, it is appropriate to ask which educational approach will be likely most strongly to produce a suitable sense of social responsibility: (1) liberal education at age eighteen to twenty-two, supplemented later by vocational and technical, education and experience; or (2) liberal education which, coming later (after thirty-five?), can supplement after school age the prior technical preparation for earning a living?

The "mixed" education typical of the programs in our colleges of business administration is not unrelated to this thought. Its "noncommerce" subject matter provides not so much a completed liberal education as a foundation upon which the student can build a liberal education. Is a four-year program of liberal education a complete education? In actual use the techniques of business administration, including accounting, have made very substantial contributions to America as we know it. Those who question education's usefulness for continuing this kind of economic and social development, and who believe that our national progress has taken place under a low sense of social responsibility, might well be asked, (1) to indicate comparable total beneficial achievements made outside of the business world and activated primarily by a high sense of social responsibility, and (2) to indicate the type of education and practical experience secured by those who seem most dissatisfied with the prospect of an America that will continue to develop within its established framework.

For the people who, for various reasons, get only a moderately early contact with liberal education, the door is no more closed for an extension than it is for those who wish to add technical education in their later years. Education of any kind and for anyone can easily be continued beyond the school age.

It may be true that a man's psychological frame of reference is pretty well established before age thirty-five. But it by no means follows that his ideas are beyond change, and they surely can be augmented. If various aspects of liberal education can confer substantial benefits when contact is made after a person is established in his work, ways and means might be sought to make this approach feasible. Classes in adult education are already widely available and special reading lists can be secured for differing needs. Self-directed study, if firmly applied, can accomplish a great deal more than most people would guess.

The most difficult time in the study of any subject is likely to occur during the first few months. The strange is always more troublesome than the familiar. Therefore it would seem that a college curriculum which gives the student a start in both the liberal and technical fields is most likely to help him launch the program of self-governed study which he must undertake if he is to be successful. This is true both in his necessary preparation for a professional goal such as the CPA and for his further education as a discriminating citizen and a participant in the cultural life of the community.

(Illinois Certified Public Accountant, December, 1951)

17. Culture in Accountancy

Would a substantial amount of accountancy in a nontechnical student's program make any contribution to his cultural education? This may seem like asking whether mathematics is a useful part of the education of someone who knows that he does not wish to become an actuary, an engineer, or an astronomer, and therefore is unlikely to use mathematics vocationally.

Not every person who is studying accountancy in a college of commerce intends to become a professional public accountant. One graduate in civil engineering became a successful advertising man; an accounting major would not be any more handicapped by his studies than this man was, if he decided after graduation to do something equally different. He could succeed as well as the engineer did, if he too had learned how to learn.

The student of business administration studies accountancy as a means of putting his mind into contact with concrete, measurable events that are typical of business activities. Seeing the concrete, measurable facts in an engineering problem is the beginning of an engineering solution. So it is in business. Accounting is quantitative and factual even when approximations must be made and estimates used. Weather predictions are estimates, revised and revised; but they have incalculable value in aviation even though they are only estimates. In spite of including some estimates, accounting data are invaluable aids in operating a business, in making investment judgments, in establishing governmental policies. A significant part of education in accountancy consists in learning to distinguish dependable estimates from arbitrary figures.

It may be popular in some quarters to believe that the businessman is typically a grasping, selfish individual, prospering at the expense of other people or not at all; and that the public accountant typically acts as his Man Friday, subservient to every wish, a willing collaborator in the promulgation of fuzzy financial statements designed to conceal rather than reveal.

It would be easy to know better. If the ready believers of the worst were to learn something real about accountancy ideals and standards, or if they were to experience the responsibilities of trying to sell goods to fussy customers in order to meet pay rolls for fidgety workers, they could see the truth more clearly about business and accountancy.

Business is a national task force with two missions: to devise ways for people to earn a living, and to develop products for people to use in living. Accounting is the navigator's chart to the task force. A specially trained man is needed to write up the log and keep the chart fully informative; but the person who issues orders must also know navigation in order to use the information wisely.

So much modern legislation affects the opportunities for people to earn their living, and so greatly influences the products available for their use in living, that the makers of statutes and the administrators of laws have a clear obligation to know something real about business as the chief instrument of living. And they have a similar obligation to know something substantial about the chief instrument of business operation— accounting.

There are other reasons for thinking there is a need for a cultural, nonvocational understanding of business and accountancy.

The student ready for college, but undecided as to the career he wishes to prepare to follow, often chooses under advice to study a variety of general topics while he makes up his mind. The subjects chosen usually are broadening; frequently they are stimulating; sometimes they are disciplinary; but they do not point in any particular direction. Can they be as educational in effect as if they had a specific focus? In what way would it be a waste of time to choose to study with a directional focus while deliberating on the choice of a career? The study of accountancy and collateral subjects during such an interval would offer a broadening, stimulating, disciplinary experience. It has much promise, for example, as an approach to the professional study of law.

Studying economics and business and accountancy in a college of commerce can be of real cultural value—cultural in the sense of contributing in a collateral and secondary way to the main theme of many educational programs. Would the time be wasted if, while undecided, a person studied accounting who, let us say, later became a social welfare worker when he found his real vocation? One priest who graduated in architecture before finding his real vocation made a splendid use of his "wasted" education when he became a bishop.

(editorial, *Accounting Review*, July, 1944)

18. Toward a Broad Course

Everyone is enthusiastic for his own specialty; and he tends to see in it broad reaches of usefulness that seem to give it universality. Thus an accountant can see that everyone has need of some knowledge of accountancy. But, he would be the first to add, not a knowledge of accounting as a technology.

If accounting is to be presented educationally other than as the technology that it is, how is this to be done? Can accounting be stripped of its techniques and still leave an adequate basis for understanding its functions and achievements? It is like asking whether the only avenue to understanding music and painting is that of learning the technique of bow and brush.

Professional accountants often see evidence of the need in various groups of laymen for an understanding of accounting; and teachers often wish they could teach it to lawyers, engineers, economists, and statisticians. But there are difficulties. Students, teachers, and practitioners in all professions know of many special areas in their own special fields that they have no time to cultivate, to say nothing of browsing through a "foreign" subject. They know or suspect that accounting is usually taught as a specialty, that instruction is focused toward business or professional accounting. Undoubtedly these "laymen" would not be interested until accounting instruction was stripped of its "know-how" approach; until the focus had been changed from bookkeeping, auditing, and CPA problems.

Can accounting be presented in the same framework to technicians and laymen? If that is to be done, extensive changes will need to be made in elementary courses so they can be terminal for some and introductory for others. Perhaps a model can be found in the typical first course in the principles of economics. On the other hand, a broad course in economic principles may itself be considered by some economists as more terminal in effect than introductory.

If the same framework of accounting instruction will not suffice for all types of students, separate courses with sharply different subject matter are indicated. In that case remodeling the usual elementary course will not be enough; compressing the procedures of several existing courses probably would still leave the emphasis on procedure. What will be needed is a fresh point of view: a new appraisal of the objectives of instruction; a clear awareness of the layman's center of interest and of the accounting matters likely to be confusing to him which therefore need explanation.

If the techniques of bookkeeping, cost accounting, auditing, and CPA problems are ruled out of the course, the principal aspects of accounting which remain are financial statements and accounting theory. Here is enough subject matter to satisfy almost any plan. But there are some questions. Can statements be presented without considering the procedures that lead up to financial statement construction? Can theory be understandably presented without being focused upon bookkeeping journal entries that express transactions technically, or upon the "good accounting practices" that form the technical basis for the auditor's judgment of items in the financial statement?

What can be said about making financial statements the central theme of such a course? And for drawing upon theory wherever it would contribute without confusion to the broad understanding of accounting that is the objective of the course?

It would seem that a study of the financial statements of a variety of different kinds of enterprises need not be technical, and could contribute a good deal to an understanding of business. Some of the reasons why this approach might be desirable are that it would tend to stress the differences among enterprises, and that it would open the way for constantly referring to the way accounting performs useful services for different people. If there is no grasp of the nature and function of business, and of business enterprises, there can be no effective understanding of accounting. And if there are groups of laymen who could benefit from a concise understanding of accounting, they could also benefit from a deeper understanding of business. Possibly the most important contribution such a course could make would be from using the study of accounting as an avenue to understanding business.

It might be a workable plan to organize the course in two parts. The first would be designed to give an understanding of what accounting means to each kind of enterprise in turn. The second would deal with the limitations of financial statements in general. In a sense this plan would show what a financial statement (and hence accounting) is and is not. If the important features of these two aspects of accounting can be made clear and convincing in this way, the course would serve a very useful purpose indeed.

There are many ways of arranging a discussion of the financial statements of each type of enterprise. But for each one, with varying emphasis as needed, it would seem useful to include the following topics somewhere: the meaning of the principal items in the statements, probably beginning with the income statement and explaining the balance sheet as a "capital statement"; the effect on statement items of the principal transactions typical of that enterprise, especially the effect on four categories—revenues, expenses, assets, liabilities; the nature of the enterprise in question, its social service, the need management has for information, the interest nonmanagement people have in the enterprise through its accounts (lenders, investors, workers, customers, government); examples of decisions that a knowledge of this enterprise's accounts can help to make-—decisions of many different people on many different matters; significance of the relationship of various important statement items and of quantitative changes in these relations—this without getting the student deeply involved in the technique of financial statement analysis.

The major instructional problem in using such an outline would be that of restraint. So much could be said about each topic for each enterprise that the objectives of the course could be met only by the most careful selection of points to be made. It would help to accomplish this selective restraint if the thought were kept continuously in mind that the student's grasp of the meaning of accounting will be cumulative. It would serve no useful purpose to try to deal comprehensively with any single enterprise, or with any single phase of accounting.

(editorial, *Accounting Review*, October, 1946)

19. Toward a Professional Course

Most college courses are compromises because it is frequently necessary to use them for more than one purpose. Courses in auditing are no exception. Yet, because the subject matter is professional, it might be of interest to speculate on the characteristics of an auditing course (and its immediate antecedent courses) if it were made as professional as possible.

The course might be designed in a manner to give students some training for their initial employment in auditing. Would it then aim at presenting internal auditing first and external auditing later? In separate semesters? Or is training for one also training for the other? Will the work of the course, under this objective, give a good deal of emphasis to the preparation of typical working papers? Are working papers standardized enough to be dependable guides to practice when they are generalized for student use? Are accounting theory and audit policy sufficiently uniform in enough particulars that the student will not have to unlearn a good deal when he joins the staff of a given firm?

Perhaps learning is more than preparing to remember. If that is the case, and if the student knows that it is, then classroom working papers need not be standard to be educationally useful; and neither theory nor policy needs to be uniformly applied in the field to be helpful to the student in class. Probably it should be one of the teacher's duties to convince his students that working papers are not standardized and theory is not uniform. For this would help the student to realize that concrete materials (working papers and data) and specific ideas of good accounting (theory and policy) were but vehicles for learning to think as an auditor thinks.

It would be a mistake to exclude concrete materials from the course. But it would be a greater mistake to focus instruction upon remembering forms and procedures.

The course might be given an objective aiming beyond the details of verifications and schedules. It might point the student, for much of his study time, toward a staff man's supervision responsibilities. Then it would be necessary to use materials and teaching methods suitable for training a person for certain particular things: to judge what evidence was satisfactory for showing reliability of documents, of ledger accounts, of accounting systems; to recognize for what they are, good, bad, and intermediate degrees of accounting treatment; to organize a field staff on a given engagement and keep the work moving; to detect the questions that need to be taken up with client or principal; to write audit reports.

Can such training be given in the classroom? In the same semester as working papers? With existing instructional materials? Or must every individual learn the techniques of supervision, if he can, by observation in the field alone? If anything is "learnable," is it not likewise "teachable?" If it is teachable, is there not economy and benefit from teaching under classroom methods?

Perhaps the plan of the course might be to teach fundamental principles in school, leaving a knowledge of applications to be gained in the field under the influence of the policies and methods of a particular firm.

Is the operation of every firm so different from that of every other one that classroom instruction in trying to be concrete will defeat its own purpose? Are the diversities of application so many and so far apart that applications cannot be usefully associated with fundamental principles in the classroom? Can methods and procedures be reduced to principles and taught as such? Can nothing be learned in the classroom of the art of fitting methods suitably to varying circumstances? Are there enough fundamental principles of auditing to constitute a course? Without including applications?

If the term "fundamental principles" is loosely defined, it may include any amount of material descriptive of methods, procedures, forms, and habits. Descriptions have a very useful place in education; but descriptions cannot help very much in developing analytical capacity or discriminating judgment. If the term is closely defined, even including auditing standards along with auditing principles, they may be so few in number that the student's task is soon finished (when applications are dealt with elsewhere).

How long would it take in class to study auditing standards? How much time for professional independence? For standards of technical competence, of objectivity in field examination, of acceptability of internal control, of due care in selecting procedures and materiality of the issues raised of full disclosure? If divorced from descriptive applications, or if given before application (procedure and methods) had been studied, the material would neither take very long nor do the student much good. Yet, skillfully integrated with other materials, standards are indispensable to the student, for they are some of the theory essence of auditing.

Much the same could be said of the fundamental principles of auditing. They can be compactly stated; they could be understandingly studied in a relatively short time; they are indispensable to the student.

All that is auditing could be brought under the application of the "principle of critical review." Expanded a little, this phrase could become a descriptive statement, such as, "auditing provides techniques for reviewing accounting methods and data." More completely phrased this statement would be as follows:

"Auditing helps to give assurance that reported accounting data will be dependable, by providing organized reviewing techniques for the use of technically trained individuals, who will critically examine the suitability and effectiveness of the details of accounting structures and who will critically judge the appropriateness of the actions taken in carrying on accounting processes."

Three more "fundamental principles": (a) "The statistical credibility of the data presented in the accounts and statements is in question until they have been tested by auditing." (b) "The external auditor seeks to substantiate the representations management makes in the accounts and statements by finding various kinds of corroborative evidence." (c) "Financial statements serve the needs for enterprise information of such a wide variety of people that a duty rests upon those responsible for statement preparation to see that a full, clear disclosure of material facts is made."

Would it take very long to analyze, illustrate, and discuss these and other principles of auditing? A semester? Without dealing with "application," except as illustrations?

Finally, what type of accounting course should precede and follow auditing (when the sole object is to present a sequence of professional courses)?

Would the prior courses give special emphasis to systems and theory? Systems, because knowledge of the anatomy of business enterprises is indispensable to the conduct of an audit? Theory, because a knowledge of good and evil, accounting-wise, is indispensable to the exercise of an auditor's critical judgment? Or could systems and theory be studied as needed in close association with procedure? In one semester? If two semesters, where to divide the courses?

Would the professional courses that follow the basic study of auditing be at the postgraduate level? Consisting of more verification procedure, systems, theory? Mixed together as in the antecedent courses? Audit peculiarities of various lines of business? Plus adaptive audit program building? Would the advanced work include corporation finance and investment analysis? Practice in writing audit reports and research reports?

Are the materials available for a series of courses in professional auditing that would be comparable in quantity and objectives to law school courses in, say, court procedures? If not now available, can the necessary material be found in needed diversity and of good quality? Are the procedures of established firms too individualistic and too confidential for publication as instructional material? Perhaps the question should not be stated in that way, since every textbook in auditing is an answer in the negative. But is there enough pooling of professional knowledge of techniques, of ways and means, so that an extensive, detailed, comprehensive professional literature may rise as fast as possible?

Every strengthening of professional competence is in the public interest; and whatever is in the public interest—accounting-wise—is in the interest of the profession.

(editorial, Accounting Review, October, 1946)

20. Economic Literacy

C. Hartley Grattan was writing of bringing about full employment after the war when he said ". . . the wise citizen will not shackle himself to either party to the argument nor bind himself to either private or government enterprise [in this connection]. He will try as best he can to tip the balance now on one side, now on the other, in accordance with his understanding of how the general welfare can be served." (*Harper's Magazine,* February, 1944.)

The author might easily have broadened the thought: A part of all good citizenship is a willingness to tip the scales in a direction that will serve the general welfare. Because this is a duty of good citizenship, it becomes the duty of education to give the individual some preparation for shifting his weight with common sense and good reason. Economic illiteracy is today one of the greatest handicaps to an intelligent attempt at "tipping of the scales." And to reduce this citizen handicap is one of the great privileges of educators, for accounting teachers as well as others.

If economics is thought of as an empty philosophy now outmoded by strong-arm governments, its real vitality is underestimated and its fundamental connection with human conduct is misunderstood. If in some quarters economics seems to be discredited, the fundamental reason probably is that its devotees have either claimed too little or promised too much. If it is linked with statistical method and promoted as a science—with the power of a science to predict—it is bound to lose face when the predictions are not fulfilled. If its legitimate claims of being able to help people understand people are submerged because the subject is presented as an abstract philosophy with a technical jargon of its own and its own way of spinning syllogisms into conclusions, then it undoubtedly deserves a good deal of neglect.

But most teachers of economics see the subject in a long perspective; they are not likely to believe that the passing show changes human nature. Nor are they likely to think of themselves as scientists—social or otherwise. Few of them are interested in prediction, or in making administrative decisions. For the most part they are teachers at heart, content to help others learn to take the complications of modern industrial life into conscious consideration—or at least try to do so.

Economic literacy derived from the teaching of economists of this caliber can be an important part of the educational preparation for a career in business or in accountancy. The student who is an accounting major is preparing both for citizenship and for rendering a technical service. His study of accountancy moves through a progressive pattern from the simple to the complex; thus he grows in technical ability. He could grow in citizenship ability from a similar presentation of economics in a progressive pattern from the simple to the complex.

Is there enough economics in the program of the typical accounting major? Is it good preparation for rendering the best kind of public service to emphasize instruction in accounting technology so much as to limit severely the desirable general education?

Let us suppose a case. It is perhaps not entirely realistic, for it could not now be achieved in many schools, if any. Yet for that very reason, it may point toward ideas that are wholly realistic.

Assume that an accounting major does not have time to secure a thorough grounding in science, literature, government, history, philosophy, and mathematics, along with an ample professional study of business and accounting. He has the idea of getting his general education principally from economics. What would his "cultural education" be like under this combination of circumstances? Could he expect to lay a foundation for intelligent citizenship in this unusual program? Would general education of this sort contribute anything to his professional career?

Clearly these are hypothetical questions, and no doubt they deserve only speculative consideration. But there is a principle involved.

In preparing the materials used below, the course offerings in undergraduate economics were listed from the catalogs of six midwestern universities. As a second step, the courses were classified by title under four heads: Human Relations, Historical Perspective, Training for Citizenship, International Affairs. It is assumed that a student who is well-grounded in these topics may be said to have obtained a pretty fair cultural education even though it may have constituted no more than about one-fifth of his program.

The next step was to select a few courses (approximately twenty-four semester hours of credit) which, from the titles, could reasonably be expected to give the student some orientation in the four aspects of education named above. These courses were as follows:

1. Development of Modern Economic Society
2. General Economic Theory
3. Public Finance
4. Current Economic Problems
5. Comparative Economic Systems
6. World Economic Policies

Preferably the first and second items would be year courses and might be taken in the first or second year of college. The others would be single-semester courses, probably taken in the third and fourth years.

The best historical perspective might be an economic one, since so many of the problems of today and tomorrow will be economic at base. A single course, named "Development of Modern Economic Society," may seem too limited to express the vast accumulation of data about economic history. Yet this limitation could easily prove an advantage in a basic course wherein perspective rather than erudition is the aim. In fact, it would be desirable for the course to include some of the history of economic doctrines, if the materials were thoughtfully selected and skillfully blended.

To be sure, a first course in the principles of economics would not cover all aspects of human relations. But economic life is a very important aspect of human affairs and one in which educated people need orientation. Furthermore, other courses in economics—perhaps we could say all economics courses—deal with human relations and thus would help make a man's education partly a study of man.

The third and fourth items aim clearly at citizenship. Taxation and government debt have always been of great concern to the citizen; that concern is now deeper than ever. Current economic problems should probably deal with other topics rather than taxation and finance, since these would usually be separately analyzed. This problem course would no doubt include something of the relationship of business and government if that topic were not available as a separate course. There are of course many other matters which prospective citizens need to know about. Yet few items are more important than those which could be brought compactly into these courses.

If "citizenship training" be broadened a little, it will need to include something about international affairs. Americans are traditionally nationally minded. But there is reason for believing that this country's destiny pushes us in the direction of a more expansive understanding— not in the sense of imperialism but within the meaning of world stability. Courses 5 and 6 are included for this reason.

The catalogs of the six universities offered many other interesting courses in economics. Some of these might be as useful, for this special purpose, in the program of an accounting major as the ones listed above. In order that the reader may be able to make substitutions and additions, another list of courses is given.

Human Relations
Theories of Price and Competition
Problems of Labor and Unionism

Historical Perspective
Evolution of Industry
Economic Development of the United States

Training for Citizenship
Economic Theory and Social Policy
Relations of Business and Government

International Affairs
Economic Relations of the United States
Latin-American Economic Problems

Other courses than these are available; no attempt is made to be exhaustive. For example, no courses are listed here which might be called business economics; these would include the topics of statistics, corporation finance, banking, transportation, insurance, etc. Obviously such topics have social as well as business connotation. And accounting majors would often take work of this kind in the department of economics since the material is closely allied to courses in business administration. Indeed, courses in business economics and business administration might be united to form another group of twenty-four semester hours, matching in size the suggested twenty-four hours of social economics.

If 24 hours of accountancy were also set in a group, and if another allotment of 24 hours were made to "tool subjects" such as English composition, business law, and the like, and if a similar block of 24 hours were given to a survey or two (the sciences, Western civilization, etc.) there would still remain an unassigned 10 semester hours of the usual minimum of 130 hours required for graduation. This remainder, plus any courses taken above 130 hours and plus any time diverted from the other groups by substitutions, would be available for increasing the work in accountancy or other subjects as choice might dictate in organizing the complete outline.

The assignment of courses in groups of twenty-four semester hours may seem mechanical and arbitrary. It is, and no argument is here made in support of that particular allotment of time. However, it is a convenient way of setting forth the major subdivisions of an accounting program and therefore contributes indirectly to the principal thought, namely, that general education, as part of the program of an accounting major, need not necessarily consist of the traditional, scattered assortment of courses in literature, language, science, mathematics, history, political science, psychology, philosophy, etc.

Such a program, while broadening the student's perspective in history, humanity, citizenship, and world affairs, would also give him a general education in certain areas of knowledge that are closely related to his field of specialization. As a result, much of his cultural education would also make a definite contribution to his technical education. Yet the program would not be called one given over to a narrowing overspecialization.

(editorial, *Accounting Review*, July, 1944)

21. Separate or Mixed Programs

Every educational program gives expression in its pattern to some educational theory. Many programs, by differentiating educational levels, seem to reflect a theory that education for living and education for working are better presented if undertaken separately. Preparation for the practice of medicine, for example, often uses four years in general college, then four years in medical school; preparation for law, four years in general college, then three years in law school; preparation for business sometimes occupies four years in general college, followed by two years in business school.

In cases like these there usually is little continuity of subject matter across school boundaries. There is perhaps some continuity where a premedical, pre-legal, or pre-business program has been followed. But even there the prior preparation is not in medicine, but in science; not in law, but in government; not in business, but in liberal arts. And science in the first case, government in the second case, and the liberal arts in the third case are usually presented as part of an education for living. The theory of educational separateness, therefore, is effectively applied even here.

Is there a justifiable basis for the theory? If the answer is in the affirmative for medicine and law, which are acknowledged professions, is it necessarily also in the affirmative for business, which is not considered a profession? Is there any reason for thinking that mixing the study of general subjects (especially science) along with medicine for eight years would produce inferior physicians, surgeons, and scientists; or for thinking that mixing the study of general subjects (especially government) along with law for seven years would produce inferior lawyers, legislators, and judges?

Most colleges of commerce follow a different educational theory from that of the professional schools. Among schools in which preparation for a career in business or accounting is stressed, all but a few express a theory different from the "stratification" that is implicit in the programs of medical and legal education.

The theory apparently underlying the typical program in business or accounting reflects a belief that education for living and education for working can be successfully integrated throughout the four years leading to a bachelor's degree, or the five years to a master's degree. This expresses the idea that working is a part of living and living involves working. It carries within it the thought that learning a technique for earning a living can itself be cultural, and that the study of well-selected cultural subjects can make a distinct contribution to the ability to earn a living.

Not all of those who would be able to benefit can spend the time or save the money to enable them to spread their advanced preparation over six, seven, or eight years beyond high school. If a longer program is out of the question, a four-year program could be made a very acceptable substitute; and a two-year alternative could be made very useful to many.

A four-year program could be constructed in two ways: to provide two years of general education (for living) and two years of technical education (for working); or to interweave education for living and working throughout four years. In the one case, the idea of separate levels of educational purpose which characterizes the professional schools would be copied on a smaller scale in a four-year college of commerce. In the other case, the idea of separation would be abandoned as not entirely appropriate to the circumstances.

If the serviceability of a two-year program is accepted, a further choice will have to be made. Shall the short program be one of education for working, based on technical courses that are usually found in the senior college; or one of education for living, based on cultural courses usually found in the general college; or, as a third choice, should the program be one of education for both living and working, based on a mixing of both types of courses throughout the limited time of two years?

No single answer can satisfy all the conditions likely to be met. Some students will have to seek maximum assistance toward learning to earn, even though in so doing they completely sacrifice education toward citizenship. For such students facilities are available and perhaps should be increased. The hope will be that in these cases some education for living and for citizenship may be secured later, perhaps in the form of adult education or even self-education. (May it not be that the years of maturity are actually the best time for study in this direction?)

But for other persons a choice may still be necessary between a short cultural program and a short mixed program. Which is likely to be the most useful?

Most of those who now go through a two-year program are students who began a four-year program but did not finish it. There is a very large population turnover in the early years of college. But it is a mistake to assume that all who do not continue for graduation are intellectually incapable of doing so if circumstances permitted. Shall it be said of those who might find the going hard in the upper division that they are failures, culls, incompetents? For the most part they are undeserving of such designation. It may be that the pace is too swift; some persons come to maturity more slowly than others; constructive imagination may be good but limited; powers of perception and memory may be workable but only moderately strong. In competition with others these students may be outdistanced. Yet they have capabilities worth developing.

Since segregation is not desirable, the first question will be: Can an educational program be prepared that will at once lay a foundation for further study toward a college degree, and provide useful terminal education for possibly one-half of those who enroll? Is a program of general education or a mixed program better suited to this double purpose?

(editorial, *Accounting Review,* July, 1944)

22. Two Programs

The two entirely hypothetical programs for accountant education indicated below offer a contrast worth discussing.

The first program illustrates a general education that might precede business education:

First Semester	*Second Semester*
English Composition	English Composition
College Algebra	Analytic Geometry
Foreign Language	Foreign Language
Physical Science	Biological Science
History of Civilization	History of Civilization

Third Semester	*Fourth Semester*
English Literature	English Literature
Foreign Language	Foreign Language
History of the United States	History of the United States
Introduction to Psychology	Introduction to Philosophy
American Government	Principles of Sociology

This hypothetical program has no obvious connection with a business education to follow. It could precede any one of a number of lines of later study. For the person who has not made a choice, it may be very suitable. A period of orientation of abilities and exploration of interests and aptitudes may be desirable for some young people. It may be questioned, however, whether such an interval and such a program is advisable for everyone.

The second hypothetical program illustrates a mixing of general education with business and accounting.

First Semester	*Second Semester*
Economic Institutions	Economic Statistics
Elementary Accounting	Financial Accounting
Business Mathematics	Marketing Methods
English Composition	English Composition
Historical Geography	History of Science

Third Semester	*Fourth Semester*
Economic Principles	Economic Principles
Factory Accounting	Typical Accounting Systems
Production Management	Business Finance
Public Speaking	Business Writing
History of Constitutional Government	History of Moral Principles

The second program is clearly vocational. Can the suggestion be defended that it is also cultural?

Learning to distinguish good reasoning from bad is not the product of any special subject matter. It can be gained from courses in economics as in this program. The power of interpreting evidence does not arise only from practice upon some particular kind of problem. It can be obtained from courses in statistics and in accountancy, among others. Accountancy is likewise a rigorous discipline, as is mathematics; and it is devoted to seeking out the truth, as is science.

Practice in writing business letters and in organizing a financial statement can be made vehicles for exercising logical processes of thought. The study of the history of science would afford many examples of the usefulness of cultivating the power of keen observation and a nonpartisan view in important matters, and thus contribute notably to the ability to earn a living.

The study of geography, of constitutional government, and of moral principles would undoubtedly be considered cultural and aimed at citizenship. But these studies are also utilitarian in connection with preparation for a career in business: the transaction of business is worldwide; business operates within a framework of government; moral principles lie at the foundation of business success. Preparation for business can be a better preparation if such elements of education for living are studied also as elements of education for working.

The cultural aim of education is to develop the person's capabilities—his ability to make choices and to compare values; his capacity for insight, understanding, discrimination; his willingness to differentiate good and bad. In fostering these aims, particular vocational subjects can be cultural as well as vocational.

In a country and in an era wherein business and industry are the major preoccupation of the people, it will be useful to know about business and industry as a part of citizenship even though one's career may turn in another direction. In a democracy wherein the major decisions are more likely than not to be concerned with economic life, an informed citizenship can hardly be said to exist if the citizens are illiterate in economics.

Having boldly adopted for my own use various phrases from another's writings, it is only fair that I quote the author verbatim.

What we should seek to impart in our colleges is not so much learning itself as the spirit of learning. You can impart that to young men; and you can impart it to them in the (two or) three or four years at your disposal. It consists of the power to distinguish good reasoning from bad, in the power to digest and interpret evidence, in a habit of catholic observation and a preference for the non-partisan point of view, in an addiction to clear and logical processes of thought and yet an instinctive desire to interpret rather than to stick to the letter of the reasoning, in a taste for knowledge and a deep respect for the integrity of the human mind. Woodrow Wilson in *Representative Phi Beta Kappa Orations*, 1915.

We cannot do in two years all that could be done in four, or compress seven into four. But in the available time, whatever it may be, it might be the part of wisdom to provide the best possible "mixture" of education because of the possibility that many students, not at first ascertainable as specific individuals, may be unable to pass through the full sequence of educational layers.

(editorial, *Accounting Review,* July, 1944)

23. Commerce and Accountancy

There are three principal ingredients in the preparation for entering a profession: general education, special education, and the education of practical experience. At various times and in different professions these ingredients have been tried in different combinations, always with the consciousness that every type of preparation is educational but with changing convictions regarding the best proportions and the most desirable sequences. In time the emphasis has shifted from apprenticeship under a practitioner to systematic study under a professor. Only in the profession of public accountancy is practical experience still emphasized over formal education as the basis for admission to the professional examination.

For forty years a high school education and three to five years of accounting experience have been the educational qualifications usually specified. And this has continued down to the present in spite of the facts that probably half of the recent candidates have had some college education and that present-day college courses in CPA problems can give a broader training of analytical powers than a short experience as a junior accountant can hope to do.

It can hardly be claimed that the enforced practice prerequisites succeed in improving the preparation of applicants. A similar percentage of candidates, on the average, pass the same test in those states which require no experience, as pass in states requiring three to five years to practice for admission to the examination. The practice requirement therefore must be a retained vestige of the past which was originally designed (1) to insure maturity and at least some experience on the part of those who were admitted to this type of public service, and (2) to offer the public this assurance that recognized practitioners had met this test as well as that of a technical examination.

If the practice requirement is, as it seems, mainly a carry-over from a period when the absence of generally available means of higher education made some such practical substitute advisable for the protection of the public against inadequately trained men, and if now there is generally available and widely used an adequate educational machinery, then perhaps the time has come to rest admission to this professional examination, as in others, upon educational standards rather than simply upon a specified period of prior contact with practice.

In place of a high school diploma and a specified period of experience, the statutory requirement might be two years of general college work and three years in a school of professional accountancy, the latter in lieu of all or part of the practice requirement.

Both of these proposals have their advocates. But no one has thought to make out a case for the existing colleges of commerce. It would be quite logical in a profession so closely related to business, to require a college degree in commerce with accountancy as a major subject for admission to the examination—due reductions being made in the practice requirements, perhaps even to the extent of dropping them entirely for those with a master's degree in accountancy.

An excellent foundation already exists for this sort of requirement in the forty-seven universities now included in the Association of Collegiate Schools of Business. At least one of these schools has been giving instruction for nearly half a century, several for at least a generation; many have included accounting as a major subject for the bachelor's degree for more than a decade, and not a few can give the student a full, five-year sequence of accounting instruction, supported and strengthened by co-ordinate work in economics, statistics, finance, and business.

In the transition from training in a craft to education for a profession there seem to be certain stages in evolution. Medicine and law have made the full transition. Engineering is approaching the stage where conditions are pressing for a separate professional school resting upon a pre-engineering education that includes mathematics, science and laboratory. But accountancy is still far from experiencing the same formative pressures. Some day, when the teaching materials at hand are vastly increased in comparison with the present and when accounting technique has grown more complicated and professional responsibilities and independence have been materially broadened, then perhaps separate accounting schools may usefully become the standard. But even then the preliminary education should contain a substantial number of commerce subjects (50 per cent?) since accounting must always rest upon economics and business as medicine and engineering rest upon science.

Until that expansion has taken place, the advancement of the profession would seem to require that the methods of educational training already available as preparation for the profession should not be neglected —that is, the work for a major in accountancy in a university college of commerce. There professional accounting is taught, or can be taught, in conjunction with indispensable collateral courses in general accounting, business administration, statistical methodology, corporation law, business finance, investment analysis. An extended education in financial statement preparation and audit procedure outside the circle of such related collateral studies may perhaps produce well-trained junior assistants and semiseniors, but it is doubtful whether this would lay the best educational foundation for developing the leadership which the profession of the future must have to bring accountancy into its full destiny.

While an occasional separate accountancy school is being formed to meet the needs of men desiring to supplement the work of a general college degree with a concentrated study of accountancy alone, it would be beneficial to the profession if constructive criticism and tangible support were given to the professional accounting work being given in the university colleges of commerce. With that in mind the following proposals are advanced as methods by which the profession can exert a steady pressure for improved educational preparation.

1. That practitioners, while giving due consideration to scholastic records in individual cases, make a consistent and concerted trial of the graduates (bachelors and masters in accounting) of the university colleges of commerce where adequate instruction is also given in closely related subjects.

2. That state societies follow the example of the New York Society in securing the amendment of their CPA law to make a college education in business a prerequisite for admission to the professional examination.

3. That state societies secure amendments to permit the separation of the examination into two parts; the first to cover accounting theory, commercial law, and business finance, and to be open to anyone with a bachelor's degree in an accounting major from a university college of commerce (without practical accounting experience); the second to consist of professional auditing and practical problems, to be open only to those

who have passed the prior examination and who have had two years of satisfactory practical experience in a public accountant's office (postgraduate work in accountancy to count as one year of this experience).

4. That a joint committee be formed from nominations by the American Institute of Accountants, the American Society of Certified Public Accountants, and the American Association of University Instructors in Accounting (American Accounting Association) with the following objectives:

    (a) To design a system of standards by which to judge the merits of the educational opportunities currently offered by colleges and universities for a career of professional accountancy.

    (b) To make a rating, based on these standards, of any school asking for that service.

    (c) To consult with individual schools upon their request, and to co-operate with the association of Collegiate Schools of Business in connection with questions related to improvements in professional education.

This method of furnishing a guide to educational institutions and an incentive toward specific improvement is not without precedent. The work of the American Bar Association and the American Medical Association in inspiring improved educational facilities is well known. The methods of building a set of standards have been worked out by universities and rating associations in connection with the interchange of credits for transfer students and could be easily adapted to the present proposal. Among other elements the rating base would, no doubt, give due weight to the education and practical experience of the teachers offering work beyond the elementary courses, to the number and types of advanced courses offered in accounting and closely allied collateral subjects, and to the success of the school's graduates in the prior five years.

Wherever the examination statutes had raised the educational requirements, state CPA boards would undoubtedly find the service of impartial ratings of considerable value to them when making up their lists of schools whose degrees would admit to the examinations.

(Accounting Review, June, 1936)

24. Schools of Law and Medicine

In urging separate and specialized schools for professional accounting with a general education prerequisite, one is tempted to reason by analogy from the example of the law school and medical school. Law and medicine, the argument runs, are professions, and the subject matter of these professions is now taught in separate professional schools with a general education prerequisite of two or more years. Accountancy is also a profession; therefore its subject matter should likewise be taught in separate professional schools following a general education. But reasoning by analogy is often fallacious when the cases are not strictly analogous. If accountancy is not directly comparable with law or medicine in certain important particulars, it will be difficult to conclude that their type of educational organization would be equally suitable for accountancy.

It may be worth while therefore to inquire why medicine and law are now taught separately from general education. Slowly formal education replaced apprenticeship. The medical student no longer "walks the wards" with a physician for his technical introduction to his career. The law student no longer "reads law," when he can find the time, in some attorney's office while serving as a clerk, thus preparing to become an attorney-at-law.

Since the best preparation for a written examination was study under men skilled in teaching and since such men congregated in educational institutions, there the prospective lawyer and prospective doctor went to learn.

The apprentice system was gradually replaced by study in educational institutions. But this fact does not explain why this relocation of educational responsibility developed separate professional schools with general educational prerequisites. Conceivably, legal and medical studies could have been pursued concurrently with general subjects. And few would dispute that students of law of today would benefit from the concurrent study of history, political science, economics, and even accountancy and finance, or that the study of medicine should go hand in hand with the study of science. Yet the mixture of general and professional education is not a part of education for medicine or law. There must have been reasons for this decision; and if the same reasons appear in connection with accountancy, they would equally well support the proposition to place accountancy instruction on the same basis as law. But if the same reasons do not exist in accountancy, the analogy to law and medicine would not hold.

The reason that law is given in a separate school is not so much because the school is professional in purpose, but rather because the enormous growth in the quantity and complexity of legal materials and problems has left no alternative. Lawyers and law teachers are not unaware of the advantages of co-ordinated education, but they also realize that an adequate foundation in the law's great complexities and in the method of attack upon its multitude of problems can only follow from an extended concentration upon its own material. In fact, they could make a strong case for extending even beyond three years the specialized study of technical law. Under these conditions it would be unwise to dilute the study of law with concurrent general studies, or to prescribe a long period of preliminary education. A practical balance must be made between the most comprehensive general and technical education, and the necessity for men to enter active practice early enough to survive those beneficial first years of struggle. Law school work probably is highly specialized by necessity rather than choice.

The reason for the separate college of medicine is similar. It needs no demonstration to convince us that the subject matter and problems of medicine, like those of law, have increased very greatly in quantity and complexity. This has been inevitable in view of the rapid strides made in pure science during the last generation or two. Separate medical schools are the result.

For the same reason the medical schools prescribe a preliminary education in the basic sciences of biology, chemistry, and physics. Since much of the medical student's later work is laboratory science, a preliminary knowledge of science and scientific methods is regarded as indispensable to good work in advanced classes. In a word, there is a high degree of continuity and necessary sequence in pre-medical courses and the later courses in the professional school.

The same cannot be said however regarding the relation of pre-law work to law courses. Recommendations for pre-law general education include history, political science, and possibly economics, as constituting excellent preparation for later life as an attorney. Pre-law studies are not, like pre-medical courses, a preliminary training which is necessary in order that the student may benefit by the studies to follow.

The next question is whether accountancy is sufficiently analogous to medicine and law that the same type of separate educational programs would be equally logical for the newer profession. It seems that the answer at this time must be in the negative.

The apprentice system has outlived its usefulness in medicine and law because of the development of organized teaching materials and experienced teachers. For the same reasons it is no longer necessary in accountancy to look exclusively to practical experience plus private reading for professional education. This condition therefore may be regarded as a sign that the time has come to change the basis of admission to the CPA examination from a practice requirement to an educational requirement.

But it does not necessarily follow that the time has also come to look upon separate professional accounting schools as the standard. The pressure of a vast growth in the quantity and complexity of materials has forced medicine and law into schools of specialization under teachers who are also specialists. But there is no comparable pressure in accountancy of accumulated special subject matter or of the subdivision of specialities.

Consider, for example, the quantity of accounting literature available for teaching purposes in comparison with the vast literature of either law or medicine. An analysis of the American publications on accounting listed in Bentley's *Bibliography* reveals only a meager professional literature.

From 1919 to 1934 about one-third of the classified titles referred to cost accounting (94 items), and two-thirds to general accounting (171 items). For the past thirty years there were, in addition to the above, thirty-five pages of titles about specialized costs, fifty-two pages for uniform systems for industry, and twenty-five pages of references to uniform systems for public utilities and railroads. In these rapidly moving times much of this must be quite out of date. In the eighteen years 1917-34 inclusive, there were published seven books on corporation accounting, thirteen on accounting problems, fifteen on special accounting topics, forty-three on general principles and practices, and five which might be called miscellaneous—a total of eighty-two volumes, many of them now over ten years old. Even if twenty-seven pamphlets of less than one hundred and twenty-five pages which might include material on higher accounting are added, the list is far from impressive.

This showing can hardly be said to indicate a rapid and extensive accumulation of complex knowledge. There is in this bibliography no material which must necessarily be presented in a separate professional school of accountancy; any of it could be presented in the accounting departments of the colleges of commerce. And few will claim that accounting technique is such as to require a separate professional school to teach it. Indeed one experienced public accountant has said in a meeting of the American Institute, "Accountancy has thus far accumulated little technique. . . ." (*Journal of Accountancy,* November, 1935.)

If there is no large body of technical literature needing the interpretation of specialists, and if there is no extensive or complicated technique in accounting to be laboriously translated into skills, then it must be clear that the same forces which produced separate law schools and medical colleges are not at present pressing accountancy in the same direction.

It is generally assumed that medical colleges and law schools accept any general educational program for admission to the specialized professional work. This is essentially true for law schools where it is considered unnecessary to exercise much control over the choice of subjects offered for admission. If an accountancy school were to follow the law school precedent, any scheme of general college education would be acceptable for admission. There is probably a place for a few schools of that kind to meet the needs of men who make their choice of a career late in their educational program. The same reasoning is the justification for graduate schools of business which admit students on the basis of any prior degree of general education. In neither case however is the implication acceptable that such an arrangement is the only or the best training for a profession.

On the other hand, the medical schools prescribe so much science for admission that pre-medical curricula hardly constitute a "general education." A man who wants the best medical training is almost under the necessity of choosing his career upon entering college. If we were intent upon selecting that program most likely to produce the best-trained men to enter professional accountancy, the medical requirements would seem to offer the better model. In that case, admission to a professional school of accountancy would require prior education in economics and business, including a considerable amount of general accounting.

(Accounting Review, June, 1936)

25. Professional Schools for Accountants

There will be little disposition among accountants to question the need for re-examining the educational prerequisites for entering the profession and the means for providing that education. Undoubtedly there will be differences of opinion regarding the particular standard to be adopted at a given time, and the best method of meeting the standards. For example, there is the specific question whether the next step in raising professional educational qualifications should be the establishment of separate professional schools of accountancy which require some general college education for admission, or the support and strengthening of the accounting departments of existing colleges of commerce.

Having watched for some time the development of colleges of commerce as an integral part of their respective universities, and noted with satisfaction the professional success of many graduates of the accounting departments of these colleges of commerce, I find a number of reasons coming to mind for doubting the need at this time for separating general education and professional education as seems implied in proposals for professional accountancy colleges.

For one thing, the profession throughout the country has not yet made a fully adequate test of existing programs of accounting instruction by a thorough trial of graduates of colleges of commerce with an accounting major. Too often in taking commerce graduates into the staff, little or no attention is paid to scholarship records as a clue to aptitude and the ability to learn; occasionally personality and college activities are allowed to outweigh the evidence of a thorough foundation in collateral subjects. Practitioners could provide an immediate and powerful stimulus to better educational preparation for accountancy if they would pledge themselves for a period of years to absorb the scholastic upper 50 per cent of the accountancy graduates of the colleges of commerce having a satisfactory accounting program.

Furthermore, we are hardly ready for separate schools of accountancy with a high degree of specialization because the literature and teaching materials are still inadequate to support a three-year program in accountancy alone. As a result of this shortage one of two things would happen in a professional school. Either collateral and related subject matter, such as economics, finance, law, and business administration, would be added to the work in accountancy in certain amounts—in which case the school would practically duplicate the present offerings of the college of commerce—or the school would be led into a degree of over-specialization that might result in excessive drilling for the development of mere skills in the technique of the work of junior assistant—hardly a suitable function for a university professional school which should train men for later professional life as well as for the beginning of their careers.

Practitioners can not hope ever to be able to transfer all responsibility to schools for training staff members even if active practitioners make up the whole faculty. No school, academic or professional, can hope to re-produce faithfully the pressure of actual engagements, the diversity of situations, or the overwhelming mass of transactions; no system of study can train men, as one accountant has said, "to remain alert after having reviewed ten thousand legitimate entries," or teach them to supervise a crew of assistants effectively. There is much skill and judgment which only later experience, after any education you choose, can bring into ex-istence.

Grant that most commerce schools now do not do as much as they could or should in laying a foundation for good professional technique. That can be remedied. But the schools must look to the practitioner to supply the teaching materials; and the practitioner must always expect to guide the novice at one time or another through his professional initia-tion into real experience, whatever his prior education.

Another reason for doubt is the thought that the ideal of a professional school manned by practitioners is too often impossible of realization be-cause of the difficulty men find in serving two masters equally well. Teaching is a profession with problems and techniques of its own just as auditing is. The problem of professional education is not to be solved by a school of professional teachers alone or by a faculty of professional prac-titioners; the real problem is to find practitioners with a feeling for the problems of teaching so they can produce a steady flow of good teaching materials, and to find teachers with such a clear perception of the prob-lems of practice that their students will always have their feet on the ground of realities.

An additional reason. One of the principal qualities desired in a profes-sional man is physical and intellectual maturity. But the layer system, wherein professional education is superimposed upon general education, is not the only way to gain that maturity. A mixture of both elements throughout the educational period can also accomplish this result. In fact, this was the early ideal in medical and legal education, but there it proved impracticable, even though desirable, largely because of the tremendous growth of teaching materials. Even if four years of college and five years of medicine, or four of college and three of law, are considered highly desirable, only a relatively small number of people can afford the cost of long training or the sacrifices of waiting to reach the stage of earning a living. Time for most people is not unlimited.

These considerations become practical matters when weighing the merits of possible combinations of educational programs in accountancy. Can enough desirable candidates be found who can give four years to general education and three to accountancy? We would probably be forced to turn to two years of general education and three of professional courses. When a man enters the profession with that background, how much better trained—or intellectually matured in his field—will he be than the man who had four years in a commerce college providing three or four years of work in accounting and well–co-ordinated collateral courses in economics and finance?

And if the commerce graduate with an accounting major should add a year or two of graduate work, he will have spent a maximum of six years against seven for the graduate of a professional accountancy school who entered with a general college degree. The commerce graduate will have spread his study of accountancy over five or perhaps six years as compared with three years for the other man; his accountancy will have been carefully graded in sequence and paralleled with co-ordinate subject matter related to business.

Training in one subject alone is not the most desirable type of professional education. What the sciences of physics, chemistry, and biology are to medicine, economics, finance, and business are to accountancy. Training in accountancy without adequate work in the related subjects is as incongruous as the study of medicine without knowledge of chemistry.

(*Accounting Review*, June, 1936)

26. Post-CPA Education

The usual educational sequence today is: study at college (with or without a major in accountancy); staff experience with a public accounting firm; certification through a state CPA examination. If education stops at that point everyone is a loser—the individual, the firm, the client, the profession. But this extreme situation seldom exists; all subsequent experience is educational and many people exert themselves to accelerate the educational effect of the day's work.

Every engagement provides not only a service for a client but also a training ground for professional personnel. We learn by doing what needs to be done. But even then all concerned will benefit if the learner has a teacher. Are staff men clearly charged by their supervisors with a collateral duty to teach those under their supervision? Are they given helpful directions as to what and how to teach? Is their willingness and ability in this duty weighed in considering promotions?

People in other lines of professional activity apparently are not content to let experience be educational when and if it can. Advanced professional education is often a matter of careful planning and persistent effort.

In medicine the future doctor spends four years in a medical college, perhaps after four years of science and general education. If he expects to be a skillful surgeon, there are four more years of training as intern, second assistant surgeon, first assistant surgeon, and resident surgeon, before he gains the status of chief, the responsible quarterback of a surgical team in action. What is he doing in these four years? Listening, watching, helping, drilling. Listening to the chief's running commentary in every operation; watching the surgical techniques called for by the circumstances; helping in small details at first, in more important ones later; drilling himself in order to improve the necessary skills.

He is willing to practice tying catgut knots that are sure to hold, even if it takes hours and hours of drill and a mile of catgut. Are there men in accountancy who subject themselves to a fraction of this much drill in the small details of their own techniques? The assistant surgeon may watch a certain type of operation 50 times, 100 times, before the responsibility falls to him. Perhaps accounting engagements, being further from life and death, do not require such rigorous or extensive preparatory field training. A slip-up may not be so disastrous, since in accounting the effect usually can be corrected without precipitating an emergency.

But certain questions still remain: Does the staff man in accounting see an important variety of procedures closely enough, and often enough, and intelligently enough, to grow professionally as he ought to do? Is well-graded sequential experience planned for him under the eye of a supervisor anxious to communicate his professional knowledge?

Journalism has some of the characteristics of a profession. The Nieman Foundation grants a certain number of fellowships at Harvard to promising journalists. The American Press Association supports several scholars in journalism studies at Columbia. Many subjects are taught in college that could benefit practicing journalists; and there are plenty of men available with field experience and the necessary professional aptitudes who would like to study. The financial support given to these scholarships and fellowships indicates that some men already high in journalism have a real vision of professional and social needs.

Most universities have a few graduate scholarships that are available to students who are accounting majors. But are there any such for men with a good variety of field experience in accounting? And would such men be willing to take time out for such study if it were made available? Would their firms grant leave-of-absence for adult education? Would the staff man reciprocate with an assured term of loyal service upon his return?

Public accounting is not so vital to this country as adequate military defense. Yet we may learn something from the way the army plans adult education.

The program at West Point is to the army what technical work in college is to the prospective professional accountant. After graduation comes field experience as a junior officer. Later the most promising officers have another term at school—in the staff and command school where lieutenants, captains, and majors study the responsibilities of higher ranks for strategy, tactics, and training. Again there is rotation through a varied experience after which some will go to the War College, where colonels and generals study to develop capacities for further planning and leadership.

Soon new subjects will be added to this program. Attention will be given to industrial mobilization and attendant problems connected with getting material, supervising labor, and building organizations. These officers will also study the national and international problems of politics, diplomacy, and economics.

Is there any stair-step progression of technical accounting education that is even in a small degree like the army plan—a program dovetailing advanced study with demonstrated ability and widening accounting experience? If adult education by way of texts, lectures, and problems can help captains to grow into colonels, would not adult education help senior accountants to grow into partners? Must recruits for the higher ranks be sought only among those who unaided show the most evidence of growth? Will that policy be sure to produce the necessary number of qualified leaders in a growing profession?

(editorial, *Accounting Review,* January, 1947)

27. Upper Staff School

Sometimes accountants look wistfully toward a college of law and wonder whether it does not afford a pattern for a college of professional accountancy.

A strictly professional school may indeed be indicated for the future: when many more people than at present decide early to devote themselves to this career whatever the length of schooling; when it has been definitely decided that professional education for accountancy must have in it a very considerable amount of business education that is neither cultural in purpose nor accounting in nature; when the idea of educational purpose shall reach beyond that of preparing to serve as a first assistant in the field and to pass the CPA examination in due time.

Until the way to a fully professional college of accountancy is clearer, perhaps there are other useful things that can be done—things which would be directly beneficial at once and would contribute in the end to the hoped-for, full-scale professional college.

Numerous schools now offer a sound program combining general, business, and accounting education in good proportions. And there are many aids in preparing to take the CPA examination. But where is there an organized program of education beyond the CPA examination and for the man who has reached the status of senior staff accountant?

Adult education is practicable. Men of experience, certified public accountants already committed to a career in accountancy, would undoubtedly welcome well-planned continuation education in suitable dosage. The summer season is usually a time of lightened pressure of accounting work. A given item of advanced study could be concentrated within a single limited topical area. And a sequential series of studies could be planned, each to cover thirty days, that would give flexibility of use without sacrificing continuity of growth for those taking several of the series.

Since numbers should be limited, admission could well be upon a scholarship basis. Appointments could rest upon such factors as prior education, technical experience, professional promise. Part of the basic information required for admission should be the results of personality tests and the scores made in aptitude examinations. For taking courses in sequence, the records made in prior courses in the series would also be considered.

In a university the organization usually is not such as to make it feasible to concentrate a broad and intensive course into one month of continuous full-time work for men on leave from the active profession. A special type of school is needed. One which could, if desired, fold its camp stool and flit to another section of the country to repeat its program. One which is something more than a program of lectures; preferably one in which small classes and the seminar method prevail. If possible, the discussion throughout the term should draw sustenance in part from a reading program carried on by the students privately for three months prior to the school session, and in part from other reading at prescribed periods throughout the current term.

It would be desirable to keep the enrollment small in each course and limit a student to one course per term. The ideal would be for each course to offer enough to constitute full-time work for four weeks.

Perhaps it would be feasible to obtain the use of a small hotel in a pleasant location with recreation facilities. Concentrated, full-time study in the summer months would be made easier for most people by using this combination in different sections of the country at different times. Joining study with recreation would help justify the individual in shaping his budget to provide some of both.

But the individual is not the only one to benefit and he should not be expected to bear the full financial load of even a nonprofit undertaking. If competitive selection were the avenue to admission, some form of subsidy would be quite appropriate. This would help to assure that the most qualified individuals had a chance. And it would enable the firms to contribute to the school's budget somewhat in proportion to the general benefits expected.

Some of these considerations suggest that the American Institute of Accountants should be a prime mover in the matter, with the firms in

supporting roles. For example, a staff man who met his firm's standards
for applying for a scholarship might be given an additional two weeks'
leave of absence (with salary) to put with his regular vacation time. With
this help he should be able to pay the transportation and living costs for
the four-week term. Teachers' salaries and other school expenses would
need to be otherwise provided. Perhaps this could be done through the
Institute, which would receive a specified sum in support of the project
from the firms for as many of their scholarship recommendations as could
be accommodated each season within the limits of the program. In case
a fully qualified individual applied personally and directly for a scholarship in the seminar, he could make a similar contribution when and if
a place was available.

Because of its entrance requirements and short-term sessions, such a
program of adult education of people already experienced in the profession would not be an encroachment upon the educational services already
provided by many colleges of commerce.

Since most college students are unable to stay for postgraduate degrees,
many who are capable and ambitious are not in a position to work for
advancement except in the course of the day's normal routine. They may
deserve help.

Fostering advanced education for men already committed to the profession and experienced in it should be a very effective way to increase
the prestige of public accountants generally and at the same time to build
wisely a deeper foundation for increasingly satisfactory professional
service in the public interest.

(editorial, *Accounting Review*, January, 1947)

28. When to Browse

It has been suggested that students of accounting do considerable browsing outside of their curriculum and thus gain acquaintance with subjects
of general and cultural interest. This is a thought worth expanding.
Browse, by all means, but do not limit that activity to college days, or
to general and nontechnical reading outside of class assignments.

Perhaps nine hours, three courses, in economics are required for an
accounting student's program. Our student might be well advised to
browse into economics much further. Three courses is hardly enough for
a young man about to be precipitated into this argumentative world.
More knowledge of economics might not enable him to defend himself
as an individual against the adverse conditions around him. But the
better he understands the busy buzz about him, the better he will be able
later to see into and behind the accounts he audits. His clients' affairs will
be carried on in the midst of economic activities and economic arguments,

and the influence of these on him and his business is inescapable. The least our student can do is to read economics beyond the limits of three courses.

The set program may call for three hours for business law and three for corporation finance which rests very much upon a legal foundation. Is this enough of the principles of law for one whose whole professional life is to be colored by concepts drawn from law and corporation practices? Accountants need more law than this, even if it is ever-changing, and more finance too. We cannot escape the impact of law any more than we can avoid economics. Perhaps one could shut his eyes and ears to both, but few of us are so fortunately situated as to be able to continue to do so for more than the length of a two-weeks' vacation. Certainly he could not do so and still be a practicing accountant.

The best programs provide that all divisions of the basic subject matter are represented throughout the four years. Some people prefer to give the first two years over to general and cultural courses in arts and science and to concentrate upon practical work in business, accounting, and law in the last two years. But this plan has always seemed to me to blink several outright facts: (1) that a good deal of the material studied in those last two years is also quite "cultural," (2) that intellectual discipline—an important cultural element—can be obtained from any well-presented subject matter, (3) that much accountancy instruction must by its nature be sequential and cannot therefore be adequately studied if too compactly presented.

There seems to be very little advantage in trying to make the first two years "cultural and disciplinary" and the last two years "utilitarian and practical." It is much better educationally to spread all four elements throughout the four years. Certainly they are well intermingled throughout later life.

In every program stress should be laid upon writing perhaps to the extent of doing some writing throughout the entire four years. Included would be report writing, presumably audit reports. The practicability may be doubted however of giving a great deal of time to the writing of technical reports. The exercise material provided there for the student will necessarily be cold, printed data which will be very lacking in the stimulation that comes from figures tested and assembled in the field. And the student has had at that time very little practical experience which will enable his imagination to picture the printed problems in their natural setting.

The larger objective of practice writing is to develop a facility for expressing the ideas one has in mind in a way "to re-create them in the mind of another." To do that takes clear thinking. Even if one never expected to write audit reports, he should write, write, write for the sake of the oil of clearness which writing and rewriting pours over the thinking process. Less time devoted to audit reports and more to general writing would not be detrimental. But audit reports should not be ignored entirely.

To write one must first have ideas; from that point on writing is but choosing words to clothe the ideas suitably—like choosing socks and ties to harmonize. To get ideas one must add experience to imagination. Reading offers vicarious experience and furnishes material for a discriminating imagination to act upon. As an introduction to actual experience therefore reading is indispensable.

This is the point where wide browsing can make a major contribution. We can all favor browsing; but when to browse, that is the question.

Many cultural subjects could be absorbed without formal classroom instruction, absorbed, that is, well enough to serve an accountant. "Learn a lot about something and something about a lot," makes a pretty good motto. Browsing fits in nicely with the last part. That's a good way for an accountant to broaden his intellectual interest. But when?

College days may not be the best time to browse up enough culture to last the next forty-five years of an active life. It may be largely a life-long task. Let's start the boy out on it; give him the technique of browsing, so to speak; lead him to taste its delights. But let him understand that he must go on from there. If he has learned to browse in connection with both his technical and nontechnical courses, he will probably have acquired a lasting taste for browsing.

Some elements of culture he cannot learn from books. Culture which is generosity is more likely to germinate on the athletic field; culture which is tolerance is more likely to rest upon close associations within a large family at home or its nearest equivalent at college, a fraternity; culture which is kindness probably derives from some sweet old grandmother, if not further back in one's ancestry. There is a lot in culture which we cannot do much about, directly and personally.

But intellectual interests can be stimulated and directed in college courses and in college browsing, and the faculty of appreciation can be uncovered and nurtured a little. In college, where there are many required courses along with many well-known distractions and attractions, there is time only for a beginning. After college—how the years stretch out ahead. That is the time to make twenty-six semester hours of "cultural electives" look like a drop in the bucket. No one can learn a little about a lot in the space of twenty-six credits, or in any other reasonable amount of time which a man following a college program could find.

But afterward—even if one used only the single night a week his wife would let him off from playing bridge—why, in forty years there are 2080 such nights. But let's be reasonable. Say two evenings per month—960 evenings—there are loads of worth-while books that can be read in two evenings—if they are not required reading for some college course or other.

(*Journal of Accountancy*, May, 1935)

29. Reading with Broad Purpose

Let's assume that you are a few years out of college and blessed with a good wife and a good job—a double prize. Now is the time to open the pasture gate and browse all over the field of broad intellectual interests. This is going to be your liberal education. It is going to continue for a long time and parallel your continued professional education through experience. It goes without saying that you are going to read the important new accounting books and the current literature of your profession.

There are two books you might well read first—a sort of introduction to browsing. They are: Martin, *The Meaning of a Liberal Education*, and Wiggam, *The Marks of an Educated Man*. After you have read the library copies, you may wish to get copies of your own; you are sure to want to reread many sections at irregular intervals.

Now to lay some other broad foundations, take history of civilization. Very well, try your teeth on some of the following: Newman, *The Nature of the World and Man*, Wells and Huxley, *The Science of Life*, Dorsey, *Man's Own Show: Civilization*, Keller, *Man's Rough Road*, Van Loon, *The Story of Mankind*. Most of them are in some dollar series or other. Or ask for suggestions at your public library. If you know someone giving "orientation" at a university, he could give you many other suggestions from which to choose.

Next, some economic perspective. The little economics included in a typical program of prescribed subjects is rather inadequate. If browsing after college is to be really liberalizing, it must include reading in economics. Incidentally, this particular reading will also help to make a better professional accountant. But even if it did not, it would still be very much worth while as general education. Our country is pre-eminently devoted to business; we possess an unusual flair for mechanics and invention; and America once was the marvel of the world in industrial productivity and high standards of living. The current depression may seem to suggest that we are slipping. But we will catch our stride presently, for the will to do is going to reassert itself; new techniques will be found. In such a country, past and future, can a man be liberally educated without possessing a reasonable economic perspective?

Choose among the following: For general background, Toutain, *Economic Life of the Ancient World*, Weber, *General Economic History*, Day, *A History of Commerce*, Rogers, *The Economic Interpretation of History*. For industrial developments, Gras, *Industrial Evolution*, Polakov, *The Power Age*, Mumford, *Technics and Civilization*, Annals of the American Academy, *The Second Industrial Revolution and its Significance*.

Top that off with a dessert of economic philosophy including the following ingredients or equivalents: Spahr, *The Economic Foundations of Business*, Commons, *Institutional Economics*. For coffee and cigars, I suggest some Americana, such, for example, as Beard's *The Rise of*

American Civilization and his outline of American government called *The American Leviathan;* perhaps you would like to add Dewey, *Financial History of the United States.*

We've had the broad sweep of historical perspective with its ever-present urge to work inward toward illuminating details. You are sure to find side roads you will want to explore. But not much has been said about browsing to deepen one's appreciations. Here compactness, intensiveness is the keynote of the initial attack; appreciativeness grows from a center outward like the widening circle about a stone cast into a still pool.

Do you aim at developing some appreciation of poetry? Choose one poet, and then only some selections from his work; but read and re-read yourself into his spirit. Concentrate; do not diversify for some time. I hold it better to know and really love one great poem than to pay lip service to half a hundred poets. Do you aim at appreciation of prose, of plot, and characterization? Choose one author, one by preference already tested for you by time, and of that author only one or two tales. Make yourself master of them; outline the plot, study the personality of the principal characters separately, read something by way of background of the times or of the historical events involved and historical persons. For example, you will find a fascinating area for study in Walter Scott's *The Abbot,* if you work in this manner from the inside outward.

The same method is recommended for appreciation of music. Select a few phonograph records of great music. Get someone's advice but make your own choices—a few movements from the great symphonies, a few concert excerpts from Wagner, played by a great orchestra. Listen repeatedly, relaxed, while the smoke from your pipe lazily curls and eddies in the air about a shaded floor lamp. Don't let anyone tell you it is too "highbrow" to understand; you are not trying to understand—just appreciate, enjoy.

Do you wish to widen your intellectual interests to include something of science, philosophy, religion? Try some of these. Dietz, *The Story of Science,* Potter, *The Story of Religion,* Durant, *The Story of Philosophy,* and if you like Durant, try his *Mansions of Philosophy* also. More? All right. Darrow, *The Story of Chemistry,* Loeb and Adams, *The Development of Physical Thought* (Physics), de Kruif, *Microbe Hunters,* Dewey, *Human Nature and Conduct,* Randall, *The Making of the Modern Mind,* Cotton, *Has Science Discovered God?*

Biography? Ludwig, *Genius and Character,* Holland and Pringle, *Industrial Explorers,* Law, *Modern Great Americans,* Wilson, *Great Men of Science,* and innumerable biographies of individuals according to taste.

Topical History? Groseclose, *Money: The Human Conflict,* Epstein, *The Automobile Industry,* Mottram, *A History of Financial Speculation.* Every field has its history. Choose if you wish, architecture, electricity, law, medicine, music, drama, education, engineering, transportation, pirates, criminology, sculpture, chemistry, steel, sugar, slavery, prehistoric man, etc. Go as far as you like.

Present-day problems? Just a sample: Beard, *Whither Mankind,* Berle and Means, *The Modern Corporation and Private Property*, Robbins, *The Great Depression,* Hall, *Government and Business*. Present-day problems seem, just now, almost unending. But do not, I beg of you in the interest of broad education, become too absorbed in them. Nor will you care to ignore them either.

Perhaps the best specific in this case is the right choice of current periodical literature. But that I leave to your own unfettered choosing. Only, browse about a bit before you choose. You can't read everything although it may seem from all this that I have been assuming that you could.

NOTE.—1959. Do not get discouraged if it seems likely that you will not get get through this list. I am still trying but new books are also attractive and can be very useful for this purpose.

(*Journal of Accountancy*, May, 1935)

30. Learning to Write

As every schoolboy knows, learning to write is not easy. Usually he is already convinced there are many other things more interesting than struggling to learn to form letters and to chain letters into words. He probably would not believe it if told that writing can become as fluent as speech; he surely would be hard to convince that his future could be strongly influenced by a laboriously acquired ability to build ideas into sentences and sentences into paragraphs.

Perforce, the student is kept in contact with exercises in written expression as long as he is in school. And his antagonism may persist, beneath a minimum of passing work, throughout college and into some career. On the other hand, many students gradually come to perceive the elements which make for good writing; and perhaps even feel a sense of pleasure in practicing the art of effective composition. This is most likely to happen if wise teachers have brought him to see the architectural features of English composition—the planned sequence of paragraphs, each contributing relevant content and visibly showing textual interrelations which give continuity of theme and unity of structure.

What of those students who have not had inspiring teachers, or have been able to sidestep available courses in writing? Some of these may have been accounting majors. Can the accounting profession do anything to help staff men toward self-development in writing ability, or to help teachers and students still in college, to realize more strongly the usefulness in an accounting career of an ability to write well?

Public accountants some years ago were slow to believe college graduates would make desirable staff members. But developments in the techniques of accounting education in the collegiate schools of business have
overcome those beliefs; and perhaps have contributed not a little to the
ability to write effectively about accounting which has for some time been
reflected in the literature.

The improved quality of accounting literature could be made an objective lesson for students by their college teachers, and an indication that
accountants do write, and well. More and more the colleges, following
the lead of the profession in recognizing communications as basic, will
succeed in improving their efforts to help accounting majors to sense the
need to prepare themselves in that direction. But the responsibility should
not be considered that of teachers' alone.

Has the CPA examination provided any stimulus to better written expression? For a long time the questions have reflected what seemed an
intangible consensus that accounting theory could not be expected to
provide satisfactory examination material; that the grading of "essay
type" questions was quite impractical for a professional test. If ability to
write clearly is professionally important, it would seem that the most
conspicuous place to make that point would be somewhere in the professional examination. The reinstatement of a paper on accounting theory in
the national examination is undoubtedly a step in the right direction,
especially since, in recent years, some questions open the doors to written
composition by asking "why," by requiring "justifications," by making
necessary a reasoned choice between alternatives.

But is this enough pressure toward developing writing ability? Other
changes could be introduced which, besides adding more encouragement
to practicing the arts of good writing, could conceivably raise the stature
of the examination as a testing of the candidate's fitness to take a stand
as a professional man.

Important and beneficial changes, in addition to the theory paper, have
been made. Notably in the collection of question materials, the choice of
the material used, the statement and timing of questions and problems,
the grading supervision, the conditional examination, etc.

It would in my opinion be a further beneficial change to make much
less use of problems about consolidated statements. There was a time some
years ago when installment liquidation of partnerships seemed to be
strongly relied upon "to separate the men from the boys." May it not be
possible that, without conscious intent, consolidated statements have inherited some of that "function?" How long is it before a typical successful
candidate meets a consolidated statement face to face in the field, even as
a senior accountant? How long is it before he has had to deal with his
first ten? Are such problems, in the extent they are found in the examinations and textbooks, indicative of their relative importance in average
professional experience? If they serve primarily to test an ability to mar-

shal complex data intelligently, are there no other problem materials adequate to that purpose? Should texts and classroom work approximate coaching in the marshaling of data, or should data-marshaling be made an instrument for training students to think? If the latter purpose prevails, why are consolidated statements so superior as to be given greatest prominence?

In fact, it might well produce a more professional testing procedure if the amount of other problem solving were also reduced so that time would be made available for two papers in auditing—surely the heart of professional practice—and for an expanded theory test—where reasoning rather than remembering was stressed.

There are of course objections. An early hesitance about objective grading of "essay" answers is one of them. Yet it would seem that this point could be met by a clearly announced policy—that of grading factual material objectively and quantitatively, and that of separate, qualitative grading for effective writing in the auditing and theory papers or designated questions therein. Literal grades could be used to express a judgment regarding quality. A value of B (satisfactory) would bring no change in the arithmetic evaluation of technical correctness; a value of A would raise the grade an announced number of points, a value of C would reduce the arithmetical grade an announced number of points.

Such qualitative judgments are not difficult to make; they are used regularly in many colleges. And of course they would be reviewed for consistency. A low amount of adjustment for effective and for ineffective writing would at most be a small penalty or premium, yet enough, when reported to the candidates, to prod the one to more effort and commend the other on a point of significance to a professional man.

Other efforts in the profession could also encourage work at improving writing ability. If it were made known that an accepted master's thesis would influence starting salary more than the degree without thesis, this kind of exercise in written expression would become part of the program at more universities. The college record of prospective staff men could provide a clue to the individual's interest in learning to write. The number of writing courses taken and the grades earned could be commented on at the time of the recruiting interview, and their significance indicated.

Men on the staff could be steadily urged to practice at writing up observations from their field experience and the results of related collateral reading. If the firm publishes a periodical, the best items submitted could be printed there. If no such publication has been established, it might prove a good investment to start one in a simple form. Not only would staff men be thus encouraged to practice writing, the staff generally could also benefit. Reading about unfamiliar aspects of accounting can be almost as broadening as direct experience.

University administrators are fully aware of the broad usefulness of a well-developed ability in written expression. But they also realize that even required courses in writing can only provide opportunities for students to practice that skill. Anything men in the profession can do to convince students the profession at large considers the art of written expression an aid to advancement will be appreciated in the colleges. It might well be that many students would trade some of the grind on consolidated statements for some stimulating exercise in learning to write better.

College teachers can urge students to take classes, but the benefits gained by being present cannot be made uniform by the teacher's exertion. For that reason a multiplication of courses may not alone suffice. The profession should strive to provide teachers with evidence which will help stir students to make the effort in class which is necessary if they are to learn to write effectively.

There are several things the collegiate schools of business could do. They could consider where the program could be adjusted to make room for more writing practice. If accounting majors are not now required to take some work in verbal expression each undergraduate year, such a requirement should be put under consideration. Freshmen themes and business letters are usually offered. A semester of public speaking could well be added and a year of English literature. The latter item is a more desirable requirement than a foreign language. The reason is that the student's writing vocabulary will be increased, his range of ideas will be broadened, and the analytical contact with good writing will improve his technical competence in effective writing. This last point is particularly important.

It would also be helpful if a course were offered in report writing. This should not be audit reports but exposition based on short research projects—a sort of course in theme writing for fourth-year students. It should not be difficult to introduce some writing of papers in several of the usual accounting courses. And it could be made current practice to announce that good or poor expression in textual matter in short quizzes and longer examinations will influence the grade. Every candidate for a master's degree should be required to write an acceptable thesis; the depth of the research would be of less importance than the quality of the writing. It may seem easier for student and faculty to permit substitution of another text-problem course, but the educational benefit to the student is far from comparable.

Most of the important aspects of a "liberal education," one of which is practice in writing, can be associated with technical work in business administration and accounting. The universities which compose the Association of Collegiate Schools of Business have for a long time been very effectively combining these two aspects of education, many of them choosing to articulate general and technical education throughout four years. If work to the bachelor degree is stratified between the first two years and the last two, the effect is to introduce a too-strong feeling among upper division students for a high degree of specialization. It seems reasonable that an approach to business technicalities could with advantage to the student in a collegiate school of business be given in the early years; and it would clearly be beneficial to such students to study some of the important parts of general education in their maturer years as upper classmen.

The administrative problems of curriculum modification are complex. This is part of the reason the profession should try to make it unmistakable that ability in written expression is a necessary aspect of a career in public accounting. It is evident in the current literature that many accountants write well; this is itself an indication that recruits should learn to write well. It may well be that the time has come somehow to make visibly desirable the capacity to use the English language effectively. I must say again, the best way I can think of is direct association of good writing with the CPA examination. The stimulus thus provided could be expected to influence university instruction, to induce college students to work at the problem, and to inspire staff men to develop projects in self-improvement with encouragement and help from their firm.

In this day, when "do-it-yourself" is so much in the advertisements, it is not unreasonable to hope some of that spirit may infect college students and younger staff men if the idea is put before them. Teachers could encourage students to take on some do-it-yourself attitude in this matter of practice writing and practice critical re-writing. All of their education does not have to carry graduation credit. Being editor of the school paper does not. Moreover, it could strengthen the individual to have learned to accomplish something worth while on his own, without pressure from classroom assignments, or prodding from short quizzes.

Staff men could be encouraged to set themselves to the task of improving their prospects by teaching themselves to write more effectively. After all, most of the educative process has to function within the individual. Probably the most important thing a student learns in college is how to go about learning. It is not necessary to attend night classes in writing. There are many things in accountancy to write about. And they can be taken in hand privately, in small doses at first. Practice makes for perfection—practice and analytical study of examples of good writing. Once you have a reasonable mastery of the art, writing is fun, and there need be no end to the fun.

(*New York Certified Public Accountant*, October, 1956)

31. Do-it-yourself Writing

An often repeated comment is that accounting majors as a group do not show very much competence in written communication. Usually it earns an implication that the collegiate schools of business might do something to improve their students' ability to write effectively. And well they might. But even such an effort would not exhaust the possibilities.

Suppose the college student does not find, does not elect, or is not required to take suitable courses in written expression. Later, having based his entry in accounting career upon his accounting courses, he may come to realize that facility in the use of words, as well as procedures, is highly desirable. If he has some of the modern do-it-yourself spirit—that attitude toward life which carried the pioneers so far—he will be handicapped only briefly. He can learn to write effectively by becoming his own teacher. After all, the educative process has to function within an individual. No outsider can "learn" him; a text and a teacher serve only as an aid to learning to learn.

To take his "deficiency" into his own hands, he needs only to feel convinced the results of the effort will be worth while and to secure a few simple tools—and use them. It would seem appropriate that assurance as to the future usefulness of writing ability should be clearly given by the voices of the profession, and that encouragement to "do-it-yourself" should come, person to person, from established members of the profession to members of their staff.

As to the tools, they are simple ones, and as to the program, you build it yourself and stick to it. A small book on common errors on English grammar; another on words often misspelled and mispronounced; a recent dictionary of synonyms. The usefulness of the first two tools will be obvious: they provide a means for checking on one's habitual usage and for forming better language habits. A dictionary of synonyms is recommended over the ordinary dictionary because good writing is likely to be greatly influenced in many situations by choosing the most appropriate word. And in order to recognize a possibility for better choice of words, it is necessary to study the distinctions between words of nearly equivalent meaning. A strong, flexible, and precise vocabulary is more to be desired than a large or a fancy vocabulary. Use of a dictionary of synonyms is in line with this idea; and besides, the distinctions described are fascinating to study.

There are two items in the program in addition to persistent study of the usefulness of these tools. They are reading and writing. Not casual reading, but reading which is selected more for its good presentation than its content. This may be drawn from a few authors famous for precise writing and from the current literature of accountancy. When a few samples are found of both kinds, they should be studied repeatedly and analytically, not in order to copy the style, but to grow in capacity to examine sentences and paragraphs critically whenever you review what you have written in draft form. For reviewing and changing and rewriting are parts of the process of giving clear expression to ideas. You would do well to become proficient, when "editing" your drafts, in reading as a stranger trying to penetrate another's real meaning. That is the way you read what someone else has written; that is the reason you should read, repeatedly and slowly, the items selected for study. Note particularly how his paragraph makes its point; practice asking how your paragraph makes its point. Material which explains will provide a more useful subject matter in your case than narrative or description. For whatever one writes as an accountant is likely to be in the nature of exposition.

Probably the most important element in such a do-it-yourself program is practice in writing. It is not necessary, and may even be undesirable, to undertake too early anything of article length. That will come before long. Start with paragraphs; not at first those needed for audit reports, but those about separate small points of usage or theory. Recommended are items which are relatively commonplace among accountants but likely not to be known or clearly understood by laymen.

It will be obvious that accountants will not always aim their phrases at other accountants when they write. Possibly too much of what they do write is unconsciously cast in language accountants would understand best. Accountancy has not, and should not, become so technical as to be intelligible only to the technician. Indeed, writing men in the profession, even when directly addressing accountants, would do well, whenever possible, to present their message in clear, correct English understandable to reasonably well informed nonaccountants. There is less mystery for the layman in accountancy than there is in medicine and in law. It would not be in the public interest, or in the interest of the profession, to let a highly technical vocabulary get established here.

Practice in writing paragraphs, in reading them analytically for structure, in rewriting them in varying phraseology, these are the keys to effective writing. Skill in writing comes as skill comes to a musician, from practice, practice, practice. Paragraphs presently become easy to review into improvement; then good paragraphs come more frequently at first trial. Before long, good expression tends to become habitual—yet never quite beyond the need for some degree of analytical review.

When paragraph construction needs less conscious attention, the important matter of bringing paragraphs into appropriate sequence becomes easier. In this longer form of expression an outline of the essential ideas involved in the whole presentation becomes a critical element. Here is a clue to another line of study of the selected reading materials. It is helpful to planning a piece of writing to have practiced reducing published articles to a compressed outline of its ideas and subideas. The authors of your study materials probably prepared some such "work program" before writing specific paragraphs; it would be the blueprint which controlled the structure of the article.

Planning an article and drafting it according to plan are writing actions which should be sharply separate tasks. Reviewing the written draft then becomes somewhat like reviewing an accounting system and the use made of it: the plan (outline) may itself have been satisfactory, but poorly applied; or the process of writing sequential paragraphs may reveal flaws in the outline. Since an outline, like a flexible financial budget, is by intention subject to change, the finished writing usually will reflect changes in outline as well as improvement in paragraph phrasing and placing.

Some of this kind of self-help program in learning to write could very profitably be begun in college. "Begun" is used advisedly, for greatest benefits come from making the practice of the arts of verbal composition an early habit which is continued after graduation. It is not necessary to wait for a course in writing exposition, or to do nothing unless pressed by academic requirements. One of the greatest of inventions was the self-starter. And it is not necessary to neglect continued practice after entering professional work. Instead of seeking diversion by way of crossword puzzles, etc., on suburban trains or out-of-town trips, construct and rework hypothetical paragraphs of exposition. Or carry a small assortment of copied paragraphs and rework them yourself, or perhaps start some friendly competition, if you have a travel companion, in rewriting better paragraphs, broader paragraphs, etc. If travel does not provide suitable opportunities for paragraph practice, other lightly occupied intervals will no doubt appear, or can be contrived. The primary question is whether you really want to improve your capacity for effective writing.

Words, like figures, are important means of communication. One of the most appreciated direct services an accountant can render is to use words effectively to make clear the message which lies within the figures. One of the most useful indirect services an accountant can render is to make his work, his techniques, his principles, his beliefs understandable to other people, accountants and laymen alike. Like other skills, the art of effective communication has to be studied and practiced persistently; wishing will not suffice.

(*Illinois Certified Public Accountant*, summer, 1957)

32. Education for Professional Accounting

Fifty years ago college education for business was relatively new. It had achieved only a modest recognition in academic circles.

That condition has gradually changed. A school of business has become a substantial factor in most universities. It has justified its status as a college by its standards of teaching, its qualified and productive faculty, its capacity for community service, its power to attract sincere, capable students, and as an expression of the flair for business which we seem to have in the United States.

Our developments in the areas of business management and business education contribute strongly to the public interest. A minority may still be of the opinion that business enterprise is merely an engine for generating profits for owners. The truth is that better business management means a more productive use of the nation's savings, increased employment resulting in greater purchasing power, and more goods and services from which come higher living standards.

Accounting "technology" contributes to this public interest. Improved internal accounting means better informed managerial decisions, more effective planning, and a reduction of inefficiency. The examination and certification of company financial statements by professional accountants form another aspect of accounting technology, one which serves the public by providing a factual basis for confident decisions in the nation's money markets. These characteristic services quite clearly justify the advances already made, and those to come, in accounting education as an area of study in schools of business.

The accounting departments in many universities are not only firmly established and rendering effective public service, but quite frequently they contribute substantially to the reputation of their university. Accounting is the language of business and finance; students majoring in that area need preparation in accounting as much as they need it in other forms of analysis, communication, economics, and the arts of business administration.

A relatively recent and continuing development of particular significance is that of postgraduate work in accounting.[1] This is noteworthy because it indicates the increasing interest in accounting as an academic subject. It also accentuates the growing recognition among businessmen that graduate work matures the individual student, thus increasing his ability to improve as he accumulates field experience. In public accounting offices it is noticeable that men with education at the graduate level usually advance more rapidly than others.

People interested in accounting education—professional accountants as well as teachers—are not content to rest on the achievements to date; they are looking toward future developments. This is clearly evident in a report prepared by a committee of twenty-two members, one half of whom were professional accountants and the other half deans of collegiate schools of business or professors of accounting.[2]

Back of the recommendations in the report stand four years of investigating into the nature of a profession, the present status of the professional accountant and the CPA examination, and the educational needs of accountants and the educational facilities now available.

The recommendations project far into the future and contemplate an

.

[1] The *Accounting Review* for July, 1957 includes a list of research projects in accountancy for the school year 1955-56. An analysis of these data shows the following facts: Master's degrees in accounting are offered in 26 universities. For the 26 schools, 14 master's theses are reported although some schools do not require such a thesis. Eighteen universities report candidates for a doctor's degree with a major in accounting, and 75 doctor's theses completed or in process during the school year.

[2] *Standards of Education and Experience for Certified Public Accountants,* published by the University of Michigan in 1956.

evolutionary approach to the further extension of accounting education. The plan calls for a period of exchange of ideas regarding objectives, and thoughtful debate over various ways and means of giving practical effect to desirable educational aims.

The essence of the committee's point of view is indicated in these words from the report:

The formal educational preparation of candidates for the profession needs to be much more advanced than that now required by most accountancy legislation and, in fact more thorough and comprehensive than is now provided by most educational institutions (p. 127).

An excellent summary of the needs of the profession and the specific recommendations of the committee has already been presented in *Western Business Review* and need not be detailed here.[3] The remainder of this article will briefly examine only one item—"the development of a type of curriculum which would be new in accounting but which has been tested for generations in other professions—a professional program. . . ."

From relevant articles which have already appeared in the current literature, it is becoming clear that one of the central problems involves the choice between two vehicles for carrying forward the next stage of accounting education visualized:

1. Professional programs within the framework of schools of business, or

2. Within a separate school of accountancy, perhaps modelled after colleges of law.

In this dilemma, the second choice would no doubt be influenced by a belief that there are similarities between the professions of law, medicine and public accountancy; the other, that it would be wise to continue a line of educational evolution which has for some time been making notable contributions to accounting progress.

On this issue there will be considerable difference of opinion and many questions will be generated, such as:

Would the needed pre-accountancy education be obtained best in a school of business, in a liberal arts college, or as the early part of a professional curriculum in a separate school for professional accounting?

Is stratification of education (highly specialized technical education on top of layers of general education) for accountancy desirable, or is a judicious mixture—economics, business administration, and nonbusiness subject matter—more desirable? [4]

Can we reasonably expect most accounting careerists to make their de-

---

[3] Clem W. Collins, "The Certified Public Accountant Enters a New Epoch," Vol. I, No. 2 (May, 1957), 76-78.
[4] In law and medicine, professional training is concentrated in the later years, and in a separate school, following pre-law studies (political science, etc.) and pre-medical studies (biological sciences, chemistry, etc.) in a nonprofessional school.

cision early enough so as to enable them to secure a bachelor's degree (in economics and business administration) in order to qualify for admission to a professional school to study accountancy? Will the numbers choosing this approach be sufficient to meet the present and growing needs for capable staff recruits?

Does the public interest indicate or require that pre-accountancy be prescribed for entrance into a separate school?

The practice of medicine is clearly related to a vital aspect of the public interest—the health of the nation's population—and, consequently, it is difficult to conceive that there could be too much technical education and research in this area. Similarly, the practice of law is clearly related to a vital aspect of the public interest—government by law rather than by decree, justice before the law for all. The complexities of human society and the difficulties in achieving even-handed justice have determined the direction in which legal education has evolved.

Accountancy is no exception to the principle that a profession should be grounded on service to the public interest. The basic public interest here involved is found principally in the nation's money markets. Dependable financial reports, certified by qualified professional certified public accountants, furnish strong support for public confidence in the reporting companies and for the investment decisions by which much of the nation's economy is maintained. The fundamental issue, therefore, becomes one of whether the extent of public interest involved in professional accounting service is of such a degree which would make the profession of accounting analogous to the professions of law and medicine.

The visible developments in accounting education which have taken place in the past twenty-five years indicate that both practitioners and teachers of accounting have long been giving careful analysis to accounting education and full consideration to the public interests involved. The same careful analysis and consideration which built business education to its present status now prompts exploration of ways and means for further advancing one section of that area—professional accountancy. *But, it would seem unlikely that any decisions arrived at could successfully divorce the study of accounting as an aid to enterprise management, and accounting as a professional service.*

What alternatives can be visualized?

1. Confine accounting instructions in the schools of business to the managerial uses of accounting data, and transfer upperclass and technical courses to a separate school of accounting specialization.

2. Keep advanced accounting courses in the school of business for the benefit of the industrial, internal and administrative accountants-to-be.

3. Duplicate all or most of these in the professional school.

The day is gone when one could develop into a fully qualified professional accountant from little more than his slowly accumulated staff experience and observation in the field, plus some private reading. Practi-

cal experience is a fine teacher in accounting as elsewhere—provided that
the learner in accounting field work has been sufficiently prepared by
prior classroom study of economics, business administration, accountancy,
etc., to understand his experiences as they materialize before him, and
prepared by a combination of study-experience to keep on learning
throughout his active lifetime. The most acceptable theory as to what
the best preparation might be should not, therefore, either rate too
highly the benefits to new recruits of early field experience, or put too
much faith in merely remembered textbook material.

Whether consciously held or not, the basic reason back of the committee's proposals for planning long-range advances in accounting education
very likely has been a conviction that good classroom experiences can
develop the individual's capabilities far beyond that of merely remembering text materials.

Because there are great differences among individuals, because an
ability to think rationally about accounting can be fostered in various
ways, and because the profession's need for recruits continues to grow,
it would seem wise to go very slowly in the matter of rigid requirements
as to the source and details of educational preparation.

Such constructive measures as setting up standards for curriculum content, teacher preparation, classroom material, testing an individual's educational progress, and for gradually broadening the examination which
leads to statutory recognition of professional status—would be cumula-
tively beneficial. It is doubtful that a single type of professional education or one kind of curriculum could be equally as beneficial, either
initially or in the long run.

Some programs of study, by virtue of their content, length of time, and
type of faculty supervision, may prove capable of developing better prepared graduates than some other arrangements. In time, these could influence other programs, thus gradually fostering progress in desirable
ways while allowing room for growth by experimentation.

Perhaps a few professional accounting schools patterned after law
schools—concentration on specialized subject matter after a substantial
general education—might very satisfactorily suit the situation of a number of individuals, particularly those who had completed a liberal arts
program before choosing a career in accounting. Their educational maturity would permit rapid progress.

At the same time it might well be that a professional program within
the framework of existing undergraduate schools of business would best
suit most individuals who presently become accounting careerists. For in
such a program it would be possible and desirable to intermix throughout four, five, or more years, the study of accountancy in a graduated
sequence of presentation with relevant and sequential studies in economics, business administration, and a suitable variety of general education subjects. This would tend to provide educational development

for the whole man. Professional education could thus move upward in steady progression and within a subject matter atmosphere similar to that in which the professional life of an accountant would fall.

(*Western Business Review,* February, 1958)